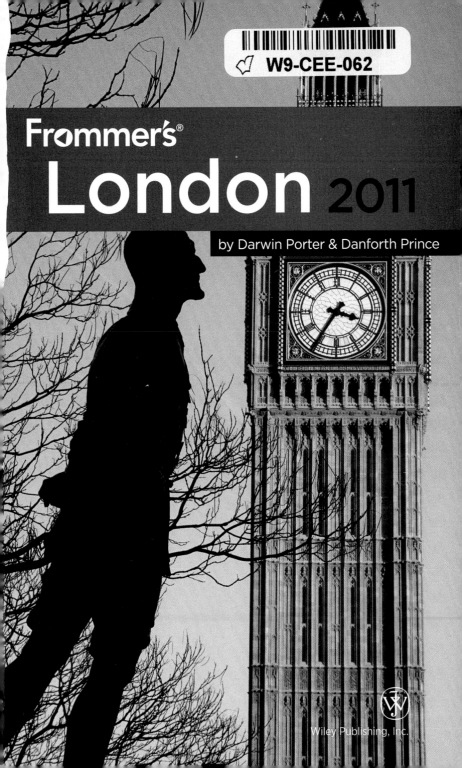

Frommer's®
London 2011

by Darwin Porter & Danforth Prince

Wiley Publishing, Inc.

Published by:
WILEY PUBLISHING, INC.
111 River St.
Hoboken, NJ 07030-5774

ISBN 978-0-470-61439-6 (paper); ISBN 978-0-470-87713-5 (paper); ISBN 978-0-470-89022-6 (ebk); ISBN 978-0-470-92643-7 (ebk); ISBN 978-0-470-94946-7 (ebk)

Editor: Jamie Ehrlich
Production Editor: Lindsay Conner
Cartographer: Andrew Murphy
Photo Editor: Richard Fox
Production by Wiley Indianapolis Composition Services

Front cover photo: Neal's Yard at Covent Garden © Steve Vidler / eStock Photo
Back cover photos: *Left:* Queen Elizabeth Gate at Hyde Park © Steve Vidler / eStock Photo; *Middle:* Street sign for Abbey Road © Paul Thomason / Eye Ubiquitous / Corbis; *Right:* London Eye and Big Ben © Pictures Colour Library / Alamy Images

For information on our other products and services or to obtain technical support, please contact our Customer Care Department within the U.S. at 877/762-2974, outside the U.S. at 317/572-3993 or fax 317/572-4002.

Wiley also publishes its books in a variety of electronic formats. Some content that appears in print may not be available in electronic formats.

Manufactured in the United States of America

5 4 3 2

CONTENTS

LIST OF MAPS

ABOUT THE AUTHORS

As a team of veteran travel writers, **Darwin Porter** and **Danforth Prince** have produced numerous titles for Frommer's, including guides to Italy, France, the Caribbean, Spain, and Germany. Together they have covered Britain for Frommer's with guides to Great Britain, Scotland, and England. Danforth Prince was previously employed by the Paris bureau of the *New York Times* and is currently the president of Blood Moon Productions and works for other media-related firms. Darwin Porter is also a film critic, columnist, broadcaster, and Hollywood biographer.

HOW TO CONTACT US

In researching this book, we discovered many wonderful places—hotels, restaurants, shops, and more. We're sure you'll find others. Please tell us about them, so we can share the information with your fellow travelers in upcoming editions. If you were disappointed with a recommendation, we'd love to know that, too. Please write to:

Frommer's London 2011
Wiley Publishing, Inc. • 111 River St. • Hoboken, NJ 07030-5774
frommersfeedback@wiley.com

AN ADDITIONAL NOTE

Please be advised that travel information is subject to change at any time—and this is especially true of prices. We therefore suggest that you write or call ahead for confirmation when making your travel plans. The authors, editors, and publisher cannot be held responsible for the experiences of readers while traveling. Your safety is important to us, however, so we encourage you to stay alert and be aware of your surroundings. Keep a close eye on cameras, purses, and wallets, all favorite targets of thieves and pickpockets.

FROMMER'S STAR RATINGS, ICONS & ABBREVIATIONS

Every hotel, restaurant, and attraction listing in this guide has been ranked for quality, value, service, amenities, and special features using a star-rating system. In country, state, and regional guides, we also rate towns and regions to help you narrow down your choices and budget your time accordingly. Hotels and restaurants are rated on a scale of zero (recommended) to three stars (exceptional). Attractions, shopping, nightlife, towns, and regions are rated according to the following scale: zero stars (recommended), one star (highly recommended), two stars (very highly recommended), and three stars (must-see).

In addition to the star-rating system, we also use seven feature icons that point you to the great deals, in-the-know advice, and unique experiences that separate travelers from tourists. Throughout the book, look for:

special finds—those places only insiders know about

fun facts—details that make travelers more informed and their trips more fun

kids—best bets for kids and advice for the whole family

special moments—those experiences that memories are made of

overrated—places or experiences not worth your time or money

insider tips—great ways to save time and money

great values—where to get the best deals

The following abbreviations are used for credit cards:

AE	American Express	**DISC**	Discover	**V**	Visa
DC	Diners Club	**MC**	MasterCard		

TRAVEL RESOURCES AT FROMMERS.COM

Frommer's travel resources don't end with this guide. Frommer's website, **www.frommers.com**, has travel information on more than 4,000 destinations. We update features regularly, giving you access to the most current trip-planning information and the best airfare, lodging, and car-rental bargains. You can also listen to podcasts, connect with other Frommers.com members through our active-reader forums, share your travel photos, read blogs from guidebook editors and fellow travelers, and much more.

THE
BEST OF
LONDON

The British capital is alive and well and culturally more vibrant than it has been in years.

The sounds of the latest music pour out of Victorian pubs, experimental theater is popping up on stages built for Shakespeare's plays, upstart chefs are reinventing the bland dishes British mums have made for generations, and Brits are even running couture houses like Dior. In food, fashion, film, music, and just about everything else, London now stands at the cutting edge, just as it did in the 1960s.

If this sea of change worries you more than it appeals to you, rest assured that traditional London still exists, essentially intact under the veneer of hip. From high tea almost anywhere to the Changing of the Guard at Buckingham Palace, the city still abounds with the tradition and charm of days gone by.

Discovering London and making it your own can be a bit of a challenge, especially if you have limited time. Even in the 18th century, Daniel Defoe found London "stretched out in buildings, straggling, confused, out of all shape,

Sunset over Houses of Parliament.

PREVIOUS PAGE: People sitting at a cafe in Neal's Yard, Covent Garden.

uncompact and unequal; neither long nor broad, round nor square." The actual City of London proper is 2.6 sq. km (1 sq. mile) of very expensive real estate around the Bank of England. All of the gargantuan rest of the city is made up of separate villages, boroughs, and corporations—each with its own mayor and administration. Together, however, they add up to a mammoth metropolis.

Luckily, whether you're looking for Dickens's house or hot designer Vivienne Westwood's flagship store, only the heart of London's huge territory need concern you. The core of London is one of the most fascinating places on earth. With every step, you'll feel the tremendous influence this city exerted over global culture back when it was the capital of an empire on which the sun never set.

London is a mass of contradictions. On the one hand, it's a decidedly royal city, studded with palaces, court gardens, coats of arms, and other regal paraphernalia; yet it's also the home of the world's second-oldest parliamentary democracy (Iceland was the first).

Today London has grown less English and more international. The gent with the bowler hat is long gone; today's Londoner might have a turban, a mohawk, or even a baseball cap. It's becoming easier to find a café au lait and a croissant than a scone and a cup of tea. The city is home to thousands of immigrants and refugees, both rich and poor, from all reaches of the world.

THE most unforgettable
TRAVEL EXPERIENCES

- **Watching the Sunset at Waterloo Bridge:** This is the ideal place for watching the sun set over Westminster. You can see the last rays of light bounce off the dome of St. Paul's and the spires in the East End.

- **Enjoying a Traditional Afternoon Tea:** At the Ritz Hotel, 150 Piccadilly, W1 (② 020/7493-8181; p. 137), the tea ritual carries on as it did in Britain's heyday. You could invite the Queen of England herself here for a "cuppa." The pomp and circumstance of the British Empire live on at the Ritz—only the Empire is missing. See p. 234.

- **Cruising London's Waterways:** In addition to the Thames, London has an antique canal system, with towpath walks, bridges, and wharves. Replaced by the railroad as the prime means of transportation, the canal system was all but forgotten until it was rediscovered by a new generation. Now undergoing a process of urban renewal, the old system has been restored, with bridges painted and repaired, and paths cleaned up, for you to enjoy. See "River Cruises Along the Thames," on p. 303.

- **Spending Sunday Morning at Speakers Corner:** At the northeast corner of Hyde Park, a British tradition carries on. Speakers sound off on every imaginable subject, and "in-your-face" hecklers are part of the fun. You might hear anything from denunciations of the monarchy to antigay rhetoric. Anyone can get up and speak. The only rules: You can't blaspheme, be obscene, or incite a riot. The tradition began in 1855—before the legal right to assembly was guaranteed in 1872—when a mob of 150,000 gathered to attack a proposed Sunday Trading Bill. See p. 300.

Tea at the Ritz.

Covent Garden.

○ **Studying the Turners at the Tate Britain:** When he died in 1851, J. M. W. Turner bequeathed his collection of 19,000 watercolors and some 300 paintings to the people of Britain. He wanted his finished works, about 100 paintings, displayed under one roof. Today you see not only the paintings but also glimpses of Turner's beloved Thames through the museum's windows. The artist lived and died on the river's banks and painted its many changing moods. See p. 251.

○ **Strolling Through Covent Garden:** George Bernard Shaw got his inspiration for *Pygmalion* here, where the cockney lass who inspired the character of Eliza Doolittle sold violets to wealthy operagoers. The old market, with its cauliflower peddlers and butchers in blood-soaked aprons, is long gone. What's left is London's best example of urban renewal and one of its hippest shopping districts. There's an antiques market on Monday and a crafts market Tuesday through Saturday. See p. 357 for market details. When you're parched, there are plenty of pubs to quench your thirst, including the **Nags Head,** 10 James St., WC2 (© **020/7836-4678;** p. 381), an Edwardian pub that'll serve you a draft of Guinness and a plate of pork cooked in cider.

○ **Rowing on the Serpentine:** When the weather's right, head to Hyde Park's 17-hectare (42-acre) man-made lake—the name derives from its winding, snakelike shape—dating from 1730. At the Boathouse, you can rent boats by the hour. It's an idyllic way to spend a sunny afternoon. Renoir must have agreed; he depicted the custom on canvas. See p. 299.

○ **Making a Brass Rubbing:** Take home some costumed ladies and knights in armor from England's age of chivalry. Make your very own brass rubbing in the crypt of St. Martin-in-the-Fields in Trafalgar Square; the staff there will be happy to show you how. See p. 271.

o **Getting to Know North London on a Sunday:** Head for Hampstead Heath off Well Walk and take the right fork, which leads to an open field with a panoramic view of London. Cap your jaunt with a visit to the **Freud Museum** (p. 310), open on Sunday until 5pm. See "Attractions on the Outskirts," on p. 308, for more information on North London.

o **Dining at Rules: Rules,** at 35 Maiden Lane, WC2 (✆ **020/7836-5314**), was established as an oyster bar in 1798; it may be the oldest restaurant in London. Long a venue for the theatrical elite and literary beau monde, it still serves the same dishes that delighted Edward VII and his mistress, Lillie Langtry, who began their meals with champagne and oysters upstairs. Charles Dickens had a regular table. If you're looking for an old-fashioned British dessert, finish off with the treacle sponge or apple suet pudding. See p. 188.

o **Spending an Evening at the Theater:** London is the theatrical capital of the world. The live stage offers a unique combination of variety, accessibility, and economy—and maybe a look at next season's Broadway hit. See "The Play's the Thing: London's Theater Scene," on p. 360.

o **Crawling the London Pubs:** Americans bar-hop; Londoners pub-crawl. With some 5,000 pubs within the city limits, you would certainly be crawling if you tried to have a drink in each of them! We have suggested the traditional pubs we think will make a worthwhile crawl in "The Best of London's Pubs: The World's Greatest Pub-Crawl," on p. 380. While making the rounds, you can partake of that quintessentially British fare known as "pub grub,"

Tour boat passing under Tower Bridge.

Drinking at a pub in Covent Garden.

which could be anything from a ploughman's lunch (a hunk of bread, cheese, and a pickle) to shepherd's pie, to nouveau British cuisine. Today, in the right places, some of that pub grub tastes better than the fare served in many restaurants.

THE best SPLURGE HOTELS

- **Covent Garden Hotel,** 10 Monmouth St., WC2 (✆ **800/553-6674** in the U.S. and Canada, or 020/7806-1000; www.firmdale.com): Once a hospital, this deluxe citadel of fine living is one of London's most charming boutique hotels, lying in one of the West End's hippest shopping districts. *Travel + Leisure* has pronounced it one of the 25 hottest addresses in the world. See p. 130.

- **One Aldwych,** 1 Aldwych, WC2 (✆ **800/745-8883** in the U.S. and Canada, or 020/7300-1000; www.onealdwych.co.uk): Once the headquarters for the London *Morning Post* at the turn of the 20th century, this luxe hotel, granted five stars by the government, attracts the fashionistas of London to its noble precincts. You're coddled in comfort here. See p. 131.

- **St. Martins Lane,** 45 St. Martin's Lane, WC2 (✆ **800/697-1791** in the U.S. and Canada, or 020/7300-5500; www.stmartinslane.com): This Covent Garden hotel was once a dull 1960s office building—now it's on the cutting edge, with its eccentric, irreverent design and whimsical touches. Refugees from New York or Los Angeles will feel at home in this ultra-sophisticated environment with state-of-the-art amenities. See p. 131.

- **Sanderson,** 50 Berners St., W1 (© **800/697-1791** in the U.S. and Canada, or 020/7300-1400; www.sandersonlondon.com): Deep in the heart of Soho, this winning choice provides a hip New York–style scene: Its owners call it an "ethereal, transparent urban spa." Everything is here, from a lush bamboo-filled roof garden to a restaurant under the general supervision of Alain Ducasse, hailed by some as the world's greatest chef. See p. 133.

- **41,** 41 Buckingham Palace Rd., SW1 (© **877/955-1515** in the U.S. and Canada, or 020/7300-0041; www.41hotel.com): Admittedly an offbeat choice in this category, this well-placed gem offers a touch of class and one of the most prestigious addresses in London (even the Queen uses the road as her mailing address). Evoking the atmosphere of a private club, it offers individually designed bedrooms with luxurious touches, modern amenities, and spoil-you-rotten service. See p. 140.

Bar at the Sanderson.   Lobby of 41.

- **Haymarket Hotel,** 1 Suffolk Place, SW1 (© **020/7470-4000;** www.firmdale.com), stands next to the historic Haymarket Theatre in the heart of the West End theater district. Completely modernized, it's been turned into a hotel of sophistication and charm while retaining much of its 19th-century John Nash architecture. See p. 133.

Haymarket Hotel.

THE best MODERATELY PRICED HOTELS

o **Windermere Hotel,** 142–144 Warwick Way, SW1 (✆ **020/7834-5480;** www.windermere-hotel.co.uk): Near Victoria Station, this award-winning small hotel, in a converted Victorian building from 1857, is imbued with English character and comfort. Rooms come in various sizes, some large enough to accommodate three or four overnighters, making them suitable for families. See p. 142.

o **The Sumner,** 54 Upper Barkeley St., Marble Arch (✆ **020/7723-2244):** This town house is part of an 1820s Georgian Terrace that has been turned into one of the finest boutique town houses in London, yet its prices are affordable. Much of the original architectural allure is intact, except for modern amenities and newly decorated bedrooms. See p. 156.

o **Twenty Nevern Square,** 20 Nevern Sq., Earl's Court, SW5 (✆ **020/7565-9555**). A redbrick Victorian house with Asian tones in its decor, even a Pasha suite with luxurious silk curtains. For what it offers, it's reasonable in price; some bedrooms feature private terraces. See p. 151.

o **Hart House Hotel,** 51 Gloucester Place, Portman Sq., W1 (✆ **020/7935-2288;** www.harthouse.co.uk): In the fashionable West End district of

Marylebone, this historic building is one of a group of Georgian mansions that was occupied by exiled French nobles during the Revolution. Today it is one of London's better small hotels, within walking distance of many theaters and offering bedrooms of comfort and character. See p. 156.

o **Lincoln House Hotel,** 33 Gloucester Place, W1 (✆ **020/7486-7630;** www. lincoln-house-hotel.co.uk): Built during the reign of King George II, this successfully converted town house lies only a 5-minute walk from Marble Arch in the center of London. Bedrooms are traditionally furnished and full of comfort and character. See p. 157.

o **St. George Hotel,** 49 Gloucester Place, W1 (✆ **020/7486-8586;** www. stgeorge-hotel.net): This privately owned hotel in a restored Georgian building overlooks one of London's most famous squares, Gloucester Square. A short walk from Oxford and Baker streets, the latter of Sherlock Holmes fame, it offers comfortably refurbished bedrooms that are well maintained. See p. 156.

THE most unforgettable
DINING EXPERIENCES

o **St. John,** 26 St. John St., EC1 (✆ **020/7251-0848;** www.stjohnrestaurant. co.uk): In a former smokehouse north of Smithfield Market, this is London's major venue for serious carnivores. Chef Fergus Henderson is England's biggest devotee of offal cuisine—meaning "nose-to-tail cookery." This earthy food obviously will not appeal to vegetarians, but it would delight a reincarnated Henry VIII. See p. 178.

Entry to Simpson's-in-the-Strand restaurant.

o **Fifteen,** 15 West Land Place, W1 (✆ **0871/ 330-1515;** www.fifteen.net/restaurants/fifteenlondon): In Shoreditch, the author of *The Naked Chef,* Jamie Oliver, takes "disadvantaged" young people and trains them from scratch. In just 4 months, they are tempting you with their modern British cuisine as chefs of the day. Amazingly, the food you're served is praiseworthy, even attracting some of London's Michelin-starred chefs. See p. 179.

o **Simpson's-in-the-Strand,** 100 the Strand, WC2 (✆ **020/7836-9112**): At least once, forsake London's trendy restaurants and dine as Sir Winston did back in the post-war '50s when he was prime minister. It's partaking of "The Deadly Sins" to dine here: roast sirloin of beef; steak, kidney, and mushroom pie; and roast saddle of mutton with red currant jelly. See p. 188.

o **Fox and Anchor,** 115 Charthouse St., EC1 (✆ **020/7250-1300**): It's like stepping back in time as you enter this traditional pub servicing traders from the nearby Smithfield meat market since 1898. A great big breakfast—called "The Full Monty"—is unique in London. But you can also visit for time-honored pub fare such as fish and chips or steak-and-kidney pie at both lunch and dinner. See p. 176.

o **Sketch,** 9 Conduit St., W1 (*©* **020/7659-4500;** www.sketch.uk.com): Hailed by the British press as a "camp wonderland," this is a restaurant, tea-room, art gallery, bar, and patisserie. There is no more chic joint at which you could be at night. The Continental and modern British cuisine are divine as well. See p. 200.

o **Club Gascon,** 57 W. Smithfield, EC1 (*©* **020/7796-0600**): Chef Pascal Aussignac is all the rage, bringing a corner of southwestern France to London—and that spells Armagnac, foie gras, and duck confit. This bistro stands next to the famous meat market in Smithfield, and it's the best place in town for a foie gras pig out. See p. 176.

THE best MUSEUMS

o **British Museum,** Great Russell Street, WC1 (*©* **020/7323-8299;** www.thebritishmuseum.ac.uk): When Sir Hans Sloane died in 1753, he bequeathed to England his vast collection of art and antiquities. This formed the nucleus of a huge collection that's come to include such remarkable objects as the Rosetta Stone and the Parthenon sculptures (which Greece wants back). See p. 238.

British Museum.

Artist drawing in statue gallery at the Victoria and Albert Museum.

○ **National Gallery,** Trafalgar Square, WC2 (✆ **020/7747-2885;** www. nationalgallery.org.uk): One of the world's greatest collections of Western art—from Leonardo da Vinci to Rembrandt to Picasso—dazzles the eye at this museum. The gallery is especially rich in Renaissance works. See p. 247.

○ **Tate Britain,** Millbank, SW1 (✆ **020/7887-8008;** www.tate.org.uk): Sir Henry Tate, a sugar producer, started it all with 70 or so paintings. The collection grew considerably when artist J. M. W. Turner bequeathed some 300 paintings and 19,000 watercolors to England upon his death. Having handed International Modernism over to the Tate Modern, the Tate Britain now concentrates on British work dating back to 1500. See p. 251.

○ **Victoria and Albert Museum,** Cromwell Road, SW7 (✆ **020/7942-2000;** www.vam.ac.uk): This is the greatest decorative arts museum in the world, boasting the largest collection of Renaissance sculpture outside Italy. It is also strong on medieval English treasures and has the greatest collection of Indian art outside India. See p. 257.

○ **National Portrait Gallery,** St. Martin's Place, WC2 (✆ **020/7306-0055**): The greats and not-so-greats in English history show their faces here, often "warts and all," to quote Oliver Cromwell. The gang's all here, from Samuel Johnson to Princess Diana, even a Holbein cartoon of Henry VIII. See p. 248.

○ **Science Museum,** Exhibition Road, SW7 (© **087/0870-4868;** www.sciencemuseum.org.uk): The collection here of scientific artifacts is among the largest, most significant, and most comprehensive in the world. Everything is here, from King George III's collection of scientific instruments in the 18th century to the *Apollo 10* space module. See p. 296.

THE best ACTIVITIES FOR FAMILIES

○ **Sightseeing:** London is filled with attractions that appeal to young and old—take **Madame Tussauds** wax museum (p. 292), that all-time favorite. There's more: everything from **London's Transport Museum** (p. 291) to the **National Army Museum** (p. 293) and, of course, the **Natural History Museum** (p. 293). A cruise along the Thames (see "River Cruises Along the Thames," on p. 303) is a great way to spend an afternoon, as is a trip to the **London Zoo** (p. 323).

○ **Trips out of London:** Board a riverboat for a **cruise to Greenwich** (p. 303), with its **National Maritime Museum** and other amusements. Part of the fun is getting there. In Greenwich you'll find many attractions, including the **Old Royal Observatory.** See "Greenwich," under "Attractions on the Outskirts," on p. 311.

Prince Frederick's Barge on display in the National Maritime Museum, Greenwich.

"Venus and Adonis" puppet show at the Little Angel Theatre.

○ **Royal London:** No kid wants to leave London without a visit to the **Tower of London** (p. 253). And, of course, children will want to see the **Changing of the Guard** (p. 242). For castles that evoke Disney, take them on a trip to **Windsor Castle** (p. 393) or **Hampton Court Palace** (p. 316).

○ **Playgrounds:** London brims with parks, nicknamed "green lungs," including **Regent's Park,** with its two boating

A lion at the London Zoo seems unperturbed by a young visitor.

lakes, one just for children. An afternoon in sprawling **Hampstead Heath** (see "Hampstead," under "Attractions on the Outskirts," on p. 308) can fill enjoyable hours, as can a stroll through **Kensington Gardens,** with its playgrounds. **Battersea Park** has a small children's zoo and adventure playground. For more information on **Regent's Park, Kensington Gardens,** and **Battersea Park,** see "Parks & Gardens," under "More Central London Attractions," on p. 299.

○ **Entertainment:** London has a number of theaters designed for children, notably **Little Angel Theatre,** which hosts regular visiting puppeteers. The minimum age is 3. See p. 319.

THE best THINGS TO DO FOR FREE (OR ALMOST)

o **Visit Museums:** London's greatest museums are now free. The world-class treasure troves where you can now roam without charge include the British Museum, National Gallery, National Portrait Gallery, Tate Britain, Tate Modern, Natural History Museum, Science Museum, Victoria and Albert Museum, Museum of London, and Sir John Soane's Museum. And don't forget the British Library, with its marvelous collection of literary gems. See chapter 7 for listings.

o **Watch the Changing of the Guard:** This Buckingham Palace event has more pomp and circumstance than any other royal ceremony on earth. See p. 242.

o **Explore Hampstead Heath:** Take the Tube north to Hampstead for the most delightful ramble in London, following in the footsteps of Keats and other luminaries. The heath's near-wilderness feel is a delicious contrast to London's other manicured parks. Drop in later for a pint at a local pub.

o **Take in a Spectacular City View:** Take the Tube to Tower Hill or Tower Gateway; then cross Tower Bridge. Wander along the South Bank of the mighty Thames at night and gaze upon London's historic landmarks and skyscrapers, floodlit in all their evening spectacle.

FROM LEFT: Summer picnic by the ponds in Hampstead Heath. Reading Room at the British Museum.

South Bank promenade.

A male and female barrister wearing wigs and gowns outside the High Courts.

- **Soak Up the Scene in Regent's Park:** Once the exclusive hunting grounds of royalty, it's now used by everyone from footballers to barefoot couples in summer. Regent's Park is home to the London Zoo, the Open Air Theatre's Shakespeare in the Park, the Prince Regent's original grand terraces, and Queen Mary's rose gardens. See p. 300.

- **Go to Court at the Old Bailey Public Gallery, Warwick Passage:** Britain's Central Criminal Court, or the "Old Bailey," was built on the foundations of the infamous Newgate Gaol. These courtrooms have seen it all, from Oscar Wilde to the Yorkshire Ripper (but never Jack). Robed and bewigged barristers and judges still administer justice with much formality and theatricality. See p. 279.

2

LONDON
IN DEPTH

NOTTING HILL GA

METRO

L ondon defined "swinging" in the '60s, and it's now rocking again, having become one of the most vibrant cities in the world. London's art, style, fashion, nightlife, and dining scenes are the stuff of tabloid headlines.

As the city gears up to host the 2012 Olympics, London changes its stripes as you move through each of its 32 boroughs. It is one of the most ethnically diverse cities in the world, with over 300 languages spoken. Its neighborhoods are eclectic: Mayfair is still a bastion of elegance, but once dilapidated neighborhoods such as Shoreditch are attracting the artistic elite and also becoming bustling after-dark diversions. The South Bank had experienced a cultural rebirth, and even once-dreary Brixton has recharged its batteries.

Today London is a place to enjoy life. With a land mass of 1,585 sq. km (612 sq. miles), 30% of which is outdoor parks, you'll never conquer London. The city is just too sprawling. By the time you take it all in, a borough will have applied new makeup to greet you anew. The energy of Londoners is inexhaustible, and so is their miraculous city.

LONDON TODAY

This giant, sprawling metropolis is one of the most intriguing cities on Earth. For about a century, one-quarter of the world was ruled from here. With every step you take, you come across some sign of the tremendous influence this city has had . . . and still wields today.

When the G-20 leaders met in 2009 for a summit on the world economy, London was their venue. Heads of government, including Barack Obama, flew in to discuss means of saving the battered world economy from collapse. The meeting of presidents, kings, and finance ministers will go down in history as the "London Summit." Like the rest of the world, London has experienced a downturn in its economy beginning in October of 2008. The Bank of England in February of 2009 reduced its base interest rate by half a percent, the lowest rate the bank has ever set since it was launched in 1694. Turmoil in the financial market has forced the Bank of England to lend £185 million to 32 banks. Retail sales fell as unemployment rose. However, the IMF has forecast that the British economy, over which London presides, will grow 2.1% in 2010.

Since 1189, London has had a Lord Mayor. The position is largely ceremonial. Beginning in 2000, the city has been presided over by an elected politician holding down the office of Mayor of London.

This officer presides over Greater London with its population of more than 7.5 million people, of which 1 out of 10 citizens is Indian, Bangladeshi, or Pakistani. Mix that with the cultures of Africa, the Caribbean, and Asia, and you have a "mixed bag" of people from all over the world, comprising today's Londoners. The citizens speak some 300 languages, and in a few years it is predicted that half of the population may no longer list themselves as Christian. The first Mayor of London, Ken Livingstone, served from 2000 to 2008. As a member of the Labour

PREVIOUS PAGE: **Commuter at Notting Hill Gate.**

Party, Livingstone dealt with the city's aging transportation infrastructure and even froze bus fares for 4 years. The new mayor reduced traffic congestion in central London by imposing a charge on cars coming into the area. Traffic fell by 20% within the zone that carried vehicular charges.

The mayor forged ahead as a "green" politician, taking significant steps to reduce pollution and other negative impacts on London's environment. He worked to reduce emissions of carbon dioxide by 20%. He also pursued a series of anti-racism policies, and presided over a city that saw a drop of 35% in racist attacks. He even issued an apology for London's historic role in the transatlantic slave trade.

In the 2008 election, Livingstone suffered one of the Labour Party's worst electoral defeats in 40 years, as the Conservative

Boris Johnson.

candidate, Boris Johnson, was swept into office, becoming the new mayor of London. An English politician and journalist, Johnson (born in 1964) was the former editor of *Spectator* magazine. Since taking office, he's become a controversial figure, and was accused of being "rude, arrogant, and disrespectful" for accepting the Olympic flag with one hand in his pocket at the 2008 Summer Olympics in Beijing. He broke tradition in 2008 by openly endorsing then-Senator Obama for the presidency of the United States. Before that, those in high political positions did not publicly comment on U.S. elections.

Critics claim London's mayor suffers from "foot-and-mouth disease," as he wanders into political incorrectness. Fairly or unfairly, he's been accused of

DATELINE

54 B.C.	Julius Caesar invades England.
A.D. 43	Romans conquer England.
410	Jutes, Angles, and Saxons form small kingdoms in England.
500–1066	Anglo-Saxon kingdoms fight off Viking warriors.
1066	William, duke of Normandy, invades England, defeats Harold II at the Battle of Hastings.
1154	Henry II, first of the Plantagenets, launches their rule (which lasts until 1399).
1215	King John signs the Magna Carta at Runnymede.
1337	Hundred Years' War between France and England begins.
1485	Battle of Bosworth Field ends the War of the Roses between the Houses of York and Lancaster; Henry VII launches the Tudor dynasty.
1534	Henry VIII brings the Reformation to England and dissolves the monasteries.

racism. Johnson claims he "loathes all forms of racism," but occasional racist remarks have not won him much appreciation in London's black communities.

Johnson's stated goals, yet to be achieved, include cutting crime by increasing police presence on public transport, removing a lot of government red tape, and ending the "waste and overspending" of his predecessor, Ken Livingstone. Johnson has praised Livingstone's contribution to London. Livingstone's comment on Johnson was short but not sweet: "A joke!"

LOOKING BACK AT LONDON

FROM MURKY BEGINNINGS TO ROMAN OCCUPATION   Britain was probably split off from the continent of Europe some 8 millennia ago by continental drift and other natural forces. The early inhabitants, the Iberians, were later to be identified with stories of fairies, brownies, and "little people." These are the people whose ingenuity and enterprise are believed to have created Stonehenge (p. 433), but despite that great and mysterious monument, little is known about them.

They were replaced by the iron-wielding Celts, whose massive invasions around 500 B.C. drove the Iberians back to the Scottish Highlands and Welsh mountains, where some of their descendants still live today.

In 54 B.C., Julius Caesar invaded England, but the Romans did not become established there until A.D. 43. They went as far as Caledonia (now Scotland), where they gave up, leaving that land to "the painted ones," or the warring Picts. The wall, built by Emperor Hadrian across the north of England, marked the northernmost reaches of the Roman Empire. During almost 4 centuries of occupation, the Romans built roads, villas, towns, walls, and fortresses; they farmed the land and introduced first their pagan religions, then Christianity. Agriculture and trade flourished.

FROM ANGLO-SAXON RULE TO THE NORMAN CONQUEST   When the Roman legions withdrew around A.D. 410, they left the country open to waves of

---

1558 The accession of Elizabeth I ushers in an era of exploration and a renaissance in science and learning.

1588 Spanish Armada defeated by England.

1603 James VI of Scotland becomes James I of England, thus uniting the crowns of England and Scotland.

1620 Pilgrims sail from Plymouth on the *Mayflower* to found a colony in the New World.

1629 Charles I dissolves Parliament, ruling alone.

1642–49 Civil War between Royalists and Parliamentarians; the Parliamentarians win.

1649 Charles I beheaded, and England is a republic.

1653 Oliver Cromwell becomes Lord Protector.

1660 Charles II restored to the throne with limited power.

1665–66 Great Plague and Great Fire decimate London.

1688 James II, a Catholic, is deposed, and William and Mary come to the throne, signing a bill of rights.

continues

invasions by Jutes, Angles, and Saxons, who established themselves in small kingdoms throughout the former Roman colony. From the 8th through the 11th century, the Anglo-Saxons contended with Danish raiders for control of the land.

By the time of the Norman Conquest, the Saxon kingdoms were united under an elected king, Edward the Confessor. His successor was to rule less than a year before the Norman invasion.

The date 1066 is familiar to every English schoolchild. It marked an epic event, the only successful military invasion of Britain in history, and one of England's great turning points: King Harold, the last Anglo-Saxon king, was defeated at the Battle of Hastings, and William of Normandy was crowned William I. To wander those ancient battlefields, visit Hastings and Battle.

One of William's first acts was to order a survey of the land he had conquered, assessing all property in the nation for tax purposes. This survey was called the *Domesday Book,* or "Book of Doom," as some pegged it. The resulting document was completed around 1086 and has been a fertile sourcebook for British historians ever since.

Norman rule had an enormous impact on English society. All high offices were held by Normans, and the Norman barons were given great grants of lands; they built Norman-style castles and strongholds throughout the country. French was the language of the court for centuries—few people realize that heroes such as Richard the Lionheart probably spoke little or no English.

FROM THE RULE OF HENRY II TO THE MAGNA CARTA   In 1154, Henry II, the first of the Plantagenets, was crowned (reigned 1154–89). This remarkable character in English history ruled a vast empire—not only most of Britain but Normandy, Anjou, Brittany, and Aquitaine in France.

Henry was a man of powerful physique, both charming and terrifying. He reformed the courts and introduced the system of common law, which

---

DATELINE continued

1727	George I, the first of the Hanoverians, assumes the throne.
1756–63	In the Seven Years' War, Britain wins Canada from France.
1775–83	Britain loses its American colonies.
1795–1815	The Napoleonic Wars lead, finally, to the Battle of Waterloo and the defeat of Napoleon.
1837	Queen Victoria begins her reign as Britain reaches the zenith of its empire.
1901	Victoria dies, and Edward VII becomes king.
1914–18	England enters World War I and emerges victorious on the Allied side.
1936	Edward VIII abdicates to marry an American divorcée.
1939–45	In World War II, Britain stands alone against Hitler from the fall of France in 1940 until America enters the war in 1941. Dunkirk is evacuated in 1940; bombs rattle London during the Blitz.
1945	Germany surrenders. Churchill is defeated; the Labour government introduces the welfare state and begins to dismantle the empire.

still operates in moderated form in England today and also influenced the American legal system. But Henry is best remembered for ordering the infamous murder of Thomas à Becket, Archbishop of Canterbury. Henry, at odds with his archbishop, exclaimed, "Who will rid me of this turbulent priest?" His knights, overhearing and taking him at his word, murdered Thomas in front of the high altar in Canterbury Cathedral.

Henry's wife, Eleanor of Aquitaine, the most famous woman of her time, was no less of a colorful character. She accompanied her first husband, Louis VII of France, on the Second Crusade, and it was rumored that she had a romantic affair at that time with the Saracen leader, Saladin. Domestic and political life did not run smoothly, however, and Henry and Eleanor and their sons were often at odds. The pair has been the subject of many plays and films, including *The Lion in Winter, Becket,* and T. S. Eliot's *Murder in the Cathedral.*

Two of their sons were crowned kings of England. Richard the Lionheart actually spent most of his life outside England, on crusades, or in France. John was forced by his nobles to sign the Magna Carta at Runnymede in 1215—another date well known to English schoolchildren.

The Magna Carta guaranteed that the king was subject to the rule of law and gave certain rights to the king's subjects, beginning a process that eventually led to the development of parliamentary democracy as it is known in Britain today. This process would have enormous influence on the American colonies many years later. The Magna Carta became known as the cornerstone of English liberties, though it only granted liberties to the barons. It took the rebellion of Simon de Montfort half a century later to introduce the notion that the boroughs and burghers should also have a voice and representation.

THE BLACK DEATH & THE WARS OF THE ROSES In 1348, half the population died as the Black Death ravaged England. By the end of the century, the population of Britain had fallen from 4 million to 2 million.

1952 Queen Elizabeth II ascends the throne.

1973 Britain joins the European Union.

1979 Margaret Thatcher becomes prime minister.

1982 Britain defeats Argentina in the Falklands War.

1990 Thatcher is ousted; John Major becomes prime minister.

1991 Britain fights with Allies to defeat Iraq.

1992 Royals jolted by fire at Windsor Castle and marital troubles of their two sons. Britain joins the European Single Market. Deep recession signals the end of the booming 1980s.

1994 England is linked to the Continent by rail via the Channel Tunnel, or Chunnel. Tony Blair elected Labour Party leader.

1996 The IRA breaks a 17-month cease-fire with a truck bomb at the Docklands that claims two lives. Charles and Di divorce. The government concedes a possible link between mad-cow disease and a fatal brain ailment afflicting humans; British beef imports face banishment globally.

continues

England also suffered in the Hundred Years' War, which went on intermittently for more than a century. By 1371, England had lost much of its land on French soil. Henry V, immortalized by Shakespeare, revived England's claims to France, and his victory at Agincourt was notable for making obsolete the forms of medieval chivalry and warfare.

After Henry's death in 1422, disputes among successors to the crown resulted in a long period of civil strife: the Wars of the Roses, between the Yorkists, who used a white rose as their symbol, and the Lancastrians with their red rose. The last Yorkist king was Richard III, who got bad press from Shakespeare, but who is defended to this day as a hero by the people of the city of York. Richard was defeated at Bosworth Field and the victory introduced England to the first Tudor, the shrewd and wily Henry VII.

THE TUDORS TAKE THE THRONE The Tudors were unlike the kings who had ruled before them. They introduced into England a strong central monarchy with far-reaching powers. The system worked well under the first three strong and capable Tudor monarchs, but it began to break down later when the Stuarts came to the throne.

Henry VIII is surely the most notorious Tudor. Imperious and flamboyant, a colossus among English royalty, he slammed shut the door on the Middle Ages and introduced the Renaissance to England. He is best known, of course, for his treatment of his six wives and the unfortunate fates that befell five of them.

Henry's first wife, Catherine of Aragon, failed to produce an heir. His ambitious mistress, Anne Boleyn, became pregnant, and he tried to annul his marriage, but the pope refused, and Catherine contested the action. Defying the power of Rome, Henry had his marriage with Catherine declared invalid and secretly married Anne Boleyn in 1533.

The events that followed had profound consequences and introduced the religious controversy that was to dominate English politics for the next

DATELINE continued

1997 London swings again. The Labour party ends 18 years of Conservative rule with a landslide election victory. The tragic death of Diana, Princess of Wales, prompts worldwide outpouring of grief.

1998 Prime Minister Tony Blair launches "New Britain"—young, stylish, and informal.

1999 England rushes toward the 21st century with the Millennium Dome at Greenwich.

2000 London presides over millennium celebration; gays allowed to serve openly in the military.

2002 Queen Elizabeth, the Queen Mother, dies at age 101.

2005 Suicide bomb attacks devastate London.

2007 Tony Blair steps down; Gordon Brown becomes prime minister.

2008 London suffers economic slowdown

2010 Labour Party continues its decline. Conservative David Cameron sweeps to victory and becomes prime minister in a coalition with his rivals, the Liberal Democrats.

Henry VIII.

4 centuries. Henry's break with the Roman Catholic Church and the formation of the Church of England, with himself as supreme head, was a turning point in English history. It led eventually to the Dissolution of the Monasteries, civil unrest, and much social dislocation. The confiscation of the Church's land and possessions brought untold wealth into the king's coffers, wealth that was distributed to a new aristocracy that supported the monarch. In one sweeping gesture, Henry destroyed the ecclesiastical culture of the Middle Ages. Among those executed for refusing to cooperate with Henry's changes was Sir Thomas More, humanist, international man of letters, and author of *Utopia*.

Anne Boleyn bore Henry a daughter, the future Elizabeth I, but failed to produce a male heir. She was brought to trial on a trumped-up charge of adultery and beheaded; in 1536, Henry married Jane Seymour, who died giving birth to Edward VI. For his next wife, he looked farther afield and chose Anne of Cleves from a flattering portrait, but she proved disappointing—he called her "The Great Flanders Mare." He divorced her the same year and next picked a pretty young woman from his court, Catherine Howard. She was also beheaded on a charge of adultery but, unlike Anne Boleyn, was probably guilty. Finally, he married an older woman, Catherine Parr, in 1543. She survived him.

Henry's heir, sickly Edward VI (reigned 1547–53), did not live long. He died of consumption—or, as rumor has it, overmedication. He was succeeded by his sister, Mary I (reigned 1553–58), and the trouble Henry had stirred up with the break with Rome came home to roost for the first time. Mary restored the Roman Catholic faith, and her persecution of the adherents of the Church of England earned her the name of "Bloody Mary." Some 300 Protestants were executed, many burned alive at the stake. She made an unpopular and unhappy marriage to Philip of Spain; despite her bloody reputation, her life was a sad one.

Elizabeth I (reigned 1558–1603) came next to the throne, ushering in an era of peace and prosperity, exploration, and a renaissance in science and learning. An entire age was named after her: the Elizabethan age. She was the last great and grand monarch to rule England, and her passion and magnetism were said to match her father's. Through her era marched Drake, Raleigh, Frobisher, Grenville, Shakespeare, Spenser, Byrd, and Hilliard. During her reign, she had to face the appalling precedent of ordering the execution of a fellow sovereign, Mary, Queen of Scots. Her diplomatic skills kept war at bay until 1588, when at the apogee of her reign, the Spanish Armada was defeated. She will be forever remembered as "Good Queen Bess."

FROM THE RESTORATION TO THE NAPOLEONIC WARS   The reign of Charles II was the beginning of a dreadful decade that saw London decimated by the Great Plague and destroyed by the Great Fire.

His successor, James II, attempted to return the country to Catholicism, an attempt that so frightened the powers that be that Catholics were for a long time deprived of their civil rights. James was deposed in the "Glorious Revolution" of 1688 and succeeded by his daughter Mary (1662–94) and William of Orange (1650–1702). (William of Orange was the grandson of Charles I, the tyrannical king whom Cromwell helped to depose.) This secured a Protestant succession that has continued to this day. These tolerant and levelheaded monarchs signed a bill of rights, establishing the principle that the monarch reigns not by divine right but by the will of Parliament. William outlived his wife, reigning until 1702.

Queen Anne then came to the throne, ruling from 1702 until her own death in 1714. She was the sister of Mary of Orange and was another daughter of James II. The last of the Stuarts, Anne marked her reign with the most significant event, the 1707 Act of Union with Scotland. She outlived all her children, leaving her throne without an heir.

Upon the death of Anne, England looked for a Protestant prince to succeed her and chose George of Hanover who reigned from 1714 to 1727. Though he spoke only German and spent as little time in England as possible, he was chosen because he was the great-grandson of James I. Beginning with this "distant cousin" to the throne, the reign of George I marked the beginning of the 174-year rule of the Hanoverians who preceded Victoria.

George I left the running of the government to the English politicians and created the office of prime minister. Under the Hanoverians, the powers of Parliament were extended, and the constitutional monarchy developed into what it is today.

The American colonies were lost under the Hanoverian George III, but other British possessions were expanded: Canada was won from the French in the Seven Years' War (1756–63), British control over India was affirmed, and Captain Cook claimed Australia and New Zealand for England. The British became embroiled in the Napoleonic Wars (1795–1815), achieving two of their greatest victories and acquiring two of their greatest heroes: Nelson at Trafalgar and Wellington at Waterloo.

THE INDUSTRIAL REVOLUTION & THE REIGN OF VICTORIA   The mid– to late 18th century saw the beginnings of the Industrial Revolution. This event changed the lives of the laboring class, created a wealthy middle class, and transformed England from a rural, agricultural society into an urban, industrial economy. England was now a world-class financial and military power. Male suffrage was extended, though women were to continue under a series of civil prohibitions for the rest of the century. To see the beginnings of the Industrial Revolution, visit Ironbridge.

Queen Victoria's reign (1837–1901) coincided with the height of the Industrial Revolution. When she ascended the throne, the monarchy as an institution was in considerable doubt, but her 64-year reign, the longest tenure in English history, was an incomparable success.

The Victorian era was shaped by the growing power of the bourgeoisie, the Queen and her consort's personal moral stance, and the perceived moral responsibilities of managing a vast empire. During this time, the first trade unions were formed, a public (state) school system was developed, and railroads were built.

Victoria never recovered from the death of her German husband, Albert. He died from typhoid fever in 1861, and the Queen never remarried. Though she had many children, she found them tiresome but was a pillar of family values nonetheless. One historian said her greatest asset was her relative ordinariness.

Middle-class values ruled Victorian England and were embodied by the Queen. The racy England of the past went underground. Our present-day view of England is still influenced by the attitudes of the Victorian era, and we tend to forget that English society in earlier centuries was famous for its rowdiness, sexual license, and spicy scandal.

Victoria's son Edward VII (reigned 1901–10) was a playboy who had waited too long in the wings. He is famous for mistresses, especially Lillie Langtry, and his love of elaborate dinners. You can actually spend the night at Langtry Manor Hotel in Bournemouth, which the king built for his favorite mistress. During his brief reign, he, too, had an era named after him: the Edwardian age. Under Edward, the country entered the 20th century at the height of its imperial power. At home, the advent of the motorcar and the telephone radically changed social life, and the women's suffrage movement began.

World War I marked the end of an era. It had been assumed that peace, progress, prosperity, empire, and even social improvement would continue indefinitely. World War I and the troubled decades of social unrest, political uncertainty, and the rise of Nazism and fascism put an end to these expectations.

THE WINDS OF WAR   World War II began in 1939, and soon thereafter Britain found a new and inspiring leader, Winston Churchill. Churchill led the nation during its "finest hour." You can visit the underground Cabinet War Rooms (p. 275) in London where he rode out parts of World War II. From the time the Germans took France, Britain stood alone against Hitler. The evacuation of Dunkirk in 1940, the Blitz of London, and the Battle of Britain were dark hours for the British people, and Churchill is remembered for urging them to hold on to their courage. Once the British forces were joined by their American allies, the tide finally turned, culminating in the D-day invasion of German-occupied Normandy. These bloody events are still remembered by many with pride, and with nostalgia for the era when Britain was still a great world power.

The years following World War II brought many changes to England. Britain began to lose its grip on an empire (India became independent in 1947), and the Labour government, which came into power in 1945, established the welfare state and brought profound social change to Britain.

QUEEN ELIZABETH RULES TO THE PRESENT DAY   Upon the death of the "wartime king," George VI, Elizabeth II ascended the throne in 1953. Her reign has seen the erosion of Britain's once-mighty industrial power, and, in recent years, a severe recession.

Political power has seesawed back and forth between the Conservative and Labour parties. Margaret Thatcher, who became prime minister in 1979,

Winston Churchill giving victory sign at rally.

seriously eroded the welfare state and was ambivalent toward the European Union. Her popularity soared during the successful Falklands War, when Britain seemed to recover some of its military glory for a brief time.

Though the Queen has remained steadfast and punctiliously has performed her ceremonial duties, rumors about the royal family abounded, and in 1992, which Queen Elizabeth labeled an *annus horribilis,* a devastating fire swept through Windsor Castle (p. 393), the marriages of several of her children crumbled, and the Queen agreed to pay taxes for the first time. Prince Charles and Princess Diana agreed to a separation, and there were ominous rumblings about the future of the House of Windsor. By 1994 and 1995, Britain's economy was improving after several glum years, but Conservative Prime Minister John Major, heir to Margaret Thatcher's legacy, was coming under increasing criticism.

The IRA, reputedly enraged at the slow pace of peace talks, relaunched its reign of terror across London in February 1996, planting a massive bomb that ripped through a building in London's Docklands, injuring more than 100 people and killing two. Shattered, too, was the 17-month cease-fire by the IRA, which brought hope that peace was at least possible. Another bomb went off in Manchester in June.

Headlines about the IRA bombing gave way to another big bomb: the end of the marriage of Princess Diana and Prince Charles. The Wedding of the Century had become the Divorce of the Century. The lurid tabloids had been right all along about this unhappy pair. But details of the $26-million divorce settlement didn't satisfy the curious: Scrutiny of Prince Charles's relationship with Camilla Parker-Bowles, as well as gossip about Princess Diana's love life, continued in the press.

In 1997, the political limelight now rested on the young Labour Leader Tony Blair. From his rock-star acquaintances to his "New Labour" rhetoric chock-full of pop-culture buzzwords, he was a stark contrast to the more staid Major. His media-savvy personality obviously registered with the British electorate. On May 1, 1997, the Labour Party ended 18 years of Conservative rule with a landslide election victory. At age 44, Blair became Britain's youngest prime minister in 185 years, following in the wake of the largest Labour triumph since Winston Churchill was swept out of office at the end of World War II.

Blair's election—which came just at the moment when London was being touted by the international press for its renaissance in art, music, fashion, and dining—had many British entrepreneurs poised and ready to take advantage of what they perceived as enthusiasm for new ideas and ventures. Comparisons to Harold Macmillan and his reign over the Swinging Sixties were inevitable, and insiders agreed that something was in the air.

However, events took a shocking turn in August 1997 when Princess Diana was killed—along with her companion, Harrods heir Dodi al-Fayed—in a high-speed car crash in Paris. The ancestral home of the late Princess at Althorp is open to the public.

"The People's Princess" still continued to dominate many headlines in 1998 with bizarre conspiracy theories about her death. But the royal family isn't the real force in Britain today.

Blair led Britain on a program of constitutional reform without parallel in the last century. Critics feared that Blair would one day preside over a "dis-united" Britain, with Scotland breaking away and Northern Ireland forming a self-government.

Of course, the future of the monarchy still remains a hot topic of discussion in Britain. There is little support for doing away with the monarchy in Britain today in spite of wide criticism of the royal family's behavior in the wake of Diana's death. Apparently, if polls are to be believed, some three-quarters of the British populace want the monarchy to continue. Prince Charles is even

[FunFACTS] IMPRESSIONS

You may call it dreary, heavy, stupid, dull, inhuman, vulgar at heart and tiresome in form . . . But for one who takes it as I take it, London is on the whole the most possible form of life.

—HENRY JAMES, 1869

Go where we may, rest where we will, Eternal London haunts us still.

—THOMAS MOORE, *Rhymes on the Road*, ca. 1820

By seeing London, I have seen as much of life as the world can show.

—SAMUEL JOHNSON in James Boswell's *Journal of a Tour to the Hebrides,* 1773

That tiresome dull place where all people under thirty find so much amusement.

—THOMAS GRAY, Letter to Norton Nicholls, 1770

It is a wonderful place, this London: a nation, not a city; with a population greater than some kingdoms, and districts as different as if they were under different governments and spoke different languages.

—BENJAMIN DISRAELI, *Lothair,* 1870

Queen Elizabeth stands with Prince Philip, Prince Charles, and princes William and Harry during the unveiling of the Princess Diana memorial fountain.

making a comeback with the British public and has appeared in public—to the delight of the paparazzi—with his longtime mistress, now wife, Camilla Parker-Bowles. The public has been fixated on the long relationship of Prince William and Kate Middleton, and the recent scandal involving Dutchess Sarah Ferguson, who attempted to sell access to her ex-husband Prince Edward.

The big news among royal watchers in Britain early in 2002 was the death of Princess Margaret at age 71, followed 7 weeks later by the death of Queen Mother Elizabeth at the age of 101. The most popular royal, the Queen "Mum" was a symbol of courage and dignity, especially during the tumultuous World War II years when London was under bombardment from Nazi Germany. The remains of the Queen Mother were laid to rest alongside her husband in the George VI Memorial Chapel at St. George's at Windsor Castle. The ashes of Princess Margaret were also interred with her parents in the same chapel.

At the dawn of the millennium, major social changes occurred in Britain. No sooner had the year 2000 begun than Britain announced a change of its code of conduct for the military, allowing openly gay men and women to serve in the armed forces. The action followed a European court ruling in the fall of 1999 that forbade Britain to discriminate against homosexuals. This change brings Britain in line with almost all other NATO countries, including France, Canada, and Germany. The United States remains at variance with the trend.

After promising beginnings, the 21st century got off to a bad start in Britain. In the wake of mad-cow disease flare-ups, the country was swept by a foot-and-mouth-disease epidemic that disrupted the country's agriculture and threatened one of the major sources of British livelihoods, its burgeoning tourist industry. After billions of pounds in tourism were lost, the panic has now subsided. The government has intervened to take whatever preventive measure it can.

Following the terrorist attacks on New York City and Washington, D.C., on September 11, 2001, Tony Blair and his government joined in a show of support for the United States, condemning the aerial bombardments and loss of life. Not only that, but the British also joined in the war in Afghanistan against the dreaded Taliban. However, by 2003 Blair's backing of George Bush's stance against President Saddam Hussein of Iraq brought his popularity to an all-time low.

Britain's involvement in Iraq remained an unpopular cause. In February of 2003, an estimated million protesters, the largest demonstration in the history of London, gathered to oppose military intervention in Iraq.

On an economic front, Britain still shies away from joining the so-called euro umbrella. In June of 2003, Tony Blair and Chancellor Gordon Brown declared that abandoning the British pound sterling in favor of the euro, prevailing on the Continent, was not right for the country at this time.

England has long endured terrorist attacks from the IRA, but was shaken on the morning of July 7, 2005, when four suicide bombs were detonated on public transportation in London, killing 52 victims. These bombs, though not the work of the IRA, were the deadliest attacks suffered by the city since the darkest days of World War II.

Following the 2005 election, Blair's popularity plummeted, and he resigned in May 2007. Succeeding him was Gordon Brown, his Chancellor of the Exchequer who became prime minister in June 2007. London joined other capitals of the world in experiencing an economic slump.

In 2008, England, like most of the rest of the world, experienced an economic slowdown, with the government at times having to intervene.

Brown's popularity with British voters continued to fall in 2009, when four of his cabinet ministers were forced to resign after using taxpayers' money to finance everything from X-rated movies to velvet-and-wool carpets.

In May 2010, David Cameron, the Conservative Party challenger, defeated Brown and became, at age 43, Britain's youngest prime minister in two centuries. Amazingly, he swept into power by forming a new coalition with a rival party, the Liberal Democrats. The coming together of the two parties is Britain's first coalition government since World War II. In an emotional farewell in front of 10 Downing Street, Brown brought an end to 13 years of rule by the Labour Party.

ART & ARCHITECTURE

You can read about London's art, but it's better, of course, to experience it first-hand in one of the city's great galleries, notably the National Gallery, Tate Britain, or Tate Modern.

No one artist, period, or museum defines England's art and architecture. You can see the country's art in medieval illuminated manuscripts, Thomas Gainsborough portraits, and Damien Hirst's pickled cows. Its architecture ranges from Roman walls and Norman castles to baroque St. Paul's Cathedral and towering postmodern skyscrapers. This section will help you make sense of it all.

Wilton Diptych.

Celtic & Medieval Art (ca. 9th C. B.C.–16th C. A.D.)

Celtic art survived the Roman conquest and medieval Christianity mainly as carved swirls and decorations on the "Celtic Crosses" peppering cemeteries. During the medieval period, colorful Celtic images and illustrations decorated the margins of Bibles and Gospels, giving the books their moniker **"illuminated manuscripts."**

The best example of this art is the **Wilton Diptych** at London's National Gallery, the first truly British painting. It was crafted in the late 1390s for King Richard II by an unknown artist. The **Lindisfarne Gospels** at London's British Library is one of the greatest illuminated manuscripts from the 7th century.

Renaissance & Baroque Art (16th–18th C.)

The **Renaissance** hit England late, but its museums contain many Old Master paintings from Italy and Germany. A few foreign Renaissance masters did come to work at the English courts and influenced some local artists, but significant Brits didn't emerge until the baroque.

The **baroque,** a more decorative version of the Renaissance approach, mixes compositional complexity and explosions of dynamic fury, movement, color, and figures with an exaggeration of light and dark, called chiaroscuro, and a kind of super-realism based on using peasants as models. The **rococo** period is baroque art gone awry, frothy and chaotic.

Significant British artists of this period include:

o **Joshua Reynolds (1723–92).** A fussy baroque painter and first president of the Royal Academy of Arts, Reynolds was a firm believer in a painter's duty to celebrate history. Reynolds spent much of his career casting his noble patrons as ancient gods in portrait compositions cribbed from Old Masters. Many of his works are in London's **National Gallery, Tate Britain, Wallace Collection,** and **Dulwich Picture Gallery;** Oxford's **Cathedral Hall;** Liverpool's **Walker Art Gallery;** and Birmingham's **Museum and Art Gallery.**

o **Thomas Gainsborough (1727–88).** Although he was a classical/baroque portraitist like his rival Reynolds, at least Gainsborough could be original. Too bad his tastes ran to rococo pastels, frothy feathered brushwork, and busy compositions. When not immortalizing noble patrons such as Jonathan Buttell (better known as "Blue Boy"), he painted a collection of landscapes just for himself. His works grace the **Victoria Art Gallery** in Bath (where he first came to fame), London's **National Gallery** and **National Portrait Gallery,** Cambridge's **Fitzwilliam Museum,** Oxford's **Cathedral Hall** and **Ashmolean Museum,** Liverpool's **Walker Art Gallery,** and Birmingham's **Museum and Art Gallery.**

Paintings by the Romantics (Late 18th to 19th C.)

The Romantics felt the Gothic Middle Ages was the place to be. They idealized the romantic tales of chivalry and had a deep respect for nature, human rights, and the nobility of peasantry.

Significant artists of this period include:

o **William Blake (1757–1827).** Romantic archetype Blake snubbed the stuffy Royal Academy of Arts to do his own engraving, prints, illustrations, poetry, and painting. His works were filled with melodrama, muscular figures, and sweeping lines. Judge for yourself at London's **Tate Britain** and Manchester's **Whitworth Art Gallery.**

o **John Constable (1776–1837).** Constable was a great British landscapist whose scenes (especially those of happy, agricultural peasants) got more idealized with each passing year—while his compositions and brushwork became freer. You'll find his best stuff in London's **National Gallery** and **Victoria and Albert Museum,** and in Liverpool's **Walker Art Gallery.**

o **J. M. W. Turner (1775–1851).** "The First Impressionist" was a prolific and multi-talented artist whose mood-laden, freely brushed watercolor landscapes influenced Monet. The River Thames and London, where he lived and died, were frequent subjects. London's **Tate Britain** displays the largest number of Turner's works.

o **Pre-Raphaelites (1848–70s).** This "brotherhood" of painters declared that art had gone all wrong with Italian Renaissance painter Raphael (1483–1520) and set about to emulate the Italian painters who preceded him. Their symbolically imbued, sweetly idealized, hyper-realistic work depicts scenes from Romantic poetry and Shakespeare as much as from the Bible. You can see pre-Raphaelite art at London's **Tate Britain,** Oxford's **Ashmolean Museum,** Liverpool's **Walker Art Gallery,** and Manchester's **City Art Gallery.**

20th-Century Art

Art of the last century often followed international schools or styles—no major ones truly originated in Britain—and artists tended to move in and out of styles over their careers.

o **Henry Moore (1898–1986).** A sculptor, Moore saw himself as a sort of reincarnation of Michelangelo. The Henry Moore Institute in Leeds, where he studied, preserves his drawings and sculpture. You'll also find his work at Cambridge's **Fitzwilliam Museum** and **Clare College.**

- o **Francis Bacon (1909–92).** A dark and brooding expressionist, Bacon presented man's foibles in formats, such as the triptych (a set of three panels, often hinged and used as an altarpiece), that were usually reserved for religious subjects. Find his works in London, Birmingham, and Manchester's **Whitworth Art Gallery.**

- o **David Hockney (b. 1937).** The closest thing to a British Andy Warhol, Hockney employs a less pop-arty style than the famous American—though Hockney does reference modern technologies and culture. His work resides in London and Liverpool.

- o **Damien Hirst (b. 1965).** Part of the YBAs (Young British Artists) movement developed in London in the '90s. The guy who pickles cows, Hirst is a celebrity/artist whose work sets out to shock. He's a winner of Britain's Turner Prize.

A Survey of Architecture

Originally, London was a collection of scattered villages and towns that were unified under the pressure of the Industrial Revolution in the 18th and 19th centuries. A little of the city's original flavor and feeling remains in such places as Whitechapel, Chelsea, Hammersmith, and Hampstead. During the 18th century, when the principles of "picturesque planning" were being evolved for a rapidly expanding London, planners consciously incorporated the best of the greens, riverbank terraces, and small-scale layouts of the original villages. These rural features (rigorously preserved by neighborhood residents today) are now completely enclosed by the bulk and congestion of urban London.

Norman Architecture (1066–1200)

The oldest surviving architectural style in London dates to when the 1066 Norman Conquest brought the Romanesque era to Britain, where it flourished as the **Norman** style.

Churches in this style were large, with a wide nave and aisles to accommodate the masses who came to hear Mass and worship at the altars of various saints. But to support the weight of all that masonry, the walls had to be thick and solid, giving Norman churches a dark, somber, mysterious, and often oppressive feeling.

The best example of Norman architecture is London's **White Tower** (1078). William the Conqueror's first building in Britain at the Tower of London, the White Tower remains one of Europe's finest examples of a Norman keep, and, as might be expected, the vital consideration of the builders at that time was defense. Naturally, as it was so long ago, not much remains from the Norman period.

The most significant Norman interior in London is found at the **Priory Church of St. Bartholomew the Great,** an Anglican Church at West Smithfield in the City of London. It once formed the chancel of a much larger monastic church from 1123. The facade, however, is from the late 19th century.

The church of St. Bartholomew with Rahere´s tomb.

Gothic Architecture (1150–1550)

The French Gothic style invaded England in the late 12th century, trading rounded arches for pointy ones—an engineering discovery that freed church architecture from the heavy, thick walls of Norman structures and allowed ceilings to soar, walls to thin, and windows to proliferate.

The Gothic proper in Britain can be divided into three overlapping periods or styles: **Early English** (1150–1300), **Decorated** (1250–1370), and **Perpendicular** (1350–1550).

Begun in 1245, Westminster Abbey is London's finest remaining medieval structure, its east arm representing the Early English style, and the nave constructed in the Perpendicular style. In the hammerbeam roof of Westminster Hall, timber roofing, one of the glories of English Gothic style, survives. London's Guildhall, on King Street in the City, has a bizarre facade from 1788 that is a mélange of 18th-century Gothic architectural ideas. Parts of the Great Hall, however, date from the 1400s.

Renaissance Architecture (1550–1650)

It wasn't until the Elizabethan era that the Brits turned to the Renaissance style sweeping the Continent. England's greatest **Renaissance** architect, **Inigo Jones** (1573–1652), brought back from his Italian travels a fevered imagination full of the exactingly classical theories of **Palladianism,** a style derived from the buildings and publications of **Andrea Palladio** (1508–80). However, most English architects at this time tempered the Renaissance style with a heavy dose of Gothic-like elements.

Jones applied his theories of Palladianism to such edifices as **Queen's House** (1616–18 and 1629–35) in Greenwich; the **Queen's Chapel** (1623–25) in St. James's Palace and the **Banqueting House** (1619–22) in Whitehall, both in London.

Guildhall.

Baroque Architecture (1650–1750)

England's greatest architect was **Christopher Wren** (1632–1723), a scientist and member of Parliament who got the job of rebuilding London after the Great Fire of 1666. He designed 53 replacement churches alone, plus the new **St. Paul's Cathedral,** which was the crowning achievement of English Baroque architecture and of Wren himself. Other proponents of Baroque architecture were **John Vanbrugh** (1664–1726) and his mentor and oft collaborator, **Nicholas Hawksmoor** (1661–1736), who sometimes worked in a more Palladian idiom. A leader of English Baroque, **Sir James Gibbs** (1682–1754) was a Scottish architect noted for bringing some of the more theatrical elements of Italian Baroque to London. The best examples of his work are in two churches—**St. Mary-le-Strand** and **St. Martin-in-the-Fields.**

Neoclassical & Greek Revival Architecture (1714–1837)

Many 18th-century architects cared little for the baroque period, and during the Georgian era (1714–1830) a restrained, simple **neoclassicism** reigned. This **Greek revival** style was practiced by architects such as **James "Athenian" Stuart** (1713–88), who wrote a book on antiquities after a trip to Greece, and the somewhat less strict **John Soane** (1773–1837).

On the south side of the Strand, **Somerset House** overlooks the Thames just east of Waterloo Bridge. The central block of this Neoclassical-style building, the **National Gallery** on Trafalgar Square was designed by William Wilkins in 1832, but only the facade opening onto the square remains essentially unchanged at this time.

The great **Robert Adam** (1728–1792), a Scotsman, was the towering Scottish architect of his era. He was the leader of the Classical revival in Britain from 1760 until his death. His younger brother, James (1732–1794), lived a bit in Robert's shadow, but achieved fame nonetheless.

Somerset House.

Victorian Gothic Revival Architecture (1750–1900)

The early Romantic Movement swept up others with rosy visions of the past. This imaginary and fairy-tale version of the Middle Ages led to such creative developments as the pre-Raphaelite painters (see "Paintings by the Romantics," earlier in this chapter) and Gothic revival architects, who really got a head of steam under their movement during the eclectic Victorian era.

Gothic "Revival" is a bit misleading, as its practitioners usually applied their favorite Gothic features at random rather than faithfully re-creating a whole structure.

The best example is the **Palace of Westminster (Houses of Parliament), London** (1835–52). Charles Barry (1795–1860) designed the wonderful British seat of government in a Gothic idiom that, more than most, sticks pretty faithfully to the old Perpendicular period's style. His clock tower, usually called "Big Ben" after its biggest bell, has become an icon of London itself.

Sir George Gilbert Scott (1811–1878), one of the most celebrated of all Victorian architects, designed the still controversial **Albert Memorial** in Hyde Park in 1864. He is also known for designing the redbrick construction, the **Midland Grand Hotel,** at London's **St. Pancras Station.** Part of his design, the St. Pancras railway station has been restored to its Victorian glory and remains known for its flamboyant Gothic Revival architecture, with elements of fantasy such as towering spires.

20th-Century Architecture

After the World War II Blitz, much of central London had to be rebuilt. Most of the new commercial buildings in the city held to a functional school of architecture aptly named Brutalism. It wasn't until the boom of the late 1970s and 1980s that **postmodern** architecture gave British architects a bold, new direction with a skyscraper motif.

Stellar examples of modern architecture include **Lloyd's Building** in London (1978–86), the masterpiece of Richard Rogers (b. 1933), and **Canary Wharf Tower** (1986), also in London, a complex designed by Cesar Pelli (b. 1926). Norman Foster designed London's new **City Hall** (2002) on the South Bank. The glass structure has an egglike shape, created to reduce surface area and improve energy efficiency.

One of the world's most controversial and most stunning skyscrapers is **30 St. Mary Axe**—nicknamed "the Gherkin"—twisting its way to the sky in the financial district of the City of London. Rising 40 floors, it opened in 2004. When you see its highly unorthodox shape, you know how the building got its nickname. In a survey of the world's largest firms of architects, the Gherkin was voted the most admired new building in the world in 2005.

Visitors take delight in walking the **London Millennium Footbridge,** a pedestrian-

The Gherkin.

only steel suspension bridge that links the City's financial district with Bankside on the south side of the river. The bridge lies between Southwark Bride and Blackfriars Bridge. It became "Wobbly Bridge" when it opened, because of its swaying motion, but it has since been stabilized. From the bridge, a magnificent view of St. Paul's emerges. The bridge has been hailed as "one of the architectural boondoggles of the turn of the century." Take the Tube to Mansion House (1986), also in London, a complex designed by Cesar Pelli (b. 1926).

LONDON IN POPULAR CULTURE: BOOKS, FILM, TV & MUSIC

BOOKS England has produced one of the world's greatest libraries of literature and drama—and not just William Shakespeare. Here is a mere preview of what's out there, at least enough to whet your appetite.

GENERAL & HISTORY Anthony Sampson's *The Changing Anatomy of Britain* (Random House) still gives great insight into the idiosyncrasies of English society; Winston Churchill's *History of the English-Speaking Peoples* (Dodd Mead) is a tour de force in four volumes; while *The Gathering Storm* (Houghton-Mifflin) captures Europe on the brink of World War II.

My Love Affair with England (Ballantine), by Susan Allan Toth, tells of England's "many-layered past" and includes such tidbits as why English marmalade tastes good only when consumed as part of a real (make that greasy) English breakfast.

Britons: Forging the Nation (1707–1837) (Yale University Press), by Linda Colley, took more than a decade to finish. Ms. Colley takes the reader from the date of the Act of Union (formally joining Scotland and Wales to England) to the succession of the adolescent Victoria to the British throne.

Children of the Sun (Basics Books), by Martin Green, portrays the "decadent" 1920s and the lives of such people as Randolph Churchill, Rupert Brooke, the Prince of Wales, and Christopher Isherwood.

In *A Writer's Britain* (Knopf), contemporary English author Margaret Drabble takes readers on a tour of the sacred and haunted literary landscapes of England, places that inspired Hardy, Woolf, Spenser, and Marvell.

Outsiders often paint more penetrating portraits than residents of any culture ever can. In England's case, many have expressed their views of the country at different periods. An early-18th-century portrait is provided by K. P. Moritz in *Journeys of a German in England in 1782* (Holt, Rinehart & Winston), about his travels from London to the Midlands. Nathaniel Hawthorne recorded his impressions in *Our Old Home* (1863), as did Ralph Waldo Emerson in *English Traits* (1856). For an ironic portrait of mid-19th-century Victorian British morals, manners, and society, seek out *Taine's Notes on England* (1872). Henry James's comments on England at the turn of the 20th century in *English Hours* are worth a read. In *A Passage to England* (St. Martin's Press), Nirad Chaudhuri analyzes Britain and the British in a delightful, humorous book—a process continued today by such authors as Salman Rushdie, V. S. Naipaul, and Paul Theroux. Among the interesting portraits written by natives are Cobbet's *Rural Rides* (1830), depicting early-19th-century England; *In Search of England* (Methuen) by H. V. Morton; and *English Journey* (Harper) by J. B. Priestley. For what's really going on behind that serene Suffolk village scene, read Ronald Blythe's *Akenfield: Portrait of an English Village* (Random House).

ART & ARCHITECTURE   For general reference, there's the huge multivolume *Oxford History of English Art* (Oxford University Press) and also the *Encyclopedia of British Art* (Thames Hudson), by David Bindman. *Painting in Britain 1530–1790* (Penguin), by Ellis Waterhouse, covers British art from the Tudor miniaturists to Gainsborough, Reynolds, and Hogarth, while *English Art, 1870–1940* (Oxford University Press), by Dennis Farr, covers the modern period.

On architecture, for sheer amusing, opinionated entertainment, try John Betjeman's *Ghastly Good Taste—the Rise and Fall of English Architecture* (St. Martin's Press). *A History of English Architecture* (Penguin), by Peter Kidson, Peter Murray, and Paul Thompson, covers the subject from Anglo-Saxon to modern times. Nikolaus Pevsner's *The Best Buildings of England: An Anthology* (Viking) and his *Outline of European Architecture* (Penguin) concentrate on the great periods of Tudor, Georgian, and Regency architecture. Mark Girouard has written several books on British architecture including *The Victorian Country House* (Country Life) and *Life in the English Country House* (Yale University Press), a fascinating social/architectural history from the Middle Ages to the 20th century, with handsome illustrations.

ABOUT LONDON   *London Perceived* (Hogarth), by novelist and literary critic V. S. Pritchett, is a witty portrait of the city's history, art, literature, and life. Virginia Woolf's *The London Scene: Five Essays* (Random House) brilliantly depicts the London of the 1930s. *In Search of London* (Methuen), by H. V.

Morton, is filled with anecdotal history and well worth reading, though written in the 1950s.

In *London: The Biography of a City* (Penguin), popular historian Christopher Hibbert paints a lively portrait. For some real 17th-century history, you can't beat the *Diary of Samuel Pepys* (written 1660–69); and for the flavor of the 18th century, try Daniel Defoe's *Tour Thro' London About the Year 1725* (Ayer).

Americans in London (William Morrow), by Brian N. Morton, is a street-by-street guide to clubs, homes, and favorite pubs of more than 250 illustrious Americans who made London a temporary home. *The Guide to Literary London* (Batsford), by George Williams, charts literary tours through London from Chelsea to Bloomsbury.

The Architect's Guide to London (Reed International), by Renzo Salvadori, documents 100 landmark buildings with photographs and maps. *Nairn's London* (Penguin), by Ian Nairn, is a stimulating discourse on London's buildings. Donald Olsen's *The City as a Work of Art: London, Paris, and Vienna* (Yale University Press) is a well-illustrated text tracing the evolution of these great cities. *London One: The Cities of London and Westminster* and *London Two: South* (Penguin) are works of love by well-known architectural writers Bridget Cherry and Nikolaus Pevsner. David Piper's *The Artist's London* (Oxford University Press) does what the title suggests—captures the city that artists have portrayed. In *Victorian and Edwardian London* (Batsford), John Betjeman expresses his great love of those eras and their great buildings. *Looking Up in London* (Wiley Academy), by Jane Peyton, offers colorful photos of some of London's architectural features.

FICTION & BIOGRAPHY   Among English writers are found some of the greatest exponents of mystery and suspense novels, from which a reader can get a good feel for English life both urban and rural. Agatha Christie, P. D. James, and Dorothy Sayers are a few of the familiar names, but the great London character is, of course, Sherlock Holmes, created by Arthur Conan Doyle. Any of these writers will give pleasure and insight to your London experience.

Evelyn Waugh.

England's literary heritage is so vast, it's hard to select particular titles, but here are a few favorites. Master storyteller Charles Dickens re-creates Victorian London in such books as *Oliver Twist, David Copperfield,* and his earlier satirical *Sketches by Boz.*

Edwardian London and the 1920s and '30s are captured wonderfully in any of Evelyn Waugh's social satires and comedies; any work from the Bloomsbury group will also prove enlightening, such as Virginia Woolf's *Mrs. Dalloway,* which peers beneath the surface of the London scene. For a portrait of wartime London, there's

Elizabeth Bowen's *The Heat of the Day;* for an American slant on England and London there's Henry James's *The Awkward Age.*

Among 18th-century figures, there's a great biography of Samuel Johnson by his friend James Boswell, whose *Life of Samuel Johnson* (Modern Library College Editions) was first published in 1791. Antonia Fraser has written several biographies of English monarchs and political figures, including Charles II and Oliver Cromwell. Her most recent is *The Wives of Henry VIII* (Knopf), telling the sad story of the six women foolish enough to marry the Tudor monarch.

Another great Tudor monarch, Elizabeth I, emerges in a fully rounded portrait: *The Virgin Queen, Elizabeth I, Genius of the Golden Age* (Addison-Wesley), by Christopher Hibbert.

Another historian, Anne Somerset, wrote *Elizabeth I* (St. Martin's Press), which was hailed by some critics as the most "readable and reliable" portrait of England's most revered monarch to have emerged since 1934.

No woman—or man, for that matter—had greater influence on London than did Queen Victoria during her long reign (1837–1901). Sarah Ferguson, the duchess of York (Prince Andrew's former wife, "Fergie"), along with Benita Stoney, a professional researcher, captures the era in *Victoria and Albert: A Family Life at Osborne House* (Prentice Hall). One reviewer said that Fergie writes about "England's 19th-century rulers not as historical figures but as a loving couple and caring parents."

Another point of view is projected in *Victoria: The Young Queen* (Blackwell), by Monica Charlot. This book has been praised for its "fresh information"; it traces the life of Victoria until the death of her husband, Prince Albert, in 1861. Queen Elizabeth II granted Charlot access to the Royal Archives.

In *Elizabeth II, Portrait of a Monarch* (St. Martin's Press), Douglas Keay drew on interviews with Prince Philip and Prince Charles.

Richard Ellman's *Oscar Wilde* (Knopf) also reveals such Victorian-era personalities as Lillie Langtry, Gilbert and Sullivan, and Henry James along the way. Quintessential English playwright Noël Coward and the London he inhabited, along with the likes of Nancy Mitford, Cecil Beaton, John Gielgud, Laurence Olivier, Vivien Leigh, Evelyn Waugh, and Rebecca West, are captured in Cole Lesley's *Remembered Laughter* (Knopf). *The Lives of John Lennon* (William Morrow), by Albert Goldman, traces the life of this most famous of all '60s musicians.

Dickens (Harper Perennial), by Peter Ackroyd, is a study of the painful life of the novelist. It's a massive volume, tracing everything from the reception of his first novel, *The Pickwick Papers,* to his scandalous desertion of his wife.

Other good reads include *Wild Spirit: The Story of Percy Bysshe Shelley* (Hodder & Stoughton), by Margaret Morley, a fictionalized biography of the poet. *Gertrude Jekyll* (Viking), by Sally Festing, paints a portrait of the woman called "the greatest artist in horticulture." *Anthony Trollope* (Knopf), by Victoria Glendinning, is a provocative portrait of the English novelist. *Lawrence and the Women: The Intimate Life of D. H. Lawrence* (HarperCollins), by Elaine Feinstein, examines involvements with the female friends and lovers of this passionately sensitive novelist.

CONTEMPORARY LITERATURE Born to a Jamaican mother and a British father, Zadie Smith is one of the most talented young authors in England. Published in 2000, her novel, *White Teeth* (Vintage), brought her early acclaim and a bestseller. She followed up with *The Autograph Man* (Vintage, 2002) and *On Beauty* (Penguin, 2005), both of which won prizes for fiction. Her writings are known for their deep penetration of the rainbow-hued races inhabiting Britain today.

Zadie Smith.

The writings of Nick Hornby have earned him the title European Ambassador of Goodness. An autobiographical work, his first book, *Fever Pitch,* was published in 1992 to both success and acclaim. In subsequent novels, he explores sports, music, "and aimless and obsessive personalities." Several of his works have been adapted for film, including *About a Boy,* starring Hugh Grant.

Influenced by the writing of his father, Sir Kingsley Amis, Martin Amis has written some of the best known works of English modern literature, especially *Money* in 1986 and *London Fields* in 1989. The *New York Times* called him the undisputed master of "the new unpleasantness." He explores the excesses of the capitalist world, plunging a sword into the heart of grotesque caricatures. His memoir, *Experience,* explores his relationship with his father, and his 2003 novel *Yellow Dog,* although praised by fans, was a disappointment in some quarters.

Monica Ali's novel *Brick Lane* (2003), named after the famous East London street, depicts the Bangladeshi community in London. Novelist Ian McEwan won the Booker Prize for his novel *Amsterdam* (1998), and his novel *Atonement* (2003) was made into wide-release film.

Hugh Grant in *Notting Hill*

FILM Some of the greatest stars came from Britain but made their mark in Hollywood, notably Charlie Chaplin, Cary Grant, and violet-eyed Elizabeth Taylor. In spite of its native-born talent, Hollywood even had to turn to Britain to cast Scarlett O'Hara in 1939's *Gone With the Wind.*

Great directors, including that master of suspense, Alfred Hitchcock, also moved from London to Hollywood for greater fame. Lord Laurence Olivier frequently was cast in Hollywood films, as were a long line of Shakespeare-trained actors who followed him—including Judi Dench, Maggie Smith, Jeremy Irons, and Ian McKellen.

Some British films seem to live on forever, as in the case of *A Hard Day's Night* (1964), depicting a "typical" day in the life of the Beatles, including many of their famous songs.

Tame by today's standards, *My Beautiful Laundrette* (1985) was a scandal upon its release. It not only brought Daniel Day-Lewis into international renown, but also dealt with homosexuality and interracial relationships.

Born in poverty in Northern Ireland, Kenneth Branagh has brought Shakespeare to mainstream audiences, notably with *Much Ado About Nothing* (1993) and a widely acclaimed *Hamlet* (1996). He's been nominated for four Oscars.

The happy household of Merchant and Ivory formed a director-producer team that turned out a series of films that achieved international fame, including *Maurice* (1987), *A Room with a View* (1985), and *Howards End* (1992).

Still a great favorite with British students, *Withnail & I* (1987) is set in London in 1969, featuring two unemployed and unemployable actors who go for an idyllic (yeah, right) holiday in the countryside.

Four Weddings and a Funeral (1994), a comedy-drama about a group of British friends, starred Hugh Grant giving his most charming performance to date. Writer Richard Curtis's other films, *Notting Hill* (1999) and *Love, Actually* (2003), are also set in London.

The ex-Mr. Madonna, Guy Ritchie, is a director-actor-producer-writer who achieved fame with such releases as *Lock, Stock & Two Smoking Barrels* (1998) and *Snatch* (2000), the latter starring Brad Pitt.

The latest film sensation from Britain is the award-winning *Atonement* (2007), in which a 13-year-old charges her older sister's lover with a crime he did not commit. The film starred Keira Knightley and James McAvoy in brilliant performances.

MUSIC The music performed at Elizabeth I's court, including compositions by Thomas Morley (ca. 1557–1602), has been recorded by the Deller Consort; one of their titles is *Now Is the Month of Maying: Madrigal Masterpieces*.

England's renaissance church music is best exemplified by English composer William Byrd (1543–1623); listen to his *Cantiones sacrae: 1575*, performed by the Choir of New College, Oxford, and recorded in the New College Chapel for London Records.

Henry Purcell's *Dido and Aeneas* is widely available in several performances. For an example of Purcell's orchestral music, listen to *The Virtuoso Trumpet*, performed by trumpeter Maurice André, who is accompanied by the Academy of St. Martin-in-the-Fields, Sir Neville Mariner conducting.

John Gay's *The Beggar's Opera*, first performed in 1728, is available in a recording by Britain's National Philharmonic Orchestra and the London Opera Chorus for Polygram Records.

The works of the beloved British team of Sir Arthur Sullivan (composer) and Sir W. S. Gilbert (librettist) are widely available. *The Mikado*, performed by the Pro Arte Orchestra and the Glyndebourne Festival Chorus, Sir Malcolm Sargent conducting, is available on CD.

The compositions of Sir Edward Elgar can be heard on the British Philharmonic Orchestra's recording of the *Pomp and Circumstance* marches, conducted by Andrew Davis.

Two fine recordings of England's modern master, Ralph Vaughan Williams, are his Symphony no. 3 ("Pastoral"), performed by the London Symphony Orchestra; and his *Sea Symphony,* performed by the London Symphony Orchestra and Chorus, with conductor André Previn.

Benjamin Britten's *Ceremony of Carols,* performed by the Choir of St. John's College, Cambridge, and his *Variations for a String Orchestra,* performed by the London Philharmonic Orchestra, with Roger Best on viola, are both fine examples of this preeminent British composer.

A recording of interest to music historians is *All Back Home,* which traces the musical themes of American and Australian folk and blues back to Irish, English, and Scottish roots. The recording includes tracks by Sinead O'Connor, the Everly Brothers, Kate Bush, Bob Dylan, Pete Seeger, the Waterboys, and Thin Lizzy.

Richard Thompson, who performs on *Amnesia,* has been

The Pigeon Detectives perform in London.

reviewed as one of the most unusual and iconoclastic of modern British folk performers. He uses guitar, mandolin, and hammered dulcimer in his melodies, and his lyrics showcase political and social satire as well as soulfully nostalgic ballads.

Of course, nothing in British musical history has equaled the popular enthusiasm that greeted the British revolution of the 1960s. Aided by improvements in acoustical technology and the changing sociology of Britain, music was suddenly the passionate interest of millions of youthful Brits, setting the scene for a cultural invasion of American shores that hadn't been seen since the 18th century.

It began with the Beatles, of course—John, Paul, George, and Ringo, who won the hearts of every schoolgirl in America when they appeared on the *Ed Sullivan Show* in February 1964. They seemed to be in the vanguard of every cultural and musical movement, and as the 1960s progressed, the Beatles didn't simply capitalize on their success or the musical styles that had originally made them popular. Their music evolved with the times and helped shape the cultural and political texture of their era.

The Beatles were only the first of many British bands who found fertile ground and a receptive audience overseas. They were soon followed by the Rolling Stones, the Who, and David Bowie.

Past Masters is a two-volume retrospective collection of Beatles music. Equally important is their milestone album *Sgt. Pepper's Lonely Hearts Club Band,* which was a musical watershed when it was released in 1967.

The Rolling Stones's *Flashpoint* is a textbook study of the spirit of rock and roll, with a guest performance by Eric Clapton on a track entitled "Little Red Rooster." Another Rolling Stone great is *Exile on Main Street.*

Britain-born icons David Bowie, Gary Glitter, the Sex Pistols, the Clash, and Faces were followed by the Neo Brit brats, Oasis. Along came Blur, Cast, and Ocean Colour Scene, acknowledging the influence of the Beatles and the Stones.

Prince Harry fell hard for the Spice Girls, an English pop group formed in 1994, but David Beckham made off with Posh.

The biggest name today is the Grammy Award–winning Amy Winehouse, mistress of soul, vocal jazz, R&B, and doo-wop. Her personal troubles and beehive hairstyle continue to make tabloid headlines. Female vocalists, such as Lily Allen, Katie Melua, Duffy, Adele, and Leona Lewis, have made a large surge in the past few years.

Way down the musical scale in pecking order are the London group the Rakes, shooting to fame in 2005 with post–punk rock music. From Leeds, the Pigeon Detectives with their indie rock were voted "the band most likely to leap to the main stage in 2007." From Brighton come the Kooks, both indie and pop rock, who released their second album, *Konk,* in the spring of 2008.

Bloc Party, another London group singing indie and rock and post-punk revival, made "Album of the Year" in 2005 with their debut, *Silent Alarm.* Yet another post-punk revival group, Franz Ferdinand originated in Glasgow as an indie favorite. The band's second album, *You Could Have It So Much Better,* topped the charts in the U.K. An alternative rock group, Coldplay, achieved worldwide fame for their hit single, "Yellow," followed by the success of their debut album, *Parachutes.*

EATING & DRINKING IN LONDON

The late British humorist George Mikes wrote that "the Continentals have good food; the English have good table manners." But the British no longer deserve their reputation for soggy cabbage and tasteless dishes. Contemporary London—and the country as a whole—boasts fine restaurants and sophisticated cuisine. If you want to see what Britain is eating today, just drop in at Harvey Nichol's Fifth Floor in London's Knightsbridge for its dazzling display of produce from all over the globe.

The buzzword for British cuisine is *magpie,* meaning borrowing ideas from global travels, taking them home, and improving on the original. A pundit once noted that to dine out in London today requires a knowledge of foreign languages. The inhabitants of London's immigrant communities have brought the food of their native lands. Indonesian restaurants are popping up more and more. Spanish tapas bars (or restaurants) are all the rage, and Japanese cuisine is going over big-time with the Londoners who flock to sushi places.

Be aware that many of the trendiest, most innovative restaurants are mind-blowingly expensive, especially in London. We've pointed out some innovative but affordable choices in this book, but if you're really trying to save on dining costs, you'll no doubt find yourself falling back on the traditional pub favorites (or better still, turning to an increasingly good selection of ethnic restaurants).

WHAT YOU'LL FIND ON THE MENU IN LONDON Of course, many who visit England want to sample the local cuisine. English cooking has been ridiculed for years (those long-boiled Brussels sprouts, for example), but the food is better than ever. The country has wonderful produce, from its Cotswold

Harvey Nichols's Fifth Floor Restaurant.

lamb to its Scottish salmon. You don't always have to dine foreign for a true gastronomic experience. English chefs, many of whom have trained on the Continent, have returned to put more flavor and flair in their native recipes.

On any pub menu, you're likely to encounter such dishes as the **Cornish pasty** (*past*-ee) and **shepherd's pie.** The first, traditionally made from Sunday-meal leftovers and taken by West Country fishermen for Monday lunch, consists of chopped potatoes, carrots, and onions mixed with seasoning and put into a pastry envelope. The second is a deep dish of chopped cooked beef mixed with onions and seasoning, covered with a layer of mashed potatoes and served hot. Another version is **cottage pie,** which is minced beef covered with potatoes and also served hot. Of course, these beef dishes are subject to availability. In addition to a pasty, Cornwall also

Cornish pasties.

gives us **Stargazy Pie**—a deep-dish fish pie with a crisp crust covering a creamy concoction of freshly caught herring and vegetables.

The most common pub meal, though, is the **ploughman's lunch,** traditional farm-worker's fare, consisting of a good chunk of local cheese, a hunk of homemade crusty white or brown bread, some butter, and a pickled onion or two, washed down with ale. You'll now find such variations as pâté and chutney occasionally replacing the onions and cheese. Or you might find **Lancashire hot pot,** a stew of mutton, potatoes, kidneys, and onions (sometimes carrots). This concoction was originally put into a deep dish and set on the edge of the stove to cook slowly while the workers spent the day at the local mill.

Among the best-known traditional English meals is **roast beef and Yorkshire pudding** (the pudding is made with a flour base and cooked under the roast, allowing the fat from the meat to drop onto it). The beef could easily be a large sirloin (rolled loin), which, so the story goes, was named by James I when he was a guest at Houghton Tower, Lancashire. "Arise, Sir Loin," he cried, as he knighted the leg of beef before him with his dagger. Another dish that makes use of a flour base is toad-in-the-hole, in which sausages are cooked in batter. Game, especially pheasant and grouse, is also a staple on British tables.

On any menu, you'll find **fresh seafood:** cod, haddock, herring, plaice, and Dover sole, the aristocrat of flatfish. Cod and haddock are used in making British **fish and chips** (chips are fried potatoes or thick french fries), which the true Briton covers with salt and vinegar. If you like **oysters,** try some of the famous Colchester variety. On the west coast, you'll find a not-to-be-missed delicacy: **Morecambe Bay shrimp.** Every region of England has its seafood specialties. In Ely, lying in the marshy fen district of East Anglia, it might be fenland eel pie with a twiggy seaweed as your green vegetable.

The **East End of London** has quite a few intriguing old dishes, among them tripe and onions. In winter, Dr. Johnson's favorite tavern, the Cheshire Cheese on Fleet Street, offers a beefsteak-kidney-mushroom-and-game pudding in a suet case; in summer, there's a pastry case. East Enders can still be seen on Sunday at the Jellied Eel stall by Petticoat Lane, eating eel, cockles (small clams), mussels, whelks, and winkles—all with a touch of vinegar.

The British call desserts **sweets,** though some people still refer to any dessert as **pudding. Trifle** is the most famous English dessert, consisting of sponge cake soaked in brandy or sherry, coated with fruit or jam, and topped with cream custard. A **fool,** such as gooseberry fool, is a light cream dessert whipped up from seasonal fruits. Regional sweets include the **northern flitting dumpling** (dates, walnuts, and syrup mixed with other ingredients and made into a pudding that is easily sliced and carried along when you're "flitting" from place to place). Similarly, **hasty pudding,** a Newcastle dish, is supposed to have been invented by people in a hurry to avoid the bailiff. It consists of stale bread, to which some dried fruit and milk are added before it is put into the oven.

Cheese is traditionally served after dessert as a savory. There are many regional cheeses, the best known being cheddar, a good, solid, mature cheese. Others are the semi-smooth Caerphilly, from a beautiful part of Wales, and Stilton, a blue-veined crumbly cheese that's often enjoyed with a glass of port.

Pear Raspberry trifle with amaretto biscuits and cream custard.

Britain Bans Public Smoking

Some 4 centuries ago King James I denounced tobacco, calling it "loathsome to the eye, hateful to the nose, harmful to the brain, and dangerous to the lungs." Britain has now heard his words, banning smoking in most public places, including restaurants and any pub that serves food. Anti-smoking activists welcomed the proposal but criticized the government for letting smokers continue lighting up in some pubs and bars. Still, it's a big step for a country that has long had a love-hate affair with tobacco. Britain's smoky pubs are at the heart of the nation's social life.

ENGLISH BREAKFASTS & AFTERNOON TEA London is famous for its enormous breakfast of bacon, eggs, grilled tomato, and fried bread. Some places have replaced this cholesterol festival with a continental breakfast, but you'll still find the traditional morning meal available.

Kipper, or smoked herring, is also a popular breakfast dish. The finest come from the Isle of Man, Whitby, or Loch Fyne, in Scotland. The herrings are split open, placed over oak chips, and slowly cooked to produce a nice pale-brown smoked fish.

Many people still enjoy afternoon tea, which may consist of a simple cup of tea or a formal tea that starts with tiny crustless sandwiches filled with cucumber or watercress and proceeds through scones, crumpets with jam or clotted cream, followed by cakes and tarts—all accompanied by a proper pot of tea. The tea at Brown's, in London, is quintessentially English, whereas the Ritz's tea is an elaborate affair, complete with orchestra and dancing.

In the country, tea shops abound, and in Devon, Cornwall, and the West Country you'll find the best cream teas; they consist of scones spread with jam and thick, clotted Devonshire cream. It's a delicious treat, indeed. People in Britain drink an average of four cups of tea a day, though many younger people prefer coffee.

WHAT TO WASH IT ALL DOWN WITH London pubs serve a variety of cocktails, but their stock-in-trade is beer: brown beer, or bitter; blond beer, or lager; and very dark beer, or stout. The standard English draft beer is much stronger than American beer and is served "with the chill off" because it doesn't taste good cold. Lager is always chilled, whereas stout can be served either way. Beer is always served straight from the tap, in two sizes: half-pint (8 oz.) and pint (16 oz.).

One of the most significant changes in English drinking habits has been the popularity of wine bars, and you will find many to try, including some that turn into discos late at night. Britain isn't known for its wine, though it does produce some medium-sweet fruity whites. Its cider, though, is famous—and mighty potent in contrast to the American variety.

Whisky (spelled without the *e*) refers to Scotch. Canadian and Irish whiskey (spelled with the *e*) are also available, but only the very best stocked bars have American bourbon and rye.

While you're in London, you may want to try the very English drink called **Pimm's,** a mixture developed by James Pimm, owner of a popular London oyster house in the 1840s. Though it can be consumed on the rocks, it's usually served as a Pimm's Cup—a drink that will have any number and variety of ingredients, depending on which part of the world (or empire) you're in. Here, just for fun, is a typical recipe: Take a very tall glass and fill it with ice. Add a thin slice of lemon (or orange), a cucumber spike (or a curl of cucumber rind), and 2 ounces of Pimm's liquor. Then finish with a splash of either lemon or club soda, 7-Up, or Tom Collins mix.

The English tend to drink everything at a warmer temperature than Americans are used to. So if you like ice in your soda, be sure to ask for lots of it, or you're likely to end up with a measly, quickly melting cube or two.

3

PLANNING YOUR TRIP TO LONDON

I f your documents are in order, flying into London is one of the most effortless undertakings in global travel. There are no shots to get, no particular safety precautions, no unusual aspects of planning a trip. With your passport, airline ticket, and enough money, you just go. In general, if you're not bringing any illegal item into the British Isles, customs officials are courteous and will speed you through entry into their country.

Of course, before you lift off the ground in your native country, you can do some advance preparation, as will be detailed in this chapter and in chapter 11. That could mean checking to see if your passport is up to date (or obtaining one if you don't already possess one), or taking care of your health needs before you go, including medication. In the case of London, you might want to make reservations at some highly acclaimed restaurants or even buy tickets in advance to hit plays in London's West End.

In the pages that follow, you'll find everything you need to know about the practicalities of planning your trip in advance: finding the best airfare, deciding when to go, figuring out British currency, and more.

VISITOR INFORMATION

Before you go, you can obtain general information from **Visit Britain** (www.visitbritain.com):

- In Australia: Level 2, 15 Blue St., North Sydney NSW 2060, Australia (© **1300/858-589**).
- In New Zealand: 17th Floor, 151 Queen St., Auckland, New Zealand, 105-652 (© **0800/700-741**).

For a full information package on London, write to **Visit London,** 2 More London Riverside, 6th Floor, Bermondsey SE1 2RR (© **020/7234-5800;** www.visitlondon.com).

The London Tourist Board's **London Visitor Centre,** 1 Lower Regent St., London SW1 (© **8701/566-366;** www.visitlondon.com; Tube: Piccadilly Circus), can help you with almost anything, from the most superficial to the most serious. Located within a 10-minute walk from Piccadilly Circus, it deals chiefly with procuring accommodations in all price categories through an on-site travel agency (www.lastminute.com), and you can also book transit on British Rail or with bus carriers throughout the U.K. There's a kiosk for procuring theater or group tour tickets, a book shop loaded with titles dealing with travel in the British Isles, a souvenir shop, and a staff that's pleasant, helpful, and friendly. It's open year-round Monday 9:30am to 6:30pm, Tuesday to Friday 9am to 6:30pm, and Sunday 9am to 5pm. Between October and May, Saturday hours are 10am to 4pm, and between June and September, Saturday hours are 9am to 5pm.

PREVIOUS PAGE: **Canary Wharf.**

A roughly equivalent organization that was conceived to help foreign visitors with their inquiries and confusion about London is the **London Information Centre,** at Leicester Square, W1 (📞 **020/7292-2333;** www.londoninformation centre.com; Tube: Leicester Sq.). The London Information Centre is a privately owned, commercially driven organization that may have a vested interest in steering you toward a particular venue.

An option that might help you navigate your way through the logistics of one of the world's biggest cities involves your call to 📞 **0800/LONDON** (566-366) for city information and to book sometimes discounted rates for London hotels, theaters, sightseeing tours, and airport transfers. A sales staff is available daily from 8am to midnight.

WHAT'S ON THE WEB? The most useful site was created by a very knowledgeable source, the British Tourist Authority itself, with U.S. visitors targeted. A wealth of information can be tapped at **www.visitbritain.com,** which lets you order brochures online, provides trip-planning hints, and even allows e-mail questions for prompt answers. All of Great Britain is covered.

Go to **www.baa.com** for a guide and terminal maps for Heathrow, Gatwick, and Stansted airports, including flight arrival times, duty-free shops, airport restaurants, and info on getting from the London airports to downtown London. Getting around London can be confusing, so you may want to visit **www.tfl.gov.uk** for up-to-the-minute info. For the latest on London's theater scene, consult **www.officiallondontheatre.co.uk.** For directions to specific places in London, consult **www.streetmap.co.uk**.

You may also wish to check out one of the following websites. **AOL members** can type in the keyword **"Britain"** and find a vibrant guide to the U.K. that gives you the skinny on arts, dining, nightlife, and more. To access the AOL London guide, type in the keyword "London."

MAPS Arriving in London, you should arm yourself with a detailed street map if you plan to do a lot of walking. London is a maze of narrow streets and "villages" within a vast city, and many addresses are obscure and hard to find.

Plot where you're going before setting out, or otherwise just walk and enjoy London as your own discovery. It's amazing what you'll come across if you have endless time. Otherwise, plot your course so you can cram as much into a precious day as your limited time will allow.

At **www.multimap.com,** you can access detailed street maps of the whole United Kingdom—just key in the location or even just the postal code, and a map of the area with the location circled will appear. For directions to specific places in London, consult **www.streetmap.co.uk**.

ENTRY REQUIREMENTS
Passports

To enter the United Kingdom, all U.S. citizens, Canadians, Australians, New Zealanders, and South Africans must have a passport valid through their length of stay. No visa is required. A passport will allow you to stay in the country for up to 6 months. The immigration officer will also want proof of your intention to return to your point of origin (usually a round-trip ticket) and of visible means of support while you're in Britain. If you're planning to fly from the United States or

Canada to the United Kingdom and then on to a country that requires a visa (India, for example), you should secure that visa before you arrive in Britain.

Your valid driver's license and at least 1 year of driving experience are required to drive personal or rented cars.

For information on how to get a passport, go to the "Passports" entry in chapter 11, "Fast Facts." The websites listed provide downloadable passport applications as well as the current fees for processing passport applications. For an up-to-date, country-by-country listing of passport requirements around the world, go to the "Foreign Entry Requirement" Web page of the U.S. Department of State at **www.travel.state.gov**.

Medical Requirements

Unless you're arriving from an area known to be suffering from an epidemic, particularly cholera or yellow fever, inoculations or vaccinations are not required for entry into the U.K.

For more information about health concerns, refer to "Health," later in this chapter.

Customs

WHAT YOU CAN BRING INTO BRITAIN

Non-E.U. nationals ages 18 and over can bring in, duty-free, 200 cigarettes, or 100 cigarillos, or 50 cigars, or 250 grams of smoking tobacco. This amount is doubled if you live outside Europe. You can also bring in 2 liters of wine and either 1 liter of alcohol more than 22% or 2 liters of wine less than 22%. In addition, you can bring in 60cc of perfume, or a quarter liter (250mL) of eau de toilette. Visitors 15 and older may also bring in other goods totaling £145; the allowance for those 14 and younger is £73. (Customs officials tend to be lenient about general merchandise, realizing the limits are unrealistically low.)

WHAT YOU CAN TAKE HOME FROM BRITAIN

U.S. CITIZENS For specifics on what you can bring back and the corresponding fees, download the invaluable free pamphlet *Know Before You Go* online at **www.cbp.gov**. Or contact the **U.S. Customs & Border Protection (CBP),** 1300 Pennsylvania Ave. NW, Washington, DC 20229 (✆ **877/ CBP-5511**), and request the pamphlet.

CANADIAN CITIZENS For a clear summary of Canadian rules, write for the booklet *I Declare,* issued by the **Canada Border Services Agency** (✆ **800/461-9999** in Canada, or 204/983-3500; www.cbsa-asfc.gc.ca).

U.K. CITIZENS For information, contact **HM Revenue & Customs** at ✆ **0845/010-9000** (from outside the U.K., 02920/501-261), or consult their website at **www.hmrc.gov.uk**.

AUSTRALIAN CITIZENS A helpful brochure available from Australian consulates or Customs offices is *Know Before You Go.* For more information, call the **Australian Customs Service** at ✆ **1300/363-263,** or log on to **www.customs.gov.au**.

NEW ZEALAND CITIZENS Most questions are answered in a free pamphlet available at New Zealand consulates and Customs offices: *New Zealand*

Customs Guide for Travellers, Notice no. 4. For more information, contact **New Zealand Customs Service,** The Customhouse, 17–21 Whitmore St., Box 2218, Wellington (☏ **04/473-6099** or 0800/428-786; **www. customs.govt.nz**).

WHEN TO GO

CLIMATE Yes, it rains, but you'll rarely get a true downpour—it's heaviest in November (2½ in. on average). British temperatures can range from 30° to 109°F (−1° to 43°C), but they rarely drop below 36°F (2°C) or go above 79°F (26°C). Evenings are cool, even in summer. Note that the British, who consider chilliness to be wholesome, like to keep the thermostats about 10°F (6°C) below the American comfort level. Hotels have central heating systems, which are usually kept just above the goose bump (in Britspeak, "goose pimple") margin.

London's Average Daytime Temperatures & Rainfall

	JAN	FEB	MAR	APR	MAY	JUNE	JULY	AUG	SEPT	OCT	NOV	DEC
TEMP. (°F)	39	39	45	48	55	61	61	64	59	52	46	43
TEMP. (°C)	4	4	7	9	13	16	16	18	15	11	8	6
RAINFALL (IN.)	2.1	1.6	1.5	1.5	1.8	1.8	2.2	2.3	1.9	2.2	2.5	1.9

CURRENT WEATHER CONDITIONS A good way to check conditions is at the Weather Channel's website: **www.weather.com**. In London, you can turn to BBC One–TV for the weather.

WHEN YOU'LL FIND BARGAINS In short, summer's warmer weather gives rise to the many outdoor music and theater festivals. But winter offers savings across the board and a chance to see Londoners going about their everyday lives largely unhindered by tourist invasions.

The cheapest time to travel to London is during the off season: from November 1 to December 12 and from December 25 to March 14. In the last few years, the airlines have offered irresistible fares during these periods. Remember that weekday flights are cheaper than weekend fares (often by 10% or more).

Rates generally increase between March 14 and June 5, then hit their peak in high travel seasons between June 6 and September 30 and December 13 and 24. July and August are also when most Britons take their holidays, so besides higher prices, you'll have to deal with crowds and limited availability of accommodations.

You can avoid crowds by planning trips for November or January through March. Sure, it may be rainy and cold—but London doesn't shut down when the tourists leave! In fact, the winter season includes some of London's best theater, opera, ballet, and classical music offerings and gives visitors a more honest view of local life. Additionally, many hotel prices drop by 20%, and cheaper accommodations offer weekly rates (unheard of during peak travel times). By arriving after the winter holidays, you can also take advantage of post-Christmas sales to buy your fill of woolens, china, crystal, silver, fashion clothing, handicrafts, and curios.

London Calendar of Events

For an exhaustive list of events beyond those listed here, check **http://events.frommers. com**, where you'll find a searchable, up-to-the-minute roster of what's happening in cities all over the world.

JANUARY

January Sales. Most shops offer good reductions at this time. Many sales start as early as late December to beat the post-Christmas slump.

London Parade. Bands, floats, and carriages contribute to the merriment as the parade wends its way from Parliament Square to Berkeley Square in Mayfair. January 1. Procession starts around noon.

London Boat Show, ExCel, Docklands, E16 XL. The largest boat show in Europe. Call ✆ **0870/906-3769** or visit www. londonboatshow.com for details. Mid-January.

Charles I Commemoration. This is the anniversary of the execution of King Charles I "in the name of freedom and democracy." Hundreds of cavaliers march through central London in 17th-century dress, and prayers are said at the Banqueting House in Whitehall. Free. Last Sunday in January.

FEBRUARY

Chinese New Year. The famous Lion Dancers appear in Soho. Free. Either late January or early February (based on the lunar calendar). Call ✆ **020/7851-6686** or see www.londonchinatown.org for schedule and event details.

Great Spitalfields Pancake Race, Old Spitalfields Market, Brushfield Street, E1. Teams of four run in relays, tossing pancakes. To join in, call ✆ **020/7375-0441,** fax 020/7375-0484, or see www. alternativearts.co.uk. At noon on Shrove Tuesday (last day before Lent).

MARCH

St. David's Day, Chelsea Barracks. A member of the Royal Family presents the Welsh Guards with the principality's national emblem, a leek. Call

✆ **020/7234-5800** for more information. March 1 (or the nearest Sun).

Oranges and Lemons Service, at St. Clement Danes, the Strand, WC2. As a reminder of the nursery rhyme "Bells of St. Clements," children are presented with the fruits during the church service, and the church bells ring out the rhyme (part of which is "Oranges and Lemons, say the bells of St. Clements") at 9am, noon, and 6pm; call ✆ **020/7242-8282** or see www.raf.mod.uk for information. Third week of March.

Westminster Abbey on Holy Week Tuesday. Call ✆ **020/7654-4900** or see www.westminster-abbey.org for information. Free. Late March or early April.

APRIL

Easter Parade. Floats, marching bands, and a full day of Easter Sunday activities enliven Battersea Park. Free. Easter Sunday.

Harness Horse Parade. A morning parade of heavy-working horses in superb gleaming brass harnesses and plumes, at Battersea Park. Call ✆ **017/3764-6132** or see www.lhhp. co.uk. Easter Monday.

Boat Race, Putney to Mortlake. Oxford and Cambridge universities' rowing teams ("eights") battle upstream with awesome power. Park yourself at one of the Thames-side pubs along the route to see the action. Early April; call ✆ **020/8971-9241** or see www.the boatrace.org.

Flora London Marathon. Thirty thousand competitors run from Greenwich Park to Buckingham Palace. Call ✆ **020/7902- 0200** or visit www.virginlondonmarathon. com for more information or to register for the marathon. Mid- to late April.

The Queen's Birthday. The Queen's birthday is celebrated with 21-gun salutes in Hyde Park and by troops in parade dress on Tower Hill at noon. April 21.

National Gardens Scheme. More than 3,000 private gardens in London are open to the public on set days, and tea is sometimes served. Pick up the NGS guidebook from most bookstores, or contact the National Gardens Scheme Charitable Trust, Hatchlands Park, East Clandon, Guildford, Surrey GU4 7RT (✆ **014/8321-1535;** fax 014/8321-1537; www.ngs.org.uk). Late April to early May.

MAY

Covent Garden May Fayre and Puppet Festival, Covent Garden. There is a procession of puppets, puppeteers, and a brass band at 10am; a service at St. Paul's on Bedford Street at 10:30am; then Punch and Judy shows until 6pm at the site where British diarist Pepys watched them in 1662. Everything is free. Call ✆ **020/7375-0441,** fax 020/7375-0484, or visit www.alternativearts.co.uk for details. Second Sunday in May.

The Royal Windsor Horse Show, Home Park, Windsor Castle, outside London. You might spot a royal at this multiday horse-racing and horse-showing event. Call ✆ **0871/230-5568** or visit www.royal-windsor-horse-show.co.uk for more details. Mid-May.

Glyndebourne Festival Opera Season, Sussex. The Glyndebourne Festival presents opera performances in a beautiful setting, with champagne picnics before and between the shows. Since the completion of the Glyndebourne opera house, one of the world's best, tickets are a bit easier to come by. Call ✆ **1273/815-000** or visit www. glyndebourne.com for a schedule and to purchase tickets. The season runs from mid-May to late August.

Chelsea Flower Show, Chelsea Royal Hospital. This show exhibits the best of British gardening, with displays of plants and flowers from all seasons. The show runs from 8am to 8pm. Tickets must be purchased in advance; they are available through the Royal Horticultural Society (www.rhs.org.uk). Call ✆ **0845/260-5000** for information. Four days in May.

JUNE

Trooping the Colour. This is the Queen's official birthday parade, a quintessential British event, with exquisite pageantry and pomp as she inspects her regiments and takes their salute, while they parade their colors before her at the Horse Guards Parade, Whitehall. Tickets for the parade and two reviews, held on preceding Saturdays, are allocated by ballot. Applicants must write between January 1 and the end of February, enclosing a self-addressed stamped envelope or International Reply Coupon to the Ticket Office, HQ Household Division, Horse Guards, Whitehall, London SW1X 6AA. Tickets are free. The ballot is held in mid-March, and only successful applicants are informed in April. Call ✆ **020/7414-2479** or see www.trooping-the-colour.co.uk for more details. Held on a day designated in June (not necessarily the Queen's actual birthday).

Vodafone Derby Stakes, Epsom Downs Racecourse, Epsom, Surrey. These famous horse races constitute the best-known event on the British horse-racing calendar. It's also a chance for men to wear top hats and women, including the Queen, to put on silly millinery creations. Visit www.epsomderby.co.uk for more information and to buy tickets, or call ✆ **0844/579-3004.** The "darby" (as it's pronounced) is run the first week in June.

Royal Academy's Summer Exhibition, Burlington House in Piccadilly Circus, W1. The Royal Academy, founded in 1768 with Sir Joshua Reynolds as president and Thomas Gainsborough as a member, has sponsored summer exhibitions of living painters' work for some 2 centuries. Visitors can browse and purchase art. Call ☎ **020/7300-8000** or visit www.royalacademy.org.uk for details. Early June to mid-August.

Royal Ascot Week, Ascot, Berkshire, SL5 7JN. Ascot Racecourse is open year-round for guided tours, events, exhibitions, and conferences. There are 25 race days throughout the year, with the feature race meetings being the Royal Meeting in June, Diamond Day in late July (p. 56), and the Ascot Festival in late September (p. 56). For Royal Ascot week, which runs from mid- to late June, everyone (including the Queen) shows up in his or her finery to watch 24 races over 4 days. For further information and tickets, call ☎ **0870/727-1234** or visit www.ascot.co.uk. Tickets should be purchased in advance. Mid- to late June.

Lawn Tennis Championships, Wimbledon, London. Ever since players took to the grass courts at Wimbledon in 1877, this tournament has attracted quite a crowd, and there's still an excited hush and a certain thrill at Centre Court. Savor the strawberries and cream that are part of the experience. Early bookings for the world's most famous tennis tournament are strongly advised. Acquiring tickets and overnight lodgings during the annual tennis competitions at Wimbledon can be difficult to arrange independently. Two outfits that book both hotel accommodations and tickets to the event include **Steve Furgal's International Tennis Tours,** 11305 Rancho Bernardo Rd., Ste. 108, San Diego, CA 92127 (☎ **800/258-3664** or 858/675-3555; www.tours4tennis.com); and **Championship Tennis Tours,** 13951 N. Scottsdale Rd., Ste. 133, Scottsdale, AZ 85254 (☎ **800/468-3664** or 480/429-7700; www.tennistours.com). Tickets for Centre and Number One courts are obtainable through a lottery. Write in from August to December to **All England Lawn Tennis Club,** P.O. Box 98, Church Road, Wimbledon, London SW19 5AE

(☎ **020/8944-1066;** www.wimbledon.org). Outside court tickets are available daily, but be prepared to wait in line. Late June to early July.

Shakespeare Under the Stars, Open Air Theatre, Inner Circle, Regent's Park, NW1 4NU. If you want to see *Macbeth, Hamlet,* or *Romeo and Juliet* (or any other Shakespeare play), our advice is to bring a blanket and a bottle of wine to watch the Bard's works performed at the Open Air Theatre. Performances are Monday through Saturday at 8pm, plus Wednesday, Thursday, and Saturday at 2:30pm. Call ☎ **0844/826-4242** or visit www.openairtheatre.org.uk for more information and to buy tickets. There is an on-site box office, but it's best to purchase tickets in advance. Previews begin in late June, and the season lasts until early September.

JULY

Kenwood Lakeside Concerts, north side of Hampstead Heath. Fireworks and laser shows enliven the excellent performances at these annual outdoor concerts on Hampstead Heath. Classical music drifts across the lake to the fans every Saturday and Sunday in summer from early July to late August. Call ☎ **0870/890-0146** or visit www.picnicconcerts.com for a schedule and information and to buy tickets. Tickets are popular, so buy yours in advance. Early July to late August.

Hampton Court Palace Flower Show, East Molesey, Surrey. This 5-day international flower show is eclipsing its sister show in Chelsea; here, you can purchase the exhibits on the last day. Call ☎ **0845/260-5000** or visit www.rhs.org.uk for exact dates and details. Early to mid-July.

The Proms, Royal Albert Hall. "The Proms"—the annual Henry Wood Promenade Concerts at Royal Albert Hall—attract music aficionados from around the world. Staged daily, the concerts were launched in 1895 and are the principal summer venue for the BBC Symphony Orchestra. Banners, balloons, and Union Jacks on parade contribute to the festive summer atmosphere. Visit www.bbc.co.uk/proms for more information and for tickets. Tickets should be bought in advance. Mid-July to mid-September.

Diamond Day, Ascot, Berkshire, SL5 7JN. This is one of the most important horse races on the international racing calendar. The major event of Ascot's summer season, it is a stylish sporting and social occasion where Brits appear in all their finery. More than £1 million in prize money is at stake at this horse race, and the world's greatest thoroughbreds are on display here. Tickets must be booked early. For more information, call ✆ **087/0727-1234** or visit www.ascot. co.uk. End of July.

AUGUST

Notting Hill Carnival, Ladbroke Grove, London. Notting Hill is the setting for one of the largest annual street festivals in Europe, attracting more than half a million people. There's live reggae and soul music, plus great Caribbean food. Call ✆ **020/7727-0072,** or see **www. nottinghillcarnival.biz** for information. Two days in late August.

SEPTEMBER

Open House, citywide. During this 2-day event, the public has access to buildings of architectural significance that are normally closed. Visit **www.londonopen house.org** or call ✆ **020/3006-7008** for a schedule and further information. Mid- to late September.

Raising of the Thames Barrier, Unity Way, SE18. Once a year, in September, a full test is done on the flood barrier. All 10 of the massive steel gates are raised out of the river for inspection, and you can get a close look at this miracle of modern engineering. Call ✆ **020/8854-8888** or visit www.greenwich.gov.uk for the exact date and time (usually a Sun near the end of Sept).

The Ascot Festival, Ascot, Berkshire, SL5 7JN. This is Britain's greatest horse-racing weekend, providing the grand finale to the summer season at Ascot. The 3-day "meeting" combines some of the most valuable racing of the year with other entertainment. A highlight of the festival is the £250,000 Watership Down Stud Sales race restricted to 2-year-old fillies. Other racing highlights include the Queen Elizabeth II Stakes, with the winning horse crowned champion miler in Europe. To book tickets, call ✆ **0870/727-1234** or visit www.ascot. co.uk. Last weekend in September.

OCTOBER

Judges Service, Westminster Abbey. The judiciary attends a service in Westminster Abbey to mark the opening of the law term. Afterward, in full regalia—wigs and all—they form a procession and walk to the House of Lords for their "Annual Breakfast." You'll have a great view of the procession from behind the Abbey. First Monday in October at 10am.

Opening of Parliament, House of Lords, Westminster. The monarch opens Parliament in the House of Lords by reading an official speech written by the prime minister's office. The Queen rides from Buckingham Palace to the House of Lords in a royal coach accompanied by the Yeoman of the Guard and the Household Cavalry. The Strangers' Gallery at the House of Lords is open to spectators on a first-come, first-served basis. Call ✆ **020/7219-3107** or visit www. parliament.uk. Late October to mid-November.

Quit Rents Ceremony, Royal Courts of Justice, WC2. The City Solicitor pays one of the Queen's officials a token rent for properties leased from the kingdom long, long ago. Two fagots of wood, a billhook, and a hatchet pay for land in Shropshire, and 61 nails and 6 horseshoes pay for a long-gone forge in the Strand. Call ✆ **020/7947-6000** or visit www.hmcourts-service.gov.uk. Tickets cost £10 or £5 for ages 13 and under. Early October.

Guy Fawkes Night. On the anniversary of the Gunpowder Plot, an attempt to blow up King James I and his Parliament, bonfires are lit and Guy Fawkes, the most famous conspirator, is burned in effigy. Today, it's more common to see elaborate fireworks displays. Free. Check *Time Out* for locations or visit www. gunpowder-plot.org. November 5.

Lord Mayor's Procession and Show, from the Guildhall to the Royal Courts of Justice, in the City of London. This annual event marks the inauguration of the new lord mayor of the City of London. The Queen must ask permission to enter the City—a right jealously guarded by London merchants during the 17th century. You can watch the procession from the street; the show is by invitation only. Call (©) **020/7222-4345** or visit www.lordmayorshow.org for more information. Second Saturday in November.

Caroling Under the Norwegian Christmas Tree. There's caroling most evenings beneath the tree in Trafalgar Square. December.

Harrods After-Christmas Sale, Knightsbridge. Call (©) **020/7730-1234** or visit www.harrods.com for dates. Truly voracious shoppers camp overnight outside the store so that they have first pickings. Late December.

Watch Night, St. Paul's Cathedral. A lovely New Year's Eve service takes place at 11:30pm. Call (©) **020/7246-8357** or visit www.stpauls.co.uk for information. December 31.

GETTING THERE & GETTING AROUND

By Plane

The major airport for arrivals from North America is **Heathrow** (LHR) outside London. This is the hub of most airlines, including British Airways and American carriers, and has the best transportation links to London. **Gatwick** (LGW) is the second major airport outside London, but it is much farther from the heart of the city, requiring longer and often more expensive hauls into the city.

Chances are you will not land at London's minor airports, certainly not if you're making a transatlantic crossing; however, you might land at one of these airports if you're winging in from the Continent. They include **Stansted** (STN), **London City** (LCY), **London Luton** (LTN), and **London Southend** (SEN).

For a full list of airlines serving London, refer to chapter 11.

THE CARRIERS

FROM THE U.S. **British Airways** (© 800/247-9297; www.britishairways. com) offers flights from 19 U.S. cities to Heathrow and Gatwick airports, as well as many others to Manchester. Nearly every flight is nonstop. With more add-on options than any other airline, British Airways can make a visit to Britain cheaper than you may have expected. Ask about packages that include both airfare and discounted hotel accommodations in Britain.

Known for consistently offering excellent fares, **Virgin Atlantic Airways** (© 800/821-5438; www.virgin-atlantic.com) flies daily to either Heathrow or Gatwick from Boston, Newark, New York's JFK, Los Angeles, San Francisco, Washington's Dulles, Miami, Orlando, and Las Vegas.

American Airlines (☎ 800/433-7300; www.aa.com) offers daily flights to Heathrow from half a dozen U.S. gateways—New York's JFK, Chicago, Boston, Miami, Los Angeles, and Dallas.

Depending on the day and season, **Delta Air Lines** (☎ 800/221-1212; www.delta.com) runs either one or two daily nonstop flights between Atlanta and Gatwick. Delta also offers nonstop daily service from Cincinnati.

Northwest Airlines (☎ 800/225-2525 or 800/447-4747; www.nwa.com) flies nonstop from Minneapolis and Detroit to Gatwick.

Continental Airlines (☎ 800/231-0856; www.continental.com) has daily flights to London from Cleveland, Houston, Newark, Orlando, and San Francisco.

United Airlines (☎ 800/864-8331; www.united.com) flies nonstop from New York's JFK and Chicago to Heathrow two or three times daily, depending on the season. United also offers nonstop service from Dulles Airport, near Washington, D.C.; Newark; Los Angeles; and San Francisco.

FROM CANADA Air Canada (☎ 888/247-2262; www.aircanada.com) flies daily to London's Heathrow nonstop from Vancouver, Montreal, and Toronto. There are also frequent direct flights from Calgary, Ottawa, and St. John's. **British Airways** (☎ 800/247-9297) has direct flights from Toronto, Montreal, and Vancouver.

FROM AUSTRALIA British Airways (☎ 1300/767-177) has flights to London from Sydney, Melbourne, Perth, and Brisbane. **Qantas** (☎ 612/131313; www.qantas.com) offers flights from Australia to London's Heathrow. Direct flights depart from Sydney and Melbourne. Some have the bonus of free stopovers in Bangkok or Singapore.

FROM NEW ZEALAND Air New Zealand (☎ 800/262-1234 in the U.S., or 0800/737-000 in New Zealand; www.airnewzealand.co.nz) has direct flights to London from Auckland. These flights depart daily.

FROM IRELAND Short flights from Dublin to London are available through **British Airways** (☎ 800/247-9297), with four flights daily into London's Gatwick airport, and **Aer Lingus** (☎ 800/IRISH-AIR [47472-247]; www.aerlingus.com), which flies into Heathrow. Short flights from Dublin to London are also available through **Ryan Air** (☎ 353-1/812-1676; www.ryanair.com) and **British Midland** (☎ 0870/607-0555; www.flybmi.com).

GETTING THROUGH THE AIRPORT

With the federalization of airport security, security procedures at U.S. airports are more stable and consistent than ever. Generally, you'll be fine if you arrive at the airport **1 hour** before a domestic flight and **2 hours** before an international flight; if you show up late, tell an airline employee and he or she will probably whisk you to the front of the line.

Bring a **current** passport. Keep your ID at the ready to show at check-in, the security checkpoint, and sometimes even the gate. (Children younger than 18 do not need government-issued photo IDs for domestic flights, but they do for international flights to most countries.)

TSA phased out **gate check-in** at all U.S. airports, and **e-tickets** have made paper tickets nearly obsolete. Passengers with e-tickets can beat the ticket-counter lines by using airport **electronic kiosks** or even **online check-in** from

Because of increased security measures, Transportation Security Administration has made changes to the prohibited items list. All liquids and gels—including shampoo, toothpaste, perfume, hair gel, suntan lotion, and all other items with similar consistency—larger than 3 oz. **are prohibited** from carry-on baggage and the security checkpoint. Pack these items in your checked baggage. All items that are 3 oz. or smaller must be packed together in a clear plastic bag, for easy viewing. Carrying liquids of any sort to the screening checkpoint may cause you delays and will result in the item being confiscated if it's not the proper size.

With the ever-changing security measures, we recommend that you check the **Transportation Security Administration**'s website, **www.tsa.gov**, as near to your departure date as possible to make sure that no other restrictions have been imposed.

your home computer. Online check-in involves logging on to your airline's website, accessing your reservation, and printing out your boarding pass—and the airline may even offer you bonus miles to do so. If you're using a kiosk at the airport, bring the credit card with which you booked the ticket, or bring your frequent-flier card. Print out your boarding pass from the kiosk and simply proceed to the security checkpoint with your pass and a photo ID. If you're checking bags or looking to snag an exit-row seat, you will be able to do so using most airline kiosks. **Curbside check-in** is also a good way to avoid lines, although a few airlines still ban curbside check-in; call before you go.

If you have trouble standing for long periods of time, tell an airline employee; the airline will provide a wheelchair. Speed up security by **not wearing metal objects** such as big belt buckles. If you've got metallic body parts, a note from your doctor can prevent a long chat with the security screeners. Keep in mind that only **ticketed passengers** are allowed past security, except for folks escorting passengers with limited mobility or children.

Federalization has stabilized **what you can carry on** and **what you can't.** The general rule is that sharp things are out. See the "Airport Security Measures" box below for information on carrying liquids on board. Bring food in your carry-on rather than checking it, as explosive-detection machines used on checked luggage have been known to mistake food (especially chocolate, for some reason) for bombs. Travelers in the U.S. are allowed one carry-on bag, plus a "personal item" such as a purse, briefcase, or laptop bag. Carry-on hoarders can stuff all sorts of things into a laptop bag; as long as it has a laptop in it, it's still considered a personal item. The Transportation Security Administration (TSA) has issued a list of restricted items; check its website (www.tsa.gov) for details.

Airport screeners may decide that your checked luggage needs to be searched by hand. You can now purchase luggage locks that allow screeners to open and relock a checked bag if hand-searching is necessary. Look for Travel Sentry certified locks at luggage or travel shops and Brookstone stores (you can buy them online at www.brookstone.com). These locks, approved by the TSA, can be opened by luggage inspectors with a special code or key. For more information on the locks, visit www.travelsentry.org. If you use something other than TSA-approved locks, your lock will be cut off your suitcase if a TSA agent needs to hand-search your luggage.

By Car from Continental Europe

If you plan to transport a rented car between London and France, check in advance with the car-rental company about license and insurance requirements and additional drop-off charges before you begin.

The English Channel is crisscrossed with "drive-on, drive-off" car-ferry services, with many operating from Boulogne and Calais in France. From either of those ports, Sealink ferries (www.ferrysmart.co.uk) will carry you; your luggage; and, if you like, your car. The most popular point of arrival along the English coast is Folkestone.

Taking a car beneath the Channel is more complicated and more expensive. Since the Channel Tunnel's opening (commonly called the "Chunnel"), most passengers have opted to ride the train alone, without being accompanied by their car. The Eurostar trains, discussed below, carry passengers only; **Eurotunnel** trains carry freight cars, trucks, and passenger cars.

The cost of moving a car on Eurotunnel varies according to the season and day of the week. Frankly, it's a lot cheaper to transport your car across by conventional ferryboat, but if you insist, here's what you'll need to know: You'll negotiate both British and French Customs as part of one combined process, usually on the English side of the Channel. You can remain within your vehicle even after you drive it onto a flatbed railway car during the 35-minute crossing. (For 19 min. of this crossing, you'll actually be underwater; if you want, you can leave the confines of your car and ride within a brightly lit, air-conditioned passenger car.) When the trip is over, you simply drive off the flatbed railway car and toward your destination. Total travel time between the French and English highway system is about 1 hour. As a means of speeding the flow of perishable goods across the Channel, the car and truck service usually operates 24 hours a day, at intervals that vary from every 15 minutes to once an hour, depending on the time of day. Neither BritRail nor any of the agencies dealing with reservations for passenger trains through the Chunnel will reserve space for your car in advance, and considering the frequency of the traffic on the Chunnel, they're usually not necessary. For information about Eurotunnel car-rail service after you reach England, call © **0844/335-3535,** or go online to **www.eurotunnel.com**.

Duty-free stores, restaurants, and service stations are available to travelers on both sides of the Channel. A bilingual staff is on hand to assist travelers at both the British and French terminals.

By Train from Continental Europe

Britain's isolation from the rest of Europe led to the development of an independent railway network with different rules and regulations from those observed on the Continent. That's all changing now, but one big difference that may affect you still remains: If you're traveling to Britain from the Continent, *your Eurailpass will not be valid when you get there.*

In 1994, Queen Elizabeth of England and President François Mitterrand of France officially opened the Channel Tunnel, or Chunnel, and the Eurostar express passenger train began twice-daily service between London and both Paris and Brussels. In 2003, the completion of a new section of high-speed rail in England, the **Channel Tunnel Rail Link,** shaved 20 minutes off the trip between London and Paris, reducing it to just 2 hours and 35 minutes (or 2 hr., 20 min. to Brussels). This extension allows Eurostar trains to go at the rate of 482kmph

(300 mph). The multibillion-pound tunnel, one of the great engineering feats of all time, is the first link between Britain and the Continent since the Ice Age.

So if you're coming to London from say, Rome, your Eurailpass will get you as far as the Chunnel. At that point, you can cross the English Channel aboard the Eurostar, and you'll receive a discount on your ticket. Once in England, you must use a separate BritRail pass or purchase a direct ticket to continue on to your destination.

Rail Europe (© 888/382-7245; www.raileurope.com) sells direct-service tickets on the Eurostar between Paris or Brussels and London. A one-way fare between Paris and London costs £297 to £549 in first class and £244 to £378 in second class. However, cheaper and restricted fares during off-peak travel times can range from £195 to £338 in first class to £122 to £248 in second class.

In London, make reservations for **Eurostar** by calling © 08705/186-186; and in the United States, it's © 800/EUROSTAR (387-67827; www.eurostar. com). Eurostar trains arrive and depart from London's Waterloo Station, Paris's Gare du Nord, and Brussels's Central Station.

By Ferry/Hovercraft from Continental Europe

P&O Ferries (© 08716/645-645; www.poferries.com) operates car and passenger ferries between Dover and Calais, France (25 sailings a day; 75 min. each way).

Getting Around
ARRIVING BY PLANE
London Heathrow Airport

West of London in Hounslow, Heathrow (© 0870/000-0123; www.baa.com) is one of the world's busiest airports. It has four terminals, each relatively self-contained. Terminal 4, the most modern, handles the long-haul and transatlantic operations of British Airways. Most transatlantic flights on U.S.-based airlines arrive at Terminal 3. Terminals 1 and 2 receive the intra-European flights of several European airlines.

GETTING TO CENTRAL LONDON FROM HEATHROW   It takes 45 to 50 minutes by the Underground (Tube) and costs £4 to make the 24km (15-mile) trip from Heathrow to the center of London. A taxi is likely to cost from £55 to £85. For more information about Tube or bus connections, call © 020/7222-1234 or go to **www.tfl.gov.uk**.

The British Airport Authority now operates **Heathrow Express** (© 0845/600-1515; www.heathrowexpress.com), a 161kmph (100-mph) train service running every 15 minutes daily from 5:10am until 11:40pm between Heathrow and Paddington Station in the center of London. Trips cost £7 to £23 each way in economy class, rising to £26 in first class. Children younger than 15 pay £8.20 in economy, £13 in first class. You can save £6.50 by booking online or by phone. The trip takes 15 minutes each way between Paddington and Terminals 1, 2, and 3; 23 minutes from Terminal 4. The trains have special areas for wheelchairs. From Paddington, passengers can connect to other trains and the Underground, or you can hail a taxi. You can buy tickets on the train with a £6.50 surcharge, or at self-service machines for £18 at Heathrow Airport. (Tickets are also available from travel agents.)

Gatwick Airport

While Heathrow still dominates, more and more scheduled flights land at relatively remote **Gatwick** (℡ 0870/574-7777; www.baa.co.uk), located some 40km (25 miles) south of London in West Sussex but only a 30-minute train ride away.

GETTING TO CENTRAL LONDON FROM GATWICK   From Gatwick, the fastest way to get to London is via the **Gatwick Express trains** (℡ 0845/850-1530; www.gatwickexpress.com), which depart approximately every 15 minutes, daily between 4:35am and 1:35am. The round-trip fare between Gatwick and Victoria Rail Station is £29 for adults and £14 for children age 10 and younger. (One-way fares cost £17 for adults and £8.45 for children.) The travel time each way is 30 minutes Monday to Saturday, and 35 minutes on Sunday.

A **taxi** from Gatwick Airport to central London costs from £95. Fares vary according to a printed price list that defines the fare from Gatwick to whichever neighborhood of London you're traveling to. Meters in this case don't apply because Gatwick lies outside the Metropolitan Police District. For further transportation information pertaining to either Gatwick or any other location within London, call ℡ 020/7222-1234.

London City Airport

Positioned 5km (3 miles) east of the bustling business community of Canary Wharf, the Docklands, and the ExCel convention center, the viability of **London City Airport** (℡ 020/7646-0088; www.londoncityairport.com) has rendered commutes from other parts of Britain and parts of Continental Europe faster and more convenient than equivalent flights into either Heathrow, Gatwick, or Stansted. Accepting flights from 23 cities throughout western Europe and Scandinavia, it services airlines that include British Airways, Cirrus Airlines, Luxair, KLM, CityJet, OLT, Lufthansa, Scot Airways, Air France, Eastern Airways, SAS, Darwin Airlines, Swiss International Airlines, and VLM.

Trains on the Docklands Light Railway make runs at 10-minute intervals from City Airport to the Underground station known as "Bank" (short for "Bank of England") in the heart of London's financial district, which is known locally as "the City." One-way passage costs £4 for adults and £1 for children younger than 16.

As a final means of getting from the airport to central London, consider boarding London Transport's bus no. 473 or 474, which makes frequent runs between the airport and various points in East London, including the Plaistow Tube (Underground) station. From here, you can make connections to virtually any other point in London.

Getting from One London Airport to the Other

Some visitors will need to transfer from one airport to the other. One bus company offers these transfers. **National Express** (℡ 0871/781-81-81; www.nationalexpress. com) buses leave from both terminals at Gatwick and from Terminals 1, 3, and 4 at Heathrow. Trip time is about an hour, with a one-way fare costing £20.

London Stansted Airport

Located some 80km (50 miles) northeast of London's West End, **Stansted,** in Essex (℡ 0844/335-1803; www.stanstedairport.com), handles mostly flights to and from the European continent.

GETTING TO CENTRAL LONDON FROM STANSTED From Stansted, your best bet to central London is the **Stansted Express train** (✆ 08457/850-0150;** www.stanstedexpress.co.uk) to Liverpool Street Station, which runs every 15 minutes from 6am to 11:45pm and every 30 minutes in the early mornings on weekends. It costs £18 for a standard ticket and £30 for first class, and it takes 45 minutes.

By bus, you can take the **A6 Airbus** (✆ 0871/781-81-81), which runs regular departures 24 hours a day to many central London locations and costs £15. If you prefer the relative privacy of a taxi, you'll pay dearly for the privilege. For a ride to London's West End, a taxi will charge from £85 to £100. Expect the ride to take around 75 minutes during normal traffic conditions, but beware of Friday afternoons, when dense traffic may double your travel time. Our advice: Stick to the Express.

BY TRAIN

Each of London's train stations is connected to the city's vast bus and Underground network, and each has phones, restaurants, pubs, luggage storage areas, and Transport for London Information Centres.

St. Pancras International (www.stpancras.com) is the new London hub for Eurostar, replacing Waterloo Station as the arrival point from the Continent. Restored and opened in 2007, it is the point where the high-speed Eurostar pulls into London, connecting England with Belgium and France through the Channel Tunnel.

The station boasts Europe's longest champagne bar, a daily farmer's market, all the Wi-Fi you'll ever need, plus dozens of boutiques—and some of the world's fastest trains. It is also served by six underground tubes, including Victoria, Northern, Piccadilly, Circle, Hammersmith & City, and Metropolitan, as well as seven other rail companies. With such a vast network of transport, you can head virtually anywhere in Greater London.

BY CAR

Once you arrive on the English side of the Channel, the M20 takes you directly into London. *Remember to drive on the left.* Two roadways encircle London: The A406 and A205 form the inner beltway; the M25 rings the city farther out. Determine which part of the city you want to enter and follow signposts.

We suggest you confine driving in London to the bare minimum, which means arriving and parking. Because of parking problems and heavy traffic, getting around London by car is not a viable option. Once there, leave your car in a garage and rely on public transportation or taxis. Before arrival in London, call your hotel and inquire if it has a garage (and what the charges are), or ask the staff to give you the name and address of a garage nearby.

By Public Transportation

The London Underground and the city's buses operate on the same system of six fare zones. The fare zones radiate in rings from the central zone 1, which is where most visitors spend the majority of their time. Zone 1 covers the area from Liverpool Street in the east to Notting Hill in the west, and from Waterloo in the south to Baker Street, Euston, and King's Cross in the north. To travel beyond zone 1, you need a multizone ticket. Note that all single one-way, round-trip, and 1-day pass tickets are valid only on the day of purchase. Tube and bus maps should be available at any Underground station. You can also download them before your trip from the excellent **London Transport (LT)** website **www.tfl.gov.uk/tfl**. There are also **LT Information Centres** at several major Tube stations: Euston, King's Cross, Oxford Circus, St. James's Park, Liverpool Street Station, and Piccadilly Circus, as well as in the British Rail stations at Euston and Victoria and in each of the terminals at Heathrow Airport. Most of them are open daily (some close Sun) from at least 9am to 5pm. A 24-hour public-transportation information service is also available at ✆ 020/7222-1234.

DISCOUNT PASSES If you plan to use public transportation a lot, investigate the range of fare discounts available. **Travelcards** offer unlimited use of buses, Underground, Docklands Light Railway, and National Rail services in Greater London for any period ranging from a day to a year. Travelcards are available from Underground ticket offices, LT Information Centres, main post offices in the London area, many news agents, and some newsstands. Children younger than age 11 generally travel free on the Tube and buses.

The **1-Day Travelcard** allows you to go anywhere throughout Greater London. For travel anywhere within zones 1 and 2, the cost is £7 for adults or £2 for children 5 to 15. The **Off-Peak 1-Day Travelcard,** which is valid after 9:30am on weekdays, is even cheaper. For two zones, the cost is £7 for adults and £2 for children 5 to 15.

The system now features a **3-Day Travelcard,** allowing adults to travel within zones 1 and 2 for £20, and allowing children to go for £6.

One-Week Travelcards cost adults £45 and children £22 for travel in zones 1 and 2. For more information, visit www.londontravelpass.com.

Consider purchasing the **Oyster Card** (www.oystercard.com), a travel discount card that's all the rage. You can prepay for single fares, which cost considerably less than a paper ticket—usually about half the price. Oysters are valid on the Tube, DLR, tram, and National Rail services within your chosen zones and across the entire London bus network. For 24-hour information, call the Oyster hot line at ✆ 020/7222-1234. The card has a daily price cap, meaning you never pay more than £3 regardless of how many trips you make in 1 day. You can buy an Oyster Card at any ticket office.

THE UNDERGROUND

The Underground, or Tube, is the fastest and easiest way to get around. All Tube stations are clearly marked with a red circle and blue crossbar. Routes are conveniently color-coded.

If you have British coins or a credit card, you can get your ticket at a vending machine. Otherwise, buy it at the ticket office. You can transfer as many times as you like as long as you stay in the Underground. Children 4 and younger travel free if accompanied by an adult.

Slide your ticket into the slot at the gate and pick it up as it comes through on the other side and hold on to it—it must be presented when you exit the station at your destination. If you're caught without a valid ticket, you'll be fined £20 on the spot. If you owe extra money, you'll be asked to pay the difference by the attendant at the exit. The Tube runs roughly from 5am to 12:30am (7:30am–10:30pm Sun). After that you must take a taxi or night bus to your destination. For information on the London Tube system, call the **London Underground** at ✆ 020/7222-1234, but expect to stay on hold for a good while before a live person comes on the line. Information is also available on **www.tfl.gov.uk**.

The Jubilee Line Extension has been extended eastward to serve the growing suburbs of the southeast and the Docklands area. This east-west axis helps ease traffic on some of London's most hard-pressed underground lines. The line also makes it much easier to reach Greenwich.

BY BUS

The comparably priced bus system is almost as good as the Underground and gives you better views of the city. To find out about current routes, pick up a free bus map at one of London Transport's Travel Information Centres, mentioned above. The map is available in person only, not by mail. You can also obtain a map at **www.tfl.gov.uk**.

As with the Underground, fares vary according to distance traveled. Generally, bus fares are £2 to £3. If you want your stop called out, simply ask the conductor or driver. To speed up bus travel, passengers have to purchase tickets before boarding. Drivers no longer collect fares on board. Some 300 roadside ticket machines serve stops in central London. You'll need the exact fare, however, as ticket machines don't make change.

Buses generally run 24 hours a day. A few night buses have special routes, running once an hour or so; most pass through Trafalgar Square. Keep in mind that night buses are often so crowded (especially on weekends) that they are unable to pick up passengers after a few stops. You may find yourself waiting a long time. Consider taking a taxi. Call the 24-hour **hot line** (✆ **020/7222-1234**) for schedule and fare information.

BY TAXI

London cabs are among the most comfortable and best-designed in the world. You can pick one up either by heading for a cab rank or by hailing one in the street. (The taxi is available if the yellow taxi sign on the roof is lit.) To **call a cab,** phone ✆ **0871/871-8710.**

The meter starts at £2.40 to £3, with increments of £2 per mile thereafter, based on distance or time. Surcharges are imposed after 8pm and on weekends and public holidays. All these tariffs include VAT. Tip 10% to 15%.

If you call for a cab, the meter starts running when the taxi receives instructions from the dispatcher, so you could find that the meter already reads a few pounds more than the initial drop of £2.20 when you step inside.

Minicabs are also available, and they're often useful when regular taxis are scarce or when the Tube stops running. These cabs are meterless, so you must negotiate the fare in advance. Unlike regular cabs, minicabs are forbidden by law to cruise for fares. They operate from sidewalk kiosks, such as those around

3

PLANNING YOUR TRIP TO LONDON

Getting There & Getting Around

Leicester Square. If you need to call one, try **Brunswick Chauffeurs/Abbey Cars** (☎ **020/8969-2555**) in west London or **Newham Minicars** (☎ **020/8472-1400**) in south London. Minicab kiosks can be found near many Tube or BritRail stops, especially in outlying areas.

If you have a complaint about taxi service or if you leave something in a cab, contact the **Public Carriage Office,** 15 Penton St., N1 9PU (Tube: Angel Station). If it's a complaint, you must have the cab number, which is displayed in the passenger compartment. Call ☎ **0845/602-7000** or 020/7222-1234 or go to www.tfl.gov.uk with complaints.

BY BICYCLE

One of the most popular bike-rental shops is **On Your Bike,** 52–54 Tooley St., London Bridge, SE1 (☎ **020/7378-6669;** www.onyourbike.com; Tube: London Bridge), open Monday to Friday 7:30am to 7pm, Saturday 10am to 6pm, and Sunday 11am to 5pm. The first-class mountain bikes, with high seats and low-slung handlebars, cost £12 for the first day and £8 for each day thereafter, or £35 per week, and require a 1p deposit on a credit card, so they will have your credit card number.

MONEY & COSTS

London is becoming one of the most expensive cities on the planet, far more expensive than New York (Brits now view the Big Apple as a bargain basement). London is not as expensive as Tokyo or Oslo, but even an average hotel rate can cost £100 or more—in many cases, much, much more.

You'll avoid lines at airport ATMs by exchanging at least some money—just enough to cover airport incidentals and transportation to your hotel—before you leave home (though don't expect the exchange rate to be ideal). You can exchange money at your local American Express or Thomas Cook office or at your bank. American Express also dispenses traveler's checks and foreign currency via www.americanexpress.com or ☎ **800/528-4800,** but they'll charge an order fee and additional shipping costs.

Pounds & Pence

Britain's decimal monetary system is based on the pound (£), which is made up of 100 pence (written as "p"). Pounds are also called **quid** by Britons. There are £1 and £2 coins, as well as coins of 50p, 20p, 10p, 5p, 2p, and 1p. Banknotes come in denominations of £5, £10, £20, and £50.

THE BRITISH POUND: The British Pound is the official currency of Great Britain. Here's how it stacks up against everything else. Because international currency ratios can and almost certainly will change prior to your arrival in Britain, you should confirm up-to-date currency rates as the time of your trip approaches.

THE VALUE OF THE BRITISH POUND VS. OTHER POPULAR CURRENCIES

UK£	US$	Can$	Euro (€)	Aus$	NZ$
£1	$1.60	C$1.70	€1.15	A$1.80	NZ$2.25

	UK£
Taxi from Heathrow to central London	50.00–80.00
Underground from Heathrow to central London	4.00
Double room at the Dorchester (very expensive)	295.00
Double room at Durrant's Hotel (expensive)	250.00
Double room at the Hallam Hotel (moderate)	105.00
Double room at Edward Lear Hotel (inexpensive)	68.00
Lunch for one at Shepherd's (expensive)	32.50
Lunch for one at Ye Olde Cheshire Cheese (inexpensive)	16.00
Dinner for one, without wine, at Bibendum, the Oyster Bay (expensive)	36.00
Dinner for one, without wine, at Porter's English Restaurant (moderate)	22.00
Dinner for one, without wine, at Cork & Bottle Wine Bar (inexpensive)	16.00
Pint of beer	3.00–4.00
Coca-Cola (large)	2.50
Cup of coffee	1.80–2.50
Admission to British Museum	Free
Movie ticket	6.00–9.00
Theater ticket	25.00–85.00

ATMs

ATMs are widely available in London. The easiest and best way to get cash away from home is from an ATM, sometimes referred to as a "cash machine," or a "cashpoint." The **Cirrus** (© **800/424-7787;** www.mastercard.com) and **PLUS** (www.visa.com) networks span the globe; look at the back of your bank card to see which network you're on; then call or check online for ATM locations at your destination. Be sure you know your personal identification number (PIN) and daily withdrawal limit before you depart.

There can be problems involved in the use of ATMs. For example, if you make a mistake and punch your secret code wrong into the machine three times, that machine will swallow your card on the assumption that it is being fraudulently used.

Users with alphabetical rather than numerical PINs may be thrown off by the lack of letters on London cash machines. If your PIN is longer than four digits, check with your bank to see if you can use the first four digits or will have to get a new number for use in Britain.

To get a cash advance by using a credit card at an ATM, ask for a PIN from your credit card company such as Visa before leaving your home country.

Note: Remember that many banks impose a fee every time you use a card at another bank's ATM, and that fee can be higher for international transactions than for domestic ones. In addition, the bank from which you withdraw cash may charge its own fee. For international withdrawal fees, ask your bank.

Credit Cards

Credit cards are another safe way to carry money, but their use has become more difficult, especially in London (see below). They also provide a convenient record of all your expenses, and they generally offer relatively good exchange rates. You can usually withdraw cash advances from your credit cards at banks or ATMs, provided you know your PIN. Keep in mind that you'll pay interest from the moment of your withdrawal, even if you pay your monthly bills on time. Also, note that many banks now assess a 1% to 3% "transaction fee" on **all** charges you incur abroad (whether you're using the local currency or your native currency).

There is almost no difference in the acceptance of a debit or a standard credit card.

Chip and PIN represents a change in the way that credit and debit cards are used. The program is designed to cut down on the fraudulent use of credit cards. More and more banks are issuing customers Chip and PIN versions of their debit or credit cards. In the future, more and more vendors will be asking for a four-digit personal identification number, or PIN, which will be entered into a keypad near the cash register. In some cases, a waiter will bring a hand-held model to your table to verify your credit card.

Warning: Some establishments in London might not accept your credit card unless you have a computer chip imbedded in it. The reason? To cut down on credit card fraud.

More and more places in London are moving from the magnetic strip credit card to the new system of Chip and PIN. In the changeover in technology, some retailers have falsely concluded that they can no longer take swipe cards or signature cards that don't have PINs.

For the time being, both the new and old cards are used in shops, hotels, and restaurants, regardless of whether they have the old credit and debit card machines or the new Chip and PIN machines installed. Expect a lot of confusion when you arrive in England or elsewhere.

Traveler's Checks

You can buy traveler's checks at most banks, and they are widely accepted in London, although frankly merchants prefer cash. Because of difficulties with credit cards (see above) or ATMs that can reject your card for no apparent reason, travelers are once again buying traveler's checks for security in case something goes wrong with their plastic. Checks are offered in denominations of $20, $50, $100, $500, and sometimes $1,000. Generally, you'll pay a service charge ranging from 1% to 4%.

The most popular traveler's checks are offered by **American Express** (© **800/528-4800,** or 800/221-7282 for cardholders—this number accepts collect calls, offers service in several foreign languages, and exempts AmEx gold and platinum cardholders from the 1% fee); **Visa** (© **800/732-1322**)—AAA members can obtain Visa checks for a $9.95 fee (for checks up to $1,500) at most AAA offices or by calling © **866/339-3378;** and **MasterCard** (© **800/ 223-9920**).

American Express, Thomas Cook, Visa, and **MasterCard** offer **foreign currency traveler's checks,** which are useful if you're traveling to one country, or to the euro zone; they're accepted at locations where dollar checks may not be.

If you carry traveler's checks, keep a record of their serial numbers separate from your checks in the event that they are stolen or lost—you'll get your refund faster.

HEALTH
Staying Healthy

Traveling to London doesn't pose any health risk. The tap water is safe to drink, the milk is pasteurized, and health services are good. The crisis regarding mad cow disease is long over, as is the foot-and-mouth disease epidemic.

London has some of the greatest medical services in the world. And get this, all the doctors speak English. It is easy to get over-the-counter medicine, and general equivalents of common prescription drugs are available throughout the British Isles.

Healthy Travels to You
The following government websites offer up-to-date health-related travel advice.
○ **Australia:** www.smartraveller.gov.au
○ **Canada:** www.hc-sc.gc.ca
○ **U.K.:** www.nathnac.org
○ **U.S.:** www.cdc.gov

General Availability of Health Care

Contact the **International Association for Medical Assistance to Travelers (IAMAT;** © **716/ 754-4883,** or 416/652-0137 in Canada; www.iamat.org) for tips on travel and health concerns in the countries you're visiting, and for lists of local doctors. The United States **Centers for Disease Control and Prevention** (© **888/232-6348;** www.cdc.gov) provides up-to-date information on health hazards by region or country and offers tips on food safety. The website **www.tripprep.com,** sponsored by a consortium of travel medicine practitioners, may also offer helpful advice on traveling abroad. You can

Avoiding "Economy-Class Syndrome"

Deep vein thrombosis, or as it's known in the world of flying, "economy-class syndrome," is a blood clot that develops in a deep vein. It's a potentially deadly condition that can be caused by sitting in cramped conditions—such as an airplane cabin—for too long. During a flight (especially a long-haul flight), get up, walk around, and stretch your legs every 60 to 90 minutes to keep your blood flowing. Other preventative measures include frequent flexing of the legs while sitting, drinking lots of water, and avoiding alcohol and sleeping pills. If you have a history of deep vein thrombosis, heart disease, or another condition that puts you at high risk, some experts recommend wearing compression stockings or taking anticoagulants when you fly; always ask your physician about the best course for you. Symptoms of deep vein thrombosis include leg pain or swelling, or even shortness of breath.

find listings of reliable clinics overseas at the **International Society of Travel Medicine** (www.istm.org).

What to Do If You Get Sick Away From Home

If you need a doctor, your hotel can recommend one, or you can contact your embassy or consulate. *Note:* U.S. visitors who become ill while they're in London are eligible only for free *emergency* care. For other treatment, including follow-up care, you'll be asked to pay.

In most cases, your existing health plan will provide the coverage you need. But double-check; you may want to buy **travel medical insurance** instead. (See the "Insurance" entry in chapter 11, "Fast Facts.") Bring your insurance ID card with you when you travel.

If you suffer from a chronic illness, consult your doctor before your departure. For conditions such as epilepsy, diabetes, or heart problems, wear a **Medic-Alert Identification Tag** (© **888/633-4298** or 209/668-3333; www.medicalert.org), which will immediately alert doctors to your condition and give them access to your records through MedicAlert's 24-hour hot line.

Pack **prescription medications** in your carry-on luggage and carry prescription medications in their original containers, with pharmacy labels—otherwise they won't make it through airport security. Also bring along copies of your prescriptions, in case you lose your pills or run out. Don't forget an extra pair of contact lenses or prescription glasses. Carry the generic name of prescription medicines, in case a local pharmacist is unfamiliar with the brand name.

SAFETY

Staying Safe

Like all big cities, London has its share of crime, but in general it is one of the safer destinations of Europe. Pickpockets are a major concern, though violent crime is relatively rare, especially in the heart of London, which hasn't seen a Jack the Ripper in a long time. Even so, it is not wise to go walking in parks at night. In London, take all the precautions a prudent traveler would in going anywhere, be it Los Angeles, Paris, or New York. Conceal your wallet or else hold onto your purse, and don't flaunt jewelry or cash. In other words, do as your mother told you.

Any unrest or protest demonstrations around London's Trafalgar Square should not concern the usual visitor, who is advised to stay out of the area during any demonstrations.

Local law enforcement officials in London have a long history of being fair and impartial to visitors, even those from Third World or Middle Eastern countries. Unlike Germany, England seems to practice great tolerance, more so than parts of America. There is little racial, ethnic, or religious discrimination, including that based on sexual preference.

Women traveling alone encounter less aggressive or so-called macho behavior than they will find in such countries as Spain and Italy. Of course, discretion is always advised—that is, don't get in a car, of course, with three lager louts at 2 o'clock in the morning.

SPECIALIZED TRAVEL RESOURCES

Travelers with Disabilities

Many London hotels, museums, restaurants, and sightseeing attractions have wheelchair ramps, although they are less common in rural England. Persons with disabilities are often granted special discounts at attractions, called "concessions" in Britain, and, in some cases, at nightclubs. Free information and advice is available from **Holiday Care Service,** the Hawkins Suite, Enham Place, Andover SP11 6JS (℃ **0845/124-9971;** fax 01539/735-567; www.holidaycare.org.uk).

Many bookstores in London carry *Access in London* (www.accessinlondon.org; £10–£15), a publication listing facilities for persons with disabilities, among other things.

The transport system, cinemas, and theaters are still pretty much off-limits, but **Transport for London** publishes a leaflet called *Access to the Underground,* which gives details of elevators and ramps at individual Underground stations; call ℃ **020/7222-1234** or visit www.tfl.gov.uk. And **London Black Cabs** (℃ **0845/108-3000;** www.londonblackcab.com) are perfectly suited for those in wheelchairs; the roomy interiors have plenty of room for maneuvering.

London's most visible organization for information about access to theaters, cinemas, galleries, museums, and restaurants is **Artsline,** 54 Chalton St., London NW1 1HS (℃ **020/7388-2227;** fax 020/7383-2653; www.artsline.org.uk). It offers free information about wheelchair access, theaters with hearing aids, tourist attractions, and cinemas. Artsline mails information to North America, but it's more helpful to contact Artsline once you arrive in London; the line is staffed Monday to Friday 9:30am to 5:30pm.

Many travel agencies offer customized tours and itineraries for travelers with disabilities. **Flying Wheels Travel** (℃ **877/451-5006** or 507/451-5005; www.flyingwheelstravel.com) offers escorted tours and cruises that emphasize sports and private tours in minivans with lifts. **Access-Able Travel Source** (www.access-able.com) offers extensive access information and advice for traveling around the world with disabilities. **Accessible Journeys** (℃ **800/846-4537** or 610/521-0339; www.disabilitytravel.com) caters specifically to slow walkers and wheelchair travelers and their families and friends.

Organizations that offer assistance to travelers with disabilities include **MossRehab** (✆ **800/CALL-MOSS** [2255-6677]; www.mossresourcenet.org), which provides a library of accessible-travel resources online; the **American Foundation for the Blind** (**AFB;** ✆ **800/232-5463** or 212/502-7600; www. afb.org), a referral resource for the blind or visually impaired that includes information on traveling with Seeing Eye dogs; and **SATH** (**Society for Accessible Travel & Hospitality;** ✆ **212/447-7284;** www.sath.org), which offers a wealth of travel resources for people with all types of disabilities and informed recommendations on destinations, access guides, travel agents, tour operators, vehicle rentals, and companion services. **AirAmbulanceCard.com** (✆ **877/424-7633**) allows you to pre-select top-notch hospitals in case of an emergency.

The "Accessible Travel" link at **Mobility-Advisor.com** (www.mobility-advisor.com) offers a variety of travel resources to persons with disabilities.

Check out the quarterly magazine **Emerging Horizons** (www.emerging horizons.com), published by SATH.

Gay & Lesbian Travelers

London has one of the most active gay and lesbian scenes in the world. Gay bars, restaurants, and centers are plentiful.

Lesbian and Gay Switchboard (✆ **020/7837-7324;** www.llgs.org.uk) is open 24 hours a day, providing information about gay-related activities in London or advice in general. London's best gay-oriented bookstore is **Gay's the Word,** 66 Marchmont St., WC1N 1AB (✆ **020/7278-7654;** http://freespace. virgin.net/gays.theword; Tube: Russell Sq.), the largest such store in Britain. The staff is friendly and helpful and will offer advice about the ever-changing scene in London. It's open Monday through Saturday from 10am to 6:30pm and Sunday from 2 to 6pm. At Gay's the Word and other gay-friendly venues, you can find a number of publications, many free, including the popular **Boyz.** Another free publication is **Pink Paper** (with a good lesbian section), and check out **9X,** filled with data about new clubs and whatever else is hot on the scene.

The International Gay and Lesbian Travel Association (**IGLTA;** ✆ **800/448-8550** or 954/630-1637; www.iglta.org) is the trade association for the gay and lesbian travel industry, and offers an online directory of gay- and lesbian-friendly travel businesses.

Many agencies offer tours and travel itineraries specifically for gay and lesbian travelers. **Above and Beyond Tours** (✆ **800/397-2681;** www.above beyondtours.com) is a gay and lesbian tour operator. **Now, Voyager** (✆ **800/255-6951;** www.nowvoyager.com) is a well-known San Francisco–based gay-owned and -operated travel service.

The following travel guides are available at many bookstores, or you can order them from any online bookseller: **Spartacus International Gay Guide** (Bruno Gmünder Verlag; www.spartacusworld.com); **Odysseus: The International Gay Travel Planner** (Odysseus Enterprises, Ltd.); and the **Damron** guides (www. damron.com), with separate, annual books for gay men and lesbians.

For more gay and lesbian travel resources, visit Frommers.com.

Senior Travel

Many discounts are available to seniors. Be advised that in Britain you often have to be a member of an association to get discounts. Public-transportation discounts, for example, are available only to holders of British Pension books.

However, many attractions do offer discounts for seniors (women 60 or older and men 65 or older). Even if discounts aren't posted, ask if they're available.

If you're older than 60, you're eligible for special 10% discounts on **British Airways (BA)** through its Privileged Traveler program. You also qualify for reduced restrictions on APEX cancellations. Discounts are also granted for BA tours and for intra-Britain air tickets booked in North America. **BritRail** offers seniors discounted rates on first-class rail passes around Britain. See "By Train from Continental Europe" in the "Getting There & Getting Around" section, earlier in this chapter.

Don't be shy about asking for discounts, but carry some kind of identification that shows your date of birth. Also, mention you're a senior when you make your reservations. Many hotels offer seniors discounts. In most cities, people older than 60 qualify for reduced admission to theaters, museums, and other attractions, and discounted fares on public transportation.

Members of **AARP,** 601 E St. NW, Washington, DC 20049 (© **888/687-2277;** www.aarp.org), get discounts on hotels, airfares, and car rentals. AARP offers members a wide range of benefits, including *AARP The Magazine* and a monthly newsletter. Anyone 50 or older can join.

Many reliable agencies and organizations target the 50-plus market. **Elderhostel** (© **800/454-5768;** www.exploritas.org) arranges worldwide study programs for those ages 55 and older.

Recommended publications offering travel resources and discounts for seniors include the quarterly magazine *Travel 50 & Beyond* (www.travel50andbeyond.com) and *Unbelievably Good Deals and Great Adventures That You Absolutely Can't Get Unless You're Over 50* (McGraw Hill), by Joann Rattner Heilman.

Frommers.com offers more information and resources on travel for seniors.

Family Travel

If you have enough trouble getting your kids out of the house in the morning, dragging them thousands of miles away may seem like an insurmountable challenge. But family travel can be immensely rewarding, giving you new ways of seeing the world through smaller pairs of eyes.

On airlines, you must request a special menu for children at least 24 hours in advance. If baby food is required, however, bring your own and ask a flight attendant to warm it to the right temperature.

Arrange ahead of time for such necessities as a crib, a bottle warmer, and a car seat (in England, small children aren't allowed to ride in the front seat).

If you're staying with friends in London, you can rent baby equipment from **Chelsea Baby Hire,** 31 Osborne House, 414 Wimbledon Park Rd., SW19 6PW (© **020/8789-9673;** www.chelseababyhire.com). **London Black Cab** (© **0845/108-3000;** www.londonblackcab.com) is a lifesaver for families; the roomy interior allows a stroller to be lifted right into the cab without unstrapping the baby.

You can find babysitting available at most hotels.

Before you go, help your kids check out London Tourist Board's **Kids Love London** at www.visitlondon.com, a site created to give kids the lowdown on kid-friendly attractions and events.

To locate those accommodations, restaurants, and attractions that are particularly kid-friendly, refer to the "Kids" icon throughout this guide.

Recommended family travel Internet sites include **Family Travel Forum** (www.familytravelforum.com), a comprehensive site that offers customized trip planning; **Family Travel Network** (www.familytravelnetwork.com), an award-winning site that offers travel features, deals, and tips; **Traveling Internationally with Your Kids** (www.travelwithyourkids.com), a comprehensive site offering sound advice for long-distance and international travel with children; and **Family Travel Files** (www.thefamilytravelfiles.com), which offers an online magazine and a directory of off-the-beaten-path tours and tour operators for families.

For a list of more family-friendly travel resources, turn to the experts at Frommers.com.

A Frommer's guide specifically for families is *Frommer's London with Kids.*

Women Travelers

Check out the award-winning website **Journeywoman** (www.journeywoman. com), a "real life" women's travel-information network where you can sign up for a free e-mail newsletter and get advice on everything from etiquette and dress to safety; or the travel guide *Safety and Security for Women Who Travel* by Sheila Swan and Peter Laufer (Travelers' Tales, Inc.), offering common-sense tips on safe travel.

For general travel resources for women, go to Frommers.com.

African-American Travelers

Black Travel Online (www.blacktravelonline.com) posts news on upcoming events and includes links to articles and travel-booking sites. **Soul of America** (www.soulofamerica.com) is a comprehensive website, with travel tips, event and family-reunion postings, and sections on historically black beach resorts and active vacations.

Agencies and organizations that provide resources for black travelers include **Rodgers Travel** (© 888/823-1775; www.rodgerstravel.com). For more information, check out the following collections and guides: *Go Girl: The Black Woman's Guide to Travel & Adventure* (Eighth Mountain Press), a compilation of travel essays; *The African American Travel Guide* by John Haggins; *Steppin' Out* by Carla Labat (Avalon); and *Pathfinders Magazine* (© 215/438-2140; www.pathfinderstravel.com), which includes articles on everything from Rio de Janeiro to Ghana, as well as information on upcoming ski, dive, golf, and tennis trips.

Student Travel

If you plan to travel outside the U.S., you'd be wise to arm yourself with an **International Student Identity Card (ISIC),** which offers substantial savings on rail passes, plane tickets, and entrance fees. It also provides you with basic health and life insurance and a 24-hour help line. The card is available for $22 from **STA Travel** (© 800/781-4040; www.sta.com), the biggest student travel agency in the world. If you're no longer a student but are still younger than 26, you can get an **International Youth Travel Card (IYTC)** for the same price from the same people, which entitles you to some discounts (but not on museum admissions).

Travel CUTS (© 800/592-2887; www.travelcuts.com) offers similar services for both Canadians and U.S. residents. Irish students should turn to **USIT** (© 01/602-1906; www.usitnow.ie).

The International Student House, 229 Great Portland St., W1W 5PN (© 020/7631-8300; www.ish.org.uk), lies at the foot of Regent's Park across from the Tube stop for Great Portland Street. It's a beehive of activity, such as discos and film showings, and rents blandly furnished, institutional rooms. Laundry facilities are available, and a key deposit is charged. Reserve way in advance.

University of London Student Union, Malet Street, WC1E 7HY (© 020/7664-2000; www.ulu.co.uk; Tube: Goodge St. or Russell Sq.), is the best place to go to learn about student activities in the Greater London area. The Union has a swimming pool, fitness center, gymnasium, general store, sports shop, ticket agency, banks, bars, inexpensive restaurants, venues for live events, an office of STA Travel, and many other facilities. It's open Monday to Thursday 8:30am to 11pm, Friday 8:30am to 1pm, Saturday 9am to 2pm, and Sunday 9:30am to 10:30pm. Bulletin boards provide a rundown on events; some you may be able to attend, others may be "closed door."

Single Travelers

Many people prefer traveling alone, and for independent travelers, solo journeys offer infinite opportunities to make friends and meet locals. Unfortunately, if you like resorts, tours, or cruises, you're likely to get hit with a "single supplement" to the base price. Single travelers can avoid these supplements, of course, by agreeing to room with other single travelers on the trip. An even better idea is to find a compatible roommate before you go, from one of the many roommate locator agencies.

Travel Buddies Singles Travel Club (© 800/998-9099; www.travel buddiesworldwide.com), based in Canada, runs small, intimate, single-friendly group trips and will match you with a roommate free of charge and save you the cost of single supplements. **TravelChums** (www.travelchums.com) is an Internet-only travel-companion matching service with elements of an online personals-type site, hosted by the respected New York–based Shaw Guides travel service.

Many reputable tour companies offer singles-only trips. **Singles Travel International** (© 877/765-6874; www.singlestravelintl.com) offers singles-only trips to London. **Backroads** (© 800/462-2848; www.backroads.com) offers more than 160 active trips to 30 destinations worldwide, including England.

For more information on traveling single, go to www.frommers.com.

SUSTAINABLE TOURISM

In 2010, "Green Tourism" in London marked its third anniversary, and in the years ahead the movement is expected to grow and gain new adherents. One of the largest impacts has been on London's carbon emissions. Mayor Boris Johnson claims that "it is absolutely fantastic to see that some of the London top tourist attractions, such as the London Zoo, are leading the way in going green." He said that London is expected to see a 60% cut in carbon emissions by 2025.

More businesses are signing on, reducing their energy and water bills and dealing with waste in a more environmentally friendly way. Activities to make London greener are being coordinated by the London Development Agency. The LDA is on a campaign to sign up more hotels, including such stellar properties as the Ritz, the Royal Lancaster Hotel, and the Cavendish. This green scheme for hotels was launched in 2007 to help improve the environment. A list of hotels

IT'S EASY BEING green

Here are a few simple ways you can help conserve fuel and energy when you travel:

o Each time you take a flight or drive a car, greenhouse gases release into the atmosphere. You can help neutralize this danger to the planet through "carbon offsetting"—paying someone to invest your money in programs that reduce your greenhouse gas emissions by the same amount you've added. Before buying carbon offset credits, just make sure that you're using a reputable company, one with a proven program that invests in renewable energy. Reliable carbon offset companies include **Carbonfund** (www.carbonfund.org), **TerraPass** (www.terrapass.org), and **Carbon Neutral** (http://coolclimate.berkeley.edu).

o Whenever possible, choose nonstop flights; they generally require less fuel than indirect flights that stop and take off again. Try to fly during the day—some scientists estimate that nighttime flights are twice as harmful to the environment. And pack light—each 15 pounds of luggage on a 5,000-mile flight adds up to 50 pounds of carbon dioxide emitted.

o Where you stay during your travels can have a major environmental impact. To determine the green credentials of a property, ask about trash disposal and recycling, water conservation, and energy use; also question if sustainable materials were used in the construction of the property. The website **www.greenhotels.com** recommends green-rated member hotels around the world that fulfill the company's stringent environmental requirements. Also consult **www.environmentally friendlyhotels.com** for more green accommodations ratings.

o At hotels, request that your sheets and towels not be changed daily. (Many hotels already have programs like this in place.) Turn off the lights and air-conditioner (or heater) when you leave your room.

o Use public transport where possible—trains, buses, and even taxis are more energy-efficient forms of transport than driving. Even better is to walk or cycle; you'll produce zero emissions and stay fit and healthy on your travels.

o If renting a car is necessary, ask the rental agent for a hybrid, or rent the most fuel-efficient car available. You'll use less gas and save money at the tank.

o Eat at locally owned and operated restaurants that use produce grown in the area. This contributes to the local economy and cuts down on greenhouse gas emissions by supporting restaurants where the food is not flown or trucked in across long distances.

participating in the green business scheme can be downloaded at **www.green-business.co.uk**.

London has long had a taste for eco-friendly fare. Those who prefer to eat locally grown and produced food increasingly call themselves "locavores." This consumption of local food is part of a collaborative effort to build more self-reliant food economies. The savings in transport alone are often astonishing. Local food networks include community gardens, food co-ops, and farmers' markets, among other entities.

As late as 1998, there was only one restaurant in London with a strict environmental agenda. Now more and more restaurants are going green. One restaurant owner predicted, "The restaurant that has always flown in the best seasonal ingredients from anywhere in the world, at any cost, will be the one earmarked for trouble in the future."

You can find some eco-friendly travel tips and statistics, as well as touring companies and associations—listed by destination under "Travel Choice"—at the TIES website, www.ecotourism.org. **Responsible Travel** (www.responsibletravel.com) is a great source of sustainable travel ideas; the site is run by a spokesperson for ethical tourism in the travel industry. **Sustainable Travel International** (www.sustainabletravelinternational.org) promotes ethical tourism practices, and manages an extensive directory of sustainable properties and tour operators around the world.

In the U.K., **Tourism Concern** (www.tourismconcern.org.uk) works to reduce social and environmental problems connected to tourism. The **Association of Independent Tour Operators** (**AITO;** www.aito.co.uk) is a group of specialist operators leading the field in making holidays sustainable.

The **Association of British Travel Agents** (**ABTA;** www.abta.com) acts as a focal point for the U.K. travel industry and is one of the leading groups spearheading responsible tourism.

PACKAGES FOR THE INDEPENDENT TRAVELER

Package tours are simply a way to buy the airfare, accommodations, and other elements of your trip (such as car rentals, airport transfers, and sometimes even activities) at the same time and often at discounted prices.

One good source of package deals is the airlines themselves. Most major airlines offer air/land packages, including **American Airlines Vacations** (✆ 800/321-2121; www.aavacations.com), **Delta Vacations** (✆ 800/654-6559; www.deltavacations.com), **Continental Airlines Vacations** (✆ 800/301-3800; www.covacations.com), and **United Vacations** (✆ 888/854-3899; www.unitedvacations.com). Several big **online travel agencies**—Expedia, Travelocity, Orbitz, and Lastminute.com—also do a brisk business in packages.

Far and away, the most options are with **British Airways Holidays** (✆ **877/4-A-VACATION** [2-82228466]; www.britishairways.com). Its offerings within the British Isles are more comprehensive than those of its competitors and can be tailored to your specific interests and budget. Many tours, such as the 9-day, all-inclusive tour through the great houses and gardens of England, include the ongoing services of a guide and lecturer. But if you prefer to travel independently, without following an organized tour, a sales representative can tailor an itinerary specifically for you, with discounted rates in a wide assortment of big-city hotels. If you opt for this, you can rent a car or choose to take the train. For a free catalog and additional information, call British Airways before you book; some of the company's available options are contingent upon the purchase of a round-trip transatlantic air ticket.

Travel packages are also listed in the travel section of your local Sunday newspaper. Or check ads in the national travel magazines such as *Arthur Frommer's Budget Travel Magazine, Travel & Leisure, National Geographic Traveler,* and *Condé Nast Traveler.*

For more information on Package Tours and for tips on booking your trip, see Frommers.com.

ESCORTED TOURS

Escorted tours are structured group tours, with a group leader. Tours most often begin and end in London. But if you want to see only London, and not the countryside of England, these tours are not your best bet. The price usually includes everything from airfare to hotels, meals, tours, admission costs, and local transportation.

Abercrombie & Kent (✆ 800/554-7016; www.abercrombiekent.com) offers extremely upscale escorted tours that are loaded with luxury. They're the best in the business.

Other contenders in the upscale package-tour business include **Maupintour** (✆ 800/255-4266; www.maupintour.com) and **Tauck World Discovery** (✆ 800/788-7885; www.tauck.com).

But not all escorted tours are so pricey. Older British folks make up a large portion of the clientele of one of the United Kingdom's largest tour operators, **Wallace Arnold Worldchoice** (✆ 0845/365-6747; www.waworldchoice.com). Most of the company's tours last between 5 and 10 days, include lodgings (at solid but not particularly extravagant hotels) and most meals, and are reasonably priced.

U.S.-based **Trafalgar Tours** (✆ 866/544-4434; www.trafalgartours.com) offers more affordable packages with lodgings in unpretentious but comfortable

FROMMERS.COM: THE COMPLETE TRAVEL resource

Planning a trip or just returned? Head to **Frommers.com,** voted Best Travel Site by *PC Magazine.* We think you'll find our site indispensable before, during, and after your travels—with expert advice and tips; independent reviews of hotels, restaurants, attractions, and preferred shopping and nightlife venues; vacation giveaways; and an online booking tool. We publish the complete contents of more than 135 travel guides in our **Destinations** section, covering more than 4,000 places worldwide. Each weekday, we publish original articles that report on **Deals and News** via our free **Frommers.com Newsletters.** What's more, **Arthur Frommer** himself blogs 5 days a week, with strong opinions about the state of travel in the modern world. We're betting you'll find our **Events** listings an invaluable resource; it's an up-to-the-minute roster of what's happening in cities everywhere—including concerts, festivals, lectures, and more. We've also added weekly **podcasts, interactive maps,** and hundreds of new images across the site. Finally, don't forget to visit our **Message Boards,** where you can join in conversations with thousands of fellow Frommer's travelers and post your trip report once you return.

hotels. It's one of Europe's largest tour operators. There may not be a lot of frills, but you can find 7-day itineraries priced from $1,075 per person, double occupancy, without airfare, that include stopovers in Stratford-upon-Avon and Bath; they also offer 8-day packages at first-class hotels in London, starting at $899 per person, double occupancy.

One of Trafalgar's leading competitors, known for roughly equivalent moderately priced tours through Britain, is **Globus & Cosmos Tours** (✆ **866/755-8581;** www.globusandcosmos.com).

Despite the fact that escorted tours require big deposits and predetermined hotels, restaurants, and itineraries, many people derive security and peace of mind from the structure they offer. Escorted tours—whether they're navigated by bus, motor coach, train, or boat—let travelers sit back and enjoy the trip without having to drive or worry about details. They take you to the maximum number of sights in the minimum amount of time with the least amount of hassle. They're particularly convenient for people with limited mobility, and they can be a great way to make new friends.

On the downside, you'll have little opportunity for serendipitous interactions with locals. The tours can be jam-packed with activities, leaving little room for individual sightseeing, whim, or adventure—plus they often focus on the heavily touristed sites, so you miss out on many a lesser-known gem.

For more information on escorted general-interest tours, and including questions to ask before booking your trip, see Frommers.com.

STAYING CONNECTED

Telephones

To call England from North America, dial **011** (international code), **44** (Britain's country code), the local area codes (usually three or four digits and found in every phone number we've given in this book), and the local phone number. The local area codes found throughout this book all begin with "0"; you drop the "0" if you're calling from outside Britain, but you need to dial it along with the area code if you're calling from another city or town within Britain. For calls within the same city or town, the local number is all you need.

For **directory assistance** in London, dial ✆ **142;** for the rest of Britain, ✆ **192.**

There are three types of **public pay phones:** those taking only coins, those accepting only phone cards (called Cardphones), and those taking both phone cards and credit cards. At coin-operated phones, insert your coins before dialing. The minimum charge is 10p.

Phone cards are available in four values—£2, £4, £10, and £20—and are reusable until the total value has expired. Cards can be purchased from newsstands and post offices. Finally, the credit card pay phone—Access (Master-Card), Visa, American Express, and Diners Club—is most common at airports and large railway stations.

To make an **international call** from Britain, dial the international access code **(00),** then the country code, then the area code, and finally the local number. Or call through one of the following long-distance access codes: **AT&T USA Direct** (✆ 1800/CALL-ATT [225-5288]), **Canada Direct** (✆ 0800/890016), **Australia** (✆ 0800/890061), and **New Zealand** (✆ 0800/890064). Common country codes are: USA and Canada, **1;** Australia, **61;** New Zealand, **64;** and South Africa, **27.**

For calling **collect** or if you need an international operator, dial ✆ **155.**

Callers beware: Some hotels routinely add outrageous surcharges onto phone calls made from your room. Inquire before you call! It may be a lot cheaper to use your own calling-card number or to find a pay phone.

Cellphones

The three letters that define much of the world's wireless capabilities are GSM (Global System for Mobiles), a big, seamless network that makes for easy cross-border cellphone use throughout England and dozens of other countries worldwide. In general, reception is good. But you'll need a Scriber Identity Module (SIM) card. This is a small chip specific to England that gives you a local phone number and plugs you into a regional network. In the U.S., T-Mobile and AT&T Wireless use this quasi-universal system; in Canada, Microcell and some Rogers customers are GSM, and all Europeans and most Australians use GSM. Unfortunately, per-minute charges can be high. Calls to the U.S. average 70p per minute.

For many, **renting** a phone is a good idea. Even worldphone owners will have to rent new phones if they're traveling to non-GSM regions. While you can rent a phone from any number of overseas sites, including kiosks at airports and at car-rental agencies, we suggest renting the phone before you leave home. North Americans can rent one before leaving home from **InTouch USA** (✆ **800/872-7626** or 703/222-7161; www.intouchglobal.com) or **RoadPost** (✆ **888/290-1616** or 905/272-5665; www.roadpost.com). InTouch will also, for free, advise you on whether your existing phone will work overseas.

Buying a phone can be economically attractive, as many nations have cheap prepaid phone systems. Once you arrive at your destination, stop by a local cellphone shop and get the cheapest package. Local calls are usually cheap, and in many countries incoming calls are free.

Internet & E-mail

WITH YOUR OWN COMPUTER

More and more hotels, cafes, and retailers are signing on as Wi-Fi (wireless fidelity) "hot spots." Mac owners have their own networking technology: Apple AirPort. **T-Mobile Hotspot** (www.t-mobile.com/hotspot or www.t-mobile.co.uk) serves up wireless connections at coffee shops nationwide. **Boingo** (www.boingo.com) and **Wayport** (www.wayport.com) have set up networks in airports and high-class hotel lobbies. iPass providers (see below) also give you access to a few hundred wireless hotel lobby setups. To locate other hot spots that provide **free wireless networks** in cities in England, go to **www.jiwire.com**.

For dial-up access, most business-class hotels offer dataports for laptop modems, and a few thousand hotels in England now offer free high-speed Internet access. In addition, major Internet service providers (ISPs) have **local access numbers** around the world, allowing you to go online by placing a local call. The **iPass** network also has dial-up numbers around the world. You'll have to sign up with an iPass provider, who will then tell you how to set up your computer for your destination(s). For a list of iPass providers, go to www.ipass.com and click on "Individuals Buy Now." One solid provider is **i2roam** (✆ **866/811-6209** or 920/233-5863; www.i2roam.com).

ONLINE TRAVELER'S toolbox

Veteran travelers usually carry some essential items to make their trips easier. Following is a selection of handy online tools to bookmark and use.

- **Airplane Food** (www.airlinemeals.net)
- **Airplane Seating** (www.seatguru.com and www.airlinequality.com)
- **Foreign Languages for Travelers** (www.travlang.com)
- **Maps** (www.mapquest.com)
- **Subway Navigator** (http://gridskipper.com/55950/subwaynavigator)
- **Time and Date** (www.timeanddate.com)
- **Travel Warnings** (http://travel.state.gov, www.fco.gov.uk/travel, www.voyage.gc.ca, or www.dfat.gov.au)
- **Universal Currency Converter** (www.xe.com)
- **Visa ATM Locator** (www.visa.com); **MasterCard ATM Locator** (www.mastercard.com)
- **Weather** (www.intellicast.com and www.weather.com)

Wherever you go, bring a **connection kit** of the right power and phone adapters, a spare phone cord, and a spare Ethernet network cable—or find out whether your hotel supplies them to guests.

WITHOUT YOUR OWN COMPUTER

To find cybercafes, check **www.cybercaptive.com** and **www.cybercafe.com**. Cybercafes are found in all large U.K. cities, especially London. But they do not tend to cluster in any particular neighborhoods because of competition. They are spread out, but can be found on almost every business street in London. **easyInternet cafes** (✆ **020/7241-9000;** www.easyinternetcafe.com) has several Great Britain locations.

Aside from formal cybercafes, most **youth hostels** and **public libraries** have Internet access. Avoid **hotel business centers** unless you're willing to pay exorbitant rates.

Most major airports now have **Internet kiosks** scattered throughout their gates. These give you basic Web access for a per-minute fee that's usually higher than cybercafe prices.

TIPS ON ACCOMMODATIONS

Reserve your accommodations as far in advance as possible, even in the so-called slow months from November to April. Travel to London peaks from May to October, and during that period, it's hard to come by a moderate or inexpensive hotel room. Sometimes you can get better rates by calling the hotel directly. Ask for the type of room you want. If you're sensitive to noise, for example, request a room that's quieter, perhaps in the rear so you won't hear traffic noise out front. Remember that in the older hotels and inns, guest rooms tend to be small and each room is different, often with different plumbing. If you need a bathtub, ask for one or else you might end up with a small shower cubicle.

For tips on surfing for hotel deals online, visit Frommers.com.

More and more visitors are looking for a more in-depth experience in a foreign city than riding around on a tour bus. The site www.like-a-local.com pairs visitors with locals in a host of European cities, including London, to get more of a local take on a destination.

This experience could range from staying with a local family to exploring the city in greater depth, including fun nightlife at the hot spots. Lodging can be arranged in a private home, B&B, or apartment. Dining arrangements can be made to taste the local cuisine at the home of a resident.

A contract is arranged between the traveler and the local, and payment is made in advance. See the website for terms of the contract.

There's the potential for problems with this arrangement. For example, what if the local and the traveler hate each other on sight? However, on the whole, Frommer's editors who have used this service have had positive experiences with it.

For more information, graphic material, and/or to book an appointment for a like-a-local experience, email the outfitter at contact@like-a-local.com.

Classifications

Unlike some countries, England has no rigid hotel classification system. The tourist board grades hotels by stars. Hotels are judged on standards, quality, and hospitality, and are rated "approved," "commended," "highly commended," and "deluxe." Five stars (deluxe) is the highest rating. A classification of "listed" refers to accommodations that are, for the most part, very modest.

All establishments from two stars upward are required to have 100% en suite (private bathroom) facilities. In a one-star hotel, buildings are required to have hot and cold running water in all rooms, but in "listed" hotels, hot and cold running water in rooms is not mandatory. Star ratings are posted outside the buildings. However, the system is voluntary, and many hotels do not participate.

All hotels once included in the room price a full English breakfast of bacon and eggs, but today that is true of only some hotels. A continental breakfast is commonly included, usually just tea or coffee and toast.

Bed & Breakfasts

In London, homeowners take in paying guests. Watch for the familiar bed-and-breakfast (B&B) signs. Generally, these are modest family homes, but sometimes they may be built like small hotels, with as many as 15 rooms. If they're that big, they are more properly classified as guesthouses. B&Bs are the cheapest places you can stay in London and still be comfortable. A good source to locate them is www.bedandbreakfast-directory.co.uk.

Reservations for bed-and-breakfast accommodations in London can also be made by writing (not calling) the **British Visitor Centre,** 1 Regent St., London SW1Y 4XT. Once in London, you can also visit their office (Tube: Piccadilly Circus).

Chain Hotels

Many American chains, such as Best Western, Hilton, and Sheraton, are found throughout London. In addition, Britain has a number of leading chains with which North American travelers are generally not familiar. **Travelodge** (② **0870/191-1600;** www.travelodge.co.uk) offers good quality, modern budget accommodations across the U.K. with a family restaurant on-site. **Thistle Hotels** (② **0871/376-9000;** www.thistle.com) is a well-regarded chain of moderate to upscale full-service hotels that cater to both business and leisure travelers. An exclusive chain of government-rated three-crown hotels is called **Malmaison** (② **0845/365-4247;** www.malmaison.com). There's not a bad hotel in their post. **Premier Travel Inn** (② **0870/242-8000;** www.premierinn. com) is a chain of modern, moderately priced accommodations across the U.K., each one featuring a licensed restaurant.

House Swapping

The market leader in home exchanges is **HomeLink International,** 2937 NW 9th Terrace, Fort Lauderdale, FL 33311 (② **800/638-3841** or 954/566-2687; www.homelink.org), which costs $80 to join. This is the oldest, largest, and best home-exchange holiday organization in the world. You'll be able to find a home away from home—the only trouble is, you've got to turn your own home over to a stranger.

A competitor is **Intervac U.S. & International,** P.O. Box 590504, San Francisco, CA 94159 (② **800/756-HOME** [4663]; www.intervacus.com). To hook up with this outfitter, you pay $65 annually. Intervac is also adept at securing a list of home exchanges throughout Great Britain, including London.

TIPS ON DINING

Contrary to popular belief (or perhaps we should say stereotype), you can indeed eat well during your trip to London. From cheap takeaway pasties or chips, to fine dining establishments that specialize in fresh, organic, and local ingredients (as part of the Modern English movement that has gripped the culinary arts), to internationally popular ethnic foods, the country today offers a little bit of everything, particularly in London or other metropolises where you would naturally expect a bit more diversity.

TAXES & TIPPING   All restaurants and cafes are required to display the prices of their food and drink in a place visible from outside. Charges for service, as well as any minimums or cover charges, must also be made clear. The prices shown must include 17.5% VAT, the so-called "value-added" tax. Most restaurants add a 15% service charge to your bill, but check to make sure. If nothing has been added, leave a 10% to 15% tip. It is by no means considered rude to tip, so feel free to leave something extra if service was good.

For more information on what to expect—and even look forward to—when dining in London, see "Eating & Drinking in London," in chapter 2.

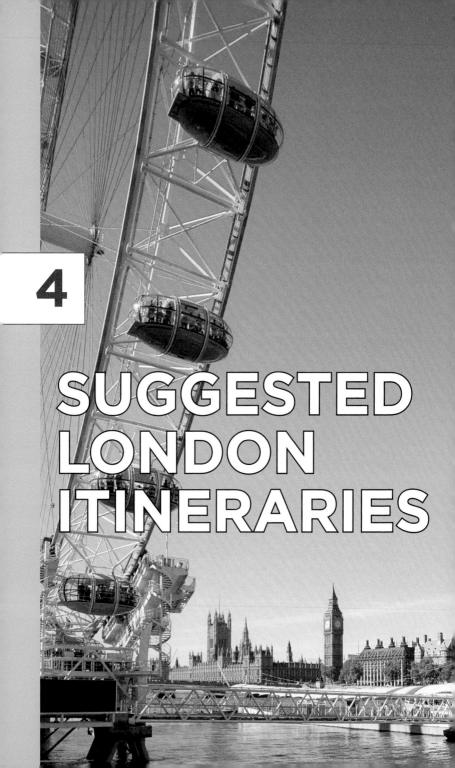

4

SUGGESTED LONDON ITINERARIES

The Queen would perhaps scoff at the idea of tackling her beloved city in just 1 day—or even 2 or 3 days. But if that's all the time you have, we want to help you make the most of it by providing a ready-made itinerary that will allow you to have a complete, unforgettable trip. Of course, there is always a hidden London that awaits discovery as you seek out its secret treasures on your own, but that can wait for another day and another trip.

You can make the most of your short time by fortifying yourself with an old-fashioned English breakfast—order "the works," perhaps skipping the blood pudding or sautéed kidneys if you're faint of heart. That way, if you sleep late (or have a "real tuck-in" as the Brits say), you might even skip lunch, so as not to lose precious daylight hours in your rushed schedule.

NEIGHBORHOODS IN BRIEF

While **central London** doesn't formally define itself, most Londoners today would probably accept the Underground's Circle Line as a fair boundary.

The **City** (the financial district) is where London began; it's the original square mile that the Romans called *Londinium,* and it still exists as its own self-governing entity. Rich in historical, architectural, and social interest, the City is one of the world's great financial areas. Even though the City is jeweled with historic sights, it empties out in the evenings and on weekends, and there are lots of better places to stay if you are looking for a hopping nightlife scene.

The **West End,** where most of London's main attractions are found, is unofficially bounded by the Thames to the south, Farringdon Road/Street to the east, Marylebone Road/Euston Road to the north, and Hyde Park and Victoria Station to the west. Most visitors will spend their time in the West End, whether at Buckingham Palace, the British Museum, or the shops and theaters of Soho. You'll find the greatest concentration of hotels and restaurants in the West End. Despite attempts to extend central London's nocturnal life to the south side of the Thames—notably the ambitious South Bank Arts Centre—London's energy fades when it crosses the river. Still, the new urban development of Docklands, the tourist attraction of the Globe Theatre, and some up-and-coming residential neighborhoods are infusing energy into the area across the river.

Farther west are the upscale neighborhoods of Belgravia, Kensington, Knightsbridge, Chelsea, Paddington and Bayswater, Earl's Court, and Notting Hill. This is also prime hotel and restaurant territory. To the east of the City is the **East End,** which forms the eastern boundary of **Inner London** (Notting Hill and Earl's Court roughly form the western boundary). Inner London is surrounded, like a doughnut, by the sprawling hinterland of **Outer London.**

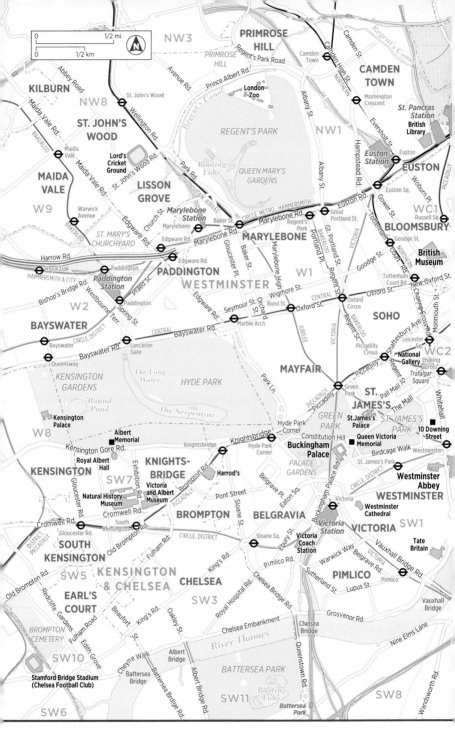

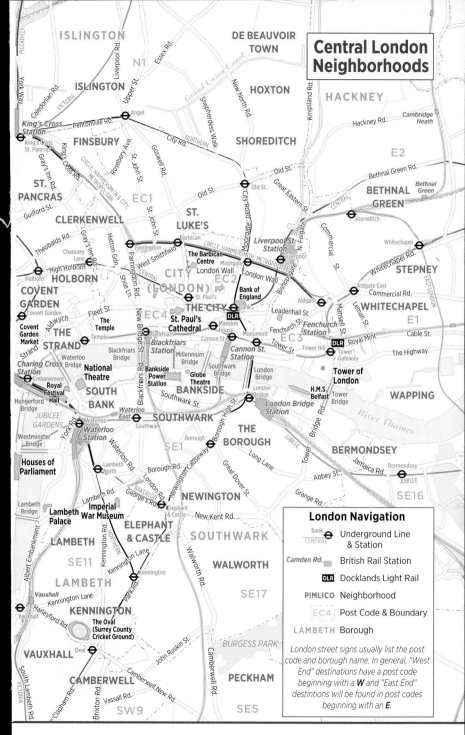

Central London Neighborhoods

The City & Environs

THE CITY   When Londoners speak of "the City" (EC2, EC3), they mean the original square mile that's now the British version of Wall Street. The buildings of this district are known all over the world: the Bank of England, the London Stock Exchange, and famed insurance company Lloyd's of London. The City was the original site of *Londinium,* the first settlement of the Roman conquerors. Despite its age, the City doesn't easily reveal its past. Although it retains some of its medieval character, much of the City has been swept away by the Great Fire of 1666, the bombs of 1940, the IRA bombs of the 1990s, and the zeal of modern developers. Landmarks include Sir Christopher Wren's masterpiece, **St. Paul's Cathedral,** which stood virtually alone in the surrounding rubble after the Blitz. Some 2,000 years of history unfold at the City's **Museum of London** and at the **Barbican Centre,** opened by Queen Elizabeth in 1982.

Following the Strand eastward from Trafalgar Square, you'll come to Fleet Street. In the 19th century, this corner of London became the most concentrated newspaper district in the world. William Caxton printed the first book in English here, and the *Daily Consort,* the first daily newspaper printed in England, was launched at Ludgate Circus in 1702. In recent times, however, most London tabloids have abandoned Fleet Street for the Docklands across the river. Where the Strand becomes Fleet Street stands Temple Bar, where the actual City of London begins. The Tower of London looms at the eastern fringe of the City, shrouded in legend, blood, and history, and permanently besieged by battalions of visitors.

The average visitor will venture into the City during the day to sample its attractions or to lunch at pubs such as **Ye Olde Cheshire Cheese,** then return to the West End for evening amusement. As a hotel district, the City wasn't even on the map until recent times. The opening of the **Great**

Fleet Street.

Hoxton Square in Shoreditch.

Eastern Hotel has brought a lot of business clients who prefer to stay here to avoid the traffic jams involved in getting into and out of the City. Stay in the City if you would prefer a hotel in a place like New York's Wall Street to a midtown address. If you can't afford the Great Eastern, consider the cheaper **Rookery** in newly fashionable Smithfield. The City lures hotel guests who prefer its quirky, quiet, offbeat flavor at night, when it's part ghost town, part movie set. There is some nightlife here, including pubs and restaurants. It's fun to wander the area when all the crowds are gone, pondering the thought that you're walking the same streets Samuel Johnson trod so long ago.

The City of London still prefers to function on its own, separate from the rest of London. It maintains its own **Information Centre** at St. Paul's Churchyard, EC4 (✆ **020/7332-1456**), which is open daily from 10am to 5:50pm.

THE EAST END   Traditionally, this was one of London's poorest districts, nearly bombed out of existence during World War II. In the words of one commentator, Hitler created "instant urban renewal" here. The East End extends east from the City Walls, encompassing Stepney, Bow, Poplar, West Ham, Canning Town, and other districts. The East End is the home of the cockney. To be a true cockney, it's said that you must be born within the sound of the Bow Bells of **St. Mary-le-Bow** church, an old church rebuilt by Sir Christopher Wren in 1670.

These days, many immigrants to London make their homes in the East End. London is pushing eastward. Today you'll find lots of trendy bars, clubs, restaurants, and boutiques or vintage clothing outlets here. Much of the fashionable life is found around Hoxton Square and its peripheries, such as Shoreditch and the northern half of Brick Lane. There is an array of contemporary galleries in the area. Brick Lane, incidentally, is a great place for some curry dishes if you can deal with all those waiters on the street trying to hustle you into their restaurants. Attractions you may want to visit if you're in the area include St. Clement Danes church, the Temple of Mithras, and Sir Christopher Wren's Monument to the Great Fire of 1666.

Since 1996, Shoreditch has attracted the most visitors from abroad, as it has become a popular and fashionable part of London. It has been the scene of major gentrification in the past decades, with the inevitable rise in property values. The district lies 4km (2½ miles) east/northeast of Charing Cross. Its historic heart is Shoreditch High Street, its landmark Shoreditch Church. The part of Shoreditch of most interest to visitors includes the area bordered to the north by Old Street; to the east by the northern stretch of Brick Lane, to the south by Old Spitalfields Market, and to the west by Old Street Station.

DOCKLANDS   In 1981, in the most ambitious scheme of its kind in Europe, the London Docklands Development Corporation (LDDC) was formed to redevelop Wapping, the Isle of Dogs, the Royal Docks, and Surrey Docks. The area is bordered roughly by Tower Bridge to the west and London City Airport and the Royal Docks to the east. Many businesses have moved here; Thames-side warehouses have been converted to Manhattan-style lofts and museums, entertainment complexes, shops, and an ever-growing list of restaurants has popped up at this 21st-century river city in the making.

Canary Wharf, on the Isle of Dogs, is the heart of Docklands. This 28-hectare (69-acre) site is dominated by a 240m-high (787-ft.) tower, which is the tallest building in the United Kingdom, and was designed by César Pelli. The Piazza of the tower is lined with shops and restaurants. On the south side of the river at Surrey Docks, Sir Terence Conran has converted the Victorian warehouses of Butler's Wharf into offices, workshops, houses, shops, and restaurants. Butler's Wharf is also home to the **Design Museum.** Chances are, you'll venture here for sights and restaurants, not for lodging, unless you've got business in the area. The area is fun during the day and home to some of London's finest restaurants, offering good food and a change of pace from the West End—this is postmillennium London, whereas the West End is the essence of tradition. See our recommendations in chapter 6, "Where to Dine." To get to Docklands, take the Underground to Tower Hill and pick up the **Docklands Light Railway** (✆ 020/7222-1234), which operates Monday to Saturday from 5:30am to 12:30am, and from 7am to 11:30pm Sunday.

SOUTH BANK   Although not officially a district, this is where you'll find the **South Bank Arts Centre,** the largest arts center in western Europe and still growing. Reached by Waterloo Bridge (or on foot by Hungerford Bridge), it lies across the Thames from the Victoria Embankment. Culture buffs flock to its galleries and halls, which encompass the **National Theatre, Queen Elizabeth Hall, Royal Festival Hall,** and the **Hayward Gallery.**

Although its day as a top hotel district in London may come in a decade or so (since there's no room left in the West End), that hasn't happened yet. The South Bank is a destination for daytime adventures and for evening cultural attractions. You may want to dine here during a day's or evening's exploration of the area. See our recommendations in chapter 6, "Where to Dine."

Nearby are such neighborhoods as Elephant and Castle, and Southwark, home to **Southwark Cathedral.** To get here, take the Tube to Waterloo Station.

Pedestrian area in front of Canary Wharf Tower, Docklands.

Southwark Cathedral.

Deptford lies south of the Thames, south of the Tower of London, in a rather inglorious corner of the Southeast, long known for its dreariness. But change is on the way and gentrification is taking place. You can take the Tube to Deptford High Street, which is still salt-of-the-earth London (the chains have not taken over here). The *New York Times* warned that "those with well-cushioned sensibilities need not make the journey." But the location, with its emerging pubs, art studios, "caffs," and hip shops, makes it a destination to those who want to experience London in the raw, a combination of what one critic called "a boisterous concoction of blue-collar aesthetics and intermittent hipsterism." A growing colony of designers and artists is moving in for cheaper rents.

CLERKENWELL This neighborhood, north and a bit west of the City, was the site of London's first hospital and is the home of several early churches. **St. Bartholomew-the-Great,** built in 1123, still stands as London's oldest church and the best example of large-scale Norman building in the city. In the 18th century, Clerkenwell declined into a muck-filled cattle yard, home to cheap gin distilleries. During a 19th-century revival, John Stuart Mill's London Patriotic Club moved here in 1872, and William Morris's socialist press called Clerkenwell home in the 1890s—Lenin worked here editing *Iskra.* The neighborhood again fell into disrepair but has recently been reinvented by the moneyed and groovy. A handful of hot restaurants and clubs have sprung up, and art galleries line St. John's Square and the border of Clerkenwell Green. Lest you think the whole area has become trendy, know that trucks still rumble into **Smithfield Market** throughout the night, unloading thousands of beef carcasses. Farringdon is Clerkenwell's central Tube stop.

KING'S CROSS   Long a seedy area in the heart of London, King's Cross is facing a massive regeneration program. Millions of pounds are going into its decaying infrastructure. The area is still far from chic, but was given renewed importance with the arrival of Eurostar, the Channel Tunnel Rail Link coming into St. Pancras instead of Waterloo. Because of this change in venue, it's estimated that some 50 million passengers will pass through King's Cross annually. Six tubes now convene underneath King's Cross Station, and it is the number-one connection hub enabling visitors to get to and from Gatwick and Heathrow airports.

ST. PANCRAS   Alongside King's Cross, St. Pancras International is the new transport hub for Eurostar, bringing renewed life to this once-decaying part of London. The station is to London what Penn Station was to New York, the finest architectural icon of the Age of Steam. British poet John Betjeman called the 1868 structure, with its gargoyles and Gothic revival towers, "too beautiful and too romantic to survive."

He almost became a prophet in the 1960s when this landmark was slated for demolition until saved by preservationists. Today the glamorous and vastly restored station is a dazzling entry point into Britain for those passengers arriving on Eurostar from the Continent. Stay tuned for hotel, shopping, and restaurant developments to blossom around the station. For more information, contact ✆ **020/7843-4250;** www.stpancras.com.

West End Neighborhoods

BLOOMSBURY   This district, a world within itself, is bound roughly by Euston Road to the north, Gower Street to the west, and Clerkenwell to the east. It is, among other things, the academic heart of London. There are three colleges in Bloomsbury, including **University College London,** the grandest and the oldest. A branch of the **University of London** is also here. Writers like Virginia Woolf, who lived in the area (it figured in her novel *Jacob's*

The Old Curiosity Shop in Bloomsbury.

The Old Bailey criminal court.

Room), have fanned the neighborhood's reputation as a place devoted to liberal thinking, arts, and "sexual frankness." The novelist and her husband, Leonard, were unofficial leaders of a group of artists and writers known as the Bloomsbury Group. However, despite its student population, Bloomsbury is a fairly staid neighborhood. The heart of Bloomsbury is **Russell Square,** whose outlying streets are lined with moderately priced to expensive hotels and B&Bs. It's a noisy but central place to stay. Most visitors come to see the **British Museum,** one of the world's greatest repositories of treasures from around the globe. The **British Telecom Tower** (1964) on Cleveland Street is a familiar landmark. The **Old Curiosity Shoppe,** said to be the oldest shop in central London and the inspiration behind Dickens's book of the same name, is found on Portsmouth Street.

Of all the areas described so far, this is the only one that could be called a hotel district. Hotel prices have risen dramatically in the past decade but are nowhere near the levels of those in Mayfair and St. James's. Bloomsbury's hotels are comparable in price to what you'll find in Marylebone to the west. But Bloomsbury is more convenient—at its southern doorstep lie the restaurants and nightclubs of Soho, the theater district, and the markets of Covent Garden. If you stay here, it's a 5-minute Tube ride to the heart of the action of the West End.

At the western edge of Bloomsbury you'll find **Fitzrovia,** bounded by Great Portland, Oxford, and Gower streets, and reached by the Goodge Street Tube. Goodge Street, with its many shops and pubs, forms the heart of the village. Charlotte Street has good and varied restaurants catering to the local media companies. Fitzrovia was once the stamping ground for writers and artists like Ezra Pound, Wyndham Lewis, and George Orwell, among others. The bottom end of Fitzrovia is a virtual extension of Soho, with a cluster of Greek restaurants.

HOLBORN The old borough of Holborn (*Ho*-burn), which abuts the City southeast of Bloomsbury, encompasses the heart of legal London—this is where you'll find the city's barristers, solicitors, and law clerks. Still Dickensian in spirit, the area preserves the Victorian author's literary footsteps in the two Inns of Court (where law students perform their apprenticeships and where barristers' chambers are located), featured in *David Copperfield,* and as the Bleeding Heart Yard of *Little Dorrit* fame. **The Old Bailey** courthouse, where judges and lawyers still wear old-fashioned wigs, has stood for English justice through the years—Fagin went to the gallows from this site in *Oliver Twist.* You might come here for some sightseeing, perhaps quenching your thirst in a historic pub. Everything in Holborn is steeped in history. For example, as you're downing a half-pint of bitter at the **Viaduct Tavern,** 126

SUGGESTED LONDON ITINERARIES

Neighborhoods in Brief

Newgate St. (Tube: St. Paul's), you can reflect on the fact that the pub was built over the notorious Newgate Prison.

COVENT GARDEN & THE STRAND The flower, fruit, and "veg" market is long gone (since 1970), but memories of Professor Higgins and his "squashed cabbage leaf," Eliza Doolittle, linger on. **Covent Garden** contains the city's liveliest group of restaurants, pubs, and cafes outside Soho, as well as some of the city's hippest shops. The restored marketplace here, with its glass and iron roofs, has been called a magnificent example of urban recycling. London's **theater district** begins in Covent Garden and spills over into Leicester Square and Soho. Inigo Jones's **St. Paul's Covent Garden** is known as the actors' church; over the years, it has attracted everybody from Ellen Terry to Vivien Leigh. The **Theatre Royal Drury Lane** was where Charles II's mistress, Nell Gwynne, made her debut in 1665 and was also where Irish actress Dorothea Jordan caught the eye of the Duke of Clarence, later William IV. **The Strand** forms the southern border of Covent Garden. It's packed with theaters, shops, first-class hotels, and restaurants. Old pubs, **Dr. Johnson's House,** and tearooms fragrant with brewing Twinings English tea evoke memories of the rich heyday of this district as the center of London's activity. The Strand runs parallel to the Thames River, and to walk it is to follow in the footsteps of Charles Lamb, Mark Twain, Henry Fielding, James Boswell, William Thackeray, and Sir Walter Raleigh, among others. The Strand's **Savoy Theatre** helped make Gilbert and Sullivan household names.

You'll probably come here for theater or dining rather than for a hotel room. Covent Garden has few hotels (although those few are very nice). We recommend the best ones (beginning on p. 130).

PICCADILLY CIRCUS & LEICESTER SQUARE Piccadilly Circus, with its statue of Eros, is the heart and soul of London. Its traffic, neon, and jostling crowds make *circus* an apt word to describe this place. Piccadilly, which was the western road out of London, was named for the "picadil," a ruffled collar created by Robert Baker, a 17th-century tailor. If you want grandeur, retreat to the Regency promenade of exclusive shops, the **Burlington Arcade,** designed in 1819. The English gentry—tired of being mud-splashed by horses and carriages along Piccadilly—came here to do their shopping. Some 35 shops, offering a treasure trove of expensive goodies, await you. A bit more tawdry is **Leicester Square,** a hub of theaters, restaurants, movie palaces, and nightlife. Leicester Square changed forever in the Victorian era, when four towering entertainment halls were opened. Over time, the old entertainment palaces changed from stage to screen; today three of them still show films.

There are a few hotels here, although they're invariably expensive. Stay here if you'd want a hotel in Times Square in New York. It's convenient for those who want to be at the center of the action. The downside is the noise, congestion, and pollution.

SOHO Soho is a confusing grid of streets crammed with restaurants. It's a great place to visit, but you probably won't want to stay here (there aren't many hotels, anyway). These densely packed streets in the heart of the West End are famous for their cosmopolitan mix of people and trades. A decade ago, much was heard about the decline of Soho with the influx of sex shops; even

Statue of Sherlock Holmes on
Baker Street in Marylebone.

the pub where Dylan Thomas used to drink himself into oblivion became a sex cinema. Since then, non-sex-oriented businesses have returned, and fashionable restaurants and shops prosper. Soho is now the heart of London's expanding gay scene.

Soho starts at Piccadilly Circus and spreads out, more or less bordered by Regent Street to the west, Oxford Street to the north, Charing Cross Road to the east, and the **theaters along Shaftesbury Avenue** to the south. Carnaby Street, a block from Regent Street, was the center of the universe in the Swinging '60s but is now a schlocky tourist trap, though a few quality stores have opened recently. Across Shaftesbury Avenue is London's **Chinatown,** centered on Gerrard Street. It's small, authentic, and packed with good restaurants. Soho's heart—featuring great delicatessens, butchers, fish stores, and wine merchants—is farther north, on Brewer, Old Compton, and Berwick streets (Berwick St. features a wonderful open-air fresh-food market). To the north of Old Compton Street, Dean, Frith, and Greek streets have fine restaurants, pubs, and clubs. The British movie industry is centered on Wardour Street. The average visitor comes to Soho to dine because many of its restaurants are convenient to the theater district. Most travelers don't stay in Soho, but a certain action-oriented visitor prefers the *joie de vivre* of the neighborhood as compared to staid Bloomsbury or swank Mayfair. Check out Soho's accommodations, starting on p. 132.

MARYLEBONE   West of Bloomsbury and Fitzrovia, Marylebone extends north from Marble Arch, at the eastern edge of Hyde Park. Most first-time visitors head here to explore **Madame Tussaud's** waxworks or walk along **Baker Street** in the footsteps of Sherlock Holmes. The streets form a near-perfect grid, with the major ones running north-south between Regent's Park and Oxford Street. Architect Robert Adam laid out **Portland Place,** one of the most characteristic squares in London, from 1776 to 1780. At **Cavendish Square,** Mrs. Horatio Nelson waited for the return of Admiral Nelson. Marylebone Lane and High Street are home to some specialist boutiques and food shops. Dickens wrote nearly a dozen books while he resided here. At **Regent's Park,** you can visit Queen Mary's Gardens or, in summer, see Shakespeare performed in an open-air theater. **Marylebone** has emerged as a major "bedroom" district for London, competing with Bloomsbury to its east. It's not as convenient as Bloomsbury, but the hub of the West End's action is virtually at your doorstep if you lodge here, northwest of Piccadilly Circus and facing Mayfair to the south. Once known only for its town houses turned into B&Bs, the district now offers accommodations in all price ranges, catering to everyone from rock stars to frugal family travelers.

MAYFAIR   Bounded by Piccadilly, Hyde Park, and Oxford and Regent streets, this is the most elegant, fashionable section of London, filled with luxury hotels, Georgian town houses, and swank shops. The area is sandwiched

Building facades in Mayfair.

between Piccadilly Circus and Hyde Park. It's convenient to London's best shopping and close to the West End theaters yet (a bit snobbily) removed from the peddlers and commerce of Covent Garden and Soho.

One of the curiosities of Mayfair is **Shepherd Market,** a village of pubs, two-story inns, restaurants, and book and food stalls, nestled within Mayfair's grandness. The hotels of Mayfair, especially those along Park Lane, are the most expensive and grand in London. This is the place if you're seeking sophisticated, albeit expensive, accommodations close to the **Bond Street** shops, boutiques, and art galleries.

Grosvenor Square (pronounced *Grov*-nor) is nicknamed "Little America" because it's home to the American Embassy and a statue of Franklin D. Roosevelt. **Berkeley Square** (*Bark*-ley) was made famous by the song "A Nightingale Sang in Berkeley Square." You'll want to dip into this exclusive section at least once.

ST. JAMES'S   Often called "Royal London," St. James's basks in its associations with everybody from the "merrie monarch" Charles II to Elizabeth II, who lives at its most famous address, **Buckingham Palace.** The neighborhood begins at **Piccadilly Circus** and moves southwest, incorporating **Pall Mall, The Mall, St. James's Park,** and **Green Park.** It's "frightfully convenient," as the English say; within its confines are American Express and many of London's leading department stores. This is the neighborhood where English gentlemen seek haven at that male-only bastion of English tradition, the gentlemen's club, where poker is played, drinks are consumed, and pipes are smoked (St. James's Club is one of the most prestigious of

View across the lake in St. James's Park.

these institutions). Be sure to stop in at **Fortnum & Mason,** 181 Piccadilly, the world's most luxurious grocery store. Launched in 1788, the store sent hams to the Duke of Wellington's army and baskets of tinned goodies to Florence Nightingale in the Crimea. Hotels in this neighborhood tend to be expensive, but if the Queen should summon you to Buckingham Palace, you won't have far to go.

WESTMINSTER   Westminster has been the seat of the British government since the days of Edward the Confessor (1042–66). Dominated by the **Houses of Parliament** and **Westminster Abbey,** the area runs along the Thames to the east of St. James's Park. **Trafalgar Square,** one of the city's major landmarks, is located at the area's northern end and remains a testament to England's victory over Napoleon in 1805. The square is home to the landmark National Gallery, which is filled with glorious paintings. Whitehall is the main thoroughfare, linking Trafalgar Square with **Parliament Square.** You can visit Churchill's Cabinet War Rooms and walk by **Downing Street** to see **Number 10,** home to Britain's prime minister (though the street itself is fenced in and guarded these days). No visit is complete without a call at **Westminster Abbey,** one of the greatest Gothic churches in the world. It has witnessed a parade of English history, beginning with William the Conqueror's coronation here on Christmas Day 1066.

Westminster also encompasses **Victoria,** an area that takes its name from bustling Victoria Station, "the gateway to the Continent." Many B&Bs and hotels have sprouted up here because of the neighborhood's proximity to the rail station. Victoria is cheap and convenient if you don't mind the noise and crowds.

Welfare recipients occupy many hotels along Belgrave Road. If you've arrived without a hotel reservation, you'll find the pickings better on the streets off Belgrave Road. Your best bet is to walk along Ebury Street, east of Victoria Station and Buckingham Palace Road. Here you'll find some of the best moderately priced lodgings in central London. Since you're near Victoria Station, the area is convenient for day trips to Oxford, Windsor, or Canterbury.

Beyond the West End

KNIGHTSBRIDGE   One of London's most fashionable neighborhoods, Knightsbridge is a top residential, hotel, and shopping district just south of Hyde Park. **Harrods** on Brompton Road is its chief attraction. Founded in 1901, Harrods has been called "the Notre Dame of department stores." Right nearby, **Beauchamp Place** (*Bee*-cham) is one of London's most fashionable shopping streets, a Regency-era, boutique-lined street with a scattering of restaurants. Most hotels here are deluxe or first class.

Knightsbridge is one of the most convenient areas of London, ideally located if you want to head east to the theater district or the Mayfair shops, or west to Chelsea or Kensington's restaurants and attractions.

BELGRAVIA   South of Knightsbridge, this area has long been an aristocratic quarter of London, rivaling Mayfair in grandeur. Although it reached its pinnacle of prestige during the reign of Queen Victoria, the Duke and Duchess of Westminster still live at **Eaton Square,** and Belgravia remains a hot area for chic hotels. The neighborhood's centerpiece is **Belgrave Square.** When town houses were built from 1825 to 1835, aristocrats followed—the Duke of Connaught, the Earl of Essex, and even Queen Victoria's mother.

Belgravia is a tranquil district. If you lodge here, no one will ever accuse you of staying on the "wrong side of the tracks." The neighborhood is convenient to the little restaurants and pubs of Chelsea, which is located to Belgravia's immediate west. Victoria Station is located to its immediate east, so Belgravia is convenient if you're planning to take day trips from London.

CHELSEA   This stylish Thames-side district lies south and to the west of Belgravia. It begins at **Sloane Square,** with **Gilbert Ledward's Venus fountain** playing watery music. The area has always been a favorite of writers and artists, including Oscar Wilde (who was arrested here), George Eliot, James Whistler, J. M. W. Turner, Henry James, and Thomas Carlyle (whose former home can be visited). Mick Jagger and Margaret Thatcher (not together) have been more recent residents, and the late Princess Diana and her "Sloane Rangers" (a term used to describe posh women, derived from Chelsea's Sloane Square) of the 1980s gave the area even more recognition. There are some swank hotels here and a scattering of modestly priced ones. The main drawback to Chelsea is inaccessibility. Except for Sloane Square, there's a dearth of Tube stops, and unless you like to take a lot of buses or expensive taxis, you may find getting around a chore.

Chelsea's major boulevard is **King's Road,** where Mary Quant launched the miniskirt in the 1960s and where the English punk look began. King's Road runs the length of Chelsea; it's at its liveliest on Saturday. The outrageous fashions of the King's Road boutiques aren't typical of otherwise upmarket Chelsea, an elegant village filled with town houses and little mews dwellings that only successful stockbrokers and solicitors can

Buildings in Chelsea.

afford to occupy. On the Chelsea/Fulham border is **Chelsea Harbour,** a luxury development of apartments and restaurants with a marina. You can spot its tall tower from far away; the golden ball on top moves up and down to indicate the tide level.

KENSINGTON   This Royal Borough (W8) lies west of Kensington Gardens and Hyde Park and is traversed by two of London's major shopping streets, **Kensington High Street** and **Kensington Church Street.** Since 1689, when asthmatic William III fled Whitehall Palace for Nottingham House (where the air was fresher), the district has enjoyed royal associations. In time, Nottingham House became Kensington Palace, and the royals grabbed a chunk of Hyde Park to plant their roses. Queen Victoria was born here. Kensington Palace, or "KP," as the royals say, was home to the late Princess Margaret (who had 20 rooms with a view) and is still home to Prince and Princess Michael of Kent, and the Duke and Duchess of Gloucester. Kensington Gardens is now open to the public, ever since George II decreed that "respectably dressed" people would be permitted in on Saturday—provided that no servants, soldiers, or sailors came (as you might imagine, that rule is long gone). During the reign of William III, Kensington Square developed, attracting artists and writers. Thackeray wrote *Vanity Fair* while living here. With all those royal associations, Kensington is a fashionable neighborhood. If you're a frugal traveler, head for South Kensington (see below) for moderately priced hotels and B&Bs. Southeast of Kensington Gardens and Earl's Court, primarily residential **South Kensington** is often called "museumland" because it's dominated by a complex of museums and colleges, including the **Natural History Museum,** the **Victoria and Albert Museum,** and the **Science Museum;** nearby is **Royal Albert Hall.** South Kensington boasts some fashionable restaurants and town-house hotels. One of the neighborhood's curiosities is the **Albert Memorial,** completed in 1872 by Sir George Gilbert Scott; for sheer excess, this Victorian monument is unequaled in the world.

A hotel room in Kensington is a prestigious address. But as Princess Margaret may have told you, you're at the far stretch of the West End, lying some 20 minutes by Tube from the heart of the theater district. As for South Kensington, it was once considered the "boondocks," although with the boundaries of the West End expanding, the neighborhood is much closer to the action than it has ever been before.

EARL'S COURT   Earl's Court lies below Kensington, bordering the western half of Chelsea. For decades a staid residential district, drawing genteel ladies wearing pince-nez glasses, Earl's Court now attracts a younger crowd (often gay), particularly at night, to its pubs, wine bars, and coffeehouses. It's a popular base for budget travelers, thanks to its wealth of B&Bs and budget hotels and its convenient access to central London: A 15-minute Tube ride takes you into the heart of Piccadilly.

WEST BROMPTON   Once regarded as a hinterland, this neighborhood is seen today as an extension of central London. It lies directly south of Earl's Court (take the Tube to West Brompton) and southeast of West Kensington. Its focal point is the sprawling **Brompton Cemetery,** a flower-filled "green lung" (park) and burial place of such famous names as Frederick Leyland, the pre-Raphaelite patron, who died in 1892. It has many good restaurants, pubs, and taverns, as well as some budget hotels.

PADDINGTON & BAYSWATER   **Paddington** radiates out from Paddington Station, north of Hyde Park and Kensington Gardens. It's one of the major B&B centers in London, attracting budget travelers who fill the lodgings in Sussex Gardens and Norfolk Square. After the first railway was introduced in London in 1836, a circle of sprawling railway terminals, including Paddington Station (which was built in 1838), spurred the growth of this middle-class area. Just south of Paddington, north of Hyde Park, and abutting more fashionable Notting Hill to the west is **Bayswater,** also filled with a large number of B&Bs that attract budget travelers. Inspired by Marylebone and elegant Mayfair, a relatively prosperous set of Victorian merchants built terrace houses around spacious squares in this area.

Paddington and Bayswater are sort of "in between" areas of London. If you've come to London to see the attractions in the east, including the British Museum, the Tower of London, and the theater district, you'll find yourself commuting a lot. Stay here for moderately priced lodgings (there are expensive hotels, too) and

Portobello Road in Notting Hill.

Primrose Hill.

for convenience to transportation. Rapidly gentrifying, this area ranges from seedy to swank.

On the other (north) side of Westway/Marylebone Road are **Maida Vale** and **St. John's Wood,** two villages that have been absorbed by central London. Maida Vale lies west of **Regent's Park,** north of Paddington, and next to the more prestigious St. John's Wood (home to the Beatles' Abbey Road Studios and Lord's Cricket ground). The area is very sports-oriented; if you take the Tube to Maida Vale, you'll find Paddington Recreation Ground, plus a smaller "green lung" called Paddington Bowling and Sports Club. The area is also home to some of the BBC studios.

PRIMROSE HILL   Londoners refer to Primrose Hill as their "quaint village." In H. G. Wells' book The War of the Worlds, Primrose Hill was the site of the final Martian encampment. Today it's the name of a pretty urban village of Victorian terrace houses and also a hill, rising 78m high (256 ft.) on the north side of Regent's Park in North London. From the hill you have a panoramic sweep of central London to the southeast and the village of Hampstead Heath to the north. In addition to the view, visitors come here to explore High Street and check out the fashionable boutiques.

NOTTING HILL   Fashionable Notting Hill is bounded on the east by Bayswater and on the south by Kensington. Hemmed in on the north by Westway and on the west by the Shepherd's Bush ramp leading to the M40, it has many turn-of-the-20th-century mansions and small houses sitting on quiet, leafy streets, plus a growing number of hot restaurants and clubs. Gentrified in recent years, it's becoming an extension of central London. Hotels are few, but increasingly chic.

Even more remote than Paddington and Bayswater, Notting Hill lies at least another 10 minutes west of those districts. In spite of that, many young professional visitors to London wouldn't stay anywhere else.

In the northern half of Notting Hill is the hip neighborhood known as **Notting Hill Gate,** home to Portobello Road, which boasts one of London's most famous street markets. The area Tube stops are Notting Hill Gate, Holland Park, and Ladbroke Grove.

Nearby **Holland Park,** an expensive residential neighborhood, promotes itself as "10 minutes by Tube from practically anywhere," a bit of an exaggeration.

SHEPHERD'S BUSH   To the immediate west of Notting Hill Gate, this increasingly fashionable area is attracting a slew of artists and photographers, and in their wake a number of trendy new hangouts. Old milk-bottling factories are being turned into chic dives, and so on. The area is close to more upscale districts such as Holland Park and Notting Hill Gate. The main BBC national office is in Shepherd's Bush, and, yes, that is Kate Moss rushing along Goldhawk Road.

Farther Afield

GREENWICH   To the southeast of London, this suburb, which contains the prime meridian—"zero" for the reckoning of terrestrial longitudes—enjoyed its heyday under the Tudors. Henry VIII and both of his daughters, Mary I and Elizabeth I, were born here. Greenwich Palace, Henry's favorite, is long gone, though. Today's visitors come to this lovely port village for nautical sights along the Thames, including visits to the tiny *Gipsy Moth IV,* a 16m (52-ft.) ketch in which Sir Francis Chichester sailed solo around the world from 1966 to 1967. Other attractions include the **National Maritime Museum.**

HAMPSTEAD   This residential suburb of north London, beloved by Keats and Hogarth, is a favorite excursion for Londoners. Everyone from Sigmund Freud and D. H. Lawrence to Anna Pavlova and John Le Carré has lived here, and it's still one of the most desirable districts in the Greater London area. It has few hotels and, of course, is quite far from central London. Nonetheless, it's an attractive residential area, and many visitors appreciate its charms. Hampstead's centerpiece is Hampstead Heath, nearly 320 hectares (791 acres) of meadows and woodland; it maintains its rural atmosphere even though it's surrounded by cityscapes on all sides. The hilltop village of Hampstead is filled with cafes, tearooms, and restaurants, and there are pubs galore, some with historic pedigrees. Take the Northern Line to Hampstead Heath station.

HIGHGATE   Along with Hampstead, Highgate in north London is another choice residential area, particularly on or near **Pond Square** and along Highgate High Street. Once celebrated for its "sweet salutarie airs," Highgate has long been a desirable place for Londoners to live; locals still flock to its taverns and pubs for "exercise and harmless merriment" as they did in the old days. Today most visitors come to see **Highgate Cemetery,** London's most famous burial ground. It's the final resting place of such figures as Karl Marx and George Eliot.

HAMMERSMITH   Sitting on the north bank of the Thames, just to the west of Kensington, Hammersmith will fool you at first into thinking it's an industrial park, thanks to the stretch of factories between Putney and Hammersmith bridges. Actually, the area is predominantly residential. Its most attractive feature is its waterfront, filled with boathouses, small businesses, some very good restaurants, and artists' studios. Beyond Hammersmith Bridge, the neighborhood blossoms with 18th-century homes behind lime and catalpa trees, more boathouses, and pubs that spill out onto the river-bank as soon as warm weather hits. Some of London's best chefs have fled the heart of the West End and its ridiculous rents to open quality dining rooms here. See p. 228.

Nearby is the delightful old village of **Barnes,** with its ironwork-decorated Barnes Terrace. **Hammersmith Terrace,** a favorite stamping ground of artists, adds color to the neighborhood. Another stretch of gracious homes lies along **Chiswick Mall,** curling into Church Street. This area imitates an English village before thrusting you back into London along Great West Road.

THE BEST OF LONDON IN 1 DAY

Touring London in a day seems ridiculous at first, considering that it's a sprawling metropolis filled with treasures, but it can be done if you get an early start and have a certain discipline, plus a lot of stamina. Since Britain is the world's most famous kingdom, this "greatest hits" itinerary focuses on royal London, monumental London, and political London, with some great art thrown in to satisfy the inner soul. After an early morning trip to Westminster Abbey, you'll want to see London's greatest plaza, Trafalgar Square, take a grand "royal stroll," visit the National Gallery, and perhaps poke into Whitehall, seeing No. 10 Downing St. (home of the prime minister). A pint of lager in a Victorian pub and a night in a West End theater will cap your day very nicely. ***Start:*** *Tube to Westminster.*

1 Westminster Abbey ★★★

This early English Gothic abbey is the shrine of the nation, and most of England's kings and queens have been crowned here—and many are buried here as well. We always like to get here when it opens at 9:30am, before the crowds descend. Architecturally, its two highlights are the fan-vaulted Henry VII's Chapel (one of the loveliest in all of Europe) and the shrine to Edward the Confessor, containing the tombs of five kings and three queens. For a final look, walk over to the Poets' Corner, where everybody from Chaucer to Robert Browning, Dr. Samuel Johnson, and Alfred Lord Tennyson rests in peace. See p. 260.

As you emerge from Westminster Abbey, you confront the virtual symbol of London itself:

2 The Houses of Parliament & "Big Ben" ★★

Guarded over by "Big Ben" (the world's most famous timepiece), the former royal Palace of Westminster shelters both the House of Lords and the House of Commons and has done so since the 11th century. Gaining admission to the debating chambers requires a long wait and a lot of red tape that the "1-Day Visitor" will have to forego, but at least you can admire the massive architectural pile from the outside before passing on your way.

If you feel you've missed something, duck into the Jewel Tower across the street (p. 245), one of only two surviving buildings from the medieval Palace of Westminster. Here you can see an exhibition of the history of Parliament and even use a touch-screen computer that takes you on a virtual tour of both Houses of Parliament. See p. 245.

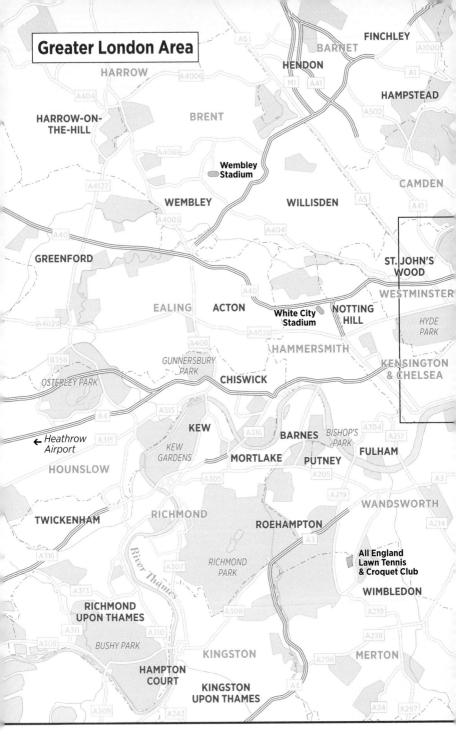

Greater London Area

FINCHLEY

BARNET

HENDON

HAMPSTEAD

HARROW

A4006

A1000

A1

A5

M1 A41

A502

HARROW-ON-
THE-HILL

BRENT

A4088

CAMDEN

A4127

A41

Wembley
Stadium

WEMBLEY

WILLISDEN

A5

A4005

ST. JOHN'S
WOOD

A404

GREENFORD

A40

WESTMINSTER

A4020

EALING

ACTON

White City
Stadium

NOTTING
HILL

HYDE
PARK

A4020

HAMMERSMITH

A406

KENSINGTON
& CHELSEA

B358

GUNNERSBURY
PARK

OSTERLEY PARK

CHISWICK

A315

A4

A315

KEW

A316

BARNES

BISHOP'S
PARK

A304

A217

← Heathrow
Airport

A315

KEW
GARDENS

MORTLAKE

PUTNEY

FULHAM

HOUNSLOW

A305

A205

A3

A219

WANDSWORTH

TWICKENHAM

RICHMOND

ROEHAMPTON

A214

A316

A3

A307

All England
Lawn Tennis
& Croquet Club

RICHMOND
PARK

RIVER THAMES

A313

WIMBLEDON

A219

RICHMOND
UPON THAMES

A308

A311

A310

BUSHY PARK

A238

KINGSTON

MERTON

HAMPTON
COURT

A298

A308

KINGSTON
UPON THAMES

A3

A309

A243

A24

A297

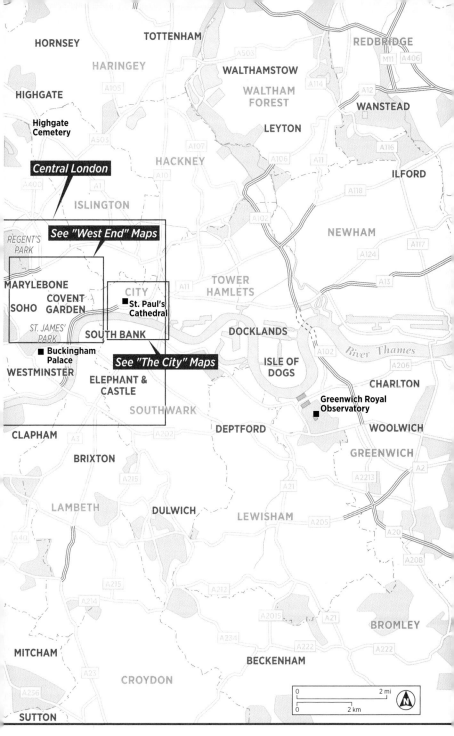

HORNSEY

TOTTENHAM

REDBRIDGE

HARINGEY

A503

M11 A406

WALTHAMSTOW

HIGHGATE

A105

WALTHAM
FOREST

A12

WANSTEAD

Highgate
Cemetery

A503

LEYTON

A116

ILFORD

HACKNEY

A107

A106

A11

A118

Central London

A400

A1

A10

A102

ISLINGTON

NEWHAM

A117

REGENT'S
PARK

See "West End" Maps

A124

MARYLEBONE

CITY

A11

TOWER
HAMLETS

A13

SOHO

COVENT
GARDEN

St. Paul's
Cathedral

ST. JAMES'
PARK

SOUTH BANK

DOCKLANDS

A102

River Thames

A206

See "The City" Maps

Buckingham
Palace

ISLE OF
DOGS

WESTMINSTER

ELEPHANT &
CASTLE

CHARLTON

Greenwich Royal
Observatory

CLAPHAM

A3

A202

SOUTHWARK

DEPTFORD

WOOLWICH

BRIXTON

A215

GREENWICH

A2

LAMBETH

DULWICH

LEWISHAM

A2213

A205

A20

A40

A215

A208

A214

A212

BROMLEY

A2015

A21

MITCHAM

A234

A222

A222

CROYDON

BECKENHAM

A23

A256

0   2 mi

SUTTON

0   2 km

Continue walking north along Whitehall until you reach:

3 No. 10 Downing St.

Hang a left and look down Downing Street to No. 10, flanked by policemen. Because of security concerns, it is no longer possible to walk down the street—you can only look down it through the gates on Whitehall. The official residence of the prime minister isn't much of a sight and is rather modest, but it's been the home of everybody from Sir Winston Churchill to Margaret Thatcher. Today David Cameron and his family call it home. Although the building is hardly palatial, it's the most famous address in Britain, other than Buckingham Palace, and all visitors seem to want to take a peek.

After that look, continue north to:

4 Trafalgar Square ★★

The hub of London, this is Britain's most famous square and the scene of many a demonstration. A 44m (144-ft.) granite statue of Horatio Viscount Nelson (1758–1805) dominates the square. As you walk around this square, noting the ferocious pigeons "dive-bombing," you'll know that you're in the very heart of London where thousands amass on New Year's Eve to ring in another year. See p. 246.

Right on this square, you can enter the:

5 National Gallery ★★★

On the north side of Trafalgar Square looms this massive gallery. All the big names, from Leonardo da Vinci to Rembrandt, from van Gogh to Cézanne, strut their stuff here. Displaying some of the most important art ever created, the panoramic galleries cover 8 centuries. This is one of the greatest art museums on the planet. On even the most rushed of schedules, you'll want to devote at least 1½ hours to its galleries. Since everybody's taste in art differs, check out our "Insider's tip" under the National Gallery review (p. 248). A computer allows you to customize your own tour. Select 10 paintings you'd most like to see, and a computer will design your own map and print it out for you.

Directly north of Trafalgar Square, you enter the precincts of:

6 Covent Garden ★

The old fruit-and-vegetable market of Eliza Doolittle fame is long gone, and the market has been recycled into one of the most bustling and exciting sections of London today. Begin with a walk around **the Piazza ★★**, the center of Covent Garden. When architect Inigo Jones designed it in 1633, it became London's first square. To its south you'll see **St. Paul's Church ★**, which Jones called "the handsomest barn in England." Immediately to the southeast of St. Paul's you can enter the **Jubilee Market** and to its immediate east the **London Transport Museum.** After wandering around the gardens and after a heavy morning of sightseeing, even with a full English breakfast, you may be ready for lunch. For our pounds sterling, there is no better place for lunch in all of London than Covent Garden.

7 ☕ **Porters English Restaurant** ★★

We suggest a visit to our dear old friend, the Earl of Bradford, who owns and runs this venerable Covent Garden favorite. Try one of Lady Bradford's old English pies (ever had lamb and apricot?), and finish off with her fabled steamed pudding, made with ginger and banana. 17 Henrietta St., WC2. ✆ **020/7836-6466.** Tube: Covent Garden or Leicester Sq. See p. 189.

The day is marching on, and you should too if you want to take in more that London has to offer.

At Covent Garden, take the Tube to Charing Cross Station to the south of Covent Garden. After disembarking here, prepare yourself for one of the grandest strolls in all of Britain, walking west along:

8 The Mall ★★ & Buckingham Palace ★★

A stroll along the Mall all the way west to Buckingham Palace is the most aristocratic walk in Britain. Passing King George IV's glorious Carlton House terrace on your right, you can enjoy the same view Elizabeth II sees when she rides in her gilded "fairy-tale" coach to open Parliament every year.

Whether you can actually go inside Buckingham Palace itself depends on the time of year. For possible visits, see the information on p. 242. We've deliberately skipped the Changing of the Guard ceremony, which isn't held every day and is often difficult to schedule. It's an overrated attraction anyway.

After viewing Buckingham Palace, walk along Constitution Hill to the Tube stop at Hyde Park Corner. Once there, head east for one big final attraction for the afternoon:

The (overrated) Changing of the Guard at Buckingham Palace.

4

SUGGESTED LONDON ITINERARIES

The Best of London in 1 Day

9 The Tower of London ★★★

We prefer to visit this attraction later in the afternoon, when some of the hordes pouring out of tour buses have departed. A first-time visitor to London wouldn't dare miss this old symbol of blood and gore standing on the Thames for 900 years. Many famous Englishmen have lost their heads at the Tower. It's been a palace, a prison, and a royal mint, but mostly it's a living museum of British history. Since you don't have a lot of time, take one of the hour-long guided tours conducted by the much-photographed Beefeaters. They make the history of the Tower come alive with their often humorous and irreverent commentary (see p. 256).

After viewing the Tower, we suggest you head back to your hotel and take a much-needed break before descending on London by night.

We like to begin our evening with a pint in an evocative London pub. Try one of the best and also one of the most famous:

10 🍺 Salisbury

This Art Nouveau pub is in the heart of the theater district. You can enjoy a drink and a quick pub dinner of home-cooked pies or freshly made salads before heading out to see the show of your choice. 90 St. Martin's Lane, WC2. **☎ 020/7836-5863.** Tube: Leicester Sq. See p. 385.

11 A Night at a London Theater

Before purchasing your ticket, read our box called "Curtain Going Up!" (p. 363), and you might save a lot of money. Unless you've got your heart set on seeing a big London hit, perhaps a musical, we suggest your one-and-only night in London be spent at **Shakespeare's Globe Theatre** (p. 363). This is a replica of the Elizabethan original where the Bard premiered many of his plays. The productions, often performed in Elizabethan costume as in Shakespeare's days, are of the highest quality, often showcasing the talents of many of Britain's greatest thespians, both young and old.

Head back to your hotel for a well-earned night of rest and promise yourself you'll come back to London soon.

THE BEST OF LONDON IN 2 DAYS

If you've already made your way through "The Best of London in 1 Day," you'll find your second full-day tour takes in a different part of London. You've seen Royal London. Now visit what might be called "Academic London" by heading to the history-rich district of Bloomsbury, following in the footsteps of Charles Dickens and Virginia Woolf. After lunch, head for "the City," London's financial district, and wander around St. Paul's Cathedral, masterpiece of Sir Christopher Wren. Then have a thrilling afternoon riding the British Airways London Eye and visiting the Tate Modern. ***Start:*** *Russell Square.*

1 The British Museum ★★★

This is the mammoth home of one of the world's greatest treasure troves—much of it plundered from other parts of the globe when Britannia ruled the waves. The most exciting of these treasures are the Parthenon Marbles,

Spring flowers and Hotel Russell at Russell Square.

stolen from Greece, and the Rosetta Stone, stolen from Egypt. You'll need at least 2 hours for even the most cursory of visits. An easy-to-follow map at the entrance will help you hit all the highlights, including the legendary Black Obelisk, dating from around 860 b.c. and exhibited in the Nimrud Gallery. You can't see everything, so don't even try. But you'll see enough to convince yourself you need to make another visit some time in the future. End your quickie tour in the modern Great Court covering the celebrated Reading Room where Karl Marx wrote *Das Kapital*. See p. 238 for more information.

The museum doesn't open until 10am, but early birds can arrive before and take a brisk morning walk, getting the feel of this famous district. Our favorite square for wandering is **Russell Square** (you can take the Tube straight there), followed by **Bedford Square** to the east and **Bloomsbury Square** to the southeast.

After the British Museum, it's time for lunch. You've already dined in Covent Garden (see Day 1), so it's time to head for "the City," the financial district of London in the East End.

2 🍵 Bow Wine Vaults

No place in the City is more evocative and atmospheric than this venerated choice for lunch. Here you can mingle with the movers and shakers of the City's financial district, enjoying well-prepared, affordable food and a drink in the bar or in the more formal street-level dining room. We always go for the Dover sole or the mixed grill (no one does this dish better than the English). 10 Bow Churchyard, EC4. ✆ **020/7248-1121.** Tube: St. Paul's. See p. 380.

Fortified for the afternoon, you can begin your descent on yet another monument:

3 St. Paul's Cathedral ★★★

Wren's Cathedral, the fifth to be built on this spot, is not filled with great art and treasures. But it's an adventure nonetheless. The thrill comes in climbing to the dome and taking in the Whispering Gallery (259 steps), the Stone Gallery (530 steps), and especially the **panoramic sweep** ★★★ from the Inner Golden Gallery on top of the dome. See p. 250.

4 Tate Modern ★★★

On the south side of the Thames, the relatively new Tate Modern (p. 252) shelters the greatest collection of international 20th-century art in Britain. You'll see all the Warhols, Picassos, and Pollocks an art devotee could ever dream of. Allow at least 1½ hours for the most cursory of visits.

St. Paul's Cathedral dome.

Head for Westminster Bridge (Tube: Westminster), the embarkation point for the:

5 British Airways London Eye ★

The world's largest observation wheel is the fourth-tallest structure in London, with panoramic views that extend on a clear day for 40km (25 miles). Each of the 32 futuristic-looking "pods" carries visitors to a bird's-eye view of London, making a complete rotation every 30 minutes. Currently, it's the most popular ride in London. See p. 306.

6 Royal National Theatre

For your final night in London (assuming you're skipping Day 3), we'd recommend a night at the Royal National Theatre. On the South Bank of the Thames, this is one of the world's great stage companies—not just one theater, but a trio of modern auditoriums, each with the latest equipment and great acoustics. Even the Queen attends for one of the new plays, comedies, or musicals. There is always a major event being presented here, often with the greatest thespians or musicians in the world. You can arrive early for a pretheater meal in one of the cultural complex's dining facilities, such as the main restaurant, the Mezzanine. See p. 363.

THE BEST OF LONDON IN 3 DAYS

Having sampled the charms of London in just 2 days, make your third and final day a little different by skipping out of town and heading for nearby Windsor Castle, which the Queen prefers as a royal residence to Buckingham Palace itself. She's got a point there—it's rather splendid. Return to London in time for a final afternoon of sightseeing in Hyde Park and elegant Mayfair, home to some of the world's most expensive real estate. **Start:** *Waterloo Station or Paddington Station (depending on your hotel location).*

1   Windsor Castle ★★★

In just half an hour, a train from London will deliver you to the royal town of Windsor (p. 389), site of England's most legendary castle. The first castle here was ordered built by William the Conqueror, and much of English history has unfolded within its walls. If you skipped the Changing of the Guard ceremony in London, you can see an even more exciting pageant here, though it takes place only from April to July Monday to Saturday at 11am (winter hours differ slightly—see p. 393 for more details). On a first visit to the castle, don't miss its greatest attraction, **St. George's Chapel ★★★**, where British monarchs are entombed, and try to budget enough time to see the state apartments, including George IV's elegant chambers. No, you can't go into the Queen's present bedchamber. Before leaving the castle

St. George's Chapel.

precincts, wander the beautifully landscaped Jubilee Garden spread over 8 hectares (20 acres).

Since you'll need 2 hours to explore Windsor Castle, this will put you in the little town for lunch, which, incidentally, is not a gourmet citadel.

2 🍷 Gilbey's Bar and Restaurant

Just across the bridge from Windsor, Gilbey's lies on the main street of Eton, serving modern English and Continental cuisine. Its fixed-price menu is one of the best bargains in either Windsor or Eton. 82–83 High St., Eton. ✆ **01753/854921.** See p. 396.

After lunch, with your precious time fading, we suggest an immediate return to London, arriving at Waterloo or Paddington Station, where you can hook up with the Tube leading to:

3 Hyde Park ★★

Adjoining Kensington Gardens, Hyde Park (p. 299; Tube: Marble Arch) was the former deer-hunting ground of Henry VIII. Allow at least 30 minutes for a stroll through the scenic grandeur of London's "green lung." Our favorite oasis in the park is a miniature lake known as the **Serpentine,** where you can row, sail model boats, or even swim. In the northeast corner of the park,

The Serpentine in Hyde Park.

at **Speakers Corner,** you can hear everything from protesters calling for the overthrow of the monarchy to sex advocates demanding legalization of child prostitution in Britain. Any point of view goes here. You can even make a speech of your own. After taking in the landmark Marble Arch (a gate originally designed as the entrance to Buckingham Palace), stroll east along Upper Brook Street to:

4 Grosvenor Square

In the heart of Mayfair, and one of the world's most famous squares, this was the grandest of all London addresses for 2 centuries. In modern times, its former allure has been diminished by Eero Saarinen's outsized and grandiose **U.S. Embassy** (1956), which led to the demolition of the west side of the square. As you cross the square through the garden, take in William Reid Dick's bronze statue of Franklin D. Roosevelt, who honeymooned with Eleanor at Brown's Hotel in Mayfair.

Time out for some ritzy shopping (or at least window shopping) along:

5 Oxford Street

From Grosvenor Square (northeast corner), cut north up Duke Street until you reach the junction of Oxford Street (p. 330), at which point you can head east, moving deeper into the heart of commercial and theatrical London. A shopping mecca since 1908 when the American retail magnate, Gordon Selfridge, opened Selfridge's Department Store, this is the most popular street in London for out-of-town shoppers. It is no longer a "lurking place for cut-throats," as an early-18th-century writer called Oxford Street, although with the present pound-to-dollar ratio, you might indeed consider some of today's merchants highway robbers. Many of the fruit-and-flower vendors you encounter along Oxford Street are the great-grandchildren of former traders, their style of making a living passed on from one generation to the next. When you come to New Bond Street, cut southeast along:

6 New & Old Bond Streets

London's most luxurious shopping street, consisting of both Old and New Bond streets (p. 331; Tube: Bond St.), links Piccadilly with Oxford Street. "The Bonds" have both traditional old English shops and outlets for the latest and hottest international designers. In the Georgian era, the beau monde of London promenaded here, window shopping. Later, the fun-loving set ranging from the Prince of Wales to the celebrated photographer Cecil Beaton and others could be seen parading up and down the tiny Old Bond Street, with its deluxe art galleries. Today this dazzling thoroughfare of shops is celebrated for haute everything, from couture to jewelry.

Once you reach the intersection with Piccadilly, continue east, passing on your left the:

7 Burlington Arcade

The Burlington Arcade (p. 331; Tube: Piccadilly Circus) closes at 5:30pm, so, of course, try to get there before then. The blueprint for all London arcades, the Burlington Arcade opened back in 1815, and it's been going strong ever since. The glass-roofed, Regency-style passage is lined with exclusive shops and boutiques and lit by wrought-iron lamps. Luxury items such as jewelry and designer cashmeres are sold here. Look for the Beadles, London's representative of Britain's oldest police force.

On the opposite side of Piccadilly, you enter the precincts of the world's most famous food department store:

8 🍵 Fortnum & Mason ★★★
Founded in 1707, this deluxe purveyor of fancy foodstuffs is still grocer to the Queen. "Mr. Fortnum" and "Mr. Mason" still present a footman's show on the outside clock every hour. See p. 232. You can enjoy an elegant tea in St. James Restaurant, 181 Piccadilly. 📞 **020/7734-8040.**

After tea, continue walking east into:

9 Piccadilly Circus ★
What Times Square is to New York, Piccadilly Circus is to London. Dating from 1819, the circus (or square) centers on a statue of Eros from 1893. That symbol of love is about the only thing that occasionally brings together the diverse group of people who converge on the circus. This is the traffic hub of London, and you're at the doorway to "theaterland" if you'd like to cap your visit to the West End with a final show.

Burlington Arcade.

Piccadilly Circus.

At the end of 3 days, realize that the time was ridiculously short to take in the allure of London—and promise yourself some future visit, when you can discover such London neighborhoods as trendy Chelsea or aristocratic Belgravia and take a day trip on a boat sailing down the river to Hampton Court.

5

WHERE TO STAY

The good news is that more than 10,000 hotel rooms have opened in London in the past decade, relieving the overcrowding that existed during peak travel months. The downside? Most of these hotels are in districts far from the city center and are of the no-frills budget-chain variety.

In recent years, some hoteliers have decided to adapt former public or institutional buildings rather than start from scratch. With all the vast improvements and upgrades made at the turn of the 21st century, chances are you'll like your room. What you won't like is the price. Even if a hotel remains scruffy, London hoteliers have little embarrassment about jacking up prices. Hotels in all categories remain overpriced.

London boasts some of the most famous hotels in the world—temples of luxury like Claridge's and the Dorchester, and more recent rivals like the Four Seasons. The problem is that there are too many of these high-priced hotels (and now there are many budget options) and not enough moderately priced options.

Even at the luxury level, you may be surprised at what you don't get. Many of the stately Victorian and Edwardian gems are so steeped in tradition that they lack modern conveniences standard in other luxury hotels around the world. A few have modernized with a vengeance, but others retain amenities from the Boer War era. London does have some cutting-edge, chintz-free hotels that seem to have been flown in straight from Los Angeles—complete with high-end sound systems and gadget-filled marble bathrooms. But these hotels are not necessarily superior; though they're streamlined and convenient, they frequently lack the personal service and spaciousness that characterize the grand old hotels.

With their charm, intimacy, and attention to detail, boutique hotels are an attractive alternative to larger, stuffier establishments. The "boutiquing" of the hotel scene continues—the city offers more personally run and privately operated hotels than ever. We've surveyed the best of them, concentrating on reasonably priced choices.

If you're looking for budget options, don't despair. London has some good-value places in the lower price ranges, and we've included the best of these. An affordable option is a bed-and-breakfast. The following reliable services will recommend and arrange a B&B room for you: The **London Bed and Breakfast Agency Limited** (☎ **020/7586-2768;** fax 020/7586-6567; www.londonbb. com) is a reputable agency that can provide inexpensive accommodations in selected private homes for £26 to £90 per person per night, based on double occupancy (although some accommodations will cost a lot more). **London B&B** (☎ **800/872-2632** in the U.S.; fax 619/531-1686; www.londonbandb.com) offers B&B accommodations in private family residences or unhosted apartments. Homes are inspected for quality and comfort, amenities, and convenience.

Instead of B&Bs, some savvy visitors prefer long-term options, including self-catering accommodations or else vacation or apartment rentals. One of the

PREVIOUS PAGE: **Room at the Covent Garden Hotel.**

best establishments for arranging this type of rental is **Coach House London Rentals** ★★, 2 Tunly Rd., London SW17 7QJ (℗ **020/8133-8332;** fax 020/8181-6152; www.rentals.chslondon.com). The agency represents more than 75 properties, ranging from modest studio flats for friendly couples to spacious homes that can sleep up to 12. The minimum length of a stay is 5 nights, and a car can be sent to the airport to pick you up.

For the upmarket traveler, the aptly named **Uptown Reservations,** 8 Kelso Place, London W8 5QD (℗ **020/7937-2001;** fax 020/7937-6660; www.uptownres.co.uk), features attractive, comfortably furnished accommodations in elegant private homes in swanky districts of the city. You share your digs with the hosts themselves, many of whom are artists, diplomats, or, in some rare cases, lords of the realm who need extra money for living expenses. A substantial breakfast is included in the price.

Amazing discounts, seemingly unavailable elsewhere, are offered by **Visit Hotels.com,** 37B New Cavendish St., London W1G 8JR (www.visithotels.com). Sometimes discounts on a room can range up to 70%.

You can also look for deals on online travel booking sites like **Travelocity, Expedia, Orbitz, Priceline,** and **Hotwire,** or you can book hotels through **Hotels.com, Quikbook** (www.quikbook.com), and **Travelaxe** (www.travelaxe.com).

HotelChatter.com is a daily webzine offering smart coverage and critiques of hotels worldwide. Go to **TripAdvisor.com** or **HotelShark.com** for helpful independent consumer reviews of hotels and resort properties. It's a good idea to **get a confirmation number** and **make a printout** of any online booking transaction.

It's true that you can almost always get a room at a deluxe hotel if you're willing to pay the price. But during certain peak periods, including the high season (roughly Apr–Oct) and during trade shows, seasonal events, and royal occasions, rooms in all kinds of hotels may be snatched up early. Book ahead. If you arrive without a reservation, begin your search for a room as early in the day as possible. If you arrive late at night, you may have to take what you can get, often at a much higher price than you'd like.

RATE REGULATIONS All hotels, motels, inns, and guesthouses in Britain with four bedrooms or more (including self-catering accommodations) must display notices listing minimum and maximum overnight charges in a prominent place in the reception area or at the entrance. The prices must include any service charge and may include VAT. If VAT isn't included, then it must be shown separately. And if meals are included, this must be stated.

SAVING ON YOUR HOTEL ROOM The **rack rate** is the maximum rate a hotel charges for a room. Hardly anybody pays this price, however, except in high season or on holidays. To lower the cost of your room:

- **Ask about special rates or other discounts.** You may qualify for corporate, student, military, senior, frequent flier, trade union, or other discounts.
- **Dial direct.** When booking a room in a chain hotel, you'll often get a better deal by calling the individual hotel's reservation desk rather than the chain's main number.
- **Book online.** Many hotels offer Internet-only discounts or supply rooms to Priceline, Hotwire, or Expedia at rates much lower than the ones you can get through the hotel itself.

- **Remember the law of supply and demand.** You can save big on hotel rooms by traveling in a destination's off season or shoulder seasons, when rates typically drop, even at luxury properties.

- **Look into group or long-stay discounts.** If you come as part of a large group, you should be able to negotiate a bargain rate. Likewise, if you're planning a long stay (at least 5 days), you might qualify for a discount. As a general rule, expect 1 night free after a 7-night stay.

- **Sidestep excess surcharges and hidden costs.** Many hotels have adopted the unpleasant practice of nickel-and-diming guests with opaque surcharges. When you book a room, ask what is included in the room rate, and what is extra. Avoid dialing direct from hotel phones, which can have exorbitant rates. And don't be tempted by the room's minibar offerings: Most hotels charge through the nose for water, soda, and snacks. Finally, ask about local taxes and service charges, which can increase the cost of a room by 15% or more.

- **Book an efficiency.** A room with a kitchenette allows you to shop for groceries and cook your own meals. This is a big money saver, especially for families on long stays.

- **Consider enrolling in hotel chains' "frequent-stay" programs,** which are upping the ante lately to win the loyalty of repeat customers. Frequent guests can now accumulate points or credits to earn free hotel nights, airline miles, in-room amenities, merchandise, tickets to concerts and events, discounts on sporting facilities—and even credit toward stock in the participating hotel, in the case of the Jameson Inn hotel group. Perks are awarded not only by many chain hotels and motels (Hilton HHonors, Marriott Rewards, Wyndham ByRequest, to name a few) but also by individual inns and B&Bs. Many chain hotels partner with other hotel chains, car-rental firms, airlines, and credit card companies to give consumers additional incentive to do repeat business.

LANDING THE BEST ROOM   Somebody has to get the best room in the house. It might as well be you. You can start by joining the hotel's frequent-guest program, which may make you eligible for upgrades. A hotel-branded credit card usually gives its owner "silver" or "gold" status in frequent-guest programs for free. Always ask about a corner room. They're often larger and quieter, with more windows and light, and they often cost the same as standard rooms. When you make your reservation, ask if the hotel is renovating; if it is, request a room away from the construction. Ask about non-smoking rooms and rooms with views. Be sure to request your choice of twin, queen- or king-size beds. If you're a light sleeper, ask for a quiet room away from vending or ice machines, elevators, restaurants, bars, and discos. Ask for a room that has been recently renovated or refurbished.

If you aren't happy with your room when you arrive, ask for another one. Most lodgings will be willing to accommodate you.

Upstairs, Downstairs

Elevators are called "lifts." Some of them are just as Victorian as the edifices in which they operate. They are, however, regularly inspected and completely safe. Many hotels (and especially B&Bs) lack even these rudimentary elevators, making those hotels inaccessible for individuals with disabilities. If you have mobility issues, call ahead and make sure there isn't a steep, narrow staircase between the lobby and your guest room.

BEST HOTEL BETS

- **Best Location:** Opposite the historic Haymarket Theatre, the **Haymarket Hotel,** 1 Suffolk Place SW1 (☎ **020/470-4000**), is the perfect choice for theatergoers. In an original 19th-century building by John Nash, a modern, sophisticated hotel in bold colors has been created. See p. 133.

- **Best in the East End:** The first luxury hotel to be built in Holborn, **Renaissance London Chancery Court,** 252 High Holborn, WC1 (☎ **800/468-3571** or 020/7829-9888; www.marriott.com), opened in 2001 and became an instant hit. A 1914 landmark building has been stunningly transformed into this citadel of luxury and plush comfort. See p. 125.

- **Best for a Romantic Getaway:** Hip couples check into the **Covent Garden Hotel,** 10 Monmouth St., WC2 (☎ **800/553-6674** or 020/7806-1000), which has been hailed as one of the 25 hottest places to stay in the world. The former hospital is now the epitome of chic comfort, with rooms so elegant and stylish that romance is inevitable. See p. 130.

- **Best Historic Hotel:** Founded by the former manservant to Lord Byron, the stylish **Brown's Hotel,** 30 Albemarle St., W1 (☎ **020/7493-6020**), dates back to Victorian times. It's one of London's most genteel hotels, with its legendary afternoon tea and paneled bar. See p. 134.

- **Best for Business Travelers:** Wheelers and dealers head to the **Langham,** 1C Portland Place, W1 (☎ **800/223-6800** or 020/7636-1000), which boasts sleek styling and grand public rooms. At times, it seems all the world's business is conducted from this nerve center. See p. 152.

- **Best Trendy Hotel: St. Martins Lane,** 45 St. Martin's Lane, WC2N (☎ **800/697-1791** or 020/7300-5500; www.stmartinslane.com), is almost without challenge in this category. Ian Schrager has brought New York cutting-edge style to a 1960s building in Covent Garden. It's his first hotel outside the U.S., and it's eccentric, irreverent, and whimsical. Would Nicole Kidman go anywhere else? See p. 131.

- **Best for Thoroughly British Ambience:** In a gaslit courtyard in back of St. James's Palace, **Dukes Hotel,** 35 St. James's Place, SW1 (☎ **800/381-4702** or 020/7491-4840), has an unsurpassed dignity. From the bread-and-butter pudding served in the clubby dining room to the impeccable service, at Dukes there will always be an England. See p. 137.

- **Best Service:** Arguably London's chicest address, **Baglioni,** 60 Hyde Park Gate, SW7 (☎ **020/7368-5700**), is a pricey citadel, opening onto Kensington Gardens. Service in the style of *la dolce vita* is topnotch and continues at high speed 24 hours per day. See p. 147.

- **Best Atmosphere:** Creaky, quirky, the **Fielding Hotel,** 4 Broad Court, Bow St., WC2 (☎ **020/7836-8305**), is in an alleyway in the center of Covent Garden—the heart of London excitement—almost opposite the Royal Opera House, with pubs, shops, markets, restaurants, even street entertainment, right outside your door. Stay here and London is at your fingertips. See p. 131.

- **Best Boutique Hotel: The Beaufort,** 33 Beaufort Gardens, SW3 (☎ **020/7584-5252;** www.thebeaufort.co.uk), is a gem that's sure to charm. Personal service and tranquillity combine for a winning choice, a private but not snobbish place 183m (600 ft.) from the famed Harrods Department Store. See p. 143.

o **Best Inexpensive Hotel:** In this price category, it's hard to be chic, but the **Pavilion,** 34–36 Sussex Gardens, W2 (© **020/7262-0905**), manages to do it. Known for its bedrooms' wacky themes, this theatrical and slightly outrageous hotel attracts models and music-industry folks. Rooms range in decor from Asian bordello ("Enter the Dragon") to 1970s kitsch ("Honky-Tonk Afro"). See p. 159.

o **Best for Families Who Don't Want to Break the Bank:** The **Colonnade,** 2 Warrington Crescent, W9 (© **020/7286-1052;** www.theetoncollection. com), stands in the canal-laced Little Venice section. Located in a safe residential area, this family-friendly hotel lets children under 12 stay free in their parent's room, and the staff can also arrange babysitting. See p. 162.

o **Best B&B:** Year after year, **Aster House,** 3 Sumner Place, SW7 (© **020/7581-5888;** www.asterhouse.com), keeps its standards high and remains one of London's best B&Bs. A friendly, inviting, welcoming place, it's safely tucked away on a tree-lined street in the heart of South Kensington. See p. 143.

o **Best for Value:** In historic Bloomsbury, site of the British Museum, the **Jenkins Hotel,** 45 Cartwright Gardens, WC1 (© **020/7387-2067**), has been hailed by London's *Mail on Sunday* as one of the city's "10 best hotel values"— and we heartily concur. This homey, Georgian-style hotel is straight out of an Agatha Christie TV show (indeed, it was featured on *Poirot*). See p. 128.

IN & AROUND THE CITY

There are precious few hotels within the confines of the City (the financial district). If you plan to do a lot of business or sightseeing in the City and you're not very interested in shopping, theater, and nightlife, then the location might be perfect for you. (For a map showing the location of the following hotels as well as restaurants in the City, see "Where to Stay & Dine in & Around the City," on p. 175.)

Very Expensive

Andaz Liverpool Street Hotel ★★   In 2007, a new and untested branch of the Hyatt group (Andaz) transformed one of the East End's most venerable hotels into a glossy and very upscale monument to relaxed chic. Strategically positioned at the junction of two trendy, arts-conscious neighborhoods (Shoreditch and Hoxton) and the financial district, it managed to gracefully incorporate respect for the cutting-edge arts with allegiance to old-fashioned British pomp and circumstance. The original hotel dates from 1884, when it was designed by architect Charles Barry, best known for his work on the Houses of Parliament. The hotel's exterior is abloom in all its Victorian glory, complete with a stained-glass dome. Bedrooms are supremely comfortable, with state-of-the-art bathrooms and color schemes of dark red and white.

40 Liverpool St., London EC2M 7QN. © **800/228-9000** or 020/7961-1234. Fax 020/7961-1235. www.hyatt.com or http://london.liverpoolstreet.andaz.hyatt.com. 267 units. £125–£360 double; £250–£460 suite. AE, DC, MC, V. Tube: Liverpool St. Station. **Amenities:** 4 restaurants; 5 bars; concierge; state-of-the-art health club; room service. *In room:* A/C, TV/DVD, CD player, hair dryer, minibar, MP3 docking station, Wi-Fi (free).

Threadneedles ★★ 🏛 Established in 2002, this was the first luxury hotel built in the City, home to many of London's major financial institutions. The building, on Threadneedle Street, was constructed in 1856 and was originally designed to be a bank, complete with solid oak doors and marble columns. Contemporary comforts are found in the midsize-to-spacious bedrooms and suites. The accommodations contain such elegant touches as Egyptian-cotton and duck-down duvets on the beds. This luxury boutique hotel lies near the Bank of England, which is also known as "the Old Lady of Threadneedle Street."

5 Threadneedle St., London EC2R 8AY. 📞 **020/7657-8080.** Fax 020/7657-8100. www.theeton collection.com. 70 units. £405–£535 double; £617 suite. Discounts of about 50% offered for stays on Fri and Sat nights. AE, DC, MC, V. Tube: Bank. **Amenities:** Restaurant; bar; babysitting; concierge; room service. *In room:* A/C, TV, hair dryer, minibar, Wi-Fi (free).

Expensive

Grange City Hotel ★ This government-rated five-star hotel is one of the best equipped in London. From its 12 floors, panoramic views over the city spread before you, with the Tower of London looming in the distance. The bedrooms are luxuriously furnished with all the latest technology, plus fully fitted kitchens and marble and granite bathrooms. Males are banned from a block of 68 rooms in a special section. Even the room service staff in this block is female. The Grange Hotel Group decided to offer these "female friendly" rooms after a survey showed that half of its customers were women, many of whom felt vulnerable when traveling alone.

8-14 Cooper's Row, London EC 3 2BQ. 📞 **020/7863-3700.** Fax 020/7863-3701. www.grange hotels.com. 317 units. £110–£300 double; from £450 suite. AE, MC, V. Parking £2.50. Tube: Tower Hill, Monument, or Aldgate. **Amenities:** 3 restaurants; 2 bars; babysitting; concierge; health club & spa; room service. *In room:* A/C, TV/DVD, CD player, CD library, hair dryer, Internet (£5), kitchen.

Malmaison London ★★ Who could imagine that this used to be a dreary nursing home? Talk about recycling. The Victorian mansion block overlooks a green cobbled square and is the first London showcase for the U.K.-only hotel chain that is known for opening up winning hotels with clever contemporary designs, state-of-the-art facilities, and, as always, a chic little brasserie serving French classics. On the southern rim of once dreary, now trendy Clerkenwell in East London, Malmaison is awash in dark teak wood; tall, glowing floor lamps; a highly polished European staff; tasteful fabrics in neutral shades; and a portrait and bust in the lobby of Napoleon and Josephine, who spent many a "wanton night" at the original Château Malmaison outside Paris. The dark-wood guest rooms are individually designed and larger than average for central London.

18–21 Charterhouse Sq., London EC1M 6AH. 📞 **020/7012-3700.** Fax 020/7012-3702. www. malmaison-london.com. 97 units. £225–£295 double; £315–£520 suite. AE, MC, V. Tube: Barbican or Farringdon. **Amenities:** Restaurant; bar; concierge; exercise room; room service. *In room:* A/C, TV/DVD, CD player, CD library, minibar, Wi-Fi (free for 30 min., then £10 per day).

The Rookery ★ 🏛 When this hotel opened in the late 1990s, it salvaged the last three remaining then-derelict antique houses in Clerkenwell, a neighborhood midway between the West End and the City. The result is a setting that's permeated with a sense of Johnson and Boswell's London, an oasis of crooked floors, labyrinthine hallways, and antique accessories and furnishings that manage to be simultaneously fun and functional. According to a spokesperson, "We went out of our way to make the floors creak," as part of its charm. Bedrooms are charming and quirky, furnished with carved 18th- and 19th-century bed frames, and lace or silk draperies. Bathrooms contain Edwardian-era fittings, including claw-foot bathtubs. Overall, this place is quirky, eccentric, and abundantly laden with a sense of the antique.

Peter's Lane, Cowcross St., London EC1M 6DS. (C) **020/7336-0931.** Fax 020/7336-0932. www. rookeryhotel.com. 33 units. £126–£185 double; £178–£354 suite. AE, DC, MC, V. Tube: Farringdon. **Amenities:** Breakfast room; concierge; room service. *In room:* A/C, TV, minibar, Wi-Fi (free).

The Zetter ★★★   Heaven will be a letdown after this. Imagine hall vending machines dispensing champagne or espresso makers providing complimentary *café* on every floor. This converted Victorian warehouse between the financial district and the West End features seven rooftop studios with patios and panoramic views of the London skyline, among other lures, including a sky-lit atrium flooding its core with natural light. Many of the features and "scars" of the original structure were retained, as tradition was blended with a chic, urban modern. Bedrooms, ranging from small to midsize, are spread across five floors. These accommodations open onto balconies that circle the atrium. Unplastered brick walls reach up to "floating" ceilings and customized wallpaper panels. Secondhand furnishings are set beside classic modern pieces. Designers achieved their goal of "a great bed, a great shower, and state-of-the-art in-room technology."

St. John's Sq., 86–88 Clerkenwell Rd., London EC1M 5RJ. (C) **020/7324-4444.** Fax 020/7324-4445. www.thezetter.com. 59 units. Mon–Thurs £180–£360 double; Fri–Sun £153–£360 double. AE, DC, MC, V. Tube: Farringdon. **Amenities:** Restaurant; bar; concierge; room service. *In room:* A/C, TV/DVD, CD player, MP3 docking station, Internet (free).

Inexpensive

The Hoxton ★ 🍴   Custom-built in 2006 in the Shoreditch neighborhood near London's financial district, the Hoxton has a stated aim of avoiding hotel rip-offs. It came up with many innovative policies—for example, instead of getting gouged if you make a phone call from your room, you are charged only 5p a minute for calls to Canada and the United States, and you'll find "supermarket prices" at the minimarket in the lobby. The main investor and figurehead, Sinclair Beecham, founder of Britain's popular Prêt-a-Manger fast-food chain, bases his price structure on policies in effect at budget airlines, offering frequent promotions to the rates noted below. Everything is simplified here: The "Lite Pret" breakfast—a bag containing freshly squeezed orange juice, granola, yogurt, and a banana—is hung on your doorknob. Bedrooms are functional and rather small but tastefully furnished, each with either queen-size or two single beds.

81 Great Eastern St., London EC2A 3HU. (C) **020/7550-1000.** Fax 020/7550-1090. www.hoxton hotels.com. 205 units. £49–£189 double. Rates include Lite Pret breakfast. AE, DC, MC, V. Tube: Old St. **Amenities:** Grill; bar; access to nearby gym (£7). *In room:* TV, fridge, hair dryer, Wi-Fi (free).

5

WHERE TO STAY

In & Around the City

THE WEST END
Bloomsbury
EXPENSIVE

The Academy ★   The Academy is in the heart of London's publishing district. If you look out your window, you see where Virginia Woolf and other literary members of the Bloomsbury Group passed by every day. Many original architectural details were preserved when these three 1776 Georgian row houses were joined. The hotel was substantially upgraded in the 1990s, with a bathroom added to every bedroom (whether there was space or not). Grace notes include glass panels, colonnades, and intricate plasterwork on the facade. With overstuffed armchairs and half-canopied beds, rooms sometimes evoke English-country-house living, but that of the poorer relations. Guests who have been here before always request rooms opening onto the garden in back and not those in front with ducted fresh air, though the front units have double-glazing to cut down on the noise. **Warning:** If you have a problem with stairs, know that no elevators rise to the four floors.

21 Gower St., London WC1E 6HG. (℃ **020/7631-4115.** Fax 020/7636-3442. www.theeton collection.com. 49 units. £235 double; £353 suite. AE, DC, MC, V. Tube: Tottenham Court Rd., Goodge St., or Russell Sq. **Amenities:** Bar; room service. *In room:* A/C, TV, CD player, hair dryer, minibar, Wi-Fi (free).

Grange Blooms Hotel ★   This restored 18th-century town house has a pedigree: It stands in what were formerly the grounds of Montague House (now the British Museum). Even though it's in the heart of London, the house has a country-home atmosphere, complete with fireplace, period art, and copies of *Country Life* in the magazine rack. Guests take morning coffee in a walled garden overlooking the British Museum. In summer, light meals are served. The small- to medium-size bedrooms are individually designed with traditional elegance, in beautifully muted tones.

7 Montague St., London WC1B 5BP. (℃ **020/7323-1717.** Fax 020/7636-6498. www.grangehotels. com. 26 units. £75–£180 double. AE, DC, MC, V. Tube: Russell Sq. **Amenities:** Restaurant; bar; room service. *In room:* TV, hair dryer, Internet (£10), minibar.

The Montague on the Gardens ★★   This member of the deluxe Red Carnation Hotel Group—others include the Rubens at the Palace (p. 140) and the Milestone (p. 147)—offers a winning combination of plush accommodations and good service. The location is right across the street from the British Museum and a short walk from the West End and the shopping on Oxford and Bond streets. The public rooms are meticulously decorated in various woods, light fabrics, and antiques, conjuring the atmosphere of an expensive manor home. Guest rooms are individually sized and decorated; most aren't huge, but all are cozy and spotless. Some beds are four-posters, and most sport half-canopies. Bi-level deluxe king rooms feature pullout couches and would be classified as suites in many other hotels.

15 Montague St., London WC1B 5BJ. (℃ **877/955-1515** in the U.S. and Canada, or 020/7637-1001. Fax 020/7637-2516. www.montaguehotel.com. 100 units. £135–£175 double; £295–£550 suite. AE, DC, MC, V. Tube: Russell Sq. **Amenities:** 2 restaurants; bar; concierge; state-of-the-art health club; room service. *In room:* A/C, TV, fax (in some rooms), hair dryer, Wi-Fi (free).

Myhotel ★ 🎁 Creating shock waves among staid Bloomsbury hoteliers, Myhotel is a London row house on the outside with an Asian *moderne*-style interior. It is designed according to feng shui principles—the ancient Chinese art of placement that utilizes the flow of energy in a space. The rooms have mirrors, but they're positioned so you don't see yourself when you first wake up—feng shui rule number one (probably a good rule, feng shui or no feng shui). Rooms are havens of comfort, taste, and tranquillity. Excellent sleep-inducing beds are found in all rooms. Tipping is discouraged, and each guest is assigned a personal assistant responsible for his or her happiness. Aimed at today's young, hip traveler, Myhotel lies within a short walk of Covent Garden and the British Museum.

11–13 Bayley St., Bedford Sq., London WC1B 3HD. ℂ **020/7667-6000.** Fax 020/7667-6044. www.myhotels.co.uk. 78 units. £148–£279 double; £566–£805 suite. AE, DC, MC, V. Tube: Tottenham Court Rd. or Goodge St. **Amenities:** Restaurant; bar; babysitting; exercise room; room service. *In room:* A/C, TV, hair dryer, Wi-Fi (free).

Renaissance London Chancery Court ★★ This opulent landmark 1914 building in the financial district opened as a hotel in 2003, and it's retained some of the best architectural features of its Edwardian heyday while becoming cutting edge in its modern comforts. The building has been used as a backdrop for such films as *Howards End* and *The Saint* because filmmakers were drawn to its soaring archways and classical central courtyard. The glamorous and exceedingly comfortable rooms are all furnished with fine linens and decorated in hues of cream, red, and blue. Some of the best accommodations are on the sixth floor, opening onto a cozy interior courtyard hidden from the busy world outside.

252 High Holborn, WC1V 7EN. ℂ **800/468-3571** in the U.S. and Canada, or 020/7829-9888. Fax 020/7829-9889. www.marriott.com. 358 units. £169–£374 double; £395–£495 suite. Rates include English breakfast. AE, DC, MC, V. Tube: Holborn. Parking £35. **Amenities:** 2 restaurants; 2 bars; babysitting; concierge; state-of-the-art health club; room service. *In room:* A/C, TV, hair dryer, Internet (£15), minibar.

MODERATE

Harlingford Hotel 🥄 This hotel comprises three town houses built in the 1820s and joined around 1900 with a bewildering array of staircases and meandering hallways. Set in the heart of Bloomsbury, it's run by a management that seems genuinely concerned about the welfare of its guests, unlike the management at many of the neighboring hotel rivals. (They even distribute little mincemeat pies to their guests during the Christmas holidays.) Double-glazed windows cut down on the street noise, and all the bedrooms are comfortable and inviting. The most comfortable rooms are on the second and third levels, but expect to climb some steep English stairs (there's no elevator). Avoid the rooms on ground level, as they are darker and have less security. You'll have use of the tennis courts in Cartwright Gardens.

61–63 Cartwright Gardens, London WC1H 9EL. ℂ **020/7387-1551.** Fax 020/7387-4616. www. harlingfordhotel.com. 43 units. £112 double; £127 triple; £137 quad. Rates include English breakfast. AE, MC, V. Tube: Russell Sq., King's Cross, or Euston. **Amenities:** Use of tennis courts in Cartwright Gardens. *In room:* TV, hair dryer, Wi-Fi (free).

Where to Stay in the West End

REGENT'S PARK

NW1

Euston Station

EUSTON

WC1

BLOOMSBURY

British Museum

Bedford Square

Tottenham Court Rd.

Soho Sqare

SOHO

Leicester Square

Leicester Sq.

National Gallery

Trafalgar Square

MARYLEBONE

WESTMINSTER

W1

Oxford Circus

Marble Arch

Speakers Corner

Grosvenor Square

MAYFAIR

Berkeley Square

Piccadilly Circus

St. James's Square

ST. JAMES'S

Pall Mall

Carlton House Terr.

Horse Guards Parade

HYDE PARK

Green Park

GREEN PARK

St. James's Palace

ST. JAMES'S PARK

Horse Guards

Hyde Park Corner

Knightsbridge

Constitution Hill

Buckingham Palace

Queen Victoria Memorial

Birdcage Walk

Anne's Gate

BELGRAVIA

Belgrave Square

Palace Gardens

WESTMINSTER

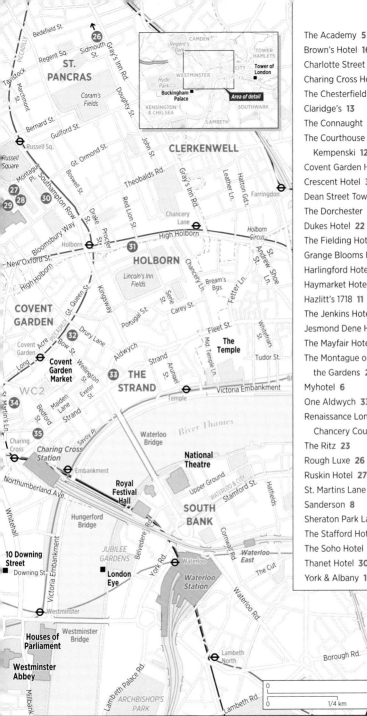

The Academy **5**
Brown's Hotel **16**
Charlotte Street Hotel **7**
Charing Cross Hotel **35**
The Chesterfield Mayfair **19**
Claridge's **13**
The Connaught **17**
The Courthouse Hotel
   Kempenski **12**
Covent Garden Hotel **15**
Crescent Hotel **3**
Dean Street Townhouse **14**
The Dorchester **18**
Dukes Hotel **22**
The Fielding Hotel **32**
Grange Blooms Hotel **29**
Harlingford Hotel **2**
Haymarket Hotel **21**
Hazlitt's 1718 **11**
The Jenkins Hotel **4**
Jesmond Dene Hotel **9**
The Mayfair Hotel **20**
The Montague on
   the Gardens **28**
Myhotel **6**
One Aldwych **33**
Renaissance London
   Chancery Court **31**
The Ritz **23**
Rough Luxe **26**
Ruskin Hotel **27**
St. Martins Lane **34**
Sanderson **8**
Sheraton Park Lane Hotel **25**
The Stafford Hotel **24**
The Soho Hotel **10**
Thanet Hotel **30**
York & Albany **1**

INEXPENSIVE

Crescent Hotel   Although Ruskin and Shelley no longer pass by, the Crescent still stands in the heart of academic London. The private square is owned by the City Guild of Skinners (who are furriers, as you might have guessed) and guarded by the University of London, whose student residential halls are across the street. You have access to the gardens and private tennis courts belonging to the City Guild of Skinners. The hotel owners view the Crescent as an extension of their home and welcome you to its comfortably elegant Georgian surroundings, which date from 1810. Some guests have been returning for 4 decades. Bedrooms range from small singles with shared bathrooms to more spacious twin and double rooms with private bathrooms.

49–50 Cartwright Gardens, London WC1H 9EL. ✆ **020/7387-1515.** Fax 020/7383-2054. www. crescenthoteloflondon.com. 27 units, 18 with bathroom (some with shower only, some with tub and shower). £99 double with bathroom; £122 family room. Rates include English breakfast. MC, V. Tube: Russell Sq., King's Cross, or Euston. **Amenities:** Babysitting; use of tennis courts at Cartwright Gardens. *In room:* TV, Wi-Fi (£6).

The Jenkins Hotel ★ 🍴   Followers of the Agatha Christie TV series *Poirot* will recognize this Cartwright Gardens residence—it was featured in the series. The antiques are gone and the rooms are small, but some of the original charm of the Georgian house remains—enough so that the *London Mail* proclaimed it one of the "10 best hotel values" in the city. All the rooms have been redecorated in traditional Georgian style, and many have been completely refurbished. The location is great, near the British Museum, theaters, and antiquarian bookshops. There are some drawbacks: no lift and no reception or sitting room. But this is a place where you can settle in and feel at home.

45 Cartwright Gardens, London WC1H 9EH. ✆ **020/7387-2067.** Fax 020/7383-3139. www. jenkinshotel.demon.co.uk. 14 units. £95 double; £110 triple. Rates include English breakfast. MC, V. Tube: Russell Sq., King's Cross, or Euston. **Amenities:** Use of tennis courts in Cartwright Gardens. *In room:* TV, fridge, hair dryer, Wi-Fi (free).

Ruskin Hotel   Although the hotel is named for author John Ruskin, the ghosts of other literary legends who lived nearby haunt you: Mary Shelley plotting her novel, *Frankenstein,* and James Barrie fantasizing about *Peter Pan.* This hotel has been managed for 2 decades by a hardworking family and enjoys a repeat clientele. Management keeps the place spick-and-span, though you shouldn't expect a decorator's flair. The furnishings, though well polished, are a bit worn.Double-glazing

---

Cheap Lodging for Students

The International Students House, 229 Great Portland St., W1W 5PN (✆ **020/7631-8310; www.ish.org.uk),** offers blandly furnished, institutional rooms within the two lowest floors of a building which rose from the ashes of World War II. It's far from glamorous, but it's hard to beat the price: £56 per person for a double with shared facilities in the hallway, and £64 per person for a double with private facilities. Per person rates in a quad with shared facilities in the hallway cost £19 per person. A £10 key deposit is charged but refunded at the end of your stay. Facilities include laundry machines, a bar, an Internet cafe, and a fitness center. Reserve way in advance, because these rooms go very quickly.

family-friendly **HOTELS**

Although the bulk of their clients are business travelers, the major hotel chains are also geared to family fun. Look for special summer packages at most hotel chains between June and August. Some of the most generous offers come from **Travelodge** (☎ **800/578-7878** in the U.S.) and **Hilton International** (☎ **800/445-8667** in the U.S.) chains. For best results, call the 800-number and ask about family packages. Here are two other family-friendly spots:

The Colonnade (p. 162)   Located in the canal-laced Little Venice section of London, this hotel lets children under 12 stay free in their parent's room, and the staff can arrange babysitting. This residential area is safe, with tree-lined avenues leading down to a canal. With its shops, cafes, and restaurants, Little Venice has a real neighborhood feel to it.

Hart House Hotel (p. 156)   This small, family-run B&B is right in the center of the West End, near Hyde Park. Many of its rooms are triples. If you need even more space, special family suites, with connecting rooms, can be arranged.

---

in the front blots out the noise, but we prefer the cozily old-fashioned chambers in the rear, as they open onto a park. Sorry, no elevator. *Note:* Prices here are kept low because only a half-dozen rooms have private bathrooms.

23–24 Montague St., London WC1B 5BH. ☎ **020/7636-7388.** Fax 020/7323-1662. 33 units, 6 with bathroom. £75 double without bathroom; £85 double with bathroom; £98 triple without bathroom, £115 triple with bathroom. Rates include English breakfast. AE, DC, MC, V. Tube: Russell Sq., Holborn, or Tottenham Court Rd. *In room:* Hair dryer.

Thanet Hotel   Most of the myriad hotels around Russell Square are indistinguishable, but the Thanet stands out. It no longer charges the same rates it did when it appeared in *England on $5 a Day,* but it's still an affordable option close to the British Museum, the theater district, and Covent Garden. It's a landmark-status building on a quiet Georgian terrace between Russell and Bloomsbury squares. For the most part, the Orchard family (third-generation hoteliers) offers small, adequately furnished rooms. However, scattered throughout the hotel are some unacceptable bedrooms. One guest reported that the foot of her lumpy bed was higher than the head. Ask to see the room before accepting it. This place is always full, so it must be doing something right, and indeed many of the bedrooms are fine.

8 Bedford Place, London WC1B 5JA. ☎ **020/7636-2869.** Fax 020/7323-6676. www.thanet hotel.co.uk. 16 units. £106 double; £125 triple; £140 quad. Rates include English breakfast. AE, MC, V. Tube: Holborn or Russell Sq. **Amenities:** Breakfast room. *In room:* TV, hair dryer, Wi-Fi (free in some).

Camden
EXPENSIVE
York & Albany ★ 🎁   The city's resident *enfant terrible*, chef Gordon Ramsay, took a derelict pub from the 19th century, a community eyesore, and fashioned it into this *restaurant avec chambres*. Sitting across from Regent's Park, the hotel is a unique way to stay in London. The luxuriously appointed bedrooms and

suites recapture the Regency elegance of a bygone era. Cutting-edge technology is combined with period antiques.

127–129 Parkway, London NW1 7PS. ℂ **020/7387-5700.** 10 units. £175–£225 double; £575 suite. AE, MC, V. Tube: Camden Town. **Amenities:** Restaurant; bar; room service. *In room:* A/C, TV/ DVD, CD player, hair dryer, Wi-Fi (free).

King's Cross

MODERATE

Rough Luxe ★ 🎁   Just minutes from St. Pancras International Station, this small boutique hotel was salvaged from the remains of one of the area's many nondescript guest houses. Set in a row of Georgian town houses, the decor is almost industrial, resembling the interior of a warehouse art gallery. No two rooms are alike. Three units come with private bathroom, with glass-enclosed showers and "rainfall" shower heads. Decades of wallpaper and paint were peeled away, leaving distressed walls of handpainted mosaic wallpaper and plaster of yesterday. Many of the antiques found throughout were purchased at an auction of the Savoy Hotel's throwaways. Modern art is displayed throughout the property.

1 Birkenhead St., London WC1H 8BA. ℂ **020/7837-5338.** www.roughluxe.co.uk. 9 units (3 with bathroom). £155 double without bathroom; £210 double with bathroom; £280 suite. Rates include continental breakfast. AE, MC, V. Tube: King's Cross. **Amenities:** Breakfast room. *In room:* TV (retro '80s sets with static), hair dryer.

INEXPENSIVE

Jesmond Dene Hotel   Well-maintained and cozy bedrooms are found at this well-run B&B in the rapidly gentrifying area of King's Cross. This is a good, convenient choice for transportation, including the Eurostar to Paris. All the small bedrooms have been refurbished and are comfortable and tasteful.

27 Argyle St., King's Cross, London WC1H 8EP. ℂ **020/7837-4654.** Fax 020/7833-1633. www. jesmonddenehotel.co.uk. 23 rooms, 20 with private bathroom. £65 double without bathroom; £90 double with bathroom; £120 triple; £135 quad. AE, DC, MC, V. Tube: King's Cross. **Amenities:** Breakfast room. *In room:* TV, Wi-Fi (free).

Covent Garden & the Strand

VERY EXPENSIVE

Covent Garden Hotel ★★★   This former hospital building lay neglected for years until it was reconfigured in 1996 by hot hoteliers Tim and Kit Kemp— whose flair for interior design is legendary—into one of London's most charming boutique hotels in one of the West End's hippest shopping neighborhoods. *Travel + Leisure* called this hotel one of the 25 hottest places to stay in the *world*. It remains so. Behind a bottle-green facade reminiscent of a 19th-century store-front, the hotel has a welcoming lobby outfitted with elaborate inlaid furniture and elegant draperies, plus a charming restaurant. Upstairs, accessible via a dramatic stone staircase, soundproof bedrooms are furnished in English style with Asian fabrics, many adorned with hand-embroidered designs. Each room has a clothier's mannequin, the hotel's decorative trademark.

10 Monmouth St., London WC2H 9HB. ☎ **800/553-6674** in the U.S., or 020/7806-1000. Fax 020/7806-1100. www.firmdale.com. 58 units. £240–£340 double; £395–£1,195 suite. AE, DC, MC, V. Tube: Covent Garden or Leicester Sq. **Amenities:** Restaurant; bar; babysitting; concierge; exercise room; room service. *In room:* A/C, TV/DVD, movie library, CD player, hair dryer, minibar, Wi-Fi (£20).

One Aldwych ★★   Just east of Covent Garden, this government-rated five-star hotel occupies a 1907 building that served as headquarters for the now-defunct *Morning Post.* Today guests enjoy an artfully simple layout that includes stylish minimalist furniture, big bay windows, masses of flowers, and lots of contemporary art. The bedrooms are sumptuous, decorated with elegant linens and rich colors, and accessorized with raw-silk curtains and deluxe furnishings. There are original works of art in every room, along with fresh fruit and flowers supplied daily. On Friday and Saturday evenings, and Sunday at brunch, movies are shown in the screening room.

1 Aldwych, London WC2B 4RH. ☎ **800/745-8883** or 020/7300-1000. Fax 020/7300-1001. www.campbellgrayhotels.com. 105 units. £390–£470 double; £645–£1,195 suite. AE, DC, MC, V. Parking £37. Tube: Temple, Covent Garden, or Embankment. **Amenities:** 2 restaurants; 3 bars; babysitting; concierge; state-of-the-art health club; pool (indoor); room service. *In room:* A/C, TV/DVD, CD player, CD library, hair dryer, minibar, Wi-Fi (free).

St. Martins Lane ★★★   "Eccentric and irreverent, with a sense of humor," is how Ian Schrager describes his cutting-edge Covent Garden hotel, which he transformed from a 1960s office building into a chic enclave. This was the first hotel that Schrager designed outside the United States, after a string of successes from New York to West Hollywood. The mix of hip design and a sense of cool has been imported across the pond. Whimsical touches abound. For example, a string of daisies replaces do not disturb signs. Rooms are all white, but you can use the full-spectrum lighting to make them any color. Floor-to-ceiling windows in every room offer panoramic views of London.

45 St. Martin's Lane, London WC2N 4HX. ☎ **800/697-1791** in the U.S., or 020/7300-5500. Fax 020/7300-5501. www.stmartinslane.com. 204 units. £215–£330 double; £380–£550 suite. AE, DC, MC, V. Tube: Covent Garden or Leicester Sq. **Amenities:** Restaurant; 2 bars; babysitting; concierge; exercise room; room service. *In room:* A/C, TV/DVD, movie library, hair dryer, minibar, Wi-Fi (£15).

MODERATE

The Fielding Hotel ★ 👜   One of London's more eccentric hotels, this rickety walk-up is cramped, quirky, quaint, and an enduring favorite. Luring media types, the hotel is named after novelist Henry Fielding of *Tom Jones* fame, who lived in Broad Court. It lies on a pedestrian street still lined with 19th-century gas lamps. The Royal Opera House is across the street, and the pubs, shops, and restaurants of lively Covent Garden are just beyond the front door. Rooms are small but charmingly old-fashioned and traditional. Some units are redecorated or at least "touched up" every year, though floors dip and sway, and the furnishings and fabrics, though clean, have known better times. With a location like this, in the heart of London, the Fielding keeps guests coming back; in fact, some love the hotel's claustrophobic charm. Children 12 and younger are not welcome; occasionally the staff makes adult patrons feel the same.

4 Broad Court, Bow St., London WC2B 5QZ. ☏ **020/7836-8305.** Fax 020/7497-0064. www.
thefieldinghotel.co.uk. 24 units. £115–£170 double. AE, DC, MC, V. Tube: Covent Garden. *In room:*
TV, Wi-Fi (free).

Trafalgar Square

EXPENSIVE

Charing Cross Hotel ★   When it was built of massive sandstone blocks in
1865, architects marveled at its location directly above the fourth largest railway
station in London, Charing Cross, and its two separate wings interconnected
with an enclosed aerial bridge spanning a pedestrian walkway (Villiers St.) below.
After a massive renovation by the Malaysia-based Guoman Group, it launched
itself as a serious contender in an attraction-packed and highly competitive
neighborhood, the Strand and Trafalgar Square. Whereas the public areas retain
their high-ceilinged Victorian flair, bedrooms are sleekly contemporary, with pricing that varies according to their view (vistas over the Strand command the highest prices) and their size. There's a well-managed restaurant on site, the Terrace
on the Strand, focusing on Continental cuisine, and an international staff well
versed in the needs of travelers.

Charing Cross Station, the Strand, London WC2N 5HX. ☏ **0871/376-9012.** Fax 0871/376-9112.
www.guoman.com. 239 units. £129–£239 double; £229–£269 junior suite. AE, DC, MC, V. Tube:
Charing Cross. **Amenities:** Restaurant; bar; concierge; exercise room. *In room:* A/C, TV, minibar,
Wi-Fi (£10).

Soho

VERY EXPENSIVE

Courthouse Hotel Kempinski ★★   Guests from Oscar Wilde to Mick
Jagger have passed through the doors of this historic courthouse. But today,
under the German hotel chain Kempinski, the hospitality is better than ever. In
a spectacular reclamation of an existing structure, the hotel retains many aspects
of its landmark building, including original Robert Adams fireplaces. A bar has
been installed inside three of the original prison cells. The judges' bench, witness
stand, and dock still occupy center stage in Silk, the hotel's deluxe dining room.
The location is among the best in London, opposite the department store Liberty's and Carnaby Street, just off Regent Street. Bedrooms are midsize to spacious,
each comfortably and tastefully decorated, with 13 suites. The best rooms are in
the new wing that was built on the site of a former police station. Our favorite
retreat here is the roof terrace, where light meals and cocktails are served.

19–21 Great Marlborough St., London W1F 7HL. ☏ **800/426-3135** in the U.S., or 020/7297-5555.
Fax 020/7297-5566. www.courthouse-hotel.com. 112 units. £169–£311 double; £314–£426 suite.
AE, DC, MC, V. Tube: Oxford Circus. **Amenities:** 2 restaurants; bar; concierge; health club and spa;
pool (indoor); room service. *In room:* A/C, TV/DVD, hair dryer, minibar, Wi-Fi (£15).

Dean Street Townhouse ★ 🎁   Deep in the heart of Soho, this boutique
hotel in a restored four-story Georgian town house is an offbeat oddity. Formerly
the home of the Gargoyle Club, it has been converted to receive paying guests,
and its Georgian architecture has been more or less preserved. Do not check in
here if you're a movie star with lots of luggage. Accommodations range from

"broom cupboard" to tiny, small, medium, and bigger. Units have four-poster beds, hand-painted wallpaper, and other retro-chic touches. Bathrooms are fitted with rainforest showers and stocked with goodies from the famous Cowshed Spa. On site is an all-day dining room with a weekly, changing menu of seasonal British food.

69–71 Dean St., London W1D 3SE. ✆ **020/7434-1775.** www.deanstreettownhouse.com. 39 units. £90–£160 standard double; £220–£270 larger double. AE, MC, V. Tube: Oxford Circus. **Amenities:** Restaurant; bar. *In room:* TV/DVD, hair dryer, minibar, Wi-Fi (free).

Haymarket Hotel ★★★ This is a chic upmarket hotel in London for those who want to avoid the grandes dames. Next to the historic Haymarket Theatre, the hotel is ideal for theatergoers. Like all Firmdale hotels, it makes a bold statement with colors of turquoise, fuchsia, mango, and even acid green. Although completely modernized and perhaps the most sophisticated small hotel of London, many satisfying proportions of the original 19th-century John Nash architecture remains. Original works of art and antiques are used, and the bedrooms are sumptuously elegant with fine linens and the latest amenities. There's even an indoor pool lounge.

1 Suffolk Place, London SW1Y 4BP. ✆ **020/7470-4000.** Fax 020/7470-4004. www.firmdale. com. 50 units. £250–£330 double; £400–£460 junior suite; £1,750–£2,250 suite. AE, DC, MC, V. Tube: Tottenham Court Rd. **Amenities:** Restaurant; bar; concierge; exercise room; pool (indoor); room service. *In room:* A/C, TV/DVD, CD player, hair dryer, Wi-Fi (£20).

Hazlitt's 1718 ★★ 🎁 This gem, housed in three historic homes on Soho Square, is one of London's best small hotels. Built in 1718, the hotel is named for William Hazlitt, who founded the Unitarian Church in Boston and wrote four volumes on the life of his hero, Napoleon. Hazlitt's is a favorite with artists, actors, and models. It's eclectic and filled with odds and ends picked up around the country at estate auctions. Some find its Georgian decor a bit spartan, but the 2,000 original prints hanging on the walls brighten it considerably. Many bedrooms have four-poster beds; some of the floors dip and sway, and there's no elevator, but it's all part of the charm. It has just as much character as the Fielding Hotel (p. 131) but is a lot more comfortable. Some rooms are a bit small, but most are spacious, all with state-of-the-art appointments. Accommodations in the back are quieter but perhaps too dark.

6 Frith St., London W1D 3JA. ✆ **020/7434-1771.** Fax 020/7439-1524. www.hazlittshotel.com. 23 units. £159–£295 double; £450–£700 suite. AE, DC, MC, V. Tube: Leicester Sq. or Tottenham Court Rd. **Amenities:** Babysitting; concierge; room service. *In room:* A/C, TV, hair dryer, minibar, Wi-Fi (free).

Sanderson ★★★ Ian Schrager, the king of New York hip, has brought Manhattan to London. For his latest London hotel, Schrager secured the help of talented partners Philippe Starck and Andra Andrei to create an "ethereal, transparent urban spa," in which walls are replaced by glass and sheer layers of curtains. The hotel, located in a former corporate building near Oxford Street, north of Soho, comes with a lush bamboo-filled roof garden, a large courtyard, and a spa. That's not all—Alain Ducasse, arguably the world's greatest chef, directs its restaurant. The accommodations are cutting edge. Although the transformation of this building into a hotel has been remarkable, the dreary grid facade of aluminum squares and glass remains. Your bed is likely to be an Italian silver-leaf sleigh attended by spidery polished stainless-steel night tables and draped with a fringed pashmina shawl.

50 Berners St., London W1T 3NG. ⓒ **800/697-1791** or 020/7300-1400. Fax 020/7300-1401. www.sandersonlondon.com. 150 units. £215–£650 double; £700–£2,800 suite. AE, DC, MC, V. Tube: Oxford Circus or Tottenham Court Rd. **Amenities:** Restaurant; 2 bars; babysitting; concierge; health club and spa. *In room:* A/C, TV/DVD, CD player, hair dryer, minibar, Wi-Fi (£15).

The Soho Hotel ★★★ A former parking garage in the heart of bustling Soho just became our favorite nest in London. When it's time to check out, we never want to leave. British hoteliers Kit and Tim Kemp have come up with a stunner here. At night we have a cocoonlike feeling entering this luxury lair in a cul-de-sac off Dean Street. The theaters of Shaftesbury are only a block or two away, as is the Ivy restaurant. All the extremely spacious bedrooms are individually designed in granite and oak. There are four penthouses on the fifth floor with tree-lined terraces opening onto panoramic sweeps of London. All the famous Kemp touches can be found, from boldly striped furnishings to deep bathtubs for a late-night soak. The glitterati, mostly actors and filmmakers, can be seen hanging out at the bar.

4 Richmond Mews, London W1D 3DH. ⓒ **020/7559-3000.** Fax 020/7559-3003. www.firmdale. com. 91 units. £290–£360 double; £400–£2,750 suite. AE, MC, V. Tube: Oxford Circus or Piccadilly Circus. **Amenities:** Restaurant; bar; concierge; exercise room; room service. *In room:* A/C, TV/DVD, CD player, hair dryer, Wi-Fi (£20).

EXPENSIVE

Charlotte Street Hotel ★★ 🎁 In North Soho, a short walk from the heartbeat of Soho Square, this town house has been luxuriously converted into a high-end hotel that is London chic at its finest, with a private screening room and a sophisticated blend of stately English manor house and contemporary decor. The latter has made the hotel a hit with the movie, fashion, and media crowd, many of whom had never ventured to North Soho before. Midsize to spacious bedrooms have fresh, modern, English interiors with strong colors. Guests can relax in the elegant drawing room and library with a log-burning fireplace.

15–17 Charlotte St., London W1T IRJ. ⓒ **800/553-6674** in the U.S., or 020/7806-2000. Fax 020/ 7806-2002. www.firmdale.com. 52 units. £230–£320 double; from £380 suite. AE, MC, V. Tube: Tottenham Court Rd. or Googe St. **Amenities:** Restaurant; bar; exercise room; room service. *In room:* A/C, TV/DVD, CD player, hair dryer, minibar, Wi-Fi (£20).

Mayfair

VERY EXPENSIVE

Brown's Hotel ★★ Almost every year a hotel sprouts up trying to evoke an English-country-house ambience with Chippendale and chintz; this quintessential town-house hotel watches these competitors come and go, and it always comes out on top. Brown's was founded by James Brown, a former manservant to Lord Byron, who knew the tastes of well-bred gentlemen and wanted to create a dignified, clublike place for them. He opened its doors in 1837, the same year Queen Victoria took the throne. Brown's occupies 14 historic houses just off Berkeley Square. Its guest rooms, completely renovated, vary considerably in decor, but all show restrained taste in decoration and appointments; even the washbasins are antiques. Accommodations range in size from small to extra spacious; some suites have four-poster beds.

30 Albemarle St., London W1S 4BP. ✆ **020/7493-6020.** Fax 020/7493-9381. www.brownshotel. com. 117 units. £475–£645 double; £885–£3,200 suite. AE, DC, MC, V. Off-site parking £50. Tube: Green Park. **Amenities:** Restaurant; bar; concierge; health club and spa; room service. *In room:* A/C, TV/DVD, hair dryer, Internet (£15), minibar, MP3 docking station.

Claridge's ★★★ That once-fading 1812 beauty has experienced a rebirth, and its staid image has changed. *Dynasty* diva Joan Collins may have staged her most recent marriage here, but now Kate Moss is spotted in the hip bar, Elizabeth Hurley strolls through the lobby, and Gordon Ramsay—Britain's most talked-about and controversial chef (and also the best)—is loud-mouthing it in the kitchen.

If you want to live in the total lap of luxury, at an even tonier address than the Connaught and the Dorchester, make it Claridge's. Much of the Art Deco style of the 1930s remains, although there are other distinctive styles as well, ranging from modern to neoclassical. The hotel's strong sense of tradition and old-fashioned "Britishness" are also intact, in spite of the gloss and the hip clientele. Afternoon tea at Claridge's remains a quintessentially English tradition. The accommodations here are the most diverse in London, ranging from the costly and stunning Brook Penthouse—complete with a personal butler—to the less expensive, so-called superior queen rooms with queen-size beds.

Brook St., London W1A 2JQ. ✆ **020/7629-8860.** Fax 020/7499-2210. www.claridges.co.uk. 203 units. £299–£400 double; £650–£3,950 suite. AE, DC, MC, V. Parking £50. Tube: Bond St. **Amenities:** 3 restaurants; 2 bars; babysitting; concierge; health club and spa; room service. *In room:* A/C, TV/DVD/VCR, hair dryer, minibar, Wi-Fi (free).

The Connaught ★★★ This elegant hotel in the heart of Mayfair is one of Europe's most prestigious. It is not the most glamorous, nor even the most fashionable in London, but it nonetheless coddles you in comfort and luxury, with a hospitality that's legendary. It has the atmosphere of an English country house—a world of fresh flowers, crystal chandeliers, Wedgwood, and antiques. There is something of an aura of aristocratic decay at the Connaught, just as the country gentry like it. In 2008, the hotel inaugurated an ambitious expansion to include an additional 30 rooms, plus a pool and spa. Rooms range from medium to large and are filled with antiques, chintz, and tasteful details such as gilt-trimmed white paneling. Sumptuous beds, marble fireplaces, ornate plasterwork, and oak paneling add to the stately allure of the rooms.

Carlos Place, London W1K 2AL. ✆ **800/63-SAVOY** (637-2869) in the U.S., or 020/7499-7070. Fax 020/7495-3262. www.the-connaught.co.uk. 122 units. £339–£369 double; from £650 suite. AE, DC, MC, V. Parking £48. Tube: Green Park. **Amenities:** 2 restaurants; 2 bars; babysitting; concierge; health club & spa; room service. *In room:* A/C, TV/DVD, hair dryer, minibar, MP3 docking station, Wi-Fi (free).

The Dorchester ★★★ One of London's best hotels, it has all the elegance of the Connaught, but without the upper-crust attitude that can verge on snobbery. Few hotels have the time-honored experience of "the Dorch," which has maintained a tradition of fine comfort and cuisine since it opened in 1931. Breaking from the neoclassical tradition, the most ambitious architects of the era designed a building of reinforced concrete clothed in terrazzo slabs. The Dorchester boasts guest rooms outfitted with Irish linen sheets on comfortable beds, plus all the electronic gadgetry you'd expect, and double- and triple-glazed windows to keep out noise, along with plump armchairs, cherrywood furnishings, and, in many cases, four-poster beds piled high with pillows.

53 Park Lane, London W1A 2HJ. ℂ **800/727-9820** in the U.S., or 020/7629-8888. Fax 020/9629-8080. www.thedorchester.com. 244 units. £295–£565 double; £720–£3,800 suite. AE, DC, MC, V. Parking £45. Tube: Hyde Park Corner or Marble Arch. **Amenities:** 3 restaurants; bar; babysitting; concierge; health club and spa; room service. *In room:* A/C, TV/DVD, CD player, fax, hair dryer, Internet (£20); minibar.

The Mayfair Hotel ★★★ Opened in 1927 by King George V, this government-rated five-star hotel, after undergoing a £70-million restoration, is better than ever. Top designers were called in to create contemporary interiors enlivened by chandeliers by Baccarat, paintings imported from St. Petersburg, and sofas and chairs by Fendi. Soft wool carpets, leather-bound beds, and triple-glazed windows are just some of the special features of the bedrooms. Accommodations range from a single to a family room for four. A deluxe way of staying here is to rent a studio suite with a private garden terrace. Memorable dining can be experienced in the luxurious Amba Bar and Grill.

Stratton St., London W1J 8LT. ℂ **800/333-3333** in the U.S., or 020/7629-7777. Fax 020/7493-0244. www.themayfairhotel.co.uk. 406 units. £207–£595 double; from £750 suite. AE, DC, MC, V. Parking £20–£55. Tube: Green Park. **Amenities:** Restaurant; bar; babysitting; concierge; room service; luxury spa. *In room:* A/C, TV/DVD, CD player, hair dryer, Wi-Fi (free).

Sheraton Park Lane Hotel ★★ Since 1924, this has been the most traditional of the Park Lane mansions, even more so than the Dorchester. The hotel was sold in 1996 to the Sheraton Corporation, which continues to upgrade it but maintains its quintessential British style. Its Silver Entrance remains an Art Deco marvel that has been used as a backdrop in many films, including the classic BBC miniseries *Brideshead Revisited*. Overlooking Green Park, the hotel offers luxurious accommodations that are a good deal—well, at least for pricey Park Lane. Many suites have marble fireplaces and original marble bathrooms. The rooms have all benefited from impressive refurbishment. The most tranquil rooms open onto a street in the rear. Rooms opening onto the court are dark. In the more deluxe rooms, you get better views.

Piccadilly, London W1J 7BX. ℂ **800/325-3535** in the U.S., or 020/7499-6321. Fax 020/7499-1965. www.starwoodhotels.com. 302 units. £189–£299; £264–£349 suite. AE, DC, MC, V. Parking £45. Tube: Hyde Park Corner or Green Park. **Amenities:** 2 restaurants; bar; concierge; state-of-the-art health club; room service. *In room:* A/C (in some), TV/DVD, movie library, hair dryer, Wi-Fi (£18).

EXPENSIVE

The Chesterfield Mayfair ★★ Just a short distance from Berkeley Square, the elegant Chesterfield serves up a traditional English atmosphere and offers a lot more bang for your buck than most hotels in pricey Mayfair. The hotel, once home to the Earl of Chesterfield, still sports venerable features that evoke an air of nobility, including richly decorated public rooms featuring woods, antiques, fabrics, and marble. The secluded Library Lounge is a great place to relax, and the glassed-in conservatory is a good spot for tea. The guest rooms are dramatically decorated and make excellent use of space—there's a ton of closet and counter space. For a more memorable experience, book one of the themed junior or executive suites. You'll get larger amounts of space, upgraded amenities (DVD players and umbrellas, for example), complimentary canapés, and theatrical decorating schemes.

35 Charles St., London W1J 5EB. ✆ **877/955-1515** in the U.S. and Canada, or 020/7491-2622. Fax 020/7491-4793. www.chesterfieldmayfair.com. 107 units. £155–£215 double; from £385 suite. AE, DC, MC, V. Tube: Green Park. **Amenities:** 2 restaurants; bar; babysitting; concierge; use of nearby health club; room service. *In room:* A/C, TV/DVD, hair dryer, minibar, Wi-Fi (free).

St. James's
VERY EXPENSIVE
The Ritz ★★★   Built in French Renaissance style and opened by César Ritz in 1906, this hotel overlooking Green Park is synonymous with luxury. Gold-leafed molding, marble columns, and potted palms abound, and a gold-leafed statue, *La Source,* adorns the fountain of the oval-shaped Palm Court. After a major restoration, the hotel is better than ever: New carpeting and air-conditioning have been installed in the guest rooms, and an overall polishing has recaptured much of the Ritz's original splendor. Still, this Ritz lags far behind the much grander one in Paris (with which it is not affiliated). The Belle Epoque guest rooms, each with its own character, are spacious and comfortable. Many have marble fireplaces, elaborate gilded plasterwork, and a decor of soft pastel hues. A few rooms have their original brass beds and marble fireplaces. Corner rooms are grander and more spacious.

150 Piccadilly, London W1J 9BR. ✆ **877/748-9536** in the U.S., or 020/7493-8181. Fax 020/7493-2687. www.theritzlondon.com. 135 units. £270–£600 double; £520–£4,500 suite. Children 15 and younger stay free in parent's room. AE, DC, MC, V. Parking £56. Tube: Green Park. **Amenities:** 2 restaurants (including the Palm Court); bar; babysitting; concierge; health club and spa; room service. *In room:* A/C, TV/DVD, fax, hair dryer, Internet (£25).

EXPENSIVE
Dukes Hotel ★★★   Dukes provides elegance without ostentation in what was presumably someone's *Upstairs, Downstairs* town house. Along with its nearest competitors, the Stafford and 22 Jermyn Street, it caters to those looking for charm, style, and tradition in a hotel. It stands in a quiet courtyard off St. James's Place; turn-of-the-20th-century gas lamps help put you into the proper mood before entering the front door. Each well-furnished guest room is decorated in the style of a particular English period, ranging from Regency to Edwardian. It's a lot cozier, more intimate, and even more clubbish than the Stafford, and Dukes is more tranquil since it's set in its own gas-lit alley.

35 St. James's Place, London SW1A 1NY. ✆ **800/381-4702** in the U.S., or 020/7491-4840. Fax 020/7493-1264. www.campbellgrayhotels.com. 90 units. £320–£390 double; from £445 suite. AE, DC, MC, V. Parking £55. Tube: Green Park. **Amenities:** Restaurant; bar; babysitting; concierge; health club & spa; room service. *In room:* A/C, TV/DVD, hair dryer, minibar, Wi-Fi (free).

The Stafford Hotel ★★★ Famous for its American Bar, its St. James's address, and the warmth of its Edwardian decor, the Stafford competes well with Dukes for a tasteful, discerning clientele. All the guest rooms are individually decorated, reflecting the hotel's origins as a private home. Many singles contain queen-size beds. Some of the deluxe units offer four-posters that will make you feel like Henry VIII. Much has been done to preserve the original style of these rooms, including preservation of the original A-beams on the upper floors. You can bet that no 18th-century horse ever slept with the electronic safes, stereo systems, and quality furnishings (mostly antique reproductions) that these rooms feature. Units on the top floor are small. In 2007, 26 luxury junior and master suites were added in the Stafford Mews, each filled with antiques and luxury facilities.

16–18 St. James's Place, London SW1A 1NJ. ✆ **800/525-4800** in the U.S., or 020/7493-0111. Fax 020/7493-7121. www.thestaffordhotel.co.uk. 107 units. £235–£440 double; £640–£1,390 suite. AE, DC, MC, V. No parking. Tube: Green Park. **Amenities:** Restaurant; bar; babysitting; concierge; exercise room; room service. *In room:* A/C, TV/DVD, CD player, hair dryer, Wi-Fi (free).

WESTMINSTER & VICTORIA

Very Expensive

The Goring ★★★ For tradition and location, the Goring is our first choice in Westminster. Just behind Buckingham Palace, it lies within easy reach of the royal parks, Victoria Station, Westminster Abbey, and the Houses of Parliament. It also offers the finest personal service of all its nearby competitors.

Built in 1910 by O. R. Goring, this was the first hotel in the world to have central heating and a private bathroom in every room. Today's guest rooms still offer all the comforts, including luxurious bathrooms with extra-long tubs and red marble walls. The beds are among the most comfortable in London. Queen Anne and Chippendale are the decor styles, and the maintenance of the highest order. The rooms overlooking the garden are best. The charm of a traditional English country hotel is conjured in the paneled drawing room, where fires crackle in the ornate fireplaces on nippy evenings.

15 Beeston Place, Grosvenor Gardens, London SW1W 0JW. ✆ **020/7396-9000.** Fax 020/7834-4393. www.goringhotel.co.uk. 71 units. £370–£650 double; from £650 suite. AE, DC, MC, V. Parking £30. Tube: Victoria. **Amenities:** Restaurant; bar; babysitting; concierge; access to nearby health club. *In room:* A/C, TV/DVD, movie library, CD player, CD library, hair dryer, Wi-Fi (£15).

Expensive

City Inn Westminster ★ Next door to Tate Britain and Parliament, this purpose-built inn with a vast array of rooms is at the nexus of elite London. The River Thames and London Eye are within a short walk. The lobby is graced with stone, oak, and leather chairs, and the on-site restaurant specializes in game and

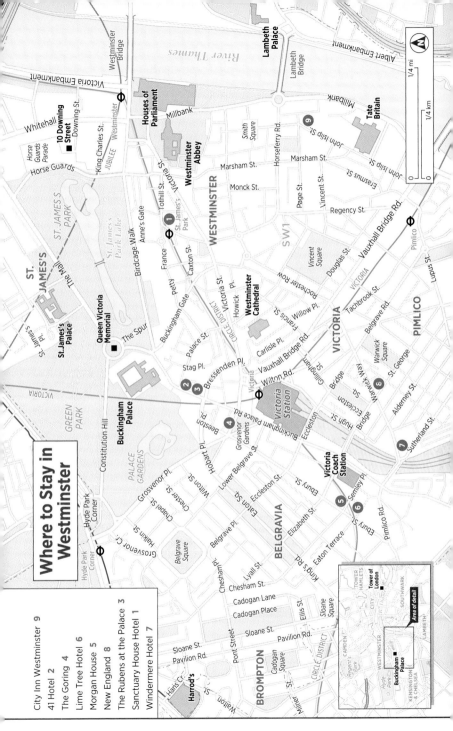

Where to Stay in Westminster

City Inn Westminster **9**
41 Hotel **2**
The Goring **4**
Lime Tree Hotel **6**
Morgan House **5**
New England **8**
The Rubens at the Palace **3**
Sanctuary House Hotel **1**
Windermere Hotel **7**

salmon, as befits the hotel's Scottish ownership. The best accommodations are the 67 City Club rooms or the 16 suites, but all units are comfortable, with a fresh, light, and contemporary design. Business clients predominate during the week, but on weekends rates are often slashed to bargain prices. Ask about this when booking. Try, if possible, for a guest room opening onto the Thames or else views of Parliament. Rooms are soundproof, with 18 inches of concrete between each unit. You can drink and dine in the City Café restaurant and bar with its alfresco terrace, and the stylish Millbank Lounge bar is a popular rendezvous point at night.

30 John Islip St., London SW1P 4DD. ✆ **020/7630-1000.** Fax 020/7233-7575. www.cityinn.com. 460 units. £119–£159 double; £139–£179 city club room; £219–£259 suite. AE, DC, MC, V. Tube: Pimlico or Westminster. **Amenities:** Restaurant; 2 bars; concierge; exercise room; room service. *In room:* A/C, TV/DVD, CD player, hair dryer, minibar, Wi-Fi (free).

41 Hotel ★★★ 🎁   This relatively unknown but well-placed gem offers the intimate atmosphere of a private club combined with a high level of personal service. Completely self-contained, it occupies the fifth (top) floor of the building whose lower floors contain an also-recommended hotel, The Rubens at the Palace. 41 Hotel is best suited to couples or those traveling alone—especially women. Public areas feature an abundance of mahogany, antiques, fresh flowers, and rich fabrics. Read, relax, or watch TV in the library-style lounge, where a complimentary continental breakfast and afternoon snacks are served each day. Guest rooms are individually sized, but all feature elegant black-and-white color schemes and magnificent beds with Egyptian-cotton linens.

41 Buckingham Palace Rd., London SW1W 0PS. ✆ **877/955-1515** in the U.S. and Canada, or 020/7300-0041. Fax 020/7300-0141. www.41hotel.com. 30 units. £275–£295 double; £525–£725 suite. Rates include continental breakfast, afternoon snacks, and evening canapés. AE, DC, MC, V. Tube: Victoria. **Amenities:** Bar; babysitting; concierge; room service. *In room:* A/C, TV/DVD, CD player, hair dryer, Internet (free), MP3 docking station.

The Rubens at the Palace ★★ 🔥   The very British Rubens is popular with Americans and Europeans seeking traditional English hospitality while enjoying the latest creature comforts. And its location is one of the best in town directly across the street from Buckingham Palace and only a 2-minute walk from Victoria Station. The public rooms are lavishly decorated with antiques, fabric wall-coverings, and fresh flowers. The size and decor of the guest rooms vary, but all feature grand comfort. Housed in a private wing, each of the eight "Royal Rooms" is named for an English monarch and is decorated in the style of that ruler's period.

39 Buckingham Palace Rd., London SW1W 0PS. ✆ **877/955-1515** in the U.S. and Canada, or 020/ 7834-6600. Fax 020/7828-5401. www.rubenshotel.com. 161 units. £139–£169 double; £189 Royal Room; £279–£579 suite. AE, DC, MC, V. Tube: Victoria. **Amenities:** 2 restaurants; bar; babysitting; concierge; access to nearby health club; room service. *In room:* A/C, TV/DVD, movie library, hair dryer, minibar, Wi-Fi (free).

Moderate

Lime Tree Hotel   The Wales-born Davies family, veterans of London's B&B business, have transformed a dowdy guesthouse into a cozy hotel for budget travelers. The simply furnished bedrooms are scattered over four floors (with no elevator) of a brick town house; each has been recently refitted with new curtains and cupboards. The front rooms have small balconies overlooking Ebury Street; units in the back don't have balconies but are quieter and feature views of the hotel's small rose garden. Rooms here tend to be larger than other hotel rooms offered at similar prices, and breakfasts are generous. Six rooms come with a tub/shower combination, the rest with shower only. Buckingham Palace, Westminster Abbey, and the Houses of Parliament are within easy reach, as is Harrods. The popular Ebury Wine Bar is nearby.

135–137 Ebury St., London SW1W 9QU. ☎ **020/7730-8191.** Fax 020/7730-7865. www.limetree hotel.co.uk. 25 units. £120–£160 double; £170–£185 triple; £185–£200 quad. Rates include English breakfast. AE, DC, MC, V. No children 4 or under. Tube: Victoria. **Amenities:** Breakfast room. *In room:* TV, hair dryer, Wi-Fi (free).

New England   A family-run business for nearly a quarter of a century, this hotel shut down at the millennium for a complete overhaul. Today it's better than ever and charges an affordable price. Its elegant 19th-century exterior conceals a completely bright and modern interior. On a corner in the Pimlico area, which forms part of the City of Westminster, the hotel is neat and clean and one of the most welcoming in the area—it justly prides itself on its clientele of "repeats." It's also one of the few hotels in the area with an elevator.

20 St. George's Dr., London SW1V 4BN. ☎ **020/7834-1595.** Fax 020/7834-9000. www.new englandhotel.com. 20 units. £85–£99 double; £129–£139 triple; £139–£149 quad. Rates include breakfast. MC, V. Tube: Victoria. *In room:* TV, hair dryer, Wi-Fi (£3/hr.).

Sanctuary House Hotel ★   Only in the new London, where hotels are bursting into bloom like daffodils, would you find a hotel so close to Westminster Abbey. And a pub hotel, no less, with rooms on the upper floors above the tavern. The building was converted by Fuller Smith and Turner, a traditional brewery in Britain. Accommodations have a rustic feel, but they have first-rate beds. Downstairs, a pub/restaurant, part of the Sanctuary, offers old-style British meals that have ignored changing culinary fashions. "We like tradition," one of the perky staff members told us. "Why must everything be trendy? Some people come to England nostalgic for the old. Let others be trendy." Actually, the food is excellent if you appreciate the roast beef, Welsh lamb, and Dover sole that pleased the palates of Churchill and his contemporaries. Naturally, there's always plenty of brew on tap.

33 Tothill St., London SW1H 9LA. ☎ **020/7799-4044.** Fax 020/7799-3657. www.fullershotels. com. 34 units. £139–£195 double. AE, DC, MC, V. Tube: St. James's Park. **Amenities:** Restaurant; pub; room service. *In room:* A/C, TV, hair dryer, Wi-Fi (£11 per day).

Windermere Hotel ★ 🍴   This award-winning small hotel is an excellent choice near Victoria Station. The Windermere was built in 1857 as a pair of private dwellings on the old Abbot's Lane linking Westminster Abbey to its abbot's residence—all the kings of medieval England trod here. A fine example of early Victorian classical design, the hotel has lots of English character. All rooms contain a private bathroom—some with shower, others with tub baths—and come in a wide range of sizes, some accommodating three or four lodgers. The ground-floor rooms facing the street tend to be noisy at night, so avoid them if you're a light sleeper.

142–144 Warwick Way, London SW1V 4JE. ℂ **020/7834-5480.** Fax 020/7630-8831. www.windermere-hotel.co.uk. 20 units. £124–£155 double; £179 family room. Rates include English breakfast. AE, MC, V. Tube: Victoria. **Amenities:** Restaurant; bar; room service. *In room:* TV, hair dryer, Wi-Fi (free).

Inexpensive

Morgan House   This Georgian house has a convenient address, but its rooms are often fully booked in summer. Morgan's finest feature is a small courtyard open to guests. Many rooms are small to midsize, while others are large enough to house up to four people. Guest rooms are individually decorated and have orthopedic mattresses. Hallway bathrooms are well maintained and adequate for guests who don't have their own private facilities. A hearty English breakfast is served in a bright, cheerful room.

120 Ebury St., London SW1W 9QQ. ℂ **020/7730-2384.** Fax 020/7730-8442. www.morgan house.co.uk. 11 units, 4 with private bathroom. £78 double without bathroom, £98 with bathroom; £98 triple without bathroom, £138 with bathroom; £148 family room with bathroom. Rates include English breakfast. MC, V. Tube: Victoria. **Amenities:** Breakfast room. *In room:* TV, hair dryer, phone only for receiving calls, Wi-Fi (free).

KNIGHTSBRIDGE TO SOUTH KENSINGTON

Knightsbridge

VERY EXPENSIVE

The Berkeley ★★★   One of London's most appealing hotels, the Berkeley is housed in a French Regency–inspired building near Hyde Park. The building, completed in 1972, replaced the original Berkeley hotel, which was built in the late 19th century. During the new construction, some of original architectural embellishments were salvaged, including what is now the popular Blue Bar. Inside you'll find an environment inspired by Art Deco and French classical design but with a contemporary edge. Each of the rooms offers high-end style, but most elegant of all are the suites, many of which have luxurious, marble-and-tile-trimmed baths.

Wilton Place, London SW1X 7RL. ℂ **800/599-6991** or 020/7235-6000. Fax 020/7235-4330. www.maybournehotelgroup.com or www.the-berkeley.co.uk. 214 units. £299–£329 double; from £490 suite. AE, DC, MC, V. Tube: Knightsbridge or Hyde Park Corner. **Amenities:** 3 restaurants; 2 bars; concierge; health club & spa; pool (outdoor rooftop). *In room:* A/C, TV/DVD, CD player, CD library, hair dryer, Wi-Fi (free).

The Capital ★★★   We'd be delighted to check in here for the season. Only 45m (148 ft.) from Harrods department store, this family-run town-house hotel is also at the doorstep of the shops of Knightsbridge and the "green lung" of Hyde Park. There are 49 bedrooms here, and while you get many of the luxuries and services of a larger hotel, warmth, intimacy, and attention to detail are the hallmarks of this oasis. Famed designer Nina Campbell furnished the spacious bedrooms with sumptuous fabrics, art, and antiques. David Linley, nephew of Her Majesty, also assisted in the design. The liveried doorman standing outside has welcomed royalty, heads of state, and international celebrities to this hotel. For dining, you don't have far to go.

22 Basil St., London SW3 1AT. ✆ **020/7589-5171.** Fax 020/7225-0011. www.capitalhotel.co.uk. 49 units. £305–£565 double; £455–£850 suite. AE, DC, MC, V. Parking £30 per night. Tube: Knightsbridge. **Amenities:** Restaurant; bar; babysitting; access to nearby health club. *In room:* A/C, TV, hair dryer, minibar, Wi-Fi (£15).

EXPENSIVE

Aster House ★★★ 🖋   This is the winner of the 2004 London Tourism Award for best B&B in London, and it's just as good now as it was then. Within an easy walk of Kensington Palace and the museums of South Kensington, it's a friendly, inviting, and well-decorated lodging on a tree-lined street. The area surrounding the hotel, Sumner Place, looks like a Hollywood stage set of Victorian London. Aster House guests eat breakfast in a sunlit conservatory and can feed the ducks in the pond outside. Since the B&B is a Victorian building spread across five floors, each unit is unique in size and shape. Rooms range from spacious to Lilliputian. Some beds are draped with fabric tents for extra drama, and each room is individually decorated in the style of an English manor-house bedroom.

3 Sumner Place, London SW7 3EE. ✆ **020/7581-5888.** Fax 020/7584-4925. www.asterhouse. com. 14 units. £180–£225 double; £250 suite. Rates include buffet breakfast. MC, V. Tube: South Kensington. **Amenities:** Breakfast room. *In room:* A/C, TV, hair dryer, Wi-Fi (free).

The Beaufort ★★   If you'd like to stay at one of London's finest boutique hotels, head here. The Beaufort, only 180m (591 ft.) from Harrods, sits in a cul-de-sac behind two Victorian porticoes and an iron/board fence. A pair of adjacent town houses from the 1870s was combined. Each guest room is tasteful and bright, individually decorated in a modern color scheme and adorned with well-chosen paintings by London artists. Rooms come with earphone radios, flowers, and a selection of books—the junior suites offer use of a mobile phone in addition to a personal fax/answering machine. Most bedrooms are small, but they're efficiently organized. The most deluxe and spacious rooms are in the front; those in the back are smaller and darker.

33 Beaufort Gardens, London SW3 1PP. ✆ **020/7584-5252.** Fax 020/7589-2834. www.the beaufort.co.uk. 29 units. £195–£235 double; £247–£275 junior suite. AE, DC, MC, V. Tube: Knightsbridge. **Amenities:** Bar; free airport transfers (for occupants of junior suites); babysitting; access to nearby health club; room service. *In room:* A/C, TV, CD player, hair dryer, Wi-Fi (free).

Claverley Hotel ★   Located on a quiet cul-de-sac, this tasteful hotel, one of the neighborhood's very best, is just a few blocks from Harrods. It's a small, cozy place accented with Georgian-era accessories. The lounge has the atmosphere of a country house, and complimentary tea, coffee, and biscuits are served all day in

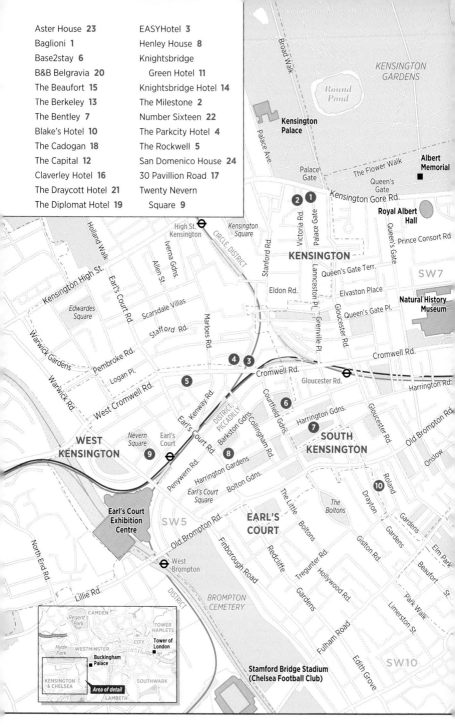

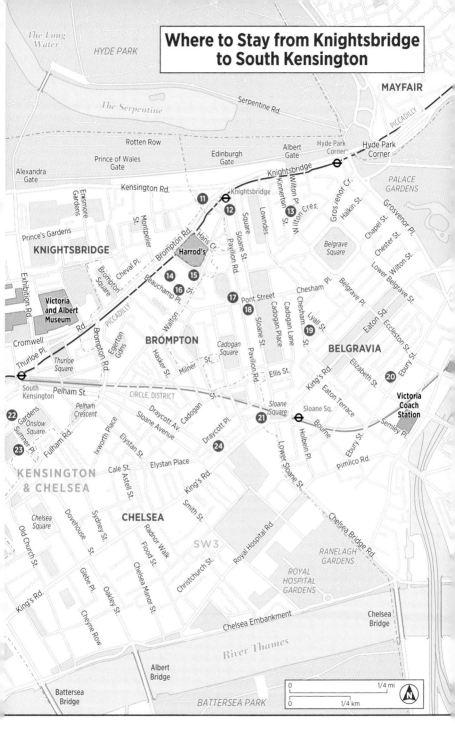

Where to Stay from Knightsbridge to South Kensington

the Reading Room. Most bedrooms have wall-to-wall carpeting and comfortably upholstered armchairs, and some open onto balconies. The rooms have marble bathrooms and power showers, and are individually decorated, some with four-poster beds.

13–14 Beaufort Gardens, London SW3 1PS. ℂ **800/747-0398** in the U.S., or 020/7589-8541. Fax 020/7584-3410. www.claverleyhotel.co.uk. 29 units. £172–£254 double. Rates include English breakfast. AE, MC, V. Parking £30 nearby. Tube: Knightsbridge. **Amenities:** Lounge. *In room:* TV, hair dryer, safe, Wi-Fi (£15).

Knightsbridge Green Hotel ★ Repeat guests from around the world view this dignified 1890s structure as their home away from home. In 1966, when it was converted into a hotel, the developers kept its wide baseboards, cove moldings, high ceilings, and spacious proportions. Even without kitchens, the well-furnished suites come close to apartment-style living. Most rooms are spacious, with adequate storage space. Bedrooms are decorated with custom-made colors and are often individualized—one has a romantic sleigh bed. This is a solid choice for lodging, just around the corner from Harrods.

10 Beaufort Gardens, London SW3 1PT. ℂ **020/7584-6300.** Fax 020/7584-6355. www.firmdale. com. 44 units. £220–£310 double; £360–£625 suite. AE, DC, MC, V. Tube: Knightsbridge. **Amenities:** Self-service bar; babysitting; room service. *In room:* TV/DVD, CD player, hair dryer, minibar, Wi-Fi (£20).

Knightsbridge Hotel ★★ ✦ The Knightsbridge Hotel attracts visitors from all over the world seeking a small, comfortable hotel in a high-rent district. It's fabulously located, sandwiched between fashionable Beauchamp Place and Harrods, with many of the city's top theaters and museums close at hand. Built in the early 1800s as a private town house, this place sits on a tranquil, tree-lined square, free from traffic. Two of London's premier hoteliers, Kit and Tim Kemp, who have been celebrated for their upmarket boutique hotels, have gone more affordable with a revamp of this hotel in the heart of the shopping district. All the Kemp "cult classics" are found here, including such luxe touches as granite-and-oak bathrooms, the Kemps' famed honor bar, and Frette linens. The hotel has become an instant hit. Most bedrooms are spacious and furnished with traditional English fabrics. The best rooms are nos. 311 and 312 at the rear, each with a pitched ceiling and a small sitting area.

10 Beaufort Gardens, London SW3 1PT. ℂ **020/7584-6300.** Fax 020/7584-6355. www.firmdale. com. 44 units. £210–£295 double; £345–£595 suite. AE, DC, MC, V. Tube: Knightsbridge. **Amenities:** Self-service bar; babysitting; room service. *In room:* TV/DVD, CD player, hair dryer, minibar, Wi-Fi (£20).

30 Pavilion Road ★ 🎁 Searcy, one of London's best catering firms, operates this recycled surprise: an old pumping station that has been turned into a hotel that's only a hop, skip, and a jump from Harrods and the boutiques of Sloane Street. At this Knightsbridge oasis, you press a buzzer and are admitted to a freight elevator that carries you to the third floor. Upstairs, you'll encounter handsomely furnished rooms with antiques, tasteful fabrics, comfortable beds (some with canopies), and often a sitting alcove. Some of the tubs are placed right in the room instead of in a separate unit. Check out the rooftop garden.

30 Pavilion Rd., London SW1X 0HJ. ☎ **020/7584-4921.** Fax 020/7823-8694. www.30pavilion
road.co.uk. 10 units. £180 double; £200 suite. Rates include continental breakfast. AE, DC, MC, V.
Tube: Knightsbridge. **Amenities:** Babysitting; room service. *In room:* A/C, TV, Wi-Fi (free).

Kensington

VERY EXPENSIVE

The Bentley ★★★ Following an 8-year renovation, this hotel is the epitome
of charm for those who prefer opulence to minimalism. Located in the heart of
Kensington, the Bentley is the Rolls-Royce (or at least the Bentley) of London
hotels. Six hundred tons of marble were imported from Turkey, Africa, and Italy
to adorn the place. Gorgeous silk fabrics fill its spacious rooms and suites, each
with a luxe marble-lined bathroom with walk-in shower and Jacuzzi. The fixtures
are gold plate, and in the bedrooms are deep pile carpets and Louis XIV accessories. The Imperial Suite even boasts a grand piano.

27–31 Harrington Gardens, London SW7 4JX. ☎ **020/7244-5555.** Fax 020/7244-5566. www.
thebentley-hotel.com. 64 units. AE, MC, V. £210–£330 double; £265–£700 suite. Tube: South
Kensington. **Amenities:** 2 restaurants; bar; babysitting; concierge; health club & spa. *In room:*
A/C, TV/DVD, hair dryer, Internet (£16), minibar.

The Milestone ★★★ This government-rated five-star boutique hotel, conveniently located in a Victorian town house across the street from Kensington Palace, offers modern luxury in an intimate, traditional setting. The Milestone's
beautiful public rooms are awash with fresh flowers, dark woods, antique furnishings, and fabric wallcoverings, creating the cozy atmosphere of a private
manor house. Guest rooms and suites are spread over six floors and vary in size,
decor, and shape (a few rooms are a bit small). The masculine Savile Row Room
is "papered" in pinstriped material and sports a tailor's dummy and books on
men's fashion; the serene Royal Studio has a small balcony and a sleigh bed; and
the bi-level Club Suite offers an English library–style lounge, complete with an
antique billiards table. You can request a room overlooking the palace and Kensington Gardens.

1 Kensington Court, London W8 5DL. ☎ **877/955-1515** in the U.S. and Canada, or 020/7917-
1000. Fax 020/7917-1010. www.milestonehotel.com. 63 units. £250–£400 double; £584–£850
suite. AE, DC, MC, V. Tube: High St. Kensington. **Amenities:** Restaurant; bar; babysitting; concierge; health club (w/Jacuzzi); room service. *In room:* A/C, TV/DVD/VCR, CD player, fax, hair
dryer, minibar, MP3 docking station, Wi-Fi (free).

EXPENSIVE

Baglioni ★★★ Arguably the city's chicest address, Baglioni, part of the Italian hotel chain, is the personification of *la dolce vita* in London. This pricey citadel attracts those who were born to shop (Harrods is a 10-min. walk away,
Kensington High St. only 5). Of the 67 stunning and luxuriously furnished bedrooms, 49 are suites. The best and most elegant bedrooms open onto Kensington
Gardens. What an enclave: Ebonized wood floors and deluxe furnishings in
mocha, taupe, and black are just part of the allure. Suites come with their own
espresso machine, and the 24-hour room service is perhaps the most skilled and
smoothly functioning in London. A chauffeur-driven Maserati Quattroporte and

a personal butler await you, as does the luxe Brunello Lounge & Restaurant inspired by the famous Tuscan wine.

60 Hyde Park Gate, London SW7 5BB. ☏ **020/7368-5700.** Fax 020/7368-5701. www.baglioni hotels.com. 67 units. £279–£329 double; from £409 suite. AE, MC, V. Parking £38. Tube: Kensington High St. **Amenities:** Restaurant; bar; babysitting; concierge; room service. *In room:* A/C, TV/DVD, movie library, CD player, CD library, hair dryer, Internet (free), minibar.

The Parkcity Hotel ★ Close to the shopping districts of Kensington and Knightsbridge, this is a very successful restoration of a Victorian structure that has been thoroughly modernized with a striking design. Contemporary furnishings grace both the public and private buildings. The town house–style hotel is rated four stars by the government because of its facilities that range from a business center to a gym. An alfresco dining terrace is open in summer. Gourmet Italian food is featured in Lessandro, and Ruby's Cocktail Bar is a sophisticated place for a rendezvous.

18–30 Lexham Gardens, Kensington, W8 5JE. ☏ **020/7341-7090.** Fax 020/7835-0189. www. theparkcity.com. 62 units. £109–£450. AE, MC, V. Tube: Gloucester Rd. **Amenities:** Restaurant; bar; concierge; exercise room; room service. *In room:* AC, TV/DVD player, Internet (£6.50), minibar.

INEXPENSIVE

Base2stay ✦ Down in Kensington a new concept in hotels has emerged, offering great value by providing "a synthesis" of what guests really need and use—minus the frills. What you get are stylish, comfortably furnished accommodations with small kitchenettes. The cheapest rooms contain bunk beds for two, and suites can be made by way of interconnecting rooms. Living may be stripped to the basics, but this is no hostel, as there is a 24-hour reception service as well as daily maid service.

25 Courtfield Gardens, London SW5 OPG. ☏ **800/511-9821** in the U.S., or 020/7244-2255. www. base2stay.com. 67 units. £93–£103 bunk beds for 2; £105–£161 double; £199 deluxe units for 4 guests. AE, MC, V. Tube: Earls Court. **Amenities:** Wi-Fi (free). *In room:* A/C, TV, kitchenette.

EASYHotel ✦ This hotel runs on the principle that guests would rather have smaller hotel rooms and pay less. If you're claustrophobic, this hotel is definitely not for you. The rooms are 6 to 7 sq. m (65–75 sq. ft.), with most of the space taken up by standard double beds. If you can get a room with a window, do so, because it makes a big difference. Just off Cromwell Road between South Kensington and Earl's Court, the hotel offers all doubles with cramped bathrooms containing a shower. There are flatscreen TVs in every unit, but a £5 fee is assessed to use the set. One staff member is permanently on-site, but no services are offered. Housekeeping service costs an optional £10 per day, there is no elevator, and checkout time is 10am. Instead of phoning the hotel, you must book by credit card through its website.

14 Lexham Gardens, Kensington, London W8 5JE. ☏ **020/7706-9911.** www.easyhotel.com. 34 units. £30–£50 double. MC, V. Tube: South Kensington or Earls Court. *In room:* A/C, TV, Wi-Fi (£10).

Belgravia

EXPENSIVE

The Diplomat Hotel ★ 🎁 Part of the Diplomat's charm is that it is a small and reasonably priced hotel located in an otherwise prohibitively expensive neighborhood. Only minutes from Harrods Department Store, it was built in 1882 as a private residence by noted architect Thomas Cubbitt. The registration desk is framed by the sweep of a partially gilded circular staircase; above it, cherubs gaze down from a Regency-era chandelier. The staff is helpful, well mannered, and discreet. The high-ceilinged guest rooms are tastefully done in Victorian style. You get good—not grand—comfort here. Rooms are a bit small and usually furnished with twin beds.

2 Chesham St., London SW1X 8DT. ✆ **020/7235-1544.** Fax 020/7259-6153. www.thediplomat hotel.co.uk. 26 units. £115–£170 double. Rates include English buffet breakfast. AE, DC, MC, V. Tube: Sloane Sq. or Knightsbridge. **Amenities:** Snack bar; babysitting. *In room:* TV, hair dryer, Wi-Fi (free).

MODERATE

B + B Belgravia ★★ In its first year of operation (2005), this elegant town house won a top Gold Award as "the best B&B in London." It richly deserves it. Design, service, quality, and comfort paid off. The prices are also reasonable, the atmosphere in this massively renovated building is stylish, and the location is grand: just a 5-minute walk from Victoria Station. The good-size bedrooms are luxuriously furnished. In the guest lounge with its comfy sofas, an open fire burns on nippy nights. There is also a DVD library, and tea and coffee are served 24 hours a day. The full English breakfast in the morning is one of the finest in the area.

64–66 Ebury St., Belgravia, London SW1W 9QD. ✆ **020/7259-8570.** Fax 020/7259-8591. www. bb-belgravia.com. 17 units. £120–£130 double; £150–£160 family room. Rates include a full English breakfast. AE, MC, V. Tube: Victoria Station. **Amenities:** Breakfast room. *In room:* TV, Wi-Fi (free).

Chelsea

EXPENSIVE

The Cadogan ★★ Best known as the spot Oscar Wilde was arrested for so-called indecent acts, this late-Victorian terra-cotta brick hotel had grown a bit stale before design doyenne Grace Leo-Andrieu stepped in. In the late 1890s, the halls rang with the laughter of Lillie Langtry, mistress of Edward VII. Today you get "stardust" wallpaper in the Drawing Room, Chanel-style tweeds on the upholstery, ostrich feathers strewn across pillows, and cheeky silver wallpaper in the very room (no. 118) where Wilde himself met his fate. The spacious and individually decorated bedrooms come in many styles and arrangements, even studios, some with two bathrooms. Rooms and suites are either contemporary with smooth lines and bold splashes of color or Edwardian style with period details and country-house furnishings.

75 Sloane St., London SW1X 9SG. ✆ **020/7235-7141.** Fax 020/7245-0994. www.cadogan.com. 50 units. £195–£260 double; £295–£385 suite. AE, DC, MC, V. Tube: Sloane Sq. or Knightsbridge. **Amenities:** Restaurant; bar; concierge; exercise room; use of tennis court in private gardens. *In room:* A/C, TV/DVD, hair dryer, minibar, Wi-Fi (free).

The Draycott Hotel ★★★ Everything about this place, radically upgraded into a government five-star rating, reeks of British gentility, style, and charm. So attentive is the staff that past clients, who have included John Malkovich, Pierce Brosnan, and Gerard Depardieu, are greeted like old friends when they enter by a staff that manages to be both hip and cordial. The hotel took its present-day form when a third brick-fronted town house was added to a pair of interconnected town houses that had been functioning as a five-star hotel since the 1980s. That, coupled with tons of money spent on English antiques, rich draperies, and an upgrade of those expensive infrastructures you'll never see, including security, has transformed this place into a gem. Bedrooms are outfitted differently, each with haute English style and plenty of fashion chic. As a special feature, the hotel serves complimentary drinks—tea at 4pm daily, champagne at 6pm, and hot chocolate at 9:30pm.

26 Cadogan Gardens, London SW3 2RP. ℂ **800/747-4942** or 020/7730-6466. Fax 020/7730-0236. www.draycotthotel.com. 35 units. £260–£315 double; £385 suite. AE, DC, MC, V. Tube: Sloane Sq. **Amenities:** Bar; access to nearby health club and spa; room service. *In room:* A/C, TV/DVD, CD player, minibar, Wi-Fi (free).

San Domenico House ★★ This "toff" (dandy) address, a redbrick Victorian-era town house that has been tastefully renovated in recent years, is located in Chelsea near Sloane Square. It combines valuable 19th-century antiques with modern comforts. Our favorite spot here is the rooftop terrace; with views opening onto Chelsea, it's ideal for a relaxing breakfast or drink. Bedrooms come in varying sizes, ranging from small to spacious, but all are opulently furnished with flouncy draperies, tasteful fabrics, and sumptuous beds. Many rooms have draped four-poster or canopied beds and, of course, antiques.

29 Draycott Place, London SW3 2SH. ℂ **800/324-9960** in the U.S., or 020/7581-5757. Fax 020/7584-1348. www.sandomenicohouse.com. 15 units. £235–£255 double; £295–£360 suite. AE, DC, MC, V. Tube: Sloane Sq. **Amenities:** Airport transfers; babysitting; room service; Wi-Fi (free in lobby). *In room:* A/C, TV, hair dryer, Internet (£9), minibar.

South Kensington

VERY EXPENSIVE

Blake's Hotel ★★★ Actress Anouska Hempel's opulent and highly individual creation is one of London's best small hotels. No expense was spared in converting this former row of Victorian town houses into one of the city's most original places to stay. It offers an Arabian Nights atmosphere: The richly appointed lobby boasts British Raj–era furniture from India, and individually decorated, elaborately appointed rooms contain such treasures and touches as Venetian glassware, cloth-covered walls, swagged draperies, and even Empress Josephine's daybed. Live out your fantasy: Choose an ancient Egyptian funeral barge or a 16th-century Venetian boudoir. Rooms in the older section have the least space and aren't air-conditioned but are chic nevertheless.

33 Roland Gardens, London SW7 3PF. ℂ **800/926-3173** in the U.S., or 020/7370-6701. Fax 020/7373-0442. www.blakeshotels.com. 48 units. £265–£375 double; from £445 suite. AE, MC, V. Parking £4 per hr. Tube: Gloucester Rd. **Amenities:** Restaurant; babysitting; exercise room; room service. *In room:* TV, hair dryer, minibar, Wi-Fi (free).

EXPENSIVE

Number Sixteen ★   This luxurious pension is composed of four early-Victorian town houses linked together. The scrupulously maintained front and rear gardens make this one of the most idyllic spots on the street. The rooms are decorated with an eclectic mix of English antiques and modern paintings, although some of the decor looks a little faded. Accommodations range from small to spacious and have themes such as tartan and maritime. Breakfast can be served in your bedroom, in the conservatory, or if the weather's good in the garden, with its bubbling fountain and fishpond.

16 Sumner Place, London SW7 3EG. © **888/559-5508** in the U.S., or 020/7589-5232. Fax 020/7584-8615. www.firmdale.com. 42 units. £165–£280 double. AE, DC, MC, V. Parking £39. Tube: South Kensington. **Amenities:** Honor bar; babysitting; access to nearby health club; room service. *In room:* TV, hair dryer, minibar, Wi-Fi (free).

The Rockwell ★★★ 🎁   One of London's latest hotels proves that high style doesn't always come with a high price tag in London. This independently owned bastion of deluxe comfort occupies a converted Georgian manse in South Kensington. Its bedrooms are tricked out with oak furnishings and Neisha Crosland wallpaper, each crafted to combine traditional English aesthetics with modern design. The bedrooms themselves are large and inviting and dressed with the finest of Egyptian cotton, feather pillows, and merino wool blankets. Each room has a solid oak cupboard and desk. Rooms are bright and airy with large windows and simple lines. We prefer the garden units with their own private patios. On site is the trendy One-Eight-One bistro whose menu is based on English fare given a contemporary twist. Yes, they serve lavender ice cream.

181 Cromwell Rd., London SW5 0SF. © **020/7244-2000.** Fax 020/7244-2001. www.therockwell.com. 40 units. £160–£180 double; £200 suites. AE, DC, MC, V. Tube: Earls Court or Gloucester Rd. **Amenities:** Restaurant; bar; access to nearby gym; room service. *In room:* A/C, TV, Internet (free), minibar.

Earl's Court

MODERATE

Twenty Nevern Square ★ 🎁   Many of the affordable hotels around Earl's Court are seedy, but not this restored hotel, a stately redbrick Victorian house with a distinctly Asian feeling, from the lounge's porcelain vases and ornate bird cages to the heavy silk draperies. The most elegant of the accommodations is the Pasha Suite, which has luxurious silk draperies printed with a peacock design. Some of the smaller rooms are made to feel much smaller by the heavy furniture, most of which was shipped in from Indonesia. Several of the bedrooms feature private terraces, and most of these are at the lower end of the price scale shown below.

20 Nevern Sq., Earls Court, London SW5 9PD. © **020/7565-9555.** Fax 020/7565-9444. www.20nevernsquare.com. 20 units. £79–£109 double; £135–£159 suite. AE, MC, V. Tube: Earls Court. **Amenities:** Bar; cafe; access to nearby gym; room service. *In room:* TV, CD player, hair dryer, Wi-Fi (free).

INEXPENSIVE

Henley House ♦ This B&B stands out from the pack around Earl's Court—and it's a better value than most. The redbrick Victorian row house is on a communal fenced-in garden that you can enter by borrowing a key from the reception desk. The staff members take a keen interest in the welfare of their guests and are happy to take bewildered newcomers under their wing, so this is an ideal place for London first-timers. A ground-floor sitting room overlooks a rear courtyard. The decor is bright and contemporary; a typical room has warmly patterned wallpaper, chintz fabrics, and solid-brass lighting fixtures. Breakfast is a cheerful event, served in a room decorated with terra-cotta accents and pots of dried flowers.

30 Barkston Gardens, London SW5 0EN. ℂ **020/7370-4111.** Fax 020/7370-0026. www.henley househotel.com. 21 units. £59 double; £69 triple. Rates include continental breakfast. AE, DC, MC, V. Tube: Earl's Court. **Amenities:** Breakfast room. *In room:* TV, hair dryer, Wi-Fi (free).

MARYLEBONE TO HOLLAND PARK

Marylebone

VERY EXPENSIVE

The Langham ★★ After it was bombed in World War II, this well-located hotel languished as dusty office space for the BBC until the early 1990s, when it was painstakingly restored. The Langham's public rooms reflect the power and majesty of the British Empire at its apex. Guest rooms are somewhat less opulent but are still attractively furnished and comfortable, featuring French Provincial furniture and red oak trim. The hotel is within easy reach of Mayfair and Soho restaurants and theaters, and shopping on Oxford and Regent streets. Plus, Regent's Park is just blocks away.

1C Portland Place, London W1B 1JA. ℂ **800/223-6800** or 020/7636-1000. Fax 020/7323-2340. http://london.langhamhotels.co.uk. 425 units. £255–£335 double; from £555 suite; £370 club room. AE, DC, MC, V. Tube: Oxford Circus. **Amenities:** 2 restaurants; bar; concierge; health club & spa; pool (indoor); room service. *In room:* A/C, TV/DVD, hair dryer, minibar, Wi-Fi (£20).

The Mandeville Hotel ★★ Call it refurbished London. In trendy Marylebone Village, just a short stroll from Selfridges and Bond Street shops, the Mandeville has been totally restored, its former 166 bedrooms restructured into 142 units. This once-staid property is now a hot address—one of London's leading decorators, Stephen Ryan, was brought in to restyle the lobby, restaurant, and bar. In the de Ville Restaurant, modern British cuisine is served against a backdrop of floral wallpaper punctuated by theatrical clear Perspex-framed paintings and Venetian-mask wall lights.

Mandeville Place, London W1U 2BE. ℂ **020/7935-5599.** Fax 020/7935-9588. www.mandeville. co.uk. 142 units. £127–£246 double; £280–£510 suite. AE, DC, MC, V. Tube: Bond St. **Amenities:** Restaurant; bar; concierge; exercise room; room service. *In room:* A/C, TV, hair dryer, minibar (in some), Wi-Fi (£13).

EXPENSIVE

Dorset Square Hotel ★★★   Just steps from Regent's Park, this is one of London's best and most stylish "house hotels"—it even overlooks Thomas Lord's (the man who set up London's first private cricket club) first cricket pitch. Hoteliers have furnished the interiors of these two Georgian town houses with a comfy mix of antiques, reproductions, and chintz that makes you feel as if you're in an elegant private home. The impressive bedrooms are decorated in a distinctly personal (and beautiful) style. Eight rooms feature crown-canopied beds, and all appointments are of a very high standard.

39–40 Dorset Sq., London NW1 6QN. © **020/7723-7874.** Fax 020/7724-3328. www.dorset square.co.uk. 37 units. £140–£160 double; from £200 suite. AE, DC, MC, V. Parking £35 daily, free on weekends. Tube: Baker St. or Marylebone. **Amenities:** Restaurant, bar, babysitting; room service. *In room:* A/C, TV, hair dryer, minibar, Wi-Fi (£7).

Durrants Hotel ★   This historic hotel off Manchester Square (established in 1789) with its Georgian-detailed facade is snug, cozy, and traditional—almost like a poor man's Brown's (p. 134). We find it to be one of the most quintessentially English of all London hotels. You could invite the queen to Durrants for tea. Over the 100 years that they have owned the hotel, the Miller family has incorporated several neighboring houses into the original structure. A walk through the pine-and-mahogany-paneled public rooms is like stepping back in time: You'll even find an 18th-century letter-writing room. The rooms are rather bland except for elaborate cove moldings and comfortable furnishings, including good beds. Some are air-conditioned, and some are, alas, small.

26–32 George St., London W1H 5BJ. © **020/7935-8131.** Fax 020/7487-3510. www.durrants hotel.co.uk. 92 units. £250 double; £265 family room for 3; £295–£425 suite. AE, MC, V. Tube: Bond St. or Baker St. **Amenities:** Restaurant; bar; babysitting; concierge; room service. *In room:* A/C (in most), TV, hair dryer, Wi-Fi (£10).

Park Plaza Sherlock Holmes Hotel   It's not located at that legendary address, 221B Baker St., but it's nearby. The converted boutique hotel was once part of Bedford College for Women and later the YWCA. Former tenants wouldn't know the place today. Modern portraits of the world's most famous detective are on display, but the decor is contemporary. Bedrooms come in a wide range of sizes and styles, ranked superior, executive, or studio. Most preferred, at least by us, is a trio of loft suites. Guests gather in Sherlock's Bar & Grill for good British beer and food.

108 Baker St., London W1U 6LJ. © **888/201-1803** or 020/7486-6161. Fax 020/7958-5211. www. parkplazasherlockholmes.com. 119 units. £109–£144 double; £139–£485 studio/loft-suite. AE, MC, V. Tube: Baker St. **Amenities:** Restaurant; bar; concierge; health club and spa. *In room:* A/C, TV, hair dryer, minibar, Wi-Fi (£15).

MODERATE

Hallam Hotel   This heavily ornamented stone-and-brick Victorian—one of the few on the street to escape the Blitz—is just a 5-minute stroll from Oxford Circus. It's the property of brothers Grant and David Baker, who maintain it well. The hotel is warm and friendly, and the central location that you get for these prices can't be beat. The guest rooms are comfortably furnished with good beds.

Where to Stay from
Marylebone to Holland Park

MAIDA VALE

W9

KENSAL TOWN

WESTBOURNE GREEN

WESTWAY A40 (M)

W10

NORTH KENSINGTON

Ladbroke Grove

Westbourne Park

BAYSWATER

W11

NOTTING HILL

Holland Park

HOLLAND PARK

HOLLAND PARK

Kensington Palace

W8

High St. Kensington

Kensington Square

SHEPHERD'S BUSH

Kensington Olympia

Kensington Olympia

KENSINGTON

CAMDEN

TOWER HAMLETS

Regent's Park

WESTMINSTER

CITY

Tower of London

Hyde Park

Area of detail

Buckingham Palace

KENSINGTON & CHELSEA

LAMBETH

SOUTHWARK

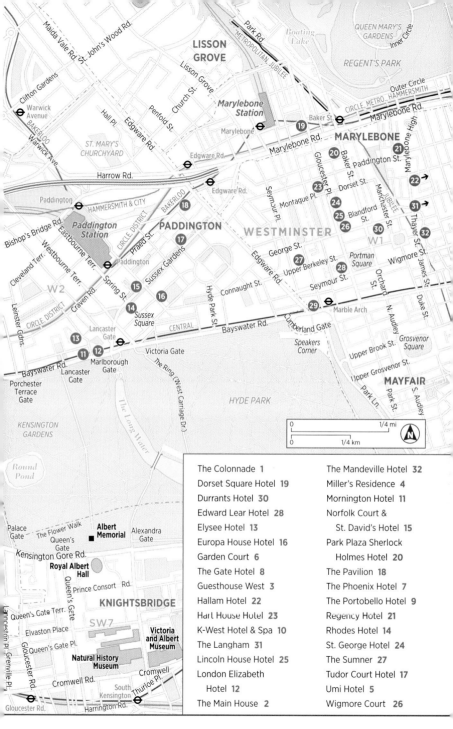

The Colonnade **1**

Dorset Square Hotel **19**

Durrants Hotel **30**

Edward Lear Hotel **28**

Elysee Hotel **13**

Europa House Hotel **16**

Garden Court **6**

The Gate Hotel **8**

Guesthouse West **3**

Hallam Hotel **22**

Hart House Hotel **23**

K-West Hotel & Spa **10**

The Langham **31**

Lincoln House Hotel **25**

London Elizabeth
   Hotel **12**

The Main House **2**

The Mandeville Hotel **32**

Miller's Residence **4**

Mornington Hotel **11**

Norfolk Court &
   St. David's Hotel **15**

Park Plaza Sherlock
   Holmes Hotel **20**

The Pavilion **18**

The Phoenix Hotel **7**

The Portobello Hotel **9**

Regency Hotel **21**

Rhodes Hotel **14**

St. George Hotel **24**

The Sumner **27**

Tudor Court Hotel **17**

Umi Hotel **5**

Wigmore Court **26**

Several of the twin-bedded rooms are quite spacious and have adequate closet space.

12 Hallam St., Portland Place, London W1N 5LF. ☎ **020/7580-1166.** Fax 020/7323-4527. www. hallamhotel.com. 25 units. £105–£120 double. Rates include English breakfast. AE, DC, MC, V. Tube: Oxford Circus. **Amenities:** Bar. *In room:* TV, hair dryer, minibar, Wi-Fi (£5).

Hart House Hotel ★ ☺   Hart House is a long-enduring favorite with Frommer's readers. In the heart of the West End, this well-preserved historic building (one of a group of Georgian mansions occupied by exiled French nobles during the French Revolution) lies within easy walking distance of many theaters. The rooms—done in a combination of furnishings, ranging from Portobello antiques to modern—are spick-and-span, each one with a different character. Favorites include no. 7, a triple with a big bathroom and shower. Ask for no. 11, on the top floor, if you'd like a brightly lit aerie. Housekeeping rates high marks here, and each bedroom is comfortably appointed with chairs, an armoire, a desk, and a large chest of drawers. Hart House has long been known as a good, safe place for traveling families. Many of its rooms are triples. Larger families can avail themselves of special family accommodations with connecting rooms.

51 Gloucester Place, Portman Sq., London W1U 8JF. ☎ **020/7935-2288.** Fax 020/7935-8516. www.harthouse.co.uk. 15 units. £110–£150 double; £130–£175 triple; £155–£185 quad. Rates include English breakfast. MC, V. Tube: Marble Arch or Baker St. **Amenities:** Babysitting. *In room:* TV, hair dryer, Wi-Fi (£5).

St. George Hotel ★ ✦   A short walk from Oxford and Baker streets, this privately owned hotel in a restored Georgian building overlooks landmark Gloucester Square. Its midsize bedrooms are attractively and comfortably refurbished in red-and-white tones, with such modern amenities as key-card doors and electronic built-in room safes. Bathrooms are well appointed, each with a tub and a shower. Two accommodations have bathrooms that are outside the room but for the sole use of occupants of a particular unit. A wide range of rooms is available, from single to quad, the latter ideal for families.

49 Gloucester Place, London W1U 8JE. ☎ **020/7486-8586.** Fax 020/7486-6567. www.stgeorge-hotel.net. 19 units. £95–£150 double; £175 triple; £200 quad. Rates include English breakfast. AE, MC, V. Tube: Marylebone Rd. or Baker St. **Amenities:** Free airport transfers. *In room:* A/C (in some), TV, fridge, hair dryer, Wi-Fi (free).

The Sumner ★ ✦   This town-house hotel, part of an 1820s Georgian terrace, has blossomed into one of the finest boutique town-house hotels in central London. It retains much of its original architectural allure from when it was a private Georgian residence. The standard rooms are midsize and attractively furnished, but you can also rent deluxe rooms with artwork and better furnishings. All the guest rooms are designer-decorated and luxuriously appointed, and there is also an elegant sitting room with a working fireplace and timber flooring.

54 Upper Berkeley St., Marble Arch, London W1H 7QR. ☎ **020/7723-2244.** Fax 087/0705-8767. www.thesumner.com. 20 units. £135–£170 double. Rates include buffet breakfast. AE, MC, V. Tube: Marble Arch. *In room:* A/C, TV, fridge, hair dryer, Wi-Fi (free).

INEXPENSIVE

Edward Lear Hotel This popular hotel, situated 1 block from Marble Arch, is made all the more desirable by the bouquets of fresh flowers in its public rooms. It occupies a pair of brick town houses dating from 1780. The western house was the London home of 19th-century artist and poet Edward Lear, famous for his nonsense verse, and his illustrated limericks adorn the walls of one of the sitting rooms. Steep stairs lead up to cozy rooms, which range from spacious to broom-closet size. Bedrooms are looking better than ever following a wholesale renovation in 2007. If you're looking for classiness, know that the bacon on your plate came from the same butcher used by the queen. One major drawback to the hotel: This is a very noisy part of town. Rear rooms are quieter.

28–30 Seymour St., London W1H 7JB. ⓒ **020/7402-5401.** Fax 020/7706-3766. www.edlear. com. 32 units, 18 with bathroom. £68–£85 double without bathroom, £94–£117 double with bathroom; £94–£117 triple without bathroom, £124–£150 triple with shower only. Rates include English breakfast and tax. AE, MC, V. Tube: Marble Arch. **Amenities:** Internet (free). *In room:* TV, Wi-Fi (free).

Lincoln House Hotel ★ Built in the late 18th century, under the reign of King George III, this refurbished and tastefully decorated hotel is a converted town house with lots of character. Only a 5-minute walk from Marble Arch Tube, it occupies one of the most central locations in London, near Oxford Street northeast of Hyde Park. Midsize bedrooms are completely modernized but decorated in a traditional fashion. You have a choice of enjoying an English breakfast downstairs or a continental breakfast served in your room.

33 Gloucester Place, London W1U 8HY ⓒ **020/7486-7630.** Fax 020/7486-0166. www.lincoln-house-hotel.co.uk. 24 units. £95–£125 double; £135–£139 triple; £145–£149 family room. AE, DC, MC, V. Tube: Marble Arch. **Amenities:** Breakfast in room. *In room:* TV, fridge (in some), hair dryer, Wi-Fi (free).

Regency Hotel The building is from the 1800s, and there has been a hotel of some kind here since the Blitz. In 1991, the place was gutted and renovated into its present form. One of the better hotels on the street, it offers simple, conservatively decorated modern bedrooms scattered over four floors and a breakfast room set in what used to be the cellar. The neighborhood is protected as a historic district, and Marble Arch, Regent's Park, and Baker Street all lie within a 15-minute walk.

19 Nottingham Place, London W1U 5LQ. ⓒ **020/7486-5347.** Fax 020/7224-6057. www.regency hotelwestend.co.uk. 20 units. £89 double; £110–£125 family room. Rates include English breakfast. AE, DC, MC, V. Parking £25 nearby. Tube: Baker St. or Regent's Park. *In room:* TV, hair dryer.

Wigmore Court ⚑ A convenient family hotel, this inn lies near the street made famous as the fictional address of Sherlock Holmes—Baker Street. It's also close to Marble Arch, Oxford Street, and Madame Tussaud's. A somber Georgian structure, it has been converted into a fine B&B suitable only for serious stair climbers, as there is no elevator. There's traffic noise outside, so request a room in the rear. Bedrooms, many quite spacious, are comfortably furnished. Most units contain double or twin beds, plus a small bathroom.

23 Gloucester Place, London W1U 8HS. ☏ **020/7935-0928.** Fax 020/7487-4254. www.
wigmore-hotel.co.uk. 19 units. £70–£89 double; £120 triple. MC, V. Tube: Marble Arch. **Amenities:** Guest kitchen. *In room:* TV, Wi-Fi (free).

Paddington & Bayswater
EXPENSIVE

London Elizabeth Hotel ★   This elegant Victorian town house is ideally situated, overlooking Hyde Park. Amid the buzz and excitement of central London,
the hotel's atmosphere is an oasis of charm and refinement. Even before the
hotel's recent £3-million restoration, it oozed character. Individually decorated
rooms range from executive to deluxe and remind us of staying in an English
country house. Deluxe rooms are fully air-conditioned, and some contain four-
poster beds. Executive units usually contain one double or twin bed. Some rooms
have special features such as Victorian antique fireplaces. Suites are pictures of
grand comfort and luxury—the Conservatory Suite boasts its own veranda, part
of the house's original 1850 conservatory.

30 John Islip St., London SW1P 4DD. ☏ **020/7630-1000.** Fax 020/7233-7575. www.cityinn.com.
460 units. £119–£159 double; £139–£179 city club room; £219–£259 suite. AE, DC, MC, V. Tube:
Pimlico or Westminster. **Amenities:** Restaurant; 2 bars; concierge; exercise room; room service.
In room: A/C, TV/DVD, CD player, hair dryer, minibar, Wi-Fi (free).

Miller's Residence ★★ 👪   Staying here is like spending a night in Charles
Dickens's Old Curiosity Shop. Others say the little hotel looks like the set of *La
Traviata.* Miller's calls itself an 18th-century rooming house, and there's nothing
quite like it in London. A roaring log fire blazes in the large book-lined drawing
room in winter. The individually designed rooms are named after romantic poets.
They vary in shape and size, but all are luxuriously furnished with antiques,
prints, and tasteful curios. In addition to its double rooms, Miller's offers two
salon-style bedrooms.

111A Westbourne Grove, London W2 4UW. ☏ **020/7243-1024.** Fax 020/7243-1064. www.millers
hotel.com. 9 units. £155–£235 double. Rates include continental breakfast. AE, MC, V. Tube: Bayswater or Notting Hill Gate. **Amenities:** Babysitting. *In room:* TV/DVD, hair dryer, MP3 docking
station, Wi-Fi (free).

The Phoenix Hotel   This hotel, a member of the Best Western chain, occupies the entire south side of Kensington Gardens Square, one of the most famous
garden squares in Europe. Well situated in an ethnically mixed neighborhood,
the Phoenix is composed of a series of 1854 town houses. The atmosphere is
welcoming. Well-furnished bedrooms keep to a smart international standard,
with a palette of muted tones. Everything is designed for comfort and ease,
including the luggage racks. The bar is a good place to unwind, and moderately
priced meals are served in the downstairs cafe. Our biggest complaint? The public areas are too small for a hotel of this size.

1–8 Kensington Gardens Sq., London W2 4BH. ☏ **800/528-1234** in the U.S., or 020/7229-2494.
Fax 020/7727-1419. www.phoenixhotel.co.uk. 130 units. £165 double; £230 triple; £255 family
room. Rates include continental breakfast. AE, DC, MC, V. Tube: Bayswater Station. **Amenities:**
Cafe; bar; room service. *In room:* TV, hair dryer, Wi-Fi (free).

MODERATE

Mornington Hotel ★ Affiliated with Best Western, the Mornington brings a touch of northern European hospitality to the center of London. Just north of Hyde Park and Kensington Gardens, the hotel has a Victorian exterior and a Scandinavian-inspired decor. The area isn't London's most fashionable, but it's close to Hyde Park and convenient to Marble Arch, Oxford Street shopping, and the ethnic restaurants of Queensway. Renovated guest rooms are tasteful and comfortable. Every year we get our annual Christmas card from "the gang," as we refer to the hotel staff—and what a helpful crew they are.

12 Lancaster Gate, London W2 3LG. ℂ **800/633-6548** in the U.S., or 020/7262-7361. Fax 020/ 7706-1028. www.bw-morningtonhotel.co.uk. 66 units. £89–£145 double. Rates include Scandinavian and English breakfast. AE, DC, MC, V. Parking £25. Tube: Lancaster Gate. **Amenities:** Bar. *In room:* TV, Wi-Fi (free).

The Pavilion ★ 🎁 Until the early 1990s, this was a rather ordinary-looking B&B. Then a team of entrepreneurs with ties to the fashion industry took over and redecorated the rooms with sometimes wacky themes, turning it into an idiosyncratic little hotel. The result is a theatrical and often outrageous decor that's appreciated by the many fashion models and music-industry folks who regularly make this their temporary home in London. Rooms are, regrettably, rather small, but each has a distinctive style. Examples include a kitschy 1970s room ("Honky-Tonk Afro"), an Asian bordello–themed room ("Enter the Dragon"), and even rooms with 19th-century ancestral themes. One Edwardian-style room, a gem of emerald brocade and velvet, is called "Green with Envy."

34–36 Sussex Gardens, London W2 1UL. ℂ **020/7262-0905.** Fax 020/7262-1324. www. pavilionhoteluk.com. 30 units. £100 double; £120 triple. Rates include continental breakfast. AE, MC, V. Parking £10. Tube: Edgeware Rd. *In room:* TV, Wi-Fi (free).

INEXPENSIVE

Elysee Hotel Finding an inexpensive hotel in central London grows harder by the year. However, this affordable choice is a good bet for the frugal traveler, facing Hyde Park and lying on Craven Terrace, famous for its Mitre Pub, location of two Woody Allen movies. Privately owned and renovated, it offers comfortable but very basic bedrooms. For those who can pay more, we recommend the more spacious and better furnished standard rooms. Guests unwind in the refurbished lounge and bar. Single, double, twin, and family rooms (sleeping up to six) are available.

25–26 Craven Terrace, London W2 3EL. ℂ **020/7402-7633.** Fax 020/7402-4193. www.hotel elysee.co.uk. 55 units. £73–£89 double; £110–£125 triple; £129–£150 quad. MC, V. Parking nearby £15. Tube: Lancaster Gate. **Amenities:** Bar. *In room:* TV, hair dryer, Wi-Fi (free).

Europa House Hotel This family-run hotel attracts visitors who want a room with a private bathroom but at shared-bathroom prices. Like most hotels along Sussex Gardens, the bedrooms are a bit cramped, but they're well maintained. Each room has color-coordinated decor, and most have been recently refurbished. Some units are custom built for groups, with three, four, or five beds per unit. A hearty English breakfast awaits you in the bright dining room every morning.

151 Sussex Gardens, London W2 2RY. ✆ **020/7723-7343.** Fax 020/7224-9331. www.europa househotel.com. 20 units. £60 double; from £128 family room. Rates include English breakfast. AE, DC, MC, V. Free parking. Tube: Paddington. **Amenities:** Breakfast room. *In room:* TV, hair dryer, Internet (free).

Garden Court You'll find this hotel on a tranquil Victorian garden square in the heart of the city. Two private houses (dating from 1870) were combined to form one efficiently run hotel, located near such attractions as Kensington Palace, Hyde Park, and the Portobello Antiques Market. Each year, rooms are redecorated and refurbished, although an overall renovation plan seems to be lacking. Most accommodations are spacious, with good lighting, generous shelf and closet space, and comfortable furnishings. If you're in a room without a bathroom, you'll generally have to share with the occupants of only one other room. There are many homelike touches throughout the hotel, including ancestral portraits and silk flowers. Each room is individually decorated and "comfy"; it's like visiting your great-aunt. Rooms open onto the square in front or the gardens in the rear.

30–31 Kensington Gardens Sq., London W2 4BG. ✆ **020/7229-2553.** Fax 020/7727-2749. www. gardencourthotel.co.uk. 34 units, 16 with bathrooms. £75 double with shared bathroom, £115 double with bathroom; £145 triple with bathroom; £165 family room. Rates include English breakfast. MC, V. Tube: Bayswater. **Amenities:** Internet (£1 per visit). *In room:* TV, hair dryer, Wi-Fi (free).

Norfolk Court & St. David's Hotel George and Foula Neokleous, two of the most welcoming hosts in this highly concentrated B&B area, run this hotel with a certain friendly, personalized style. Only a 2-minute walk from Paddington Station, the hotel was built when Norfolk Square knew a grander age. The bluebloods are long gone, but the area is still safe and recommendable. The refurbished bedrooms are well maintained and furnished comfortably, and you can't beat the price. In the rooms that do have showers, a cubicle shower does the job.

14–20 Norfolk Sq., London W2 1RS. ✆ **020/7723-4963.** Fax 020/7402-9061. www.stdavids hotels.com. 75 units, 70 with bathrooms. £65 double without bathroom, £80 double with bathroom; £90 triple with shower; £100–£130 quad with shower. Rates include English breakfast. AE, MC, V. Tube: Paddington. *In room:* TV, Wi-Fi (free).

Rhodes Hotel This elegant late-Georgian house, just a short stroll from Hyde Park, is decorated with a certain theatrical flair. The owners, Chris and Maria Crias, have poured many pounds into their hotel to give it a cozy charm, with a Victorian curtained lounge, Greek murals, lacquered walls, and *trompe l'oeil* bambini on puffy clouds. Creature comforts weren't ignored, either. You'll find air-conditioning—a bit of a rarity in the neighborhood, especially at these prices—plus Asian rugs and up-to-date bathrooms. The superior accommodations have Jacuzzi baths and private terraces, and there's a good bunkroom for families.

195 Sussex Gardens, London W2 2RJ. ✆ **020/7262-0537.** Fax 020/7723-4054. www.rhodes hotel.com. 36 units. £90–£110 double; £105–£115 triple; £125–£145 family. Rates include buffet breakfast. MC, V. Tube: Paddington or Lancaster Gate. **Amenities:** Breakfast room. *In room:* A/C, TV, fridge, hair dryer, Internet (free).

Tudor Court Hotel   Originally built in the 1850s and much restored and altered, this Victorian structure is now a boutique hotel of tranquillity and comfort, lying only a 3-minute walk from Paddington Station. It is a standout in a section of less desirable hotels. Bedrooms are midsize, completely restored, and comfortably furnished, with a choice of single, double (or twin), triple, and family rooms available. Rooms without bathrooms have a washbasin, with facilities right outside the door. The hotel's maintenance and affordable price make this one a winner—that, plus a helpful staff.

10–12 Norfolk Sq., London W2 1RS. ☎ **020/7723-6553.** Fax 020/7723-0727. www.tudorcourt paddington.co.uk. 36 units. £89 double w/bathroom; £78 triple without bathroom, £108 triple w/bathroom. Rates include English breakfast. AE, DC, MC, V. Limited street parking. Tube: Paddington. **Amenities:** Breakfast room. *In room:* TV, Wi-Fi (in rooms w/bathroom; free).

Notting Hill Gate

EXPENSIVE

Guesthouse West ★ 🍴   In the heart of Notting Hill, this hip, upmarket B&B lies in a stucco-fronted Edwardian house in the fashionable part of Westbourne Grove. Much of the family atmosphere of the original private home has been retained, and midsize bedrooms are comfortable, with understated style. Even if you're not a guest, drop into the ground-floor 1950s-style bar, created by the savvy entrepreneurs of Woody's and the Bush Bar and Grill.

163–165 Westbourne Grove, London WII 2RS. ☎ **020/7792-9800.** Fax 020/7792-9797. www. guesthousewest.com. 20 units. £140–£200 double. Rates include breakfast. AE, MC, V. Tube: Notting Hill Gate. **Amenities:** Restaurant; bar; babysitting; room service. *In room:* A/C, TV, Wi-Fi (free).

The Portobello Hotel ★   On an elegant Victorian terrace near Portobello Road, two 1850s-era town houses have been combined to form a quirky property that has its devotees. We remember these rooms when they looked better, but they still have plenty of character. Who knows what will show up in what nook? Perhaps a Chippendale, a claw-foot tub, or a round bed tucked under a gauze canopy. Try for no. 16, with a full-tester bed facing the garden. Some of the cheaper rooms are so tiny that they're basically garrets, but others have been combined into large doubles. An elevator goes to the third floor; after that, it's the stairs. Since windows are not double-glazed, request a room in the quiet rear. Some rooms are air-conditioned. Service is erratic at best, but this is still a good choice.

22 Stanley Gardens, London W11 2NG. ☎ **020/7727-2777.** Fax 020/7792-9641. www.portobello hotel.co.uk. 24 units. £190–£225 double; £265–£630 suite. Rates include continental breakfast. AE, MC, V. Tube: Notting Hill Gate or Holland Park. **Amenities:** Restaurant; bar; room service. *In room:* A/C (some rooms), TV, hair dryer, Internet (free), minibar.

MODERATE

The Main House ★★ 🎁   Each beautifully appointed room takes up a whole floor of this Victorian town house in Notting Hill, close to Portobello Road, the antiques markets, art galleries, and designer shops. Kensington Palace and Albert Hall are within walking distance. Russian princesses, Japanese pop stars, and Los Angeles film producers have already discovered this spot. Owner and creator

Caroline Main is a former African explorer, Mayfair nightclub owner, and DJ. To furnish the house, she shopped "quirky" on Portobello Road, picking up gilded mirrors, watercolors of elegantly dressed 1930s women, and similar antiques. The ceilings are dramatically high, and the gleaming wood floors are swathed in animal skins.

6 Colville Rd., London W11 2BP. ☎ **020/7221-9691.** www.themainhouse.co.uk. 4 suites. £110–£140 suite. MC, V. Parking £2.50 per hour. Tube: Notting Hill Gate. Bus: 23, 27, 52, 94, or 328. **Amenities:** Bikes; access to health club & spa; Internet (free); room service. *In room:* TV, hair dryer.

INEXPENSIVE

The Gate Hotel   This antiques-hunters' favorite is the only hotel along the length of Portobello Road—and because of rigid zoning restrictions, it will probably remain the only one for years to come. It was built in the 1820s as housing for farmhands at the now-defunct Portobello Farms and has functioned as a hotel since 1932. It has two cramped but cozy bedrooms on each of its three floors. Be prepared for some *very* steep English stairs. Rooms are color coordinated, with a bit of style, and have such extras as full-length mirrors and built-in wardrobes. Housekeeping is excellent. Especially intriguing are the wall paintings that show the original Portobello Market: Every character looks like one straight from a Dickens novel. The on-site manager can direct you to the attractions of Notting Hill Gate and nearby Kensington Gardens, both within a 5-minute walk.

6 Portobello Rd., London W11 3DG. ☎ **020/7221-0707.** Fax 020/7221-9128. www.gatehotel. co.uk. 7 units. £80–£100 double; £105–£125 triple. Rates include continental breakfast (served in room). AE, MC, V. Tube: Notting Hill Gate or Holland Park. **Amenities:** Room service. *In room:* TV, minibar, hair dryer, Wi-Fi (£5).

Umi Hotel ★   Location, location, location. This charming little hotel would be a steal in most of London, but given its proximity to Hyde Park, Portobello Road, and hip (and very pricey) Notting Hill's shopping and dining, it's a true find. Located in side-by-side row houses on a quiet square, Umi offers a bit of character that is often missing in budget hotels. Still, don't expect luxury—although the decor is modern and inviting, it's pretty basic. But that's just fine, given that the basics are done so well here. Rooms are small (this is London after all) but spotless, and the staff is warm and helpful. Added bonus: The hotel offers both single and family rooms that can sleep four. Ask for one of the rooms in front, as the view of the square's garden is gorgeous.

16 Leinster Sq., London, W2 4PR. ☎ **020/7221-9131.** Fax 020/7221-4073. www.umihotel.com. 117 units. £150–£165 double; £165 triple; £180 quad. AE, DISC, MC, V. Tube: Bayswater or Queensway. **Amenities:** Restaurant; cafe; bar; concierge. *In room:* TV, Wi-Fi (£3 per hour).

In Nearby Maida Vale

EXPENSIVE

The Colonnade ★ ☺   Tired of large chain hotels? Head for this boutique charmer in the canal-laced "Little Venice" (an appellation bestowed by Lord Byron) area of London. A handsome Victorian edifice, the hotel was built in 1886 as two different structures, one of which was a hospital. An unusually shaped elevator, which was used to transport stretchers, still remains. Before he purchased his own place in Hampstead, Sigmund Freud stayed here in 1938. Each midsize bedroom is individually decorated, and many feature four-poster beds and small terraces. Tasteful fabrics and antiques evoke town-house living. The least desirable units are two small basement bedrooms. They are impeccably furnished but subject to rumblings from the Underground. Families might want to opt for the spacious two-level JFK suite.

2 Warrington Crescent, London W9 1ER. ☏ **020/7286-1052.** Fax 020/7286-1057. www.theeton collection.com. 43 units. £294–£329 double; £364–£411 suite. AE, DC, MC, V. Tube: Warwick Ave. **Amenities:** Room service; Wi-Fi (free). *In room:* A/C, TV, CD player, hair dryer.

Shepherd's Bush

EXPENSIVE

K-West Hotel & Spa ★★ 🎒   A hotel as modern as tomorrow has been fashioned out of the former home of the BBC administration center. In spite of its off-center Shepherd's Bush location, it attracts cool guests, especially media mavens and touring musicians. The latter can be seen rocking all night long in the chic K Lounge and recovering the next day with an Asian head massage in the spa. Swanky suites and elegant bedrooms in an avant-garde neutral style await this cosmopolitan crowd of guests. Room decor uses soft taupes, creams, and browns with stainless steel and sandblasted glass. Creative modern dishes are served at the stylish Kanteen (which is anything but) with its luxurious leather seating and rich blues and reds.

Richmond Way, London W14 0AX. ☏ **020/8008-6600.** Fax 020/8008-6650. www.k-west. co.uk. 220 units. £119–£169 double; £250–£450 suite. AE, DC, MC, V. Parking £5 for 3 hrs., £1.50 per hour after that. Tube: Shepherd's Bush. **Amenities:** Restaurant; bar; health club and spa. *In room:* A/C, TV/DVD, CD player, hair dryer, Wi-Fi (free).

THE SOUTH BANK

Near London Bridge

EXPENSIVE

Hilton London Tower Bridge ★   Set against the backdrop of the historic Tower Bridge, on the south side of the Thames, this hotel fills up with business travelers during the week and families and couples on the weekends. You're only a 10-minute walk from the Tower of London, Tate Modern, or Shakespeare's Globe. Rooms are spacious and sleekly tailored, with dark wood furnishings, Japanese lantern-inspired light fixtures, and patches of color like scarlet or plum. The large, airy lounge is perfect for a rendezvous with friends, who can sip cappuccinos and some of the best cocktails on the South Bank.

Tower Bridge, 5 More London Place, Tooley St., London, SE1 2BY. ☏ **020/3002-4300.** Fax 020/ 3002-4350. www1.hilton.com. 245 units. £109–£329 double; £500 suite. AE, DC, MC, V. Parking £12. Tube: Tower Hill. **Amenities:** Restaurant; bar; babysitting; concierge; exercise room; room service. *In room:* A/C, TV/DVD, hair dryer, Internet (£15), minibar.

London Bridge Hotel ★   Many guests to London today prefer to stay in a hotel on the emerging South Bank, near many sightseeing and cultural attractions. If you're among them, you can't do much better than lodging at this independently owned, government-rated four-star hotel. A former telephone exchange building, this 1915 structure was successfully recycled into a bastion of comfort and charm. Bedrooms are completely up to date and offer homelike comfort and plenty of amenities. Rooms in the front have double glazing on windows to cut down on noise. The best luxuries are found on the executive floor, in the deluxe rooms, and in the executive kings and suites.

8–18 London Bridge St., London SE1 9SG. © **020/7855-2200.** Fax 020/7855-2233. www.london bridgehotel.com. 140 units. £125–£240 double. Children 11 and under stay free in parent's room. AE, DC, MC, V. Tube: London Bridge. **Amenities:** 2 restaurants; bar; babysitting; access to nearby health club. *In room:* A/C, TV/DVD, hair dryer, minibar, Wi-Fi (free).

Bermondsey

MODERATE

Bermondsey Square Hotel ★ 🎁 Time was when no one would think of staying in Bermondsey in southeast London. But the times are changing, and galleries, boutiques, bars, and restaurants are opening. This hotel, the first boutique hotel in the area, is part of the neighborhood's renaissance. Overlooking one of London's largest antiques markets, the cool hotel caters to both foodies drawn to its Alfie's Bar & Kitchen and fashionistas attracted to its designer chic bedrooms. Rooms on the penthouse floor are named for hit songs from the '60s, including "Lucy" and "Jude." A rooftop terrace is a special feature of the Bermondsey.

Bermondsey Sq., Tower Bridge, SE1. © **0870/111-2525.** www.bermondseysquarehotel.co.uk. 79 units. £129 standard double; £350 deluxe double; £500 junior suite. AE, MC, V. Tube: London Bridge, then bus 78. **Amenities:** Restaurant; bar; concierge; room service. *In room:* A/C, TV/ DVD, hair dryer, minibar, MP3 docking station, Wi-Fi (free).

NEAR THE AIRPORTS

The reason for staying at one of the hotels below is obvious: You either want to catch an early plane or are arriving too late to search for a hotel in central London. Unless you like plane-spotting, there isn't much reason to hang out. The hotels below provide transportation to and from the airport.

Near Heathrow

EXPENSIVE

Heathrow Airport Hilton ★ This first-class hotel, with a five-story atrium that evokes a hangar, is linked to Heathrow's Terminal 4 by a covered walkway. A glass wall faces the runways, so you can see planes land and take off. You can take buses to terminal 1, 2, or 3. Medium-size bedrooms are standard, decorated with built-in wood furniture and comfortable sofas. The best accommodations are on the fifth floor because they offer better extras (bathrobes and so forth) as well as a private lounge with airport vistas. All rooms are soundproofed.

Terminal 4, Hounslow TW6 3AF. © **800/774-1500** in the U.S., or 020/8759-7755. Fax 020/8759-7579. www1.hilton.com. 395 units. £149–£259 double; £425–£475 suite. AE, DC, MC, V. Parking £16. Tube: Heathrow Terminal 4. **Amenities:** 3 restaurants; 2 bars; babysitting; state-of-the-art health club; pool (indoor); room service. *In room:* A/C, TV/DVD, movie library, hair dryer, Internet (£15).

Radisson Edwardian Heathrow ★ The poshest digs at Heathrow, this deluxe hotel lies just south of the M4 about 5 minutes east of the highway that leads to terminals 1, 2, and 3. Since 1991, it has housed tired air travelers from all over the world. The grand spa has a swimming pool and two whirlpools. You'll enter the hotel through a courtyard with potted trees. Persian rugs, brass-railed staircases, and chandeliers live up to the "Edwardian" in the hotel's name. Rooms are medium in size but adorned with hand-painted hardwood furnishings. The bathrooms are in tile and marble, with robes, a shower, and a tub. All in-room televisions have a channel reserved to broadcast flight information. Car hire is also available.

140 Bath Rd., Hayes, Middlesex UB3 5AW. ✆ **800/333-3333** in the U.S., or 020/8759-6311. Fax 020/8759-4559. www.radisson.com. 459 units. £65–£181 double; £170–£275 suite. AE, DC, MC, V. Parking £10. Hotel Hoppa bus service. **Amenities:** 2 restaurants; bar; health club; room service. *In room:* A/C, TV/DVD, hair dryer, minibar, Wi-Fi (free).

INEXPENSIVE

Holiday Inn London-Heathrow This is your best bet in the inexpensive-to-moderate range at London's major airport. The decor is bland but not unpleasant. Rooms are midsize, with immaculate bathrooms containing shower stalls.

Sipson Way, Bath Rd., Hayes, Middlesex UB7 0DP. ✆ **800/465-4329** in the U.S., or 020/8990-0000 in the U.K. Fax 020/8564-7744. www.ichotelsgroup.com. 230 units. Mon–Thurs £79–£109 double; Fri–Sun £52–£82 double. Children 18 and under stay free in parent's room. AE, DC, MC, V. Parking £9–£15. Tube: Heathrow Terminals 1, 2, 3. **Amenities:** Restaurant; bar; babysitting; concierge; room service. *In room:* A/C, TV, hair dryer, minibar (in executive rooms), Wi-Fi (£15).

Near Gatwick

MODERATE

Hilton London Gatwick Airport ★ This deluxe five-floor hotel—Gatwick's most convenient—is linked to the airport terminal by a covered walkway; an electric buggy service transports people between the hotel and the airport. The most impressive part of the hotel is the first-floor lobby. Its glass-covered portico rises four floors. The reception area has a lobby bar and lots of greenery. The well-furnished, soundproof rooms have triple-glazed windows.

South Terminal, Gatwick Airport, West Sussex RH6 0LL. ✆ **800/774-1500** in the U.S., or 01293/518080. Fax 01293/579072. www.hilton.co.uk/gatwick. 821 units. £99–£124 double; £149–£189 suite. AE, DC, MC, V. Parking £16. **Amenities:** 2 restaurants; 2 bars; babysitting; concierge; exercise room; room service. *In room:* A/C, TV, hair dryer, Wi-Fi (£15).

INEXPENSIVE

The Manor House Owners Mark and Beverly Jeffries include transportation from Gatwick as part of the price. There is a courtesy pickup from the airport operating in the morning between 6 and 10am. Their home is a sprawling neo-Tudor affair on .8 hectares (2 acres) of land, surrounded by fields on all sides. It was built in 1894 as a supplemental home for the lord of Ifield, who occupied a larger house nearby and never actually moved in. Two of the rooms—a single and a triple—share a bathroom; the others have bathrooms with showers. Each of the accommodations has flowered wallpaper and simple, traditional accessories.

Bonnetts Lane, Ifield, Crawley, Sussex RH11 0NY. (*)/fax **01293/518046.** www.manorhouse-gatwick.co.uk. 6 units, 4 (doubles) with private bathroom. £50 double; from £55 family unit; £55 triple. Rates include continental breakfast. MC, V. Parking £2. *In room:* TV, no phone.

Yotel (*) The first Yotel, an affordable Japanese-style "capsule hotel," operates at the South Terminal. One guest said it was like a spaceship designed by Ian Schrager. The hotel offers two types of cabins—standard at 7 sq. m (75 sq. ft.) and eight premium cabins with 2.8 sq. m of extra space (30 sq. ft.). For such a small area, you still have a private bathroom and room to store small bags and a minimum of suitcases. There's even a TV. There is also 24-hour room service for light meals and drinks, including beer and wine. An elevator across from the Gatwick arrivals area takes you one floor up to Yotel's entrance.

South Terminal, Arrivals Concourse, Gatwick Airport, West Sussex RH6 0NP. (*) **0207/100-1100.** www.yotel.com. 46 cabins. Standard cabin £37 for 4 hr., plus £7 for each additional hour; premium cabin £40 for 4 hr. plus £7 per extra hour. AE, MC, V. **Amenities:** Room service. *In room:* TV.

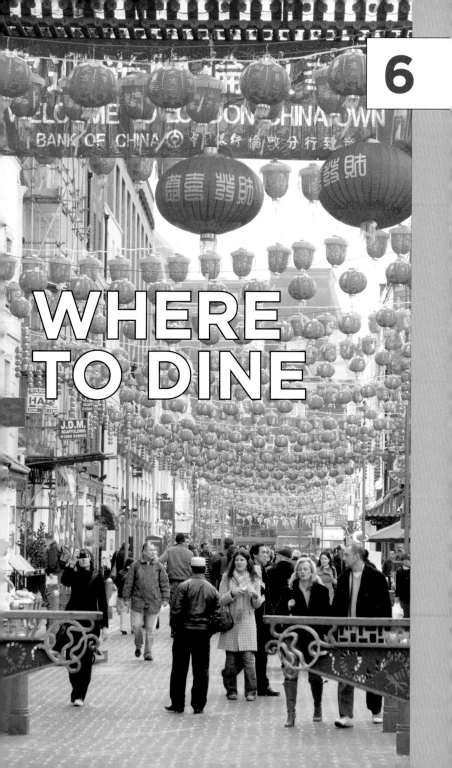

WHERE TO DINE

n 1946, George Mikes, Britain's famous Hungarian-born humorist, wrote about the cuisine of his adopted country: "The Continentals have good food. The English have good table manners." Quite a lot has happened since.

London has emerged as one of the great food capitals of the world. Both its veteran and upstart chefs have fanned out around the globe for culinary inspiration and returned with innovative dishes, flavors, and ideas that London diners have never seen before. These chefs are pioneering "Modern British" style, which is innovative, yet familiar in many ways.

Traditional British cooking has made a comeback, too. The dishes that British mums have been forever feeding their families are fashionable again. We're talking British soul food: bangers and mash, Norfolk dumplings, cottage pie. This may be a rebellion against the minimalism of the nouvelle cuisine of the 1980s, but maybe it's just plain nostalgia. Pig's nose with parsley-and-onion sauce may not be your idea of cutting-edge cuisine, but Simpson's-in-the-Strand is serving it for breakfast.

If you want a lavish meal, London is the place: Gourmet havens such as Le Gavroche and a half-dozen others are reviewed in the following pages. We've also included many affordable restaurants where you can dine well and still pay off your mortgage. You'll find that London's food revolution has infiltrated every level of the dining scene—even the lowly pub has entered the culinary sweepstakes. Believe the unthinkable: At certain pubs, you can now dine better than in many restaurants. In some, standard pub grub has given way to Modern British and Mediterranean-style fare; in others, oyster bars have taken hold.

SOME DINING NOTES

HOURS Restaurants in London keep varied hours, but in general, lunch is offered from noon to 2pm and dinner from 7:30 to 9:30pm, although more restaurants are staying open later. Sunday is the usual closing day for restaurants, but there are exceptions. (Many also close for a few days around Christmas, so call ahead during the holidays.) We've listed serving hours in the descriptions below.

PRICES When restaurants are classified as Moderate or Inexpensive, most main courses are at the lower end of the price scale. That doesn't mean the chefs don't prepare some expensive dishes. Often they do, especially if they offer shellfish. But if you avoid the highest-priced dishes, you can dine moderately or inexpensively at our selections.

RESERVATIONS Nearly all places, except pubs, cafeterias, and fast-food joints, prefer or require reservations. Almost invariably, you get a better table if you book in advance. For a few of the famous places, you might need to reserve weeks in advance, even before leaving home. (Reservations should always be confirmed when you get to London.) However, if you don't have reservations, even at a "reservations required" restaurant, it's worth trying to walk in; if they have room, you won't be turned down.

TAXES & TIPPING   All restaurants and cafes are required to display the prices of their food and drink in a place visible from outside. Charges for service, as well as any minimums or cover charges, must also be made clear. The prices shown must include 17.5% VAT. Most restaurants add a 10% to 15% service charge to your bill, but check to make sure. If nothing has been added, leave a 10% to 15% tip. It is not considered rude to tip, so feel free to leave something extra if service was good.

BEST DINING BETS

o **Best Spot for a Celebration:** There's no spot in all of London that's more fun than **Quaglino's,** 16 Bury St., SW1 (℗ 020/7930-6767), which serves Continental cuisine. On some nights, as many as 800 diners show up at Sir Terence Conran's gargantuan Mayfair eatery. It's the best place in London to celebrate almost any occasion—and the food's good, too. There's live jazz every evening and on Sunday at lunch. See p. 206.

o **Best Newcomer:** A self-styled "restless Aussie," Syke Gyngell is luring London's most serious foodies to **Petersham Nurseries Café,** south of the Thames on Church Lane in Richmond in Surrey (℗ 020/8605-3527). The author of two best-selling cookbooks, she is one of the most acclaimed chefs in Greater London. Her dishes are not fussy but utterly captivating. See p. 229.

o **Best Place for Spotting Celebrities:** If virtually any visiting celebrities are in town, chances are they'll be hiding out behind a translucent silk curtain in the center of London's hot new restaurant, **Alain Ducasse at the Dorchester,** on the lobby level of the chic Dorchester hotel, on Park Lane (℗ 020/7629-8866). A chef *maestro* many critics hail as the world's greatest has crossed the Channel to open this citadel of haute cuisine. See p. 198.

o **Best Seafood:** After a long slumber, the famous **Scott's,** 20 Mount St., W1 (℗ 020/7495-7309), has reopened in a swank restaurant in Mayfair. It began as an oyster warehouse in 1851, but has gone from that rustic beginning to Mayfair glitter, peddling market-fresh Dover sole and "cockles and mussels." See p. 202.

o **Best Gastro Pub:** At last London's *enfant terrible* chef, Gordon Ramsay, has entered the gastro-pub sweepstakes by opening **the Narrow,** 44 Narrow St., E14 (℗ 020/7592-7950). Pub grub never tasted like this. Some of the dishes will put hair on your chest even if you don't want it—whole baked gilthead bream or braised Gloucester pig cheeks with neeps (turnips). See p. 181.

o **Best English Breakfast:** Serving traders at the Smithfield meat market since 1898, **Fox and Anchor,** 115 Charterhouse St., EC1 (℗ 020/7250-1300), offers the "Full House" breakfast, a plate with eight items ranging from black pudding to kidneys and bacon. With a Black Velvet (champagne with Guinness), the day is yours. See p. 176.

o **Best American Cuisine:** A favorite with homesick expats, **Automat,** 33 Dover St., W1 (℗ 020/7499-3033), is Mayfair's slice of the Big Apple, serving perhaps the best U.S. beef in London, including New York strip sirloin. All those familiar favorites are dished up here, even chili con carne. See p. 204.

○ **Best Continental Cuisine: Le Gavroche,** 43 Upper Brook St., W1 (✆ 020/7408-0881), was one of the first London restaurants to serve modern French cuisine, and it's lost none of its appeal. If you want to know why, order *pigeonneau de Bresse en vessie aux deux celeris:* The whole bird is presented at your table, enclosed in a pig's bladder; the pigeon is removed, and then carved and served on a bed of braised fennel and celery. Trust us—it's fabulous. See p. 199.

○ **Best for Value:** The long-enduring **Stockpot,** 38 Panton St., off Haymarket, SW1 (✆ 020/7839-5142), may not serve the finest food in London, but no one complains about the prices. It's good, solid, and filling fare. See p. 193.

○ **Best Modern British Cuisine:** Just north of Smithfield Market, **St. John,** 26 St. John St., EC1 (✆ 020/7251-0848), serves a modern interpretation of British cuisine like none other in town. The chefs here believe in using offal (those parts of the animal usually discarded)—after all, why use just parts of the animal when you can use it all? Although some diners are a bit squeamish at first, they're usually hooked once they get past the first bite. Book ahead of time. See p. 178.

○ **Best Traditional British Cuisine:** There is no restaurant in London quite as British as **Simpson's-in-the-Strand,** 100 the Strand, WC2 (✆ **020/7836-9112**), which has been serving the finest English roast beef since 1828. Henry VIII, were he to return, would surely pause for a feast here. This place is such a British institution that you'll think they invented roast saddle of mutton. See p. 188.

○ **Best for Kids:** The owner, the Earl of Bradford, feeds you well and affordably at **Porters English Restaurant,** 17 Henrietta St., WC2 (✆ **020/7836-6466**). Kids of all ages dig Lady Bradford's once secretly guarded recipe for banana-and-ginger pudding, along with classic English pies, including such old-fashioned favorites as lamb and apricot; and ham, leek, and cheese. See p. 189.

○ **Best Indian Cuisine:** London's finest Indian food is served at **Café Spice Namaste,** in a landmark Victorian hall near Tower Bridge, 16 Prescot St., E1 (✆ **020/7488-9242**). You'll be tantalized by an array of spicy southern and northern Indian dishes. We like the cuisine's Portuguese influence; the chef, Cyrus Todiwala, is from Goa (a Portuguese territory absorbed by India), where he learned many of his culinary secrets. See p. 174.

○ **Best Italian Cuisine:** At **Zafferano,** 15 Lowndes St., SW1 (✆ **020/7235-5800**), chefs prepare delectable meals with ingredients that conjure up the Mediterranean. The most refined palates of Knightsbridge come to this chic, rustic trattoria for dishes like pheasant and black-truffle ravioli with rosemary. See p. 209.

○ **Best Innovative Cuisine:** In the heart of Mayfair, Irish chef Richard Corrigan brings his imaginative cuisine to **Corrigan's Mayfair,** 28 Upper Grosvenor St., W1 (✆ **020/7499-9943**). The menu is dependent on what looks good at the market that day and the chef's inspiration. After you've sampled his steamed Cornish scallops with ginger and coconut, or his buttered poached pheasant, you'll want to kidnap him for your own kitchen. See p. 200.

○ **Best Wine-Bar Food: Cork & Bottle Wine Bar,** 44–46 Cranbourn St., WC2 (✆ **020/7734-7807**), serves the best wine-bar food in London. The ham-and-cheese pie alone is worth the trek across town—it's hardly your typical quiche. Also try the prawns with garlic and asparagus, or the lamb in ale. The wine selection is superb, with a strong emphasis on Australian selections. See p. 192.

o **Best Cantonese Cuisine: Fung Shing,** 15 Lisle St., WC2 (℗ **020/7437-1539**), is a culinary landmark, serving the finest Cantonese cuisine in London, both traditional and innovative. The seasonal specials are the way to go. Stewed duck with yams, tender ostrich in yellow-bean sauce, and a delectable whole sea bass are some of the delicious treats. See p. 191.

o **Best Japanese Cuisine:** Robert De Niro and his gang have generated much excitement about **Nobu,** in the Metropolitan Hotel, 19 Old Park Lane, W1 (℗ **020/7447-4747**). The sushi chefs create gastronomic pyrotechnics with their raw dishes. See p. 202.

RESTAURANTS BY CUISINE

AMERICAN
Automat (p. 204, $)
Ed's Easy Diner (p. 197, $)
Hard Rock Cafe (p. 203, $$)

ASIAN
(See also Cantonese, Chinese, Japanese, Szechuan, and Thai)
E&O (p. 227, $$)
Imperial City ★ (p. 176, $$)
Yauatcha ★ (p. 197, $)

BELGIAN
Belgo Centraal (p. 188, $$)

BENGALI
Meraz Café (p. 180, $)

BRITISH—MODERN
Admiral Codrington ★ (p. 217, $$)
Balans (p. 196, $)
Bumpkin (p. 226, $$)
Clarke's ★ (p. 216, $$$)
The Collection ★ (p. 212, $$)
Corrigan's Mayfair (p. 200, $$$)
The Cow ★ (p. 226, $$)
The Criterion Brasserie ★ (p. 194, $$)
Fifteen ★ (p. 179, $$$)
The Ivy ★★ (p. 191, $$$)
Launceston Place ★ (p. 217, $$$)
The Narrow ★ (p. 181, $)
Odette's ★ (p. 224, $$)
The Portrait Restaurant ★ (p. 198, $$)

Prism ★★ (p. 174, $$$)
Rex Whistler ★★ (p. 207, $$)
St. John ★★ (p. 178, $$)
Simpson's-in-the-Strand ★★ (p. 188, $$$)
Sketch ★★ (p. 200, $$$$)

BRITISH—TRADITIONAL
Acorn House (p. 185, $$)
Arbutus Restaurant (p. 193, $$)
Bob Bob Ricard (p. 193, $$)
Brown's Bar and Restaurant Covent Gardens (p. 192, $)
Butler's Wharf Chop House ★ (p. 181, $$$)
The Enterprise (p. 218, $$)
Fox and Anchor ★ (p. 176, $)
The George (p. 190, $)
The George & Vulture (p. 177, $)
Greens Restaurant & Oyster Bar (p. 205, $$)
Langan's Bistro (p. 223, $$)
Langan's Brasserie (p. 203, $$)
The National Dining Rooms (p. 198, $$)
The Pig's Ear ★ (p. 215, $)
Porters English Restaurant ★★ (p. 189, $$)
Rules ★ (p. 188, $$$)
Shepherd's (p. 207, $$$)
Simpson's-in-the-Strand ★★ (p. 188, $$$)
The Stockpot (p. 193, $)

Tom's Kitchen ★ (p. 215, $$$)
Ye Olde Cheshire Cheese (p. 178, $)

CANTONESE

Fung Shing ★★ (p. 191, $$$)
Jenny Lo's Teahouse (p. 207, $)
Royal China ★ (p. 225, $$$)

CHINESE

(See also Cantonese and Szechuan)
Chuen Cheng Ku ★ (p. 194, $$)
Hakkasan ★ (p. 194, $$)

CONTINENTAL

Admiral Codrington ★ (p. 217, $$)
Arbutus Restaurant (p. 193, $$$)
Brown's Bar and Restaurant Covent
    Gardens (p. 192, $)
Cantina Vinopolis ★ (p. 183, $$)
hush (p. 201, $$$)
L'Autre Pied ★★ (p. 201, $$$)
Quaglino's ★ (p. 206, $$)
Shampers (p. 196, $$)
Sketch ★★ (p. 200, $$$$)
The Stockpot (p. 193, $)
Tom Aikens ★★★ (p. 216, $$$$)
Union Cafe (p. 224, $$)
Villandry ★ (p. 224, $$)
The Wolseley ★★ (p. 206, $$)

CYPRIOT

Halepi ★ (p. 226, $$)
Sarastro ★ (p. 190, $)

ENGLISH TEA

The Blue Room (p. 233, $)
Claridge's ★ (p. 231, $$$)
The Georgian Restaurant (p. 232, $$$)
The Lanesborough (p. 232, $$$)
The Orangery ★ (p. 233, $)
The Palm Court (p. 232, $$$)
Richoux (p. 233, $$)
Ritz Palm Court ★★★ (p. 232, $$$)
St. James Restaurant & the Fountain
    Restaurant (p. 232, $$$)
The Tearoom at the Chelsea Physic
    Garden (p. 234, $)

EUROPEAN

The Engineer ★ (p. 229, $$)
The Enterprise (p. 218, $$)

Greenhouse (p. 201, $$$)
Kensington Place (p. 218, $$)
The Ledbury ★★ (p. 226, $$$)
Texture (p. 222, $$$)
Wild Honey ★ (p. 204, $$)

FRENCH

Alain Ducasse at the Dorchester ★★
    (p. 198, $$$$)
Aubergine ★★ (p. 213, $$$$)
Bibendum/The Oyster Bar ★
    (p. 216, $$$)
Café des Amis (p. 189, $$)
Club Gascon ★★ (p. 176, $$)
The Criterion Brasserie ★
    (p. 194, $$)
Galvin ★ (p. 223, $$)
Gordon Ramsay ★★★
    (p. 214, $$$$)
Langan's Bistro (p. 223, $$)
Langan's Brasserie (p. 203, $$)
Le Cercle ★★ (p. 214, $$$)
Le Gavroche ★★★ (p. 199 $$$$)
Les Trois Garçons ★★ (p. 179, $$$)
Marcus Wareing at the Berkeley
    (p. 209, $$$$)
Mon Plaisir (p. 189, $$)
Oriel (p. 215, $)
Orrery ★★ (p. 222, $$$)
Pied-à-Terre ★★★ (p. 184, $$$)
Plateau (p. 182, $$$)
Racine (p. 212, $$)
Roussillon ★★ (p. 214, $$$$)
The Square ★★★ (p. 200, $$$$)
Vertigo 42 ★ (p. 177, $)

GREEK

Halepi ★ (p. 226, $$)

HUNGARIAN

The Gay Hussar ★ (p. 194, $$)

INDIAN

Amaya ★ (p. 209, $$$)
The Bengal Clipper ★ (p. 182, $$)
Café Spice Namaste ★★ (p. 174, $$)
Cinnamon Kitchen (p. 176, $$)
Empress of India ★ (p. 180, $)
Kasturi (p. 181, $$)
Masala Zone (p. 197, $)

Mela ★ (p. 195, $$)
Rasa Samudra ★ (p. 195, $$)
Tamarind ★ (p. 203, $$$)
Veeraswamy (p. 196, $$)
Zaika ★★ (p. 219, $$)

INTERNATIONAL
The Collection ★ (p. 212, $$)
Cork & Bottle Wine Bar ★★
    (p. 192, $)
Greens Restaurant & Oyster Bar
    (p. 205, $$)
The Ivy ★★ (p. 191, $$$)
Le Metro (p. 212, $)
Le Pont de la Tour ★ (p. 182, $$$)
Maze ★★ (p. 202, $$$)
Odin's ★ (p. 222, $$$)
Orrery ★★ (p. 222, $$$)
Oxo Tower Restaurant ★
    (p. 183, $$$)
Petersham Nurseries Café (p. 229, $)
Prince Bonaparte (p. 227, $)
Villandry ★ (p. 224, $$)

ITALIAN
Assaggi ★ (p. 219, $$$)
Caldesi (p. 223, $$)
Joe's Café ★ (p. 218, $$)
L'Anima (p. 174, $$$)
Locanda Locatelli ★★ (p. 223, $$$)
The River Café ★★ (p. 228, $$$)
Salt Yard ★ (p. 185, $)
Theo Randall at the InterContinental
    ★★ (p. 203, $$$)
Zafferano ★★ (p. 209, $$$$)

JAPANESE
Nobu ★★ (p. 202, $$$)
Satsuma (p. 195, $$)
Wagamama (p. 185, $)

MEDITERRANEAN
Bibendum/The Oyster Bar ★
    (p. 216, $$$)
Bluebird ★ (p. 214, $$$)
Leon ★ (p. 205, $)

MOROCCAN
Momo (p. 204, $$)
Pasha (p. 219, $$)

NORTH AFRICAN
Momo (p. 204, $$)
Moro ★★ (p. 178, $$)

PACIFIC RIM
Suze (p. 205, $)

PORTUGUESE
Eyre Brothers ★ (p. 179, $$)

SEAFOOD
Greens Restaurant & Oyster Bar
    (p. 205, $$)
J. Sheekey ★ (p. 191, $$$)
Randall & Aubin ★ (p. 192, $$)
Scott's ★★ (p. 202, $$$)

SPANISH
Moro ★★ (p. 178, $$)
Salt Yard ★ (p. 185, $)

STEAK
Black & Blue ★ (p. 212, $$)
The Bountiful Cow ★★ (p. 190, $$$)
Notting Grill ★ (p. 228, $$)

SZECHUAN
Jenny Lo's Teahouse (p. 207, $)
Royal China ★ (p. 225, $$$)

THAI
Blue Elephant ★ (p. 217, $$)
The Engineer ★ (p. 229, $$)
Sri Nam ★ (p. 183, $$)

TURKISH
Sarastro ★ (p. 190, $)

VEGAN
Rootmaster (p. 180, $)

VEGETARIAN
Mildreds ★ (p. 197, $)

KEY TO ABBREVIATIONS:
$$$$** = Very Expensive   **$$$** = Expensive   **$$** = Moderate   **$ = Inexpensive

IN & AROUND THE CITY
The City

EXPENSIVE

L'Anima ★★ ITALIAN   The name of this restaurant means "soul" in Italian, and that's what Francesco Mazzei puts into his creative Italian cuisine. When his restaurant opened in 2009, several organizations voted L'Anima best restaurant newcomer of the year. Although that has passed, of course, his standards seem even higher as each year goes by. Many of his dishes are native to his homeland in the south of Italy, especially Calabria, Puglia, and Sicily. From his starters such as octopus with cannellini to his homemade soups, risottos, and pastas, his cuisine reaches the summit. So do his main courses, including sea-salt crusted sea bass or Sicilian rabbit, and especially his spit-roasted leg of lamb or the slow-roasted black pig belly in a cantarata sauce. You can finish off with one of the luscious desserts such as a cappuccino tiramisu.

1 Snowden St., Broadgate West, EC2. ✆ **020/7422-7000.** www.lanima.co.uk. Main courses £12–£32; 2-course set lunch £24, 3-course set lunch £27. AE, DC, MC, V. Mon–Fri 11:45am–1am; Sat 5:30–11pm. Tube: Liverpool Station.

Prism ★★ MODERN BRITISH   In the financial district, called the City, this restaurant attracts London's movers and shakers and their demanding palates. Harvey Nichols—known for his chic department store in Knightsbridge—took this 1920s neo-Grecian hall and installed Mies van der Rohe chairs in chrome and lipstick-red leather. In this setting, traditional British dishes from the north are given a light touch—try the tempura of Whitby cod, or cream of Jerusalem artichoke soup with roasted scallops and truffle oil. For a first course, you may opt for a small, seared calf's liver with a mushroom risotto, or try a salad of Parmesan-seasoned Savoy cabbage and Parma ham. The menu reveals that the chef has traveled a bit—note such dishes as Moroccan spiced chicken livers, lemon and parsley couscous, and a zesty chili sauce.

147 Leadenhall St., EC3. ✆ **020/7256-3875.** www.harveynichols.com. Reservations required. Main courses £18–£32. AE, DC, DISC, MC, V. Mon–Fri 11:30am–3pm and 6–10pm. Tube: Bank or Monument.

MODERATE

Café Spice Namaste ★★ INDIAN   This is our favorite Indian restaurant in London, where the competition is stiff. It's cheerfully housed in a landmark Victorian hall near Tower Bridge, just east of the Tower of London. The Parsi chef, Cyrus Todiwala, concentrates on southern and northern Indian dishes, with a strong Portuguese influence. Chicken and lamb are prepared a number of ways, from mild to spicy-hot. As a novelty, Todiwala occasionally even offers a menu of emu dishes; when marinated, the meat is rich and spicy and evocative of lamb. Emu is not the only dining oddity here. Ever have ostrich gizzard kebab, alligator tikka, or minced moose, bison, or blue boar? Many patrons journey here just for the complex chicken curry known as *xacutti*. Lambs' livers and kidneys are also cooked in the tandoor.

16 Prescot St., E1. ✆ **020/7488-9242.** www.cafespice.co.uk. Reservations required. Main courses £5.50–£19. AE, DC, MC, V. Mon–Fri noon–3pm and 6:15–10:30pm; Sat 6:30–10:30pm. Tube: Tower Hill.

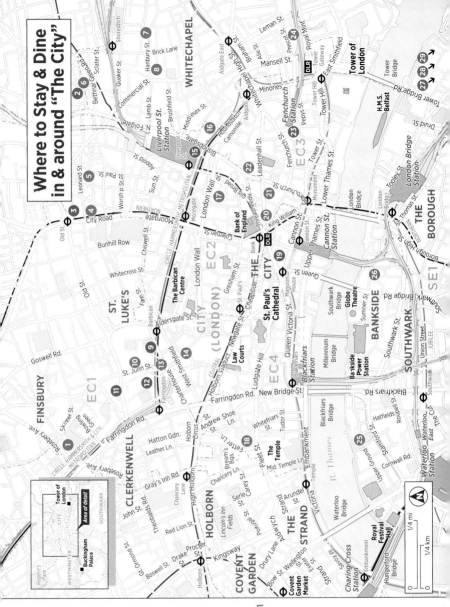

Where to Stay & Dine in & around "The City"

Cinnamon Kitchen ★ INDIAN   In a bright, airy space, converted from a historic East India Company spice warehouse, this restaurant near Liverpool Street has been compared to a New York steakhouse in atmosphere. But the food is strictly from India, a refined cuisine using first-rate ingredients. The waitstaff is top of the line. You can pop in throughout the day for a spicy breakfast or brunch and stick around for lunch or dinner from the Indian grill and tandoor bar. There is also an all-weather al fresco terrace. One of the best starters in the City is duck with sesame and tamarind glaze. This could be followed by such mains as black leg chicken with fresh fenugreek or tandoori king prawns with kedgeree. The sides are especially good, including a selection of three Indian breads.

9 Devonshire Sq., EC21. ✆ **020/7626-5000.** Reservations recommended. Main courses £8.50–£20; set menus £15 for 2 courses, £18 for 3 courses. AE, MC, V. Mon–Fri 11am–midnight; Sat 6pm–midnight. Tube: Liverpool St. Station.

Club Gascon ★★ 🍴 FRENCH   This slice of southwestern France serves such tasty treats as foie gras, Armagnac, and duck confit. Chef Pascal Aussignac is all the rage in London, ever since he opened his bistro next to the meat market in Smithfield. He dedicates his bistro to his favorite ingredient: foie gras. Foie gras appears in at least nine different incarnations on the menu, and most of the first-class ingredients are imported from France. His menu is uniquely divided into these categories—the Salt Route, Ocean, and Kitchen Garden. The best way to dine here is to arrive in a party of four or five and share the small dishes, each harmoniously balanced and full of flavor. Each dish is accompanied by a carefully selected glass of wine. After a foie gras pig out, proceed to such main courses as a heavenly quail served with pear and rosemary honey. A cassoulet of morels and truffles transforms a plain but perfectly cooked steak.

57 W. Smithfield, EC1. ✆ **020/7796-0600.** www.clubgascon.com. Reservations required. Main courses £13–£72. AE, MC, V. Mon–Fri noon–2pm and 7–10pm; Sat 7–10:30pm. Tube: Barbican.

Imperial City ★ ASIAN   In the undercroft of the Royal Exchange Building, this restaurant, with its sleek modern interior and exotic fish tanks, serves authentic East and Southeast Asian cuisine. High-quality food and a first-rate presentation keep a stream of diners flowing in. There are familiar starters such as mandarin spareribs or razor clams with chili-laced black beans, but also unusual ones, such as crispy seaweed with walnuts. A whole or half Peking duck is served, as is a braised mixed seafood pot for two. Chilean sea bass with sea cucumber and star anise is a delight, as is wok-fried duck breast with cherries and wild ginger. Vegetarians will be delighted here, but so will meat eaters. The wok-fried venison with black pepper and snow peas is a winner, as is the beef with lemon grass. The typical rice and noodle dishes are also served, topped off by such desserts as a mango-and-toffee cheesecake.

Royal Exchange, Cornhill EC3. ✆ **020/7256-3437.** www.orientalrestaurantgroup.co.uk. Reservations recommended. Main courses £12–£40; fixed-price menu £34–£32. AE, DC, MC, V. Mon–Fri noon–3pm and 5–11pm. Tube: Bank or Monument.

INEXPENSIVE

Fox and Anchor ★ 🍴 TRADITIONAL BRITISH   For British breakfast at its best, try this place, which has been serving traders from the nearby Smithfield meat market since 1898. Breakfasts are gargantuan, especially if you order the

"Full House"—a plate with at least eight items, including sausage, bacon, kidneys, eggs, beans, black pudding, and fried bread, along with unlimited tea or coffee, toast, and jam. Add a Black Velvet or the more fashionable Bucks Fizz (orange juice and champagne, known in the U.S. as a mimosa). The staff serves an even bigger breakfast called "the Full Monty" including a Guinness. Of course, more delicate stomachs might settle for smoked salmon and scrambled eggs. The Fox and Anchor is noted for its fine English ales, which are all available at breakfast. Butchers from the market, spotted with blood, still appear, as do clerks and City tycoons who've been making millions all night. For lunch and dinner the food is standard pub fare, including fish and chips, steak-and-kidney pie, and a choice of steaks, followed by such classic British desserts as sticky toffee pudding or chocolate fudge cake.

115 Charterhouse St., EC1. ✆ **020/7250-1300.** www.foxandanchor.co.uk. Reservations recommended. "Full house" breakfast £6.50; "Full Monty" breakfast £11; main courses £11–£14. AE, MC, V. Mon–Sat 8–10pm, Sun 12-5pm. Tube: Barbican or Farringdon.

The George & Vulture TRADITIONAL BRITISH   Dickens enthusiasts seek out this Pickwickian place. Founded in 1660, it claims that it's "probably" the world's oldest tavern, referring to an inn that operated on this spot in 1175. While they no longer put up overnight guests here, the George & Vulture does serve English lunches (but no dinners) in a warren of small dining rooms scattered over the tavern's three floors. The menu includes a mixed grill, a loin chop, a lamb-based hot pot, and a grilled Dover-sole filet with tartar sauce. Potatoes and buttered cabbage are the standard vegetables, and the apple tart is always reliable. Arrive and give your name, and then retire to any of the three different pubs (Simpson's Bar, the Cross Key's Pub, or the Jamaican Pub across the way) on the same narrow street for a drink; you're "fetched" when your table is ready. Afterward, be sure to explore the mazes of pubs, shops, wine houses, and other old buildings near the tavern. The Pickwick Club, a private literary group, meets here four times a year for reunion dinners.

3 Castle Court, Cornhill, EC3. ✆ **020/7626-9710.** Reservations accepted before 12:45pm. Main courses £6.90–£12. AE, MC, V. Mon–Fri noon-2:30pm. Tube: Bank or Monument.

Vertigo 42 ★ 🍴 MODERN/FRENCH   This is a relatively unknown little spot, on the 42nd floor of Tower 42 in the heart of the City, that offers one of London's most beautiful views. After securing a special security pass downstairs, you're taken to Vertigo 42 in a high-speed elevator. Dining here is like being on top of the world—you take in a bird's-eye view of London, from the Canada Tower to the Law Courts. We prefer to come here as the sun sets and the city lights begin to twinkle. Blue binoculars are provided if you want a more intimate view of the cityscape. Appetizers feature the likes of layered smoked salmon with herb butter and a mustard dressing, followed by seared scallops or a filet steak with Roquefort butter and caramelized onions. The food is more of a bar menu, and there isn't a large choice of main courses. You must be 18 or older to patronize this restaurant.

Tower 42, 25 Old Broad St., EC2. ✆ **020/7877-7842.** www.vertigo42.co.uk. Reservations required. Main courses £9.50–£32. AE, DC, MC, V. Mon–Fri noon–3pm and 5–11pm. Closed weekends. Tube: Liverpool St.

Ye Olde Cheshire Cheese ☺ TRADITIONAL BRITISH   The foundation of this carefully preserved building was laid in the 13th century, and it holds the most famous of the old City chophouses and pubs. Established in 1667, it claims to be the spot where Dr. Samuel Johnson (who lived nearby) entertained admirers with his acerbic wit. Charles Dickens and other literary lions also patronized the place. Later, many of the ink-stained journalists and scandalmongers of 19th- and early-20th-century Fleet Street made it their watering hole. You'll find five bars and two dining rooms here. The house specialties include Ye Famous Pudding (steak, kidney, mushrooms, and game) and Scottish roast beef with Yorkshire pudding and horseradish sauce. Sandwiches, salads, and standby favorites such as steak-and-kidney pie are also available, as are dishes such as Dover sole. The Cheshire is the best and safest venue to introduce your children to an English pub.

Wine Office Court, 145 Fleet St., EC4. ✆ **020/7353-6170.** Main courses £8–£12. AE, DC, MC, V. Meals Mon–Fri noon–10pm; Sat noon–2:30pm and 6–9:30pm; Sun noon–2:30pm. Drinks and bar snacks Mon–Sat 11am–11pm; Sun noon–6pm. Tube: St. Paul's or Blackfriars.

Clerkenwell

MODERATE

Moro ★★ NORTH AFRICAN/SPANISH   If you've been hearing about all the trendy restaurants in Clerkenwell and want to try one, make it Moro. The aroma of delicious meats on the charcoal grill will attract carnivores, but vegetarian meals are also available. At the long zinc bar, you can fill up on some of the city's best tapas, or a Maghreb-inspired dinner of impeccable quality. The restaurant's recipes were inspired by the epoch when Arab culture met European culture in southern Spain (8th–15th c.). The charcoal-grilled lamb chops with peppers are tantalizing. Desserts are always tempting and made fresh daily, including Málaga raisin ice cream with sherry or a yogurt cake with pistachios and pomegranates. Tapas are available at the bar Monday to Saturday 12:30 to 10:30pm, including quail eggs, Manchego cheese, and octopus salad.

34-36 Exmouth Market, EC1. ✆ **020/7833-8336.** www.moro.co.uk. Reservations recommended. Main courses £18–£20; tapas £3.50–£15. AE, DC, MC, V. Mon–Sat 12:30–2:30pm and 7–10:30pm. Tube: Farringdon.

St. John ★★ MODERN BRITISH   Located in a former smokehouse just north of Smithfield Market, this air-conditioned, canteenlike dining room is the restaurant of choice for carnivores. It is a showcase for the talents of owner/chef Fergus Henderson, a leader in the offal movement, which advocates the use of all animal parts in cuisine. In true British tradition, he uses the entire animal— we're talking neck, trotters, tail, liver, heart, the works. It's called nose-to-tail cookery. But don't think you'll be served warmed-over haggis: The food is excellent and flavor-packed. The grilled lamb chops, garnished with sliced pig's tongue, bacon, salsify, and dandelion, are matchless. Roast bone marrow appears with a parsley salad, and pork chops are called pig chops. It's hard these days to find an eel, bacon, and clam stew, but you'll discover one here. French wines wash it all down.

26 St. John St., EC1. ✆ **020/7251-0848.** www.stjohnrestaurant.co.uk. Reservations required. Main courses £160–£25. AE, DC, MC, V. Mon–Fri noon–3pm; Mon–Sat 6–11pm. Tube: Farringdon.

Shoreditch

EXPENSIVE

Les Trois Garçons ★★ 👔 FRENCH   As trendy London moves east, and once-seedy districts like Shoreditch (north of the City) become cutting edge, eye-popping restaurants like Les Trois Garçons are bound to follow. The three "garçons" of the restaurant's name are Hassan Abdullah, Michel Lassere, and Stefan Karlson. They took this pub, which opened early in Victoria's reign, and turned it into one of the hottest reservations for London's young, fashionable set. Inside, stuffed animals, including a British bulldog, are adorned with glittering tiaras. That's Quentin the crocodile balanced on top of the baby grand. In such a setting, the cuisine could be second to the entertainment. But, happily, the restaurant serves an excellent and modern French menu. Making an excellent starter is the parsnip veloute with Roquefort-filled tortellini or a carpaccio of Scottish beef with a cabernet sauvignon vinaigrette and poached quail eggs. For main courses, we've enjoyed both the wild Scottish turbot and langoustines with a Jerusalem artichoke purée and sautéed chanterelles and the seared lamb filet with lamb kidneys and braised endives.

1 Club Row, E1. ✆ **020/7613-1924.** www.lestroisgarcons.com. Reservations essential. Tasting menu £62; fixed-price menu £40 2 courses, £46 3 courses. AE, MC, V. Mon–Sat 7pm–midnight. Tube: Liverpool St.

MODERATE

Eyre Brothers ★ 👔 PORTUGUESE   As more and more of trendy London flocks to Shoreditch, their destination is often this elegant and refined restaurant, inaugurated by David Eyre, who virtually revolutionized pub grub in London at the dawn of the millennium. The chef is often inspired by Portuguese cuisine—and by the cuisine of former Portuguese colonies like Mozambique. A typical example: tiger prawns piri-piri (in a hot chili marinade). Succulent T-bones are grilled on the open fire here as in the style of Lisbon. The fresh catch of the day, perhaps yellowfin tuna, is also grilled to one's request. The house specialty is a marvelous banquet of roast suckling pig flavored to perfection. For starters, try the Spanish garlic and ham soup with smoked paprika and sherry, or octopus with green peppers, coriander, and sherry vinegar. Other tempting mains include salt cod filet cooked with tomatoes, peppers, and onions or slow-cooked lamb shank with dried Choricero peppers and garbanzos.

70 Leonard St., EC2. ✆ **020/7613-5346.** www.eyrebrothers.co.uk. Reservations required. Main courses £15–£27. AE, DC, MC, V. Mon–Fri noon–3pm; Mon–Sat 6:30–10:45pm. Tube: Old St.

Fifteen ★★ MODERN BRITISH   When Jamie Oliver, author of *The Naked Chef*, opened this restaurant, it created a media blitz, thanks to a six-part TV show on the Food Network called "Jamie's Kitchen." Oliver takes disadvantaged young people and trains them from scratch in just 4 months before turning them loose as your chef for the day, with all the profits going to charity. In a redbrick Victorian building, convenient for touring the trendy Hoxton Square art galleries, the decor is contemporary and clean cut, not unduly gussied up. Although a bit hyped in the media, the food is quite sumptuous and has won the praise of London's battle-toughened critics. Even Michelin-starred chefs have shown up here raving about the dishes, especially the succulent pastas. There are two dining venues here—a ground-floor trattoria and a downstairs restaurant, the latter the only place to order the set menus quoted below. Among some of the more delectable main dishes you are likely to enjoy are chargrilled halibut in a lemon crème fraîche or loin of pork pot roasted with balsamic vinegar flavoring and bay leaves.

15 Westland Place, N1. © **0871/330-1515.** www.fifteen.net. Reservations required as far in advance as possible. Main courses £14–£21; breakfast £2–£11; fixed-price 2- or 3-course lunch Mon–Fri £22–£25; fixed-price 6-course dinner £60. AE, MC, V. Mon–Sat 7:30–11am; Sun 9–11am; daily noon–3pm and 6–10pm. Tube: Old St.

Meraz Café 🍴 BENGALI   When you're shopping around Brick Lane, pass the tourist-trap Indian restaurants with their tired luncheon buffets and head for this cafe. For more than 35 years, it has been offering authentic home-cooked food in a sleek atmosphere with designer seating areas and kitschy art. Some specialties include beef on the bone cooked with a citrus fruit native to Bangladesh, or roast lamb with chickpea-based dal. A spicy chicken is cooked with fresh tomatoes, and you can also enjoy steaming vegetable and meat samosas.

56 Hanbury St., El. © **020/7247-2588.** www.themeraz.co.uk. Reservations not needed. Main courses £4.50–£5.50. MC, V. Daily noon–3pm and 6–11:30pm. Tube: Aldgate East.

Rootmaster 🍴 VEGAN   This is a real dining oddity, drawing vegans from across greater London since its opening in 2006. The restaurant is housed in one of the city's famous double-decker red Routemaster buses, with candlelit dining upstairs at night, and the kitchen and cafe on the main level. The upstairs contains three separate tables plus a communal table, with a cramped yet convivial vibe. Specialties include oven-braised tofu and caramelized onion tart, or red lentil kofta, as well as organic nutlet cutlets and maple-glazed butternut squash salad. The juicy stuffed mushrooms are a delight, as are the coconut curried vegetables. Call it lunch (or dinner) on a bus.

Elys Yards, the Old Truman Brewery, Hanbury St, E1. © **07912/389314.** www.root-master.co.uk. Reservations not required. Main courses £9–£14. MC, V. Mon–Sat 11am–11pm; Sun 11am–10:30pm. Tube: Aldgate East.

Hackney

INEXPENSIVE

Empress of India ★ 🍴 INDIAN   This brasserie is drawing foodies to Hackney, or more specifically Victoria Park in an up-and-coming section of East London. It's worth the trip. The restaurant is named after one of Queen Victoria's titles, and the smart-looking brasserie was converted from an old nightclub. A long zinc bar is cooled by brass fans, and there's a mural of Mogul India of the 18th century along with mussel-shell chandeliers. Some dishes would appeal to the heart of Samuel Johnson—skewered duck hearts, saddle of venison, and filet of gilthead. The day's market-fresh specialties are posted on a blackboard, and are likely to include such delights as roast suckling pig, Cornish fish stew, or battered monkfish with aioli. Finish off with such old-fashioned desserts such as baked egg custard tart with nutmeg ice cream.

130 Lauriston Rd., E9. © **020/8533-5123.** www.theempressofindia.com. Reservations recommended. Main courses £9–£14. AE, MC, V. Mon–Sat noon–3pm and 6–10pm; Sun noon–10:30pm. Tube: Hackney Central.

Whitechapel

MODERATE

Kasturi INDIAN Kasturi is a strong-smelling secretion found in rare musk deer. But the name has nothing to do with the Indian Pakhtoon cuisine served here. Originating in the northwest frontier province of India, the essence of Pakhtoon cuisine is the preparation of kabob and grilled food utilizing the juices of meat and vegetables, cutting down on the ghee and butter. Delight in such dishes as ginger-flavored lamb chops or chicken kabob from Bharatpur, even yogurt-flavored vegetables. Our favorite bread is *Methi ki roti* (with fenugreek). One of the best vegetarian dishes is baby eggplant with peanut and poppy seeds. Rajsi Pilau (basmati with fruit) is the perfect rice complement to spicy dishes.

57 Aldgate High St., Whitechapel, EC3. 📞 **020/7480-7402.** www.kasturi-restaurant.co.uk. Reservations recommended. Main dishes £3.50–£12; set menus £16–£19. AE, MC, V. Mon–Sat 11am–11pm. Tube: Aldgate.

Limehouse

INEXPENSIVE

The Narrow ★ 🏨 MODERN BRITISH London's most celebrated chef, Gordon Ramsay, has launched an East End gastro-pub standing on a bend of the Thames in the Limehouse district. Warmed by open fires, the restaurant and pub are chicly decorated in nautical navy and white. The menu is a modernized version of a nostalgic English kitchen—for example, with such delights "on toast" as soft herring roes or deviled lamb's kidneys. In how many places today can you find braised Gloucester pig cheeks with mashed neeps (turnips)? Other tempting mains include whole baked gilthead bream with fennel and watercress and a Hereford sirloin with portobello mushrooms and anchovy butter. For dessert, there's a good version of the famous Bakewell Tart.

44 Narrow St., E14. 📞 **020/7592-7950.** www.gordonramsay.com. Reservations required for the restaurant. Main courses £12–£17; fixed-price lunch 2 courses for £18, 3 courses for £22; bar snacks £3.50–£12. AE, MC, V. Mon–Fri 11:30am–3pm and 6–10:30pm; Sat noon–10pm; Sun noon–9pm. Tube: Limehouse.

Docklands

EXPENSIVE

Butler's Wharf Chop House ★ TRADITIONAL BRITISH Of the four restaurants housed in Butler's Wharf (other Butler's Wharf restaurants are listed below), this one is the closest to Tower Bridge. It maintains its commitment to moderate prices. The Chop House was modeled after a large boathouse, with banquettes, lots of exposed wood, flowers, candles, and windows overlooking Tower Bridge and the Thames. Dishes are largely adaptations of English recipes such as fish and chips with mushy peas or steak-and-kidney pudding with oysters, even roast pork loin with applesauce. The bar, among other offerings, features several English wines, plus a half-dozen French clarets by the jug.

36E Shad Thames, SE1. 📞 **020/7403-3403.** www.chophouse.co.uk. Reservations recommended. Main courses £14–£20; fixed-price 2-course lunch £25, 3-course lunch £28. AE, DC, MC, V. Mon–Fri noon–3pm; Sat–Sun noon–4pm; Mon–Sat 6–11pm (6–10pm May–Oct); Sun 6–10pm. Tube: Tower Hill or London Bridge.

Le Pont de la Tour ★ INTERNATIONAL   Built in the mid–19th century as a warehouse, Le Pont de la Tour is another of Terrence Conran's restaurants. From its windows, diners and shoppers enjoy sweeping views of some of the densest river traffic in Europe. The **Bar and Grill**'s live piano music (on evenings and weekends), together with a wide choice of wines and cocktails, creates one of the most convivial atmospheres in the area. The culinary star is a heaping platter of fresh shellfish—perfect when shared with a friend, accompanied by a bottle of wine. In bold contrast is the large, more formal room known simply as the **Restaurant.** Filled with burr oak furniture and decorated with framed lithographs of early-20th-century Parisian cafe society, it offers excellent food and a polite but undeniable English reserve. One especially winning selection is end of lamb, with a black olive- and-herb-crust in a red-pepper sauce. All the fish is excellent, but none better than the Dover sole, which can be ordered grilled or meunière.

36D Shad Thames, Butler's Wharf, SE1. ℂ **020/7403-8403.** www.dandlondon.com. Reservations highly recommended in the Bar and Grill; recommended in the Restaurant. Bar and Grill main courses £8.50–£20; Restaurant 2-course lunch £27, 3-course lunch £32; 3-course dinner £43. AE, DC, MC, V. Bar and Grill Mon–Fri noon–3pm and 6–11pm; Sat noon–11pm; Sun noon–10:30pm. Restaurant daily noon–3pm and 6–11pm. Tube: Tower Hill or London Bridge.

MODERATE

The Bengal Clipper ★ INDIAN   This former spice warehouse by the Thames serves what it calls "India's most remarkable dishes." The likable and often animated restaurant is outfitted with cream-colored walls, tall columns, and modern artwork inspired by the Moghul Dynasty's depictions of royal figures, soaring trees, and well-trained elephants. Seven windows afford sweeping views over the industrialized Thames-side neighborhood, and live piano music plays in the background. The cuisine includes many vegetarian choices derived from the former Portuguese colony of Goa and the once-English colony of Bengal. There is a zestiness and spice to the cuisine, but it's never overpowering. A tasty specialty is stuffed *murgh masala,* a tender breast of chicken with potatoes, onions, and apricots. The duckling (off the bone) comes in a tangy sauce with a citrus bite. One of the finest dishes we tasted in North India is served here and has lost nothing in the transfer: marinated lamb simmered in cream with cashew nuts.

11–12 Cardamom Buildings, Shad Thames, Butler's Wharf, SE1. ℂ **020/7357-9001.** www.bengal clipper.co.uk. Reservations recommended. Main courses £7.50–£13; set menu £15 (July–Apr); Sun buffet £9. AE, DC, MC, V. Mon–Sat noon–2:30pm and 6–11:30pm; Sun noon–4pm and 6–11pm. Tube: Tower Hill.

Canary Wharf

EXPENSIVE

Plateau FRENCH   Entrepreneur Terence Conran has succeeded again with the opening of this trendsetting restaurant at Canary Wharf, serving a modern French cuisine. The chef proudly boasts that he appeals to both high- and low-brow palates—and so he does, succeeding admirably. The atmosphere is retro chic with Harry Bertoia chrome chairs and Eero Saarinen tables. The location is on the fourth floor at the top of the Canada Place building, with panoramic views of London. There are two different dining sections divided by a semi-open-to-view kitchen. One is a chic bar and grill, the other a more formal restaurant, each with its own terrace. In the bar and grill, partake of food enjoyed in the 1920s and 1930s, notably Colchester native oysters followed by Billingsgate fish pie. The upgraded cuisine in the main restaurant is quite sumptuous—a foie gras terrine with champagne jelly followed by such main courses as venison stew with spaetzle and savoy cabbage.

Canada Place, Canary Wharf, E14. ✆ **020/7715-7100.** www.danddlondon.com. Reservations recommended. Bar and grill main courses £10–£20. 2-course dinner £32; 3-course dinner £32–£35. AE, DC, MC, V. Bar and grill Mon–Sat noon–11pm; Sun noon–4pm. Restaurant Mon–Fri noon–3pm; Mon–Sat 6–10:30pm; Sun noon–4pm. Tube: Canary Wharf.

MODERATE

Sri Nam ★ 👫 THAI   Celebrity chef Ken Hom is the chief exponent of Thai cookery in London, and even the Thai community agrees he's the best. Some of his culinary secrets are revealed in his book, *Foolproof Thai Cookery.* At Canary Wharf, Sri Nam brings an authentic and very spicy (read: hot) cuisine to foodies who like to dine on the Thames. There's a buzz-filled cafe-bar on the ground floor and a more formal restaurant upstairs. The Thai cuisine served here is a fusion of modern and traditional, the latter in theory the type served to the "King of Siam." Served here (and rarely seen on other London menus) is lamb masaman, flavored with peanuts and potatoes. The signature dish—and is it ever good—is the Thai green chicken curry with chilis, coconut milk, bamboo shoots, baby eggplant, and lime leaves.

N. Colonnade, 10 Cabot Sq., Canary Wharf, E14. ✆ **020/7715-9515.** www.orientalrestaurant group.co.uk. Reservations required. Main courses £6.25–£14; fixed-price menus £25–£30. AE, DC, MC, V. Mon–Fri noon–3pm and 5–11pm. Tube: Canary Wharf

South Bank

EXPENSIVE

Oxo Tower Restaurant ★ INTERNATIONAL   In the South Bank complex, on the eighth floor of the Art Deco Oxo Tower Wharf, you'll find this dining sensation. It's operated by the department store Harvey Nichols. Down the street from the rebuilt Globe Theatre, this 140-seat restaurant could be visited for its view alone, but the cuisine is also stellar. You'll enjoy a sweeping view of St. Paul's Cathedral and the City, all the way to the Houses of Parliament. The decor is chic 1930s-style. The cuisine, under chef David Sharland, is rich and prepared with finesse. Menu items change based on the season and the market. Count on a modern interpretation of British cookery, as well as the English classics. The fish is incredibly fresh here. The whole sea bass for two is delectable, as is the roast rump of lamb with split pea, mint purée, and balsamic vinegar sauce. We were also impressed with the roast filet of plaice with olive oil and truffle cabbage cream.

22 Barge House St., South Bank, SE1. ✆ **020/7803-3888.** www.harveynichols.com. Main courses £20–£32; fixed-price lunch £23–£29. AE, DC, MC, V. Mon–Sat noon–2:30pm and 6–11pm; Sun noon–3pm and 6:30–10pm. Tube: Blackfriars or Waterloo.

MODERATE

Cantina Vinopolis ★ 👫 CONTINENTAL   Not far from the re-created Globe Theatre of Shakespeare's heyday, this place has been called a "Walk-Through Wine Atlas." In the revitalized Bankside area, south of the Thames near

family-friendly RESTAURANTS

Hard Rock Cafe (Mayfair; p. 203) This is a great place for kids old enough to busy themselves with rock-and-roll memorabilia as they wait for their familiar burgers, fries, and salads with Thousand Island dressing.

Porters English Restaurant (Covent Garden & the Strand; p. 189)   This restaurant serves traditional English meals that most kids love—especially the pies, stews, and steamed "spuds." They'll get a kick out of ordering the wonderfully named bubble-and-squeak (that's cabbage and potatoes) and mushy peas.

Royal China (Paddington & Bayswater; p. 225)   If there's a dim sum lover in your family, head for this eatery. We saw a young brother and sister devouring a dish of seafood golden cups—stir-fried scallops, prawns, water chestnuts, and mushrooms in crispy puff pastry.

Simpson's-in-the-Strand (Covent Garden & the Strand; p. 188)   If your offspring is an aspiring Henry VIII, take him here for the best roasts in London, including tender roast sirloin of beef. For dessert, he might be introduced to such English favorites as treacle rolls.

Ye Olde Cheshire Cheese (the City; p. 178)   Fleet Street's famous chophouse, established in 1667, is an eternal favorite. If "ye famous pudding" turns your kids off, sandwiches and roasts will tempt them.

Southwark Cathedral, this bricked, walled, and high-vaulted brasserie was converted from long-abandoned Victorian railway arches. Inside you can visit both the Vinopolis Wine Gallery and the Cantina Restaurant. Although many come here just to drink the wine, the food is prepared with very fresh, quality ingredients, and the menu is sensibly priced. Start with a bit of heaven such as the pea and ham soup. Pan-fried snapper, with crushed new potatoes and salsa verde, won us over. Many of the dishes have the good country taste of a trattoria you'd find in the countryside of southern Italy. Naturally, the wine list is the biggest in the U.K.

1 Bank End, London Bridge, SE1. (✆) **020/7940-8333.** www.cantinavinopolis.com. Reservations required. Main courses £13–£23; 3-course fixed-price menu £26–£30. AE, DC, MC, V. Mon–Sat noon–3pm and 6–10:30pm; Sun noon–4pm. Tube: London Bridge.

THE WEST END
Bloomsbury
EXPENSIVE

Pied-à-Terre ★★★ FRENCH   A meticulously rendered French cuisine is served at the most acclaimed restaurant in Bloomsbury. The interior is stylish, with intimate tables; we prefer those in the rear. Chef Shane Osborn cleverly combines a classical technique with his own modern inventiveness in the kitchen. He demonstrates a flair for flavorful "marriage" of ingredients. Try his seared and poached foie gras with borlotti beans or his steamed halibut with a tomato fondue. Blackleg chicken breast from Landes arrives with a garlic purée, or else you can order kid goat with caramelized endive and roasted shallots, or certainly the roasted Devonshire loin of venison with a quince purée and walnuts.

34 Charlotte St., W1. ✆ **020/7636-1178.** www.pied-a-terre.co.uk. Set-price 2-course lunch £25; set-price 2-course dinner £51; 10-course dinner £87; 5-course dinner with wine £145. Mon–Fri 12:15–2:30pm; Mon–Sat 6:15–11pm. Tube: Goodge St.

INEXPENSIVE

Salt Yard ★ SPANISH/ITALIAN   Calling itself a "charcuterie bar and restaurant," this is a fashionable choice with a bustling downstairs. The chefs here specialize in affordable plates of tasty Spanish and Italian dishes which are often shared. This joint is far superior to most tapas houses. How many places do you know that serve truffle-laced honey? Its Serrano ham, 18 months in "curing," is arguably the finest in London. Braised beef cheek comes with broad beans, and zucchini flowers are stuffed with Monte Enebro cheese and drizzled with honey. Fresh squid arrives with aioli, and bar snacks are also served.

54 Goodge St., W1. ✆ **020/7637-0657.** www.saltyard.co.uk. Reservations recommended. Tapas £3.50–£7.50; charcuterie platters £7.60–£13. AE, MC, V. Mon–Fri noon–11pm (3–6pm bar snacks only); Sat 5–11pm. Tube: Goodge St.

Wagamama JAPANESE   This noodle joint, in a basement just off New Oxford Street, is noisy and overcrowded, and you'll have to wait in line for a table. It calls itself a "nondestination food station" and caters to some 1,200 customers a day. Many dishes are built around ramen noodles with your choice of chicken, beef, or salmon. Try the tasty *gyoza*, light dumplings filled with vegetables or chicken. Vegetarian dishes are available, but skip the so-called Korean-style dishes.

4 Streatham St., WC1. ✆ **020/7323-9223.** www.wagamama.com. Reservations not accepted. Main courses £7–£11. AE, MC, V. Mon–Sat noon–11pm; Sun noon–10pm. Tube: Tottenham Court Rd.

King's Cross

MODERATE

Acorn House ★ 🍃 BRITISH/TRADITIONAL   Near St. Pancras Station, this is one of the most eco-friendly restaurants in London. The chefs are dedicated to healthy eating from their fresh seasonal menus, and they call themselves "environmentally responsible from design to delivery." For its weekday lunches you face a large display of plates and trays filled with meats and fish, fresh vegetables, cured meats, chilled salads, ripe fruits, and homemade breads and desserts—all laid out on a counter for your selection. A warm menu can be cooked to order as well. Hot soups, take-away sandwiches, and salads to go are also sold. Dinner is more formal, with a larger and more structured menu, including four seasonal starters, three "mid-courses," and four main dishes such as duck confit with braised bok choy or basil-scented sea bream with pancetta.

69 Swanton St., WC1. ✆ **020/7812-1842.** www.acornhouserestaurant.com. Reservations recommended. Main courses £13–£18. Fixed-price menus £30–£40. MC, V. Mon–Fri noon–3pm and 6–10pm; Sat 6–9:30pm. Tube: King's Cross.

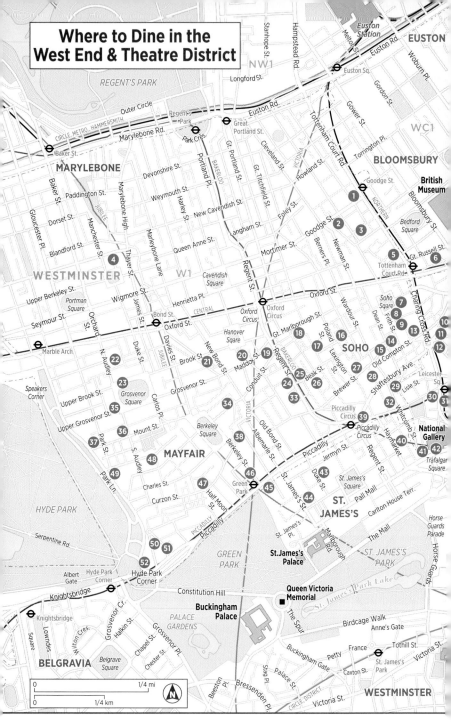

Where to Dine in the West End & Theatre District

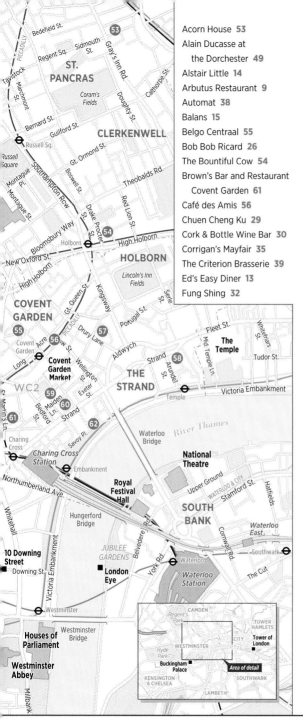

Covent Garden & the Strand

The restaurants in and around Covent Garden and the Strand are the most convenient choices when you're attending theaters in the West End.

EXPENSIVE

Rules ★ TRADITIONAL BRITISH   If you're looking for London's most quintessentially British restaurant, eat here. London's oldest restaurant was established in 1798 as an oyster bar; today, the antler-filled Edwardian dining rooms exude nostalgia. You can order such classic dishes as Irish or Scottish oysters, jugged hare, and mussels. Game and fish dishes are offered from mid-August to February or March, including wild Scottish salmon; wild sea trout; wild Highland red deer; and game birds such as grouse, snipe, partridge, pheasant, and woodcock. As a finale, the "great puddings" continue to impress.

35 Maiden Lane, WC2. ✆ **020/7836-5314.** www.rules.co.uk. Reservations recommended. Main courses £17–£28. AE, DC, MC, V. Mon–Sat noon–11:30pm; Sun noon–10:30pm. Tube: Covent Garden.

Simpson's-in-the-Strand ★★ ☺ TRADITIONAL AND MODERN BRITISH   Simpson's is more of an institution than a restaurant. Long a family favorite with lots of large tables, it has been in business since 1828, and as a result of a recent £2-million renovation, it's now better than ever with its Adam paneling, crystal, and an army of grandly formal waiters serving traditional English fare. The owners object to the word "menu" here—"too French." It's called "bill of fare." Men and women can now dine together. Before 1904 such an "outrage" was forbidden. Through the years the dress code has become more relaxed—in other words, Elizabeth Taylor in trousers would no longer be forbidden to enter. Famous diners of yesterday include everyone from Charles Dickens to Charles Chaplin, and the restaurant is often used as a film setting, including one for Alfred Hitchcock's *Sabotage.* Most diners agree that Simpson's serves the best roasts in London, an array that includes roast sirloin of beef; roast saddle of mutton with red-currant jelly; roast Aylesbury duckling; and steak, kidney, and mushroom pie.

100 the Strand (next to the Savoy Hotel), WC2. ✆ **020/7836-9112.** www.simpsonsinthestrand. co.uk. Reservations required. Main courses £16–£33; 3-course fixed-price pretheater dinner £30; 2-course meal £25; breakfast £12–£21. AE, DC, MC, V. Mon–Fri 7:15–10:30am; Mon–Sat 12:15–2:45pm and 5:45–10:45pm; Sun noon–2:45pm and 5:45–9pm. Tube: Charing Cross or Embankment.

MODERATE

Belgo Centraal BELGIAN   Chaos reigns supreme in this cavernous basement, where mussels *marinières* with fries, plus 100 Belgian beers, are the raison d'être. Take a freight elevator past the busy kitchen and into a converted cellar, divided into two large eating areas. One section is a beer hall seating about 250; the menu here is the same as in the restaurant, but you don't need reservations. The restaurant side has three nightly seatings: at 5:30, 7:30, and 10pm. Although heaps of fresh mussels are the big attraction, you can opt for fresh Scottish salmon, roast chicken, a perfectly done steak, or one of the vegetarian specialties. Gargantuan plates of wild boar sausages arrive with *stoemp*—Belgian mashed spuds and cabbage. Belgian stews, called *waterzooï*, are also served.

50 Earlham St., WC2. ✆ **020/7813-2233.** www.belgo-restaurants.co.uk. Reservations required for the restaurant. Main courses £11–£13. AE, DC, MC, V. Mon–Sat noon–11pm; Sun noon–10:30pm. Closed Christmas. Tube: Covent Garden.

Café des Amis FRENCH For more than half a century, Café des Amis has been entertaining theatergoers with the two-fisted drinks at its bar and fine Gallic cuisine in its restaurant. With service by French waiters and sophisticated Continental decor, it brings a touch of Paris to the heart of London. Dishes are both traditional and modern, but with reduced calories since the days of Escoffier. The wine list from France is one of the best in Covent Garden. The cafe is a good choice for a pre- or post-theater meal, or a romantic dinner even if you're not attending a play or musical. The menu is not completely conventional. There are modern touches as well, such as soupe au chocolat with black-pepper ice cream. You might begin with French onion soup or shellfish bisque, perhaps seared scallops with chorizo and roasted hazelnuts. Among the mains we've savored are roasted sea bass in a vinaigrette with palourd clams, and pot-roasted lamb flavored with cinnamon and cloves. Desserts are more English than French, such as poached Yorkshire rhubarb flavored with ginger and served with a cream custard.

11–14 Hanover Place (off Long Acre), WC2. ✆ **020/7379-3444.** www.cafedesamis.co.uk. Reservations recommended. Main courses £7.50–£22; fixed-price menus £15 (2 courses), £17 (3 courses). AE, DC, MC, V. Mon–Sat noon–11:30pm. Tube: Covent Garden.

Mon Plaisir ✦ FRENCH Serving fine French cuisine for more than half a century, Mon Plaisir is London's oldest French restaurant. It's so authentic that its pewter topped bar once graced the lounge of a Lyonnais bordello. The menu wanders into nostalgia with its *classiques* but has been modernized as well. Its pretheater fixed-price menu is one of the best deals in the West End. Pigs' trotters stuffed with foie gras and langoustines evoke the old markets of Les Halles in Paris. Of course, there are snails with garlic and a traditional French onion soup. The fish dishes are fresh and tantalizing, including coquilles Saint-Jacques (scallops). A delicious coq au vin, another classic, is cooked in burgundy. For dessert, why not the pan-fried brioche with poached pear and—get this—beer ice cream?

21 Monmouth St., WC2. ✆ **020/7836-7243.** www.monplaisir.co.uk. Reservations recommended. Main courses £17–£36; pretheater menu £14–£16. AE, DC, MC, V. Mon–Fri noon–2:15pm; Mon–Sat 5:45–11:15pm. Tube: Covent Garden.

Porters English Restaurant ★★ ☺ TRADITIONAL BRITISH The seventh earl of Bradford serves "real English food at affordable prices." He succeeds notably—and not just because Lady Bradford turned over her carefully guarded recipe for banana-and-ginger steamed pudding. This comfortable, two-story restaurant is family-friendly, informal, and lively. Porters specializes in classic English pies, including Old English fish pie; lamb and apricot; and, of course, bangers and mash. The overwhelming favorite is steak, Guinness, and mushroom pie. Main courses are so generous—and accompanied by vegetables and side dishes—that you hardly need appetizers. They have also added grilled English fare to the menu, including sirloin and lamb steaks and marinated chicken. Porters is famous for its mouthwatering puddings. Where can you find a good spotted dick these days? It's a steamed syrup sponge cake with sultanas (raisins). Another favorite is a dark-chocolate-chip pudding made with steamed chocolate sponge, chocolate chips, and chocolate custard. Even the ice cream is homemade. The bar does quite a few exotic cocktails, as well as beers, wine, or English mead. A traditional English tea is served from 2:30 to 5:30pm.

17 Henrietta St., WC2. © **020/7836-6466.** www.porters.uk.com. Reservations recommended. Main courses £11–£19; fixed-price lunch and pretheater menu £12; fixed-price dinner menu £23. AE, MC, V. Mon–Sat noon–11:30pm; Sun noon–10:30pm. Tube: Covent Garden or Leicester Sq.

INEXPENSIVE

The George TRADITIONAL BRITISH   Although the George's half-timbered facade would make you believe it's older than it is, this pub has been around *only* since 1723, when it was built as a coffeehouse. Set on the Strand, at the lower end of Fleet Street opposite the Royal Courts of Justice, the George is a favorite of barristers, their clients, and the handful of journalists who haven't moved to other parts of London. The pub's illustrious history saw Samuel Johnson having his mail delivered here and Oliver Goldsmith enjoying many tankards of what eventually became draught Bass. Today the setting seems only slightly changed, as much of the original architecture is still intact. Hot and cold platters, including bangers and mash, fish and chips, steak-and-kidney pie, and lasagna, are served from a food counter at the back of the pub. Other main dishes include Cumberland sausages with mashed potatoes and red-onion gravy or chicken Parmagiana. A headless cavalier is said to haunt the basement, where he enjoyed his liquor in an earlier (and less headless) day. Although the place has long hours (see below), the actual food service is Monday to Thursday 11am to 3pm, Friday and Saturday noon to 9pm, and Sunday noon to 6:30pm.

213 the Strand, WC2. © **020/7353-9638.** www.capitalpubcompany.com/the-george. Reservations not needed. Main courses £6.95–£9.95. AE, MC, V. Mon–Sat noon–9pm; Sun noon–8pm. Tube: Temple.

Sarastro ★ CYPRIOT/TURKISH   The setting here makes you feel like you're in the prop room of an opera house. As the manager says, "We're the show after the show." The decor is sort of neo-Ottoman, and the cuisine celebrates the bounty of the Mediterranean, especially Turkey and Cyprus. In a Victorian building behind the Theatre Royal, the restaurant is decorated with battered urns, old lamps, fading lampshades, and knickknacks—it looks like an old Turkish curiosity shop. Ten opera boxes adorn the restaurant; the royal box is the most desired. The restaurant takes its name from a character in Mozart's *The Magic Flute.* Live opera performances are staged from time to time. You can begin your meal with such starters as grilled Mediterranean prawns with garlic mushrooms or stuffed grape leaves and hummus. The best mains include a filet or sirloin steak with a red-wine sauce; lamb meatballs; or perhaps fettuccine with cream, mushrooms, and Parma ham. The fish dishes are fresh, including grilled lemon sole and monkfish with tomatoes and onions.

126 Drury Lane, WC2. © **020/7836-0101.** www.sarastro-restaurant.com. Reservations required. Main courses £9–£16; fixed-price menu £27; pretheater menu £15. AE, DC, MC, V. Daily noon–11:45pm. Tube: Covent Garden.

Holborn

EXPENSIVE

The Bountiful Cow ★★ STEAK   This 1960s pub has been turned into a "public house" devoted to top beef. In the Holborn district, or from far beyond, it's harder to find better steaks and burgers than those found here. All the steaks come from select beef hung for at least 2 weeks. The owner, Roxy Beaujolais, is the author of the classic pub cookbook, *Home from the Inn Contented*. Five cuts of beefsteak are featured on the menu: onglet or flank steak, rib-eye, sirloin, filet, and T-bone. These steaks are tender and full of flavor. You can select from such sauces as Béarnaise or green peppercorn. Vegetarian dishes are also served, and there are daily market specials. You can down cask-conditioned ales such as Adams, taking in such poster art as Barbara Stanwyck and Ronald Reagan in *Cattle Queen of Montana*.

51 Eagle St., WC1. ✆ **020/7404-0200.** Reservations required. Main courses £9.50–£21. AE, MC, V. Mon–Sat 11am–11pm; Sun noon–8pm. Tube: Holborn.

Piccadilly Circus & Leicester Square

Piccadilly Circus and Leicester Square lie at the doorstep of the West End theaters. All the choices below (along with those in the "Covent Garden & the Strand" and "Soho" sections) are good candidates for dining before or after a show.

EXPENSIVE

Fung Shing ★★ CANTONESE   In a city where the competition is stiff, Fung Shing emerges as London's finest Cantonese restaurant. Firmly established as a culinary landmark, it dazzles with classic and nouvelle Cantonese dishes. Look for the seasonal specials. Some of the dishes may be a bit experimental—notably stir-fried fresh milk with scrambled egg white—but you'll feel right at home with the soft-shell crab sautéed in a light batter and served with tiny rings of red-hot chili and deep-fried garlic. Chinese gourmets come here for the fried intestines; you may prefer the hotpot of stewed duck with yam. The spicy sea bass and the stir-fried crispy chicken are worthy choices. There are more than 150 dishes from which to choose, and most are moderate in price.

15 Lisle St., WC2. ✆ **020/7437-1539.** www.fungshing.co.uk. Reservations required. Main courses £8–£26. AE, DC, MC, V. Daily noon–11:30pm. Tube: Leicester Sq.

The Ivy ★★ MODERN BRITISH/INTERNATIONAL   Effervescent and sophisticated, the Ivy is the dining choice of visiting theatrical luminaries and has been intimately associated with the theater district ever since it opened in 1911. With its ersatz 1930s look and tiny bar near the entrance, this place is fun and hums with the energy of London's glamorous scene. The kitchen has a solid appreciation for fresh ingredients and a talent for preparation. Some appetizers may be a bit much, like wild rabbit salad with black pudding, whereas others are more appealing, such as Bang Bang chicken. The crispy duck and watercress salad is another favorite. Mains feature a chargrilled fish of the day, and carnivores take to the sautéed veal kidneys or the escalope of veal Holstein. Desserts are familiar, including chocolate pudding soufflé or rhubarb sponge pudding with custard.

1–5 West St., WC2. ✆ **020/7836-4751.** www.the-ivy.co.uk. Reservations required. Main courses £8–£40; Sat–Sun fixed-price lunch £29. AE, DC, MC, V. Mon–Sat noon–3pm; Sun noon–3:30pm; daily 5:30pm–midnight (last order). Tube: Leicester Sq.

J. Sheekey ★ SEAFOOD   English culinary tradition lives on at this fish joint, long a favorite of West End actors. The jellied eels that delighted Laurence Olivier and Vivien Leigh are still here, along with an array of fresh oysters from the coasts of Ireland and Brittany, plus that Victorian favorite, fried whitebait. Sheekey's fish pie is still on the menu, as is Dover sole. The old "mushy" peas still appear, but the chefs also offer the likes of steamed organic sea beet. Opt for the traditional dishes or specials based on the fresh catch of the day. The double chocolate pudding soufflé is a delight, and many favorite puddings remain.

28–32 St. Martin's Court, WC2. ✆ **020/7240-2565.** www.j-sheekey.co.uk. Reservations recommended. Main courses £13–£40. AE, DC, MC, V. Mon–Sat noon–3pm and 5:30pm–midnight; Sun noon–3:30pm and 6pm–midnight. Tube: Leicester Sq.

MODERATE

Randall & Aubin ★ 🎁 SEAFOOD   Past the sex boutiques of Soho you stumble upon this real discovery, whose consultant is TV chef Ed Baines, an ex-Armani model who turned this butcher shop into a cool, hip champagne-and-oyster bar. The impressive shellfish display of the night's goodies is the "bait" used to lure you inside. Chances are you won't be disappointed. Loch Fyne oysters, lobster with chips, pan-fried fresh scallops—the parade of seafood we've sampled here has in each case been genuinely excellent. The *soupe de poisson* (fish soup) is the best in Soho, or else you might want one of the hors d'oeuvres such as delightful Japanese-style fish cakes or fresh Cornish crab. Yes, they still have Sevruga caviar for lotto winners. For the rare meat-only eater, there is a limited array of dishes such as a perfectly roasted chicken on the spit that has been flavored with fresh herbs. The lemon tart with crème fraîche rounds out a perfect meal.

16 Brewer St., W1. ✆ **020/7287-4447.** www.randallandaubin.com. Reservations not accepted. Main courses £8–£17. AE, DC, MC, V. Mon–Sat noon–11pm; Sun 4–10pm. Tube: Piccadilly Circus or Leicester Sq.

INEXPENSIVE

Brown's Bar and Restaurant Covent Gardens CONTINENTAL/TRADI-TIONAL BRITISH   The decor of this popular restaurant is reminiscent of an Edwardian brasserie, with mirrors, dark-wood trim, and cream-colored walls. The staff is attentive, hysterically busy, and high spirited. The most amazing thing about the restaurant is its size. It's a cavernous labyrinth of tables complemented by a bar where (often single) patrons tend to be good-looking, happy-go-lucky, and usually up for a chat. Without ever rising to greatness, mains are well prepared and rather tasty, especially the chargrilled chicken with air-dried ham, melted Taleggio cheese, and hollandaise sauce, and the salmon with an herby mustard crust. The braised lamb shank is another good dish, served in a beer sauce, or order whole lemon sole in a burnt butter sauce.

82–84 St. Martin's Lane, WC2. ✆ **020/7497-5050.** www.browns-restaurants.com. Reservations not needed. 2-course fixed-price pretheater menu £15 available 4–6:30pm Mon–Sat; main courses £8.95–£19. AE, DC, MC, V. Mon–Wed 9am–11pm; Thurs–Fri 9am–11:30pm; Sat 10am–11:30pm; Sun 10am–10:30pm.

Cork & Bottle Wine Bar ★★ 🍷 INTERNATIONAL   Don Hewitson, a connoisseur of fine wines for more than 30 years, presides over this trove of blissful fermentation. The ever-changing wine list features an excellent selection of Beaujolais Crus from Alsace, 30 selections from Australia, 30 champagnes, and a good selection of California labels. If you want something to wash down, the most successful dish is a raised ham-and-cheese pie, with a cream cheese–like filling and crisp, well-buttered pastry—not your typical quiche. There's also chicken and apple salad, black pudding, Mediterranean prawns with garlic and asparagus, lamb in ale, and a Thai chicken wings platter.

44–46 Cranbourn St., WC2. ✆ **020/7734-7807.** www.corkandbottle.net. Reservations not accepted after 6:30pm. Fixed-price menu £11–£14; main courses £8–£16. AE, DC, MC, V. Mon–Sat 11am–midnight; Sun noon–11pm. Tube: Leicester Sq.

The Stockpot 🍴 CONTINENTAL/TRADITIONAL BRITISH   Pound for pound (British pounds, that is), we'd hazard a guess that this cozy little restaurant offers one of the best dining bargains in London. Mains include such familiar favorites as beef Stroganoff or penne with ham and broccoli. You might also opt for the fish cakes with chips and salad or else a vegetable moussaka. Desserts include Jell-O and ice cream (if you're feeling nostalgic for childhood) or else a rhubarb crumble with vanilla custard. At these prices, the food is hardly refined, but it's filling and satisfying nonetheless. During peak hours, the Stockpot has a share-the-table policy in its dining room.

38 Panton St. (off Haymarket, opposite the Comedy Theatre), SW1. ✆ **020/7839-5142.** Reservations accepted for groups for dinner. Main courses £3.50–£6.95; fixed-price 2-course meal £6.50, 3-course £8.60. No credit cards. Mon–Tues 11:30am–11:30pm; Wed–Sat 11:30am–midnight; Sun noon–11:30pm. Tube: Piccadilly Circus or Leicester Sq.

Soho

The restaurants of Soho are conveniently located for those rushing to have dinner before an evening at one of the West End theaters.

MODERATE

Arbutus Restaurant ★ 🍴 BRITISH/TRADITIONAL/CONTINENTAL   This Soho eatery was the brainchild of Anthony Demetre and Will Smith, who have operated other Michelin-starred restaurants elsewhere. They now bring their quality cooking and service to the heart of Soho in rather unpretentious surroundings. They don't please all diners, but not for lack of effort. Sometimes they use parts of the pig not seen since the days of Henry VIII—pig's head, for example, but this may be too rich for some diners who'd prefer the wintery beef daube in a dark but flavorful sauce. Ever had a squid and mackerel burger? It's an oddity but won't put McDonald's out of business. Other winning dishes include smoked eel risotto or pork rillettes with a celeriac remoulade. A traditional bouillabaisse also scores points (it's made with regular fish, not shellfish).

63–64 Frith St., W1. ✆ **020/7734-4545.** Reservations required. Main courses £15–£20; 3-course lunch £17; pre- and post-theater fixed-price menu £19. AE, DC, MC, V. Mon–Sat noon–2:30pm and 5–11pm; Sun noon–3pm and 5:30–10:30pm. Tube: Tottenham Court Rd.

Bob Bob Ricard BRITISH/TRADITIONAL   From early morning to the wee hours (a rarity in London), this eatery serves a sophisticated but old-fashioned version of English comfort food. How many places in London can you find a prune milkshake on the menu? You can start with quail eggs and go on to poached Loch Duart salmon. Sir Winston Churchill, should he return, might delight in the pork cheeks braised in port or the 28-day aged Aberdeenshire beef cutlet. For dessert, we'd opt for the piña colada soufflé flavored with 7-year-old Havana rum.

At tea time, crumpets and tea cakes are served. Why not a spread of rose petal jelly on your crumpet?" For some diners, the decor evokes Liberace's living room.

1 Upper James St., W1. © **020/3145-1000.** www.bobbobricard.com. Reservations not needed. English breakfast £14; main dishes £13–£29. MC, V. Mon–Fri 7am–1am; Sat 10am–3am; Sun 10am–midnight. Tube: Piccadilly Circus.

Chuen Cheng Ku ★ CHINESE   This is one of the finest places in Soho's New China. Chuen Cheng Ku has the longest Cantonese menu in town. Specialties include paper-wrapped prawns, rice in lotus leaves, steamed spareribs in black-bean sauce, and shredded pork with cashew nuts—all served in generous portions. Other featured dishes include lobster with ginger and spring onion, sliced duck in chili and black-bean sauce, and Singapore noodles (thin, rich noodles, mixed with curry and pork, or with shrimp and red and green pepper). Dim sum is served from 11am to 6pm. We must note, however, that the standard of service has slipped over the years.

17 Wardour St., W1. © **020/7734-3281.** www.chuenchengku.co.uk. Reservations recommended on weekend afternoons. Main courses £7.80–£16; fixed-price menus £9.80–£23. AE, DC, MC, V. Mon–Sat 11am–11:45pm; Sun 11am–11:15pm. Closed Dec 24–25. Tube: Piccadilly Circus or Leicester Sq.

The Criterion Brasserie ★ FRENCH/MODERN BRITISH   Designed by Thomas Verity in the 1870s, this palatial neo-Byzantine mirrored marble hall is a glamorous backdrop for a superb cuisine, served under a golden ceiling, with theatrical peacock-blue draperies. The menu is wide ranging, offering everything from Paris brasserie food to "nouvelle-classical," a combination of classic French cooking techniques with some of the lighter, more experimental leanings of modern French cuisine. The food is excellent but falls short of sublime. Start with beef carpaccio in a mustard dressing or else spaghetti with clams and chili peppers, to be followed by such fish as wild sea bass with a shellfish fondue or else roast suckling pig in applesauce.

224 Piccadilly, W1. © **020/7930-0488.** www.criterionrestaurant.com. Main courses £16–£26; lunch special 2- to 3-course £16–£19. AE, MC, V. Mon–Sat noon–2:30pm and 5:30–11:30pm; Sun noon–3:30pm and 5:30–6:30pm. Tube: Piccadilly Circus.

The Gay Hussar ★ HUNGARIAN   Is this still the best Hungarian restaurant in the world? That's what some say. We can't agree until we've sampled every Hungarian restaurant in the world, but we're certain Gay Hussar would be near the top. Since 1953, it's been an intimate place with authentic cuisine, a loyal clientele of politicians, and a large international following, especially among visiting Hungarians. Begin with chilled wild-cherry soup or mixed Hungarian salami. Gutsy main courses include cabbage stuffed with minced veal and rice, half a perfectly done chicken in mild paprika sauce with cucumber salad and noodles, roast duck with red cabbage and caraway potatoes, and, of course, veal goulash with egg dumplings. Expect gigantic portions. For dessert, go with either the poppy-seed strudel or the walnut pancakes.

2 Greek St., W1. © **020/7437-0973.** www.gayhussar.co.uk. Reservations recommended. Main courses £12–£17; 2-course lunch £19; 3-course lunch £21. AE, DC, MC, V. Mon–Sat 12:15–2:30pm and 5:30–10:45pm. Tube: Tottenham Court Rd.

Hakkasan ★ 🍴 CHINESE   Asian mystique and pastiche are found in this offbeat restaurant in a seedy alley off Tottenham Court Road. This is another

London venture created by Alan Yau, who became a citywide dining legend because of his Wagamama noodle bars. Come here for great dim sum and tantalizing cocktails. Feast on such dishes as *har gau* (steamed prawn dumplings) and strips of tender barbecued pork. The spring roll is refreshing with the addition of fried mango and a delicate prawn-and-scallop filling. Steamed scallop *shumai* (dumplings) with *tobiko* caviar are fresh and meltingly soft. Desserts in most of London's Chinese restaurants are hardly memorable, but the offerings here are an exception to that rule, especially the layered banana sponge with chocolate cream.

8 Hanway Place, W1. © **020/7927-7000.** www.hakkasan.com. Reservations recommended. Main courses £10–£68. AE, MC, V. Lunch Mon–Fri noon–3pm, Sat noon–5pm; dinner Mon–Wed 6–11:30pm, Thurs–Sat 6–11:30pm, Sun 6–11pm. Tube: Tottenham Court Rd.

Mela ★ 🍴 INDIAN   Serious foodies know you'll likely be served some of London's finest Indian cuisine at this address. The *London Evening Standard* named this the best Indian restaurant in Britain in 2004, and it is as good now as it was back then. Expect robust aromas and earthy flavors. Our spiced duck flavored with spring onions, ginger, and coriander evoked some of the best country dining in India. Eggplant came stuffed with a spicy lamb mince and was superb, as was the whole fresh fish of the day in a spicy marinade flavored with saffron and cooked whole in a charcoal oven. Tawa cookery (which in India is street food, cooked on a hot plate) is a specialty. At Mela, the fresh meats and other ingredients are cooked straight on a hot plate. Look for the chef's special Tawa dish of the day, perhaps queen prawns cooked with onions and fresh tomatoes. Save room for one of their special desserts.

152–156 Shaftesbury Ave., WC2. © **020/7836-8635.** www.melarestaurant.co.uk. Reservations required. Main courses £5.95–£22; 3-course fixed-price meal (available before 7pm) £11. AE, MC, V. Mon–Thurs noon–11:30pm; Fri noon–11:45pm; Sat 1–11:45pm; Sun noon–10:30pm. Tube: Tottenham Court Rd. or Leicester Sq.

Rasa Samudra ★ 🍴 INDIAN   This outpost offers the best southern Indian cuisine in town, and all the dishes are fish or vegetable based—no red meat or poultry. Rasa Samundra features cookery of the southern state of Kerala, focusing on specialties from the sea. Owner Das Sreedharan's mother has trained all the chefs, and the results are delectable. Try *malslam pattichathu* (kingfish cooked in fresh spices, with green chili and coconut paste), *para konju nirachathu* (lobster cooked with black pepper, garlic, and Indian shallots, and served with whole-lemon and beet-root curry), *masala dosa* (paper-thin rice and black-grain pancakes filled with potato and ginger masala), and *moru kachlathu* (green bananas and mangoes cooked in a yogurt sauce with turmeric and onions). Rasa also offers a range of appetizers, side orders, breads, rice, and desserts. Most dishes are at the lower end of the price scale.

5 Charlotte St., W1. © **020/7637-0222.** www.rasarestaurants.com. Reservations required. Main courses £6.50–£13; fixed-price dinner £23–£30. AE, DC, MC, V. Mon–Sat noon–3pm and 6–11pm; Sun 6–11pm. Tube: Tottenham Court Rd.

Satsuma JAPANESE   This funky Japanese canteen is all the rage in London. The clean lines, stark white walls, and long wooden tables suggest an upmarket youth hostel. But patrons come for good food at reasonable prices. The restaurant is ideal for a pretheater visit. Your meal comes in a lacquered bento box on a matching tray. Try the chicken teriyaki or fresh chunks of tuna and salmon. The dumplings are excellent, as is the miso soup. A specialty is the large bowl of seafood ramen, with noodles swimming in a well-seasoned broth studded with mussels, scallops, and prawns. Tofu steaks are a delight, as are udon noodles with wok-fried chicken and fresh vegetables. You can finish with deep-fried tempura ice cream.

56 Wardour St., W1. ☎ **020/7437-8338.** www.osatsuma.com. Reservations not accepted. Main courses £6–£16. AE, DC, MC, V. Mon–Tues noon–11pm; Wed–Thurs noon–11:30pm; Fri–Sat noon–midnight; Sun noon–10:30pm. Tube: Piccadilly Circus or Leicester Sq.

Shampers CONTINENTAL This is a favorite of West End wine-bar aficionados. In addition to the street-level wine bar serving snacks, there's a more formal basement-level restaurant. In either venue, you can order such main dishes as grilled calves' liver with bacon, chips, and salad; pan-fried large prawns with ginger, garlic, and chili; and platters of cheeses. Salads are popular, including spicy chicken salad or the grilled eggplant salad with tomato, avocado, buffalo mozzarella, and pesto. The platter of Irish mussels cooked in a cream-and-tarragon sauce is everybody's favorite. The restaurant is now open in the evening, but the wine bar also serves an extensive menu, offering fresh squid, tuna steak, pan-fried tiger prawns, free-range chicken, and other tasty specialties. There is also a daily specials menu.

4 Kingly St. (btw. Carnaby and Regent sts.), W1. ☎ **020/7437-1692.** www.shampers.net. Reservations recommended. Main courses £9–£15. AE, DC, MC, V. Restaurant and wine bar Mon–Sat noon–11pm. Closed Dec 24–Jan 2. Tube: Oxford Circus or Piccadilly Circus.

Veeraswamy 🍴 INDIAN The oldest Indian restaurant in England, originally established in the 1920s, Veeraswamy has been restyled and rejuvenated and is looking better than ever. Today it serves some of the most affordable fixed-price menus in central London, the heart of the city. Shunning the standard fare offered in most London-based Indian restaurants, Veeraswamy features authentic, freshly prepared dishes—the kind that would be served in a private Indian home. Try almost anything: spicy oysters, brochette of monkfish, or tender and flavorful lamb curry. One of our favorite dishes is lamb with turnips from Kashmir, flavored with large black cardamoms, powdered fennel, and a red chili powder, giving the dish a savory flavor and a vivid red color.

Victory House, 99 Regent St., W1. ☎ **020/7734-1401.** www.veeraswamy.com. Reservations recommended. Main courses £16–£21; lunch and pre-/post-theater menu Mon–Sat £38–£55; Sun 2- or 3-course set menus £22. AE, DC, MC, V. Mon–Fri 12:30–2:15pm and 5:30–10:30pm; Sat 12:30–2:30pm and 5:30–10:30pm; Sun 12:30–2:30pm and 6–10pm. Tube: Piccadilly Circus.

INEXPENSIVE

Balans MODERN BRITISH On one of London's most gay-friendly streets, Old Compton Street, Balans is the city's best-known gay restaurant and has been since its inauguration in 1993. Some diehard fans take all their meals here. Its extensive hours of service are almost without equal in London. Although the food is deemed "British," it is an eclectic cuisine, borrowing freely from whatever kitchen the chef chooses, from the Far East to America. For starters, try the smoked duck salad with quail eggs or pan-seared scallops with a cauliflower cheese gratin. Main dish temptations include pumpkin ravioli in a shallot and truffle sauce or swordfish steak with black-bean rice and a lime and coriander salsa. Rump of lamb is a tasty dish flavored with garlic and rosemary. Balans has a party pub atmosphere and is a good place to meet people.

60 Old Compton St., W1. 📞 **020/7439-2183.** www.balans.co.uk. Reservations recommended. Main courses £11–£17. AE, MC, V. Mon–Thurs 8am–5am; Fri–Sat 8am–6am; Sun 8am–2am. Tube: Piccadilly Circus or Leicester Sq.

Ed's Easy Diner AMERICAN   This is one of four branches of this popular retro American diner. It's the kind of place Michael J. Fox might have walked into in *Back to the Future*. Featuring 1950s and 1960s rock 'n' roll on the jukebox, a horseshoe-shaped counter with the kitchen in the middle, and a staff that fits the theme, the restaurant offers not only good diner staples such as burgers, onion rings, waffles, corned-beef hash, and cheesecake, but also good people-watching, with a broad cross-section of fashion trends on parade around the counter. The milkshakes and malts are popular items, as are the bowls of chili and five different types of fries with five sauces on the side. Other locations include Piccadilly and Leicester Square.

12 Moor St., W1. 📞 **020/7434-4439.** www.edseasydiner.co.uk. Reservations not accepted. Main courses £4.95–£6.35. Mon–Sat 10am–midnight; Sun 10am–11pm. Tube: Leicester Sq. or Tottenham Court Rd.

Masala Zone 🍴 INDIAN   One of the best, most popular, and most affordable Indian restaurants in the heart of London is this bustling eatery, serving authentic Indian home-style cookery. There's even a food-to-go concession if you've always wanted to sample Indian street fare from vendors. Order fresh Indian lemonade or a mango and coconut lassi while you study the menu. The noodle bowls are especially recommended, especially the chicken madras. The specialty, though, are their thalis, a balanced meal on a large platter with several bowls of different dishes, including chapatis (freshly made bread eaten in Indian homes).

9 Marshall St., W1. 📞 **020/7287-9966.** www.masalazone.com. Main courses £7–£11. MC, V. Mon–Fri noon–3:30pm and 5:30–11pm; Sat 12:30–11pm; Sun 12:30–3:30pm and 5–10:30pm. Tube: Oxford Circus.

Mildreds ★ 👜 VEGETARIAN   Mildreds may sound like a 1940s Joan Crawford movie, but it's one of London's most enduring vegetarian and vegan dining spots. It was vegetarian long before such restaurants became trendy. Jane Muir and Diane Thomas worked in various restaurants together before opening their own place. Today they run a busy, bustling diner with casual, friendly service. Sometimes it's a bit crowded and tables are shared. They do a mean series of delectable stir-fries. The ingredients in their dishes are organically grown, and they strongly emphasize the best seasonal produce. The menu changes daily but always features an array of homemade soups, casseroles, and salads. Organic wines are served, and portions are very large.

45 Lexington St., W1. 📞 **020/7494-1634.** www.mildreds.co.uk. Reservations not accepted. Main courses £7–£9.25. No credit cards. Mon–Sat noon–11pm. Tube: Tottenham Court Rd.

Yauatcha ★ ASIAN   This Asian eatery is a showcase for Alan Yau, who won Britain's first Michelin star for his Chinese cooking at London's Hakkasan. This is a more informal dim sum outlet where service is casual, and it's so popular you're practically rushed through your meal to make way for newly arriving patrons. But the food is worth it if you don't mind a slight hassle. The ground floor is a chic teahouse and patisserie, and the restaurant is in the basement. Dim sum, among the finest in London, is served for both lunch and dinner. The roast venison dim sum is spectacular. The prawn and date dumplings literally melt in your mouth. Other notable specialties include har gau—scallops and prawns with fish eggs or a pan-fried bean curd roll with prawns and yellow chives. The uniforms of the waiters are by Tim Yip, who won an Oscar for art direction in *Crouching Tiger, Hidden Dragon.*

15 Broadwick St., W1. ✆ **020/7494-8888.** www.yauatcha.com. Main courses £5–£24. AE, MC, V. Mon–Sat noon–midnight; Sat noon–11:45pm; Sun noon–10:30pm. Tube: Oxford Circus.

Trafalgar Square
MODERATE

The National Dining Rooms ENGLISH   In the National Gallery, this dining choice lies over the foyer of the Sainsbury Wing, providing a panoramic view of fabled Trafalgar Square. Classic dishes using market-fresh ingredients go into the starters such as warm watercress mousse with braised pearl onions or smoked mackerel pâté with apple and chicory. Try main dishes such as monkfish, mullet, and mussel stew or else baked lemon chicken with Savoy cabbage and creamed potatoes. The cheese selection from Great Britain is amazing in its variety, everything from traditionally aged Stilton to soft goat cheese from the Cotswolds. Finish off with one of the freshly baked cakes such as layered chocolate or walnut and banana. There is a cafe offshoot in the basement of the main building, which is a good choice for sandwiches, pastas, soups, and pastries.

In the National Gallery, Trafalgar Sq., WC2. ✆ **020/7747-2525.** www.peytonandbyrne.com. 2-course menu £23; 3-course menu £26. AE, MC, V. Thurs–Tues 10am–5:30pm; Wed 10am–8:45pm. Tube: Charing Cross.

The Portrait Restaurant ★ MODERN ENGLISH   This rooftop restaurant is a sought-after dining ticket on the fifth floor of the National Portrait Gallery's Ondaatje Wing. Along with the view (Nelson's Column, the London Eye, Big Ben, and the like), you get superb meals. Patrons usually go for lunch, not knowing that the chefs also cook on Thursday and Friday nights. In spring, there's nothing finer than the green English asparagus. All the main courses are filled with flavor. The high quality of the produce really shines through in such dishes as roast breast of guinea fowl with truffles and wild mushrooms, or pan-fried filet of Scotch salmon with bacon-and-onion potato cakes. For your "pudding," nothing is finer than steamed chestnut and honey pudding with toffee and pecan sauce. Chefs aren't afraid of simple preparations, mainly because they are assured of the excellence of their ingredients. The wine list features some organic choices.

In the National Portrait Gallery, Trafalgar Sq., WC2. ✆ **020/7312-2490.** www.searcys.co.uk/nationalportraitgallery/101/restaurant. Reservations recommended. 2-course meal £15, 3-course meal £19. AE, MC, V. Daily 11:45am–2:45pm; Thurs–Fri 5:30–8:30pm. Tube: Leicester Sq. or Charing Cross.

Mayfair
VERY EXPENSIVE

Alain Ducasse at the Dorchester ★★ FRENCH   In 2007, the maestro of upper-strata French cuisine reached across the Channel and planted a bulkhead in England with the establishment of this ultrachic corner of gastronomy.

Outfitted in tones of pastels and grays, it's rather startlingly arranged around a circular central table for six, which is surrounded with a translucent silk curtain and illuminated with a "waterfall" of illuminated fiber-optic cables. Collectively, it seems to conceal the patrons in a gauzy cloud. What, pray, does someone order in an environment this rarified? Consider prawns wrapped in a hot and spicy cocoon of seaweed; steamed crayfish with hearts of artichoke, served in a potato and truffle shell; steamed halibut with yogurt, spicy condiments, and beans; or a filet of beef Rossini-style, with seared foie gras, root veggies, and Perigueux sauce. Can you expect to see the maestro himself whipping up sauces in the kitchen? It's unlikely, since he's farmed many of the day-to-day operations to his long-term disciple, Jocelayn Herland. Nonetheless, he keeps a tight rein on the place from other parts of his empire.

On the lobby level of the Dorchester Hotel, Park Lane. ℂ 020/7629-8866. www.alainducasse-dorchester.com. Reservations required 2 weeks in advance. Set-price menus £75 for 3 courses, £95 for 4 courses, £115 for 7 courses. AE, DC, MC, V. Tues–Fri noon–2pm; Tues–Sat 6:30–10pm. Tube: Green Park, Hyde Park Corner, or Marble Arch.

Le Gavroche ★★★ FRENCH   Although challengers come and go, this luxurious "gastro-temple" remains the number-one choice in London for classical French cuisine. It may have fallen off briefly in the early 1990s, but it's fighting its way back to stellar ranks. There's always something special coming out of the kitchen of Michel Roux, Jr., the son of the chef who founded the restaurant in 1966. The service is faultless, and the ambience formally chic without being stuffy. The menu changes constantly, depending on the fresh produce that's available and the current inspiration of the chef. But it always remains classically French, though not of the "essentially old-fashioned bourgeois repertoire" that some critics suggest. Signature dishes honed over years of unswerving practice include the town's grandest cheese soufflé (Soufflé Suissesse); warm foie gras with crispy, cinnamon-flavored crepes; and Scottish filet of beef with port-wine sauce and truffled macaroni. Depending on availability, game is often served as well. A truly Gallic dish is the cassoulet of snails with frog thighs or the mousseline of lobster in a champagne sauce.

43 Upper Brook St., W1. ℂ **020/7408-0881.** Fax 020/7491-4387. www.le-gavroche.co.uk. Reservations required as far in advance as possible. Main courses £30–£60; fixed-price lunch £48; *Le Menu Exceptional* £95 without wine, £150 with wine. AE, MC, V. Mon–Fri noon–2pm; Mon–Sat 6:30–11pm. Tube: Marble Arch.

The Best Charcuterie in Mayfair

Born-to-shop aficionados who spend hours trawling Oxford Street, Bond Street, and South Moulton often retreat to **Truc Vert,** 42 North Audley St., W1 (ℂ **020/7491-9988;** www.trucvert. co.uk). This is a combination grocery store and dining room. In an elegantly casual atmosphere, it offers an array of some of the finest charcuterie products in Mayfair, along with cheese, wines, tasty sandwiches, salads, and daily quiches and soups. You can also order main courses from £15 to £18, or secure the makings of a picnic here. Make sure to try the chocolate-orange mousse tart. Open Monday to Friday 7:30am to 10pm, Saturday 9am to 10pm, Sunday 9am to 5pm. Tube: Bond Street.

Sketch ★★ CONTINENTAL/MODERN BRITISH   In a converted 18th-century building in Mayfair, Mourad ("Momo") Mazouz, along with a team of chefs and designers, masterminds this fashionable creation. You can come here to dine elegantly but also to bar-hop, as Sketch is actually a number of venues that, to confuse matters, change their agendas as the day progresses. For example, one section is an art gallery by day and "gastro-brasserie" by night. Whimsical and informal, the Parlour is for light lunches and delectable teas. In the Lecture Room and Library, each dish represents different sensations. The Art Gallery becomes a restaurant and bar at night. The East Bar is a popular late-night rendezvous, and the Glade is open for lunches and light snacks. The menu showcases a cuisine that is both bold and imaginative—and also delicious. For starters, you get fresh Tsarskaya oysters with lemon, shallots, vinegar, and warm rye bread pudding. The fresh pumpkin soup is always invigorating, and the well-flavored, tender lamb is served with a beet-root cake, white cabbage, and dried fruits.

9 Conduit St., W1. ✆ 020/7659-4500. www.sketch.uk.com. Reservations essential for dining. Main courses £15–£30; snacks and small meals £8–£24. Lecture Room and Library 3-course fixed-price dinner £35; 7-course vegetarian fixed-price dinner £70. AE, MC, V. Art Gallery Mon–Sat 7pm–2am (last food order 11pm Mon–Wed and 1am Thurs–Sat). Lecture Room and Library Tues–Fri noon–2:30pm and Tues–Sat 6:30–10:30pm. Parlour Mon–Fri 8am–9pm; Sat 10am–9pm. The Glade Mon–Sat noon–3pm. East Bar daily 6:30pm–2am. Tube: Oxford Circus.

The Square ★★★ FRENCH   Hip, chic, casual, sleek, and modern, the Square still isn't scaring Le Gavroche as a competitor for first place on London's dining circuit, but it is certainly a restaurant to visit on a serious London gastronomic tour. Chef Philip Howard delivers the goods at this excellent restaurant. You get creative, personalized cuisine in a cosseting atmosphere with abstract modern art on the walls. The chef has a magic touch, with such concoctions as a starter of terrine of partridge with smoked foie gras and pear with cider jelly, or else a lasagna of Cornish crab with a champagne foam. For a main course we urge you to try the peppered aged rib-eye of Ayrshire beef with smoked shallots, Tuscan snails, and a red-wine sauce, or else the roast saddle of hare with port-glazed endive. The fish dishes, such as steamed turbot with buttered langoustine claws and poached oysters, are always fresh, and Bresse pigeon is as good as it is in its hometown in France.

6-10 Bruton St., W1. ✆ 020/7495-7100. www.squarerestaurant.org. Reservations required. Fixed-price lunch £60–£75, dinner £100. AE, DC, MC, V. Mon–Fri noon–3pm; Mon–Sat 6:30–10:45pm; Sun 6:30–10pm. Tube: Bond St. or Green Park.

EXPENSIVE

Corrigan's Mayfair ★★ 🍴 BRITISH-MODERN   Exclusive Mayfair has become the latest home for the acclaimed Irish chef Richard Corrigan. The press has hailed him for "redefining" the concept of a quintessential British cuisine, combining the best of seasonal produce with his vast and imaginative culinary skills. His fixed-price lunches offer exceptional value. The chef offers one of the best list of starters in Mayfair, everything from octopus carpaccio to rose veal tongue with wild celery and truffles. A selection of market-fresh fish is also presented daily—try the steamed sea bass and bouillabaisse for a real treat. Corrigan is especially adept at his meat selections, and is skilled at game dishes such as poached pheasant, venison chop (with a serving of rhubarb), or saddle of wild rabbit with dates and orange segments.

28 Upper Grosvenor St., W1. ✆ **020/7499-9943.** Reservations required. Main courses £22–£28. AE, DC, MC, V. Mon–Fri noon–3pm and 6–11pm; Sat 6–11pm; Sun noon–4pm and 6–9:30pm. Tube: Marble Arch.

Greenhouse EUROPEAN   Head chef Antonin Bonnet is inspired, producing first-class dishes without destroying the natural flavor of his ingredients. Regrettably, all this good food comes at a price, and the Greenhouse is no longer the moderate restaurant it used to be but rather an expensive one.

Peerless technique goes into such starters as Cornish crab with coconut dressing, or shellfish flavored with kaffir lime leaves. Fine ingredients are also reflected in the main dishes such as Limousin filet of beef flavored with mustard and served with fondant potatoes. The Shetland organic cod appears with hummus, and a Bresse mallard duckling comes with spicy endives and an orange marmalade. For many diners, cheese is their dessert specialty; it's one of the largest selections in London. You can order yummy confections as well. The menu is backed up by a very large wine list with some 500 selections.

27A Hays Mews, W1. ✆ **020/7499-3331.** www.greenhouserestaurant.co.uk. Reservations required. 3-course fixed-price dinner £70; fixed-price lunch £25–£29. AE, DC, MC, V. Mon–Fri noon–2:30pm; Mon–Sat 6:45–11pm. Closed Christmas and bank holidays. Tube: Green Park.

hush CONTINENTAL   It's charming, it's trendy, and it's a retreat with lots of attractive people and not a tourist in sight; hush is one of a number of outdoor restaurants in a cul-de-sac. The terrace outside on a summer day seats up to 60 and offers some of London's best alfresco dining. On the ground floor expect a chic decor with a combination of lightwood tables and limestone floors, the color provided by "warm" spice colors. The well-chosen menu features traditional brasserie food—in this case, such items as smoked haddock fishcakes, lobster and chips with garlic butter, and most definitely the Hush Hamburger, which some critics have hailed as the best in London. Start with Andalusian gazpacho or a meze platter (a selection of Greek hors d'oeuvres). Such classic dishes are offered as sautéed calves' liver or Toulouse sausages with creamed potatoes and a mustard sauce. The desserts are hard to resist, especially the champagne jelly with mixed berries or the lemon cheesecake with raspberries.

8 Lancashire Court, Brook St., W1. ✆ **020/7659-1500.** www.hush.co.uk. Reservations recommended. Fixed-price menus £35–£55; brasserie main courses £9–£24. AE, DC, MC, V. Restaurant daily noon–3pm and 6:30–11pm. Brasserie Mon–Fri 7:30am–11pm; Sat noon–11pm; Sun noon–4pm. Bar daily 11am–midnight. Tube: Bond St.

L'Autre Pied ★★ CONTINENTAL   A young chef, Marcus Eaves, showcases his modern Continental cuisine at this restaurant ideal for Bond Street shoppers. The decor is sort of retro, but not the cuisine. Eaves likes "foams" and purées, and his menus are tantalizing. One of the best examples of his style of cuisine is a delectable red mullet with flap mushrooms and Jerusalem artichokes. For a whole table, he'll prepare a tasting menu of seven courses, including such delights as roasted breast of Gressingham duck with a carrot and orange purée. For dessert, you might try the rhubarb and pistachio crumble with rhubarb sorbet.

5-7 Blandford St., W1. ✆ **020/7486-9696.** www.lautrepied.co.uk. Reservations required. Fixed-price lunch or pretheater (6–7pm) set menu £18 for 2 courses, £21 for 3 courses; main courses £22–£30; tasting menu £55 per person. AE, MC, V. Mon–Fri noon–2:45pm; Sat noon–2:30pm; Sun noon–3:30pm; Mon–Sat 6–10:45pm (Sun until 9:30pm). Tube: Bond St.

Maze ★★ INTERNATIONAL   Gordon Ramsay may be the leading chef of London, but our nominee for the most promising chef is Jason Atherton, a one-time protégé of Ramsay. Atherton learned his master's secrets and has plenty of creative culinary imagination all on his own. One reviewer claimed Atherton combined "Spain's progressive technique with Gallic voluptuousness and a dash of British wit." And so he does. His combinations may sound a bit bizarre, but the resulting flavors and ingredients taste sublime.

He's a chef that appeals to "grazers" (that is, those diners liking a series of small plates or tapas). The changing seasons are reflected by what rests on your plate. In a New York–inspired interior by the American architect David Rockwell, Atherton enthralls with dish after dish. Take his starters: Go for the Orkney scallops roasted with spices and served with a peppered golden raisin purée, or else the foie gras marinated in pinot noir. For a main, we'd recommend the roasted partridge with plum preserves or the roast Scottish filet of beef with Landes foie gras and an ox-cheek cottage pie.

10–13 Grosvenor Sq., W1. ✆ **020/7107-0000.** www.gordonramsay.com. Reservations required. Fixed-price lunch £29–£43; main dishes (small platters) £13–£14. AE, DC, MC, V. Daily noon–2:30pm and 6–10:30pm. Tube: Bond St.

Nobu ★★ JAPANESE   London's innovative restaurant, a celebrity haunt, owes much to its founders, actor Robert De Niro and chef Nobu Matsuhisa. The kitchen staff is brilliant and as finely tuned as their New York counterparts. The sushi chefs create gastronomic pyrotechnics. Those on the see-and-be-seen circuit don't seem to mind the high prices that go with these incredibly fresh dishes. Elaborate preparations lead to perfectly balanced flavors. Where else can you find an excellent sea urchin tempura? Salmon tartare with caviar is a brilliant appetizer. Follow with a perfectly done filet of sea bass in a sour bean paste or soft-shell crab rolls. The squid pasta is sublime, as is the incredibly popular suki-yaki. Cold sake arrives in a green bamboo pitcher.

In the Metropolitan Hotel, 19 Old Park Lane, W1. ✆ **020/7447-4747.** www.noburestaurants.com. Reservations required 1 month in advance. Main courses £11–£33; sushi and sashimi £3–£8.25 per piece; fixed-price lunch £26, dinner £11–£33. AE, DC, MC, V. Mon–Fri noon–2:15pm and 6–10:15pm; Sat–Sun 12:30–2:30pm; Sat 6–11pm; Sun 6–9:30pm. Tube: Hyde Park Corner.

Scott's ★★ SEAFOOD   In business after a long slumber, Scott's has regained its position as one of London's great seafood restaurants. Opened as an oyster warehouse in 1851 by a young fishmonger, John Scott, the restaurant first earned its fame at its Haymarket site where it resided until 1968. Now filled with cosmopolitan glitter in Mayfair, it doesn't rest on its long-ago fame but has made its reputation anew.

Once a favorite of Ian Fleming, creator of the James Bond character, it was the setting in the '50s and '60s where he discovered the dry martini—"shaken, not stirred." It is dear to the seafood lover's heart, from market-fresh Dover sole to "cockles and mussels." Always ask about the fresh catch of the day, or else order filet of halibut with chervil butter or Scottish lobster thermidor. For meat eaters there's rib steak or braised pork cheeks.

20 Mount St., W1. ✆ **020/7495-7309.** www.scotts-restaurant.com. Reservations required. Main courses £16–£40. AE, DC, MC, V. Mon–Sat noon–10:30pm; Sun noon–10pm. Tube: Green Park or Bond St.

Tamarind ★ INDIAN   In favor with critics as well as the lunchtime business crowd, Tamarind is the most popular Indian restaurant in Mayfair. The basement dining room has gold pillars and a tandoor window so that you can watch the chefs pull their flavorful dishes from the ovens. Chef Alfred Prasad leads a culinary brigade from Delhi that maintains the style of cooking they knew at home. The team selects the best, freshest ingredients in the markets each day. The kitchen prides itself on nouvelle dishes but also excels at traditional Indian fare. The monkfish marinated in saffron and yogurt is delectable, and the mixed kabob platter, with all the kabobs cooked in a charcoal-fired tandoor, is extraordinary— these chefs are the kings of kabobs. Your best bet for a curry? Opt for the prawns in a five-spice mixture. Vegetarians will find refuge here, especially if they go for the *dal Bukhari,* a black-lentil specialty of northwest India.

20–22 Queen St., W1. ✆ **020/7629-3561.** www.tamarindrestaurant.com. Reservations required. Main courses £13–£26; fixed-price dinner menu £56; 3-course fixed-price lunch £15–£25. AE, DC, DISC, MC, V. Sun–Fri noon–2:45pm; Mon–Sat 6–11:30pm; Sun 6:30–10:30pm. Tube: Green Park.

Theo Randall at the InterContinental ★★ ITALIAN   No longer the head chef at the River Café, where he made a name for himself, Theo Randall now operates from this namesake restaurant at this swanky Mayfair hotel. His dishes represent some of the best of northern Italian fare, and are deliberately rustic, although the upmarket decor might be described as "corporate." Randall is a disciple of the famed chef Alice Waters and her belief in fresh food. "My menu is always determined by what's at the market that morning," he said. Only after shopping does he print his menu for the day, including such sublime dishes as the custard-like buffalo mozzarella in a spinach ravioli. Other best examples of his cuisine include a fleshy seabass roasted in a wood-burning oven or slow-cooked shoulder of lamb with polenta. For starters, try, if featured, the fresh crab with herb aioli and garlic bruschetta.

In the InterContinental Hotel, 1 Hamilton Place, W1. ✆ **020/7318-8747.** www.theorandall.com. Reservations required. Main courses £10–£34. AE, DC, MC, V. Mon–Fri noon–3:30pm and 6–11pm; Sat 6–11pm. Tube: Hyde Park Corner.

MODERATE

Hard Rock Cafe ☺ AMERICAN   This is the original Hard Rock, and it's served more than 12 million people since it opened in 1971. Just like every other Hard Rock Cafe, there's usually a line (or, in this case, a queue) of people waiting to get in, plus an equally long line of people buying T-shirts. You'll find better-than-average burgers and a good selection of beers here. The collection of rock memorabilia at the original is a far sight better than the collections at later facsimiles. The restaurant also accepts U.S. dollars.

150 Old Park Lane, W1. ✆ **020/7514-1700.** www.hardrock.com. Reservations not accepted. Main courses £8–£21. AE, DC, MC, V. Sun–Thurs 11:30am–12:30am; Fri–Sat 11:30am–1am. Closed Dec 25–26. Tube: Green Park or Hyde Park Corner.

Langan's Brasserie FRENCH/TRADITIONAL BRITISH   In its heyday in the early 1980s, this was one of the hippest restaurants in London, and the upscale brasserie still welcomes an average of 700 diners a day. The 1976 brainchild of actor Michael Caine and chef Richard Shepherd, Langan's sprawls over two noisy floors filled with potted plants and ceiling fans that create a 1930s feel.

The menu is "mostly English with a French influence," and includes spinach soufflé with anchovy sauce, quail eggs in a pastry case served with a sautéed hash of mushrooms and hollandaise sauce, and prawn salad with Marie-Rose sauce. There's also a selection of English pub fare, including bangers and mash, and fish and chips. The dessert menu is a journey into nostalgia: bread-and-butter pudding, treacle tart with custard, apple pie with clotted cream . . . wait, how did mango sorbet slip in here?

Stratton St., W1. ℭ 020/7491-8822. www.langansrestaurants.co.uk. Reservations recommended. Main courses £14–£20. AE, DC, MC, V. Mon–Thurs 12:15–11pm; Fri and Sat 12:15–11:30pm. Tube: Green Park.

Momo MOROCCAN/NORTH AFRICAN   You'll be greeted here by a friendly, casual staff member, and the setting is like Marrakesh, with stucco walls, a wood-and-stone floor, patterned wood window shades, burning candles, and banquettes. You can fill up on the freshly baked bread, along with appetizers such as garlicky marinated olives and pickled carrots spiced with pepper and cumin—all gifts from the chef. Other appetizers are also tantalizing, especially the *briouat:* paper-thin and very crisp triangular packets of puffed pastry filled with saffron-flavored chicken and other treats. One of the chef's specialties is *pastilla au pigeon,* a traditional poultry pie with almonds. Many diners visit for the *couscous maison,* among the best in London. Served in a decorative pot, this aromatic dish of raisins, meats (including merguez sausage), chicken, lamb, and chickpeas is given added flavor with *marissa,* a powerful hot sauce from the Middle East. There is also a tearoom and a bazaar based on a Moroccan souk, plus a terrace in summer. The on-site Kemia Bar serves Arabic tapas—called Kemia—for £4 to £6 per dish.

25 Heddon St., W1. ℭ **020/7434-4040.** www.momoresto.com. Reservations required. Main courses £15–£42; fixed-price lunch £15–£19. AE, DC, MC, V. Mon–Sat noon–2:30pm and 6:30–11:30pm; Sun 6:30–11pm. Tube: Piccadilly Circus or Oxford Circus.

Wild Honey ★ EUROPEAN   In the gilded environs of Mayfair, chef Anthony Demetre rules in the oak-paneled former digs of a gentleman's club. Those gents never ate food like that served here. The chef is at the top of his form, treating fresh local products with loving care as he fashions them into temptations for your palate. The menu specializes in game, but other dishes are equally fine, including English snails scattered over a thick pancake. Another specialty is buttery Scottish Buccleuch beef. Roast Norfolk hare appears with caramelized endive; the wild duck with Armagnac sauce, and line-caught cod with Cornish cockles. Finish with the namesake "Wild Honey" ice cream with the actual honeycomb.

12 St. George St., WC1. ℭ **020/7758-9160.** www.wildhoneyrestaurant.co.uk. Reservations required. Main courses £14–£27. AE, MC, V. Mon–Sat noon–2:30pm and 6–11pm; Sun noon–3pm and 6–10:30pm. Tube: Oxford Circus, Bond St., Green Park, or Piccadilly Circus.

INEXPENSIVE

Automat ★ AMERICAN   The famous faces who flocked to this Mayfair eatery when it opened aren't seen too much anymore, but a clientele of Yankees patronizes the modern precincts, enjoying everything from macaroni and cheese to a soft-shell po' boy sandwich with fries. Some of the best U.S. beef in London is also offered, including New York strip sirloin. London food critics have called it "Mayfair's slice of the Big Apple," after digging into the crab cakes with guacamole or the chili con carne. Salad is a wedge of iceberg lettuce with blue-cheese dressing. Perhaps the most popular item on the menu is the Automat hamburger with fries.

33 Dover St., W1. ℂ **020/7499-3033.** www.automat-london.com. Reservations recommended. Main courses £8–£28. AE, DC, MC, V. Mon–Fri 7–11am and noon–3pm; Sat–Sun 11am–4pm; Mon–Sat 6pm–midnight. Tube: Green Park.

Leon ★ 🍴 MEDITERRANEAN   Its biggest fans call it "gourmet fast food." While gourmet it is not, this is a great place to just sit and eat without being rushed during a day of shopping on Oxford Street. It does what its nearby competitors don't do: It produces fresh, wholesome food at affordable prices. Everything is freshly cooked, and that means certain dishes may be variable, but we find ourselves returning in spite of a flaw here and there. Everything on the menu is fresh, often organic. The salads, chicken nuggets, and hearty stews are good. The nuggets are made with succulent breast meat and doused in a creamy yogurt-and-garlic sauce. Even the chili con carne is different. It's a bowl of spicy, tender minced beef with black kidney beans, and is served with a fluffy organic brown rice speckled with pumpkin, sunflower, and sesame seeds, and accompanied by a tasty cabbage and beet slaw. Your drink of choice might be a ginger and carrot juice. Save room for the chocolate brownie "zinged" up with orange zest and swaddled in sinful scoops of ice cream made from Jersey cream. Leon is also the best place in the area for breakfast—try the organic porridge.

35 Great Marlborough St., W1. ℂ **020/7437-5280.** Reservations not required. Breakfast from £2.50; main courses £5.10–£7. AE, MC, V. Mon–Fri 8am–10:30pm; Sat 9:30am–10:30pm; Sun 10:30am–6:30pm. Tube: Oxford Circus.

Suze PACIFIC RIM   The owners of this wine bar attach equal importance to their food and to their impressive wine list. On the ground floor, you can enjoy fine wines along with a well-chosen selection of bar food. Upon your arrival, a basket of homemade bread, along with olives, goat cheese, salami, and roasted peppers, is placed before you. The menu has been upgraded and made more sophisticated and appealing. Begin perhaps with the timbale of plum tomato and peppercorn mousse with an avocado salad, or else New Zealand green shell mussels with lime leaf, coriander, and ginger broth. For a main we'd suggest fresh Australian fish with chips and a salad, or New Zealand lamb filet with a vegetable medley.

41 N. Audley St., W1 (btw. Upper Brook and Oxford sts.). ℂ **020/7491-3237.** www.suze inmayfair.com. Reservations recommended. Main courses £11–£32. AE, MC, V. Mon–Sat noon–11pm. Tube: Bond St.

St. James's

MODERATE

Greens Restaurant & Oyster Bar INTERNATIONAL/SEAFOOD/TRADITIONAL BRITISH   Critics say it's a triumph of tradition over taste, but as far as seafood in London goes, this is a tried-and-true favorite, thanks to an excellent menu with moderately priced dishes, a central location, and a charming staff. This place has a cluttered entrance leading to a crowded bar where you can sip fine wines and, from September to April, enjoy oysters. The oyster bar is run by Simon Parker-Bowles, Camilla's ex-brother-in-law. In the faux-Dickensian dining room, you can choose from a long menu of fresh seafood dishes, which changes monthly depending on what is in season. Starters are vibrant, yet earthy fare, including Dorset crab salad, potted shrimp with whole meal toast, and pan-fried foie gras with apple purée. The chefs are at the top of their form in turning out such mains as seafood platters, filet of halibut with a mussel veloute, or grilled Dover sole with hollandaise sauce. Meat dishes are also superb, including rump of lamb with roast garlic polenta or steak tartare.

36 Duke St., St. James's, SW1. ℂ **020/7930-4566.** www.greens.org.uk. Reservations required. Main courses £17–£48; most dishes are moderately priced. AE, DC, MC, V. Mon–Sat 11:30am–3pm and 5:30–11pm. Tube: Green Park.

Quaglino's ★ CONTINENTAL   Come here for fun, not culinary subtlety and finesse, and be prepared to wear your best duds. In 1993, noted restaurateur and designer Sir Terence Conran brought this restaurant—first established in 1929 by Giovanni Quaglino—into the postmodern age with a vital new decor. Menu items have been criticized for their quick preparation and standard format; but considering that on some nights up to 800 people might show up, the marvel is that this place functions as well as it does. That's not to say there isn't an occasional delay. The menu changes often, but your choice of an appetizer might include wild mushroom and truffle soup or else a goat-cheese tart with caramelized onions. You can settle for an old favorite for a main dish—haddock and chips—or else go for the whole roasted sea bass with braised fennel. Their oyster selection is one of the best in central London. Although some diners shy away from organ meats these days, the English still order calves' liver with bacon here. Desserts are mostly favorites such as apple and blackberry crumble or sticky toffee pudding with walnut ice cream. ***Note:*** A mezzanine with bar features live jazz every night and Sunday at lunch.

16 Bury St., SW1. ℂ **020/7930-6767.** www.quaglinos.co.uk. Reservations recommended. Main courses £14–£55; fixed-price menu (available only for lunch and pretheater dinner from 5:30–6:30pm) 2 courses £15, 3 courses £20. AE, DC, MC, V. Daily noon–3pm; Mon–Thurs 5:30pm–midnight; Fri–Sat 5:30pm–1am; Sun 5:30–11pm. Tube: Green Park.

The Wolseley ★★ CONTINENTAL   Two of London's top restaurateurs, Jeremy King and Chris Corbin, formerly of the Ivy, offer one of the finest and most serviceable restaurants in London. With its vaulted ceilings and pillars, polished marble, wrought-iron chandeliers, and Art Deco interior, the Wolseley recalls a Viennese cafe, but for much of the past century it was a bank and later an automobile showroom. Now it's the idyllic spot for afternoon tea (second only to the Palm Court of the Ritz Hotel). We often duck out of our hotel for breakfast here (served from 7am), ordering such old favorites as fried duck eggs with Ayrshire bacon or smoked fish cakes with poached eggs. There is an all-day menu offering light fare. For dinner, the menu grows more elaborate, including such dishes as Weiner Holstein with fried egg and anchovies, grilled lobster with butter, and even roast Landaise chicken with Lyonnaise potatoes. A specialty is the spit-roasted suckling pig with apple sauce. The most expensive breakfast (see below) features caviar.

160 Piccadilly, St. James's, W1. ℂ **020/7499-6996.** www.thewolseley.com. Reservations required. Main courses £10–£29; afternoon tea £9.75–£20; breakfast £2.75–£53. AE, DC, MC, V. Mon–Fri 7am–midnight; Sat 8am–midnight; Sun 8am–11pm. Tube: Green Park.

WESTMINSTER & VICTORIA

Expensive

Shepherd's TRADITIONAL BRITISH   Some observers claim that many of the inner workings of the English government operate from the precincts of this conservative, likable restaurant. Set in the shadow of Big Ben, it enjoys a regular clientele of barristers, members of Parliament, and their constituents from far-flung districts. So synchronized is this place to the goings-on at Parliament that a Division Bell rings in the dining room, calling MPs back to the House of Commons when it's time to vote. Even the decor is designed to make them feel at home, with leather banquettes, sober 19th-century accessories, and a worthy collection of European portraits and landscapes.

The menu reflects years of English culinary tradition, and dishes are prepared intelligently, with fresh ingredients. In addition to the classic roast, dishes include a cream-based mussel stew; hot salmon-and-potato salad with dill dressing; salmon and prawn fish cakes in spinach sauce; and roast leg of lamb with mint sauce.

Marsham Court, Marsham St. (at the corner of Page St.), SW1. ✆ **020/7834-9552.** Reservations recommended. Fixed-price menu 2 courses £33, 3 courses £37. AE, DC, MC, V. Mon–Fri 12:15–2:45pm and 6:30–11pm (last order at 11pm). Tube: Pimlico or St. James's.

Moderate

Rex Whistler ★★ 🕊 MODERN BRITISH   The Tate Britain's restaurant is particularly attractive to wine fanciers. It offers what may be the best bargains for superior wines anywhere in Britain. Bordeaux and burgundies are in abundance, and the management keeps the markup between 40% and 65%, rather than the 100% to 200% added in most restaurants. In fact, the prices here are lower than they are in most wine shops. Wine begins at £15 per bottle, or £4 per glass. Oenophiles frequently come for lunch. The restaurant offers an English menu that changes about every month. Dishes might include pheasant casserole, pan-fried skate with black butter and capers, and vegetarian selections. One critic found the staff and diners as traditional "as a Gainsborough landscape." Access to the restaurant is through the museum's main entrance on Millbank.

Tate Britain, Millbank, SW1. ✆ **020/7887-8825.** www.tate.org.uk. Reservations recommended. 2-course fixed-price menu £16; 3-course fixed-price menu £20; breakfast from £3.95; afternoon tea £7.25. AE, DC, MC, V. Mon–Fri 11:30am–3pm; Sat–Sun 10am–3pm; daily 3:30–5pm for afternoon tea. Tube: Pimlico. Bus: 77 or 88.

Inexpensive

Jenny Lo's Teahouse CANTONESE/SZECHUAN   London's noodle dives don't get much better than this. Before its decline, Ken Lo's Memories of China offered the best Chinese dining in London. The late Ken Lo, whose grandfather was the Chinese ambassador to the court of St. James, made his reputation as a cookbook author. Jenny Lo is Ken's daughter, and her father taught her many of his culinary secrets. Belgravia matrons and young professionals come here for perfectly prepared, reasonably priced fare. Ken Lo cookbooks contribute to the dining room decor of black refectory tables set with paper napkins and chopsticks. Opt for such fare as a vermicelli rice noodle dish (a large plate of noodles

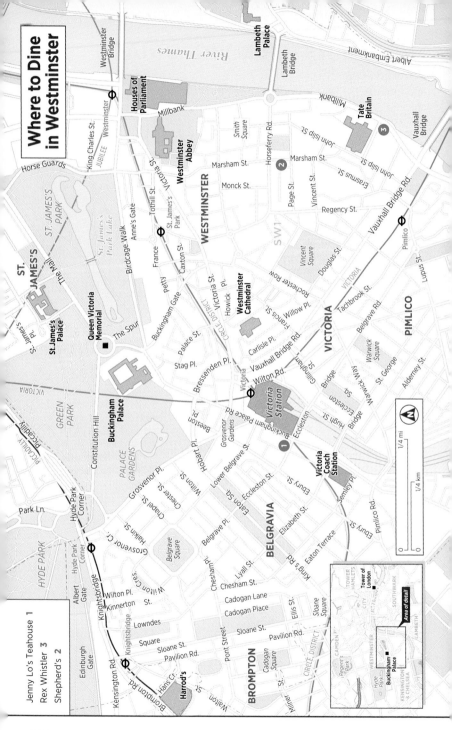

Where to Dine in Westminster

Jenny Lo's Teahouse **1**
Rex Whistler **3**
Shepherd's **2**

River Thames

Lambeth Palace

Westminster Bridge

Houses of Parliament

Millbank

Lambeth Bridge

Albert Embankment

Tate Britain **3**

Vauxhall Bridge

Horse Guards

King Charles St.

Westminster

JUBILEE

Smith Square

Horseferry Rd.

John Islip St.

Millbank

Westminster Abbey

Marsham St.

Marsham St. **2**

Erasmus St.

John Islip St.

Vauxhall Bridge Rd.

ST. JAMES'S PARK

St. James's Park Lake

The Mall

Birdcage Walk

Anne's Gate

St. James's Park

Tothill St.

Victoria St.

France

Caxton St.

WESTMINSTER

Monck St.

Page St.

Vincent St.

Regency St.

Pimlico

SW1

VICTORIA

St. James's Palace

St. James's Pl.

ST. JAMES'S

Queen Victoria Memorial

St. James's Park

Buckingham Gate

Petty France

Palace St.

CIRCLE, DISTRICT

Victoria St.

Howick Pl.

Westminster Cathedral

Carlisle Pl.

Francis St.

Willow Pl.

Vauxhall Bridge Rd.

Vincent Square

Rochester Row

Douglas St.

VICTORIA

Tachbrook St.

Belgrave Rd.

PIMLICO

Lupus St.

GREEN PARK

PICCADILLY

Constitution Hill

PALACE GARDENS

The Spur

Buckingham Palace

Stag Pl.

Bressenden Pl.

Beeston Pl.

Victoria St.

Wilton Rd.

Gillingham St.

Victoria Station **1**

Eccleston Bridge

Hugh St.

Warwick Square

St. George

Warwick Way

St. George's Sq.

Alderney St.

VICTORIA

Hyde Park Corner

Park Ln.

Park Lane

Hyde Park Corner

Grosvenor Cr.

Halkin St.

Grosvenor Pl.

Chapel St.

Chester St.

Wilton St.

Hobart Pl.

Grosvenor Gardens

Buckingham Palace Rd.

Lower Belgrave St.

Eccleston St.

Eaton Sq.

Belgrave Pl.

Ebury St.

Elizabeth St.

Eccleston St.

Victoria Coach Station

Sennley Pl.

Ebury St.

Pimlico Rd.

HYDE PARK

Albert Gate

Edinburgh Gate

Hyde Park Corner

Knightsbridge

Wilton Pl.

Kinnerton St.

Lowndes Square

Sloane St.

Pavilion Rd.

Belgrave Square

Chesham Pl.

Chesham St.

Lyall St.

BELGRAVIA

King's Rd.

Eaton Terrace

Cadogan Lane

Cadogan Place

Ellis St.

Sloane Square

Sloane St.

Pont Street

Cadogan Square

Pavilion Rd.

Kensington Rd.

Brompton Rd.

Hans Cr.

Walton St.

Harrod's

BROMPTON

CIRCLE, DISTRICT

Minera St.

Sloane St.

Minera

Regent's Park

CAMDEN

TOWER HAMLETS

Tower of London

CITY

SOUTHWARK

Area of detail

WESTMINSTER

Buckingham Palace

KENSINGTON & CHELSEA

LAMBETH

1/4 mi

1/4 km

0

0

topped with grilled chicken breast and Chinese mushrooms) or white noodles with minced pork. Rounding out the menu are stuffed Peking dumplings, chili-garnished spicy prawns, and wonton soup with slithery dumplings. The black bean–seafood noodle dish is a delight, as is the chili-beef soup.

14 Eccleston St., SW1. ☎ 020/7259-0399. Reservations not accepted. Main courses £6.95–£8.50. No credit cards. Mon–Fri noon–3pm; Mon–Sat 6–10pm. Tube: Victoria Station.

KNIGHTSBRIDGE TO SOUTH KENSINGTON

Knightsbridge

VERY EXPENSIVE

Marcus Wareing at the Berkeley ★★★ FRENCH   Clubby and not at all stuffy, this is the domain of Marcus Wareing, a former boxer from Lancashire. The restaurant serves a modern French cuisine in the grand tradition of Wareing's mentor (and London's hottest chef) Gordon Ramsay. You'll find excellent food prepared with market-fresh ingredients and technical precision, even a touch of whimsy, served in an opulent setting. The chef's set reflects his culinary ambitions. Start with tea-smoked mackerel and a duck-egg tart or else pan-fried foie gras with glazed black figs and hazelnuts. For your main, perhaps try the wild sea bass with sea urchin or the Dorset turbot with frogs' legs and lemon confit.

In the Berkeley Hotel, Wilton Place, SW1. ☎ 020/7235-1200. www.the-berkeley.co.uk. Reservations required. Fixed-price menu £75. AE, MC, V. Mon–Fri noon–2:30pm; Mon–Sat 6–11pm. Tube: Knightsbridge.

Zafferano ★★ ITALIAN   There's something honest and satisfying about this restaurant, where decor consists of little more than ochre-colored walls, immaculate linens, and a bevy of diligent staff members. The modernized interpretation of Italian cuisine features such dishes as ravioli of pheasant with black truffles, wild pigeon with garlic purée, sea bream with spinach and balsamic vinegar, and monkfish with almonds. Other choice dishes include linguine with lobster and fresh tomatoes or a crayfish risotto. The owners pride themselves on one of the most esoteric and well-rounded collections of Italian wine in London: You'll find as many as 20 different vintages each of Brunello and Barolo and about a dozen vintages of Sassecaia.

15 Lowndes St., SW1. ☎ 020/7235-5800. www.zafferanorestaurant.com. Reservations required. Main courses £17–£25; set-price dinner menu £35–£55. AE, MC, V. Mon–Fri noon–2:30pm; Sat–Sun 12:30–3pm; daily 7–11pm (until 10:30pm Sun). Tube: Knightsbridge.

EXPENSIVE

Amaya ★ INDIAN   This chic restaurant, a hot dining ticket, is credited with introducing the small-plates concept to Indian food. Dishes are shared, hopefully with a party of friends. This is no mere curry house, but an ambitious restaurant with skilled chefs standing over grills and tandoor ovens in the eye-catching open kitchen. After devouring the rock oysters in a ginger-studded coconut sauce, we knew we were in for a special meal. Our table shared grilled baby eggplant sprinkled with mango powder. Chicken tikka is one of the signature dishes, the lamb chops are fork tender, and the lobster beautifully spiced. Vegetarians delight in the tandoor-cooked broccoli in a yogurt sauce or artichoke biryani (basmati rice

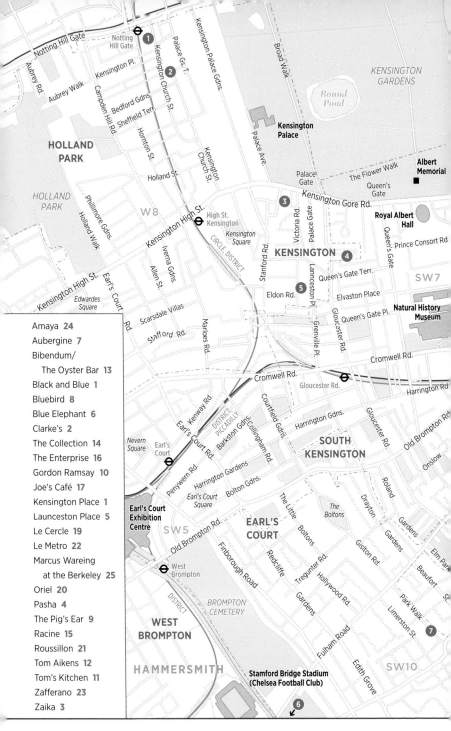

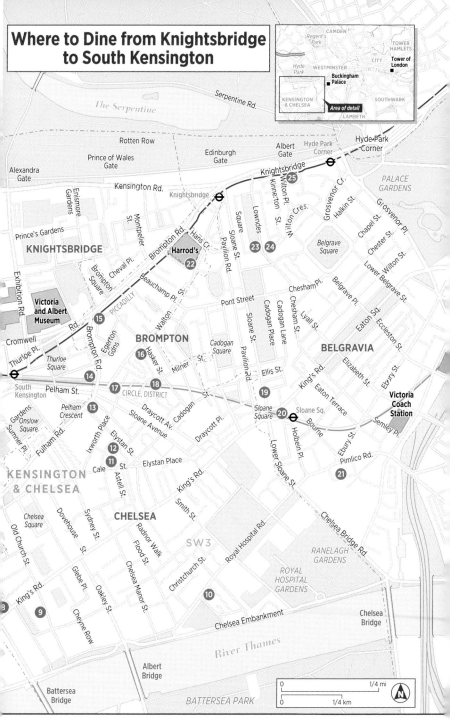

Where to Dine from Knightsbridge to South Kensington

The Serpentine

Serpentine Rd.

Rotten Row

Prince of Wales Gate

Edinburgh Gate

Albert Gate

Hyde Park Corner

Hyde Park Corner

PALACE GARDENS

Alexandra Gate

Knightsbridge — 25

Kensington Rd.

Kinnerton St.

Wilton Pl.

Grosvenor Cr.

Halkin St.

Grosvenor Pl.

Exhibition Rd.

Enismore Gardens

Knightsbridge

Square

Lowndes

Wilton Cres.

Wilton St.

Chapel St.

Chester St.

Lower Belgrave St.

Prince's Gardens

KNIGHTSBRIDGE

Montpelier

Brompton Rd.

Hans Cr.

Sloane St.

Pavilion Rd.

23 24

Belgrave Square

Belgrave Pl.

Lower Belgrave St.

Cheval Pl.

Harrod's 22

Chesham Pl.

Lyall St.

Eaton Sq.

Eccleston St.

Victoria and V&A Museum

Brompton Square

Beauchamp Pl.

PICCADILLY

Walton St.

Pont Street

Cadogan Lane

Cadogan Place

Chesham St.

BELGRAVIA

Cromwell Rd.

15

Egerton Gdns.

BROMPTON

Hasker St.

Milner St.

Cadogan Square

Sloane St.

Pavilion Rd.

King's Rd.

Elizabeth St.

Ebury St.

Thurloe Pl.

Thurloe Square

16

Ellis St.

Eaton Terrace

South Kensington

14

Pelham St.

17 18 CIRCLE, DISTRICT

Draycott Av.

Cadogan St.

Sloane Square 19

20 Sloane Sq.

Bourne

Victoria Coach Station

Semley Pl.

Gardens

Onslow Square

Pelham Crescent

13

Ixworth Place

Sloane Avenue

Holbein Pl.

Ebury St.

Summer Pl.

Fulham Rd.

12

Elystan St.

11

Cale St.

Elystan Place

King's Rd.

Lower Sloane St.

Pimlico Rd.

21

KENSINGTON & CHELSEA

Astell St.

Smith St.

Chelsea Square

Dovehouse St.

Sydney St.

CHELSEA

Radnor Walk

SW 3

Chelsea Bridge Rd.

RANELAGH GARDENS

Old Church St.

Flood St.

Christchurch St.

Royal Hospital Rd.

ROYAL HOSPITAL GARDENS

King's Rd.

9

Glebe Pl.

Oakley St.

Chelsea Manor St.

10

Chelsea Embankment

Chelsea Bridge

Cheyne Row

Albert Bridge

River Thames

Battersea Bridge

BATTERSEA PARK

| 0 | | 1/4 mi |
| 0 | | 1/4 km |

cooked with spices) baked in a pastry-sealed pot. For dessert, try the fresh pome-granate granita, which is sugar-free.

Halkin Arcade, Motcomb St., Knightsbridge SW1. ℂ **020/7823-1166.** www.amaya.biz. Reservations required. Main courses £9.50–£36; set-price lunch £16–£25, dinner £45. AE, DC, MC, V. Mon–Sat 12:30–2:15pm and 6:30–11:30pm; Sun 12:45–2:45pm and 6–10:30pm. Tube: Knightsbridge.

MODERATE

Black & Blue ★ STEAK   The atmosphere is marvelously informal, the prices affordable, and the steaks of high quality, each from a traditionally reared, grass-fed Scottish cow. Take your pick—Scottish sirloin, rib-eye, T-bone. We especially like the *cote de boeuf,* a hefty rib of beef for two to share. The sauces served with the steaks are divine. Burgers, chargrilled chicken, and fish dishes are also on offer on the changing menu, and even freshly made salads and platters for the vegetarian.

215–217 Kensington Church St., W8. ℂ **020/7727-0004.** www.blackandbluerestaurants.com. Reservations required. Main courses £9–£26. MC, V. Mon–Thurs noon–11pm; Fri–Sat noon–11:30pm. Tube: Notting Hill Gate.

The Collection ★ INTERNATIONAL/MODERN BRITISH   This is a temple to voyeurism and the vanities, catering to the aesthetics and preoccupations of the fashion industry. It occupies an echoing warehouse; the only access is by a 9m (30-ft.) catwalk that feels like it should have couture models striding along it. Yummy menu items include appetizers like Thai spiced chicken and coconut soup, and artichoke hearts salad with fresh fennel and Pecorino cheese, followed by such mains as grilled tiger prawns in coriander oil with couscous, and honey-roasted duck with Asian pear and bok choi. You might also order the grilled swordfish with pickled Asian vegetables, followed by such desserts as banana tarte tatin, and English strawberries with mascarpone. Don't overlook this place as a stop on your after-dark bar-hop.

264 Brompton Rd., SW3. ℂ **020/7225-1212.** www.the-collection.co.uk. Reservations recommended. Main courses £12–£55; early-dinner 3-course menu Mon–Fri 6–7:15pm £36–£42. AE, MC, V. Mon–Sat 6–11:30pm. Tube: South Kensington.

Racine FRENCH   The chef, Henry Harris, may be as English as they get, but the cuisine at this bustling French brasserie puts you across the Channel in Paris. Francophiles flock to this bistro with its wooden floors, dark-leather banquettes, and black-and-white-clad waiters. Seasonal dishes are featured on the ever-changing menu composed by Harris, who serves what he loves to cook and eat. That means such bistro favorites as rabbit in mustard sauce or salad lyonnaise, even *ris de veau* (sweetbreads) with wild mushrooms or sauerkraut Alsacienne. A veal head is served in the classic sauce ravigote. Expect true, robust flavors and a minimum of pretentiousness.

239 Brompton Rd., SW3. ℂ **020/7584-4477.** www.racine-restaurant.com. Main courses £15–£26; set-price 2-course lunch £15, 3-course £18. MC, V. Daily noon–3pm and 6–10:30pm. Tube: Knightsbridge.

INEXPENSIVE

Le Metro INTERNATIONAL   Located just around the corner from Harrods, Le Metro draws a fashionable crowd to its basement precincts. The place serves good, solid, reliable food prepared with flair. The menu changes frequently. You

Dining Green on Eco-Friendly Fare

More and more Londoners are seeking out eco-friendly fare. At most of these cafes, gastro-pubs, or small restaurants, more than three-quarters of the fresh produce served comes from the "Home Counties," those areas bordering London. Diners in these places tend to ask the provenance of the meat, or how the fish was caught. Many chefs in these restaurants claim that "eating green doesn't have to be a culinary sacrifice."

Some of the leading green restaurants include **The Duke of Cambridge,** 30 St. Peter's St., N1 (✆ **020/7359-3066;** www.dukeorganic.co.uk; Tube: Angel) in Islington. This modern Brit restaurant is an all-organic extravaganza.

In Southwest London, **Daylesford Organic's Cookery School,** 44B Pimlico Rd., SW1 (✆ **020/7881-8060;** www.daylesfordorganic.com; Tube: Sloane Square), specializes in seasonal produce, including vegetables from their own kitchen gardens along with organic cakes, pastries, and breads.

Water House Restaurant, 10 Orsman Rd., N1 (✆ **020/7033-0123;** www.waterhouserestaurant.co.uk; Tube: Old St. (but a long walk to the restaurant), is tucked away behind apartment houses close to the Regent's Canal. It calls itself the world's first carbon-neutral restaurant. Try such dishes as a risotto with pumpkin, ricotta cheese, and Parmesan or linguine with freshly caught mussels.

might choose the homemade soup of the day with freshly baked bread or the twice-baked cheese soufflé with an arugula salad as your starting point. For a main, opt for such dishes as salmon fish cakes with horseradish mayonnaise or else pork, leek, and herb sausages with red-onion gravy.

28 Basil St., SW3. ✆ **020/7589-6286.** Main courses £11–£16. AE, DC, MC, V. Mon–Sat 8am–10pm; Sun 8am–4pm. Tube: Knightsbridge.

Chelsea

VERY EXPENSIVE

Aubergine ★★ FRENCH "Eggplant" is luring savvy diners down to the lower reaches of Chelsea where chef William Drabble took over from the renowned Gordon Ramsay. Although popular with celebrities, the restaurant remains unpretentious and refuses to pander to the whims of the rich and famous. (Madonna was once refused a late-night booking!) Every dish is satisfyingly flavorsome, from warm salad of truffled vegetables with asparagus purée to roasted monkfish served with crushed new potatoes, roasted leeks, and red-wine sauce. Starters continue to charm and delight palates, ranging from ravioli of crab with mussels, chili, ginger, and coriander *nage* to terrine of foie gras with confit of duck and pears poached in port. A stunning main course is a tranche of sea bass with bouillabaisse potatoes. There are only 14 tables, so booking is imperative.

11 Park Walk, SW10. ✆ **020/7352-3449.** http://atozrestaurants.com/auberginechelsea. Reservations required and accepted as many as 4–8 weeks in advance. Fixed-price 3-course lunch £29; fixed-price 3-course dinner £68; 8-course menu gourmand £85 or £145 with wine. AE, DC, MC, V. Tues–Sat noon–2:30pm and 7–11pm. Tube: South Kensington.

Gordon Ramsay ★★★ 🏠 FRENCH   One of the city's most innovative and talented chefs is Gordon Ramsay. All of London is rushing to sample Mr. Ramsay's wares, and he has had to turn away some big names. Every dish from this kitchen is gratifying, reflecting subtlety and delicacy without any sacrifice to the food's natural essence. Try, for example, Ramsay's celebrated cappuccino of white beans with grated truffles. His appetizers are likely to dazzle: salad of crispy pigs' trotters with calves' sweetbreads, fried quail eggs and a cream vinaigrette, or foie gras three ways—sautéed with quince, *mi-cuit* with an Earl Grey consommé, or pressed with truffle peelings. From here, you can grandly proceed to the main courses, such as oven-roasted pigeon from Anjou wrapped in Parma ham with foie gras.

68 Royal Hospital Rd., SW3. ✆ **020/7352-4441.** www.gordonramsay.com. Reservations essential (1 month in advance). Fixed-price 3-course lunch £45, 3-course dinner £90, 7-course dinner £120. AE, DC, MC, V. Mon–Fri noon–2:30pm and 6:30–11pm. Tube: Sloane Sq.

Roussillon ★★ FRENCH   In a quiet corner of Pimlico, near Sloane Square, British produce meets a French chef. The rage of trendy Chelsea, Roussillon serves a cuisine called "vegecentric," featuring seven-course tasting menus, each a delight. No one seems to prepare fresh vegetables in London better than chef Alexis Gauthier, who changes his menu twice a season, using local ingredients whenever possible. Roast monkfish is served with braised chicory, and meat choices include a sublime filet of beef with purple artichokes. You might settle for one of the French cheese board selections at the end of the meal, but few can resist the Louis XV praline concoction, using Weiss chocolate from St-Etienne.

16 St. Barnabas St., SW1. ✆ **020/7730-5550.** www.roussillon.co.uk. Reservations required. 3-course lunch £35; tasting menu at lunch £48–£58; 3-course dinner £60; tasting menu at dinner £78. AE, MC, V. Mon–Fri noon–2:30; Mon–Sat 6:30-10:30pm. Tube: Sloane Sq.

EXPENSIVE

Bluebird ★ MEDITERRANEAN   Before it was a restaurant, the site was a garage that repaired the legendary Bluebird, an English sports car that is, alas, no longer produced. Today, this enormous space resounds with clinking silverware and peals of laughter from a loyal clientele. You'll find a color scheme of red-and-blue canvas cutouts in the shape of birds in flight. Tables are close together, but the scale of the place makes dining private and intimate. The massive menu emphasizes savory, precisely cooked cuisine, some emerging from a wood-burning stove used to roast everything from lobster to game. An immense shellfish bar stocks every crustacean you can think of, and the liquor bar does a thriving business with the Sloane Square subculture. Starter temptations include Serrano ham with fresh tomato tostados or chopped steak tartare, or perhaps wild mushrooms on brioche. We're fond of the venison shank in a bitter chocolate sauce (don't knock it until you've tried it). You might also try the lamb with lentils and cepe mushrooms.

350 King's Rd., SW3. ✆ **020/7559-1000.** www.danddlondon.com. Reservations recommended. Main courses £10–£24; fixed-price lunch menu £17–£21. AE, DC, MC, V. Mon–Fri noon–2:30pm; Sat–Sun noon–3:30pm; Mon–Sat 6-10:30pm; Sun 6–9:30pm. Tube: Sloane Sq.

Le Cercle ★★ FRENCH   The owners of Club Gascon have come up with another winner in this chic subterranean dining room, a sort of Chelsea speakeasy. At last Sloane Street has a restaurant that is to food what the boulevard has long been to fashion. Service may not be the most efficient, and the noise level is at times deafening, but the food is absolutely amazing. You make your menu selection among an occasional famous face and a lot of lesser mortals. For us, the best dish was tuna carpaccio with crispy pork cubes. The French-styled dishes are served as tapas-size portions, and the menu is divided into seven sections according to principal ingredients. The chefs turn out one of the most succulent cuts of beef in London—it appears as *onglet* on the menu. Particularly memorable was the duck and fig combo and the chestnut risotto. For dessert, the chocolate fondant may arguably be the best served in London. It's served with vanilla and pepper (you heard right) ice cream.

1 Wilbraham Place, SW1. ℂ **020/7901-9999.** www.lecercle.co.uk. Reservations required. Fixed-price lunch (noon–3pm Tues–Sat) £15–£20; French tapas £5–£25. AE, MC, V. Tues–Sat noon–10:45pm (snacks only 3–6pm). Tube: Sloane Sq.

Tom's Kitchen ★ TRADITIONAL BRITISH   Down in Chelsea, a former pub has been stylishly converted into this chic restaurant, which from the moment of its opening attracted a loyal following of the local smart set. Today a bright, bustling brasserie with an open kitchen in back, it's the dream come true for Tom Aikens, who is assisted by his twin brother, Rob. Stop in for breakfast if you crave brioche French toast with caramelized apples, cinnamon ice cream, and maple syrup. Or else make a luncheon rendezvous to tuck in Tom's seductive fish and chips.

27 Cale St., SW3. ℂ **020/7349-0202.** www.tomskitchen.co.uk. Reservations required. Main courses £14–£30. AE, MC, V. Mon–Fri 7–10am, noon–3pm, and 6pm–midnight; Sat 10am–3pm and 6pm–midnight; Sun 11am–3pm and 6pm–midnight. Tube: Fulham Broadway.

INEXPENSIVE

Oriel FRENCH   Right on the corner of Sloane Square in the heart of Chelsea, this brasserie has long been a favorite of shoppers hitting the boutiques along Kings Road. The upstairs is in the French-brasserie style, rather classic with large mirrors and high ceilings. The atmosphere downstairs is more informal, and there are a few sidewalk tables for those who want to check out the Chelsea scene. If you arrive early for coffee and newspaper reading, you could mistake Oriel for a Parisian cafe. The food is fine but not excellent, including such brasserie standards as tuna niçoise or steak and *pommes frites*. Other dishes include steak au poivre with a very peppery sauce, or perhaps a traditional béarnaise. Mussels marinara is another classic dish, and the salads are always freshly tossed. Vegetarians won't go hungry here either.

50–51 Sloane Sq., SW1. ℂ **020/7730-2804.** Reservations not required. Main courses £10–£23. AE, DC, MC, V. Mon–Sat 8:30am–11pm; Sun 9am–10pm. Tube: Sloane Sq.

The Pig's Ear ★ 👕 TRADITIONAL BRITISH   The staff are still talking about the surprise visit of Prince William—he may be heir to one of the world's most fabled fortunes, but at the end of the evening here he split the bill among his friends, paying only his fair share at this, one of the best gastro-pubs in Chelsea. It might be called the Pig's Ear, but it's really the silk purse when it comes to food. Start with such dishes as Jerusalem artichoke soup with truffle oil, or chicken livers flavored with sherry vinegar. Other dishes include seared tuna with black olives and chicory or else foie gras ballantine with an onion marmalade. In honor of its namesake, the chefs deep-fry pigs' ears. Filet of sea bass appears with beet and baby leeks, and a roast wood pigeon is stuffed with garlic-laced porto-bello mushrooms. The atmosphere is friendly and unpretentious in either the ground-floor pub area or in the wood-paneled restaurant upstairs.

35 Old Church St., SW3. ℂ **020/7352-2908.** www.turningearth.co.uk/thepigsear. Reservations required in restaurant. Main courses £12–£16. AE, DC, MC, V. Mon–Sat noon–11pm; Sun noon–10:30pm. Tube: Sloane Sq.

Kensington & South Kensington

VERY EXPENSIVE

Tom Aikens ★★★ CONTINENTAL The amazingly skilled Tom Aikens is one of the truly top-flight Gallic chefs of London. Aikens certainly was trained well, working in Paris under Joël Robuchon during the time he was proclaimed as France's greatest chef. Aikens also ran the prestigious Pied-à-Terre in London. In elegant surroundings in chic Knightsbridge, the food at this namesake restaurant is basically a modern interpretation of high French cuisine, with a great deal of flourish and some very elaborately worked dishes. Regardless of the contrast in ingredients, main courses show harmony and cohesion, as exemplified by the poached sea bass with saffron risotto and a bouillabaisse sauce. Everything sounds like an unlikely combination, but the end result is most satisfying. The menu's voluptuous side is evoked by braised suckling pig with roasted fresh almonds, apple purée, and a pork lasagna.

43 Elystan St., Knightsbridge, SW3. ℂ **020/7584-2003.** www.tomaikens.co.uk. Reservations required. Fixed-price lunch 2-course £23, 3-course £29; dinner main courses £25–£40; tasting menu £80 or £140 with wine pairings. AE, DC, MC, V. Tues–Fri noon–2:30pm and Mon–Sat 6:45–11pm. Tube: South Kensington.

EXPENSIVE

Bibendum/The Oyster Bar ★ FRENCH/MEDITERRANEAN In trendy Brompton Cross, this still-fashionable restaurant occupies two floors of a garage that's now an Art Deco masterpiece. Though its heyday came in the early 1990s, the white-tiled room with stained-glass windows, lots of sunlight, and a chic clientele is still an extremely pleasant place. The eclectic cuisine, known for its freshness and simplicity, is based on what's available seasonally. Dishes might include roast pigeon with celeriac purée and apple sauté, rabbit with artichoke and parsley sauce, or grilled lamb cutlets with a delicate sauce. Some of the best dishes are for splitting between two people, including Bresse chicken flavored with fresh tarragon and grilled veal chops with truffle butter. Simpler meals and cocktails are available in the **Oyster Bar** on the building's street level. The bar-style menu stresses fresh shellfish presented in the traditional French style, on ice-covered platters adorned with strands of seaweed.

81 Fulham Rd., SW3. ℂ **020/7581-5817.** www.bibendum.co.uk. Reservations required in Bibendum, not accepted in Oyster Bar. Main courses £17–£46; fixed-price 2-course lunch £25, 3-course £30; cold seafood platter in Oyster Bar £30. AE, DC, MC, V. Bibendum Mon–Fri noon–2:30pm and 7–11pm; Sat 12:30–3pm and 7–11pm; Sun 12:30–3pm and 7–10:30pm. Oyster Bar daily noon–11pm. Tube: South Kensington.

Clarke's ★ MODERN BRITISH Sally Clarke is one of the finest chefs in London, and this is one of the hottest restaurants around. *Still.* She opened it in the Thatcher era, and it's still going strong. In this excellent restaurant, everything is bright and modern, with wood floors, discreet lighting, and additional space in the basement where tables are more spacious and private. Some people are put off by the fact that there is only a fixed-price menu, but the food is so well prepared that diners rarely object to what ends up in front of them. The menu, which changes daily, emphasizes chargrilled foods with herbs and seasonal veggies. You might begin with an appetizer salad of blood orange with red onions, watercress, and black olive–anchovy toast; then follow that with roasted breast of chicken with black truffle, crisp polenta, and arugula.

124 Kensington Church St., W8. ✆ **020/7221-9225.** www.sallyclarke.com. Reservations recommended. Main courses £15–£18 lunch; main courses £19–£20 dinner; fixed-price 3-course dinner £40; Sun brunch 3-course £32. AE, DC, MC, V. Mon–Fri 12:30–2pm; Sat noon–2:30pm; Sun 12:30–2pm, Mon–Sat 6:30–10pm. Tube: High St. Kensington or Notting Hill Gate.

Launceston Place ★ MODERN BRITISH   Launceston Place is in an almost village-like neighborhood where many Londoners would like to live, if only they could afford it. This stylish restaurant lies within a series of uncluttered Victorian parlors, the largest of which is illuminated by a skylight. Each room contains a collection of Victorian-era oils and watercolors, as well as contemporary paintings. The restaurant has been known for its new British cuisine since 1986. The menu changes every 6 weeks, but you're likely to be served such appetizers as langoustines and herb gnocchi with roast cauliflower or a Jerusalem artichoke soup. For a tempting main course, try the grilled rump of veal with mushrooms and sweet potato or mackerel with a sauté of artichokes and salsify. Another specialty is herb-crusted plaice with shellfish linguine.

1A Launceston Place, W8. ✆ **020/7937-6912.** www.launcestonplace-restaurant.co.uk. Reservations required. 3-course lunch £20; 3-course dinner £46; 6-course dinner £60; 3-course Sun lunch £24. Tues–Sat noon–2:30pm; Sun noon–3pm; daily 6:30–10:30pm. AE, DC, MC, V. Tube: Gloucester Rd. or Kensington High St.

MODERATE

Admiral Codrington ★ 🍴 CONTINENTAL/MODERN BRITISH   Once a lowly pub, this stylish bar and restaurant is now all the rage. The exterior has been maintained, but the old "Cod," as it is affectionately known, has emerged to offer plush dining with a revitalized decor by Nina Campbell and a glass roof that rolls back on sunny days. The bartenders still offer a traditional pint, but the sophisticated menu features such delectable fare as grilled calves' liver and crispy bacon, or pan-fried rib-eye with a truffled horseradish cream. Opt for the charbroiled tuna with eggplant caviar and a red-pepper vinaigrette.

17 Mossop St., SW3. ✆ **020/7581-0005.** www.theadmiralcodrington.co.uk. Reservations recommended. Main courses £11–£20. AE, MC, V. Mon–Sat 11:30am–midnight; Sun noon–10:30pm. Tube: South Kensington.

Blue Elephant ★ THAI   This is the counterpart of the famous L'Eléphant Bleu restaurant in Brussels. In a converted factory building in West Brompton, the Blue Elephant has been wildly popular since 1986. It remains the leading Thai restaurant in London, where the competition seems to grow daily. In an almost magical garden setting of tropical foliage, diners are treated to an array of MSG-free Thai dishes. You can begin with a "Floating Market" (shellfish in clear broth, flavored with chili paste and lemon grass), then go on to a splendid selection of main courses, for which many of the ingredients have been flown in from Thailand. We recommend the roasted-duck curry served in a clay cooking pot.

You might also try a spicy fish stew with mussels, prawns, crab, and scallops, or else a chicken curry with coconut milk and sweet basil.

3–6 Fulham Broadway, SW6. ☎ **020/7385-6595.** www.blueelephant.com. Reservations required. Main courses £12–£28; Royal Thai banquet £35–£53; fixed-price lunch menu Mon–Fri £18–£21; Sun buffet £25. AE, DC, MC, V. Daily noon–2:30pm; Mon–Thurs 7–11:30pm; Sat 6–11:30pm; Fri–Sat 6:30–10:30pm. Tube: Fulham Broadway.

The Enterprise EUROPEAN/TRADITIONAL BRITISH The Enterprise's proximity to Harrods attracts both regulars and out-of-town shoppers. Although the joint swarms with singles at night, during the day it attracts the ladies-who-lunch. With banquettes, white linen, and fresh flowers, you won't mistake it for a lowly boozer. The kitchen serves respectable traditional English fare as well as European favorites. Featured dishes include fried salmon cakes with butter spinach, golden calamari, and grilled steak with fries and salad. The juicy, properly aged, flavorful entrecôte slice of beef is about the best you can find in London.

35 Walton St., SW3. ☎ **020/7584-3148.** www.theenterprise.co.uk. Reservations accepted for lunch only Mon–Fri. Main courses £8–£18. AE, MC, V. Mon–Fri noon–3pm and 6–10:30pm; Sat–Sun noon–3:30pm and 6–10pm (Sat until 10:30pm). Tube: South Kensington or Knightsbridge.

Joe's Café ★ 🏛 ITALIAN One of three London restaurants established by fashion designer Joseph Ettedgui, it's often filled at breakfast and lunch with well-known names from the British fashion and entertainment industries, thanks to its sense of glamour and fun. No one will mind if your meal is composed exclusively of appetizers. There's a bar near the entrance, a cluster of tables for quick meals near the door, and more leisurely (and gossipy) dining available in an area a few steps up. The atmosphere remains laid-back and unstuffy, just as trendsetters in South Ken prefer it. With a name like Joe's, what else could it be? You can sample such starters as crab ricotta pancake with orange dressing and baby spinach or a goat terrine with cherry tomato marmalade. Main-dish allures include homemade pappardelle with a wild rabbit ragout and Pecorino cheese, and a lamb shank in a red-wine sauce. A specialty is chargrilled lobster with king prawns, squid, and langoustines with a tomato concasse.

126 Draycott Ave., SW3. ☎ **020/7225-2217.** Reservations required on weekdays, not accepted on weekends. Main courses £11–£18. AE, MC, V. Mon–Sat 9am–6pm and 7–11pm; Sun 10:30am–6pm. Tube: South Kensington.

Kensington Place EUROPEAN Rowley Leigh, the chef here, has attracted a devoted following of regulars. But word of his delicious cuisine is spreading, and now more and more visitors are rushing here to sample some of his signature dishes. For starters, try the risotto verde with mozzarella and roast peppers or the pickled herring salad with boiled eggs and potatoes. Grilled wild boar chops with polenta and herbs is another specialty. Also look for Leigh's innovative seasonal dishes. The chef has a marvelous way with grouse, venison, roast partridge, and sea bass. For dessert, you can take delight in the grilled pineapple with chili syrup (you heard that right) and coconut ice cream or the hot, bitter chocolate mousse with coffee ice cream. Everybody from pop stars to Kensington dowagers flocks to this animated, noisy bistro. The set lunch is one of the best values in the area. Save room for the steamed chocolate pudding with custard.

201 Kensington Church St., W8. ☎ **020/7727-3184.** www.danddlondon.com. Reservations required. Fixed-price dinner £22–£25; fixed-price lunch £20. Daily noon–3pm; Mon–Thurs 6:30–10:30pm; Fri–Sat 6:30–11pm; Sun 6:30–10pm. Tube: Notting Hill Gate.

Pasha MOROCCAN   You'll find virtually every kind of ethnic restaurant within London, but few boast the zest and stylishness of this re-creation of a palace within the medina at Marrakech. Each of the two dining rooms is outfitted with Bedouin colors, rich upholsteries, flickering candles, and belly-dancing music. You'll enjoy regional specialties that were once sampled only by cherished royal-family guests. If you wish, you can begin your meal with Moroccan tapas, including pigeon with spices and roasted almonds in a cinnamon-flavored pastry or baked baby eggplant with cumin-flavored shallots, even chargrilled king prawns. Main dish specialties include a slow-cooked whole lamb shoulder with apricots, figs, dates, and prunes served with a cinnamon-flavored couscous and sultanas. A tagine Djaj is chicken with preserved lemon, onion confit, saffron potatoes, and green olives. The chargrilled swordfish is a very special dish flavored with pomegranates, fresh mint, and cinnamon.

1 Gloucester Rd., SW7. ☎ **020/7589-7969.** www.pasha-restaurant.co.uk. Reservations recommended. Tapas £4.50–£8; main courses £14–£20; feast menu £35. AE, DC, MC, V. Sun–Wed noon–12:30am; Thurs–Sat noon–1:30am. Tube: Gloucester Rd.

Zaika ★★ INDIAN   Although a dish might miss here and there, this place nonetheless continues to receive accolades as one of the most accomplished of its type in Britain. In a former bank building in Kensington, the restaurant serves one innovative dish after another in flavors and combinations that may be new to you. Zaika lives up to its name, which, translated, means "sophisticated flavors." Of course, you can also order traditional dishes such as lamb and lentil patties stuffed with egg and onion. Main courses feature some sublime harmonies of flavor such as pan-fried and spicy sea bass with Indian couscous, raw mango, and a turmeric sauce, and—one of our favorites—"butter chicken," a classic tandoori chicken breast, with a buttery tomato sauce flavored with fenugreek, with saffron rice and stir-fried spinach. For a true feast, order the tasting menu, *Jugalbandi*.

1 High St., Kensington, W8. ☎ **020/7795-6533.** www.zaika-restaurant.co.uk. Reservations required. Main courses £15–£21; 2-course lunch £20; 3-course lunch £25; *Jugalbandi* menu without wine £39. Mon 6-10:45pm; Tues–Sat noon-2:45pm, 6-10:45pm; Sun noon-2:45pm, 6–9:45pm. Tube: High St. Kensington.

MARYLEBONE TO NOTTING HILL GATE

Marylebone

EXPENSIVE

Assaggi ★ 🍴 ITALIAN   You wouldn't think of heading to the second floor of a very ordinary pub in Bayswater for fine Italian cuisine, but we urge you to do so in this case to sample chef Nino Sassu's take on Italian classics, especially those from the south. Serious London foodies have discovered this low-key venue, and flock here for food prepared with flair and passion, using market-fresh and top-quality ingredients. The chef sets out to prove that straightforward dishes can often be the best when simply handled. Grilled Mediterranean vegetables in

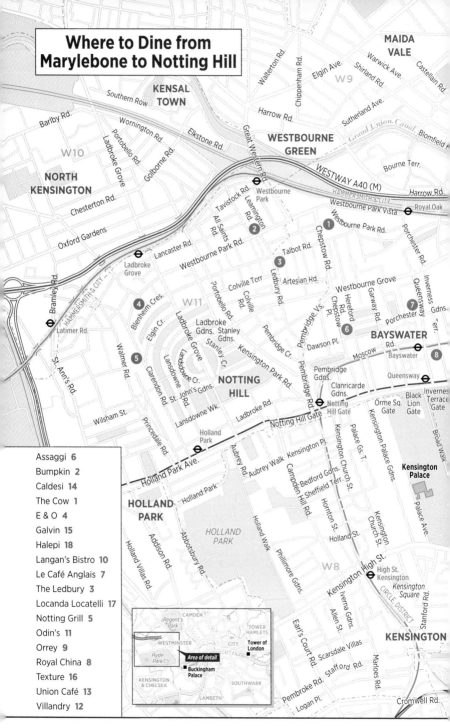

Where to Dine from Marylebone to Notting Hill

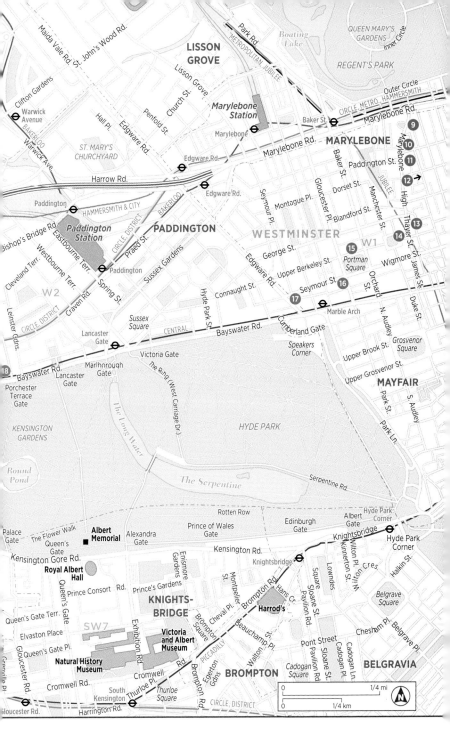

virgin olive oil and fresh herbs are an always winning appetizer, followed by such mains as grilled sea bass or filet of pork with black truffles. The menu is short but long on flavor if you try such dishes as a butter-and-sage ravioli, tender calves' liver, or panna cotta.

39 Chepstow Place, W2. ✆ **020/7792-9033.** Reservations required. Main courses £19–£32. AE, MC, V. Mon–Sat 12:30–2:30pm and 7:30–11pm. Tube: Bayswater.

Odin's ★ INTERNATIONAL   Set adjacent to its slightly less expensive twin, Langan's Bistro, Odin's features ample space between tables and an eclectic decor that includes evocative paintings and Art Deco accessories. As other restaurants nearby have come and gone, the cookery here remains solid and reliable. The standard of fresh ingredients and well-prepared dishes is always maintained. The menu changes with the seasons: Typical fare may include forest mushrooms in brioche, braised leeks glazed with mustard and tomato sauce, roast duck with applesauce and sage-and-onion stuffing, or roast filet of sea bass with a juniper cream sauce.

27 Devonshire St., W1. ✆ **020/7935-7296.** www.langansrestaurants.co.uk. Reservations required. Fixed-price 2-course meal £33; fixed-price 3-course meal £37. AE, DC, MC, V. Mon–Fri noon–2:30pm; Mon–Sat 6:30–11pm. Tube: Regent's Park.

Orrery ★★ FRENCH/INTERNATIONAL   With ingredients imported from France, this is one of London's classic French restaurants. Sea bass from the shores of Montpellier, olive oil from Maussane-les-Alpilles, mushrooms from the fields of Calais, and poultry from Bresse—they all turn up on a highly refined menu, the creation of chef Andre Garret. On the second floor of the Conran Shop in Marylebone, Orrey changes its menu seasonally to take advantage of the best produce. Garret is a purist in terms of ingredients. Everything has a brilliant, often whimsical touch, as evoked by the sautéed leeks in pumpkin oil. We ended with a cheese plate featuring a Banton goat cheese so fresh that it oozed onto the plate. Enjoy summer evenings on a fourth-floor terrace while drinking and ordering light fare from the bar menu.

55 Marylebone High St., W1. ✆ **020/7616-8000.** www.orreryrestaurant.co.uk. Reservations required. Fixed-price 3-course lunch £29; fixed-price 2-course dinner £44; fixed-price 3-course dinner £50. AE, DC, MC, V. Daily noon–2:30pm; daily 6:30–10pm. Tube: Baker St.

Texture ★★ EUROPEAN   This extraordinary restaurant treats us to the sensuous flavors of a talented chef, Iceland-born Agnar Sverrisson, who worked for the celebrated Raymond Blanc at La Manoir Aux Quat' Saisons outside Oxford. He is assisted by French-born Xaviar Rousset, acclaimed as the U.K.'s best sommelier. Their 60-seat restaurant and 30-seat champagne bar are the toast of London foodies. The chef's Icelandic roots are evident in such good-tasting signature dishes as lamb from Skagafjördur or Icelandic cod. Vegetables change with the season—in autumn, for example, they feature wild mushrooms, hazelnuts, and Umbrian black truffles. Another specialty is chargrilled Anjou pigeon with a red-wine sauce and "bacon popcorn."

34 Portman St., W1. ✆ **020/7224-0028.** www.texture-restaurant.co.uk. Reservations required. Main courses £22–£29; fixed-price 2-course lunch £19; fixed-price 3-course lunch £22; tasting menus £59; fish tasting menu £53. AE, MC, V. Tues–Sat noon–2:30pm; Tues–Sat 6:30–11pm. Tube: Marble Arch.

MODERATE

Caldesi ITALIAN   Good food, reasonable prices, fresh ingredients, and authentic Tuscan family recipes attract a never-ending stream of patrons to this eatery founded by owner and head chef Giancarlo Caldesi. The extensive menu includes a wide array of pasta, fish, and meat dishes. Start with the excellent *insalata Caldesi,* made with tomatoes slow-roasted in garlic and rosemary oil, and served with mozzarella flown in from Tuscany. Pasta dishes include an especially flavor-filled homemade tortellini stuffed with salmon. Monkfish and prawns are flavored with wild fennel and fresh basil, or you might sample the tender duck breast *à l'orange,* steeped in white wine, honey, thyme, and rosemary.

118 Marylebone Lane, W1 ℭ **020/7935-1144.** www.caldesi.com. Reservations required. Main courses £17–£22. AE, MC, V. Mon–Fri noon–2:30pm; Mon–Sat 6–11pm. Tube: Bond St.

Galvin ★ FRENCH   Evoking the fabled bistros of Paris, this Gallic-inspired *bistro de luxe* has brought foodies to the once gastro wasteland along Baker Street. Chris and Jeff Galvin, two brothers, provide straightforward French cuisine at a decent price (at least for London). The French classics appear in full-flavored combinations using the finest of seasonal ingredients. In an unpretentious setting, you can dine on a superb *soupe de poisons* (fish soup) or a classic endive salad with Roquefort, pear, and walnuts. That old-fashioned starter, salad of poached lamb's tongue with sauce ravigote, also appears on the menu. For robust eaters, there is an array of such dishes as roasted veal brains in *beurre noisette,* part of a platter that also includes roast rump of veal and melt-in-the-mouth braised cheeks.

6 Baker St., W1. ℭ **020/7935-4007.** www.galvinrestaurants.com. Reservations required. Main courses £13–£20; fixed-price menu £18. AE, MC, V. Mon–Sat noon–2:30pm and 6–11pm; Sun noon–9:30pm. Tube: Baker St.

Langan's Bistro FRENCH/TRADITIONAL BRITISH   This unpretentious bistro is still around—although perhaps it's not quite the happening scene it was when actor Sir Michael Caine founded it back in the 1960s. Of the restaurants in this chain (Langan's Brasserie, p. 203), it's the least expensive but the most visually appealing. Set behind a brightly colored storefront, the dining room is decorated with clusters of Japanese parasols, mirrors, surrealistic paintings, and old photographs. The menu is "mostly English with a French influence." Dishes change with the seasons but might include such starters as roast figs and goat cheese tart with walnut salad or sardines in sauce. Longtime brasserie favorites like mussels marinara, barbecued spareribs, and baked salmon in pastry are reassuringly familiar and as good as they ever were. Only fixed-price menus are served here.

26 Devonshire St., W1. ℭ **020/7935-4531.** www.langansrestaurants.co.uk. Reservations recommended. Fixed-price 2-course lunch or dinner £23, 3 courses £26. AE, DC, MC, V. Mon–Fri 12:30–2:30pm; Mon–Sat 6:30–11pm. Tube: Regent's Park or Baker St.

Locanda Locatelli ★★ ITALIAN   Inside the Hyatt Regency Churchill Hotel, this Italian restaurant is the success of the moment. Its charismatic owner, Giorgio Locatelli, is something of a celebrity himself these days. In a sleek, modern dining room with etched-glass panels and leather banquettes, you are served some of London's finest Italian fare. Beginning with the appetizers, dishes burst with flavor. We are especially fond of the artichoke and ham-hock salad, and the pan-fried scallops with saffron, both served as starters. The food is superbly cooked and beautifully presented, especially the succulent homemade pastas, such as homemade chestnut tagliatelle with wild mushrooms and another homemade pasta stuffed with pheasant and served with a rosemary jus. We give high praise to such mains as steamed filet of hake with a garlic and parsley sauce or roast leg of rabbit with Parma ham and polenta.

8 Seymour St., W1. ℭ **020/7935-9088.** www.locandalocatelli.com. Reservations required. Main courses £9.50–£30. AE, MC, V. Mon–Fri noon–3pm; Sat–Sun noon–3:30pm; Mon–Thurs 6:45–11pm; Fri–Sat 6:45–11:30pm; Sun 6:45–10:15pm. Tube: Marble Arch.

Union Cafe CONTINENTAL   After shopping along Oxford Street, restore your spirits with the exceptional food served at this sleek spot. The chefs use the finest-quality ingredients in every season. Everything from farmhouse English cheeses to free-range meat will tempt you. Rarely is any item oversauced, so natural, fresh flavors come to the fore. In most cases, the fresh fish and meat are chargrilled just right. Some of the best starters include stuffed peppers with feta cheese or fish soup with rouille. Especially good mains include roast cod filet with chives and grain mustard, and homemade crab cakes with chili jam. Linguine is flavorful with tiger prawns, mussels, and chili flavoring.

96 Marylebone Lane, W1. ℭ **020/7486-4860.** www.brinkleys.com/unioncafe.asp. Reservations recommended. Main courses £12–£23. AE, MC, V. Mon–Fri noon–3:30pm and 6:30–10:30pm; Sat 11am–4pm and 6:30–11pm; Sun 11am–4pm. Tube: Bond St.

Villandry ★ CONTINENTAL/INTERNATIONAL   Food lovers and gourmands flock to this food store, delicatessen, and restaurant, where racks of the world's finest meats, cheeses, and produce are displayed and changed virtually every hour. The best of the merchandise is whimsically transformed into the restaurant's menu choices. The setting is an oversize Edwardian-style storefront north of Oxford Circus. The inside is a kind of minimalist temple dedicated to the glories of fresh produce and esoteric foodstuffs. Ingredients here change so frequently that the menu is rewritten twice a day—during our latest visit, it proposed such perfectly crafted dishes as breast of duck with fresh spinach and a gratin of baby onions; and pan-fried turbot with deep-fried celery, artichoke hearts, and hollandaise sauce.

170 Great Portland St., W1. ℭ **020/7631-3131.** Reservations recommended. Main courses £15–£23. AE, MC, V. Restaurant Mon–Sat noon–3pm and 6–10:30pm; Sun 11:30am–4pm. Food store Mon–Sat 8am–10pm; Sun 10am–4pm. Tube: Great Portland St.

Primrose Hill

MODERATE

Odette's ★ MODERN BRITISH   No longer a stodgy choice for ladies-who-lunch, Odette's has been taken over by Bryn Williams, one of London's top chefs. He gained prominence when he won the fish course for Queen Elizabeth's 80th birthday celebration. Born in Wales, he still uses inspiration from that kitchen along with Gallic influences picked up on the Continent. In a contemporary setting of white tablecloths and white brick, Williams gives every dish his distinctive style. He proves his talent with such dishes as curried scallops with cauliflower

Eating at Authentic Chippies

Déclassé or not, Britain's national dish of fish and chips was called "the good companions" by Sir Winston Churchill. Introduced to London by Murano Jews, this dish has been Britain's fast food since the mid–19th century. Those slightly limp chips (fries to Americans) burst open with flavor with a squirt of malt vinegar, and each dish is accompanied by a "wally," in chippy vernacular (a pickled gherkin). Britons consume some 300 million fish-and-chips meals per year. The staunchest of devotees claim that the fish has to be cooked in beef drippings, but there is much disagreement on that in recent years.

We always head for **Rock & Sole Plaice,** 47 Endell St., WC2 (✆ **0871/426-3380;** Tube: Covent Garden), for our fish-and-chips fix. The cooks here prefer to fry the fish, such as sweet, delicate lemon sole, in clean peanut oil instead of beef drippings. This is London's oldest chippy, having existed under one name or another since 1871. Fish here is cooked in a puffy, ale-colored batter. Count on spending from £10 to £15 for a dinner, served Monday to Saturday 11:30am to 10:30pm and Sunday noon to 10pm.

Another authentic choice is the **Golden Hind,** 73 Marylebone Lane, W1 (✆ **0871/332-7803;** Tube: Bond St.), tucked away on this side street since 1914. Fresh fish arrives daily from the port of Grimsby on the western coast. Locals claim that "haddock is for heroes, cod for zeroes," so haddock is the way to go here. It's concealed in a thin batter (not overpuffed like at most chippies). A dinner ranges from £5 to £7.40, and service is Monday to Friday noon to 3pm and Monday to Saturday 6 to 10pm.

purée, roasted wild sea trout with a pea and mint puree, grilled baby squid in wild garlic, or Elwy Valley lamb with pine nuts and zucchini.

130 Regent's Park Rd., NW1. ✆ **020/7586-8569.** www.odettesprimrosehill.com. Reservations required. Main courses £15–£22; set lunch £12 for 2 courses, £16 for 3 courses; set dinners £50; tasting menu £50–£60. AE, MC, V. Tues-Sat noon-2:30pm, 6:30-10:30pm; Sun noon-3pm, 6-10:30pm; closed Mon. Tube: Chalk Farm.

Paddington & Bayswater

EXPENSIVE

Royal China ★ ☺ CANTONESE/SZECHUAN   Unexpectedly delightful Cantonese and Szechuan specialties are available at this popular eatery, a family favorite. Come here for the best dim sum in London. Forget the garish decor and concentrate on what's on your plate—you'd probably have to go to Hong Kong to find Chinese cooking as authentic as this. The eight-page menu is overwhelming in its choices, and many of the classic dishes are known only to true students of Chinese cuisine. We were delighted by the Shanghai dumplings, steamed on one side and sautéed on the other. Various whole ducks and chickens are prepared with skill passed down through centuries. We noticed a table of London Chinese raving about the jellyfish with sesame oil, although we opted for the sautéed prawns with fresh mango.

13 Queensway, W2. ✆ **020/7221-2535.** www.royalchinagroup.co.uk. Reservations recommended. Main courses £8–£55; fixed-price dinner £30–£38. AE, DC, MC, V. Mon–Thurs noon–11pm; Fri–Sat noon–11:30pm; Sun 11am–10pm. Tube: Bayswater or Queensway.

MODERATE

Halepi ★ 🍴 CYPRIOT/GREEK   Run by the Kazolides family since 1966, this establishment is hailed by the *Automobile Association of America Guide* as the best Greek restaurant in the world. Despite its reputation, the atmosphere is informal, with rows of brightly clothed tables, *bouzouki* background music, and a large native Greek clientele. Portions are generous. Menu items rely heavily on lamb and include kabobs, *klefticon* (baby lamb prepared with aromatic spices), moussaka (minced lamb and eggplant with béchamel sauce), and *dolmades* (vine leaves stuffed with lamb and rice). Other main courses include scallops; sea bass; Scottish halibut; huge Indonesian shrimp with lemon juice, olive oil, garlic, and spring-onion sauce; and *afelia* (filet of pork cooked with wine and spices, served with potatoes and rice). The homemade baklava is recommended for dessert. Most dishes are moderate in price.

18 Leinster Terrace, W2. ✆ **020/7262-1070.** www.halepi.co.uk. Reservations required. Main courses £12–£46. AE, DC, MC, V. Daily noon–12:15am. Closed Dec 25–26. Tube: Queensway.

Notting Hill Gate

EXPENSIVE

The Ledbury ★★ EUROPEAN   Australian-born Brett Graham deserves his culinary acclaim. As befits a chef born down under, he subtly incorporates Asian staples such as shiso and soy into his cookery. He's not a fancy, prissy chef, but likes to gut a squid and other such horrors. His ballotine of foie gras with a refreshing date purée is about the best version of this starter you are likely to have. Save room for his eggplant braised with miso and garlic, or his ravioli of chicken and morels in a white asparagus fondue. He's also skilled at fish, especially his monkfish roasted with fresh rosemary. For dessert, we'd recommend the date-and-vanilla tart.

127 Ledbury Rd., W11. ✆ **020/7792-9090.** www.theledbury.com. Reservations recommended. Set lunch £23–£28 Mon–Sat; set lunch Sun £40; set dinners £60. AE, MC, V. Mon–Sat noon–2:30pm and 6:30–10:30pm; Sun noon–3pm and 7–10pm. Tube: Westbourne Park.

MODERATE

Bumpkin MODERN BRITISH   Even the most fashion-conscious residents of chic Notting Hill like a taste of the country every now and then, heading for this bit of a rural idyll. This gastro-pub is one of the finest in the area in both its service and choice of fresh ingredients deftly handled by a skilled kitchen staff. The food is above average, especially in its well-prepared steak and chicken dishes. Feast on such mains as a juicy pork chop flavored with cider and fresh tarragon, or an appetizer such as seared tuna carpaccio with wild arugula. For the whisky drinker, there are some rare vintages on the menu such as Springbank 1968, but a single shot would set you back £28.

209 Westbourne Park Rd., W11. ✆ **020/7243-9818.** www.bumpkinuk.com. Reservations recommended. Main courses £12–£20; 2-course lunch £12. AE, MC, V. Mon–Fri noon–3pm; Sat 11am–4pm; Sun 11am–4pm; daily 6–11pm. Tube: Ladbroke Grove or Westbourne Park.

The Cow ★ 🍴 MODERN BRITISH   You don't have to be a young fashion victim to enjoy the superb cuisine served here (although many of the diners are). This increasingly hip Notting Hill watering hole looks like an Irish pub, but the accents you'll hear are "trustafarian" rather than street-smart Dublin. With a pint of Fuller's or London Pride, you can linger over the modern European menu, which changes daily but is likely to include ox tongue poached in milk; mussels in curry and cream; or a mixed grill of lamb chops, calves' liver, and sweetbreads. The seafood selections are delectable. The Cow Special—a half-dozen Irish rock oysters with a pint of Guinness or a glass of wine for £11—is the star of the show. A raw bar downstairs serves other fresh seafood choices.

89 Westbourne Park Rd., W2. ℂ **020/7221-0021.** Reservations required. Main courses £9.50–£19. MC, V. Daily noon–midnight. Tube: Westbourne Grove.

Le Café Anglais ★★ BRITISH/MODERN   This exciting restaurant evokes the spirit of an Art Deco Parisian brasserie, but fundamentally the cookery is firmly rooted in Britain. The extensive menu looks like dinner on the Titanic, but you won't sink regardless of what you order. To get into the spirit, start perhaps with a fresh elderflower cordial for an aperitif and then dazzle your palate with starters, everything from kipper pâté to mackerel teriyaki or salsify fritters. Chef Rowley Leigh is one of the founding fathers of contemporary British cookery and writes a food column for The Financial Times. He specializes in the most tantalizing rotisserie dishes in London—saddle of roebuck, English partridge, wild duck, whatever. Ever had roast hare with chili and pumpkin? The setting is in an offbeat location in West London, adjoining Notting Hill, on the second floor of Whiteleys Shopping Mall.

8 Porchester Gardens, W2. ℂ **020/7221-1415.** www.lecafeanglais.co.uk. Reservations required. Main courses £14–£25; fixed-price lunch £17–£20; set dinner £20–£25. AE, MC, V. Daily noon–3:30pm; Mon–Thurs 6–11pm, Fri–Sat 6–11:30pm; Sun 6:30–10:15pm. Tube: Bayswater or Queensway.

INEXPENSIVE

Prince Bonaparte INTERNATIONAL   This offbeat restaurant serves great pub grub in what used to be a grungy boozer before Notting Hill Gate became fashionable. Now pretty young things show up, spilling onto the sidewalk when the evenings are warm. The pub is filled with mismatched furniture; and CDs of jazz and lazy blues fill the air, competing with the babble. It may seem at first that the staff doesn't have its act together, but once the food arrives, you won't care— the dishes served here are very good. The menu roams the world for inspiration: Moroccan chicken with couscous is as good or better than any you'll find in Marrakech, and the seafood risotto is delicious.

80 Chepstow Rd., W2. ℂ **020/7313-9491.** www.theprincebonapartew2.co.uk. Main courses £12–£22. AE, MC, V. Mon–Sat noon–10:30pm. Tube: Notting Hill Gate or Westbourne Park.

Ladbroke Grove
MODERATE

E&O ASIAN   Nicole Kidman comes here to nibble on the succulent pumpkin and litchi curry, Kate Moss to devour prawn-and-chive dumplings without fear of weight gain, and Richard Branson to feast on the barbecue roasts. In an offbeat, out-of-the-way location, E&O is hailed as the "new Ivy," a reference to the most famous restaurant in the West End theater district, also a celeb favorite (after all these years). Melbournian restaurant guru Will Ricker is known for having created several hot east-London dining spots. We sampled the crispy fried fish and pronounce it a winner, as is the crispy-skin chicken and the *char siu* pork—baby pork spareribs crusted with sesame seeds and served with a garlic-and-ginger sauce. Succulent sushi and sashimi appear on the menu. One London reviewer found the patrons "comically trendy," although we'd call them more fashionable instead. At least they were insiderish enough to book a table at this place.

14 Blenheim Crescent, W11. © **020/7229-5454.** www.rickerrestaurants.com. Reservations required. Main courses £7.50–£25. AE, DC, MC, V. Mon–Fri 12:15–3pm and 6:15–11pm; Sat 12:30–4pm and 6:15–11pm; Sun 12:30–4pm and 6:15–10:30pm. Tube: Ladbroke Grove or Notting Hill Gate.

Notting Grill ★ 🍴 STEAK   Notting Grill owner Anthony Worrall-Thompson looks for well-bred, well-fed animals in his search for "the Holy Grail of British meats." His dream of creating the best grill house in London, using the *crème de la crème* of beef and fish, is more or less coming true in this out-of-the-way, offbeat rendezvous for serious foodies. Since Britain is known for its great breeds of beef cattle, Worrall-Thompson features a different purebred steak each month, ranging from Welsh Black to Aberdeen Angus, from Hereford to Ruby Red. With little fuss or bother, he also offers succulent scallops, "Big Daddy" prawns, organic sausages, and calves' liver. Celebs, media types, and the arty crowd show up here. If they're not chowing down on the steaks, they're likely to be seen dining on the rare-breed Middle White pork or organic chicken with hand-cut chips. Middle White suckling pig and the 24-ounce T-bone steak are the chef's specialties.

123A Clarendon Rd., W11. © **020/7229-1500.** Reservations required. Main courses £5.50–£49. AE, MC, V. Tues–Fri noon–3:30pm; Sat 1–4pm; Mon–Fri 6:30–10:30pm; Sat 6:30–11:30pm; Sun noon–10pm. Tube: Ladbroke Grove (a bit of a hike from the station).

A BIT FARTHER AFIELD
Hammersmith

To see where Hammersmith lies in relation to central London, refer to the map "Greater London Area" (p. 104).

EXPENSIVE

The River Café ★★ ITALIAN   For the best Italian cuisine in London, head to this Thames-side bistro operated by Ruth Rogers and Rose Gray. The charmingly contemporary establishment, with a polished steel bar, was designed by Ruth's husband, Richard, who also designed the Pompidou Centre in Paris. The cafe attracts a trendy crowd that comes to eat fabulous food and to see and be seen. The menu changes regularly. The owners' goal was to re-create the kind of cuisine they'd enjoyed in private homes in the Italian countryside, and they've succeeded. Some of London's chefs can be seen shopping in local markets—but not the River Café's chefs. The market comes to them: first-spring asparagus harvested in Andalusia and arriving in London within the day, live scallops and langoustines taken by divers in the icy North Sea, and a daily shipment of the finest harvest of Italy, ranging from radicchio to artichokes. Even tiny bulbs of fennel are zipped across the Channel from France. Britain's own rich bounty appears on the menu as well—in the form of pheasant and wild salmon. The best dishes are either slowly roasted or quickly seared.

Thames Wharf, Rainville Rd., W6. ☎ **020/7386-4200.** www.rivercafe.co.uk. Reservations required. Main courses £12–£35. AE, DC, MC, V. Mon–Fri 12:30–2:15pm and 7–9pm (to 9:15 Fri.); Sat 12:30–2:30pm and 7–9:15pm; Sun noon–3pm. Tube: Hammersmith.

Camden Town

MODERATE

The Engineer ★ 🏠 EUROPEAN/THAI   This temple to north London chic is another one of our favorites. The stylishly converted pub is owned by Abigail Osborne and Tamsin Olivier, daughter of Sir Laurence Olivier (or "Larry's Daughter," as she's called locally), and is named for Victorian bridge, tunnel, and railway builder Isambard Kingdom Brunel. It sits beside Regent's Canal, one of Brunel's creations. The pub is divided into a bar, a dining room, and a garden area for warm days. Cuisine is modern European with a Thai influence and relies on seasonal produce and organic meat and eggs. For an appetizer, try a crispy potato and onion tart with truffle oil or the tequila-cured salmon. For mains, we'd recommend the baked salmon filet wrapped in Parma ham and served with a saffron and anchovy sauce, or the Moroccan spiced lamb flavored with coriander and served with dates and couscous. For dessert, nothing is richer than the baked banana and toffee cheesecake, although you might opt for the pear and almond tart with pistachio crème fraîche.

65 Gloucester Ave., NW1. ☎ **020/7722-0950.** www.the-engineer.com. Reservations recommended. Main courses £13–£21. MC, V. Mon–Fri noon–3pm and 7–10:30pm; Sat 12:30–4pm and 7–11:30pm; Sun 12:30–4pm and 7–10pm. Tube: Chalk Farm or Camden Town.

In Richmond

INEXPENSIVE

Petersham Nurseries Café ★★★ INTERNATIONAL   South of the Thames in Richmond, Surrey, an easy commute from Central London, a "restless Aussie," Skye Gyngell is the hottest dining reservation in London. She may remain in that lofty position for years to come, because there's no one quite like her. She became known as a chef when she wrote two best-selling cookbooks, including *A Year in My Kitchen* and *My Favorite Ingredients*. Her restaurant is

---

🎁 The Brew House

Unknown to most visitors, there's a charming little place in North London for breakfast, afternoon tea, and lunches at one of Hampstead Heath's most alluring attractions. It's the **Brew House,** in Kenwood House (p. 311), Hampstead Lane, NW3 (☎ 020/8341-5384; www.companyofcooks.com), open in summer daily from 9am to 6pm (until 4pm in winter). There is always a freshly made soup of the day and at least one vegetarian dish. Main courses are likely to include freerange sausages or else fresh Scottish salmon, and even free-range chicken. You can partake of the breakfast buffet for between £4 and £9.50; at lunch main courses cost £6.50 to £12. Tube: Northern line to Archway Station, then bus no. 210.

simplicity itself, even though she's a media darling. "I just love to cook—that's all." That's not all. She's modest but supremely talented. Her dishes may be "unfussy," but they are utterly captivating, including a tomatoey chowder of clams and monkfish or rabbit cooked with duck fat, verjuice, and mustard. Sitting on her al fresco summer terrace, eating one of her homemade desserts, such as rhubarb ice cream, is about as good as it gets. There is no alcohol—just jugs of homemade lemon cordial.

Church Lane, Richmond. (🕿 **020/8605-3527.** Reservations required (as far in advance as possible). 2 courses for £28; 3 courses for £30. AE, DC, MC, V. Wed–Sun noon–2:30pm. Tube: Richmond Station.

TEATIME

Everyone should indulge in a formal afternoon tea at least once while in London. It's a relaxing, drawn-out, civilized affair that usually consists of three courses, all elegantly served on delicate china: first, dainty finger sandwiches (with the crusts cut off, of course), then fresh-baked scones served with jam and deliciously decadent clotted cream (Devonshire cream), and then an array of bite-size sweets. All the while, an indulgent server keeps the pot of tea of your choice fresh at hand. Sometimes ports and aperitifs are on offer to accompany your final course. High tea, popular with the before-theater crowd, includes an extra serving or two, including a sandwich, making it, in essence, a light supper. Having tea is a quintessentially British experience, and we've listed our favorite tea venues below. Note that for the most popular hotels (especially the Ritz), you should make reservations as far in advance as possible. If you go to a place that doesn't take reservations, show up at least half an hour early, especially between April and October. Jacket and tie are often required for gentlemen, and jeans and sneakers are usually frowned upon.

The British Empire no longer comes to a grinding halt at 4pm with all of England rushing for their cuppa. The English still like a cup of tea in the afternoon, but in workaday London it's often consumed at desks piled high with papers. A proper sit-down tea is reserved mainly for those ladies-who-lunch who like to indulge in fattening but delectable pastries in the late afternoon. Visitors are also fond of participating in this ritual.

London is now awash in coffee-bar chains, and many Londoners have abandoned the time-honored custom of afternoon tea altogether. But not all—some are returning to this quaint custom, and the city is experiencing a tea-drinking revival.

There are variations in tea drinking, as today's London is a rainbow-hued city. Take **Mômô**, at 23 Heddon St., W1 (🕿 **020/7434-4040**). At this offshoot of a North African restaurant, you'll think you're in Morocco as you're served mint tea in gold-encrusted glasses against a backdrop of hanging lanterns and embroidered cushions. Quite different from the traditional afternoon tea Queen Victoria enjoyed!

If drinking tea with your pinky extended just isn't your style, we've also included a handful of less formal (and less expensive) alternatives. A full high tea costs more than £24 at the finest hotels.

Be careful when you make reservations that you are booking at the right "Palm Court," as there are several of them.

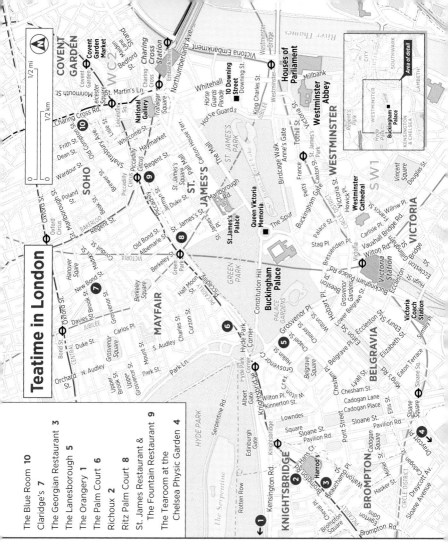

Teatime in London

The Blue Room **10**
Claridge's **7**
The Georgian Restaurant **3**
The Lanesborough **5**
The Orangery **1**
The Palm Court **6**
Richoux **2**
Ritz Palm Court **8**
St James Restaurant &
The Fountain Restaurant **9**
The Tearoom at the
Chelsea Physic Garden **4**

High Tea

MAYFAIR

Claridge's ★   Claridge's teatime rituals have managed to persevere through the years with as much pomp and circumstance as the British Empire itself. The experience is never stuffy, though; you'll feel very welcome. Tea is served in the Reading Room. A portrait of Lady Claridge gazes from above as your choice of over 30 kinds of tea is served ever so politely. The courses, served consecutively, include finger sandwiches with cheese savories, apple-and-raisin scones, and yummy pastries.

55 Brook St., W1. *②* **020/7629-8860.** www.claridges.co.uk. Reservations essential. Jacket and tie required for men after 6pm. High tea £35, £40–£50 including champagne. AE, DC, MC, V. Daily 3–5:30pm. Tube: Bond St.

The Palm Court This is one of the great London favorites for tea. Restored to its former charm, the lounge has an atmosphere straight from 1927, with a domed yellow-and-white glass ceiling, *torchères*, and palms in Compton stoneware *jardinières*. A delightful afternoon repast that includes a long list of teas is served daily against the background of live harp music.

In the Sheraton Park Lane Hotel, Piccadilly, W1. ☎ **020/7290-7328.** www.palmcourtlondon. co.uk. Reservations recommended. Afternoon tea £27–£36, with a glass of Park Lane champagne £36. AE, DC, MC, V. Daily 3–6pm. Tube: Hyde Park Corner or Green Park.

ST. JAMES'S

Ritz Palm Court ★★★ This is the most fashionable place in London to order afternoon tea—and the hardest to get into without reserving way in advance. The spectacular setting is straight out of *The Great Gatsby*, complete with marble steps and columns, and a baroque fountain. You can choose from a wide range of teas served with delectable sandwiches and luscious pastries.

In the Ritz Hotel, 150 Piccadilly, W1. ☎ **020/7493-8181.** www.theritzlondon.com. Reservations required at least 8 weeks in advance. Jeans and sneakers not accepted. Jacket and tie required for men. Afternoon tea £39–£50. Champagne afternoon tea with 2 complimentary glasses of champagne is offered at 7:30pm sitting. AE, DC, MC, V. 5 seatings daily at 11:30am, and at 1:30, 3:30, 5:30, and 7:30pm. Tube: Green Park.

St. James Restaurant & the Fountain Restaurant This pair of tea salons functions as a culinary showplace for London's most prestigious grocery store, Fortnum & Mason. The more formal of the two, the St. James, on the store's fourth floor, is a pale green-and-beige homage to formal Edwardian taste. More rapid and less formal is the Fountain Restaurant, on the street level, where a sense of tradition and manners is very much a part of the dining experience, but in a less opulent setting. There is no longer an "official" afternoon tea at the Fountain, but you can order pots of tea plus food from an a la carte menu that includes sandwiches, scones, and the like.

In Fortnum & Mason, 181 Piccadilly, W1. The Fountain ☎ **020/7973-4140.** www.fortnumand mason.com. St. James **020/7734-8040,** ext. 2241. St. James afternoon tea £32–£38. The Fountain a la carte menu £13–£32. AE, DC, MC, V. St. James Mon–Sat noon–6:30pm; Sun noon–4:30pm. The Fountain Mon–Sat 7:30am–11am, noon–3pm, 6–11pm; Sun 11am–3pm and tea 3–5:30pm. Tube: Piccadilly Circus.

KNIGHTSBRIDGE

The Georgian Restaurant For as long as anyone can remember, tea at Harrods has been a distinctive feature of Europe's most famous department store. A flood of visitors is gracefully herded into a high-volume but elegant room. Many come here for the ritual of the tea service, as staff members haul silver pots and trolleys laden with pastries and sandwiches through the cavernous dining hall.

On the 4th floor of Harrods, 87–135 Brompton Rd., SW1. ☎ **020/7225-6800.** Reservations recommended. High tea £25 or £42 with Harrods champagne, per person. AE, DC, MC, V. Daily 3:30–5:30pm (last order). Tube: Knightsbridge.

The Lanesborough You'll suspect that many of the folks sipping exotic teas here have dropped in to inspect the public areas of one of London's most expensive hotels. The staff offers a selection of seven teas that include the Lanesborough special blend, and herbal esoterica like Rose Congou. The focal point for this ritual is the Conservatory, a glass-roofed Edwardian fantasy filled with potted plants and a sense of the long-gone majesty of the Empire. The finger sand-wiches, scones, and sweets are all appropriately lavish and endlessly correct. Live piano music plays during afternoon tea.

Hyde Park Corner, SW1 (in the Lanesborough Hotel). ℂ **020/7259-5599.** www.lanesborough. com. Reservations required. High tea £35; high tea with strawberries and champagne £80. Min. charge £9.50 per person. AE, DC, MC, V. Mon–Sat 3:30–6pm; Sun 4–6pm. Tube: Hyde Park Corner.

Richoux   There's an old-fashioned atmosphere at Richoux, established in the 1920s. You can order four hot scones with strawberry jam and whipped cream or choose from a selection of pastries. Of course, tea is obligatory; always specify lemon or cream, one lump or two. A full menu, with fresh salads, sandwiches, and burgers, is served all day. There are three other locations, open Monday to Friday 8am to 11pm, Saturday 8am to 11:30pm. There's a branch at the bottom of Bond Street, 172 Piccadilly (ℂ **020/7493-2204;** Tube: Piccadilly Circus or Green Park); one at 41A S. Audley St. (ℂ **020/7629-5228;** Tube: Green Park or Hyde Park Corner); and one at 3 Circus Rd. (ℂ **020/7483-4001;** Tube: St. John's Wood).

86 Brompton Rd. (opposite Harrods), Knightsbridge, SW3. ℂ **020/7584-8300.** www.richoux. co.uk. Full tea £17. AE, MC, V. Mon–Sat 8am–9pm; Sun 10am–9pm. Tube: Knightsbridge.

KENSINGTON

The Orangery ★ 🎁   In its way, the Orangery is the most amazing place for afternoon tea in the world. Set 46m (151 ft.) north of Kensington Palace, it occu-pies a long, narrow garden pavilion built in 1704 by Queen Anne. In homage to her original intentions, rows of potted orange trees bask in sunlight from soaring windows, and tea is served amid Corinthian columns, ruddy-colored bricks, and a pair of Grinling Gibbons woodcarvings. There are even some urns and statuary that the royal family imported from Windsor Castle. The menu includes soups and sandwiches, with a salad and a portion of upscale potato chips known as kettle chips. The array of different teas is served with high style, accompanied by fresh scones with clotted cream and jam, and Belgian chocolate cake.

In the gardens of Kensington Palace, W8. ℂ **020/7376-0239.** Reservations not accepted. Pot of tea only £1.95–£5; cakes and puddings £3.50–£8.75; afternoon tea £13–£35; champagne tea £22. MC, V. Daily 3–5pm. Tube: High St. Kensington or Queensway.

Casual Tearooms

SOHO

The Blue Room   Nothing about this place will remind you of the grand tea-rooms above, where tea drinking is an intricate and elaborate social ritual. What you'll find here is a cozy, eccentric enclave lined with the artwork of some of the regular patrons, battered sofas that might have come out of a college dormitory, and a gathering of likeable urban hipsters to whom very little is sacred. You can enjoy dozens of varieties of tea, including herbals, served in steaming mugs. Lots of arty types gather here during the late afternoon, emulating some of the rituals of old-fashioned tea service with absolutely none of the hauteur.

3 Bateman St., W1. ℂ **020/7437-4827.** Reservations recommended. Cup of tea £2; cakes and pastries £2.50–£5.50; sandwiches £3.50–£8.75. No credit cards. Mon–Fri 8am–10:30pm; Sat 10am–10:30pm; Sun noon–10pm. Tube: Leicester Sq.

CHELSEA

The Tearoom at the Chelsea Physic Garden   The garden encompasses a small area, crisscrossed with gravel paths and ringed with a high brick wall that shuts out the roaring traffic of Royal Hospital Road. These few spectacular acres honor the memory of industries that were spawned from seeds developed and tested within the garden's walls. Founded in 1673 as a botanical education center, the Chelsea Physic Garden's list of successes includes the exportation of rubber from South America to Malaysia and tea from China to India.

On the 4 days a week that it's open, the tearoom is likely to be filled with botanical enthusiasts sipping cups of tea as fortification for their garden treks. The setting is a banal-looking Edwardian building. Since the tearoom is secondary to the garden itself, don't expect the lavish pomp of some other teatime venues. But you can carry your cakes and cups of tea out into a garden that, despite meticulous care, always looks a bit unkempt. (Herbaceous plants within its hallowed precincts are left untrimmed to encourage bird life and seed production.) Botanists and flower lovers in general find the place fascinating.

66 Royal Hospital Rd., SW3. © **020/7352-5646.** www.chelseaphysicgarden.co.uk. Tea with cake £7.50–£11. MC, V (in shop only). Wed–Fri 12:30–5pm; Sun noon–6pm. Closed Nov–Mar. Tube: Sloane Sq.

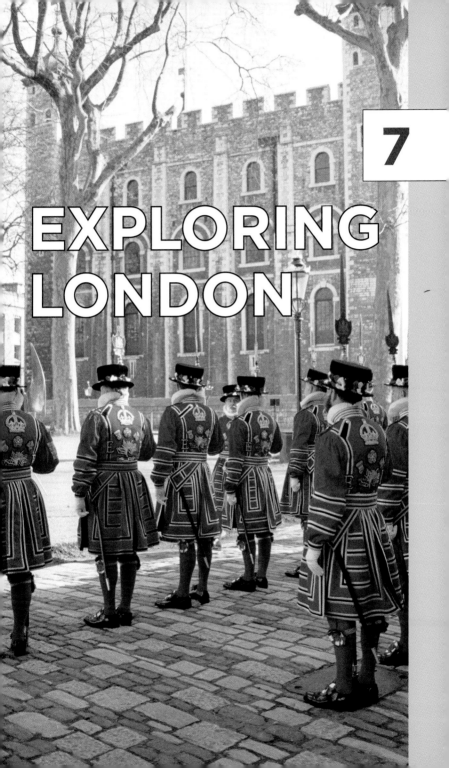

7

EXPLORING LONDON

S amuel Johnson said, "When a man is tired of London, he is tired of life, for there is in London all that life can afford." It would take a lifetime to explore every alley, street, and square in this city. Since you don't have a lifetime to spend, we've chosen the best London has to offer.

For visitors, the question is not what to do, but what to do first. The suggested itineraries in chapter 4 and "The Top Attractions," below, should help.

A note about admission and open hours: In the listings below, children's prices generally apply to those 16 and under. To qualify for a senior discount, women must be 60 or older, men 65 or older. Students must present a student ID to get discounts, where available. In addition to closing on bank holidays, many attractions close around Christmas and New Year's (and, in some cases, early in May), so always call ahead if you're visiting in those seasons. All museums are closed Good Friday, December 24 through 26, and New Year's Day.

SIGHTS & ATTRACTIONS BY NEIGHBORHOOD

BELGRAVIA
Apsley House, The Wellington Museum ★ (p. 283)

BLOOMSBURY
British Library ★★ (p. 284)
British Museum ★★★ (p. 238)
Dickens House (p. 281)
St. Pancras Station (p. 280)

CHELSEA
Carlyle's House (p. 280)
Chelsea Physic Garden (p. 301)
Chelsea Royal Hospital ★★ (p. 275)
National Army Museum ★ (p. 293)
Saatchi Gallery ★★ (p. 295)

THE CITY
All Hallows Barking-by-the-Tower (p. 266)
Guildhall Art Gallery ★ (p. 288)
London Bridge (p. 304)
Museum of London ★★ (p. 293)

Old Bailey (p. 279)
St. Bride's ★ (p. 266)
St. Giles Cripplegate ★ (p. 270)
St. Mary-le-Bow ★★ (p. 272)
St. Paul's Cathedral ★★★ (p. 250)
Samuel Johnson's House ★★ (p. 283)
Temple Church ★★ (p. 272)
Tower Bridge ★★ (p. 253)
Tower of London ★★★ (p. 253)

CLERKENWELL
St. Etheldreda's (p. 266)
Wesley's Chapel, House & Museum of Methodism (p. 273)

COVENT GARDEN & THE STRAND
Courtauld Gallery (p. 286)
London's Transport Museum ★ (p. 291)
St. Paul's Church (the Actors' Church) ★ (p. 272)

PREVIOUS PAGE: **Tower of London Beefeaters**

7

EXPLORING LONDON

Sights & Attractions by Neighborhood

THE TOP ATTRACTIONS

British Museum ★★★   Set in scholarly Bloomsbury, this immense museum grew out of a private collection of manuscripts purchased in 1753 with the proceeds of a lottery. It grew and grew, fed by legacies, discoveries, and purchases, until it became one of the most comprehensive collections of art and artifacts in the world. It's impossible to take in this museum in a day.

The museum is divided basically into the national collections of antiquities; prints and drawings; coins, medals, and banknotes; and ethnography. Even on a cursory first visit, be sure to see the Asian collections (the finest assembly of

Roman sculpture at the British Museum.

Grand Staircase at Buckingham Palace.

Timesaver

With 4km (2½ miles) of galleries, the **British Museum** is overwhelming. To get a handle on it, we recommend taking a 1½-hour overview tour for £9, £6 for students and children under 11 and held daily at 10:30am or 3pm. Afterward, you can return to the galleries that most interest you. If you have limited time to spend on the museum, concentrate on the Greek and Roman rooms (nos. 11–23, 69–73, and 77–85), which hold the golden hoard of booty both bought and stolen from the Empire's once far-flung colonies. For information on the British Library, see p. 284.

Islamic pottery outside the Islamic world), the Chinese porcelain, the Indian sculpture, and the prehistoric and Romano-British collections. Special treasures you might want to seek out on your first visit include the **Rosetta Stone,** in the Egyptian Room, the discovery of which led to the deciphering of hieroglyphics; the **Parthenon Sculptures,** a series of pediments, metopes, and friezes from the Parthenon in Athens, in the Duveen Gallery; and the legendary **Black Obelisk,** dating from around 860 b.c., in the Nimrud Gallery. Other treasures include the contents of Egyptian royal tombs (including mummies); fabulous arrays of 2,000-year-old jewelry, cosmetics, weapons, furniture, and tools; Babylonian astronomical instruments; and winged lion statues (in the Assyrian Transept) that guarded Ashurnasirpal's palace at Nimrud. The exhibits change throughout the year, so if your heart is set on seeing a specific treasure, call to make sure it's on display.

Insider's tip: If you're a first-time visitor, you will, of course, want to concentrate on some of the fabled treasures previewed above. But what we do is duck into the British Museum several times on our visits to London, even if we have only an hour or two, to see the less heralded but equally fascinating exhibits. We recommend wandering rooms 33 and 34, and 91 to 94, to take in the glory of the Orient, covering Taoism, Confucianism, and Buddhism. The Chinese collection is particularly strong. Sculpture from India is as fine as anything at the Victoria and Albert. The Mexican Gallery in room 33C traces that country's art from the 2nd millennium b.c. to the 16th century a.d. A gallery for the North American collection is also nearby. Another section of the museum is devoted to the **Sainsbury African Galleries ★**, one of the finest collections of African art and artifacts in the world, featuring changing displays selected from more than 200,000 objects. Finally, the Money Gallery in room 68 traces the story of (what else?) money. You'll learn that around 2000 b.c. in Mesopotamia, grain was used as currency, and that printed money came into being in the 10th century in China.

The museum's inner courtyard is now canopied by a lightweight, transparent roof, transforming the area into a covered square that houses a Centre for Education, exhibition space, bookshops, and restaurants. The center of the Great Court features the Round Reading Room, which is famous as the place where Karl Marx hung out while writing *Das Kapital.*

Warning: Watch your wallets when you're standing in crowds, particularly in front of the Rosetta Stone. The museum is free and tends to attract a few grab-happy drifters. For information on the British Library, see p. 284.

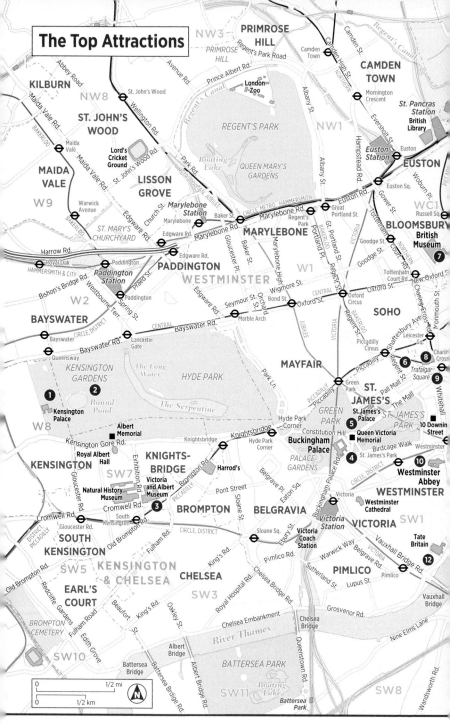

The Top Attractions

NW3
PRIMROSE HILL

PRIMROSE HILL

Regent's Park Road

NW8

KILBURN

ST. JOHN'S WOOD

London Zoo

REGENT'S PARK

CAMDEN TOWN

St. Pancras Station

British Library

MAIDA VALE

Lord's Cricket Ground

LISSON GROVE

Queen Mary's Gardens

Boating Lake

NW1

Euston Station

EUSTON

W9

Paddington Station

PADDINGTON

Marylebone Station

MARYLEBONE

BLOOMSBURY

British Museum ❼

WESTMINSTER

W2

SOHO

BAYSWATER

KENSINGTON GARDENS

HYDE PARK

The Long Water

The Serpentine

Piccadilly Circus

Leicester Sq.

❻ ❽

Charing Cross

Trafalgar Square ❾

MAYFAIR

Round Pond

❶

❷

ST. JAMES'S

Green Park

St. James's Palace

10 Downing Street

Kensington Palace

Albert Memorial

Knightsbridge

Hyde Park Corner

Buckingham Palace ❹

Queen Victoria Memorial ❺

WESTMINSTER

Westminster Abbey ❿

W8

Royal Albert Hall

KNIGHTS-BRIDGE

Harrod's

PALACE GARDENS

Westminster Cathedral

KENSINGTON

Natural History Museum

Victoria and Albert Museum ❸

BROMPTON

BELGRAVIA

Victoria Station

VICTORIA

SW1

SOUTH KENSINGTON

KENSINGTON & CHELSEA

Victoria Coach Station

PIMLICO

Tate Britain ⓬

EARL'S COURT

CHELSEA

SW3

BROMPTON CEMETERY

SW5

Albert Bridge

River Thames

Chelsea Bridge

Vauxhall Bridge

SW10

Battersea Bridge

BATTERSEA PARK

Boating Lake

Battersea Park

SW11

SW8

0   1/2 mi

0   1/2 km

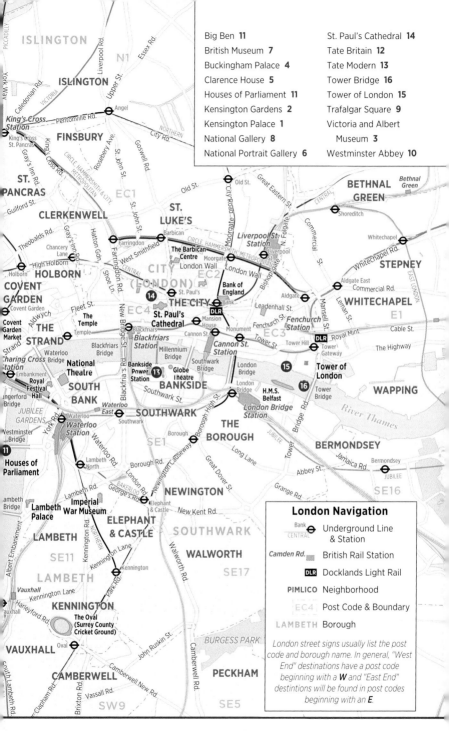

Great Russell St., WC1. ☏ **020/7323-8299** or 020/7636-1555 for recorded information. www. britishmuseum.org. Free admission. Sat–Wed 10am–5:30pm; Thurs–Fri 10am–8:30pm. Tube: Holborn, Tottenham Court Rd., Goodge St., or Russell Sq.

Buckingham Palace ★★ ☺   This massive, graceful building is the official residence of the Queen. The redbrick palace was built as a country house for the notoriously rakish Duke of Buckingham. In 1762, King George III, who needed room for his 15 children, bought it. It didn't become the official royal residence, though, until Queen Victoria took the throne; she preferred it to St. James's Palace. From George III's time, the building was continuously expanded and remodeled, faced with Portland stone, and twice bombed (during the Blitz). Located in a 16-hectare (40-acre) garden, it's 108m (354 ft.) long and contains 600 rooms. You can tell whether the Queen is at home by checking to see if the Royal Standard is flying from the mast outside. For most of the year, you can't visit the palace without an official invitation. Since 1993, though, much of it has been open for tours during an 8-week period in August and September, when the royal family is usually vacationing outside London. Elizabeth II agreed to allow visitors to tour the State Room, the Grand Staircase, the Throne Room, and other areas designed by John Nash for George IV, as well as the Picture Gallery, which displays masterpieces by Van Dyck, Rembrandt, Rubens, and others. You have to buy a timed-entrance ticket the same day you plan to tour the palace. Tickets go on sale at 9am, but rather than lining up at sunrise with all the other tourists—this is one of London's most popular attractions—book by phone with a credit card and give yourself a few more hours of sleep.

During the 8 weeks of summer, visitors are also allowed to stroll through the royal family's garden, along a 4.5km (2¾-mile) walk on the south side of the grounds, with views of a lake and the usually off-limits west side of the palace. The garden is home to 30 types of birds, plus 350 varieties of wildflowers.

Buckingham Palace's most famous spectacle is the vastly overrated **Changing of the Guard** (daily Apr–July and on alternating days for the rest of the year). The new guard, marching behind a band, comes from either the Wellington or Chelsea barracks and takes over from the old guard in the forecourt of the palace. The ceremony begins at 11:30am, although it's frequently canceled because of bad weather, state events, and other, harder-to-fathom reasons. We like the changing of the guard at Horse Guards better (p. 277) because you can actually see the men marching and you don't have to battle such tourist hordes. However, few first-time visitors will resist the lure of the Buckingham Palace Changing of the Guard. If that includes you, arrive as early as 10:30am and claim territorial rights to a space in front of the palace. If you're not firmly anchored here, you'll miss much of the ceremony.

> ## The Guard Doesn't Change Every Day
>
> **The schedule for the Changing of the Guard ceremony is variable, at best. In theory, at least, the guard is changed daily from May to mid-July, at which time it goes on its "winter" schedule—that is, alternating days. Always check locally with the tourist office to see if it's likely to be staged at the time of your visit. The ceremony has sometimes been cut at the last minute, leaving thousands of visitors feeling they have missed out on a London must-see (though we say it's overrated anyway).**

Clarence House

At end of the Mall (on the road running from Trafalgar Sq.). © **020/7766-7300.** www.royal collection.org.uk. Palace tours £17 adults, £16 61 and older and students, £9.75 16 and younger, family ticket £45, free for ages 4 and younger; Changing of the Guard free. Aug 1–Sept 27 (dates can vary), and additional dates may be added. Daily 9:45am–6pm. Changing of the Guard daily Apr–July at 11:30am and alternating days for the rest of the year at 11am. Tube: St. James's Park, Green Park, or Victoria.

Clarence House ★★   From 1953 until her death in 2002, the Queen Mother lived at Clarence House in a wing of St. James's Palace. It was constructed between 1825 and 1927 to the designs of John Nash. Today it is the official residence of the Prince of Wales, and is open to the public only during a specified period of the year (see below). The present Queen Elizabeth and the Duke of Edinburgh lived here following their marriage in 1947.

After the death of the Queen Mother, the house was refurbished and redecorated with antiques and art from the royal collection. Visitors are taken on a guided tour of five of the staterooms, where much of the Queen's collection of art and furniture is on display, along with pieces added by Prince Charles. The Queen Mother had an impressive collection of 20th-century British art, including works by John Piper, Augustus John, and Graham Sutherland. She also was known for her superb collection of Fabergé and English porcelain and silver, especially pieces from her family collection (the Bowes-Lyon family).

Stable Yard Gate, SW1. © **020/7766-7303.** www.royalcollection.org.uk. Admission £8.50 adults, £4.50 ages 5–16, free for children 4 and under. Aug 1–Sept 30 (dates subject to change—call first) daily 10am–5:30pm. Tube: Green Park or St. James's Park.

Houses of Parliament & Big Ben ★★   The Houses of Parliament, along with their trademark clock tower, Big Ben, are the ultimate symbols of London.

They're the strongholds of Britain's democracy, the assemblies that effectively trimmed the sails of royal power. Both the House of Commons and the House of Lords are in the former royal Palace of Westminster, which was the king's residence until Henry VIII moved to Whitehall. The current Gothic Revival buildings date from 1840 and were designed by Charles Barry. (The earlier buildings were destroyed by fire in 1834.) Assisting Barry was Augustus Welby Pugin, who designed the paneled ceilings, tiled floors, stained glass, clocks, fireplaces, umbrella stands, and even the inkwells. There are more than 1,000 rooms and 3km (1¼ miles) of corridors. The clock tower at the eastern end houses the world's most famous timepiece. **"Big Ben"** refers not to the clock tower itself, but to the largest bell in the chime, which weighs close to 14 tons and is named for the first commissioner of works, Sir Benjamin Hall.

You may observe debates for free from the **Stranger's Galleries** in both houses. Sessions usually begin in mid-October and run to the end of July, with recesses at Christmas and Easter. The chances of getting into the House of Lords when it's in session are generally better than for the more popular House of Commons. Although we can't promise you the oratory of a Charles James Fox or a William Pitt the Elder, the debates in the House of Commons are often lively and controversial (seats are at a premium during crises).

For years, London tabloids have portrayed members of the House of Lords as a bunch of "Monty Pythonesque upper-class twits," with one foreign secretary calling the House of Lords "medieval lumber." Today, under Gordon Brown's Labour government, the House of Lords is being shaken up as lords lose their inherited posts. Panels are studying what to do with this largely useless house, its members often descendants of royal mistresses and ancient landowners.

Those who'd like to book a tour can do so, but it takes a bit of work. Both houses are open to the general public for guided tours only for a limited season

The Jewel Tower.　　　　Kensington Palace.

in July and August. The palace is open Monday, Tuesday, Friday, and Saturday from 9:15am to 4:30pm during that season. All tour tickets cost £12 for adults; £8 for seniors, students, and children 15 and younger; and £30 for a family ticket. Children 3 years old and younger may enter free. For advance tickets call 𝄐 **08709/063773** (www.parliament.uk/visiting/visiting.cfm).

If you arrive just to attend a session, these are free, but you need a card of introduction. Foreign and Commonwealth visitors should apply to their embassy or High Commission in the U.K. for a card of introduction, which will normally permit entry during the early afternoon. Embassies and High Commissions may issue no more than four cards on any day, so visitors from certain countries may find cards are booked for several weeks ahead. Please note that such cards do not guarantee entry. Quite often, it will not be possible to admit their bearers until *after* Prime Minister's Question Time. British embassies abroad do not issue such cards.

With your card of introduction in hand, you line up at Stephen's Gate, heading to your left for the entrance into the Commons or to the right for the Lords. The London daily newspapers announce sessions of Parliament.

Insider's tip: The hottest ticket and the most exciting time to visit is during Prime Minister's Question Time on Wednesdays, which is only from noon to 12:30pm, but which must seem like hours to Gordon Brown, who is on the hot seat. It's not quite as thrilling as it was back when Margaret Thatcher exchanged barbs with the MPs (members of Parliament), but still worth a viewing.

Across the street is the **Jewel Tower ★**, Abingdon Street (𝄐 **020/7222-2219;** www.english-heritage.org.uk), one of only two surviving buildings from the medieval Palace of Westminster. It was constructed in 1365 as a place where Edward III could stash his treasure-trove. The tower hosts an exhibition on the history of Parliament and makes for a great introduction to the inner workings of the British government. The video presentation on the top floor is especially informative. A touch-screen computer allows visitors to take a virtual tour of both Houses of Parliament. The tower is open daily from 10am to 5pm April to October and 10am to 4pm November to March. Admission is £3.20 for adults, £2.60 for students and seniors, and £1.60 for children.

Westminster Palace, Old Palace Yard, SW1. House of Commons 𝄐 **020/7219-4272;** House of Lords 𝄐 **020/7219-3107.** www.parliament.uk. Free admission. Mid-Oct to Aug Mon–Tues 9am–noon; Wed 9–9:20am; Fri 3:30–5pm. Both houses open for tours (see above). Join line at St. Stephen's entrance. Tube: Westminster.

Kensington Palace ★ ☺   Once the residence of British monarchs, Kensington Palace hasn't been the official home of reigning kings since George II, who died in 1760. William III and Mary II acquired it in 1689 to escape the damp royal rooms along the Thames. Since the end of the 18th century, the palace has housed various members of the royal family, and the State Apartments are open for tours.

It was here in 1837 that a young Victoria was awakened with the news that her uncle, William IV, had died and she was now the Queen of England. You can view a collection of Victoriana here, including some of her memorabilia. In the apartments of Queen Mary II is a striking 17th-century writing cabinet inlaid with tortoiseshell. Paintings from the Royal Collection line the walls. A rare 1750 lady's court dress and splendid examples of male court dress from the 18th century are on display in rooms adjacent to the State Apartments, as part of the Royal

Ceremonial Dress Collection, which features royal costumes dating as far back as 200 years.

Kensington Palace was the London home of the late Princess Margaret, and is the current home of the Duke and Duchess of Kent. The palace was also the home of Diana, Princess of Wales, and her two sons. (William and Harry now live with their father at St. James's Palace.) The palace is probably best known for the millions of flowers placed in front of it during the days following Diana's death. The former apartment of the late Princess Margaret has been opened to the public as an education center and an exhibition space for royal ceremonial dress.

Warning: You don't get to see the apartments where Princess Di lived or where both Di and Charles lived until they separated. Many visitors think they'll get to peek at these rooms and are disappointed. Charles and Di lived on the west side of the palace, still occupied today by minor royals.

The **Kensington Gardens** are open to the public for leisurely strolls through the manicured grounds and around the Round Pond. One of the most famous sights is the controversial Albert Memorial, a lasting tribute not only to Victoria's consort, but also to the questionable artistic taste of the Victorian era. There's a wonderful afternoon tea offered in the Orangery (p. 233).

The Broad Walk, Kensington Gardens, W8. ✆ **0844/482-7777.** www.hrp.org.uk. Admission £13 adults, £11 seniors and students, £6.25 children 5–15, £34 family ticket. Mar–Oct daily 10am–6pm; Nov–Feb daily 10am–5pm. Tube: Queensway or Notting Hill Gate; High St. Kensington on south side.

trafalgar: LONDON'S MOST FAMOUS SQUARE

London is a city full of landmark squares. Without a doubt, the best-known is **Trafalgar Square ★★**; www.london.gov.uk/trafalgarsquare (Tube: Charing Cross), which honors one of England's great military heroes, Horatio Viscount Nelson (1758–1805). Although he suffered from seasickness, he went to sea at the age of 12 and was an admiral by age 39. Nelson was a hero of the Battle of Calvi in 1794, where he lost an eye; the Battle of Santa Cruz in 1797, where he lost an arm; and the Battle of Trafalgar in 1805, where he lost his life. He is also famous for his affair with Lady Hamilton, the subject of books and films (including *That Hamilton Woman,* with Laurence Olivier and Vivien Leigh).

The square is dominated by the 44m (144-ft.) granite *Nelson's Column,* built by E. H. Baily in 1843. The column looks down Whitehall toward the Old Admiralty, where Lord Nelson's body lay in state. The figure of the naval hero towers 5m (16 ft.) high—not bad for a man who stood 5'4" in real life. The capital is of bronze, cast from cannons recovered from the wreck of the *Royal George,* which sank in 1782. Queen Victoria's favorite animal painter, Sir Edward Landseer, added the four lions at the base of the column in 1868. The pools and fountains weren't added until 1939; they were the last work of Sir Edwin Lutyens.

Political demonstrations take place in the square and around the column, which has the most aggressive pigeons in London. Much of the world focuses on the square via TV cameras on New Year's Eve, as revelers jump into the chilly waters of the fountains. The Christmas tree that's installed here

National Gallery ★★★   This stately neoclassical building contains an unrivaled collection of Western art spanning 7 centuries—from the late 13th to the early 20th—and covering every great European school. For sheer skill of display and arrangement, it surpasses its counterparts in Paris, New York, Madrid, and Amsterdam.

The largest part of the collection is devoted to the Italians, including the Sienese, Venetian, and Florentine masters. They're now housed in the Sainsbury Wing, which was designed by noted Philadelphia architects Robert Venturi and Denise Scott Brown and opened by Queen Elizabeth II in 1991. On display are such works as Leonardo's *Virgin of the Rocks;* Titian's *Bacchus and Ariadne;* Giorgione's *Adoration of the Magi;* and unforgettable canvases by Bellini, Veronese, Botticelli, and Tintoretto. Botticelli's *Venus and Mars* is eternally enchanting. The Sainsbury Wing is also used for large temporary exhibits.

Of the early Gothic works, the Wilton Diptych (French or English school, late 14th c.) is the rarest treasure; it depicts Richard II being introduced to the Madonna and Child by John the Baptist and the Saxon kings, Edmund and Edward the Confessor. Then there are the Spanish giants: El Greco's *Agony in the Garden* and portraits by Goya and Velázquez. The Flemish-Dutch school is represented by Bruegel, Jan van Eyck, Vermeer, Rubens, and de Hooch; the Rembrandts include two of his immortal self-portraits. None of van Eyck's art creates quite the stir that the **Arnolfini Portrait** does. You probably studied this

every December is a gift from Norway to the British people, in appreciation of Britain's sheltering the Norwegian royal family during World War II. The tree is surrounded by carolers most December evenings. Year-round, street performers (now officially licensed) entertain in hopes of receiving a token of appreciation for their efforts.

To the southeast of the square, at 36 Craven St., stands a house that was occupied by Benjamin Franklin from 1757 to 1774. On the north side of the square rises the National Gallery, constructed in the 1830s. In front of the building is a copy of a statue of George Washington by J. A. Houdon.

To the left of St. Martin's Place is the National Portrait Gallery, a collection of portraits of famous Brits—from Chaucer and Shakespeare to Nell Gwynne,

Margaret Thatcher, and Lady Diana. Also on the square is the steeple of St. Martin-in-the-Fields, the final resting place of Sir Joshua Reynolds, William Hogarth, and Thomas Chippendale.

Fountain in Trafalgar Square.

Le Chapeau de Poil by Sir Peter Paul Rubens in the National Gallery.

painting from 1434 in your Art History 101 class. The stunning work depicts Giovanni di Nicolao Arnolfini and his wife (who is not pregnant as is often thought; she is merely holding up her full-skirted dress in the contemporary fashion). There's also an immense French Impressionist and post-Impressionist collection that includes works by Manet, Monet, Degas, Renoir, and Cézanne. Particularly charming is the peep-show cabinet by Hoogstraten in one of the Dutch rooms: It's like spying through a keyhole.

British and modern art are the specialties of the Tate galleries (see listings below), but the National Gallery does have some fine 18th-century British master-pieces, including works by Hogarth, Gainsborough, Reynolds, Constable, and Turner.

Long written off as a "fake," a painting of Mary Queen of Scots (1542–87) is on display. The portrait, purchased for less than £100 (at today's exchange rate) was acquired by the gallery in 1916 at a Christie's auction. It has gathered dust in a warehouse until it was rediscovered and authenticated. The wood on which the image of Mary was painted turned out to be from the late 16th century. Today the painting is believed to be one of the only two paintings made in the lifetime or shortly after the death of the Queen.

Guided tours of the National Gallery are offered twice daily at 11:30am and 2:30pm. A Gallery Guide soundtrack is also available. A portable CD player provides audio information on paintings of your choice with the mere push of a button. Although this service is free, contributions are appreciated.

Insider's tip: The National Gallery has a computer information center where you can design your own personal tour map for free. The computer room, located in the Micro Gallery, includes a dozen hands-on workstations. The online system lists 2,200 paintings and has background notes for each work. Using a touch-screen computer, you can design your own personalized tour by selecting a maximum of 10 paintings you would like to view. Once you have made your choices, you print a personal tour map with your selections.

North side of Trafalgar Sq., WC2. © **020/7747-2885.** www.nationalgallery.org.uk. Free admission. Thurs–Tues 10am–6pm; Wed 10am–9pm. Tube: Charing Cross or Leicester Sq.

National Portrait Gallery ★★ In a gallery of both remarkable and unremarkable portraits (they're collected for their subjects rather than their artistic quality), a few paintings tower over the rest, including Sir Joshua Reynolds's first portrait of Samuel Johnson ("a man of most dreadful appearance"), Nicholas Hilliard's miniature of handsome Sir Walter Raleigh, a full-length of Elizabeth I, and a Holbein cartoon of Henry VIII. There's also a portrait of William Shakespeare (with a gold earring) by an unknown artist that bears the claim of being the "most authentic contemporary likeness" of its subject. One of the most famous pictures in the gallery is the group portrait of the Brontë sisters (Charlotte, Emily, and Anne) by their brother, Bramwell. An idealized portrait of Lord Byron by Thomas Phillips is also on display.

The galleries of Victorian and early-20th-century portraits were radically redesigned. Some of the more flamboyant personalities of the past 2 centuries are on show: T. S. Eliot; Disraeli; Macmillan; Sir Richard Burton (the explorer, not the actor); Elizabeth Taylor; and our two favorites, G. F. Watts's famous portrait of his great actress wife, Ellen Terry, and Vanessa Bell's portrait of her sister, Virginia Woolf. Perhaps not surprisingly, a portrait of the late Princess Diana on the Royal Landing seems to attract the most viewers.

In 2000, Queen Elizabeth opened the Ondaatje Wing of the gallery, increasing the gallery's exhibition space by more than 50%. The most intriguing new space is the splendid Tudor Gallery, featuring portraits of Richard III and Henry VII. There's also a portrait of Shakespeare that the gallery acquired in 1856. A Balcony Gallery taps into the cult of celebrity, displaying more recent figures whose fame has lasted longer than Warhol's 15 minutes. These include everybody from Mick Jagger to Joan Collins, and, of course, the Baroness Thatcher. The Gallery operates a cafe and art bookshop.

St. Martin's Place, WC2. ℰ **020/7306-0055.** www.npg.org.uk. Free admission; fee charged for certain temporary exhibitions. Sat–Wed 10am–6pm; Thurs–Fri 10am–9pm. Tube: Charing Cross or Leicester Sq.

A portrait by Angela Reilly (R) on display at the National Portrait Gallery.

Interior of St. Paul's Cathedral.

Gardens outside St. Paul's Cathedral.

St. Paul's Cathedral ★★★   During World War II, newsreel footage reaching America showed St. Paul's Cathedral standing virtually alone among the rubble of the City, its dome lit by fires caused by bombings all around it. That the cathedral survived at all is a miracle, since it was badly hit twice during the early years of the bombardment of London. But St. Paul's is accustomed to calamity, having been burned down three times and destroyed by invading Norsemen. The old St. Paul's was razed during the Great Fire of 1666, making way for a new structure designed by Sir Christopher Wren and built between 1675 and 1710. The cathedral is architectural genius Wren's ultimate masterpiece.

The classical dome of St. Paul's dominates the City's square mile. The golden cross surmounting it is 110m (361 ft.) above the ground; the golden ball on which the cross rests measures 2m (6½ ft.) in diameter, though it looks like a marble from below. In the interior of the dome is the **Whispering Gallery,** an acoustic marvel in which the faintest whisper can be heard clearly on the opposite side. Sit on one side, have your traveling companions sit on the other, and whisper away. You can climb to the top of the dome for a 360-degree view of London. A second steep climb leads from the Whispering Gallery to the **Stone Gallery,** which opens onto a panoramic view of London. Another 153 steps take you to the **Inner Golden Gallery,** situated at the top of the inner dome. Here an even more panoramic view of London unfolds.

St. Paul's Churchyard, EC4. ✆ **020/7246-8350.** www.stpauls.co.uk. Cathedral and galleries £13 adults, £12 seniors and students, £4.50 children 6–16, £30 family

Roses Are Red

One of the most enjoyable activities of a spring visit to London is a stroll through the gardens of St. Paul's when the roses are in bloom.

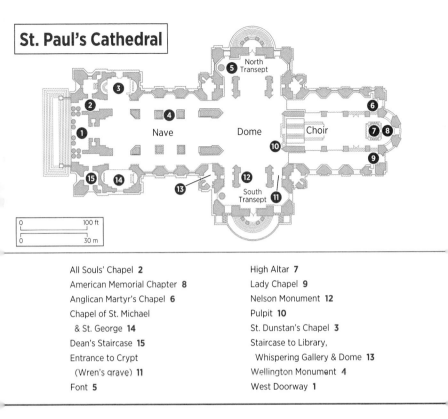

St. Paul's Cathedral

North Transept **5**

Nave

Dome

Choir

South Transept

0 — 100 ft
0 — 30 m

All Souls' Chapel **2**	High Altar **7**
American Memorial Chapter **8**	Lady Chapel **9**
Anglican Martyr's Chapel **6**	Nelson Monument **12**
Chapel of St. Michael	Pulpit **10**
& St. George **14**	St. Dunstan's Chapel **3**
Dean's Staircase **15**	Staircase to Library,
Entrance to Crypt	Whispering Gallery & Dome **13**
(Wren's grave) **11**	Wellington Monument **4**
Font **5**	West Doorway **1**

ticket, free for children 5 and younger; guided tours £3 adults, £2.50 students and seniors, £1 children; recorded tours £4, free for children 5 and younger. Cathedral (excluding galleries) Mon–Sat 8:30am–4pm; galleries Mon–Sat 9:30am–4pm. No sightseeing Sun (services only). Tube: St. Paul's, Mansion House, Cannon St., or Blackfriars.

Tate Britain ★★★   Fronting the Thames near Vauxhall Bridge in Pimlico, the Tate looks like a smaller and more graceful relation of the British Museum. The most prestigious gallery in Britain, it houses the national collections, covering British art from the 16th century to the present day, as well as an array of international works. The Tate's collection of 20th- and 21st-century art is housed at **Tate Modern** (see below), but the collection at Tate Britain is still much too large to be displayed all at once, so the works on view change from time to time.

The older works include some of the best of Gainsborough, Reynolds, Stubbs, Blake, and Constable. William Hogarth is well represented, particularly by his satirical *O the Roast Beef of Old England* (also known as the *Gate of Calais*). You'll find the illustrations of William Blake, the incomparable mystical poet, including such works as *The Book of Job, The Divine Comedy,* and *Paradise Lost.* The collection of works by J. M. W. Turner is the Tate's largest by a single artist—Turner himself willed most of his paintings and watercolors to the nation.

Also on display are pieces by many major 19th- and 20th-century painters, including Paul Nash, Matisse, Dalí, Modigliani, Munch, Bonnard, and Picasso.

Truly remarkable are the several enormous abstract canvases by Mark Rothko, the group of paintings and sculptures by Giacometti, and the paintings by one of England's best-known modern artists, Francis Bacon.

Insider's tip: After you've seen the grand art, don't hasten away. Drop in to the Tate Gallery Shop for some of the best art books and postcards in London. The gallery sells whimsical T-shirts with art masterpieces on them. Those ubiquitous Tate Gallery canvas bags seen all over London are sold here, as are the town's best art posters. Invite your friends for tea at the Coffee Shop, with its excellent cakes and pastries, or lunch at the Tate Gallery's restaurant (p. 207). You'll get to enjoy good food, Rex Whistler art, and the best and most reasonably priced wine list in London.

Millbank, SW1. ✆ **020/7887-8008.** www.tate.org.uk. Free admission; special exhibitions sometimes incur a charge of £5–£15. Daily 10:30am–5:50pm. Tube: Pimlico.

Tate Modern ★★★   In the transformed Bankside Power Station in Southwark, this museum draws some two million visitors a year to see the greatest collection of international 20th-century art in Britain. How would we rate the collection? At the same level of the Pompidou in Paris, with a slight edge over New York's Guggenheim. Tate Modern is viewer-friendly, with eye-level hangings. All the big painting stars are here—a whole galaxy ranging from Dalí to Duchamp, from Giacometti to Matisse and Mondrian, from Picasso and Pollock to Rothko and Warhol. The Modern is also a gallery of 21st-century art, displaying new and exciting works.

Hall in the Tate Britain.

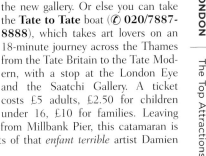

The Tate Modern makes extensive use of glass for both its exterior and interior, offering panoramic views. Galleries are arranged over three levels and provide a variety of spaces for display. Instead of exhibiting art chronologically and by school, the Tate Modern, in a radical break from tradition, takes a thematic approach. This allows displays to cut across movements.

You can cross the Millennium Bridge, a pedestrian-only walk from the steps of St. Paul's, over the Thames to the new gallery. Or else you can take the **Tate to Tate** boat (✆ **020/7887-8888**), which takes art lovers on an 18-minute journey across the Thames from the Tate Britain to the Tate Modern, with a stop at the London Eye and the Saatchi Gallery. A ticket costs £5 adults, £2.50 for children under 16, £10 for families. Leaving from Millbank Pier, this catamaran is

Embankment by Rachel Whiteread at the Tate Modern.

decorated by the trademark colorful dots of that *enfant terrible* artist Damien Hirst.

Bankside, SE1. ✆ **020/7887-8888.** www.tate.org.uk. Free admission. Sun–Thurs 10am–6pm; Fri–Sat 10am–10pm. Tube: Southwark or Blackfriars.

Tower Bridge ★★   This is one of the world's most celebrated landmarks and possibly the most photographed and painted bridge on earth. Despite its medieval appearance, Tower Bridge was built in 1894.

In 1993, the Tower Bridge Exhibition opened inside the bridge to commemorate its century-old history; it takes you up the north tower to high-level walkways between the two towers with spectacular views of St. Paul's, the Tower of London, and the Houses of Parliament. You're then led down the south tower and into the bridge's original engine room, containing the Victorian boilers and steam engines that used to raise and lower the bridge for ships to pass. Exhibits in the bridge's towers use animatronic characters, video, and computers to illustrate the history of the bridge.

At Tower Bridge, SE1. ✆ **020/7403-3761.** www.towerbridge.org.uk. Tower Bridge Experience £7 adults, £5 students and seniors, £3 children 5–15, £14 family ticket, free for children 4 and younger. Tower Bridge Experience Apr–Sept daily 10am–6:30pm; off season daily 9:30am–6pm. Closed Christmas Eve and Christmas Day. Tube: Tower Hill, London Bridge, or Fenchurch St.

Tower of London ★★★ ☺   This ancient fortress continues to pack in the crowds with its macabre associations with the legendary figures imprisoned and/or executed here. There are more spooks here per square foot than in any other building in the whole of haunted Britain. Headless bodies, bodiless heads, phantom soldiers, icy blasts, clanking chains—you name them, the Tower's got them.

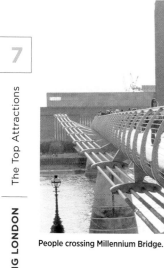

People crossing Millennium Bridge.

Centuries after the last head rolled on Tower Hill, a shivery atmosphere of impending doom still lingers over the Tower's mighty walls. Plan on spending a lot of time here.

The Tower is actually a compound of structures built through the ages for varying purposes, mostly as expressions of royal power. The oldest is the **White Tower,** begun by William the Conqueror in 1078 to keep London's native Saxon population in check. Later rulers added other towers, walls, and fortified gates, until the buildings became like a small town within a city. Until the reign of James I (beginning in 1603), the Tower was also a royal residence. But above all, it was a prison for important captives.

Every stone of the Tower tells a story—usually a gory one. In the **Bloody Tower,** according to Shakespeare, Richard III's henchmen murdered the two little princes (the young sons of his brother, Edward IV). Richard knew his position as king could not be secure as long as his nephews were alive, and there seems no reasonable doubt that the princes were killed on his orders. Attempts have been made by some historians to clear his name, but Richard remains the chief suspect, and his deed caused him to lose the "hearts of the people," according to the *Chronicles of London* at the time.

Sir Walter Raleigh spent 13 years in the Bloody Tower before his date with the executioner. On the walls of the **Beauchamp Tower,** you can still read the last messages scratched by despairing prisoners. Through **Traitors' Gate** passed such ill-fated, romantic figures as Robert Devereux, the

> ### Tower Tips
>
> You can spend the shortest time possible in the Tower's long lines if you buy your ticket at the kiosk at Tower Hill Tube station before emerging above ground. Even so, choose a day other than Sunday—crowds are at their worst then—and arrive as early as you can in the morning or late afternoon.

second Earl of Essex and a favorite of Elizabeth I. A plaque marks the eerie place at **Tower Green** where two wives of Henry VIII, Anne Boleyn and Catherine Howard, plus Sir Thomas More, and the 9-day queen, Lady Jane Grey, all lost their lives.

The Tower, besides being a royal palace, a fortress, and a prison, was also an armory, a treasury, a menagerie, and, in 1675, an astronomical observatory. Reopened in 1999, the White Tower holds the **Armouries,** which date from the reign of Henry VIII, as well as a display of instruments of torture and execution that recall some of the most ghastly moments in the Tower's history. In the Jewel House, you'll find the Tower's greatest attraction, the **Crown Jewels**—some of the world's most precious stones set into robes, swords, scepters, and crowns. The Imperial State Crown is the most famous crown on earth; made for Victoria in 1837, it's worn today by Queen Elizabeth II when she opens Parliament. Studded with some 3,000 jewels, it includes the Black Prince's Ruby, worn by Henry V at Agincourt. The 530-carat Star of Africa, a cut diamond on the Royal Sceptre with Cross, would make Harry Winston turn over in his grave. You'll have to stand in long lines to catch just a glimpse of the jewels as you and hundreds of others scroll by on moving sidewalks, but the wait is worth it.

The presumed prison cell of Sir Thomas More is open to the public. More left this cell in 1535 to face his executioner after he'd fallen out with King Henry VIII over the monarch's desire to divorce Catherine of Aragon, the first of his six wives. More is believed to have lived in the lower part of the Bell Tower, here in

Tower Bridge.

this whitewashed cell, during the last 14 months of his life, although some historians doubt this claim.

A **palace** inhabited by King Edward I in the late 1200s stands above Traitors' Gate. It's the only surviving medieval palace in Britain. Guides at the palace are dressed in period costumes, and reproductions of furniture and fittings, including Edward's throne, evoke the era, along with burning incense and candles.

In 2004 several improvements were made, including the opening of a visitor center and the restoration of a 13th-century wharf. To the west of the Tower is the newly created Tower Hill Square, designed by Stanton Williams, with a series of pavilions housing ticketing facilities, a gift shop, and a cafeteria.

Oh, yes—don't forget to look for the ravens. Six of them (plus two spares) are all registered as official Tower residents. According to a legend, the Tower of London will stand as long as those black, ominous birds remain, so to be on the safe side, one of the wings of each raven is clipped.

One-hour guided tours of the entire compound are given by the Yeoman Warders (also known as "Beefeaters") every half-hour, starting at 9:30am, from the Middle Tower near the main entrance. The last guided walk starts about 3:30pm in summer, 2:30pm in winter—weather permitting, of course.

You can attend the nightly **Ceremony of the Keys,** the ceremonial locking-up of the Tower by the Yeoman Warders. For free tickets, write to the Ceremony of the Keys, Waterloo Block, Tower of London, London EC3N 4AB, and

Entry to the Traitors' Gate at the Tower of London.

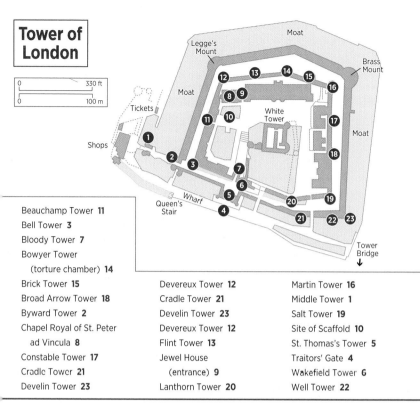

Tower of London

0		330 ft
0		100 m

Moat
Legge's Mount
Brass Mount
Moat
Tickets
White Tower
Moat
Shops
Wharf
Queen's Stair
Tower Bridge ↓

Beauchamp Tower **11**

Bell Tower **3**

Bloody Tower **7**

Bowyer Tower
  (torture chamber) **14**

Brick Tower **15**

Broad Arrow Tower **18**

Byward Tower **2**

Chapel Royal of St. Peter
  ad Vincula **8**

Constable Tower **17**

Cradle Tower **21**

Develin Tower **23**

Devereux Tower **12**

Cradle Tower **21**

Develin Tower **23**

Devereux Tower **12**

Flint Tower **13**

Jewel House
  (entrance) **9**

Lanthorn Tower **20**

Martin Tower **16**

Middle Tower **1**

Salt Tower **19**

Site of Scaffold **10**

St. Thomas's Tower **5**

Traitors' Gate **4**

Wakefield Tower **6**

Well Tower **22**

request a specific date, but also list alternate dates. At least 6 weeks' notice is required. Accompany all requests with a stamped, self-addressed envelope (British stamps only) or two International Reply Coupons. With ticket in hand, a Yeoman Warder will admit you at 9:35pm. Frankly, we think it's not worth the trouble you go through to see this rather cheesy ceremony, but we know some who disagree with us.

Tower Hill, EC3. ☎ **0844/482-7777.** www.hrp.org.uk. Admission £17 adults, £15 students and seniors, £9.50 children ages 5–15, family ticket £47, free for children 4 and under. Mar–Oct Tues–Sat 9am–5:30pm, Sun–Mon 10am–5:30pm; Nov–Feb Tues–Sat 9am–4:30pm, Sun–Mon 10am–4:30pm. Tube: Tower Hill.

Victoria and Albert Museum ★★★   The Victoria and Albert is the greatest decorative-arts museum in the world. It's also one of the liveliest and most imaginative museums in London—where else would you find the quintessential "little black dress"—made famous by Coco Chanel—in the permanent collection?

The medieval holdings include such treasures as the Early English Gloucester Candlestick; the Byzantine Veroli Casket, with its ivory panels based on Greek plays; and the Syon Cope, a unique embroidery made in England in the early 14th century. An area devoted to Islamic art houses the Ardabil Carpet from 16th-century Persia.

The V&A boasts the largest collection of Renaissance sculpture outside Italy. A highlight of the 16th-century collection is the marble group *Neptune with Triton* by Bernini. The cartoons by Raphael, which were conceived as designs for tapestries for the Sistine Chapel, are owned by the queen and are on display here. A most unusual, huge, and impressive exhibit is the Cast Courts, life-size plaster models of ancient and medieval statuary and architecture.

The museum has the greatest collection of Indian art outside India, plus Chinese and Japanese galleries. In complete contrast are suites of English furniture, metalwork, and ceramics, and a superb collection of portrait miniatures, including the one Hans Holbein the Younger made of Anne of Cleves for the benefit of Henry VIII, who was again casting around for a suitable wife. The Dress Collection includes a representation of corsets through the ages that's sure to make you wince. There's also a remarkable collection of musical instruments.

V&A has 15 modern galleries—the **British Galleries ★★★**—telling the story of British design from 1500 to 1900. No other museum in the world houses such a diverse collection of British design and decorative art. From Chippendale to Morris, all of the top British designers are featured in some 3,000 exhibits, ranging from the 5m-high (16-ft.) Melville Bed (1697) with its luxurious wild-silk damask and red-velvet hangings, to 19th-century classics such as furniture by Charles Rennie Mackintosh. One of the most prized possessions is the "Great Bed of Ware," mentioned in Shakespeare's *Twelfth Night*. Also on exhibit is the wedding suite of James II. And don't miss the V&A's most bizarre gallery, Fakes and Forgeries. The impostors here are amazingly authentic—in fact, we'd judge some of them as better than the Old Masters themselves. The interactive displays hold special interest. Learning about heraldry is far more interesting when you're designing your own coat of arms.

On view is a suite of five painting galleries that were originally built in 1850. A trio of these galleries focuses on British landscapes as seen through the eyes of Turner, Constable, and others. Constable's oil sketches were donated by his daughter, Isabel, in 1888. Another gallery showcases the bequest of Constantine Ionides, a Victorian collector, with masters such as Botticelli, Delacroix, Degas, Tintoretto, and Ingres. There's even a piano here designed by the famous Edward Burne-Jones, which once belonged to Ionides's brother. In 2009, the **Gilbert Collection ★★★**, one of the most important bequests of the decorative arts ever made in England, was moved to a suite of galleries in the V&A. Sir Arthur Gilbert made his gift of gold, silver, mosaics, and gold snuffboxes to the nation in 1996, at which time the value was estimated at £75 million. The collection of some 800 objects in

The Annunciation (early 14th century) at the Victoria and Albert Museum.

Artifacts in the British Galleries at the Victoria and Albert Museum.

three fields is among the most distinguished in the world. The array of mosaics is among the most comprehensive ever gathered, with Roman and Florentine examples dating from the 16th to the 19th centuries. The gold and silver collection, the most exceptional in London, has exceptional breadth, ranging from the 15th to the 19th centuries, spanning India to South America. It is strong in masterpieces of great 18th-century silversmiths, such as Paul de Lamerie. Such exhibits as the Maharajah pieces, the "Gold Crown," and Catherine the Great's Royal Gates are fabulous. The gallery also displays one of the most representative collections of gold snuffboxes in the world, with some 200 examples. Some of the snuffboxes were owned by Louis XV, Frederick the Great, and Napoleon.

Cromwell Rd., SW7. ℭ **020/7942-2000.** www.vam.ac.uk. Free admission. Temporary exhibitions often £12. Daily 10am–5:45pm (until 10pm every Wed and the last Fri of each month). Tube: South Kensington.

Westminster Abbey ★★★   With its identical square towers and superb archways, this early-English Gothic abbey is one of the greatest examples of ecclesiastical architecture on earth. But it's far more than that: It's the shrine of a nation, the symbol of everything Britain has stood for and stands for, and the place in which most of its rulers were crowned and where many lie buried.

Nearly every figure in English history has left his or her mark on Westminster Abbey. Edward the Confessor founded the Benedictine abbey in 1065 on this spot overlooking Parliament Square. The first English king crowned in the Abbey may have been Harold, in January 1066. The man who defeated him at the Battle of Hastings later that year, William the Conqueror, had the first recorded coronation in the Abbey on Christmas Day that same year. The coronation tradition has continued to the present day. The essentially early-English Gothic structure existing today owes more to Henry III's plans than to those of any other sovereign, although many architects, including Wren, have contributed to the Abbey.

Built on the site of the ancient Lady Chapel in the early 16th century, the **Henry VII Chapel** is one of the loveliest in Europe, with its fan vaulting, Knights of Bath banners, and Torrigiani-designed tomb for the king himself, near which hangs a 15th-century Vivarini painting, *Madonna and Child.* Also here, ironically buried in the same tomb, are Catholic Mary I and Protestant Elizabeth I (whose archrival, Mary Queen of Scots, is entombed on the other side of the Henry VII Chapel). In one end of the chapel, you can stand on Cromwell's memorial stone and view the **Royal Air Force Chapel** and its Battle of Britain memorial window, unveiled in 1947 to honor the Royal Air Force.

You can also visit the most hallowed spot in the abbey, the **shrine of Edward the Confessor** (canonized in the 12th c.). Near the tomb of Henry V is the Coronation Chair, made at the command of Edward I in 1300 to display the mystical Stone of Scone (which some think is the sacred stone mentioned in Genesis and known as Jacob's Pillar). Scottish kings were once crowned on the stone. (It has since been returned to Scotland.)

When you see a statue of the Bard, with one arm resting on a stack of books, you've arrived at **Poets' Corner.** Shakespeare himself is buried at Stratford-upon-Avon, but resting here are Chaucer, Samuel Johnson, Tennyson, Browning, and Dickens. There's even an American, Henry Wadsworth Longfellow, as well as monuments to just about everybody: Milton, Keats, Shelley, Henry James, T. S. Eliot, George Eliot, and others. The most stylized monument is Sir Jacob

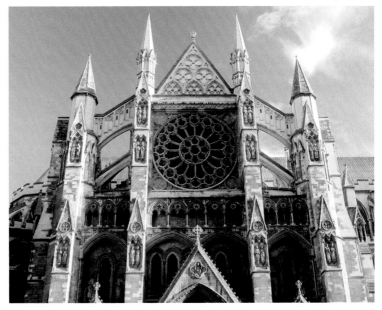

North front of Westminster Abbey.

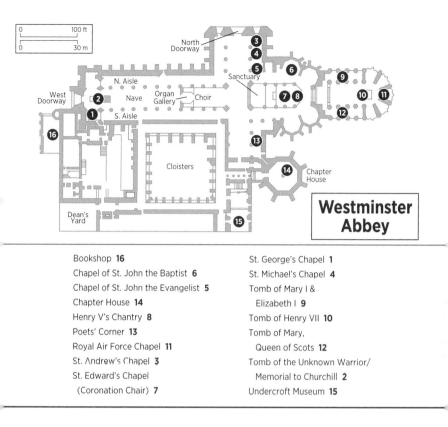

Bookshop **16**	St. George's Chapel **1**
Chapel of St. John the Baptist **6**	St. Michael's Chapel **4**
Chapel of St. John the Evangelist **5**	Tomb of Mary I &
Chapter House **14**	Elizabeth I **9**
Henry V's Chantry **8**	Tomb of Henry VII **10**
Poets' Corner **13**	Tomb of Mary,
Royal Air Force Chapel **11**	Queen of Scots **12**
St. Andrew's Chapel **3**	Tomb of the Unknown Warrior/
St. Edward's Chapel	Memorial to Churchill **2**
(Coronation Chair) **7**	Undercroft Museum **15**

Epstein's sculptured bust of William Blake. More recent tablets commemorate poet Dylan Thomas and Sir Laurence Olivier.

Statesmen and men of science—Disraeli, Newton, Charles Darwin—are also interred in the abbey or honored by monuments. Near the west door is the 1965 memorial to Sir Winston Churchill. In the vicinity of this memorial is the tomb of the **Unknown Warrior,** commemorating the British dead of World War I.

Although most of the Abbey's statuary commemorates notable figures of the past, 10 new statues were unveiled in July 1998. Placed in the Gothic niches above the West Front door, these statues honor 10 modern-day martyrs drawn from every continent and religious denomination. The sculptures include Elizabeth of Russia, Janani Luwum, and Martin Luther King, Jr., representatives of those who have sacrificed their lives for their beliefs.

Off the Cloisters, the **College Garden** is the oldest garden in England, under cultivation for more than 900 years. Established in the 11th century as the abbey's first infirmary garden, this was once a magnificent source of fruits, vegetables, and medicinal herbs. Five of the trees in the garden were planted in 1850, and they continue to thrive today. Surrounded by high walls, flowering trees dot the lawns, and park benches provide comfort where you can hardly hear the roar of passing traffic. The garden is open only Tuesday through Thursday April

Poets' Corner at Westminster Abbey.

through September from 10am to 6pm, and October through March from 10am to 4pm.

Insider's tip: Far removed from the pomp and glory is the **Abbey Treasure Museum,** which displays a real bag of oddities in the undercroft—or crypt—part of the monastic buildings erected between 1066 and 1100. You'll find royal effigies that were used instead of the real corpses for lying-in-state ceremonies because they smelled better. You'll see the almost lifelike effigy of Admiral Nelson (his mistress arranged his hair) and even that of Edward III, his lip warped by the cerebral hemorrhage that felled him. Other oddities include Henry V's funeral armor, a unique corset from Elizabeth I's effigy, and the Essex Ring that Elizabeth I gave to her favorite (Robert Devereux, the Earl of Essex) when she was feeling good about him.

On Sundays, the Abbey is not open to visitors; the rest of the church is open unless a service is being conducted. For times of services, phone the **Chapter Office** (✆ **020/7222-5152**).

Broad Sanctuary, SW1. ✆ **020/7222-5152.** www.westminster-abbey.org. Admission £15 adults, £12 students and seniors, £6 children 11–18, £32 family ticket, free for children 10 and younger. Mon–Tues and Thurs–Fri 9:30am–3:45pm; Wed 9:30am–6pm; Sat 9:30am–2:45pm. Tube: Westminster or St. James's Park.

MORE CENTRAL LONDON ATTRACTIONS

See the "Sights & Attractions by Neighborhood" list on p. 236 for more information on which attractions are in which neighborhood.

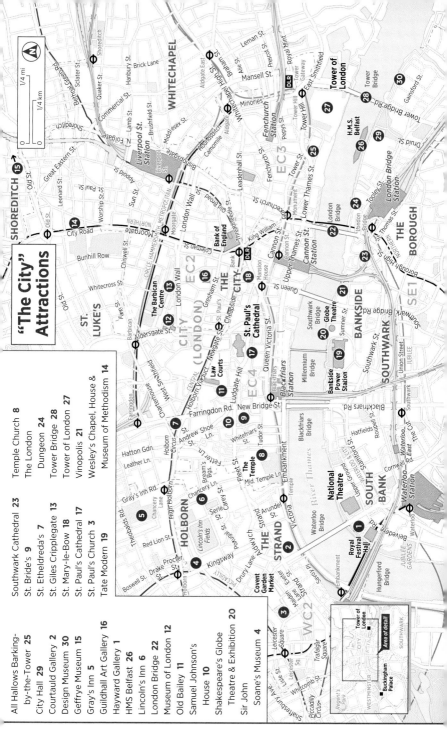

"The City" Attractions

All Hallows Barking-
by-the-Tower **25**
City Hall **29**
Courtauld Gallery **2**
Design Museum **30**
Geffrye Museum **15**
Gray's Inn **5**
Guildhall Art Gallery **16**
Hayward Gallery **1**
HMS Belfast **26**
Lincoln's Inn **6**
London Bridge **22**
Museum of London **12**
Old Bailey **11**
Samuel Johnson's
House **10**
Shakespeare's Globe
Theatre & Exhibition **20**
Sir John
Soane's Museum **4**

Southwark Cathedral **23**
St. Bride's **9**
St. Etheldreda's **7**
St. Giles Cripplegate **13**
St. Mary-le-Bow **18**
St. Paul's Cathedral **17**
St. Paul's Church **3**
Tate Modern **19**

Temple Church **8**
The London
Dungeon **24**
Tower Bridge **28**
Tower of London **27**
Vinopolis **21**
Wesley's Chapel, House &
Museum of Methodism **14**

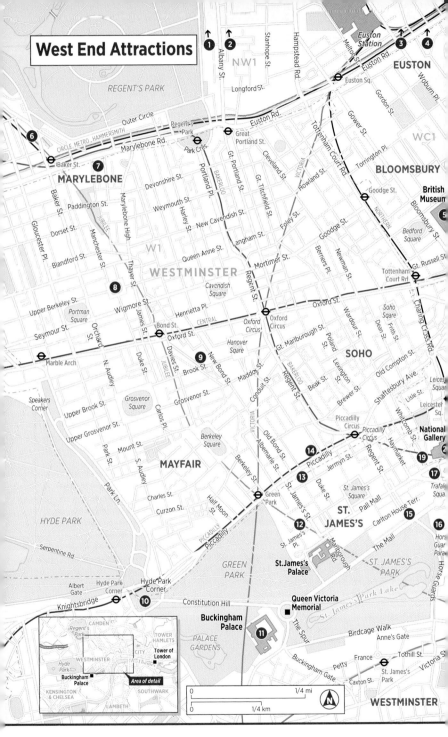

West End Attractions

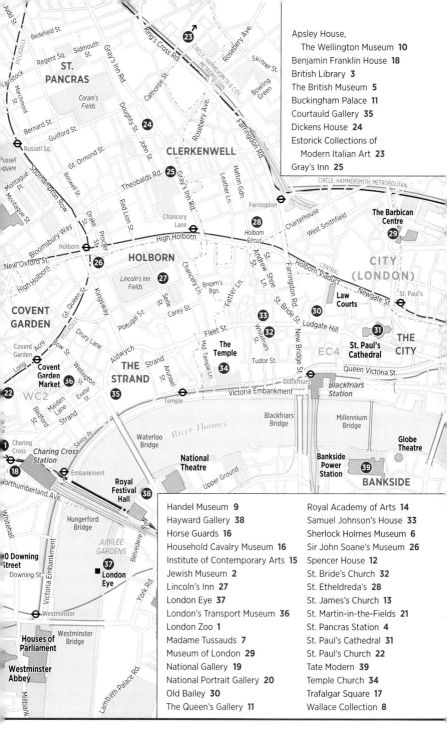

Apsley House,
The Wellington Museum **10**
Benjamin Franklin House **18**
British Library **3**
The British Museum **5**
Buckingham Palace **11**
Courtauld Gallery **35**
Dickens House **24**
Estorick Collections of
Modern Italian Art **23**
Gray's Inn **25**

Handel Museum **9**
Hayward Gallery **38**
Horse Guards **16**
Household Cavalry Museum **16**
Institute of Contemporary Arts **15**
Jewish Museum **2**
Lincoln's Inn **27**
London Eye **37**
London's Transport Museum **36**
London Zoo **1**
Madame Tussauds **7**
Museum of London **29**
National Gallery **19**
National Portrait Gallery **20**
Old Bailey **30**
The Queen's Gallery **11**

Royal Academy of Arts **14**
Samuel Johnson's House **33**
Sherlock Holmes Museum **6**
Sir John Soane's Museum **26**
Spencer House **12**
St. Bride's Church **32**
St. Etheldreda's **28**
St. James's Church **13**
St. Martin-in-the-Fields **21**
St. Pancras Station **4**
St. Paul's Cathedral **31**
St. Paul's Church **22**
Tate Modern **39**
Temple Church **34**
Trafalgar Square **17**
Wallace Collection **8**

265

Churches & Cathedrals

Many of London's churches offer free lunchtime concerts; a full list is available from the London Tourist Board. It's customary to leave a small donation.

All Hallows Barking-by-the-Tower   This fascinating church, which houses a brass-rubbing center, is located next door to the Tower of London. It features a crypt museum, Roman remains, and traces of early London, including a Saxon arch predating the Tower. Samuel Pepys, the famed diarist, climbed the spire of the church to watch the raging fire of London in 1666. In 1644, William Penn was baptized here, and in 1797, John Quincy Adams was married here. Bombs destroyed the church in 1940, leaving only the tower and walls standing. The church was rebuilt from 1949 to 1958. See "The City Attractions" map (p. 263).

Byward St., EC3. (*C*) **020/7481-2928.** www.allhallowsbythetower.org.uk. Free admission; crypt museum tour £6. Museum Mon–Fri 10am–5:30pm; Sat 10am–5pm; Sun 1–5pm. Church Mon–Fri 9am–6pm; Sat–Sun 10am–5pm. Tube: Tower Hill.

St. Bride's ★   Known as the "the church of the press," thanks to its location at the end of Fleet Street, St. Bride's is a remarkable landmark. The current church is the eighth one that has stood here. After it was bombed in 1940, an archaeologist excavated the crypts and was able to confirm much of the site's legendary history: A Roman house was discovered, and it was established that in the 6th century, St. Brigit of Ireland founded the first Christian church that was built here. In addition, a crypt with evidence of six subsequent churches was discovered. Diarist Samuel Pepys was baptized here, and novelist Samuel Richardson and his family are buried here. After the Great Fire destroyed it, Christopher Wren rebuilt the church with a spire that's been described as a "madrigal in stone." The crypt was a burial chamber and charnel house for centuries; today it's a museum. Evensong is every Sunday at 6:30pm, and choral concerts are sometimes staged—call for information or check the website below. See "The City Attractions" map (p. 263).

Fleet St., EC4. (*C*) **020/7427-0133.** www.stbrides.com. Free admission. Mon–Fri 8am–6pm; Sat 11am–3pm; Sun 10am–1pm and 5–7:30pm. Choral concerts are Feb–July and Sept–Nov at 1:15pm Tues and Fri. Tube: Blackfriars.

St. Etheldreda's   The oldest Roman Catholic church in London, St. Etheldreda's stands on Ely Place, off Charterhouse Street, at Holborn Circus. Built in 1251, it was mentioned by the Bard in both *Richard II* and *Richard III*. A survivor of the Great Fire of 1666, the church and the area surrounding it were the property of the diocese of the city of Ely, in the days when many bishops had Episcopal houses in London, as well as in the cathedral cities in

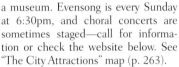

The Steeple at St. Bride's.

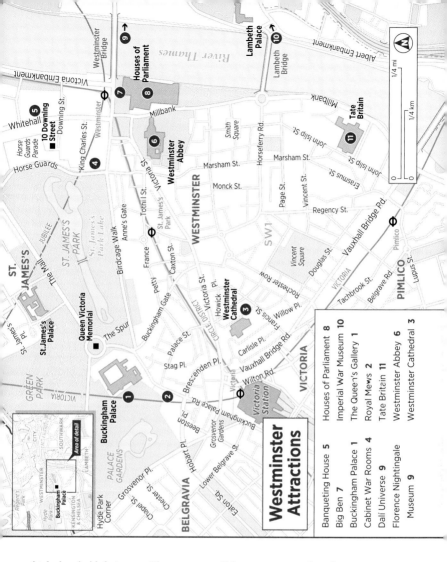

Westminster Attractions

Banqueting House 5
Big Ben 7
Buckingham Palace 1
Cabinet War Rooms 4
Dalí Universe 9
Florence Nightingale Museum 9
Houses of Parliament 8
Imperial War Museum 10
The Queen's Gallery 1
Royal Mews 2
Tate Britain 11
Westminster Abbey 6
Westminster Cathedral 3

which they held their sees. The property still has a private road, with impressive iron gates and a lodge for the gatekeeper.

St. Etheldreda, whose name is sometimes shortened to St. Audrey, was a 7th-century king's daughter who left her husband and established an abbey on the Isle of Ely. St. Etheldreda's has a distinguished musical tradition, with the 11am Mass on Sunday sung in Latin. Other Masses are on Sunday at 9am, Monday to Friday at 8am and 1pm, and Saturday at 9:30am. Lunch, with a varied choice of hot and cold dishes, is served Monday to Friday from noon to 2:30pm in the Crypt Café. See "The City Attractions" map (p. 263).

14 Ely Place, Holborn Circus, EC1. ✆ **020/7405-1061.** www.stetheldreda.com. Free admission. Daily 7:30am–6pm; Sat Mass 9:30am; Sun Masses 9 and 11am; weekday Masses Mon–Fri 8am and 1pm. Tube: Farringdon or Chancery Lane.

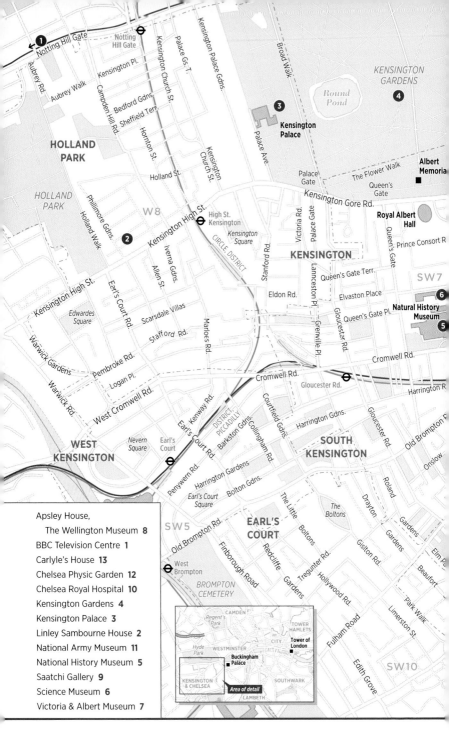

1 Notting Hill Gate

HOLLAND PARK

Notting Hill Gate

Kensington Pl.

Aubrey Rd.

Aubrey Walk

Campden Hill Rd.

Bedford Gdns.

Sheffield Terr.

Hornton St.

Kensington Church St.

Palace Gs. T.

Kensington Palace Gdns.

HOLLAND PARK

Phillimore Gdns.

Holland Walk

W 8

Holland St.

Kensington Church St.

Kensington Square

3 **Kensington Palace**

Palace Ave.

Palace Gate

Broad Walk

KENSINGTON GARDENS

Round Pond

4

The Flower Walk

Queen's Gate

Albert Memoria

Kensington Gore Rd.

Royal Albert Hall

Victoria Rd.

Palace Gate

Queen's Gate

Prince Consort R

KENSINGTON

SW7

Kensington High St.

Iverna Gdns.

Allen St.

Edwardes Square

Scarsdale Villas

Stafford Rd.

Marloes Rd.

Pembroke Rd.

Logan Pl.

Warwick Gardens

Warwick Rd.

West Cromwell Rd.

Nevern Square

Earl's Court

WEST KENSINGTON

Penywern Rd.

Harrington Gardens

Earl's Court Square

Bolton Gdns.

SW 5

Old Brompton Rd.

Earl's Court Rd.

Earl's Court Rd.

2

High St. Kensington

CIRCLE DISTRICT

Stanford Rd.

Eldon Rd.

Lancaston Pl.

Palace Gate

Grenville Pl.

Gloucester Rd.

Queen's Gate Terr.

Elvaston Place

Queen's Gate Pl.

Queen's Gate

Natural History Museum

6

5

Cromwell Rd.

Cromwell Rd.

Gloucester Rd.

Harrington R

Harrington Gdns.

Gloucester Rd.

Old Brompton Rd.

Onslow

Barkston Gdns.

Collingham Rd.

Courtfield Gdns.

DISTRICT PICCADILLY

SOUTH KENSINGTON

Roland

Gardens

Elm Pa

Drayton

The Little Boltons

The Boltons

Gilston Rd.

Beaufort

EARL'S COURT

Old Brompton Rd.

Finborough Road

West Brompton

BROMPTON CEMETERY

Redcliffe Gardens

The Boltons

Tregunter Rd.

Hollywood Rd.

Fulham Road

Limerston St.

Park Walk

Edith Grove

SW10

Regent's Park

Hyde Park

WESTMINSTER

Buckingham Palace

KENSINGTON & CHELSEA

CAMDEN

CITY

R. Thames

Area of detail

LAMBETH

TOWER HAMLETS

Tower of London

SOUTHWARK

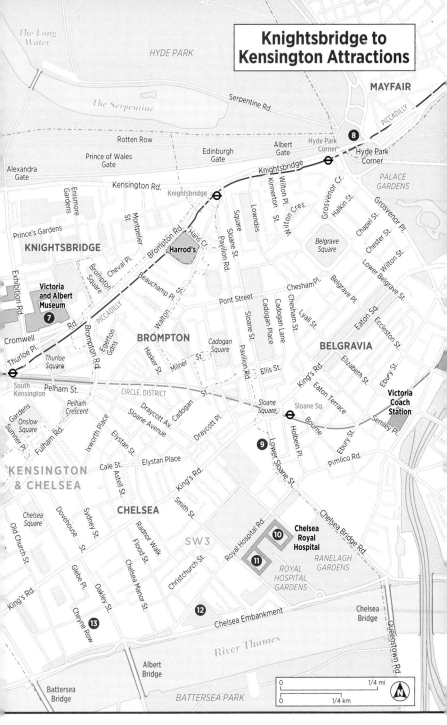

St. Giles Cripplegate ★   Named for the patron saint of cripples, St. Giles was founded in the 11th century. The church survived the Great Fire, but the Blitz left only the tower and walls standing. In 1620, English revolutionary Oliver Cromwell was betrothed to Elizabeth Bourchier here, and in 1674, John Milton, author of *Paradise Lost,* was buried here. More than a century later, someone opened the poet's grave, knocked out his teeth, stole a rib bone, and tore hair from his skull. Guided tours are available most Tuesday afternoons. Call to confirm. See "The City Attractions" map.

At Fore and Wood sts., London Wall, EC2. (*) **020/7638-1997.** www.stgilescripplegate.com. Free admission. Mon–Fri 10am–4pm; Sat–Sun 8am–noon for services, 4pm for evensong. Tours most Tues afternoons 2–5pm. Tube: Moorgate, St. Paul's, or Barbican.

St. James's Church ★   When the aristocratic area known as St. James's was developed in the late 17th century, Sir Christopher Wren was commissioned to build its parish church. Diarist John Evelyn wrote of the interior, "There is no altar anywhere in England, nor has there been any abroad, more handsomely adorned." Wren's master carver Grinling Gibbons created the reredos (a screen decorated with religious icons and placed behind the altar), organ case, and font. This church has rich historical associations: The poet William Blake was baptized here, as was William Pitt, who became England's youngest prime minister at age 24. Caricaturist James Gillray, auctioneer James Christie, and coffeehouse founder Francis White are all buried here. One of the more colorful marriages celebrated here was that of explorer Sir Samuel Baker and the woman he had bought at a slave auction. St. James's Church is a radical, inclusive Anglican church. It's also the Centre for Health and Healing and holds seminars on New Age and Creation Spirituality. There's a Bible Garden and a crafts market in the courtyard. The Wren Café is open daily, and

St. Giles.

Back view of St. Martin-in-the-Fields.

lunchtime and evening concerts are presented. There is an antiques market at St. James's on Tuesday from 10am to 6pm, and a crafts market Wednesday to Saturday 10am to 6pm.

197 Piccadilly, W1. ℭ **020/7734-4511.** www. st-james-piccadilly.org. Free admission. Lunchtime concerts are held on Mon, Wed, and Fri at 1:10pm. Suggested donation £4. Evening concerts are on an irregular schedule; check at the church for a poster listing the current slate of evening concerts. Tube: Piccadilly Circus or Green Park.

St. Martin-in-the-Fields ★ Designed by James Gibbs, a disciple of Christopher Wren, and completed in 1726, this classical church stands at the northeast corner of Trafalgar Square, opposite the National Gallery. Its spire, added in 1824, towers 56m (184 ft.) higher than Nelson's Column, which also rises on the square. The steeple became the model for many churches in colonial America. Since the first year of World War I (1914), the homeless have sought "soup and shelter" at St. Martin, a tradition that continues.

At one time, the crypt held the remains of Charles II (he's in Westminster Abbey now), who was christened here, giving St. Martin a claim as a royal parish church. His mistress, Nell Gwynne, and the highwayman Jack Sheppard are both interred here. The floors of the crypt are actually gravestones, and the walls date from the 1500s. The little restaurant, **Café in the Crypt,** is still called "Field's" by its devotees. Also in the crypt is the **London Brass Rubbing Centre** (ℭ 020/7930-9306; www2.stmartin-in-the-fields.org/page/visiting/brass. html), with 88 exact copies of bronze portraits ready for use. Paper, rubbing materials, and instructions on how to begin are furnished, and there's classical music for you to enjoy as you proceed. Fees to make the rubbings start at £4.50. There's also a gift shop with brass-rubbing kits for children, ready-made rubbings, Celtic jewelry, miniature brasses, and model knights. The center is open Monday to Wednesday 10am to 7pm, Thursday to Saturday 10am to 10pm, and Sunday noon to 7pm. See the "West End Attractions" map (p. 264).

Insider's tip: In the back of the church is a crafts market. Also, lunchtime and evening concerts are staged Monday, Tuesday, and Friday at 1:05pm, and Tuesday and Thursday through Saturday at 7:30pm. Lunch concerts are free, but evening tickets cost £6 to £24.

Trafalgar Sq., WC2. ℭ **020/7766-1100.** www.stmartin-in-the-fields.org. Mon–Fri 9am–6pm; Sat–Sun 8:45am–7:30pm as long as no service is taking place. Concerts Mon, Tues, and Fri 1:05pm; Tues and Thurs–Sat 7:30pm. Tube: Charing Cross.

St. Mary-le-Bow ★★   It's said that a true Cockney must be born within range of the sound of this church's famous Bow bells. The church has a sometimes-gruesome history. In 1091, its roof was ripped off in a storm; in 1271, the church tower collapsed and 20 people were killed; in 1331, Queen Philippa and her ladies-in-waiting fell to the ground when a balcony collapsed during a joust celebrating the birth of the Black Prince. Wren rebuilt the church after the Great Fire of 1666 engulfed it. The original "Cockney" Bow bells destroyed in the Blitz have been replaced. The church was rededicated in 1964 after extensive restoration work. See "The City Attractions" map (p. 263).

Cheapside, EC2. ℭ **020/7248-5139.** www.stmarylebow.co.uk. Free admission. Mon–Fri 6:30am–6pm. Tube: St. Paul's or Bank.

St. Paul's Church (the Actors' Church) ★   With the Drury Lane Theatre, the Royal Opera House, and many other theaters within its parish, St. Paul's has long been associated with the theatrical arts. Inside you'll find memorial plaques dedicated to such luminaries as Vivien Leigh, Boris Karloff, Margaret Rutherford, and Noel Coward, to name only a few. Designed by Inigo Jones in 1631, this church has been substantially altered over the years, but has retained a quiet garden-piazza in the rear. Among the famous people buried here are woodcarver Grinling Gibbons, writer Samuel Butler, and actress Ellen Terry. Landscape painter J. M. W. Turner and librettist W. S. Gilbert were both baptized here. The church often opens on Saturday at some point, but hours vary. There are free lunchtime piano recitals, most often scheduled on Thursday or Friday at 1pm—check before heading here if you want to attend one. See "The City Attractions" map (p. 263).

Bedford St., Covent Garden, WC2. ℭ **020/7836-5221.** www.actorschurch.org. Free admission. Mon–Fri 8:30am–5:30pm; Sun service 11am. Tube: Covent Garden.

Southwark Cathedral ★★   There's been a church on this site, in the heart of London's first theater district, for more than a thousand years. The present one dates from the 15th century and was partly rebuilt in 1890. The previous one was the first Gothic church to be constructed in London (in 1106). A wooden effigy of a knight dates from 1275. Shakespeare and Chaucer worshiped here, and inside is a memorial to the playwright. In 1424, James I of Scotland married Mary Beaufort here. During the reign of Mary Tudor, Stephen Gardiner, the Bishop of Winchester, held a consistory court in the retro choir that condemned seven Protestants—the Marian martyrs—to death. Organ concerts are presented on Monday from 1:10 to 1:50pm, and classical music concerts on Tuesday from 3:15 to 4pm. Both are free. See "The City Attractions" map (p. 263).

Montague Close, London Bridge, SE1. ℭ **020/7367-6700.** www.southwark.anglican.org/cathedral. Free admission; suggested donation £4. Mon–Fri 7:30am–6pm; Sat–Sun 8:30am–6pm. Tube: London Bridge.

Temple Church ★★   One of three Norman "round churches" left in England, this one was first completed in the 12th century. Not surprisingly, it has been restored. Look for the knightly effigies and the Norman door, and take note of the circle of grotesque portrait heads, including a goat in a mortarboard. Free organ recitals are presented Wednesday from 1:15 to 1:35pm. On Inner Temple Lane, about where the Strand becomes Fleet Street going east, you'll see the memorial pillar called **Temple Bar,** which marks the boundary of the City of London. See "The City Attractions" map.

Close-up of a statue at Southwark Cathedral.

The Temple (within the Inner Temple), King's Bench Walk, EC4. ℂ **020/7353-3470.** www.temple church.com. Free admission. Mon–Tues and Fri 11am–12:30am and 1–4pm; Wed 2–4pm; Thurs 11am–12:30pm and 2–3:30pm; Sat 11am–12:30pm and 1–3pm; Sun 1–3:30pm. Tube: Temple.

Wesley's Chapel, House & Museum of Methodism John Wesley, the founder of Methodism, established this church in 1778 as his London base. Wesley, who rode on horseback throughout the English countryside and preached in the open air, lived at no. 47, next door to the chapel. He's buried in a grave behind the chapel. The house contains many of Wesley's belongings and his study chair. While it survived the Blitz, the church later fell into disrepair; major restoration was completed in the 1970s. In the crypt, a museum traces the history of Methodism to present times.

Across the road in Bunhill Fields is the **Dissenters Graveyard,** where Daniel Defoe, William Blake, and John Bunyan are buried. See "The City Attractions" map (p. 263).

49 City Rd., EC1. ℂ **020/7253-2262.** www.wesleyschapel.org.uk. Chapel free. House and museum are also free, but a donation of £2 per person is expected. House and museum Mon–Sat 10am–4pm; Sun noon–1:45pm. Tube: Old St. or Moorgate.

Westminster Cathedral ★ This spectacular brick-and-stone church (1903) is the headquarters of the Roman Catholic Church in Britain. Adorned in early-Byzantine style, it's massive: 108m (354 ft.) long and 47m (154 ft.) wide. One hundred marbles compose the richly decorated interior, and eight marble columns support the nave. Eight yellow-marble columns hold up the huge canopy over the high altar. Mosaics emblazon the chapels and the vaulting of the sanctuary. If you take the elevator to the top of the 82m (269-ft.) campanile, you'll be rewarded with sweeping views that take in Buckingham Palace, Westminster Abbey, and St. Paul's Cathedral. There is a cafe serving light snacks and soft drinks from 9am to 5pm and a gift shop open Monday to Saturday from 9:30am to 5:15pm, Sunday from 10am to 4:45pm. See the "Westminster Attractions" map (p. 267).

Temple Bar Griffin monument on the Strand.

Interior of Westminster Cathedral.

Ashley Place, SW1. ✆ **020/7798-9055.** www.westminstercathedral.org.uk. Cathedral free. Audio tours £2.50. Tower £3. Cathedral services Mon–Sat 7am–7pm; Sun 8am–8pm. Tower daily 9:30am–12:30pm and 1–5pm. Tube: Victoria.

Historic Buildings

Banqueting House ★★   The feasting chamber in Whitehall Palace is probably the most sumptuous dining hall on earth. (Unfortunately, you can't dine here unless you're a visiting head of state.) Designed by Inigo Jones and decorated with original ceiling paintings by Rubens, the hall is dazzling enough to make you forget food altogether. Among the historic events that took place here were the beheading of King Charles I, who stepped to his execution through a window onto the scaffold outside, and the restoration ceremony of Charles II, marking the return of monarchy after Cromwell's brief Puritan Commonwealth. The house often closes on short notice for official events, so it's best to call in advance if you want to see it. See the "Westminster Attractions" map (p. 267).

Whitehall Palace, Horse Guards Ave., SW1. ✆ **0894/482-7777.** www.hrp.org.uk. Admission £4.80 adults, £4 seniors and students, £2.25 children 15 and under. Mon–Sat 10am–5pm (last admission 4:30pm). Tube: Westminster or Embankment.

Benjamin Franklin House ★   The only surviving home of Benjamin Franklin in London opened as a museum in 2006. Off Trafalgar Square, the modest four-story brick building was Franklin's residence from 1757 to 1775, when he was a diplomat on behalf of American colonists. Curators call the house "the first de facto U.S. Embassy." The building was also the site of many of Franklin's scientific experiments. It was here that he invented bifocal glasses and created the ethereal-sounding musical instrument, the glass harmonica. Franklin lived here in "serene comfort and affection," often having a full household of friends or relatives. Visitors can view the parlor where Franklin—a great fan of fresh air—sat "air bathing" naked by the open windows. The museum stages a "Historical Experience" every 45 minutes throughout the day. Visitors are taken through the various rooms by actors presenting a re-creation of Franklin's last night in London.

36 Craven St., WC2. ✆ **020/7839-2006.** www.benjaminfranklinhouse.org. Admission £7 adults, free children 16 and under. Wed–Sun 10am–5pm. Tube: Trafalgar Sq.

Cabinet War Rooms ★ Visitors today can see the **Cabinet War Rooms,** the bombproof bunker suite of rooms, just as they were when abandoned by Winston Churchill and the British government at the end of World War II. You can see the Map Room with its huge wall maps; the Atlantic map is a mass of pinholes (each hole represents at least one convoy). Next door is Churchill's bedroom-cum-office, which has a bed and a desk with two BBC microphones on it—he used these to broadcast the now-famous speeches that stirred the nation. Other rooms on the tour include the Chiefs of Staff map room, Churchill's kitchen and dining room, Sir Winston's private detectives' room, and Mrs. Churchill's bedroom. There's everything here from a pencil cartoon of Hitler, to a mousetrap in the kitchen, to the original chamber pots under the beds (they had no flush toilets). The **Transatlantic Telephone Room** is little more than a broom closet, but it housed the Bell Telephone Company's special scrambler phone, called *Sigsaly,* and it was where Churchill conferred with Roosevelt. Visitors are provided with a step-by-step personal sound guide, providing a detailed account of each room's function and history.

Painted ceiling of the Banqueting House.

Also in the war rooms is the **Churchill Museum,** the world's first major museum dedicated to the life of Sir Winston Churchill. It explores in various exhibits and photographs the saga of Britain's wartime prime minister. The opening marked the 40th anniversary of the prime minister's death. The museum, through its memorabilia, introduces visitors to the private man but also traces his development as a world leader.

Clive Steps, at end of King Charles St. (off Whitehall near Big Ben), SW1. ✆ **020/7930-6961.** http://cwr.iwm.org.uk. Admission £15 adults, £12 seniors and students, free for children 15 and under. Daily 9:30am–6pm (last admission at 5pm). Tube: Westminster or St. James's.

Chelsea Royal Hospital ★★ This dignified institution, founded by Charles II in 1682 as a home for veterans, was designed and completed by Sir Christopher Wren in 1692. It consists of a main block containing the hall and the chapel, flanked by east and west wings. There's been little change to Wren's design, except for minor work done by Robert Adam in the 18th century and the addition of stables by Sir John Soane in 1814. The Duke of Wellington lay in state here from November 10 to 17, 1852. So many people thronged to see him that two were crushed to death. Today, the hospital is home to bachelor pensioners who fought in World War II or other conflicts. See the "Knightsbridge to Kensington Attractions" map (p. 268).

Royal Hospital Rd., SW3. (℗ **020/7881-5200.** www.chelsea-pensioners.co.uk. Free admission. Mon–Sat 10am–noon and 2–4pm; Sun 2–4pm. Museum and shop closed Sun Oct–Mar. Tube: Sloane Sq.

City Hall On the South Bank of the Thames, adjacent to Tower Bridge, the mayor of London and the London Assembly got a new home in 2002. A gleaming, 10-story, egg-shaped, steel-and-glass structure, it was dedicated by Her Majesty.

A City of Wine

At **Vinopolis,** 1 Bank End, Park St., SE1 (℗ **0870/241-4040**; www.vinopolis. co.uk), you can partake of London's largest selection of wine by the glass. On the South Bank, this "city of wine" lies under cavernous railway arches created in Victoria's era. The bacchanalian attraction was created in a multimedia format, at the cost of £23 million. You can journey virtually through some of the earth's most prestigious wine regions, driving a Vespa through the Tuscan countryside or taking a "flight" over the vineyards of Australia. The price of entrance includes free tastings of five premium wines, and a shop sells almost any item related to the grape. The site also boasts a good restaurant (see "Cantina Vinopolis," p. 183). Depending on the ticket and package purchased, admission ranges from £24 to £100. Hours are Monday, Thursday, Friday, and Saturday noon to 9pm, Wednesday and Sunday noon to 6pm. Closed Tuesday.

Cantina Vinopolis restaurant.

City Hall.

The new home for city government has become London's latest—some say, most controversial—landmark. Half of City Hall is open to the public, and the views from its rooftop gallery are worth the trek over to the South Bank. An exhibition space highlights changing cultural exhibits, and there is also a cafe on-site.

The Queen's Walk, SE1. *© 020/7983-4100.* www.london.gov.uk. Free admission. Visitor information desk Mon–Fri 9am–5pm; cafe Mon–Fri 8am–8pm. Tube: London Bridge.

Gray's Inn ★   Gray's Inn is one of four ancient Inns of Court still in operation. As you enter, you'll see a late-Georgian terrace lined with buildings that serve as both residences and offices. Gray's was restored after suffering heavy damage in World War II. It contains a rebuilt Tudor Hall, but its greatest attraction is the tree-shaded lawn and handsome gardens. A 17th-century atmosphere exists today in the square. Scientist-philosopher Francis Bacon (1561–1626) was the inn's most eminent tenant. See "The City Attractions" map (p. 263).

Gray's Inn Rd. (north of High Holborn; entrance on Theobald's Rd.), 8 South Sq., WC1. *© 020/7458-7800.* www.graysinn.org.uk. Free admission to squares and gardens. Gardens Mon–Fri noon–2:30pm; squares Mon–Fri 6:30am–midnight. Tube: Chancery Lane, Holborn, or Farrington.

Horse Guards ★   North of Downing Street, on the west side of Whitehall, is the Horse Guards building, which is the headquarters of the British Army. The real draw here is the Horse Guards themselves: the Household Cavalry Mounted Regiment, a combination of the oldest and most senior regiments in the British Army—the Life Guards and the Blues and Royals. In theory, their duty is to protect the sovereign. Life Guards wear red tunics and white plumes, and Blues and Royals are attired in blue tunics with red plumes. Two mounted members of the Household Cavalry keep watch daily from 10am to 4pm. The mounted sentries

Gray's Inn.   Trooping the Colour.

change duty every hour as a benefit to the horses. Foot sentries change every 2 hours. The chief guard rather grandly inspects the troops here daily at 4pm. The guard, with flair and fanfare, dismounts at 5pm.

We prefer the once-daily **changing of the guards** here to the more famous ceremony at Buckingham Palace. Beginning around 11am Monday through Saturday and 10am on Sunday, a new guard leaves the Hyde Park Barracks on horseback, rides down Pall Mall, and arrives at the Horse Guards building, all in about 30 minutes. The old guard then returns to the barracks.

If you pass through the arch at Horse Guards, you'll find yourself at the **Horse Guards Parade,** which opens onto St. James's Park. This spacious court provides the best view of the various architectural styles that make up Whitehall. Regrettably, the parade ground itself is now a parking lot.

The military pageant—the most famous in Britain—known as **Trooping the Colour,** celebrating the Queen's birthday, takes place in June at the Horse Guards Parade (see "London Calendar of Events," in chapter 3). The "Colour" refers to the flag of the regiment. For devotees of pomp and circumstance, "Beating the Retreat" is staged here two successive evenings in June. It's only a dress rehearsal, though, for Trooping the Colour. See the "West End Attractions" map (p. 264).

Whitehall, SW1. ☎ **020/7414-2479.** www.trooping-the-colour.co.uk. Free admission. Tube: Charing Cross, Westminster, or Embankment.

Lincoln's Inn ★★   Lincoln's Inn is the oldest of the four Inns of Court (see the box "Legal London," below). Between the City and the West End, Lincoln's Inn comprises 4.4 hectares (11 acres), including lawns, squares, gardens, a 17th-century chapel (Mon–Fri noon–2pm), a library, and two halls. One of these, Old Hall, dates from 1490 and has remained almost unaltered, with its linenfold paneling, stained glass, and wooden screen by Inigo Jones. It was once the home of Sir Thomas More, and it was where barristers met, ate, and debated 150 years before the *Mayflower* sailed on its epic voyage. Old Hall is the scene for the opening chapter of Charles Dickens's *Bleak House*. The other hall, Great Hall, remains one of the finest Tudor Revival buildings in London and was opened by Queen Victoria in 1843. See "The City Attractions" map (p. 263).

Lincoln's Inn Fields, WC2. ✆ **020/7405-1393.** www.lincolnsinn.org.uk. Free admission to grounds. Mon–Fri 10am–4pm. Tube: Holborn or Chancery Lane.

Old Bailey   This courthouse replaced the infamous Newgate Prison, once the scene of hangings and other forms of "public entertainment." It's affectionately known as "Old Bailey" after a street that runs nearby. It's fascinating to watch the bewigged barristers presenting their cases to the high-court judges. Entry is strictly on a first-arrival basis, and guests line up outside; security will direct you to one of the rooms where cases are being tried. It's impossible to predict how long a line you might face. If there's a sensational trial, forget about it—you'll never get in. On a day with trials attracting little attention, you can often enter after only 15 minutes or so. The best time to line up is 10am. You enter courts 1 to 4, 17, and 18 from Newgate Street, and the others from Old Bailey Street. See "The City Attractions" map (p. 263).

Newgate St., EC4. ✆ **020/7248-3277.** www.oldbaileyonline.org. Free admission. Court in session Mon–Fri 10am–1pm and 2–4pm. Children 13 and under not admitted; those 14–16 must be accompanied by a responsible adult. No cameras, video equipment, large bags, food, tape recorders, or cellphones (and there are no coat-checking facilities). To get here from the Temple, travel east on Fleet St., which becomes Ludgate Hill; cross Ludgate Circus and turn left at the Old Bailey, a domed structure with the figure of *Justice* atop it. Tube: St. Paul's.

Legal London

The smallest borough in London, bustling **Holborn** (*Ho*-burn) is often referred to as "Legal London." It's home to the majority of the city's barristers, solicitors, and law clerks, as well as the ancient **Inns of Court** (Tube: Holborn or Chancery Lane), the beautiful complexes where barristers have their chambers and law students perform their apprenticeships. All barristers (litigators) must belong to one of these institutions: **Gray's Inn, Lincoln's Inn** (the best preserved), the **Middle Temple,** or the **Inner Temple** (both just over the line inside the City). The area was severely damaged during World War II, and some razed buildings were replaced with modern offices, but the borough still retains pockets of architecture of former days. See "The City Attractions" map (p. 263).

St. Pancras Station   The London terminus for the Eurostar trains, St. Pancras Station (built from 1863–67) is a masterpiece of Victorian engineering. Designed by W. H. Barlow, the 207m-long (679-ft.) glass-and-iron train station spans 72m (236 ft.) in width and rises to a peak of 30m (98 ft.) above the rails. The platforms were raised 6m (20 ft.) above the ground because the tracks ran over the Regent's Canal before entering the station. The pièce de résistance, though, is Sir George Gilbert Scott's fanciful St. Pancras Chambers. Done in high Gothic style, it's graced with pinnacles, towers, and gables; it now functions as office space. The facade runs 170m (558 ft.) and is flanked by a clock tower and a west tower. See the "West End Attractions" map (p. 264).

Euston Rd., NW1. *©* **020/7843-4250.** www.stpancras.com. Mon–Fri 3:45am–12:30am; Sat 5am–12:30am; Sun 6am–12:30am. Tube: King's Cross/St. Pancras.

Spencer House ★★   This is one of the city's most beautiful buildings. It was constructed in 1766 for the first Earl Spencer, who intended it as a shrine to Georgiana Poyntz, his childhood sweetheart whom he had secretly married the year before. It hasn't been a private residence since 1927, and it had something of a checkered history until it was restored and opened as a museum in 1990. Rooms are filled with period furniture and art, some even loaned by the Queen herself. The most spectacular salon is the Palm Room, all in white, gold, and green. See the "West End Attractions" map (p. 264).

27 St. James's Place, SW1. *©* **020/7499-8620.** www.spencerhouse.co.uk. Admission £9 adults; £7 students, seniors and children 10–16; children 9 and under not allowed. Garden admission £3.50. Sun only 10:30am–5:45pm (last admission 4:45pm). Closed Jan and Aug. Tube: Green Park.

Literary & Musical Landmarks

Besides the homes of the authors and composers listed below, you can visit the abodes of other celebrated Londoners (detailed in other sections of this chapter), including Apsley House, the former mansion of the Duke of Wellington (p. 283). The homes of John Keats and Sigmund Freud are also open to the public; both are north of London in Hampstead (p. 308). Finally, the fascinating home of legendary architect Sir John Soane (p. 298) is open to the public and houses a museum about Soane.

Carlyle's House   From 1834 to 1881, Thomas Carlyle, author of *The French Revolution,* and Jane Baillie

St. Pancras Station.

Welsh Carlyle, his noted letter-writing wife, resided in this modest 1708 terraced house. Furnished essentially as it was in Carlyle's day, the house is located about half a block from the Thames, near the Chelsea Embankment, along King's Road. It was described by his wife as being "of most antique physiognomy, quite to our humour; all wainscoted, carved, and queer-looking, roomy, substantial, commodious, with closets to satisfy any Bluebeard." The most interesting chamber is the not-so-soundproof "soundproof" study in the skylit attic. Filled with Carlyle memorabilia—his books, a letter from Disraeli, personal effects, a writing chair, even his death mask—this is where the author did his work. See the "Knightsbridge to Kensington Attractions" map (p. 268).

Exterior and sign for Ye Olde Cheshire Cheese pub.

24 Cheyne Row, SW3. ℂ **020/7352-7087.** Admission £4.90 adults, £2.50 children 6–16, free for children 5 and under. Mar 14–Oct Wed–Fri 2–5pm; Sat–Sun and bank holidays 2–5pm. Closed Nov–Mar 13. Tube: Sloane Sq. or South Kensington.

Dickens House Here in Bloomsbury stands the simple abode in which Charles Dickens wrote *Oliver Twist* and finished *The Pickwick Papers* (his American readers actually waited at the dock for the ship that brought in each new installment). The place is almost a shrine: Its reconstructed interiors contain his study, manuscripts, and personal relics. During Christmas week (including Christmas Day), the museum is decorated in the style of Dickens's first Christmas there. During Christmas, the raised admission prices of £10 for adults and £5 for children include hot mince pies and a few glasses of "Smoking Bishop," Dickens's favorite hot punch, as well as a copy of the museum's guidebooks. See the "West End Attractions" map (p. 264).

48 Doughty St., WC1. ℂ **020/7405-2127.** www.dickensmuseum.com. Admission £6 adults, £4.50 students and seniors, £3 children, £15 family ticket. Mon–Sat 10am–5pm; Sun 11am–5pm. Tube: Russell Sq., Chancery Lane, or Holborn.

Handel Museum This is the first composer museum to open in London. George Frederic Handel lived in this town house until his death in 1759, and it was here that he composed *Messiah*. Most of his organ concerts were written here, as well as "Israel in Egypt" and "Coronation Anthems." Handel settled in London in 1710 but didn't move to this Georgian house until 1723. The house has been restored to its original 18th-century styling, with furniture and fabrics accurate (though not original) to the time Handel lived here. The museum is hung with portraits and prints of Handel, his colleagues, and his patrons. On display are two harpsichords, which are played frequently by professionals when

A NEIGHBORHOOD OF ONE'S OWN: THE HOMES OF Virginia Woolf

Born in London in 1882, author and essayist Virginia Woolf used the city as the setting for many of her novels, including *Jacob's Room* (1922). The daughter of Sir Leslie Stephen and his wife, Julia Duckworth, Virginia spent her formative years at **22 Hyde Park Gate,** off Kensington Road, west of Royal Albert Hall. Her mother died in 1895 and her father in 1904.

After the death of their father, Virginia and her sister Vanessa left Kensington for Bloomsbury, settling near the British Museum. It was an interesting move, as Bloomsbury was a neighborhood that upper-class Victorians didn't view as "respectable." But Virginia was to make it her own, and in the process, make the district world-famous as the hub of literary London. From 1905, the Stephens lived at **46 Gordon Sq.,** east of Gower Street and University College. It was here that the celebrated literary and artistic circle known as the "Bloomsbury Group" came into being. In time, the group would embrace art critic Clive Bell and author Leonard Woolf, future husbands of Vanessa and Virginia, respectively. Later, Virginia went to live at **29 Fitzroy Sq.,** west of Tottenham Court Road, in a house once occupied by George Bernard Shaw.

During the next 2 decades, Virginia resided at several more Bloomsbury addresses, including **Brunswick Square, Tavistock Square,** and **Mecklenburg Square.** These homes have disappeared or been altered beyond recognition. During this time, the Bloomsbury Group

reached out to include the artists Roger Fry and Duncan Grant, and Virginia became a friend of economist John Maynard Keynes and author E. M. Forster (*A Passage to India*). At Tavistock Square (1924–39) and at Mecklenburg Square (1939–40), she operated the Hogarth Press with Leonard. She published her own early work here, as well as T. S. Eliot's *The Waste Land*.

the museum is open. Precious objects include Mozart's handwritten arrangement of a Handel fugue, and furnishings such as a canopied bedroom from 1720 on loan from the Victoria and Albert Museum. Visit is by guided tour only. There are recitals every Thursday evening between 6:30 and 7:30pm and on occasional other days as well. Concerts cost £9 for adults or £7.50 for students and seniors. See the "West End Attractions" map.

25 Brook St., W1. ℂ **020/7495-1685.** www.handelhouse.org. Admission £5 adults, £4.50 students and seniors, £2 children 5–15. Free for children on Saturday. Tues–Sat 10am–6pm (until 8pm Thurs); Sun noon–6pm. Tube: Bond St.

Samuel Johnson's House ★★   Dr. Johnson and his copyists compiled his famous dictionary in this Queen Anne house, where the lexicographer, poet, essayist, and fiction writer lived from 1748 to 1759. Although Johnson also lived at Staple Inn in Holborn and at a number of other places, the Gough Square house is the only one of his residences remaining in modern London. The 17th-century building has been painstakingly restored, and it's well worth a visit.

After you're done touring the house, you might want to stop in at **Ye Olde Cheshire Cheese,** Wine Office Court, 145 Fleet St. (ℂ **020/7353-6170**), Johnson's favorite locale. He must have had some lean nights at the pub because by the time he had compiled his dictionary, he'd already spent his advance of 1,500 guineas. G. K. Chesterton, author of *What's Wrong with the World* (1910) and *The Superstition of Divorce* (1920), was also a patron of the pub. See "The City Attractions" map (p. 263).

17 Gough Sq., EC4. ℂ **020/7353-3745.** www.drjohnsonshouse.org. Admission £4.50 adults, £3.50 students and seniors, £1.50 children, £10 family ticket, free for children 10 and under. Oct–Apr Mon–Sat 11am–5pm; May–Sept Mon–Sat 11am–5:30pm. Tube: Blackfriars, Chancery Lane, Temple, or Holborn. Walk up New Bridge St. and turn left onto Fleet St.; Gough Sq. is tiny and hidden, north of Fleet St.

FROM TOP: **Harpsicord at the Handel Museum; Samuel Johnson's House.**

Museums & Galleries

Apsley House, the Wellington Museum ★   This was the mansion of the Duke of Wellington, the "Iron Duke," one of Britain's greatest generals, who defeated Napoleon at Waterloo. Later, for a short period while he was prime minister, the duke had to have iron shutters fitted to his windows to protect him from a mob outraged by his autocratic opposition to reform. (His unpopularity soon passed, however.)

A MONEY-SAVING PASS

The **London Pass** provides admission to more than 55 attractions in and around London, "timed" admission at some attractions (bypassing the queues), plus free travel on public transport (buses, Tubes, and trains) and a pocket guidebook. It costs £39 for 1 day, £63 for 3 days, and £87 for 6 days (children ages 5–15 pay £22, £39, or £55), and includes admission to St. Paul's Cathedral, HMS *Belfast,* the Jewish Museum, and the Thames Barrier Visitor Centre—and many other attractions. This rather pricey pass is useful to persons who try to cram 2 days' worth of sightseeing into a single day. But if you're a slow-moving visitor, who likes to stop and smell the roses, you may not get your money's worth. Decide how much transportation and sightseeing you hope to get done, and, using this guide, calculate what the costs will be. It's a bit of paper work, but it will help you decide whether the London Pass is a good deal for you. You can also purchase the pass without the transportation package. Visit the website at **www. londonpass.com**.

The house is crammed with art treasures, including three original Velázquez paintings, and mementos that include the duke's medals and battlefield orders. Apsley House also holds some of the finest silver and porcelain pieces in Europe, displayed in the Plate and China Room. European monarchs grateful to Wellington for saving their thrones showered him with treasures. The collection includes a Sèvres Egyptian service originally intended as a divorce present from Napoleon to Josephine (she refused it); Louis XVIII eventually presented it to Wellington. Another treasure, the Portuguese Silver Service, has been hailed as the single greatest artifact of Portuguese neoclassical silver. See the "West End Attractions" map (p. 264).

149 Piccadilly, Hyde Park Corner, W1. ☎ **020/7499-5676.** www.english-heritage.org.uk. Admission £6 adults, £5.10 seniors, £3 children 15 and under. Apr–Oct Tues–Sun 11am–5pm; Nov–Mar Tues–Sun 11am–4pm. Tube: Hyde Park Corner.

BBC Television Centre   Have you ever wanted to go backstage to take a look at one of the most famous television studios in the world? The behind-the-scenes tours of this news center include visits to the weather center, the prop storehouse, and the production galleries. Because this is a working studio, no tours are exactly the same. Those looking for souvenirs, books, or videos will find an on-site shop. There is also a cafe. You must book in advance, and visitors must be 10 years of age or over. *Tip:* Because this is such a popular attraction, make reservations 2 to 3 days in advance.

Television Centre, Wood Lane, W12. ☎ **0870/603-0304.** www.bbc.co.uk/tours. Admission £9.30 adults, £8.30 seniors, £6.85 students and children ages 9–15, £27 family ticket. Mon–Sat tours are at 10, 10:20, and 10:40am, and 1:15, 1:30, 1:45, 3:30, 3:45, and 4pm. Tube: White City.

British Library ★★   In 1996, one of the world's great libraries began moving its collection of some 12 million books, manuscripts, and other items from the British Museum to its very own home in St. Pancras. In the new building, you get modernistic beauty rather than the fading glamour and the ghosts of Karl Marx, William Thackeray, and Virginia Woolf of the old library at the British Museum.

You are also likely to get the book you want within an hour instead of 3 days. Academics, students, writers, and bookworms from all over the world come here. On a recent visit, we sat next to a student researching the history of pubs.

The bright, roomy interior is far more inviting than the rather dull redbrick exterior suggests. The most spectacular room is the Humanities Reading Room, constructed on three levels with daylight filtered through the ceiling.

The fascinating collection includes such items of historic and literary interest as two of the four surviving copies of the *Magna Carta* (1215), a Gutenberg Bible, Nelson's last letter to Lady Hamilton, and the journals of Captain Cook. Almost every major author—Dickens, Jane Austen, Charlotte Brontë, Keats, and hundreds of others—is represented in the section devoted to English literature. Beneath Roubiliac's 1758 statue of Shakespeare stands a case of documents relating to the Bard, including a mortgage bearing his signature and a copy of the First Folio of 1623. There's also an unrivaled collection of stamps and stamp-related items.

Using headphones set around the room, you can hear thrilling audio snippets such as James Joyce reading a passage from *Finnegan's Wake*. Particularly intriguing is an exhibition called "Turning the Pages," where you can, for example, electronically read a complete Leonardo da Vinci notebook by putting your hands on a special computer screen that flips from one page to another. There is a copy of *The Canterbury Tales* from 1410, and even manuscripts from *Beowulf* (ca. 1000). In the Historical Documents section are letters by everybody from Henry VIII to Napoleon, from Elizabeth I to Churchill. In the music displays, you can seek out original sheet music by Beethoven, Handel, Stravinsky, and Lennon and McCartney. An entire day spent here will only scratch the surface.

Though self-guided admission to the library is free, walking tours cost £8 for adults and £6.50 for seniors, students, and children. They are conducted Monday, Wednesday, and Friday at 3pm, and Saturday at 10:30am and 3pm. Library tours that include a visit to one of the reading rooms take place on Sundays and bank holidays at 11:30am and 3pm; they cost £8 adults, £6.50 for seniors and students. Reservations can be made up to 2 weeks in advance.

96 Euston Rd., NW1. ✆ **020/7412-7332.** www.bl.uk. Free admission. Mon and Wed–Fri 9:30am–6pm; Tues 9:30am–8pm; Sat 9:30am–5pm; Sun 11am–5pm. Tube: King's Cross/St. Pancras, or Euston Sq.

FROM LEFT: BBC weatherman discussing new forecasting methods; *The Wardington Hours* at the British Library.

Exhibit at the Design Museum.   Detail of arches at the Dulwich Picture Gallery.

Courtauld Gallery   The nucleus of this collection was acquired by Samuel Courtauld, who upon his death in 1947 left it to the University of London. Today it houses the biggest collection of Impressionist and post-Impressionist paintings in Britain, with masterpieces by Monet, Manet, Degas, Renoir, Cézanne, van Gogh, and Gauguin. The gallery also has a superb collection of old-master paintings and drawings, including works by Rubens and Michelangelo; early-Italian paintings, ivories, and majolica; the Lee collection of old masters; and early-20th-century English, French, and British paintings. Second-floor galleries display paintings and sculptures from the late 19th and 20th centuries, including an outstanding group of Fauve works and art by everybody from Matisse to Dufy. We come here at least once every season to revisit one work in particular: Manet's exquisite *A Bar at the Folies-Bergère* ★. Many of the paintings are displayed without glass, giving the gallery a more intimate feeling than most.

Somerset House, the Strand, WC2. ✆ **020/7848-2526.** www.courtauld.ac.uk. Admission £5 adults, £4 seniors and international students, free for British students and children 17 and under. Daily 10am–6pm; last admission 5:15pm. Tube: Temple, Covent Garden, Charing Cross, or Holborn.

Design Museum   The Design Museum is a showcase of modern design—kind of like West Elm without the price tags. It's the only museum in Europe that explains why and how mass-produced objects work and look the way they do and how design contributes to the quality of our lives. The collection of objects includes cars, furniture, domestic appliances, graphics, and ceramics, as well as changing displays of new products and prototypes from around the world. The cafe offers panoramic views of Tower Bridge and the Thames. See "The City Attractions" map (p. 263).

28 Shad Thames, SE1. ✆ **0870/833-9955.** http://designmuseum.org. Admission £8.50 adults, £5 students, £6.50 seniors, free for children 11 and under. Daily 10am–5:45pm. Tube: Tower Bridge or London Bridge.

Dulwich Picture Gallery ★ 🏛

Just 12 minutes by train from Victoria Station, this rarely visited museum houses one of the world's most significant collections of European old masters from the 17th and 18th centuries. In a purpose-built gallery designed by Sir John Soane in 1811, the collection is one of the oldest in Britain, having been assembled in the 1790s. Many of the paintings were collected by Stanislaus Augustus of Poland for shipment to his homeland. Before that happened, his kingdom was partitioned out of existence, and the paintings remained in London. You can view works by such old masters as Rembrandt, Rubens, Canaletto, Gainsborough, Watteau, Pousin, and others. The *Sunday Telegraph* has hailed Dulwich as "the most beautiful small art gallery in the world."

Gallery Road, Dulwich Village, SE21. ✆ **020/8693-5254.** www.dulwichpicturegallery.org.uk. Admission £9 adults, £8 seniors, free for students and children 17 and under. Tues–Fri 10am–5pm; Sat–Sun 11am–5pm. Tube: W. Dulwich Station.

Estorick Collection of Modern Italian Art

Long dismissed as "unfashionable," early-20th-century Italian art is given a showcase in London. Eric Estorick (1913–93) was an American political scientist and writer who was a passionate collector. The year he died, he established a foundation to display his collection and to stage temporary-loan exhibitions. His is one of the finest 20th-century Italian art collections in the world. Powerful images by the main protagonists of the early-20th-century Italian avant-garde Futurist movement, including Balla, Boccioni, Carrá, Serverini, and Russolo, are on permanent view. The collection includes works by figurative artists like Modigliani, Sironi, and Campigli, plus works by the metaphysical painter de Chirico. See the "West End Attractions" map (p. 264).

39A Canonbury Sq., N1. ✆ **020/7704-9522.** www.estorickcollection.com. Admission £5 adults, £3.50 seniors and children. Wed–Sat 11am–6pm; Sun noon–5pm. Tube: Victoria Line to Highbury and Islington.

Modern Idol by Umberto Boccioni (1911) at the Estorick Collection.

Florence Nightingale Museum

The life and work of one of England's most influential women of the 1800s is celebrated here. You'll learn that her most famous accomplishment—nursing soldiers during the Crimean War—was only part of a career spanning half a century. Nightingale raised the image of the British soldier (from a brawling lowlife to a heroic working man) and made nursing a respectable profession. Before the "Lady with the Lamp," nursing was seen as a job fit only for prostitutes.

In 1896, Nightingale "retired to her bed" but didn't slow down. She continued to write on public health. Much of her advice is still valid today.

By the time she died in 1910 at the age of 90, she had become so reclusive that the general public assumed she was already dead. The collection at this museum includes many objects owned or used by Nightingale, including 63 letters written by her. There are also exhibits relating to the Crimean War. See the "Westminster Attractions" map (p. 267).

St. Thomas' Hospital, 2 Lambeth Palace Rd., SE1. ✆ **020/7620-0374.** www.florence-nightingale. co.uk. Admission £6 adults; £5 seniors, students, children ages 5–16, and persons with disabilities; free for children 4 and under; £18 family ticket. Mon–Fri 10am–5pm; Sat–Sun 10am–4:30pm. Last admission 1 hr. before closing. Tube: Westminster or Waterloo.

Geffrye Museum ★ If you'd like an overview of British interiors and lifestyles of the past 4 centuries, head to this museum, housed in a series of restored 18th-century almshouses that escaped Hitler's Blitz. Period rooms are arranged chronologically, allowing you to follow changing tastes in the days of the Empire. You'll see the development of furnishings and objets d'art in English middle-class homes. The collection is rich in Jacobean and Georgian interiors and strongest in the Victorian period. In the 20th-century rooms, you'll see the richness of the Art Deco style and the bleakness of the utilitarian designs that followed in the aftermath of World War II. Newer galleries showcase the decor of the later 20th century.

The museum architecture alone is worth a visit. Gardens in front attract much attention, especially the herb garden. There is a design center, which showcases changing exhibitions of the latest works from contemporary British designers. There is also a cafe/restaurant. See "The City Attractions" map (p. 263).

136 Kingsland Rd., E2. ✆ **020/7739-9893.** www.geffrye-museum.org.uk. Free admission to gallery, £2 to Almshouses (free for children 15 and under). Tues–Sat 10am–5pm; Sun and bank holidays noon–5pm. Gardens Apr–Oct only. Closed Good Friday, Dec 24–26, New Year's Day. Tube: Liverpool St., then bus 149 or 242; or Old St. Tube, then bus 243.

Guildhall Art Gallery ★ Since the 1999 reopening of the Guidhall (the original burned down in a 1941 air raid) many famous and much-loved pictures, which for years were known only through temporary exhibitions and reproductions, are again available for the public to see in a permanent setting. The art ranges from classical to modern. A curiosity is the huge double-height wall built to accommodate Britain's largest independent oil painting, John Singleton Copley's *The Defeat of the Floating Batteries at Gibraltar, September 1782.* The Corporation of London in the City owns these works and has been collecting them since the 17th century. The most popular art is in the Victorian collection, including such favorites as Millais's *My First Sermon* and *My Second Sermon*, and Landseer's *The First Leap.* There is also a landscape of Salisbury Cathedral by John Constable. Since World War II, all paintings acquired by the gallery concentrate on London subjects. See "The City Attractions" map (p. 263).

Guildhall Yard, EC2. ✆ **020/7332-3700.** www.guildhall-art-gallery.org.uk. Admission £2.50 adults, £1 seniors and students, free for children 15 and under. Free Fri and after 3:30pm on all other days. Mon–Sat 10am–5pm; Sun noon–4pm. Tube: Bank, St. Paul's, Mansion House, or Moorgate.

Hayward Gallery Opened by Elizabeth II in 1968, this gallery presents a changing program of major contemporary and historical exhibits. It's managed by the South Bank Board, which also includes Royal Festival Hall, Queen Elizabeth

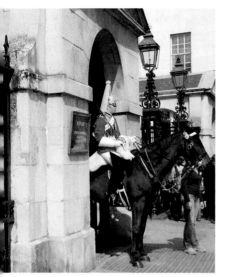
Horse guards at the Household Cavalry Museum.

Hall, and the Purcell Room. Every exhibition is accompanied by a variety of educational activities, including tours, workshops, lectures, and publications. The gallery closes between exhibitions, so call before crossing the Thames.

Belvedere Rd., South Bank, SE1. ☏ **0871/663-2500.** www.southbank centre.co.uk. Admission varies but usually £10 adults, £6.50 students and seniors, free for children 11 and under. Tickets half-price Mon. Hours subject to change, depending on the exhibit: Thurs and Sat–Mon 10am–6pm; Fri 10am–9pm; Tues–Wed 11am–8pm. Tube: Waterloo or Embankment.

Household Cavalry Museum

The Queen herself showed up in 2008 to open this museum installed in the Whitehall stables, which are still in use. The Household Cavalry consists of the True Life guards and the Blues and Royals, the oldest and most senior regiments in the British Army. This is a living museum, and you can, for example, see troopers working with horses in their original stables from the 1700s. Founded in 1661, on orders of King Charles II, the cavalry guards Her Majesty on ceremonial occasions. Some of the men in the regiment are also deployed on active service in Afghanistan and Iraq. In the museum visitors can see regimental collections of arms and militaria.

Horse Guards, Whitehall SW1. ☏ **020/7930-3070.** www.householdcavalrymuseum.co.uk. Admission £6 adults, £4 ages 5–6, £15 family ticket. Mar–Sept daily 10am–6pm; Oct–Feb daily 10am–5pm. Tube: Charing Cross, Westminster, or Embankment.

Imperial War Museum ★　One of the few major sights south of the Thames, this museum occupies 1 city block the size of an army barracks, greeting you with 38cm (15-in.) guns from the battleships *Resolution* and *Ramillies*. The large domed building, constructed in 1815, was the former Bethlehem Royal Hospital for the insane, known as "Bedlam."

　A wide range of weapons and equipment is on display, along with models, decorations, uniforms, posters, photographs, and paintings. You can see a Mark V tank, a Battle of Britain Spitfire, and a German one-man submarine, as well as a rifle carried by Lawrence of Arabia. In the Documents Room, you can view the self-styled "political testament" that Hitler dictated in the chancellery bunker in the closing days of World War II, witnessed by henchmen Joseph Goebbels and Martin Bormann, as well as the famous "peace in our time" agreement that Neville Chamberlain brought back from Munich in 1938. It's a world of espionage and clandestine warfare in the major permanent exhibit known as the "Secret War Exhibition," where you can discover the truth behind the image of James Bond—and find out why the real secret war is even stranger and more fascinating than fiction. Displays include many items never before seen in public: coded

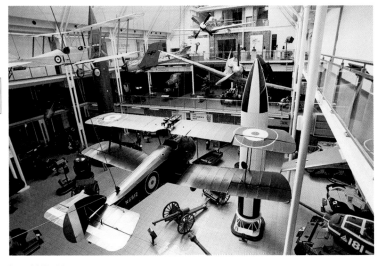

Imperial War Museum.

messages, forged documents, secret wirelesses, and equipment used by spies from World War I to the present day.

Supported by a £13-million grant from the Heritage Lottery Fund, a permanent Holocaust exhibition now occupies two floors. Through original artifacts, documents, film, and photographs, some lent to the museum by former concentration camps in Germany and Poland, the display poignantly relates the story of Nazi Germany and the persecution of the Jews. In addition, the exhibit brings attention to the persecution of other groups under Hitler's regime, including Poles, Soviet prisoners of war, people with disabilities, and homosexuals. Among the items on display are a funeral cart used in the Warsaw Ghetto, a section of railcar from Belgium, a sign from the extermination camp at Belzec, and the letters of an 8-year-old French Jewish boy who hid in an orphanage before being sent to Auschwitz.

Another exhibition, called "Crimes Against Humanity," explores the theme of genocide. See the "Westminster Attractions" map (p. 267).

Lambeth Rd., SE1. ☎ **020/7416-5320** (info line). www.iwm.org.uk. Free admission. Daily 10am–6pm. Closed Dec 24–26. Tube: Baker Line to Lambeth North, Elephant and Castle, or Southwark.

Institute of Contemporary Arts   London's liveliest cultural program takes place in this temple to the avant garde, launched in 1947. It keeps Londoners and others up-to-date on the latest in the worlds of cinema, theater, photography, painting, sculpture, and other visual and performing arts. Classics and cult favorites are frequently dusted off here. On Saturday and Sunday at 3pm, the cinema offers screenings for kids. Experimental plays are also presented. Sun Microsystems, the American Internet pioneer, donated money to build a state-of-the-art New Media Centre in 1998. The photo galleries, showing the latest from British and foreign photographers, probably wouldn't win the approval of the people who set up "decency" panels for the arts. There is a popular cafe/bar at ICA, and it often hosts club nights and musical performances in the evening. It's open until 11pm Monday, 1am Tuesday to Saturday, and 10:30pm Sunday. It opens daily when the museum does. See the "West End Attractions" map (p. 264).

The Mall, SW1. ℂ **020/7930-3647.** www.ica.org.uk. Free admission. Galleries daily noon–7pm; bookstore daily noon–9pm. Film screenings daily. Tube: Piccadilly Circus or Charing Cross.

Linley Sambourne House ★ 🎒 You'll step back into the days of Queen Victoria when you visit this house, which has remained unchanged for more than a century. Built in the late 1860s, this five-story Suffolk brick structure was the home of Linley Sambourne, a legendary cartoonist for *Punch.* In the entrance hall, you'll see the mixture of styles and clutter that typifies Victorian decor, with a plush portière, a fireplace valance, stained glass, and a large set of antlers vying for attention. The drawing room alone contains an incredible number of Victorian items. An actor in period costume leads tours. Allow about 1½ hours for your visit. *Insider's tip:* It's best to prebook your tour by phone. See the "Knightsbridge to Kensington Attractions" map (p. 268).

18 Stafford Terrace, W8. ℂ **020/7602-3316.** www.rbkc.gov.uk/linleysambournehouse. Admission £6 adults, £4 seniors and students, £1 children 17 and under. Sat–Sun 11am–3:30pm, guided tours only (11:15am, and 1, 2:15, and 3:30pm). Closed mid-Mar to mid-June. Tube: High St. Kensington.

London's Transport Museum ★ ☺ After a vast restoration and expansion, this museum has increased its display space by 25%. A collection of nearly 2 centuries of historic vehicles is displayed in a splendid Victorian building that

formerly housed the Flower Market at Covent Garden. The museum shows how London's transport system evolved, and a representative collection of road vehicles includes a reconstruction of George Shillibeer's Omnibus of 1829. A steam locomotive that ran the world's first underground railway, a knifeboard bus, London's first trolleybus, and a Feltham tram are also of particular interest. The museum's galleries consider the future of London's transport as well as the past. For the first time, Harry Beck's original 1930s artwork for the world-famous Underground map is now on public display, along with gems from the museum's valuable poster collections, including some by such famous artists as Man Ray.

Covent Garden Piazza, WC2. ℂ **020/7379-6344.** www.ltmuseum.co.uk. Admission £10 adults, £8 seniors, £6 students, free for children 15 and under. Sat–Thurs 10am–6pm. Tube: Covent Garden, Leicester Sq., Holburn, or Charing Cross.

Fireplace in master bedroom of the Linley Sambourne House.

Madame Tussauds ✋ ☺︎   Madame Tussauds is not so much a wax museum as an enclosed amusement park. A weird, moving, sometimes terrifying (to children) collage of exhibitions, panoramas, and stage settings, it manages to be most things to most people, most of the time.

Madame Tussaud attended the court of Versailles and learned her craft in France. She personally took the death masks from the guillotined heads of Louis XVI and Marie Antoinette (which you'll find among the exhibits). She moved her original museum from Paris to England in 1802. Her exhibition has been imitated in every part of the world, but never with the realism and imagination on hand here. Madame herself molded the features of Benjamin Franklin, whom she met in Paris. All the rest—from George Washington to John F. Kennedy, Mary Queen of Scots to Sylvester Stallone—have been subjects for the same painstaking (and often breathtaking) replication.

In the well-known Chamber of Horrors—a kind of underground dungeon— are all kinds of instruments of death, along with figures of their victims. The shadowy presence of Jack the Ripper lurks in the gloom as you walk through a Victorian London street. Present-day criminals are portrayed within the confines of prison. The latest attraction to open here is "The Spirit of London," a musical ride that depicts 400 years of London's history, using special effects that include audio-animatronic figures that move and speak. Visitors take "time-taxis" that allow them to see and hear "Shakespeare" as he writes and speaks lines, to be received by "Queen Elizabeth I," and to feel and smell the Great Fire of 1666 that destroyed London.

We've seen these changing exhibitions so many times over the years that we feel they're a bit cheesy, but we still remember the first time we were taken here as kids. We thought it fascinating back then.

Insider's tip: To avoid the long lines—sometimes more than an hour in summer—call in advance and reserve a ticket for fast pickup at the entrance. If

Wax replica of the Beatles at Madame Tussaud's.

you don't want to bother with that, be aggressive and form a group of nine people waiting in the queue. A group of nine or more can go in almost at once through the "group door." Otherwise, go when the gallery first opens or late in the afternoon when crowds have thinned.

Marylebone Rd., NW1. ✆ **0870/999-0046.** www.madame-tussauds.com. Admission £22–£41 adults, £18–£30 children 15 and younger. *Note:* Admission prices can go higher or lower during the year. Mon–Fri 9:30am–5:30pm; Sat–Sun 9am–6pm. Tube: Baker St.

Museum of London ★★ In London's Barbican district, near St. Paul's Cathedral and overlooking The City's Roman and medieval walls, this museum traces the history of London from prehistoric times to the 20th century through archaeological finds; paintings and prints; social, industrial, and historic artifacts; and costumes, maps, and models. Exhibits are arranged so that you can begin and end your chronological stroll through 250,000 years at the main entrance to the museum. The museum's pièce de résistance is the Lord Mayor's Coach, a gilt-and-scarlet fairy-tale coach built in 1757 and weighing in at 3 tons. You can also see the Great Fire of London in living color and sound thanks to an audiovisual presentation; the death mask of Oliver Cromwell; cell doors from Newgate Prison, made famous by Charles Dickens; and most amazing of all, a shop counter showing pre–World War II prices. The World City Gallery examines life in London between 1789 and 1914, the beginning of World War I. Some 2,000 objects are on view. See the "West End Attractions" map (p. 264).

150 London Wall, EC2. ✆ **020/7001-9844.** www.museumoflondon.org.uk. Free admission. Mon–Sat 10am–5:50pm; Sun 11:30am–5:50pm. Tube: St. Paul's or Barbican.

National Army Museum ★ 😊 The National Army Museum occupies a building adjoining the Royal Hospital, a home for retired soldiers. Whereas the Imperial War Museum is concerned with wars of the 20th century, the National Army Museum tells the colorful story of British armies from 1485 on. Here you'll find uniforms worn by British soldiers in every corner of the world, plus weapons and other gear, flags, and medals. Even the skeleton of Napoleon's favorite charger is here. Also on display are Florence Nightingale's jewelry, the telephone switchboard from Hitler's headquarters (captured in 1945), and Orders and Medals of HRH the Duke of Windsor. "The Rise of the Redcoats" contains exhibitions detailing the life of the British soldier from 1485 to 1793 and includes displays on the English Civil War and the American War of Independence. See the "Knightsbridge to Kensington Attractions" map (p. 268).

Royal Hospital Rd., SW3. ✆ **020/7730-0717.** www.national-army-museum.ac.uk. Free admission. Daily 10am–5:30pm. Closed Good Friday, 1st Mon in May, and Dec 24–26. Tube: Sloane Sq.

Natural History Museum ★★ 😊 This is the home of the national collections of living and fossil plants, animals, and minerals, with many magnificent specimens on display. The zoological displays are quite wonderful—not up to the level of the Smithsonian in Washington, D.C., but still definitely worthwhile. Exciting exhibits designed to encourage people of all ages to learn about natural history include "Human Biology—An Exhibition of Ourselves," "Our Place in Evolution," "Origin of the Species," "Creepy Crawlies," and "Discovering Mammals." The Mineral Gallery displays marvelous examples of crystals and gemstones. Visit the Meteorite Pavilion, which exhibits fragments of rocks that have crashed into the earth, some from the farthest reaches of the galaxy. The dinosaur exhibit attracts the most attention, displaying 14 complete skeletons. "Earth

Galleries" is an exhibition outlining humankind's relationship with planet Earth. Here, in the section "Earth Today and Tomorrow," visitors are invited to explore the planet's dramatic history from the big bang to its inevitable death. The latest development here is the new Darwin Centre. Dedicated to the great naturalist Charles Darwin, the center reveals the museum's scientific research and out-reach facilities and activities. You're given an insider look at the storage facili-ties—including 22 million preserved specimens—and the laboratories of the museum. Fourteen behind-the-scenes free tours (ages 10 and up only) are given daily; you should book immediately upon entering the museum if you're inter-ested. See the "Knightsbridge to Kensington Attractions" map (p. 268).

Cromwell Rd., SW7. ✆ 020/7942-5000. www.nhm.ac.uk. Free admission. Mon–Sat 10am–5:50pm; Sun 11am–5:50pm. Tube: S. Kensington.

The Queen's Gallery ★★   The refurbished gallery on the grounds of Buck-ingham Palace reopened to the public in 2002 in time for the Golden Jubilee celebration of Queen Elizabeth II. The 1831 building by John Nash was con-verted to a chapel for Queen Victoria in 1843 and later destroyed in an air raid in 1940. Today, the gallery is dedicated to changing exhibitions of the wide-ranging treasure trove that forms the Royal Collection. You'll find special showings of paintings, prints, drawings, watercolors, furniture, porcelain, miniatures, enam-els, jewelry, and other works of art. At any given time, you may see such artistic peaks as Van Dyck's equestrian portrait of Charles I; the world-famous *Lady at the Virginal*, by Vermeer; a dazzling array of gold snuffboxes; paintings by Monet from the collection of the late Queen Mother; personal jewelry; studies by Leon-ardo da Vinci; and even the recent and very controversial portrait of the current queen by Lucian Freud.

Buckingham Palace, Buckingham Palace Rd., SW1. ✆ 020/7766-7301. www.royalcollection.org.uk. Admission £5 adults, £4.50 students and seniors, £3 children 5–16, free for children 4 and under. Daily 10am–5:30pm. Tube: Hyde Park Corner, Green Park, or Victoria.

Royal Academy of Arts   Established in 1768, this organization counted Sir Joshua Reynolds, Thomas Gainsborough, and Benjamin West among its found-ing members. Since its beginning, each member has had to donate a work of art, and so, over the years, the academy has built up a sizable collection. The

Sign at the entrance of the Museum of London.

Tyrannosaurus Rex at the Natural History Museum.

Close-up of exhibit at the Queen's Gallery.

outstanding treasure is Michelangelo's beautiful relief of *Madonna and Child.* The annual Summer Exhibition has been held for more than 200 years; see the "London Calendar of Events" in chapter 3 for details. The main focus of the gallery, however, is on temporary exhibitions which are not related to the Royal Academicians. See the "West End Attractions" map (p. 264).

Burlington House, Piccadilly, W1. ℂ **020/7300-8000.** www.royalacademy.org.uk. Admission varies from £7–£10 depending on the exhibition. Sat–Thurs 10am–6pm (last admission 5:30pm); Fri 10am–10pm (last admission 9:30pm). Tube: Piccadilly Circus or Green Park.

Royal Mews ★★   This is where you can get a close look at Her Majesty's State Coach, built in 1761 to the designs of Sir William Chambers and decorated with paintings by Cipriani. Traditionally drawn by eight gray horses, it was used by sovereigns when they traveled to open Parliament and on other state occasions; Queen Elizabeth traveled in it to her 1953 coronation and in 1977 for her Silver Jubilee Procession. You can also pay a visit to the Queen's carriage horses, which are housed here. See the "Westminster Attractions" map (p. 267).

Buckingham Palace, Buckingham Palace Rd., SW1. ℂ **020/7766-7302.** www.royalcollection.org. uk. Admission £7.75 adults, £7 seniors and students, £5 children 5–17, free for children 4 and under. Mar 25–July 26 and Sept 26–Oct 31 Mon–Thurs and Sat–Sun 11am–4pm; July 27–Sept 25 daily 10am–5pm. Tube: Green Park or Victoria.

Saatchi Gallery ★★   This world-famous gallery has settled into its latest home in the former Royal Military Asylum building in 1801. British mega-collector Charles Saatchi is known for shocking the world with his stunningly avant-garde exhibitions of art. Art lovers define the controversial collector as the vision of the 21st century—or else demand that he be jailed at once and the key thrown away. If you're offended at the revered Madonna (no, not *that* one) with elephant dung, or Damien Hirst's pickled sharks, then go look at a Rembrandt. This former

The State Coach at the Royal Mews.

ad man has been called everything from a "modern-day Medici" to a "Machiavellian mogul." Saatchi's aim is to bring contemporary art to the widest possible audience. He presents works by unseen young artists or by established international artists whose work is rarely if ever exhibited in the U.K. Regardless of what's on display at the time of your visit, it's liable to be controversial.

Duke of York's Headquarters, Kings Rd., SW3. ✆ **020/7811-3070.** www.saatchi-gallery.co.uk. Free admission. Daily 10am–6pm. Tube: Sloane Sq.

Science Museum ★★★ ☺ This museum traces the development of science and industry and their influence on everyday life. These scientific collections are among the largest and most significant anywhere. On display is Stephenson's original rocket and the tiny prototype railroad engine; you can also see Whittle's original jet engine and the *Apollo 10* space module. The King George III Collection of scientific instruments is the highlight of a gallery on 18th-century science. The museum has two hands-on galleries, as well as working models and video displays.

The museum also presents a behind-the-scenes look at the science and technology that went into making the film trilogy *The Lord of the Rings*. Exhibitions showcase the artifacts and animatronics, costumes, and characters from the fable. The exhibition also offers a number of interactive displays—for example, you are given the chance to be shrunk to the size of a hobbit.

Insider's tip: A large addition to this museum explores such topics as genetics, digital technology, and artificial intelligence. Four floors of a new Welcome Wing shelter half a dozen exhibition areas and a 450-seat IMAX theater. On an upper floor, visitors can learn how DNA was used to identify living relatives of the Bleadon Man, a 2,000-year-old Iron Age man. On the third floor is the computer that Tim Berners-Lee used to design the World Wide Web outside Geneva, writing the first software for it in 1990.

Saatchi Gallery.

Note also the marvelous interactive consoles placed strategically in locations throughout the museum. These display special itineraries, including directions to the various galleries for families, teens, adults, and those with special interests.

Exhibition Rd., SW7. (© **087/0870-4868.** www.sciencemuseum.org.uk. Free admission. Daily 10am–6pm. Closed Dec 24–26. Tube: S. Kensington.

Shakespeare's Globe Theatre & Exhibition ★ This is a recent re-creation of what was probably the most important public theater ever built, Shakespeare's Globe, on the exact site where many of Shakespeare's plays opened. The late American filmmaker Sam Wanamaker worked for some 20 years to raise funds to re-create the theater as it existed in Elizabethan times, thatched roof and all. A fascinating exhibit tells the story of the Globe's construction, using the material (including goat hair in the plaster), techniques, and craftsmanship of 400 years ago. The new Globe isn't an exact replica: It seats 1,500 patrons, not the 3,000 who regularly squeezed in during the early 1600s, and this thatched roof has been specially treated with a fire retardant. Guided tours of the facility are offered throughout the day. See "The City Attractions" map (p. 263).

See "The Play's the Thing: London's Theater Scene" on p. 360 for details on attending a play here.

21 New Globe Walk, SE1. (© **020/7902-1400.** www.shakespeares-globe.org. Admission £11 adults, £8.50 seniors and students, £6.50 children 15 and under. Oct–Apr daily 10am–7:30pm; May–Sept daily 9am–noon and 12:30–5pm. Tube: Mansion House or London Bridge.

Sherlock Holmes Museum ✋ Where but on Baker Street would there be a museum displaying mementos of this famed fictional detective? Museum officials call it "the world's most famous address" (although No. 10 Downing St. is a rival for the title). Mystery writer Sir Arthur Conan Doyle created a fictional residence on Baker Street for Sherlock Holmes and his faithful Dr. Watson, and the famous sleuths "lived" here from 1881 to 1904. In Victorian rooms, you can examine a range of exhibits, including published Holmes adventures and letters written to Holmes. This is a very commercial and artificial museum, and strikes us as a tourist trap. Holmes fans might be better off just visiting the gift shop downstairs and buying a postcard or a deerstalker. Some of the merchandise is interesting, though no Persian slippers—for shame. See the "West End Attractions" map (p. 264).

221B Baker St., NW1. (C) **020/7935-1127.** www.sherlock-holmes.co.uk. Admission £6 adults, £4 children 16 and under. Daily 9:30am–6pm. Tube: Baker St.

Sir John Soane's Museum ★   This is the former home of Sir John Soane (1753–1837), an architect who rebuilt the Bank of England (although not the present structure). With his multiple levels, fool-the-eye mirrors, flying arches, and domes, Soane was a master of perspective and a genius of interior space (his picture gallery, for example, is filled with three times the number of paintings that a room of similar dimensions would normally hold). One prize of the collection is William Hogarth's satirical series *The Rake's Progress,* which includes his much-reproduced *Orgy and the Election,* a satire on mid-18th-century politics. Soane also filled his house with classical sculpture: The sarcophagus of Pharaoh Seti I, found in a burial chamber in the Valley of the Kings, is here. See the "West End Attractions" map (p. 264).

13 Lincoln's Inn Fields, WC2. (C) **020/77440-4263.** www.soane.org. Free admission (donations invited). Tues–Sat 10am–5pm; 1st Tues of each month also 6–9pm. Tours given Sat at 2:30pm; £5

Performance at Shakespeare's Globe Theatre.

Sir John Soane's Museum.

tickets distributed at 2pm, first-come, first-served (group tours by appointment only). Tube: Holborn.

Wallace Collection ★★ 🏛 Located in a palatial setting (the modestly described "town house" of the late Lady Wallace), this collection is a contrasting array of art and armaments. The collection is evocative of the Frick Museum in New York and the Musée d'Jacque André in Paris. The art collection includes works by Watteau, Boucher, Fragonard, and Greuze, as well as such classics as Frans Hals's *Laughing Cavalier* and Rembrandt's portrait of his son Titus. The paintings of the Dutch, English, Spanish, and Italian schools are outstanding. The collection also contains important 18th-century French decorative art, including furniture from royal palaces, Sèvres porcelain, and gold boxes. The European and Asian armaments, on the ground floor, are works of art in their own right.

Manchester Sq., W1. ✆ **020/7563-9500.** www.the-wallace-collection.org.uk. Free admission (some exhibits charge admission). Daily 10am–5pm. Tube: Bond St. or Baker St.

Parks & Gardens

London's parks are the most advanced system of "green lungs" in any large city on the globe. Although not as rigidly maintained as those of Paris (Britons traditionally prefer a more natural look), they're cared for with a loving and lavishly artistic hand that puts their American counterparts to shame.

The largest of the central London parks is **Hyde Park** ★★ (Tube: Marble Arch, Hyde Park Corner, or Lancaster Gate), once a favorite deer-hunting ground of Henry VIII. With the adjoining Kensington Gardens (see below), it covers 246 hectares (608 acres) of central London with velvety lawns interspersed with ponds, flower beds, and trees. Running through its width is a 17-hectare (42-acre) lake known as the **Serpentine,** where you can row, sail model boats, or swim (provided you don't mind sub-Florida water temperatures). **Rotten Row,** a 2.5km (1.5-mile) sand riding track, attracts some skilled equestrians on Sunday. You can rent a paddleboat or a rowboat from the boathouse (open Mar–Oct) on the north side of **Hyde Park's Serpentine** (✆ **020/7262-1330**).

At the northeastern tip of Hyde Park, near Marble Arch, is **Speakers Corner**. Since 1855 (before the legal right to assembly was guaranteed), people have been getting on their soapboxes about any and every subject under the sun. In the past you might have heard Karl Marx, Frederick Engels, or Lenin, and almost certainly William Morris and George Orwell. The corpse of Oliver Cromwell was hung here in a cage for the public to gape at or throw rotten eggs at. The king wanted to warn others against what might happen to them if they wished to abolish the monarchy. Hecklers, often aggressive, are part of the fun. Anyone can speak; just don't blaspheme, use obscene language, or start a riot.

Blending with Hyde Park and bordering the grounds of Kensington Palace, well-manicured **Kensington Gardens** (Tube: High St. Kensington or Queensway) contains the famous statue of Peter Pan, with bronze rabbits that toddlers are always trying to kidnap. The park is also home to that Victorian extravaganza, the Albert Memorial. The Orangery is an ideal place to take afternoon tea (p. 233).

East of Hyde Park, across Piccadilly, stretch **Green Park ★** (Tube: Green Park) and **St. James's Park ★** (Tube: St. James's Park), forming a chain of landscaped beauty. These parks are ideal for picnics; you'll find it hard to believe that this was once a swamp near a leper hospital. There's a lake stocked with ducks and pelicans, descendants of the pair the Russian ambassador presented to Charles II in 1662.

Regent's Park ★★★ (Tube: Regent's Park or Baker St.) covers most of the district of that name, north of Baker Street and Marylebone Road. Designed by 18th-century genius John Nash to surround a palace for the prince regent (the palace never materialized), this is the most classically beautiful of London's parks. Its core is a rose garden planted around a small lake alive with waterfowl and spanned by Japanese bridges; in early summer, the rose perfume is heady in the air. The park is home to the **Open-Air Theatre** (p. 362) and the **London Zoo** (see "Especially for Kids" on p. 323). As at all the local parks, hundreds of chairs are scattered around the lawns, waiting for sunbathers. The deck-chair

Equestrians in Rotten Row.

Regent's Park rose garden.

A man on his soapbox at Speakers Corner.

attendants, who rent the chairs for a small fee, are mostly college students on break. Rowboats and sailing dinghies are available in **Regent's Park** (② **020/7724-4069;** www.royalparks.org.uk). Sailing and canoeing cost £6.50 per adult and £4.40 per child for 1 hour.

   Chelsea Physic Garden, 66 Royal Hospital Rd., SW3 (② **020/7352-5646;** www.chelseaphysicgarden.co.uk; Tube: Sloane Sq.), founded in 1673 by the Worshipful Society of Apothecaries, is the second-oldest surviving botanical garden in England. Sir Hans Sloane, doctor to George II, required the apothecaries of the Empire to develop 50 plant species a year for presentation to the Royal Society. The objective was to grow plants for medicinal study. Plant specimens and even trees arrived at the gardens by barge, many to grow in English soil for the first time. Cottonseed from this garden launched an industry in the

---

Where to In-Line Skate

London's parks are great places to skate. Rental skates are available at **Slick Willies,** 12 Gloucester Rd., SW7 (② **020/7225-0004;** www.slickwillies.co.uk; Tube: Gloucester Rd.), costing £10 per day for skates and wrist guards, with a £100 credit card deposit required. Hours are Monday to Saturday 10am to 6:30pm, Sunday noon to 5pm.

Memorial to Princess Diana

The life of the Princess of Wales was troubled, and so is the **Diana Princess of Wales Memorial Fountain** in the center of Hyde Park. The £3.6-million ring-shape water sculpture weighs 700 tons, and water flows from the highest point down both sides, through a 210m (689-ft.) trough, and into a basin called the Tranquil Pool. The fountain was originally opened by Queen Elizabeth in 2004 but had to be shut down after several people were injured swimming in it. After repairs, it was later reopened. You're not allowed to swim, but you can put your hands and feet into the fountain.

Diana's mother, the late Frances Shand Kydd, criticized the memorial for its "lack of grandeur," and other critics have branded it a "storm drain." Culture Secretary Tessa Jowell said that the public has thrown garbage, including diapers, into the water and has also allowed dogs to paddle in the flow.

Not all criticism has been harsh. Jonathan Glancey, of the *Guardian,* likened the memorial to "the cycle of a princess's life, with all its ups and downs, and their ultimate draining away."

new colony of Georgia. Some 7,000 plants still grow here, everything from pomegranate to exotic cork oak, and the garden also houses England's earliest rock garden. The garden is open April to October Wednesday noon to dusk, Thursday and Friday noon to 5pm, and Sunday noon to 6pm. Admission is £8 for adults and seniors, £5 for children 5 to 15 and students. The garden is a perfect setting for a well-recommended afternoon tea—you can carry your cuppa on promenades through the garden (p. 234).

Battersea Park, SW11 (© **020/8871-7530;** www.batterseapark.org; Tube: Sloane Sq.), is a vast patch of woodland, lakes, and lawns on the South Bank of the Thames, opposite Chelsea Embankment, between Albert Bridge and Chelsea Bridge. Formerly known as Battersea Fields, the park was laid out between 1852 and 1858 on an old dueling ground. (The most famous duel was between Lord Winchelsea and the Duke of Wellington in 1829.) There's a lake for boating, a deer field with fenced-in deer and wild birds, and tennis and soccer areas. There's also a children's zoo, open from Easter to October 1 daily from 10am to 5pm, and weekends only in winter from 1 to 3pm. The park's architectural highlight is the Peace Pagoda, built by Japanese craftspeople in cooperation with British architects. The park is open from dawn to dusk. From the Sloane Square Tube stop, it's a brisk 15-minute walk to the park, or you can pick up bus no. 137 (get off at the first stop after the bus crosses the Thames).

Knot garden at London Physics Garden.

The hub of England's—and perhaps the world's—horticulture is in Surrey, at the **Royal Botanic Gardens at Kew** (also known as Kew Gardens). See "Attractions on the Outskirts," below.

EXPLORING LONDON BY BOAT

All of London's history and development is linked with the River Thames: This winding ribbon of water connects the city with the sea, from which London first drew its wealth and power. The Thames was London's chief commercial thoroughfare and royal highway. Every royal procession was undertaken on gorgeously painted and gilded barges (which you can still see at the National Maritime Museum in Greenwich). Important state prisoners were delivered to the Tower of London by water, eliminating the chance of an ambush in one of the narrow, crooked alleys surrounding the fortress. Much commercial traffic on the water ceased when London's streets were widened enough for horse-drawn coaches to maintain a decent pace.

River Cruises Along the Thames

A trip up or down the river will give you an entirely different view of London than the one you get from land. You'll see how the city grew along and around the Thames and how many of its landmarks turn their faces toward the water. Several companies operate motor launches from the Westminster piers (Tube: Westminster), offering panoramic views of one of Europe's most historic waterways.

Thames River Services, Westminster Pier, Victoria Embankment, SW1 (© **020/7930-4097;** www.westminsterpier.co.uk), concerns itself only with downriver traffic from Westminster Pier to such destinations as Greenwich. The most popular excursion departs for Greenwich (a 50-min. ride) at half-hour intervals between 10am and 4pm daily in April, May, September, and October, and between 10am and 5pm from June to August; from November to March, boats depart from Westminster Pier at 40-minute intervals daily from 10:40am to 3:20pm. One-way fares are £9 for adults and £4.50 for children 15 and younger. Round-trip fares are £12 for adults, £6 for children. A family ticket for two adults and as many as three children 14 and younger costs £30 round-trip.

Westminster Passenger Association (Upriver) Ltd., Westminster Pier, Victoria Embankment, SW1 (© **020/7930-2062** or 020/7930-4721; www.wpsa.co.uk), offers the only riverboat service upstream from Westminster Bridge to Kew, Richmond, and Hampton Court, with regular daily sailings from the

Monday before Easter until the end of October on traditional riverboats, all with licensed bars. Trip time, one-way, can be as little as 1½ hours to Kew and between 2½ and 4 hours to Hampton Court, depending on the tide. Cruises from Westminster Pier to Hampton Court via Kew Gardens leave daily at 10:30 and 11:15am, and noon. Round-trip tickets are £20 for adults, £13 for seniors, £9.75 for children ages 4 to 14, and £49 for a family ticket; one child 3 or younger accompanied by an adult goes free.

Thames-Side Sights
THE BRIDGES
Some of the Thames bridges are household names. **London Bridge,** contrary to the nursery rhyme, never fell down, but it has been replaced a number of times and is vastly different from the original London Bridge, which was lined with houses and shops. The one that you see now is the ugliest of the versions; the previous incarnation was dismantled and shipped to Lake Havasu, Arizona, in the 1960s.

Also on the Thames, you can visit London's newest park, **Thames Barrier Park,** SE1, which is the city's first new riverside park in years. It lies on the north bank of the Thames alongside the Thames Barrier, a steel-and-concrete movable flood barrier inaugurated in 1982. The park is spread across 8.8 hectares (22 acres), and has fountains that flow into a channel in the 390m (1,280-ft.) sunken landscaped garden. There's also a riverside promenade and a children's playground here. The park is open daily from sunrise to sunset (reached via the no. 474 bus from the Canning Town Tube station). It's also possible to take the DLR from Canning Town to Pontoon Dock, a 5-minute walk from the park—travel time is about 15 minutes shorter than the bus.

The Green Dock at Thames Barrier Park.

St. Katharine's Dock.

HMS *BELFAST*

An 11,500-ton cruiser, the **HMS *Belfast*,** Morgan's Lane, Tooley Street, SE1
((&) **020/7940-6300;** http://hmsbelfast.iwm.org.uk; Tube: Tower Hill or London Bridge), is a World War II ship preserved as a floating museum. It's moored
opposite the Tower of London, between Tower Bridge and London Bridge. During the Russian convoy period and on D-day, the *Belfast* saw distinguished service, and in the Korean War it was known as "that straight-shootin' ship." You can
explore all its decks, right down to the engine room; exhibits above and below
show how sailors lived and fought over the past 50 years. It's open daily from
10am, with last boarding at 5:15pm in summer, 4:15pm in winter. Admission is
£13 adults, £10 seniors and students, and free for children under 16.

DOCKLANDS ★

What was a dilapidated wasteland surrounded by water—some 89km (55 miles)
of waterfront acreage within a sailor's cry of London's major attractions—has
been reclaimed, restored, and rejuvenated. **Docklands** is coming into its own as
a leisure, residential, and commercial lure.

Next to the Tower of London, **St. Katharine's Dock** was the first of the
docks to be given an entirely new role. Originally built from 1827 to 1828, this
was for many years a leading dock, with the advantage of being closest to the
City. Today, as a residential center and yacht marina, St. Katharine's again profits
from its proximity to the City. The modern World Trade Centre looks down on
the brick-brown sails of barges and gleaming hulls of moored luxury yachts.
Blocks of fashionable Manhattan-style loft apartments sit between the docks and
the river.

Canary Wharf, on the Isle of Dogs, is the heart of Docklands. This huge
site is dominated by a 240m (787-ft.) tower, the tallest building in the United

7

EXPLORING LONDON | Exploring London by Boat

bird's-"eye" **VIEW OF LONDON**

The world's largest observation wheel, the **British Airways London Eye** ★, Millennium Jubilee Gardens ((℃ **0870/5000-600;** www.ba-londoneye.com), opened in 2000. It is the fourth-tallest structure in London, offering panoramic views that extend for some 40km (25 miles) if the weather's clear. Passengers are carried in 32 "pods" that make a complete revolution every half-hour. Along the way you'll see some of London's most famous landmarks from a bird's-eye view.

Built out of steel by a European consortium, it was conceived and designed by London architects Julia Barfield and David Marks, who claim inspiration from the Statue of Liberty in New York and the Eiffel Tower in Paris. Some 2 million visitors are expected to ride the Eye every year.

The Eye lies close to Westminster Bridge (you can hardly miss it). Tickets are £18 for adults, £14 for seniors and students, £9.50 for children 4 to 15. October to May daily 10am to 8pm; June to September daily 10am to 9pm. Tube: Westminster or Waterloo.

Kingdom, designed by César Pelli. The **Piazza** is lined with shops and restaurants. A visit to the **Exhibition Centre** gives you an overview of the Docklands—past, present, and future. Already the area has provided welcome space for the overflow from the City of London's square mile, and its development is more than promising.

On the south side of the river at Surrey Docks, the Victorian warehouses of **Butler's Wharf** have been converted into offices, houses, shops, and restaurants; this area is home to the **Design Museum** (p. 286).

Docklands can be reached via the **Docklands Light Railway,** which links the Isle of Dogs to two London Underground stations. If you're coming from the Tower of London, you can pick up the DLR at the Tower Hill station. To see the whole complex, take the railway at Tower Gateway near Tower Bridge for a short journey through Wapping and the Isle of Dogs. You can get off at Island Gardens and then cross through the 100-year-old Greenwich Tunnel under the Thames to see the attractions at Greenwich (see "Attractions on the Outskirts," below).

The other DLR terminal in central London is Bank, which has even better Tube connections than Tower Hill. (It has links to five lines rather than two.) Also, to visit Canary Wharf/Greenwich, it is better to go from Bank as it offers direct trains. From Tower Gateway, it is necessary to change trains at Westferry.

London Waterbus in Little Venice.

Butler's Wharf.

Exploring London's Canals by Boat

Boat trips on London's canals, especially Regent's Canal in London's canal-laced "Little Venice," are an increasingly popular way to seeing the city. Bus no. 6 takes you to Little Venice, where you can board one of several boats for a tour along the canals. You can return either by boat or by Tube at the end of a one-way trip— Warwick Avenue on the Bakerloo line is only a couple of minutes' walk from where the canal boats dock.

Since the Festival of Britain in 1951, some of the traditional painted canal boats have been resurrected for Venetian-style trips through the waterways. One of them is *Jason,* which takes you on a 90-minute round-trip ride from Bloomfield Road in Little Venice through the long Maida Hill tunnel under Edgeware Road, through Regent's Park, past the Mosque, the London Zoo, Lord Snowdon's Aviary, and the Pirate's Castle, to Camden Lock, and finally back to Little Venice. Passengers who opt to make the 45-minute one-way journey disembark at Camden Lock.

The season runs April to October, with daily trips at 12:30 and 2:30pm. A canalside seafood specialty restaurant/cafe at *Jason*'s mooring offers lunches, dinners, and teas, all freshly made. The round-trip fare is £8.50 for adults, £7.50 for seniors and children 14 and under, free for children 4 and under. One-way fares are £7.50 for adults, £6.50 for seniors and children 14 and under. Family tickets cost £20 to £24. For reservations, contact **Jason's,** Jason's Wharf, opposite 60 Bloomfield Rd., Little Venice, London W9 (© **020/7286-3428;** www.jasons. co.uk; Tube: Warwick Ave.).

Singer at Camden Lock.

ATTRACTIONS ON THE OUTSKIRTS

These sights are perfect for a morning or afternoon jaunt and are easily accessible by Tube, train, boat, or bus.

Hampstead ★

About 6.5km (4 miles) north of the center of London lies the lovely village of Hampstead (Tube: Northern Line to Hampstead) and scenic Hampstead Heath.

The 320-hectare (791-acre) expanse of high heath known as **Hampstead Heath** is a chain of formal parkland, woodland, heath, meadowland, and ponds. On a clear day, you can see St. Paul's Cathedral and even the hills of Kent. Londoners would certainly mount the barricades if Hampstead Heath were imperiled; for years, they've come here to sun-worship, fly kites, fish the ponds, swim, picnic, and jog. In good weather, it's also the site of big 1-day fairs. At the shore of Kenwood Lake, in the northern section, is a concert platform devoted to symphony performances on summer evenings. In the northeast corner, in Waterlow Park, ballets, operas, and comedies are staged at the Grass Theatre in June and July.

Once the Underground reached **Hampstead Village** in 1907, writers, artists, architects, musicians, and scientists were among those who decamped for the leafy village. Keats, D. H. Lawrence, Shelley, Robert Louis Stevenson, and Kingsley Amis all once lived here, and John Le Carré still does.

The Regency and Georgian houses of the village and the rolling greens of the heath are just 20 minutes by Tube from Piccadilly Circus. The village has a quirky mix of historic pubs, toy shops, and chic boutiques along **Flask Walk,** a

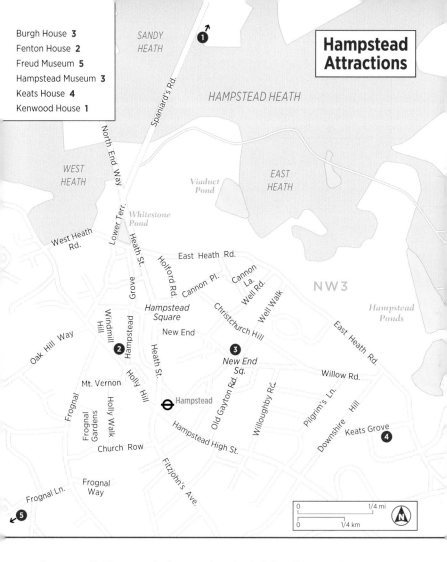

Hampstead Attractions

SANDY HEATH

HAMPSTEAD HEATH

Spaniard's Rd.

North End Way

WEST HEATH

Viaduct Pond

EAST HEATH

West Heath Rd.

Lower Terr.

Whitestone Pond

Heath St.

Grove

Holford Rd.

East Heath Rd.

Cannon Pl.

Cannon La.

Well Rd.

Well Walk

NW 3

Hampstead Ponds

Oak Hill Way

Windmill Hill

Hampstead

Hampstead Square

New End

Heath St.

Christchurch Hill

New End Sq.

East Heath Rd.

Willow Rd.

Mt. Vernon

Holly Hill

Holly Walk

Hampstead

Old Gayton Rd.

Willoughby Rd.

Pilgrim's Ln.

Downshire Hill

Keats Grove

Frognal

Frognal Gardens

Church Row

Hampstead High St.

Fitzjohn's Ave.

Frognal Ln.

Frognal Way

0   1/4 mi

0   1/4 km

N

pedestrian mall. The original village, on the side of a hill, still has old alleys, steps, courts, and groves ideal for strolling.

Burgh House This Queen Anne home (1703), in the center of the village, was the residence of the daughter and son-in-law of Rudyard Kipling, who often visited here. It's now used for local art exhibits, concerts, recitals, talks, and public meetings on many subjects. The house is the headquarters of several local societies, including the Hampstead Music Club and the Hampstead Scientific Society. **Hampstead Museum,** in Burgh House, illustrates the local history of the area. It has a room devoted to reproductions of works by the great artist John Constable, who lived nearby for many years and is buried in the local parish church. There's

Flask Walk.

also a licensed **Buttery Café** (✆ **020/7794-2905**) that's popular for lunch or tea, with lunches for just £4 to £10. In pricey Hampstead, it's a real bargain.

New End Sq., NW3. ✆ **020/7431-0144** or 020/7794-2905 for Buttery reservations. www.burghhouse.org.uk. Free admission. House and museum Wed–Sun noon–5pm; Sat by appt. Buttery Tues–Fri 11am–5:30pm; Sat–Sun 9:30am–5:30pm. Tube: Northern Line to Hampstead.

Fenton House This National Trust property is on the west side of Hampstead Grove, just north of Hampstead Village. Built in 1693, its paneled rooms contain furniture and pictures; 18th-century English, German, and French porcelain; and an outstanding collection of early keyboard musical instruments.

Windmill Hill, NW3. ✆ **020/7435-3471.** Admission £6 adults, £3 children, £14 family ticket. Mar Sat–Sun 2–5pm; Apr–Oct Sat–Sun 11am–5pm, Wed–Fri 2–5pm. Closed Nov–Feb. Tube: Northern Line to Hampstead.

Freud Museum After he and his family left Nazi-occupied Vienna as refugees, Sigmund Freud lived, worked, and died in this spacious three-story house in northern London. In view are rooms with original furniture, letters, photographs, paintings, and the personal effects of Freud and his daughter, Anna. In the study and library, you can see the famous couch and Freud's large collection of Egyptian, Roman, and Asian antiquities.

20 Maresfield Gardens, NW3. ✆ **020/7435-2002.** www.freud.org.uk. Admission £6 adults, £4.30 seniors, £3 students, free for children 11 and under. Wed–Sun noon–5pm. Tube: Jubilee Line to Finchley Rd.

Freud Museum.

Keats House ★★ The poet lived here for only 2 years, but that was approximately two-fifths of his creative life; he died of tuberculosis in Rome at the age of 25 (in 1821). In Hampstead, Keats wrote some of his most celebrated odes, including "Ode on a Grecian Urn" and "Ode to a Nightingale." His Regency house possesses the manuscripts of his last sonnet ("Bright star, would I were steadfast as thou art") and a portrait of him on his deathbed in a house on the Spanish Steps in Rome.

Keats Grove, NW3. ✆ **020/7332-3868.** www.cityoflondon.gov.uk/keats. Admission £5 adults, £3 students and seniors, free for children 15 and under. Tues–Sun 1–5pm. Tube: Northern Line to Hampstead or Belsize Park.

Funerary statue at Highgate Cemetery.

Kenwood House ★★ Kenwood House was built as a gentleman's country home and was later enlarged and decorated by the famous Scottish architect Robert Adam, starting in 1764. The house contains period furniture and paintings by Turner, Frans Hals, Gainsborough, Reynolds, and more.

Hampstead Lane, NW3. ✆ **020/8348-1286.** www.english-heritage.org.uk. Free admission. Apr–Oct daily 11am–5pm; Nov–Mar daily 11am–4pm. Tube: Northern Line to Golders Green, then bus 210.

IN NEARBY HIGHGATE

Highgate Cemetery A stone's throw east of Hampstead Heath, Highgate Village has a number of 16th- and 17th-century mansions and small cottages, lining three sides of the now-pondless Pond Square. Its most outstanding feature, however, is this beautiful cemetery, laid out around a huge 300-year-old cedar tree and laced with serpentine pathways. The cemetery was so popular and fashionable in the Victorian era that it was extended on the other side of Swain's Lane in 1857. The most famous grave is that of Karl Marx, who died in Hampstead in 1883; his grave, marked by a gargantuan bust, is in the eastern cemetery. In the old western cemetery—accessible only by guided tour, given hourly in summer—are scientist Michael Faraday and poet Christina Rossetti.

Swain's Lane, N6. ✆ **020/8340-1834.** http://highgate-cemetery.org. Western Cemetery guided tour £5. Eastern Cemetery admission £3. Western Cemetery: Mar–Oct guided tours only Mon–Fri 2pm, Sat–Sun hourly 11am–4pm; Nov–Feb, tours Sat–Sun hourly 11am–3pm. Eastern Cemetery: Apr–Oct Mon–Fri 10am–4:30pm, Sat–Sun 11am–4:30pm; Nov–Mar Mon–Fri 10am–3:30pm, Sat–Sun 11am–3:30pm. Both cemeteries closed at Christmas and during funerals. Tube: Northern Line to Archway, then walk or take bus 143, 210, or 271.

Greenwich ★★★

When London overwhelms you and you'd like to escape for a beautiful, sunny afternoon on the city's outskirts, make Greenwich your destination.

Greenwich Mean Time is the basis of standard time throughout most of the world, and Greenwich has been the zero point used in the reckoning of terrestrial longitudes since 1884. But this lovely village—the center of British seafaring when Britain ruled the seas—is also the home of the Royal Naval College, the National Maritime Museum, and the Old Royal Observatory. Greenwich also has some wonderful shopping, including a famous weekend market. (See the "GST: Greenwich Shopping Time" box on p. 332.)

Greenwich was the site of Britain's Millennium Dome, a multimedia extravaganza mixing education and entertainment. Most of the project's cost, estimated at more than £1.3 billion, came from a national lottery. Then the much-heralded Dome bombed with audiences and the project became a national joke. Prince Charles ridiculing it as a monstrous *blanc mange,* that unattractive milky gelatin dessert, didn't help matters, and it finally closed. But the much-maligned Millennium Dome reopened in the summer of July 2007 as **"The 02,"** featuring an 11-screen cinema, a live music venue, exhibition spaces, theaters, bars, and restaurants. It will also host sports evenings during the 2012 Olympics. See the "Greater London Area" map on p. 104 to see Greenwich's location in relation to central London.

ESSENTIALS

GETTING THERE   The fastest way to get to Greenwich is to take the Tube in central London to Waterloo Station, where you can take a fast train to Greenwich Station.

The Tube is for speed, taking only 15 minutes, but if you'd like to travel the 6.5km (4 miles) to Greenwich the way Henry VIII did, you still can. In fact, getting to Greenwich is half the fun. The most appealing way involves boarding any of the frequent ferryboats that cruise along the Thames at intervals that vary from every half-hour (in summer) to every 45 minutes (in winter). Boats that leave from Charing Cross Pier (Tube: Embankment) and Tower Pier (Tube: Tower Hill) are run by **City Cruises** (✆ **020/7740-0400**). A single ticket to Greenwich costs £9 for adults or £12 return. A kid's ticket goes for £4.50 one-way or £6 return.

VISITOR INFORMATION   The **Greenwich Tourist Information Centre** is at 2 Cutty Sark Gardens (✆ **0870/608-2000;** www.greenwich.gov.uk); it's open daily from 10am to 5pm. The Tourist Information Centre conducts **walking tours** of Greenwich's major sights. Tours cost £6 for adults and £5 for students, seniors, and children; depart daily at 12:15 and 2:15pm; and last 1¼ to 1½ hours. Advance reservations aren't required, but you may want to phone in advance to find out any last-minute schedule changes.

SEEING THE SIGHTS

The **National Maritime Museum, Old Royal Observatory,** and **Queen's House** stand together in a beautiful royal park, high on a hill overlooking the Thames. All three attractions are free to get into and open daily from 10am to 5pm (until 6pm in summer). For more information, call ✆ **020/8858-4422** or visit **www.nmm.ac.uk**.

From the days of early seafarers to 20th-century sea power, the **National Maritime Museum ★★** illustrates the glory that was Britain at sea. The cannon, relics, ship models, and paintings tell the story of a thousand naval battles and a thousand victories, as well as the price of those battles. Look for some

Old Royal Observatory.

oddities here—everything from the dreaded cat-o'-nine-tails used to flog sailors until 1879 to Nelson's Trafalgar coat, with the fatal bullet hole in the left shoulder clearly visible. In time for the millennium, the museum spent £20 million in a massive expansion that added 16 new galleries devoted to British maritime history and improved visitor facilities.

Old Royal Observatory ★ is the original home of Greenwich Mean Time. It has the largest refracting telescope in the United Kingdom and a collection of historic timekeepers and astronomical instruments. You can stand astride the meridian and set your watch precisely by the falling time-ball. Sir Christopher Wren designed the Octagon Room. Here the first royal astronomer, Flamsteed, made his 30,000 observations that formed the basis of his *Historia Coelestis Britannica.* Edmond Halley, he of the eponymous Halley's Comet, succeeded him. In 1833, the ball on the tower was hung to enable shipmasters to set their chronometers accurately.

Designed by Inigo Jones, **Queen's House ★★** (1616) is a fine example of this architect's innovative style. It's most famous for the cantilevered tulip staircase, the first of its kind. Carefully restored, the house contains a collection of royal and marine paintings and other objets d'art.

The **Wernher Collection at Ranger's House ★★**, Chesterfield Walk (*©* **020/8853-0035;** www.english-heritage.org.uk), is a real find and one of the finest and most unusual 19th-century mixed-art collections in the world. Acquired by a German diamond dealer, Sir Julius Wernher, the collection contains some 650 exhibits, some dating as far back as 3 b.c. It's an eclectic mix of everything, including jewelry, bronzes, ivory, antiques, tapestries, porcelain pieces, and classic paintings. Hanging on the walls of the gallery are rare works by such old masters as Hans Memling and Filippino Lippi, along with portraits by such English painters as Reynolds and Romney. One salon is devoted to the biggest collection of Renaissance jewelry in Britain. Look also for the carved medieval, Byzantine, and Renaissance ivories, along with Limoges enamels and Sèvres porcelain. The most unusual items are enameled skulls and a miniature coffin complete with 3-D skeleton. Don't expect everything to be beautiful—Wernher's taste was often bizarre. Admission is £6 adults, £5.10 seniors and students, £3 children, free for children 4 and younger. The attraction is open only March 1 to September Sunday to Wednesday 10am to 5pm.

Nearby is the **Royal Naval College ★★**, King William Walk, off Romney Road (☎ **020/8269-4747**; www.oldroyalnavalcollege.org). Designed by Sir Christopher Wren in 1696, it occupies 4 blocks named after King Charles, Queen Anne, King William, and Queen Mary. Formerly, Greenwich Palace stood here from 1422 to 1640. It's worth stopping in to see the magnificent Painted Hall by Thornhill, where the body of Nelson lay in state in 1805, and the Georgian chapel of St. Peter and St. Paul. It's open daily from 10am to 5pm; admission is free.

Painted Hall at the Royal Naval College.

Kew ★★★

About 15km (9½ miles) southwest of central London, Kew is home to one of the best-known botanical gardens in Europe. It's also the site of **Kew Palace ★★** (☎ **0844/482-7777**), former residence of George III and Queen Charlotte. A dark redbrick structure, it is characterized by its Dutch gables. The house was constructed in 1631, and at its rear is the Queen's Garden in a very formal design and filled with plants thought to have grown here in the 17th century. The interior is very much an elegant country house of the time, fit for a king, but not as regal as Buckingham Palace. You get the feeling that someone could have actually lived here as you wander through the dining room, the breakfast room, and upstairs to the queen's drawing room where musical evenings were staged. The rooms are wallpapered with designs actually used at the time. Perhaps the most intriguing exhibits are little possessions once owned by royal occupants here—everything from snuffboxes to Prince Frederick's gambling debts. The palace is open April 2 to September 26 daily 10am to 5pm, charging an admission of £5 adults, £4.50 seniors, and free ages 15 and under. The most convenient way to get to Kew is to take the **District Line** Tube to the Kew Gardens stop, on the South Bank of the Thames. Allow about 30 minutes.

Royal Botanic Gardens, Kew ★★★ These world-famous gardens offer thousands of varieties of plants. But Kew Gardens, as it's known, is no mere pleasure garden—it's essentially a vast scientific research center that happens to be beautiful. The gardens, on a 121-hectare (299-acre) site, encompass lakes, greenhouses, walks, pavilions, and museums, along with examples of the architecture of Sir William Chambers. Among the 50,000 plants are notable collections of ferns, orchids, aquatic plants, cacti, mountain plants, palms, and tropical water lilies.

No matter what season you visit, Kew always has something to see, from the first spring flowers through to winter. Gigantic hothouses grow species of shrubs, blooms, and trees from every part of the globe, from the Arctic Circle to tropical rainforests. Attractions include a newly restored Japanese gateway in traditional landscaping, as well as exhibitions that vary with the season. The newest greenhouse, the Princess of Wales Conservatory (beyond the rock garden), encompasses 10 climatic zones, from arid to tropical; it has London's most thrilling collection of miniature orchids. The Marianne North Gallery (1882) is an absolute gem, paneled with 246 different types of wood that the intrepid Victorian artist collected on her world journeys; she also collected 832 paintings of exotic and tropical flora, all displayed on the walls. The Visitor Centre at Victoria Gate houses an exhibit telling the story of Kew, as well as a bookshop.

Kew. (℃ **020/8332-5655.** www.rbgkew.org.uk. Admission £13 adults, £11 students and seniors, free for children 16 and younger. Apr–Aug Mon–Fri 9:30am–6pm, Sat–Sun 9:30am–7pm; Sept–Oct daily 9:30am–5:30pm; Nov–Jan daily 9:30am–3:45pm; Feb–Mar daily 9:30am–5pm. Tube: District Line to Kew Gardens.

KEW FOR TEA

Across the street from the Royal Botanic Gardens is one of the finest tearooms in the area, the **Original Maids of Honour Tearooms,** 288 Kew Rd. (℃ **020/8940-2752;** www. theoriginalmaidsofhonour.co.uk). Oak paneling and old leaded-glass windows give the place a cozy warmth. The homemade cakes are delectable, as are the delightfully light scones. The Maids of Honour (flavored with jam, cottage cheese, golden raisins, almond extract, and almonds) is their pastry specialty, originally baked for Henry VIII, who liked it so much that its secret recipe has been passed along through the centuries. Afternoon tea is £8.95 per person. The tearoom is open Monday 9:30am to 1pm and Tuesday to Saturday 9:30am to 6pm, and tea is served 2:30 to 5:30pm.

Royal Botanic Gardens.

Kew Palace.

Hampton Court

Hampton Court, on the north side of the Thames, 21km (13 miles) west of London in East Molesey, Surrey, is easily accessible and is one of the great palaces of England. But if you have very limited time, we'd save it for a future visit. If you're going to be in London for perhaps a week, then we'd recommend a stop, but only after you've spent a day at Windsor. Frequent **trains** (☎ **08457/484950** in the U.K., or 01603/764776) run from Waterloo Station (Network Southeast) to Hampton Court Station. **London Transport** (☎ **020/7222-5600**) bus nos. 111, 131, 216, 267, and 461 make the trip from Victoria Coach Station on Buckingham Palace Road (just southwest of Victoria Station). Boat service is offered to and from Kingston, Richmond, and Westminster (see "River Cruises Along the Thames," on p. 303). If you're **driving** from London, take A308 to the junction with A309 on the north side of Kingston Bridge over the Thames. See the "Side Trips from London" map on p. 391 to find Hampton Court in relation to London.

Hampton Court Palace ★★★   The 16th-century palace of Cardinal Wolsey can teach us a lesson: Don't try to outdo your boss, particularly if he happens to be Henry VIII. The rich cardinal did just that, and he eventually lost his fortune, power, and prestige, and ended up giving his lavish palace to the Tudor monarch. Henry took over, even outdoing the Wolsey embellishments. The Tudor additions included the Anne Boleyn gateway, with its 16th-century astronomical clock that even tells the time of high tide at London Bridge. From Clock Court, you can see one of Henry's major contributions, the aptly named Great Hall, with its hammer-beam ceiling. Also added by Henry were the tiltyard (where jousting competitions were held), a tennis court, and a kitchen.

Although the palace enjoyed prestige and pomp in Elizabethan days, it owes much of its present look to William and Mary—or rather to Sir Christopher Wren, who designed and had built the Northern or Lion Gates, intended to be the main entrance to the new parts of the palace. The fine wrought-iron screen at the south end of the south gardens was made by Jean Tijou around 1694 for William and Mary. You can parade through the apartments today, filled as they were with porcelain, furniture, paintings, and tapestries. The King's Dressing Room is graced with some of the best art, mainly paintings by old masters on loan from Queen Elizabeth II. Finally, be sure to inspect the royal chapel (Wolsey wouldn't recognize it). To confound yourself totally, you may want to get lost in the serpentine shrubbery maze in the garden, also the work of Wren. More and more attention is now focused on improving and upgrading the famous gardens here—the formal gardens are among the last surviving examples of garden methods and designs from several important periods of history.

The 24-hectare (59-acre) gardens—including the Great Vine, King's Privy Garden, Great Fountain Gardens, Tudor and Elizabethan Knot Gardens, Board Walk, Tiltyard, and Wilderness—are open daily year-round from 7am until dusk (but not later than 9pm) and, except for the Privy Garden, can be visited free. A garden cafe and restaurant are located in the Tiltyard Gardens.

Hampton Court, on the north side of the Thames and 21km (13 miles) west of London, is easily accessible. Frequent trains run from Waterloo Station (Network Southeast) to **Hampton Court Station** (ⓒ **0845/748-4950**). Once you're at the station, buses will take you the rest of the way to the palace. If you're driving from London, take the A308 to the junction with the A309 on the north side of Kingston Bridge over the Thames.

East Molesey, Surrey. ⓒ **0844/482-7777.** www.hrp.org.uk. Palace admission £14 adults, £12 students and seniors, £7 children 5–15, family ticket £38, free for children 4 and younger; general gardens free admission; south and east formal gardens £4.60 adults, £4 students and seniors, free children without palace ticket during summer months. Cloisters, courtyards, state apartments, great kitchen, cellars, and Hampton Court exhibition Mar–Oct daily 10am–6pm; Nov–Feb daily 10am–4:30pm. Gardens year-round daily 7am–dusk (no later than 9pm).

Hampton Court Palace.

Shrubbery maze at Hampton Court Palace.

ESPECIALLY FOR KIDS

London has fun places for kids of all ages. In addition to the attractions listed below, kids love to explore **Buckingham Palace, Kensington Palace, Madame Tussaud's,** the **National Army Museum,** the **National Maritime Museum** (in Greenwich), the **Natural History Museum,** the **Science Museum,** and the **Tower of London,** all discussed above or earlier in this chapter.

Bethnal Green Museum of Childhood   This branch of the Victoria and Albert specializes in toys. The variety of dolls alone is staggering; some have such elaborate period costumes that you don't even want to think of the price tags they would carry today. With the dolls come dollhouses, from simple cottages to miniature mansions, complete with fireplaces, grand pianos, kitchen utensils, and carriages. You'll also find optical toys, marionettes, puppets, a considerable exhibit of soldiers and war toys from both world war eras, trains and aircraft, and a display of clothing and furniture relating to the social history of childhood.

Cambridge Heath Rd., E2. ✆ **020/8983-5200.** www.vam.ac.uk/moc. Free admission. Daily 10am–5:45pm. Tube: Central Line to Bethnal Green.

Horniman Museum   This century-old museum set in 6.5 hectares (16 acres) of landscaped gardens is quirky, funky, and fun. The collection was accumulated by Frederick Horniman, a Victorian tea trader. A full range of events and activities takes place here, including storytelling and art-and-crafts sessions for kids, along with workshops for adults. The museum owns some 350,000 objects ranging from a gigantic, overstuffed walrus to such oddities as oversize model insects. There are also displays of live insects and a small aquarium constructed in waterfall-like tiers. The torture chair thought to have been an original used at the Spanish Inquisition was proven to be a fake, but the instruments are genuine.

100 London Rd., Forest Hill, SE23. ✆ **020/8699-1872.** www.horniman.ac.uk. Free admission except for temporary exhibitions. Museum daily 10:30am–5:30pm. Library Wed–Sat 10:30am–5pm; Sun 2–5:30pm. Gardens Mon–Sat 7:30am–dusk; Sun 8am–dusk. Tube: London Bridge.

Little Angel Theatre ☺ Puppetry in all its forms is presented at this charming small theater in Islington, north of the city. There are homegrown shows that tour nationally and internationally as well as performances by a variety of visiting companies. The range of puppetry is wide, from marionettes (string puppets) to rod-and-glove puppets. Most of the work is targeted at children; age limits are stated for every show presented (for example, "no under-3s allowed"); grown-ups will enjoy them, too. There's a coffee bar and an adjacent workshop where the puppets, sets, and costumes are made.

14 Dagmar Passage, N1. ✆ **020/7226-1787.** www.littleangeltheatre.com. Admission £8 adults, £6 children 12 and under. Showtimes Wed–Sun 11am and 2pm (sometimes 4:30pm Fri). Tube: Northern Line to Angel or Victoria Line to Highbury and Islington.

London Aquarium ★ One of the largest aquariums in Europe, this South Bank attraction boasts 350 species of fish, everything from British freshwater species to sharks that once patrolled the Pacific. Observe the bountiful riches of the coral reefs of the Indian Ocean and what lurks in the murky depths of the Atlantic and Pacific oceans, including an array of eels, sharks, piranhas,

Bethnal Green Museum of Childhood.

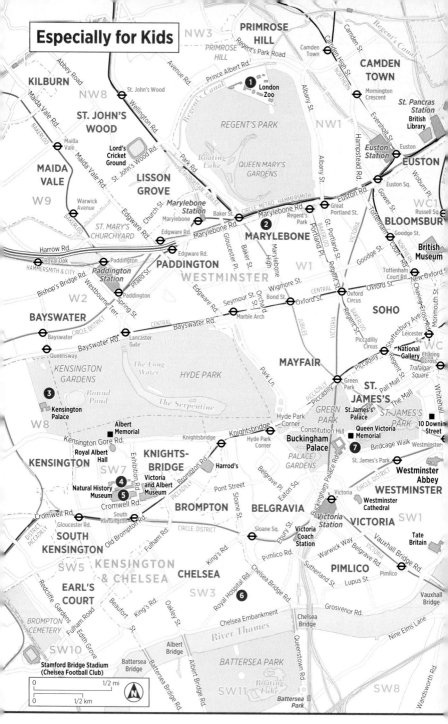

Especially for Kids

PRIMROSE HILL
NW3
PRIMROSE HILL
Regent's Park Road
Prince Albert Rd.

Camden St.
Camden High St.
Camden Town
CAMDEN TOWN

KILBURN
NW8
St. John's Wood
Abbey Road

ST. JOHN'S WOOD

Wellington Rd.
St. John's Wood Rd.
Avenue Rd.

Albany St.
London Zoo ❶

REGENT'S PARK
NW1

Mornington Crescent
St. Pancras Station
British Library
Eversholt St.

MAIDA VALE
Maida Vale
W9
Maida Vale Rd.

Lord's Cricket Ground

Park Rd.

Boating Lake
QUEEN MARY'S GARDENS

Hampstead Rd.

Euston Station
Euston
EUSTON
Euston Sq.
Woburn Pl.

Warwick Avenue

LISSON GROVE
St. John's Wood Rd.
Church St.

ST. MARY'S CHURCHYARD

Marylebone Station
Marylebone
Baker St.

Marylebone Rd.
Marylebone Rd.
❷

Regent's Park

Gt. Portland St.
Great Portland St.
Euston Rd.
Gower St.
Tottenham Court Rd.

WC1
Russell Sq.
BLOOMSBUR
Goodge St.

British Museum

Harrow Rd.

Edgware Rd.
Edgware Rd.
Gloucester Pl.
Baker St.

MARYLEBONE
Portland Pl.
Marylebone High

Wigmore St.
Bond St.
Oxford St.
Oxford St.
Oxford Circus

New Oxford St.
Charing Cross Rd.
Monmouth

Royal Oak
HAMMERSMITH & CITY
Paddington Station
Paddington

PADDINGTON
W1
WESTMINSTER

Seymour St.
Orchard St.
Marble Arch

Regent St.

SOHO

Shaftesbury Ave.
Leicester Sq.

Bishop's Bridge Rd.
Westbourne Terr.
Spring St.
Praed St.
W2
Paddington

Lancaster Gate

Bayswater Rd.
Bayswater Rd.
CENTRAL

Piccadilly Circus
Regent St.
National Gallery
Charing Cross

BAYSWATER
Bayswater
CIRCLE, DISTRICT
Bayswater Rd.

Queensway

KENSINGTON GARDENS
Round Pond

The Long Water

HYDE PARK

Park Ln.

MAYFAIR

Green Park
Piccadilly

Piccadilly
ST. JAMES'S
The Mall
Trafalgar Square
WC
Charing Cross

❸ **Kensington Palace**

The Serpentine

PICCADILLY Piccadilly
GREEN PARK
St. James's Palace
St. James's Palace
ST. JAMES'S PARK
10 Downing Street
Whitehall

W8

Albert Memorial
Hyde Park Corner
Hyde Park Corner
Constitution Hill
Buckingham Palace
Queen Victoria Memorial
❼
Birdcage Walk
PALACE GARDENS

Westminster

Kensington Gore Rd.
Knightsbridge
Knightsbridge

KENSINGTON
Royal Albert Hall
SW7
KNIGHTS-BRIDGE
Harrod's

Belgrave Rd.

Westminster Abbey

Westminster Cathedral

CIRCLE, DISTRICT
WESTMINSTER

Natural History Museum
❹
❺
Victoria and Albert Museum
Exhibition Rd.
Brompton Rd.
Pont Street
Sloane St.
Eaton Sq.

BROMPTON
BELGRAVIA

Buckingham Palace Rd.

Victoria
Victoria Station
VICTORIA
SW1
Tate Britain

Cromwell Rd.
Cromwell Rd.
South Kensington
Gloucester Rd.
DISTRICT PICCADILLY
Old Brompton Rd.

SOUTH KENSINGTON
Fulham Rd.
CIRCLE, DISTRICT

Sloane Sq.
Ebury St.
Victoria Coach Station
Pimlico Rd.

PIMLICO
Pimlico
Vauxhall Bridge Rd.

SW5
KENSINGTON & CHELSEA

King's Rd.
CHELSEA
SW3
Chelsea Bridge Rd.
Warwick Way
Belgrave Rd.
Sutherland St.
Lupus St.

Vauxhall Bridge Rd.
Vauxhall

EARL'S COURT
Redcliffe Gardens
Fulham Road
Edith Grove
Beaufort St.
King's Rd.
Oakley St.
Royal Hospital Rd.
Chelsea Bridge Rd.
❻
Grosvenor Rd.
Grosvenor Rd.
SW8

SW10
BROMPTON CEMETERY
Nine Elms Lane

Stamford Bridge Stadium (Chelsea Football Club)
Battersea Bridge
Battersea Bridge Rd.
Albert Bridge
Albert Bridge Rd.
Chelsea Embankment
River Thames
Chelsea Bridge
Queenstown Rd.
Wandsworth Rd.

BATTERSEA PARK
Boating Lake
SW11
Battersea Park

0   1/2 mi
0   1/2 km

N

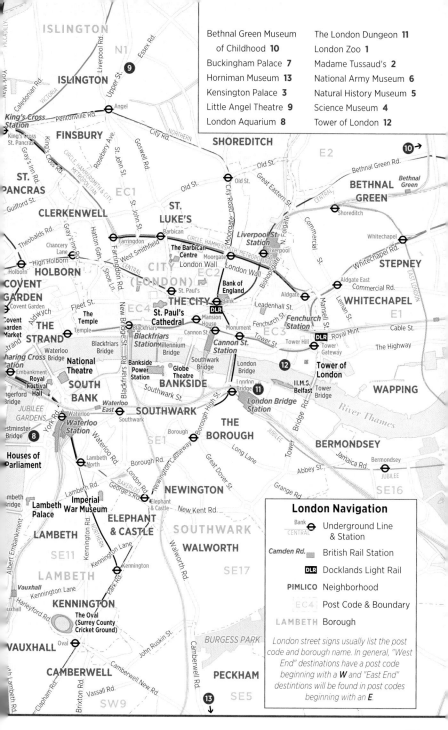

Bethnal Green Museum of Childhood **10**	The London Dungeon **11**
Buckingham Palace **7**	London Zoo **1**
Horniman Museum **13**	Madame Tussaud's **2**
Kensington Palace **3**	National Army Museum **6**
Little Angel Theatre **9**	Natural History Museum **5**
London Aquarium **8**	Science Museum **4**
Tower of London **12**	

London Navigation

Bank — Underground Line & Station

Camden Rd. — British Rail Station

DLR — Docklands Light Rail

PIMLICO — Neighborhood

EC4 — Post Code & Boundary

LAMBETH — Borough

*London street signs usually list the post code and borough name. In general, "West End" destinations have a post code beginning with a **W** and "East End" destinations will be found in post codes beginning with an **E**.*

rays, jellyfish, and other denizens of the deep. You ford a freshwater stream into a mangrove swamp to reach a tropical rainforest. The seawater, incidentally, is just normal Thames water mixed with 8 tons of salt at a time.

County Hall, Westminster Bridge Rd., SE1. © **020/7967-8000.** www.londonaquarium.co.uk. Admission £18 adults, £16 students and seniors, £12 ages 3–14, £54 family ticket. Sept–July daily 10am–6pm; Aug daily 10am–7pm. Closed Christmas Day. Tube: Waterloo.

The London Dungeon   This ghoulish place was designed to chill the blood while reproducing the conditions of the Middle Ages. Set under the arches of London Bridge Station, the dungeon is a series of tableaux more grisly than those at Madame Tussaud's. The rumble of trains overhead adds to the atmosphere, and tolling bells bring a constant note of melancholy; dripping water and caged rats make for even more atmosphere. Naturally, it offers a burning at the stake as well as a torture chamber with racking, branding, and fingernail extraction, and a spine-chilling "Jack the Ripper Experience." The special effects were originally conceived for major film and TV productions. They've recently added a new show called "Boat Ride to Hell." You're sentenced to death (by actors, of course) and taken on a boat ride to meet your fate. If you survive, a Pizza Hut is on-site, and a souvenir shop sells certificates that testify you made it through the works. New in 2007, "Extremis: Drop Ride to Doom" is a thrill attraction that simulates a hanging (only without those pesky nooses): When the trapdoor opens, you plummet down into the dark. Visitors to the dungeon should use discretion with young children.

28–34 Tooley St., SE1. © **020/7403-7221.** www.thedungeons.com. Admission £23 adults, £21 students and seniors, £17 children 5–14, free for children 4 and younger. Nov 1–Mar 18 daily 10:30am–5pm; Mar 19–Apr 3 daily 9:30am–5:30pm; Apr 4–May 27 daily 10am–5pm; May 28–Oct daily 10am–7:30pm. Tube: London Bridge.

Kids check out a tank at the London Aquarium.

London Zoo ★ ☺   One of the greatest zoos in the world, the London Zoo is more than 1½ centuries old. This 14-hectare (35-acre) garden houses about 8,000 animals, including some of the rarest species on earth. There's an insect house (incredible bird-eating spiders), a reptile house (huge, dragonlike monitor lizards), and others, such as the Sobell Pavilion for Apes and Monkeys and the Lion Terraces. In the Moonlight World, special lighting simulates night for the nocturnal beasties while rendering them visible to onlookers, so you can see all the night rovers in action.

The Millennium Conservation Centre combines animals, visuals, and displays to demonstrate the nature of life on this planet. Many families budget almost an entire day here, watching the penguins being fed, enjoying an animal ride in summer, and meeting elephants on their walks around the zoo.

Regent's Park, NW1. ✆ **020/7722-3333.** www.zsl.org. Admission £19 adults, £18 students and seniors, £16 children 3–15, £63 family ticket (2 adults and 2 children or 1 adult and 3 children). Mar 5–Oct daily 10am–5:30pm; Nov–Feb 10 daily 10am–4pm; Feb 11–Mar 4 daily 10am–4:30pm. Tube: Regent's Park or Camden Town. Bus: C2 or 274.

ORGANIZED TOURS

Bus Tours

For the first-timer, the quickest and most economical way to bring the big city into focus is to take a bus tour. One of the most popular is the **Original London Sightseeing Tour,** which passes by all the major sights in just about 1½ hours. The tour—which uses a traditional double-decker bus with live commentary by a guide—costs £24 for adults, £12 for children 15 and younger, free for those 4 and younger. A family ticket costs £84. The tour, valid for 48 hours, allows you to hop on or off the bus at any point in the tour at no extra charge.

Departures are from convenient points within the city; you can choose your departure point when you buy your ticket. Tickets can be purchased on the bus or at a discount from any London Transport or London Tourist Board Information Centre. Most hotel concierges also sell tickets. For information or phone purchases, call ✆ **020/8877-1722.** It's also possible to book online at **www.the originaltour.com**.

Big Bus Company Ltd., Waterside Way, London SW17 (✆ **020/7233-9533;** www.bigbus.co.uk), operates a 2-hour tour in summer, departing frequently between 8:30am and 4:30pm daily from Marble Arch by Speakers Corner, Green Park by the Ritz Hotel, and Victoria Station (Buckingham Palace Rd. by the Royal Westminster Hotel). Tours cover the highlights—18 in all—ranging from the Houses of Parliament and Westminster Abbey to the Tower of London and Buckingham Palace (exterior looks only), accompanied by live commentary. The cost is £25 for adults, £10 for children; a family ticket (two adults with two children) is £60. A 1-hour tour follows the same route but covers only 13 sights. Tickets are valid all day; you can hop on and off the bus as you wish.

Walking Tours

The **Original London Walks,** 87 Messina Ave., P.O. Box 1708, London NW6 4LW (✆ **020/7624-3978;** www.walks.com), the oldest established walking-tour company in London, is run by an Anglo-American journalist/actor couple, David and Mary Tucker. Their hallmarks are variety, reliability, reasonably sized groups, and—above all—superb guides. The renowned crime historian Donald Rumbelow, the leading authority on Jack the Ripper and author of the classic guidebook *London Walks,* is a regular guide, as are several prominent actors (including classical actor Edward Petherbridge). Walks are regularly scheduled daily and cost £7 for adults, £5 for students and seniors; children 14 and younger go free. Call for a schedule; no reservations are needed.

LONDON LIDOS

London is not exactly known as a beach town, but you can go swimming in summer at one of its large freshwater ponds, amusingly called "Lidos" for Italian chic. Fed by the Fleet River flowing into Hampstead in North London, the **Hampstead Ponds ★** are usually called "Highgate Ponds." They date from the 17th and 18th centuries, when they were dug as reservoirs. The trio of ponds is designated for men or for women only, and one mixed.

The **Kenwood Ladies' Pond,** Highgate Rd., NW5 (✆ **020/7485-4491**) has the purest water because it's fed by natural springs. Women are protected from Peeping Toms by sprawling foliage. Bus 210 also runs by here.

The **Hampstead Mixed Pond** (no phone) lies in the middle of the Heath (Tube: Hampstead Heath, then a 15-minute walk along South End Rd.). The men's and women's ponds are open in summer 7am to 7:30pm (sometimes 8:30pm), the mixed pond daily 7am to 6:30pm. Admission is £2 for adults or £1 for students and seniors.

The **Highgate Men's Pond,** Highgate, NW3 (✆ **020/7485-4491**) is accessed via Millfield Lane. Bus 210 from the Archway tube stop goes here. The pond attracts a lot of boxers and weightlifters—and those who'd like to meet them. Incidentally, nudity is de rigeur in the fenced-in enclosure of the men's pond.

Lifeguard at Brockwell Lido.

The **Brockwell Lido** in Brockwell Park, SE2, one of London's last remaining open-air swimming pools, lies in Herne Hill off Dulwich Road in South London. The park commands panoramic views of the skyline of London. The park (✆ **020/7346-5955**) is open June to August Monday to Friday 6:30am to 8pm, Saturday and Sunday 10am to 6pm. Off-season hours are Monday to Friday 6:30am to 10am and 4 to 8pm, Saturday and Sunday 10am to 6pm. This is the best lido for children as it offers a paddling pool and a play area plus amusements. Other facilities here include a gym, hydrotherapy pool, and a spin studio; dance and yoga classes are also offered. You can even hire a personal trainer here; costs depend on what activities you select. Tube: Brixton.

The more accessible and more famous **Regent's Park** is not recommended for swimming, but you can rent boats or canoes here and go sailing on the park's lake (see p. 300). Ever since 1867 when 40 people died in an accident on the lake, the water was drained and reduced to 1.2m (4 ft.) before the lake was reopened.

SPECTATOR SPORTS

CRICKET   In summer, attention turns to cricket, played either at **Lord's,** St. John's Wood Road, NW8 (✆ **020/432-1000;** www.lords.org; Tube: Jubilee Line to St. John's Wood), in north London, or at the somewhat less prestigious **Oval Cricket Ground,** The Oval, Kensington, London SE11 (✆ **020/7582-6660;** www.allinlondon.co.uk/the-oval-cricket-ground.php; Tube: Northern Line to the Oval or Vauxhall), in south London. During the international test matches between Britain and Australia, the West Indies, India, or New Zealand (as important as the World Series in the United States), Britons go into a collective trance, with everyone glued to the nearest radio or TV.

FOOTBALL (SOCCER)   The season runs from August to April and attracts fiercely loyal fans. Games usually start at 3pm and are great to watch, but the stands can get very rowdy, so think about reserving seats. Centrally located premier division football clubs include **Arsenal,** Emirates Stadium, Ashburton Grove, N7 (✆ **020/7704-4000,** box office 020/7704-4040; www.arsenal.com; Tube: Piccadilly Line to Arsenal); **Tottenham Hotspur,** 748 High Rd., N17 (✆ **0844/844-0102,** box office 0844/499-5000; www.tottenhamhotspur.com; Tube: Victoria Line to Seven Sisters); and **Chelsea,** Stamford Bridge, Fulham Road, SW6 (✆ **0871/984-1955,** box office 0871/984-1905; www.chelseafc.com; Tube: District Line to Fulham Broadway). Tickets cost £20 to £110.

HORSE RACING   Within reach of central London are horse-racing tracks at Kempton Park, Sandown Park, and the most famous, Epsom, where the Derby is the main event of early June. Contact **United Racecourses Ltd.** (✆ **01372/470047;** www.jcrtickets.com) for information on the next race at one of these tracks.

TENNIS   Fans from around the world focus on **Wimbledon** (Tube: District Line to Wimbledon). At Wimbledon's All England Lawn Tennis & Croquet Club, you'll see some of the world's best tennis players. The famous annual championship spans roughly the last week in June to the first week in July,

Test match at Lord's Cricket Ground.   Roger Federer serving at Wimbledon.

with matches lasting from about 2pm until dark. (The gates open at 10:30am.) Tickets usually range in price from £20 to £120. Coveted center-court seats are sold by lottery. A limited number of tickets for the outside courts are available at the gate. For recorded ticket information, call ✆ **020/8944-1066,** go to www.wimbledon.org, or send a self-addressed stamped envelope to the **All England Lawn Tennis & Croquet Club,** P.O. Box 98, London, SW19.

8

SHOPPING

When Prussian Field Marshal Blücher, Wellington's stout ally at Waterloo, first laid eyes on London, he allegedly slapped his thigh and exclaimed, "Herr Gott, what a city to plunder!" He was gazing at what, for the early 19th century, was a phenomenal mass of shops and stores. Since those days, other cities may have equaled London as a shopping mecca, but none has surpassed it.

SHOPPING IN LONDON

Although London is one of the world's best shopping cities, it often seems made solely for wealthy visitors. To find real values, do what most Londoners do: Wait for sales or search out discount stores.

American-style shopping has taken Britain by storm, in concept—warehouse stores and outlet malls—and in actual name: One block from Hamleys, you'll find the Disney Store. Gap is everywhere, and Tiffany sells more wedding gifts than Asprey these days. Still, your best bet is to concentrate on British goods. You can also do well with French products; values are almost as good as in Paris.

TAXES & SHIPPING   Value-added tax (VAT) is the British version of sales tax. VAT is a whopping 17.5% on most goods, but it's included in the price, so the number you see on the price tag is exactly what you'll pay at the register. Non-E.U. residents can get back much of the tax by applying for a VAT refund (see "How to Get Your VAT Refund," below).

In Britain, the minimum expenditure needed to qualify for a refund on value-added tax is £50. Not every single store honors this minimum, but it's far easier to qualify for a tax refund in Britain than almost any other country in the European Union.

Vendors at flea markets may not be equipped to provide the paperwork for a refund, so if you're contemplating a major purchase and are counting on a refund, ask before you buy. Be suspicious of any dealer who tells you there's no VAT on antiques. This was once true, but things have changed—the European Union has made the British add VAT to antiques, and pricing should reflect this. So ask if it's included—before you bargain. Get to a price you're comfortable with first, then ask for the VAT refund.

VAT is not charged on goods shipped out of the country. Many London shops will help you beat the VAT by shipping for you. But watch out: Shipping may be even more expensive than the VAT, and you might also have to pay U.S. duties when the goods get to you at home.

You can ship your purchases on your flight home by paying for excess baggage (rates vary by airline) or have your packages shipped independently,

PREVIOUS PAGE: Colorful Wellington boots, or "Wellies," at Camden Lock Market.

which is generally less expensive than shipping it through the airlines. To ship independently, try **Burns International Facilities,** at Heathrow Airport Terminal 1 (📞 **020/8745-5301**). You can avoid the VAT upfront *only* if you have the store ship directly for you. If you ship via excess baggage or an independent shipping company, you still have to pay the VAT upfront and apply for a refund.

HOURS   London keeps fairly uniform store hours, mostly shorter than American equivalents. The norm is a 10am opening and 6pm closing Monday to Saturday, with a late Thursday night until 7pm. Most stores on Oxford Street and in Covent Garden don't close until 7pm every day. However, more upmarket stores on Bond Street usually shut earlier—around 6pm.

Sunday shopping is now legal. Stores are allowed to be open for 6 hours; usually they choose 11am to 5pm. Stores in designated tourist areas and flea markets are exempt from this law and may stay open all day on Sunday. Therefore, Covent Garden, Greenwich, and Hampstead are big Sunday destinations for shoppers.

SALES   Traditionally, stores in Britain held only two sale periods: January and July. Now, whenever they need cash they have a sale, although January and July sales are still prevalent. July sales begin in June—or earlier—and promotions are commonplace. The January sale is still the big event of the year. Boxing Day in England (Dec 26), following the Christmas shopping spree, marks the beginning of year-end clearance sales, which often run through January. On Boxing Day itself, many merchants take an additional 10% off

HOW TO GET YOUR VAT refund

You *must* get your VAT refund form from the retailer. Several readers have reported that merchants have told them they can get refund forms at the airport as they leave the country. *This is not true.* Don't leave the store without a form—it must be completed by the retailer on the spot. After you have asked if the store does VAT refunds and determined their minimum, request the paperwork.

Global Refund (www.globalrefund. com) is your best bet for getting VAT refunds at the airport. Shop where you see the Global Refund Tax-Free Shopping sign, and ask for a Global Refund Tax-Free check when you purchase your items.

Fill out your form and then present it—with the goods, receipts, and passports—at the Customs office in the airport. Allow an hour to stand in line.

Remember: You're required to show the goods, so put them in your carry-on.

Once the paperwork has been stamped, you have two choices: You can mail the papers (remember to bring a stamp) and receive your refund as a British check (no!) or a credit card refund (yes!), or go to the Cash VAT Refund desk at the airport and get your refund in cash. Know that if you accept cash other than British pounds, you will lose money on the conversion.

Many stores charge a fee for processing your refund, so £3 to £5 may be deducted from the total you receive. But since the VAT in Britain is 17.5%, it's worth the trouble to get the money back.

Note: If you're heading to other countries in the European Union, you should file all of your VAT refunds at once at your final E.U. destination.

merchandise that has already been marked down. Though some stores start their after-Christmas sales on December 26, most start after the first week in January, when round-trip airfares are in the low range, and savings on sale items might earn your travel money back if you find enough bargains.

Discounts can range from 25% to 50% at leading department stores. Depending on their inventories and their sense of timing, Harrods produces some very visible sales events, spending large amounts on promotions and publicity. Depending on the sale, extra discounts might apply to souvenirs with Harrods logos, furniture and gift items, English china (seconds are trucked in from factories in Stoke-on-Trent), and English designer brands like Jaeger. But while the Harrods sale is the most famous in London, it's not the only game in town. Just about every other store—except Boots—also has big sales in January and June. Beware, though: There's a huge difference in the quality of the finds at genuine sales, when stores are actually clearing the shelves, and the goods bought at "produced" sales, when special merchandise has been hauled in just for the sale.

DUTY-FREE AIRPORT SHOPPING Shopping at airports is big business. Terminal 4 at Heathrow is a virtual shopping mall, and each of the other terminals at Heathrow has a wide range of shopping outlets, with not a lot of crossover between brands. Prices at the airport for items like souvenirs and candy bars are, of course, higher than on the streets of London, but duty-free prices on luxury goods are usually fair. There are often promotions and coupons that allow for pounds off at the time of purchase. Most of the sales at these airport shops are made for passengers passing through Heathrow en route to other destinations, usually home. Most passengers, by the end of their stay in London, have at least some grasp of what items are available in London shops and at what prices, and therefore have some basis of comparison to prices of equivalent goods outside the airports.

CENTRAL LONDON SHOPPING

Thankfully for those pressed for time, several key streets offer some (or even all) of London's best retail stores, compactly located in a niche or neighborhood so you can just stroll and shop.

THE WEST END As a neighborhood, the West End includes Mayfair and is home to the core of London's big-name shopping. Most of the department stores, designer shops, and multiples (chain stores) have their flagships in this area.

The key streets are **Oxford Street** (in either direction) for affordable shopping (start at Marble Arch Tube station if you're ambitious, or Bond St. station if you care to see only some of it), and **Regent Street,** which intersects Oxford Street at Oxford Circus (Tube: Oxford Circus). The Oxford Street flagship (at Marble Arch) of the private-label department store Marks & Spencer ("Marks & Sparks" in the local parlance) is worth visiting for quality goods. Regent Street, which leads all the way to Piccadilly, has more upscale department stores (including the famed Liberty of London), chains (Laura Ashley), and specialty dealers.

Busy shoppers on Oxford Street.

Parallel to Regent Street, **Bond Street** (Tube: Bond St.) connects Piccadilly with Oxford Street and is synonymous with the luxury trade. Divided into New and Old, it has experienced a recent revival and is the hot address for international designers—Donna Karan has two shops here. A slew of international hotshots, from Chanel to Ferragamo to Versace, have digs nearby.

Burlington Arcade (Tube: Piccadilly Circus), the famous glass-roofed, Regency-style passage leading off Piccadilly, looks like a period exhibition and is lined with intriguing shops and boutiques. Lit by wrought-iron lamps and decorated with clusters of ferns and flowers, its small, smart stores specialize in fashion, jewelry, Irish linen, cashmere, and more. If you linger there until 5:30pm, you can watch the beadles (the last London representatives of Britain's oldest police force), in their black-and-yellow livery and top hats, ceremoniously place the iron grills that block off the arcade until 9am, at which time they just as ceremoniously remove them to start a new business day (There are only 3 beadles remaining.) Also at 5:30pm, a hand bell called the Burlington Bell is sounded, signaling the end of trading.

For a total contrast, check out **Jermyn Street** (Tube: Piccadilly Circus), on the far side of Piccadilly, a tiny 2-block-long street devoted to high-end men's haberdashers and toiletries shops; many have been doing business for centuries. Several hold royal warrants, including Turnbull & Asser, where HRH Prince Charles has his pj's made. A bit to the northwest, Savile Row (btw. Regent and New Bond sts.) is synonymous with the finest in men's tailoring.

The West End theater district borders two more shopping areas: the still-not-ready-for-prime-time **Soho** (Tube: Tottenham Court Rd.), where the sex shops are slowly converting into cutting-edge designer boutiques, and **Covent Garden** (Tube: Covent Garden), a shopping masterpiece full of fashion, food, books, and everything else. The original Covent Garden marketplace has overflowed its boundaries and eaten up the surrounding neighborhood; it's fun to wander the narrow streets and shop. Covent Garden is mobbed on Sundays.

Just a stone's throw from Covent Garden, **Monmouth Street** is somewhat of a London shopping secret: Londoners know they can find a wide array of stores in a space of only 2 blocks. Many shops here are outlets for British designers, and some along this street sell both used and new clothing. In addition, stores specialize in everything from musical instruments from the Far East to palm and crystal-ball readings.

Though many London shops are now open on Sundays, the best Sunday shopping is in the stalls of the flea and craft markets in the royal city of Greenwich.

The ideal way to enjoy the trip is to float downstream on a boat from Charing Cross or Westminster Pier (service begins at 10:30am on Sun; see "River Cruises Along the Thames," under "Exploring London by Boat," p. 303). The trip takes about a half-hour, and you'll get a knowledgeable commentary on the Docklands development and the history of the river. You'll also be able to view the Tower and much of London from the water along the way.

The boat leaves you in the heart of Greenwich, minutes from the craft market held on Saturday and Sunday. Follow the signs—or the crowd. After you're done, follow the crowd again to Greenwich's several antiques markets, which fall under the general category of the **Greenwich Market** (© **020/8923-3110;** www.greenwichmarket.net), open Thursday to Sunday 10am to 6pm. First

is **Canopy Market,** which isn't under a canopy at all, but sprawls through several parking lots where junk and old books abound, and then onto **High Street,** where the fancier flea market is held. It's possible that there will be yet another antiques market at **Town Hall,** across the street, but these shows usually charge an admission fee.

You're only a half-block from the Greenwich rail station now, which is on Greenwich High Road, and there's a train back to London every half-hour until about 11:30pm.

Olives at Greenwich Market.

KNIGHTSBRIDGE & CHELSEA   Knightsbridge (Tube: Knightsbridge), the home of Harrods, is the second-most-famous London retail district. (Oxford St. edges it out.) Nearby Sloane Street is chock-a-block with designer shops.

Walk southwest on **Brompton Road** (toward the Victoria and Albert Museum) and you'll find **Cheval Place,** lined with designer resale shops, and Beauchamp (*Bee*-cham) Place. It's only a block long, but it's very "Sloane Ranger" or "Sloanie" (as the Brits say), featuring the kinds of shops where young British aristocrats buy their clothing for the "season."

If you walk farther along Brompton Road, you'll connect to **Brompton Cross,** another hip area for designer shops made popular when Michelin House was rehabbed by Sir Terence Conran, becoming the Conran Shop. Seek out **Walton Street,** a tiny snake of a street running from Brompton Cross back toward the museums. Most of the shops here specialize in nonessential luxury products, the kind a severe and judgmental Victorian moralist might dismiss as vanities and fripperies. This is where you'll find aromatherapy from Jo Malone, needlepoint, and costume jewelry. **King's Road** (Tube: Sloane Sq.), the main street of Chelsea, will forever remain a symbol of the Swinging '60s. It's still popular with the young crowd, but there are fewer mohawk haircuts, Bovver boots, and Edwardian ball gowns these days. More and more, King's Road is a lineup of markets and "multistores," conglomerations of indoor stands, stalls, and booths within one building or enclosure. About a third of King's Road is devoted to "multistore" antiques markets, another third houses design-trade showrooms and stores of household wares, and the remaining third is faithful to the area's teeny-bopper roots.

Finally, don't forget all those museums in nearby **South Kensington**—they all have great gift shops.

KENSINGTON, NOTTING HILL & BAYSWATER **Kensington High Street** (Tube: High St. Kensington) is the hangout of the classier breed of teen, the one who has graduated from Carnaby Street and is ready for street chic. While there are a few staples of basic British fashion here, most of the stores feature items that stretch and are very, very short; very, very tight; and very, very black.

From Kensington High Street, you can walk up **Kensington Church Street,** which, like Portobello Road, is one of the city's main shopping avenues for antiques, selling everything from antique furniture to Impressionist paintings.

Kensington Church Street dead-ends at the Notting Hill Gate Tube station, jumping-off point for Portobello Road, whose antiques dealers and weekend market are 2 blocks beyond.

Not far from Notting Hill Gate is **Whiteleys of Bayswater,** 151 Queensway, W2 (© **020/7229-8844;** www.whiteleys.com; Tube: Bayswater or Queensway), an Edwardian mall whose chief tenant is Marks & Spencer. Whiteleys also contains 75 to 85 other shops, mostly specialty outlets, plus restaurants, cafes, bars, and an eight-screen movie theater.

THE DEPARTMENT STORES

Contrary to popular belief, Harrods is not the only department store in London. The British invented the department store, and they have lots of them, mostly in Mayfair, and each has its own customer profile.

DAKS Opened in 1936 as the home of DAKS clothing, DAKS has been going strong ever since. It's known for menswear—its basement-level men's shoe department is a model of the way quality shoes should be fitted and sold—as well as women's fashions, perfume, jewelry, and lingerie. Many of the clothes are lighthearted, carefully made, and casually elegant. Solid and dependable, this is a well-established store whose core market is male and female clients ages 30 to 50. Clothes aren't particularly cutting edge (and indeed, many of the regular clients here aren't looking for that), except for the youth line, Daks E1. 10 Old Bond St., W1. © 020/7409-4000. www.daks.com. Tube: Green Park.

Fenwick of Bond Street Fenwick (the *w* is silent), dating from 1891, is a stylish store that offers an excellent collection of designer womens wear, ranging from moderately priced ready-to-wear items to more expensive designer fashions. An extensive selection of lingerie in all price ranges is also sold. 63 New Bond St., W1. © 020/7629-9161. www.fenwick.co.uk. Tube: Bond St.

Fortnum & Mason ★★★ Catering to well-heeled clients as a full-service department store since 1707, Fortnum & Mason is better than ever. Offerings

Fortnum & Mason interior.

include one of the most comprehensive delicatessens and food markets in London, as well as stationery; gift items; porcelain and crystal; and lots and lots of clothing for men, women, and children. 181 Piccadilly, W1. ✆ **020/7734-8040.** www. fortnumandmason.com. Tube: Piccadilly Circus.

Harrods Harrods remains an institution, but in the last decade or so, it has grown increasingly dowdy and is not nearly as cutting edge as it used to be. For the latest trends, shop elsewhere. However, we always stop here during our visits to London. As entrenched in English life as Buckingham Palace and the Ascot Races, it's still an elaborate emporium. Goods are spread across 300 departments, and the range, variety, and quality will still dazzle the visiting out-of-towner.

The whole fifth floor is devoted to sports and leisure, with a wide range of equipment and attire. Toy Kingdom is on the fourth floor, along with children's wear. The Egyptian Hall, on the ground floor, sells crystal from Lalique and Baccarat, plus porcelain.

There are also a barber, a jewelry department, and a fashion department for younger customers. You'll have a choice of 18 restaurants and bars. Best of all are the **Food Halls,** with a huge variety of foods and several cafes. Harrods began as a grocer in 1849, and food and drinks are still the heart of the business. The motto remains "If you can eat or drink it, you'll find it at Harrods." 87–135 Brompton Rd., SW1. ✆ **020/8479-5100.** www.harrods.com. Tube: Knightsbridge.

Harvey Nichols Locals call it "Harvey Nicks." Once a favorite of the late Princess Di, this store is large, but it doesn't compete directly with Harrods because it has a more upmarket, fashionable image. Harvey Nicks has its own gourmet food hall and fancy restaurant, **the Fifth Floor,** and is crammed with the best in designer home furnishings, gifts, and fashions for all, although women's clothing is the largest segment of its business. The store carries many American designer brands; avoid them, as they're more expensive in London than they are in the U.S. 109–125 Knightsbridge, SW1. ✆ **020/7235-5000.** www.harveynichols.com. Tube: Knightsbridge.

John Lewis This department store remains one of the most tried-and-true outlets in London. Their motto is that they are never knowingly undersold, and they mean it. We've always found great bargains here, most recently in a clearance sale of fine earthenware by Royal Stafford. Whatever you're looking for, ranging from Egyptian towels to clothing and jewelry, it's likely to be for sale here. 278–306 Oxford St., W1. © **020/7629-7711.** www.johnlewis.com. Tube: Oxford St.

Liberty ★★ This department store is celebrated for its Liberty Prints: top-echelon fabrics, often in floral patterns, prized by decorators for the way they add a sense of English tradition to a room. The front part of the Regent Street store isn't particularly distinctive, but don't be fooled: Other parts of the place have been restored to Tudor-style splendor that includes half-timbering and interior paneling. There are six floors of fashion, china, and home furnishings, including the famous Liberty Print fashion fabrics, upholstery fabrics, scarves, ties, luggage, gifts, and more. 210–220 Regent St., W1. © **020/7734-1234.** www.liberty.co.uk. Tube: Oxford Circus.

Peter Jones Founded in 1877 and rebuilt in 1936, Peter Jones is known for household goods, household fabrics and trims, china, glass, upholstered furniture, and linens. The linen department is one of the best in London. Sloane Sq., SW1. © **020/7730-3434.** www.peterjones.co.uk. Tube: Sloane Sq.

Primary ★ For low-cost high fashion, this remarkable store is hard to rival. Opened in 2009, Primary carries fashionable, yet affordable, clothing for men, women, and children, plus a vast array of household wares. The collection features the latest styles. One shopper reported on the web that it was "amazing" what she purchased for only £55. The store's specialty is providing inexpensive imitations of catwalk designs. Look for great deals in the lingerie or shoe departments as well. 499–517 Oxford St., W1. © **020/7495-0420.** Tube: Marble Arch.

Selfridges ★★ In recent years, this mammoth department store has made a name for itself in fashion. It is so vast that seemingly it could clothe the denizens of the British Empire. It is a clothing outlet for the entire family—the kids, mom, and dad or the roving bachelor or single girl. In addition to affordable garments, it also offers all the "catwalk name" designers as well. Since it was founded by an American in 1858, Selfridges has adapted to changing times. Wander the ground floor "Wonder Room" for luxurious jewelry and unusual giftware. Supposedly, the cosmetics department has the widest range of that merchandise in Europe. Sports gear, lingerie, beauty items, food, exotic teas, accessories, and household items—it's all here. 400 Oxford St., W1. © **0800/123-400.** Tube: Bond St.

GOODS A TO Z
Antiques

Also check out the description of **Portobello Market** on p. 356.

Alfie's Antique Market This is the biggest (and one of the best-stocked) conglomerates of antiques dealers in London, crammed into the premises of a 19th-century store. It has more than 370 stalls, showrooms, and workshops in over 3,252 sq. m (35,004 sq. ft.) of floor space. You'll find the biggest Susie Cooper (a well-known designer of tableware and ceramics for Wedgwood) collection in Europe here. A whole antiques district has grown up around Alfie's along Church

Street. 13–25 Church St., NW8. ☏ **020/7723-6066.** Fax 020/7724-0999. www.alfies antiques.com. Tube: Marylebone or Edgware Rd.

Antiquarius   This market echoes the artistic diversity of King's Road. More than 120 dealers offer specialized merchandise, usually of the small, domestic variety, such as antique and period jewelry, porcelain, silver, first-edition books, boxes, clocks, prints, and paintings, with an occasional piece of antique furniture and many items from the 1950s. 131–141 King's Rd., SW3. ☏ **020/7823-3900.** www. antiquarius.co.uk. Tube: Sloane Sq. or S. Kensington.

Grays Antiques and Grays Mews   These markets have been converted into walk-in stands with independent dealers. Here, the term *antiques* covers items from oil paintings to, say, the 1894 edition of the *Encyclopedia Britannica*. Also sold are antique jewelry; silver; gold; maps and prints; bronzes and ivories; arms and armor; Victorian and Edwardian toys; furniture; Art Nouveau and Art Deco items; antique lace; scientific instruments; craft tools; and Asian, Persian, and Islamic pottery, porcelain, miniatures, and antiquities. There's a cafe in each building. Check out the 1950s-style **Victory Cafe** on Davies Street for their homemade cakes. 58 Davies St. and 1–7 Davies Mews, W1. ☏ **020/7629-7034.** www.grays antiques.com. Tube: Bond St.

Art & Crafts

ACAVA 🎁   This London-based visual-arts organization provides studios and other services for professional artists, and represents about 250 artists working in spaces around London. Call for individual open-studio schedules, as well as dates for the annual Open Studios weekend. 54 Blechynden St., W1. ☏ **020/8960-5015.** www.acava.org. Tube: Perivale.

Antique plates at Portobello Market.

Camden Arts Centre ★   Hailed by *The Times of London* as "the best place to see contemporary art in north London," the Camden Arts Centre has a cafe, bookstore, and studios in addition to its exhibition galleries, where the displays are frequently changed. Arkwright Rd., NW3. © **020/7472-5500.** www.camdenarts centre.org. Tube: Finchley Rd.

Cecilia Colman Gallery   One of London's most established crafts galleries, Cecilia Colman features decorative ceramics, studio glass, jewelry, and metalwork. Among the offerings are glass sculptures by Lucien Simon, jewelry by Caroline Taylor, and pottery by Simon Rich. Exhibitions of contemporary original works are featured. There's also a large selection of mirrors and original-design perfume bottles. 67 St. John's Wood High St., NW8. © **020/7722-0686.** www.cecilia colmangallery.com. Tube: Jubilee Linc to St. John's Wood.

Contemporary Applied Arts ★   This association encourages traditional and progressive contemporary artwork. Many of Britain's best-established craftspeople, as well as promising talents, are represented within this contemporary-looking space. The gallery houses a diverse display of glass, ceramics, textiles, wood, furniture, jewelry, and metalwork—all by contemporary artisans. A program of special exhibitions, including solo and small-group shows, focuses on innovations in craftwork. There are new exhibitions every 6 weeks. 2 Percy St., W1. © **020/ 7436-2344.** www.caa.org.uk. Tube: Tottenham Court Rd.

England & Co.   Under the guidance of Jane England, this gallery specializes in Outsider Art and Art in Boxes (that is, art that incorporates a box structure into the composition or frame of a 3-D work). The gallery focuses attention on neglected postwar British artists such as Tony Stubbings and Ralph Romney. One-person and group shows are mounted frequently, and many young artists get early exposure here. 216 Westbourne Grove, W11. © **020/7221-0417.** www.englandgallery. com. Tube: Notting Hill Gate.

Gabriel's Wharf   This South Bank complex of shops, restaurants, and bars is open Tuesday to Sunday 11am to 6pm (dining and drinking establishments are open later). Lying 2 minutes by foot from Oxo Tower Wharf, it is filled with some of London's most skilled craftspeople, turning out original pieces of sculpture, jewelry, ceramics, art, and fashion. From food to fashion, from arts to crafts, it awaits you here. The place is a lot of fun to poke around in. 56 Upper Ground, SE1. © **020/7021-1686.** www.coinstreet.org. Tube: Blackfriars, Southwark, Waterloo, or Embankment.

Gong   One of the best selections of furniture and offbeat crafts and jewelry in England awaits you here. The merchandise is the work of both Asian and other international artisans. 172 Fulham Rd., W11. © **020/7370-7176.** www.gong.co.uk. Tube: S. Kensington.

Grosvenor Prints   London's largest stock of antique prints, ranging from the 17th up to the 20th centuries, is on sale here. Obviously, views of London are the biggest-selling items. Some prints depict significant moments in the city's history, including the Great Fire. Of course, the British are great animal lovers, so expect plenty of prints of dogs and horses. 19 Shelton St., WC2. © **020/7836-1979.** www. grosvenorprints.com. Tube: Covent Garden.

Kelly Hoppen   The British press has labeled interior designer Kelly Hoppen as their own minimalist Martha Stewart (prescandal, of course). Hoppen's designer emporium on Fulham Road opened to great fanfare, and even Hoppen herself

GO EAST, art lover

The East End neighborhood of Hoxton was a tawdry backwater until very recently, when artists starting flocking here and opening studios, cleaning up the discarded mattresses and rejuvenating abandoned buildings.

Success was ensured with the opening of **White Cube,** 48 Hoxton Sq., N1 (✆ **020/7930-5373;** www.whitecube. com), owned by Jay Jopling, the leading dealer in modern English art, whose artists include Britain's most contentious, Damien Hirst. The other hot gallery is **Victoria Miro Gallery,** 16 Wharf Rd., N1 (✆ **020/7336-8109;** www.victoria-miro. com). Some of London's most controversial art appears here. Miro represents Chris Ofili, whose "Madonna and Dung" painting enraged former New York mayor and art critic Rudolph Giuliani.

These art dealers and the artists themselves (that is, those who've sold a painting) can be found dining at **Cantaloupe,** 35–42 Charlotte Rd., EC2 (✆ **020/7729-5566;** www.cantaloupe london.co.uk), which serves Mediterranean cuisine and great tapas. This informal bar/restaurant, with its wooden tables and industrial fittings, prepares such superb dishes as chargrilled Aberdeen Angus steak with rosemary butter, and fried *halloumi* (a white cheese from Cyprus) with olive salsa. It's open Monday to Friday noon to 3pm and 6 to 11pm, and Saturday 7 to 11pm.

Take the Tube to Old Street to arrive near the doorsteps of all of these establishments.

has been pleased with the "stock just flying out." Expect a little bit of everything here, including her own charming medley of ceramics (some designed for Wedgwood), furniture, and original accessories such as giant horn buttons or pony-skin bags from Argentina. 102A Chepstow Rd., St. Stephen's Yard, W2. ✆ **020/7471-3350.** www.kellyhoppenretail.com. Tube: Westbourne Park.

Whitechapel Art Gallery This century-old "artists' gallery for everyone" has greatly expanded, with new collection displays, new galleries, and ever-changing exhibitions. Close to Brick Lane in the East End, the gallery has been hailed as "the most vibrant artistic community in Europe" by the *Financial Times.* It is cutting edge in its contemporary art exhibitions, and has premiered such artists in days of yore as Picasso or Frida Kahlo. The gallery also promotes artists who live and work in the East End. 77-82 Whitechapel High St., E1. ✆ **020/7522-7888.** www. whitechapelgallery.org. Tube: Aldgate East.

Bath & Body

The Body Shop There's a branch of the Body Shop in every shopping area and tourist zone in London. Some are bigger than others, but all are filled with politically and environmentally friendly beauty, bath, and aromatherapy products. Prices are much lower in the U.K. than they are in the U.S. There's an entire children's line, a men's line, and lots of travel sizes and travel products. 374 Oxford St., W1. ✆ **020/7409-7868.** www.bodyshop.com. Tube: Bond St. Other locations throughout London.

Boots the Chemist This store has branches all over Britain. The house brands of beauty products are usually the best, including the original Boots line (try the cucumber facial mask); Boots's versions of the Body Shop; and Boots's versions of Chanel makeup (called No. 7). They also sell film, sandwiches, and all of life's other little necessities. 490 Oxford St., W1G. ✆ **020/7491-8546.** www.boots. com. Tube: Marble Arch. Other locations throughout London.

Culpeper the Herbalist ★ You'll have to put up with a cramped space to check out all the food, bath, and aromatherapy products, but it's worth it. Stock up on essential oils, or go for the dream pillows, candles, and sachets. The Market, Covent Garden, WC2. ✆ **020/7379-6698.** www.culpeper.co.uk. Tube: Covent Garden.

Floris ★★ A variety of toilet articles and fragrances fill Floris's floor-to-ceiling mahogany cabinets, which are architectural curiosities in their own right. They were installed relatively late in the establishment's history—that is, 1851—long after the shop had received its royal warrants as suppliers of toilet articles to the King and Queen. 89 Jermyn St., SW1. ✆ **0845/702-3239.** www.florislondon.com. Tube: Piccadilly Circus.

Lush In our view, the handmade soaps and cosmetics sold here are the most intriguing in London. The store is always launching something new, and their products include Rock Star Soap, which is very pink and smells like candy. Among the extensive selection is Tam O'Santa, an allspice, sandalwood, and frankincense bubble bath, and Banana Moon, a creamy banana soap. The products are made with fresh fruit and vegetables, the finest essential oils, and safe synthetics—no animal ingredients. 11 The West Piazza, Covent Garden. ✆ **020/7240-4570.** www.lush.co.uk. Tube: Covent Garden. Other locations throughout London.

Neal's Yard Remedies Noted the world over for their cobalt-blue bottles, these chic bath, beauty, and aromatherapy products are must-haves for those who pooh-pooh the Body Shop as too common. Prices are higher in the United States, so stock up here. 15 Neal's Yard, WC2. ✆ **020/7379-7222.** www.nealsyard remedies.com. Tube: Covent Garden.

Penhaligon's ★★★ This Victorian perfumery offers a large selection of perfumes, after-shaves, soaps, and bath oils for women and men. Gifts include antique silver scent bottles and leather traveling requisites. 41 Wellington St., WC2. ✆ **020/7836-2150.** www.penhaligons.co.uk. Tube: Covent Garden.

Books, Maps & Engravings

In addition to the bookstores below, **Waterstone's ★★★**, 203–206 Piccadilly, SW1 (✆ **020/7851-2400;** www.waterstones.com), is the largest bookstore in Europe—and it even has a bar.

Foyle's Bookshop Claiming to be the world's largest bookstore, Foyle's has an impressive array of hardcovers and paperbacks, as well as travel maps, new records, CDs, videotapes, and sheet music. The store also has a cafe and "jazz shop," which sometimes hosts live performances. Foyles also has a tradition of rehousing local independent bookstores forced to close because of high rents—for example, it now carries the stock of Silver Moon, once the best-known women's bookstore in London. 113-119 Charing Cross Rd., WC2. ✆ **020/7437-5660.** www.foyles. co.uk. Tube: Tottenham Court Rd. or Leicester Sq.

Gay's the Word Britain's leading gay and lesbian bookstore offers a large selection of books, as well as magazines, cards, and guides. There's also a used-books section. 66 Marchmont St., WC1. ✆ **020/7278-7654.** http://freespace.virgin.net/ gays.theword. Tube: Russell Sq.

Once a haven for immigrant jews, **Brick Lane,** E1 (Tube: Liverpool St. Station), today is a thriving street in East London, catering to London's burgeoning Indian and Bangladeshi community.

Some of London's most fashionable and trendsetting shoppers are trekking over to Brick Lane, the main drag along "Banglatown," known for its low-cost curry restaurants and sari stores. Almost overnight, funky little boutiques and home furnishing stores started moving in. On Sundays, it erupts into one of London's most exciting flea markets. If you are in the market for a mango *lassi* or handmade jewelry, you'll find it here. Vintage clothing outlets also abound.

Today you can seek out such shopping delights as **Beyond Retro,** 110–112 Cheshire St. (② **020/7613-3636;** www. beyondretro.com), where the managers keep the displays interesting by adding 300 new vintage pieces daily. At **Mar Mar Co.,** 16 Cheshire St. (② **020/7729-1494;** www.marmarco.com), you'll find Scandinavian ceramics and china boxes. **At Work Gallery,** 156 Brick Lane (② **020/7377-0597;** www.atwork gallery.co.uk), offers a collection of quirky jewelry.

The highlight of Brick Lane is the 4.5-hectare (11-acre) **Backyard Market** (also called The Old Truman Brewery), 91 Brick Lane, E1 (② **020/7770-6028**). This market contains some 142 stalls created from a former warehouse on a 4.5-hectare (11-acre) site. Expect edgy women's wear, tailored clothing for guys, kiddie wear, and lots of handmade jewelry. The food market has everything from Spanish paella to sushi. The stalls are open Sunday 10am to 5pm.

While shopping Brick Lane, you can also pick up some rare treats for your lunch, notably at **Beigle Bake,** 159 Brick Lane, E1 (② **020/7729-0616;** Tube: Aldgate East). The oldest and best of the bagel shops of London, this social

mecca is open 24 hours, turning out 7,000 bagels a night. The best is stuffed with mountains of salt beef, which aficionados claim is also the best in London. A bagel is 12p; those with fillings cost from £1.50.

In the Old Truman Brewery, **Story Deli,** 3 Dray Walk, E1 (② **020/7247-3137;** Tube: Aldgate East), serves the best pizzas in Shoreditch, and each one 100% organic. The pizzas are inventive, with thin, crispy oven-baked dough. Toppings range from five cheese to ham and artichoke (the ham is air dried) with a mound of arugula. Expect to pay £10 for a pizza. You can also order freshly made soups and salads. Open Monday to Saturday 8am to 7pm, Sunday 9am to 7pm.

Finally, for your dessert, head for **Rajmahal Sweets,** 57 Brick Lane, E1 (② **020/7375-3536;** Tube: Aldgate East). Try such delights as pistachio *borfey* (like a marzipan) or a *jalebi* (pretzel-like fried dough covered with syrup—it tastes a lot better than it sounds). The shop sells take-away boxes of mixed cookies, cakes, and fruits, as well as marzipan-based sweets. It opens for breakfast daily at 7am, usually closing around 7 or 8pm.

Nearby **Columbia Road** on Sunday (8am–2pm) becomes a virtual greenhouse of shrubs and blooms in all shapes and sizes. This is London's main plant and flower market (Tube: Liverpool St. Station).

Secondhand bookshop on Charing Cross Road.

Hatchards On the south side of Piccadilly, Hatchards offers a wide range of books on all subjects and is particularly renowned in the areas of fiction, biography, travel, cookery, gardening, art, history, and finance. In addition, Hatchards is second to none in its range of books on royalty. 187 Piccadilly, W1. ℂ **020/7439-9921.** www.hatchards.co.uk. Tube: Piccadilly Circus or Green Park.

The Map House of London An ideal place to find an offbeat souvenir. The Map House sells antique maps and engravings, plus a vast selection of old prints of London and England, both original and reproduction. The cost of a century-old original engraving begins at £24. 54 Beauchamp Place, SW3. ℂ **020/7589-4325.** www.themaphouse.com. Tube: Knightsbridge.

Stanfords Established in 1852, Stanfords is the world's largest map shop. Many maps, including worldwide touring and survey maps, are unavailable elsewhere. It's also London's best travel bookstore (with a complete selection of Frommer's guides!). 12-14 Long Acre, WC2. ℂ **020/7836-1321.** www.stanfords.co.uk. Tube: Covent Garden.

Cashmere & Woolens

Berk This store boasts one of the largest collections of cashmere sweaters in London—at least the top brands. The outlet also carries capes, stoles, scarves, and camelhair sweaters. 46 Burlington Arcade, W1. ℂ **020/7493-0028.** www.berk cashmere.co.uk. Tube: Piccadilly Circus or Green Park.

China, Glass & Silver

London Silver Vaults ★ 🎁 Don't let the out-of-the-way location or the facade's lack of charm slow you down. Downstairs you'll enter vaults—40 in all—filled with tons of silver and silverplate, plus collections of jewelry. It's a staggering selection of old and new, with excellent prices and friendly dealers. Chancery House, 53–64 Chancery Lane, WC2. ✆ 020/7242-3844. www.thesilvervaults. com. Tube: Chancery Lane.

Royal Doulton ★★★ Founded in the 1930s, this company has one of the largest inventories of china in Britain. A wide range of English bone china, as well as crystal and giftware, is sold. The firm (www.royaldoulton.com) no longer operates its own outlet in London. But its products are sold in many upmarket stores, notably **Selfridges** at 400 Oxford St., W1 (✆ 0800/123-400; Tube: Bond St.), and **John Lewis,** 278–306 Oxford St., W1 (✆ 020/7629-7711; Tube: Bond St.).

Thomas Goode ★★ This is one of the most famous emporiums in Britain; it's worth visiting for its architectural interest and nostalgic allure alone. Originally built in 1876, Goode's has 14 rooms loaded with porcelain, gifts, candles, silver, tableware, and even a private museum. There's also a tearoom-cum-restaurant tucked into the corner. 19 S. Audley St., W1. ✆ 020/7499-2823. www.thomasgoode. co.uk. Tube: Bond St., Green Park, Marble Arch, or Hyde Park.

Chocolates

Melt These chocolatiers are called "bespoke," meaning custom made. Their chocolate delicacies come from recipes and concoctions from five different countries. The moment you enter you smell the fruity aromas, and many of the chocolates are made from cocoa from the heartland of Columbia, perhaps the finest in the world. You can even watch the chocolates being made. Our favorite treat? Marzipan and cherry Kirsch. 59 Ledbury Rd., Notting Hill, W11. ✆ 020/7727-5030. www.melt chocolates.com. Tube: Notting Hill Gate.

Handmade chocolates at Paul A. Young.

Paul A. Young Since 2006, these chocolaterie guys have been turning out some of the finest artisan chocolates in the U.K. Making the treats on site by hand, the team finds inspiration for its concoctions on a daily basis. They use only the finest natural ingredients to create products from artisan bars to brownies. In the heart of Islington, you can close your eyes and let your nose lead you to this high-quality shop. 33 Camden Passage, Islington, N1. ✆ 020/7424-5750. www.paulayoung.co.uk. Tube: Angel.

Rococo Chocolates Anyone with a dangerous passion for chocolate might want to come here to indulge in this remarkable store. It was inspired by a visit to the spice island of Grenada in the Caribbean. Today an island farm supplies all of its harvest of organic Trinitario cocoa beans, which are made into some of the finest chocolate in London. In 2008, the Academy of Chocolate Awards granted Rococo its highest honor for "changing the way people think about chocolate." 45 Marylebone High St., W1. ✆ **020/7935-7780.** http://rococo chocolates.com. Tube: Bond St.

Fashion

We have divided this category into "Classic," "Cutting Edge," and "Vintage & Secondhand," below.

CLASSIC

While every internationally known designer worth his or her weight in Shantung silk has a boutique in London, the best buys are on the sturdy English styles that last forever. See also the separate sections on "Cashmere & Woolens," "Handbags," "Jewelry," and "Shoes."

Alfred Dunhill's Bourdon House This is the epitome of London chic and luxury for gents. Alfred Dunhill's lies in the 18th-century residence of the Duke of Westminster. The store is known for its leather goods and tailored menswear. It is both a retail shop and a private club, the latter with four suites and a luxury restaurant. In addition, it's the place to go for accessories, gifts, and gadgets. 2 Davies St., Mayfair, W1. ✆ **0845/458-0779.** www.dunhill.com. Tube: Oxford St.

Austin Reed Austin Reed has long stood for superior-quality clothing and excellent tailoring. Chester Barrie's off-the-rack suits, for example, are said to fit like tailor-made. The polite employees are unusually honest about telling you what looks good. The store always has a wide variety of top-notch jackets and suits, and men can outfit themselves from dressing gowns to overcoats. For women, there are carefully selected suits, separates, coats, shirts, knitwear, and accessories. 103–113 Regent St., W1. ✆ **020/7534-7777.** www.austinreed.co.uk. Tube: Piccadilly Circus.

Beau Monde This outlet earns its fame selling chic "nouvelle couture" for women—fitted and adjusted to your body. All designs are by the locally famous London designer Sylvia Young. Her design philosophy is that a busy woman should be conscious of fashion, but not a victim of its whims, and clothes should work for her—not against her. Her womens wear is comfortable and fashionable, but not stuffy. 20 Kingly St., W1. ✆ **020/7734-6563.** www.beaumonde.uk.com. Tube: Piccadilly Circus.

Burberry ★★★ The name has been synonymous with raincoats ever since Edward VII ordered his valet to "bring my Burberry" when the skies threatened. An impeccably trained staff sells the famous raincoats, plus excellent men's shirts, sportswear, knitwear, and accessories. Raincoats are available in women's sizes and styles as well. Prices are high, but you get quality and prestige. 157–167 Regent St., SW1. ✆ **020/7806-1328.** www.burberry.com. Tube: Piccadilly Circus.

Designer Sale UK 🏷 Amazingly, you can sometimes get 90% off designer clothing for both men and women at this outlet. Of course, you've got to sift through 140 rails of clothing and accessories, much of which had a good reason for not selling in the first place. The shop claims it caters to both the discerning label lover and the devoted bargain hunter. Yes, those rails carry Stella McCartney, Vivienne Westwood, and a lot of the lesser lights in designer fashion. A £2 admission is charged to attend the sale. Studio 85, Old Truman Brewery, 95A Brick Lane, E1. ✆ **01273/858-464** in Lewes. www.samplesaleslondon.co.uk. Tube: Aldgate E. or Liverpool St.

Emmett ★   Some of the finest men's shirts in London are sold at this outlet. Shirt styles are sold in limited editions of about two dozen each, so chances are, you'll never run into another man wearing the same garb as you. Complementary patterns line collars and cuffs, and the look is very British, very Prince Charles sophisticated. Beautiful woven silk ties are also featured. 112 Jermyn St., SW1. ✆ **020/7247-1563.** www.emmettlondon.com. Tube: Piccadilly Circus.

Gieves & Hawkes ★★★   This men's clothing store has a prestigious address and a list of clients that includes the Prince of Wales, yet its prices aren't as lethal as others on this street. They're high, but you get good quality. Cotton shirts, silk ties, Shetland sweaters, and exceptional ready-to-wear and tailor-made suits are sold. 1 Savile Row, W1. ✆ **020/7434-2001.** www.gievesandhawkes.com. Tube: Piccadilly Circus or Green Park.

Hilditch & Key ★★   The finest name in men's shirts, Hilditch & Key has been in business since 1899. The two shops on this street both offer men's clothing (including a custom-made shirt service) and women's ready-made shirts. There's also an outstanding tie collection. Shirts go for half-price during the twice-yearly sales (Jan and June); men fly in from all over the world for them. 37 and 73 Jermyn St., SW1. ✆ **020/7734-4707.** www.hilditchandkey.co.uk. Tube: Piccadilly Circus or Green Park.

Jigsaw   Branches of this fashion chain are numerous and feature trendy, middle-market womens wear. 21 Long Acre, WC2. ✆ **020/7240-3855.** www.jigsaw-online.com. Tube: Covent Garden.

Next   This chain of "affordable fashion" stores saw its heyday in the 1980s, when it was celebrated for its success in marketing avant-garde fashion ideas to a wide spectrum of the British public. No longer at its peak, it still merits a stop. The look remains very contemporary, with a Continental flair, and there are clothes for men, women, and kids. 15–17 Long Acre, WC2. ✆ **0844/844-5325.** www.next.co.uk. Tube: Covent Garden. Other locations throughout London.

Reiss   In a city where men's clothing often sells at exorbitant prices, Reiss is a haven of reasonable sporty and casual wear. Take your pick from everything from pullovers to rugged cargo pants. Reis also stocks womens wear and has become quite a sophisticated and trendy label, with more than 15 stores in London. 114 King's Rd., SW3. ✆ **020/7225-4910.** www.reiss.co.uk. Tube: Sloane Sq.

Thomas Pink ★★★   This Jermyn Street shirt-maker, named after an 18th-century Mayfair tailor, gave the world the phrase "in the pink." It has a prestigious reputation for well-made cotton shirts for both men and women. The shirts are created from the finest two-fold Egyptian and Sea Island pure-cotton poplin. Some patterns are classic, others new and unusual. All are generously cut with long tails and finished with a choice of double cuffs or single-button cuffs. A small pink square in the tail tells all. 85 Jermyn St., SW1. ✆ **020/7930-6364.** www.thomaspink.com. Tube: Green Park or Piccadilly Circus.

Turnbull & Asser ★★   Over the years, everyone from David Bowie to Ronald Reagan has been seen in custom-made shirts from Turnbull & Asser. Excellent craftsmanship and simple lines—plus bold colors—distinguish these shirts. The outlet also sells shirts and blouses for an upscale female clientele. Note that T&A shirts come in only one sleeve length and are then altered to fit, a ritual that takes only a few days and costs £10. If you want custom shirts created from scratch, the made-to-measure service takes 10 to 12 weeks, and you must order at least a

Turnbull and Asser shop on Jermyn Street.

half-dozen. Of course, the monograms are included. 71–72 Jermyn St., SW1. ✆ **020/7808-3000.** www.turnbullandasser.com. Tube: Green Park.

CUTTING EDGE

Warning: Cutting-edge fashion can be out of reach for the average shopper, unless you're married to Bill Gates. If you demand the very best, at least look for sales, or else patronize some of our more democratically priced establishments, even secondhand stores. Sometimes still fashionable dresses or gowns have been worn only two or three times at the most.

Currently, the most cutting-edge shopping area in London is **Conduit Street,** W1, in Mayfair (Tube: Oxford Circus or Green Park). Once known for its dowdy airline offices, it is now London's smartest fashion street. Trendy shops are opening between Regent Street and the "blue-chip" boutiques of New Bond Street. Current stars include **Vivienne Westwood** (see below), who has left her punk origins behind and is now the grande dame of English fashion. See below for her flagship store. **Krizia,** 25 Conduit St., W1 (✆ **020/7491-4987;** www.krizia.net), the fashion rage of Rome since the 1950s, displays not only Krizia's clothing lines, but her luxury home goods as well.

For muted elegance, **Yohji Yamamoto,** 14–15 Conduit St., W1 (✆ **020/7491-4129**), is hard to beat, and **Issey Miyake,** 52 Conduit St., W1 (✆ **020/7851-4620;** www.isseymiyake.com), is the Japanese master of minimalism.

Accessorize ✦ This aptly named store is often packed with women who have an eye for bargains but want top-notch style. The store stays abreast of the latest fads and trends, especially in evening bags, which range from antique to high fashion. All sorts of treasures are stocked here, everything from hologram-flecked nail polish to silk scarves. 123A Kensington High St., W8. ✆ **020/7937-1433.** www.monsoon.co.uk. Tube: High St. Kensington.

Display of Marc Jacobs shoes and handbags.

Anya Hindmarch   Although her fashionable bags are sold at Harvey Nichols, Liberty, Harrods, and throughout the U.S. and Europe, this is the only place to see the complete range of Anya Hindmarch's handbags, wallets, purses, and key holders. Smaller items start at £45, whereas handbag prices start at £165, with alligator being the most expensive. The outlet is famous for its "Be a Bag" merchandise. You supply them with a photo, which they print onto a bag of your choice. It takes 6 weeks to deliver, but they will ship overseas. The shop will also print personal inscriptions onto bags. 15–17 Pont St., SW3. ℂ **020/7838-9177.** www.anyahindmarch.com. Tube: Sloane Sq. or Knightsbridge.

Browns ★★   Sought after by trend-conscious Londoners, this cluster of boutiques offers inventories from the "heavily edited" collections of designers who include, among others, the late Alexander McQueen. We're told that the store will continue to offer through the lifetime of this edition McQueen's revealing, feminine women's couture and ready-to-wear pieces. Browns (no relation to the famous hotel of the same name) also stocks designers including Marc Jacobs and Dolce & Gabbana. In addition to clothing, the store offers lifestyle products such as scents, books, jewelry, and gift objects. Across the street, **Browns Focus,** 38–39 S. Molton St. (ℂ **020/7514-0063**), stocks younger, more daring designs. Menswear is concentrated at a separate storefront a few steps away, **"23,"** at 23 S. Molton St. (tel. **020/7514-0038**). Just down the street, **Browns Labels for Less,** 50 S. Molton St. (ℂ **020/7514-0052**), is a discount outlet designer store. 24-27 S. Molton St., W1. ℂ **020/7514-0016.** www.brownsfashion.com. Tube: Bond St.

Dover Street Market   This trendy showcase for many designers, especially Comme des Garçons, is a fashion-filled six-story emporium with an organic cafe crowning it all. The market showcases some of the world's youngest and most talented new designers, including those from Japan, and also sells an array of other items from perfumes to wallets, even Speedos. 17–18 Dover St., W1. ℰ **020/7518-0680.** www.doverstreetmarket.com. Tube: Green Park.

Equa ★ 🎁👕 This womens-wear boutique is a bit of a no-frills type of place. If there's such a thing as an eco-friendly shop, this is it. You'll find organic cotton collections, clothing made from sustainable fabrics such as bamboo and soya, and shoes that have been created by using reconstituted leather. 28 Camden Passage, N1. ℰ **020/7359-0955.** www.equaclothing.com. Tube: Angel.

Joseph Joseph Ettedgui, a fashion retailer born in Casablanca, is a maverick in the fashion world. He's known for his daring designs and his ability to attract some of the most talented designers in the business to work with him. The stretch jeans with flair ankles are the label's best-selling items.

The most complete collection of Joseph Ettedgui clothing anywhere, with clothes for both men and women (including suits, knitwear, suede, and leather clothing), is available within the two largest branches of his empire. Three smaller branches of Joseph (www.joseph.co.uk) lie clustered close to one another, each of them within a very short walk of the South Kensington Tube stop. They're at 315 Brompton Rd., SW3 (ℰ 020/7225-3335), and 77 Fulham Rd., SW4

THE comeback OF CARNABY STREET

What happened to Carnaby Street? Is it just a faded echo left over from the Swinging '60s? That was true for a long time. But Carnaby is rising again. A new influx of talented designers and offbeat shops are popping up not only on Carnaby, but also along its offshoot streets—Newburgh, Foubert's Place, Kingly Street, Marlborough Court, and Lowndes Court. Innovative boutiques seem to open each week behind small Georgian shop fronts.

Among the many shops are such favorites as **Lambretta Clothing,** 29 Carnaby St., W1 (ℰ **020/7437-7078;** www.lambrettaclothing.co.uk), which retains the mod lifestyle philosophy and has launched a range of casual wear for men and footwear for men and women. The line has a retro feel but uses the latest fibers and fabric finishes of today. **Stella McCartney,** 30 Bruton St., W1 (ℰ **020/7518-3100;** www.stellamc cartney.com; Tube: Bond St.) is a show-case for the clothing designs of Paul McCartney's daughter. Vegetarians and animal lovers adore her "no leather, no suede, and no fur" policy.

To reach the stores above, take the Tube to Oxford Circus.

Carnaby Street in 1967.

347

(☎ 020/7823-9500). Close by, and focusing only on menswear, is a Joseph boutique at 74 Sloane Ave., SW3 (☎ 020/7591-0808). Newest of all is a branch in Notting Hill selling clothes for men and women at 236 Westbourne Grove, W11 (☎ 020/7243-9920; Tube: Notting Hill Gate). 23 Old Bond St., W1. ☎ **020/7629-3713.** Tube: Green Park. Also at 16 Sloane St., SW1X. ☎ **020/7235-1991.** Tube: Knightsbridge.

The Laden Showroom ★ Even celebrity shoppers such as Posh Beckham or Noel Gallagher show up here to check out the trendy clothing for both men and women, including jewelry, handbags, belts, and shoes—all sold at moderate tariffs. What makes the place so special is that it is one of the best showcases in London for untried, independent designers who are struggling to make a name for themselves. You may walk out wearing something by the Vivienne Westwood of tomorrow. 103 Brick Lane, E1. ☎ **020/7247-2431.** www.laden.co.uk. Tube: Whitechapel.

The Library Despite its name, this is a showcase for some of the best young designers for men. It's cutting edge without dipping into the extremes of male fashion. The Library is famous for having introduced Helmut Lang to London and now features such designers as Fabrizio del Carlo and Kostas Murkudis. 268 Brompton Rd., SW3. ☎ **020/7589-6569.** Tube: S. Kensington.

Paul Smith's Westbourne House This shop was converted from a stately three-story Edwardian town house into a showcase for the clothing of Paul Smith, whose well-made ready-to-wear men's (and, to a lesser extent, women's and children's) clothing defies the preconceptions of Savile Row tailors who believe that only custom-made garments will fit well. Preferred colors, with occasional exceptions, include grays, browns, and blacks, though there is a medley of velvet prints inspired by Carnaby Street in the 1960s. Look for women's clothes and accessories on the building's street level, men's clothes and accessories on the two floors above street level. 122 Kensington Park Rd., W11. ☎ **020/7727-3553.** www.paulsmith.co.uk. Tube: Notting Hill Gate or Kensington Park Rd.

Topshop ★★ This is the largest fashion store in the world. It is similar to Miss Selfridge but with better design and quality, although Topshop remains quite affordable. Its versatile and ever-changing merchandise is aimed at younger shoppers, but that doesn't stop many women in their 30s and 40s from shopping here. The outlet was the first to release a range of designs from Kate Moss. The shop, though aimed mainly at women, also has a men's floor. Women's shoes, vintage clothing, and other designer labels are sold in the basement. 216 Oxford St., W1. ☎ **0844/848-7487.** www.topshop.co.uk. Tube: Bond St.

Vivienne Westwood ★★ No one in British fashion is hotter than the unstoppable Vivienne Westwood. While it's possible to purchase some Westwood pieces around the world, her U.K. shops are the best places to find her full range of designs. The flagship location (on Conduit St.) concentrates on her couture line, known as the Gold Label. One of the U.K.'s most watched designers, Westwood creates clothes that manage to be elegant, alluring, and stylish all at the same time. Westwood's Anglomania line of clothing focuses on casual designs for youthful bodies, including T-shirts, jeans, and sportswear. The outlet also carries a line of clothing for men. 44 Conduit St., W1. ☎ **020/7287-3188.** Tube: Oxford Circus. Also at 430 King's Rd., SW3. ☎ **020/7352-6551.** www.viviennewestwood.com. Tube: Sloane Sq.

VINTAGE & SECONDHAND

Note that there's no VAT refund on used clothing.

Annie's Vintage Clothes 🎁 This shop concentrates on carefully preserved dresses from the 1920s and 1930s but also has a range of clothing and textiles from the 1880s through the 1960s. A 1920s fully beaded dress will run you about £335, but there are scarves for £21, camisoles for £30, and a range of exceptional pieces priced between £50 and £70. Clothing is located on the main floor; textiles, including old lace, bed linens, and tapestries, are upstairs. 12 Camden Passage, N1. 📞 020/7359-0796. www.anniesvintageclothing.co.uk. Tube: Northern Line to Angel.

Pandora 🥢 A London institution since the 1940s, Pandora stands in fashionable Knightsbridge, a stone's throw from Harrods. Several times a week, chauffeurs drive up with bundles packed anonymously by England's gentry. One woman voted best-dressed at the Ascot Horse Races several years ago was wearing a secondhand dress acquired here. Prices are generally one-third to half the retail value. Chanel and Anne Klein are among the designers represented. Outfits are usually no more than two seasons old. 16–22 Cheval Place, SW7. 📞 020/7589-5289. Tube: Knightsbridge.

Pop Boutique For the best in original streetwear from the 1950s, 1960s, and 1970s, this clothing store is tops. Right next to the chic Covent Garden Hotel, it sells fabulous vintage wear at affordable prices: Leather jackets that would run in the hundreds in the vintage shops of downtown New York are affordable here. 6 Monmouth St., WC2. 📞 020/7497-5262. www.pop-boutique.com. Tube: Covent Garden.

Rokit There are three locations for this small chain, but the most central and best stocked is in Covent Garden. The media have weighed in, calling it everything from "painfully hip" to "automatically suspect with shoe prices that are criminal." The trick here is to browse at leisure, looking for that steal in retro or vintage clothing. The stock is imported from a mother company in Canada. Fetishists of old uniforms will love it here. 42 Sheldon St., WC2. 📞 020/7836-6547. www.rokit.co.uk. Tube: Covent Garden.

Steinberg & Tolkien London's leading dealer in vintage costume jewelry and clothing also offers some used designer clothing that's not old enough to be vintage but is prime for collectors; other pieces are merely secondhand designer thrills. 193 King's Rd., SW3. 📞 020/7376-3660. www.urbanpath.com. Tube: Sloane Sq.

Pop Boutique.

Food

English food has come a long way, and it's worth enjoying and bringing home. Don't miss the Food Halls in Harrods. Consider the Fifth Floor at Harvey Nicks if Harrods is too crowded—it isn't the same, but it'll do. Also check out the internationally famous Fortnum & Mason food emporium. See "The Department Stores," earlier in this chapter, for descriptions, plus other options.

Charbonnel et Walker ★   Charbonnel et Walker is famous for its hot chocolate in winter (buy it by the tin) and its chocolate-covered strawberries, available whenever strawberries are available or in season. The company will send messages of thanks or love spelled out on the chocolates themselves. Ready-made presentation boxes are also available. 1 The Royal Arcade, 28 Old Bond St., W1. *C* **020/7491-0939.** www.charbonnel.co.uk. Tube: Green Park.

Neal's Yard Dairy   Specializing in British and Irish cheeses, this shop occupies the very photogenic premises of what was originally built as a warehouse for the food stalls at Covent Garden. Today you'll see a staggering selection of artisanal cheeses, including cloth-bound cheddars and a wide selection of mild farmer's cheeses, set in big display windows behind an antique, dark-blue Victorian facade. There are also olive oils, breads, fresh produce, and a lot of the fixings of a picnic. 17 Shorts Gardens, WC2. *C* **020/7240-5700.** www.nealsyarddairy.co.uk. Tube: Covent Garden.

Gifts & Souvenirs

Asprey & Garrard   This is as well-known and well-respected a name in luxury gift giving as anything you're likely to find in all of Britain, with a clientele that includes the likes of the Sultan of Brunei and Queen Elizabeth. Scattered over four floors of a dignified Victorian building, it's filled with antiques, porcelain, leather goods, crystal, clocks, and enough unusual objects of dignified elegance to stock an entire English country house. 167 New Bond St., W1. *C* **020/7493-6767.** www.asprey.com. Tube: Green Park.

Muji   An emporium for Japanese wares, this store is known for its bargain offerings. Among its merchandise, the frugal shopper will find everything from "simple and functional chic" clothing to flatware, most of it in avant-garde, minimalist styles completely devoid of any traditional or baroque influences of Olde England. The bath soaps are a delight, coming in such unusual scents as grapefruit and mandarin orange. Funky umbrellas and a host of other ever-changing wares tempt shoppers. 157 Kensington High St., W8. *C* **020/376-2484.** www.muji.co.uk. Tube: High St. Kensington.

Handbags

Bill Amberg's   Most famous for his logo-free classic handbags, Amberg has opened his own shop and expanded his line to include luggage, picture frames, and furniture. Fans of Amberg's designs include Donna Karan, Romeo Gigli, Jerry Hall, and Christy Turlington. Given those celebrity clients, fashion-conscious shoppers may consider the £45 to £450 price range of most items a steal. 14 Burlington Arcade, W1. *C* **020/7499-0962.** www.billamberg.com.

Lulu Guinness   This self-taught British handbag designer, who launched her business in 1989, is known as the finest such designer in London. Many of the world's greatest retail outlets, such as Neiman Marcus, sell her handbags. Her signature handbags, such as the "Florist Basket" and the "House Bag," are immortalized in the fashion collection at the Victoria and Albert Museum. Seen about

London carrying Lulu Guinness handbags are such celebrities as Madonna and Elizabeth Hurley. 3 Ellis St., SW1. ✆ **020/7823-4828.** www.luluguinness.com. Tube: Sloane Sq.

Home Design, Furnishings & Housewares

Also see "Art & Crafts."

Caravans In the mood for a white rabbit lamp or an owl money box? Then head for the showroom of interior stylist Emily Chalmers, who oversees this beautiful collection in flea market–style chic in Shoreditch. This shop, however, is not for Second Hand Rose, since everything is newly made. Chalmers is also the author of three books on interiors. 3 Redchurch St., E2. ✆ **020/7033-3532.** www.caravanstyle.com. Tube: Liverpool St.

The Conran Shop You'll find Sir Terence Conran's high style at reasonable prices at this outlet. The fashion press cites Conran as "the director" of British middle-class taste since the 1960s. This place is great for gifts, home furnishings, and tabletop ware—or just for gawking. Michelin House, 81 Fulham Rd., SW3. ✆ **020/7589-7401.** www.conranshop.co.uk. Tube: S. Kensington.

The Couverture Shop This is an emporium of the unexpected, with original products for both adults and children as well as the home. It's strongest on what they call "bedroom must-haves," embracing bed linen, throws, cushions, and the like. Vintage finds along with designer pieces—often handmade—are also sold. 310 King's Rd., SW3. ✆ **020/7229-2178.** www.couverture.co.uk. Tube: Sloane Sq.

David Linley Furniture ★★★ This is a showcase for the remarkable furniture of Viscount Linley, son of the late Princess Margaret. His designs are complex. For example, his Apsley House Desk is done in French walnut with ebony and nickel-plated detailing, contains secret drawers, and is rimmed with a miniature of the neoclassical Apsley House. Linley's clients include Elton John, Mick Jagger, and Nina Campbell. The director at the Victoria and Albert Museum predicts that Linley's furnishings and accessories will become "the antiques of the future." 60 Pimlico Rd., SW1. ✆ **020/7730-7300.** www.davidlinley.com. Tube: Sloane Sq.

Designers Guild After more than 3 decades in business, creative director Tricia Guild and her young designers still lead the pack in all that's bright and whimsical. They are often copied but never outdone. There's an exclusive line of handmade furniture and accessories at the no. 267–271 location, and wallpaper and more than 2,000 fabrics at the neighboring no. 275–277 shop. The colors remain vivid forever, and the designs are always irreverent. Also available are children's accessories, toys, crockery, and cutlery. 267–271 and 275–277 King's Rd., SW3. ✆ **020/7351-5775.** www.designersguild.com. Tube: Sloane Sq.

Eco ★ 🎁 In a converted Chiswick town house, actor Colin Firth operates this store devoted to home design. Firth calls himself an "eco-warrior." For example, he sells home furnishings such as lampshades that were made out of shaved wood of fallen Norwegian trees. The wallpaper sold here is biodegradable. Downstairs his shelves contain the likes of everything from poppy organic face cream to floral-printed recycled stationery. 213 Chiswick High Rd., W4. ✆ **020/8995-7611.** www.eco-age.com. Tube: Turnham Green.

Gallery Fumi ★ 🎁 Some of the smartest home designers in London are trekking over to Shoreditch to check out the ever-changing showroom at Fumi. Is it an art gallery or a furniture showroom—perhaps both? Partners Valerio Capo and Sam Pratt prefer to call it "a collection of beautiful things," which might include furniture from the hip Lebanese brand Bokja. This outfit reupholsters retro pieces from the '60s and '70s and recycles them in vintage Asian textiles. Savvy shoppers have noted everything here from sculpture to Paul Cocksedge's polystyrene and neon hanging lamps. The space itself is all bare brick walls designed to showcase the collection, not the house decor. 87–89 Tabernacle St., EC2. ✆ **020/7490-2366.** www.galleryfumi.com. Tube: Old St.

Habitat   There are several branches of Terence Conran's popular store, but the massive flagship building is at the address below. If you're looking for household wares and contemporary furnishings, chances are you'll find it here—most items at an affordable price. Chain buyers roam the globe for merchandise to fill this store. 196–199 Tottenham Court Rd., W1. ✆ **08444/991-1122.** www.habitat.co.uk. Tube: Goodge St.

Laboru and Wait ★ 🎁   This store at the Spitalfields market might be called the Old Curiosity Shop. Established in 2003 in East London, it offers useful items that have gone out of style in many households—enamel bread bins, rope doorstops, galvanized steel watering cans and buckets, stylish (yes, stylish) brooms, whatever. The shop is a showcase for specialist makers from around the world, many of whom manufacture items based on their traditional and original designs. Items are both new and vintage. The shop lies around the corner from Brick Lane. Open only Saturday 1 to 5pm, and Sunday 10am to 5pm. 18 Cheshire St., E2. ✆ **020/7729-6253.** www.labourandwait.co.uk.

Summerill & Bishop   Some of London's most sophisticated kitchenware is sold here—items that may not be available in your hometown store. The range is from Edward S. Wohl's charming bird's-eye maple breadboards to John Julian Sainsbury's black granite mortar with a stainless steel–handled pestle. Some of the top designers in Britain created the unusual wares at this outlet. 100 Portland Rd., W11. ✆ **020/7221-4566.** www.summerillandbishop.com. Tube: Holland Park.

Jewelry

Asprey & Garrard   Previously known as Garrard & Co., this recently merged jeweler specializes in both antique and modern jewelry, and silverware. The in-house designers also produce pieces to order and do repairs. You can have a pair of pearl earrings or silver cufflinks made for £60—but the prices go nowhere but up from there. 167 New Bond St., W1. ✆ **020/7493-6767.** www.asprey.com. Tube: Green Park.

Butler & Wilson   This Mayfair store built its reputation on retro costume jewelry, but offers so much more. In addition to bracelets, brooches, earrings, and necklaces, it also sells jewelry for men along with handbags, accessories, and gift items. 20 S. Molton St., W1. ✆ **020/7409-2955.** www.butlerandwilson.co.uk. Tube: Bond St.

Dinny Hall   In business for 20 years, Dinny Hall likes to say that she makes jewelry to be worn—not put in the bank. For much of her inspiration, she turns to nature itself, with many ideas originating from grasses, buds, berries, seeds, and pods. Much of her jewelry is in gold and silver with simple designs. 200 Westbourne Grove, Notting Hill, W11. ✆ **020/7792-3913.** www.dinnyhall.com. Tube: Notting Hill Gate.

Lesley Craze Gallery/Textiles This complex has developed a reputation as a showcase of the best contemporary British jewelry and textile design. The gallery shop focuses on precious metals and includes pieces by such renowned designers as Wendy Ramshaw. Prices start at £60. The gallery also features costume jewelry in materials ranging from bronze to paper. Textiles feature contemporary designs, including wall hangings, scarves, and ties by artists such as Jo Barker, Dawn DuPree, and Victoria Richards. 33–35A Clerkenwell Green, EC1. © **020/7608-0393** (jewelry), **020/7251-9200** (textiles). www.lesleycrazegallery.co.uk. Tube: Farringdon.

Sanford Brothers Ltd. In business since 1923, this family firm sells all styles of jewelry (Victorian through modern), silver, and a fine selection of clocks and watches. Old Elizabeth Houses, 3 Holborn Bars, EC1. © **020/7405-2352.** www.sanfords.co.uk. Tube: Chancery Lane.

Stephen Webster ★ This is the flagship store of this jeweler, lying in the heart of the West End in Mayfair. Here you get glamour with a rock and roll edge. Funky jewelry is a specialty. For example, to celebrate the opening of an oyster and chop house, the store designed gold and enamel lamb chop pendants. From "fire earrings" to diamond enamel bracelets, it's all on display here. 93 Mount St., W1. © **020/486-6576.** www.stephenwebster.com. Tube: Bond St.

Luggage

Mulberry Company This flagship store offers a complete line of the town's most cutting-edge designer luggage. Their signature grosgrain luggage begins at £295. Mulberry is also earning a name in fashion for its English country–style ready-to-wear clothes for men and women. Plus, it carries fashionable furnishings and accessories for the home, including throws and cushions in chenille and damask. 11–12 Gees Court, W1. © **020/7629-3830.** www.mulberry.com. Tube: Bond St.

Museum Shops

Victoria and Albert Museum Gift Shop ★★ This is the best museum shop in London—indeed, one of the best in the world. It sells cards, a fabulous selection of art books, and the usual items, along with reproductions from the design museum archives. Cromwell Rd., SW7. © **020/7942-2696.** www.vandashop.com. Tube: S. Kensington.

Music

Collectors should browse **Notting Hill** because there are a handful of good shops near the Notting Hill Gate Tube stop. Also browse **Soho** in the Wardour Street area, near the Tottenham Court Road Tube stop. Sometimes dealers show up at Covent Garden on the weekends.

Dress Circle This store is unique in London in that it's devoted to musical theater and standard vocalists such as Frank Sinatra or Judy Garland. After half a century, recordings in the U.K. enter the public domain—hence the lower prices on re-released CDs of West End and Broadway musicals from the 1950s. They are priced very low, since royalties don't have to be paid. New releases, of course, cost at least three times more. Karaoke recordings, even theatrical souvenirs are sold—perhaps a Bette Davis doll as Margo Channing in *All About Eve*. 57–59 Monmouth St., WC2. © **020/7240-2227.** www.dresscircle.co.uk. Tube: Covent Garden.

Flashback ★ 🎁 This small, cramped store deep in the heart of Islington is devoted to golden oldies. For the music lover, especially the devotee of the hits of yesterday, it's a gem and a discovery—and one of the best places in London to spend an afternoon browsing. 50 Essex Rd., N1. ✆ **020/7354-9356.** www.flashback. co.uk. Tube: Angel.

HMV ★ This is the U.K.'s leading specialist retailer in music, DVD/video, computer games, and other products. The celebrated composer, Sir Edward Elgar, launched the first store in 1921. Here at this vast emporium of entertainment you'll have the widest possible range of recorded music titles, including the latest releases, along with computer games and other temptations such as titles on both CD and vinyl. From rock to pop, from indie to R&B, from reggae to hip-hop, it's all here. Check downstairs for classical and jazz, and avail yourself of any listening post to check out the CD before buying it. 150 Oxford St., W1. ✆ **020/7631-3423.** http://hmv.com. Tube: Oxford Circus.

Shoes

Also see **DAKS** in "The Department Stores," earlier in this chapter.

Natural Shoe Store A range of shoes for men and women is stocked in this shop, which also does repairs. The selection includes all comfort and quality footwear, from Birkenstock to the British classics. 21 Neal St., WC2. ✆ **020/7836-5254.** www.thenaturalshoestore.com. Tube: Covent Garden.

Office In spite of its dull name, this is an excellent store for style-setters on a budget. Its imitations of some of the world's leading shoe designers have earned it the reputation of being the "Madame Tussaud's of footwear." Within the store is a section devoted to Poste Mistress, a more upmarket section of designer shoes for girls and women. The shoes are more sophisticated than the regular line, everything from almond-toed shoes to multi-strap, and also more expensive. 107 Queensway, W2. ✆ **020/7792-4000.** www.office.co.uk. Tube: Queensway or Bayswater.

Sporting Goods

Harrods (see "The Department Stores," earlier in this chapter) has a surprising collection of sporting goods, including everything you'll need for a polo match.

Stationery & Paper Goods

Paperchase This flagship store has three floors of paper products, including handmade paper, wrapping paper, ribbons, picture frames, and a huge selection of greeting cards. It's the best of its kind in London. 213–215 Tottenham Court Rd., W1. ✆ **020/7467-6200.** www.paperchase.co.uk. Tube: Goodge St. or Tottenham Court Rd. Other locations throughout London.

Tea

Of course, don't forget to visit **Fortnum & Mason** for tea as well (see "The Department Stores," earlier in this chapter).

The Tea House This shop sells everything associated with tea, tea drinking, and teatime. It boasts more than 70 quality teas and tisanes, including whole-fruit blends and the best teas of China (Gunpowder, and jasmine with flowers); India (Assam leaf, and choice Darjeeling); Japan (Genmaicha green); and Sri Lanka (pure Ceylon), plus such longtime-favorite English blended teas as Earl

Inside Hamleys toy shop on Regent's Street.

The Tea House in Covent Garden.

Grey. The shop also offers novelty teapots and mugs. 15A Neal St., WC2. ℂ **020/7240-7539.** www.covent garden.co.uk. Tube: Covent Garden.

Toys

Hamleys   This flagship is the finest toy shop in the world—more than 35,000 toys and games on seven floors of fun and magic. The huge selection includes soft, cuddly stuffed animals as well as dolls, radio-controlled cars, train sets, model kits, board games, outdoor toys, computer games, and more. 188–196 Regent St., W1. ℂ **0844/855-2424.** www.hamleys.com. Tube: Oxford Circus or Piccadilly Circus. Also at Covent Garden and Heathrow Airport.

STREET & FLEA MARKETS

If Mayfair stores are not your cup of tea, don't worry; you'll have more fun, and find a better bargain, at any of the city's street and flea markets. A general website for all the markets, including information and opening hours, is at www.london tourist.org/markets.html.

CAMDEN   London's famous Camden Markets ★ (www.camden-market.org; Tube: Camden Town or Chalk Farm) sprawl along Camden High Street and Chalk Farm Road in north London, stretching for a mile from the Chalk Farm tube station. The main market is by Regent's Canal. Whatever you're looking for from books to musical instruments, from handcrafts to clothing and jewelry, is for sale here. Bric-a-brac, fast food, and plenty of snacks both hot and cold are also sold. Some 100,000 shoppers frequent the market every weekend. The market has moved from being a weekend event to a 7-days-a-week happening. The best visiting hours are daily from 9am to

Camden Lock market railway bridge.

4pm. By coming on a weekday you miss the hordes of shoppers, although not all traders are open.

THE EAST END At the gentrified **Spitalfields Market** ★★ (www.visit spitalfields.com; Tube: Liverpool St.), you'll meet the true cockney of the East End. No doubt the hawker will have some merchandise to sell, perhaps a hidden gem of fashion or something tatty from grandmother's attic. It is both cutting-edge and vintage in this modernized shopping center with plenty of merchants and eateries (the old market hall was torn down). From the quirky to the trend-setting, it's all here—fashion, antiques, whatever. Shops and restaurants are open daily 11am to 7pm. Thursday is best for antiques and vintage items, Friday for fashion and art.

We also highly recommend the eclectic market at Brick Lane; see p. 340 for more details.

NOTTING HILL **Portobello Market** (www.portobelloroad.co.uk; Tube: Notting Hill Gate) is a magnet for collectors of virtually everything. It's mainly a Saturday happening, from 6am to 5pm. You needn't be here at the crack of dawn; 9am is fine. Once known mainly for fruit and vegetables (still sold here throughout the week), in the past 4 decades Portobello has become synonymous with antiques. But don't take the stallholder's word for it that the fiddle he's holding is a genuine Stradivarius left to him by his Italian great-uncle; it might just as well have been "nicked" from an East End pawnshop.

The market is divided into three major sections. The most crowded is the antiques section, running between Colville Road and Chepstow Villas to the south. (**Warning:** There's a great concentration of pickpockets in this area.) The second section (and the oldest part) is the "fruit and veg" market, lying between Westway and Colville Road. In the third and final section is a flea market, where Londoners sell bric-a-brac and lots of secondhand goods they didn't really want in the first place. But looking around still makes for interesting fun.

Note: Some 90 antiques and art shops along Portobello Road are open during the week when the street market is closed. This is actually a better time for the serious collector to shop because you'll get more attention from dealers, and you won't be distracted by the organ grinder.

SOUTH BANK   Open on Fridays only, **New Caledonian Market** is commonly known as the **Bermondsey Market** because of its location on the corner of Long Lane and Bermondsey Street (Tube: London Bridge, then bus no. 78 or walk down Bermondsey St.). The market is at the extreme east end, beginning at Tower Bridge Road. It's one of Europe's outstanding street markets for the number and quality of the antiques and other goods. The stalls are well known, and many dealers come into London from the country. Prices are generally lower here than at Portobello and the other markets. It gets underway at 5am—with the bargains gone by 9am—and closes at noon. Bring a "torch" (flashlight) if you go in the wee hours.

SOUTHWARK   In Southeast London, **Borough Market ★★**, Southwark St., SE1 (✆ 020/7407-1002; www.boroughmarket.org.uk), is one of the largest food markets in the world, selling a mammoth variety of delectables from across the globe. Savvy London foodies have long known you can get a virtual free lunch on Friday and Saturday by simply enjoying the samples on display. The market of small shops lies only a few blocks from the London Bridge Tube station. You'll find fish and chips galore, plus so much more. If you want more elegant fare, try **Roast,** 6 Southwark St, SE1 (✆ 020/7940-1300; www.roast-restaurant.com), open 7 days a week. Sample their free-range Banham chicken or slow-roasted pork belly. Mains start at £19. The market is open Thursday 11am to 5pm, Friday noon to 6pm, and Saturday 9am to 5pm.

THE WEST END   Covent Garden Market (✆ 020/7836-9136; www.coventgarden londonuk.com; Tube: Covent Garden) offers several markets Monday to Saturday 10am to 6pm (we think it's most fun to come on Sun 11am–6pm). It can be a little confusing until you dive in and explore. **Apple Market** is the bustling market in the courtyard, where traders sell—well, everything. Many of the items are what the English call collectible nostalgia: a wide array of glassware and ceramics, leather goods, toys, clothes, hats,

Food stall serving organic seafood curry at Borough Market.

and jewelry. Some of the merchandise is truly unusual. Many items are handmade, with some of the craftspeople selling their own wares—except on Monday, when antiques dealers take over. Some goods are new, some are very old. Out back is **Jubilee Market** (ℂ **020/7836-2139**), also an antiques market on Monday. Tuesday to Sunday, it's sort of a fancy hippie market with cheap clothes and books. Out front there are a few tents of cheap stuff, except on Monday.

At the indoor market section of Covent Garden Market (in a superbly restored hall) specialty shops sell fashions and herbs, gifts and toys, books and dollhouses, cigars, and much more. There are bookshops and branches of famous stores (Hamleys, the Body Shop), and prices are kept moderate.

St. Martin–in-the-Fields Market (Tube: Charing Cross) is good for teens and those who don't want to trek all the way to Camden Market and are interested in imports from India and South America, crafts, and local football (soccer) souvenirs. It's located near Trafalgar Square and Covent Garden; hours are Monday through Saturday from 11am to 5pm and Sunday from noon to 5pm.

The thriving neighborhood of Marylebone continues to blossom with chic boutiques, restored Victorian pubs, designer shops, markets, and epicurean emporiums. One of our favorites is the amusingly named **Cabbages and Frocks** in the churchyard of St. Marylebone Parish Church, Marylebone High St., W1 (ℂ **020/7794-1636;** www.cabbagesandfrocks.co.uk; Tube: Baker St.). Here you are tempted by an array of clothing from new designers, as well as vintage clothing, along with jewelry, blown glass, and cute duds for kids. The market opens Saturday 11am to 5pm, at which time it also offers a number of food specialties, ranging from Japanese delicacies to Argentinian steak sandwiches.

Berwick Street Market (Tube: Oxford Circus or Tottenham Court Rd.) may be the only street market in the world that's flanked by rows of strip clubs, porno stores, and adult-movie dens. Don't let that put you off. Humming 6 days a week in the scarlet heart of Soho, this array of stalls and booths sells the best and cheapest fruit and vegetables in town. It also hawks ancient records, tapes, books, and old magazines, any of which may turn out to be a collector's item one day. It's open Monday to Saturday 8am to 5:30pm.

On Sunday mornings artists hang their work on the railings along a 1.5km (1-mile) stretch of **Bayswater Road,** along the edge of Hyde Park and Kensington Gardens. If the weather's right, start at Marble Arch and walk. You'll see the same thing on the railings of Green Park along Piccadilly on Saturday afternoons.

9

LONDON AFTER DARK

F rom the fringes of the East End to the bowels of West Brompton and beyond, London pulsates with more nightlife than any other capital of Europe. Bette Midler once said that when it's three o'clock in the morning in New York, it's 1938 in London. But she said that a long time ago. Times have changed, and London is an all-night party town.

The draconian liquor laws of yesterday have been relaxed a bit. Even if your favorite pub closes at 11pm, there are still bars and late-night joints awaiting your business. Bars, in fact, are no longer places to drop in for a drink, but often all-night venues unto themselves. Many bars are attached to fashionable restaurants with dinner menus, dance floors, and even DJs, so they are looking more and more like nightclubs.

There is such diversity here: a night at the theater, a supper club, a dance club, a fashionable bar, an old-fashioned pub with literary associations, an evening at a Covent Garden opera or the Royal Ballet, a classical music concert at Albert Hall, an intimate jazz club, even a first-run movie or a gay time at a cruisy bar. You name it: London has it.

The Tube may shut down early, but there are always night buses to get you back to your hotel. Taxis are available 24 hours but are expensive.

Weekly publications such as *Time Out* carry full entertainment listings, including data on restaurants, nightclubs, and bars. You'll also find listings in daily newspapers, notably the *Times* and the *Telegraph*.

THE PLAY'S THE THING: LONDON'S THEATER SCENE

Even more than New York, London is the theater capital of the world. Few things here are as entertaining and rewarding as the theater. The number and variety of productions, and the standards of acting and directing, are unrivaled. The London stage accommodates both the traditional and the avant-garde and is, for the most part, accessible and reasonably affordable. You'll also find most of the theaters listed in this section on the "Central London Theaters" color map at the beginning of this book.

Getting Tickets

To see specific shows, especially hits, purchase your tickets in advance. The best method is to buy your tickets from the theater's box office, which you can do over the phone using a credit card. You'll pay the theater price and pick up the tickets the day of the show. You can also go to a ticket agent, especially for discount tickets such as those sold by the **Society of London Theatre** (© **020/7557-6700;**

www.officiallondontheatre.co.uk) on the southwest corner of Leicester Square, open Monday to Saturday 10am to 7pm and Sunday noon to 3pm. A £2 service fee is charged. You can purchase all tickets here, although the booth specializes in half-price sales for shows that are undersold. These tickets must be purchased in person—not over the phone. For phone orders, you have to call **Ticketmaster** at ✆ **0870/060-2340;** www.ticketmaster.co.uk.

For tickets and information before you go, try **Keith Prowse,** 234 W. 44th St., Ste. 1000, New York, NY 10036 (✆ **800/669-8687** or 212/398-4175; www. keithprowse.com). Their London office (which operates under the name of both Global Tickets and First Call Tickets) is at the British Visitors Center, 1 Regent St., SW1 (✆ **0870/906-3860**). They'll mail your tickets, fax a confirmation, or leave your tickets at the appropriate production's box office. Instant confirmations are available for most shows. A booking and handling fee of up to 20% is added to the price of all tickets.

Applause Theatre and Entertainment Service, 311 W. 43rd St., Ste. 601, New York, NY 10036 (✆ **800/451-9930** or 212/307-7050; fax 212/397-3729; www.applause-tickets.com), can sometimes get you tickets when Prowse can't. In business for some 2 decades, it is a reliable and efficient company.

Another option is **Theatre Direct International** (**TDI;** ✆ **800/ BROADWAY** [276-2392] or 212/541-8457 in the U.S.; www.broadway.com). TDI specializes in providing London fringe theater tickets but also has tickets to major productions, including those at the Royal National Theatre and the Barbican. The service allows you to arrive in London with your tickets or have them held for you at the box office.

If you're staying at a first-class or deluxe hotel with a concierge, you can also call and arrange tickets before you arrive, putting them on a credit card.

London theater tickets are priced quite reasonably when compared with those in the United States. Prices vary greatly depending on the seat—from £25 to £85. Sometimes gallery seats (the cheapest) are sold only on the day of the performance, so you'll have to head to the box office early in the day and return an hour before the performance to queue up because they're not reserved seats.

Many of the major theaters offer reduced-price tickets to students on a standby basis, but not to the general public. When available, these tickets are sold 30 minutes prior to curtain. Line up early for popular shows, as standby tickets go fast and furious. Of course, you must have a valid student ID.

Warning: Beware of scalpers who hang out in front of theaters with hit shows. Many report that scalpers sell forged tickets, and their prices are outrageous.

Major Theaters & Companies

We have listed some of the most popular theaters and companies below. To find out what's on currently in all of the major and fringe theaters, pick up *Time Out London, Where,* a London daily newspaper, or "The Official London Theatre Guide" pamphlet (online at www.officiallondontheatre.co.uk), available at ticket brokers and all West End theaters. For locations, see the "Central London Theaters" color map at the beginning of this book.

One of the world's finest theater companies, the **Royal Shakespeare Company ★★★**, performs at various theaters throughout London. Check its website at **www.rsc.org.uk** for current shows and venues, or call ✆ **0844/800-1110** Monday to Saturday 9am to 8pm. The theater troupe performs in London during the winter months, specializing in the plays of the Bard. In summer, it tours England and abroad.

Cadogan Hall   Nestled in the heart of Chelsea, this decommissioned church was the first Christian Science church in the world, founded in 1893. It has now been turned into a concert hall for the Royal Philharmonic Orchestra. Completely restored and massively altered, the building now boasts a 900-seat auditorium and all the acoustics of the 21st century. The box office is open Monday to Saturday from 10am to 7pm and Sunday from 10am to 7pm on performance days only. 5 Sloane Terrace, SW1. ✆ **020/7730-4500.** www.cadoganhall.com. Tickets vary according to the event. Tube: Sloane Sq.

Open-Air Theatre   This outdoor theater is in Regent's Park; the setting is idyllic, and both seating and acoustics are excellent. Presentations are mainly of Shakespeare, usually in period costume. Its theater bar, the longest in London, serves both drink and food. In the case of a rained-out performance, tickets are offered for another date. The season runs from June to mid-September Monday to Saturday at 8pm, plus Wednesday, Thursday, and Saturday matinees at 2:30pm. Inner Circle, Regent's Park, NW1. ✆ **0844/826-4242.** www.openairtheatre.org. Tickets £10–£33. Tube: Baker St.

NEW venues FOR LONDON OPERA LOVERS

Frank Matcham, famed designer of the Coliseum, built **Hackney Empire,** 291 Mare St., E8 (✆ **020/8985-2424;** www.hackneyempire.co.uk), an Italian-style rococo opera house that opened in 1901. Today its cultural offerings range from opera to the Bard.

The **Savoy Theatre,** the Strand, WC2 (✆ **0870/164-8787;** www.savoy-theatre.co.uk), also presents operas and other musicals such as a revival of *Porgy and Bess.* This was the famous opera theater built in 1880 by Richard D'Oyly Carte that specialized in Gilbert & Sullivan musicals. Today, the 1,100-seat theater has been completely refurbished and is one of the few West End theaters with an orchestra pit; this one holds the Royal Philharmonic Opera Orchestra.

Hackney Empire.

Royal Court Theatre This theater has always been a leader in producing provocative, cutting-edge, new drama. In the 1950s, it staged the plays of the angry young men, notably John Osborne's then-sensational *Look Back in Anger;* earlier it debuted the plays of George Bernard Shaw. The theater is home to the English Stage Company, formed to promote serious stage writing. Box-office hours are Monday to Saturday from 10am to 6pm. Sloane Sq., SW1. ℂ **020/7565-5000.** www.royalcourt theatre.com. Tickets £10–£25; call for the latest information. Tube: Sloane Sq.

Royal National Theatre Home to one of the world's greatest stage companies, the Royal National Theatre is not one but three theaters—the Olivier, reminiscent of a Greek amphitheater with its open stage; the more traditional Lyttelton; and the Cottesloe, with its flexible stage and seating. The National presents the finest in world theater, from classic drama to award-winning new plays, including comedies, musicals, and shows for young people. A choice of at least six plays is offered at any one time.

It's also a full-time theater center, with an amazing selection of bars, cafes, restaurants, free foyer music and exhibitions, short early-evening performances, bookshops, backstage tours, riverside walks, and terraces. You can have a three-course meal in Mezzanine, the National's restaurant; enjoy a light meal in the brasserie-style Terrace cafe; or have a snack in one of the coffee bars. Box office hours are Monday to Saturday 10am to 8pm. South Bank, SE1. ℂ **020/7452-3000.** www.nationaltheatre.org.uk. Tickets £10–£38; midweek matinees, Sat matinees, and previews cost less. Tube: Waterloo, Embankment, or Charing Cross.

Shakespeare's Globe Theatre In May 1997, the new Globe Theatre—a replica of the Elizabethan original, thatched roof and all—staged its first slate of plays (*Henry V* and *A Winter's Tale*) yards away from the site of the 16th-century theater where the Bard originally staged his work.

Productions vary in style and setting; not all are performed in Elizabethan costume. In keeping with the historic setting, no lighting is focused just on the stage, but floodlighting is used during evening performances to replicate daylight in the theater—Elizabethan performances took place in the afternoon. Theatergoers sit on wooden benches of yore—in thatch-roofed galleries, no less—but these days you can rent a cushion to make yourself more comfortable. About 500 "groundlings" can stand in the uncovered yard around the stage, just as they did when the Bard was here.

From May to September, the company intends to hold performances Tuesday to Saturday at 2 and 7pm. There will be a limited winter schedule. In any season, the schedule may be affected by weather because this is an outdoor theater. Performances last 2½ to 4 hours, depending on the play.

For details on the exhibition that tells the story of the painstaking re-creation of the Globe, as well as guided tours of the theater, see p. 297. New Globe Walk, Bankside, SE1. ℂ **020/7902-1400** for box office. www.shakespeares-globe.org. Tickets £5 for groundlings, £15–£32 for gallery seats; exhibition tickets £9 adults, £7.50 seniors and students, £6.50 ages 5–15. Tube: Mansion House or Blackfriars.

Theatre Royal Drury Lane   Drury Lane is one of London's oldest and most prestigious theaters, crammed with tradition—not all of it respectable. This, the fourth theater on this site, dates from 1812; the first was built in 1663. Nell Gwynne, the rough-tongued Cockney lass who became Charles II's mistress, used to sell oranges under the long colonnade in front. Nearly every star of London theater has taken the stage here at some time. It has a wide-open repertoire but leans toward musicals, especially long-running hits. Guided tours of the backstage area and the front of the house are given most days at 10:15am, noon, and 2:15 and 4:45pm. The box office is open Monday to Saturday from 10am to 8pm. Evening performances are held Monday to Saturday at 7:30pm, with matinees on Wednesday and Saturday at 2:30pm. Catherine St., Covent Garden, WC2. ℂ **0844/412-2955** www.theatreroyaldrurylane.co.uk. Tickets £27–£60. Tube: Covent Garden.

Fringe Theater

Some of the best theater in London is performed on the "fringe"—at the dozens of theaters devoted to alternative plays, revivals, contemporary dramas, and musicals. These shows are usually more adventurous than established West End productions, and they're cheaper. Most offer discounted seats to students and seniors. Fringe theaters are scattered around London, so check listings in *Time Out* and www.officiallondontheatre.co.uk and www.londontheatre.co.uk.

Almeida Theatre   The Almeida is known for its adventurous stagings of new and classic plays. The theater's legendary status is validated by consistently good productions at lower-than-average prices. Performances are usually held Monday to Saturday. The Almeida is also home to the Festival of Contemporary Music (also called the Almeida Opera) from mid-June to mid-July, featuring everything from atonal jazz to 12-tone chamber orchestra pieces. Box office is open Monday through Saturday 10am to 6pm. Almeida St., N1. ℂ **020/7359-4404.** www.almeida. co.uk. Tickets £6–£30. Tube: Northern Line to Angel or Victoria Line to Highbury & Islington.

The Gate   This tiny room above a Notting Hill pub is one of the best alternative stages in London. Popular with local cognoscenti, the Gate specializes in translated works by foreign playwrights. Performances are held Monday to Friday at 7:30pm, Saturday at 3pm. Call for shows and times. Box office is open Monday to Friday 10am to 6pm. 12 Pembridge Rd., W11. ℂ **020/7229-0706.** www. gatetheatre.co.uk. Tickets £10–£16. Tube: Notting Hill Gate.

The King's Head   London's most famous fringe locale, the King's Head is also the city's oldest pub-theater. Despite its tiny stage, the theater is heavy on musicals; several have gone on to become successful West End productions. Matinees are held on Saturday and Sunday at 3:30pm. Evening performances are held Tuesday to Saturday at 7:30 or 8pm. Box office is open daily 10am to 8pm. 115 Upper St., N1. ℂ **0844/209-0326.** www.kingsheadtheatre.org. Tickets £15–£20. Tube: Northern Line to Angel.

Young Vic   Long known for presenting both classical and modern plays, the famous theater company is back at its home base following a 2-year restoration. The acoustics, the seating, and the stage equipment are better than ever. The Young Vic nurtures younger talent than its sister theater, **Old Vic** (www.oldvictheatre.com), which puts on productions by more established artists. Productions at the Young Vic could be almost anything and are priced depending on the show. Prices are usually £7.50 and £25, and note that discounted tickets are available for students and others 26 and under. The box office is open Monday to Saturday 10am to 7pm. 66 The Cut, SE1. ✆ **020/7922-2922.** www.youngvic.org. Tube: Oval.

CLASSICAL MUSIC, DANCE & OPERA
The Rest of the Performing Arts Scene

Currently, London supports five major orchestras—the **London Symphony,** the **Royal Philharmonic,** the **Philharmonia Orchestra,** the **BBC Symphony,** and the **BBC Philharmonic**—several choirs, and many smaller chamber groups and historic instrument ensembles. Look for the **London Sinfonietta,** the **English Chamber Orchestra,** and, of course, the **Academy of St. Martin in the Fields.** Performances are in the South Banks Arts Centre and the Barbican. Smaller recitals are at Wigmore Hall and St. John's Smith Square.

Barbican Centre (home of the London Symphony Orchestra and more) The largest art and exhibition center in western Europe, the roomy and comfortable Barbican complex is the perfect setting for enjoying music and theater. Barbican Hall is the permanent home address of the London Symphony Orchestra, as well as host to visiting orchestras and performers of all styles, from classical to jazz, folk, and world music.

In addition to its hall and two theaters, Barbican Centre encompasses the Barbican Art Gallery, the Curve Gallery, and foyer exhibition spaces; Cinemas One and Two, which show recently released mainstream films and film series; the Barbican Library, a general lending library that places a strong emphasis on the arts; the Conservatory, one of London's largest greenhouses; and restaurants, cafes, and bars. The box office is open Monday to Saturday from 9am to 8pm. Silk St., EC2. ✆ **020/7638-8891.** www.barbican.org.uk. Ticket prices depend on the event. Tube: Barbican or Moorgate.

London Coliseum (home of the English National Opera) Built in 1904 as a variety theater and converted into an opera house in 1968, the London Coliseum is the city's largest theater. For its 100th birthday, the renowned opera house received a multimillion-pound restoration fit for a diva. Today not only is the Edwardian splendor restored, but there are roomier foyers, plus a two-story lobby and bar with views of Trafalgar Square. The 2,358-seat Coliseum still remains the largest proscenium theater in England. One of two national opera companies, the English National Opera performs a range of works here, from classics to Gilbert and Sullivan to new experimental works. All performances are in English. The Opera presents a repertory of 18 to 20 productions 5 or 6 nights a week for 10 months of the year (the theater is dark mid-July to mid-Sept). The theater also hosts touring companies. Although balcony seats are cheaper, many visitors seem to prefer the upper circle or dress circle. The box office is open Monday to Saturday from 10am to 6pm. London Coliseum, St. Martin's Lane, WC2. ✆ **0870/145-0200.** www.eno.org. Tickets from £10 balcony, £26–£84 upper or dress circle or stalls; about 100 discount balcony tickets sold on the day of performance from 10am. Tube: Charing Cross or Leicester Sq.

Royal Albert Hall   Opened in 1871 and dedicated to the memory of Victoria's consort, Prince Albert, this circular building holds one of the world's most famous auditoriums. With a seating capacity of 5,200, it's a popular place to hear music by stars. Occasional sporting events (especially boxing) figure strongly here, too.

Since 1941, the hall has hosted the BBC Henry Wood Promenade Concerts, known as "the Proms," an annual series that lasts for 8 weeks between mid-July and mid-September. The Proms, incorporating a medley of rousing, mostly British orchestral music, have been a British tradition since 1895. Although most of the audience occupies reserved seats, true aficionados usually opt for standing room in the orchestra pit, with close-up views of the musicians on stage. Newly commissioned works are often premiered here. The final evening is the most traditional; the rousing favorites "Jerusalem" or "Land of Hope and Glory" echo through the hall. After its 8-year restoration, the Albert Hall now allows tours every 30 minutes, starting at 10:30am Friday to Tuesday and ending at 2:30pm, at a cost of £7.50. Limited to only 15 participants, tours take in such sights as the Queen's Box and the Royal Retiring Room used by royals during intermission. Those on tour are also shown the Royal Albert Hall organ with it 9,999 pipes. The box office is open daily 9am to 9pm. Kensington Gore, SW7. ✆ **020/7589-8212.** www.royalalberthall.com. Tickets £5–£150, depending on the event. Tube: S. Kensington.

The Royal Opera House (home of the Royal Ballet and the Royal Opera)   The Royal Ballet and the Royal Opera are at home again in this magnificently restored theater. Opera and ballet aficionados hardly recognize the renovated place, with its spectacular public spaces, including the Floral Hall (a chamber-music venue), a rooftop restaurant, and bars and shops. The entire

Royal Albert Hall.

Kenwood Lakeside Concerts.

Ballet Nacional de Cuba performing *Don Quixote* at Sadler's Wells.

northeast corner of one of London's most famous public squares has been transformed, finally realizing Inigo Jones's original vision for this colonnaded plaza.

Performances of the Royal Opera are usually sung in the original language, but supertitles are projected. The Royal Ballet, which ranks with top companies such as the Kirov and the Paris Opera Ballet, performs a repertory with a tilt toward the classics, including works by its earlier choreographer-directors Sir Frederick Ashton and Sir Kenneth MacMillan. The box office is open Monday to Saturday from 10am to 8pm. Bow St., Covent Garden, WC2. ✆ 020/7304-4000. www. royalopera.org. Tickets £6–£200. Tube: Covent Garden.

Sadler's Wells Theatre   This is a premier venue for dance and opera. It occupies the site of a series of theaters, the first built in 1683. In the early 1990s, the turn-of-the-20th-century theater was mostly demolished, and construction began on an innovative new design completed at the end of 1998. The turn-of-the-20th-century facade has been retained, but the interior has been completely revamped with a stylish cutting-edge theater design. The new theater offers classical ballet, modern dance of all degrees of "avant-garde-ness," and children's theatrical productions, including a Christmas ballet. Performances are usually at 7:30pm. The box office is open Monday to Saturday from 9am to 8:30pm. Rosebery Ave., EC1. ✆ 020/7863-8198. www.sadlers-wells.com. Tickets £10–£60. Tube: Northern Line to Angel.

Southbank Centre   Three of the most acoustically perfect concert halls in the world were erected here between 1951 and 1964: the Royal Festival Hall, the Queen Elizabeth Hall, and the Purcell Room, all located in this complex. Together, the halls present more than 1,200 performances a year, including classical music, ballet, jazz, popular music, and contemporary dance. Also here is the internationally renowned Hayward Gallery (p. 288).

The Southbank Centre, which usually opens daily at 10am, offers an extensive array of things to see and do, including free exhibitions in the foyers and occasional free lunchtime music at 12:30pm. On Friday, "Commuter Jazz" in the foyer from 5:15 to 6:45pm is free. The Poetry Library is open Tuesday to Sunday 11am to 8pm, and shops display a selection of books, records, and crafts. Food and drink are also served at various venues. Head to the Skylon Bar and Grill (www.skylonrestaurant.co.uk), a new restaurant on Level 3, serving a modern Continental cuisine with panoramic views of the London skyline. Less formal dining is available at the Riverside Terrace Café on Level 2, where guests dine outdoors in fair weather, watching boat traffic on the Thames. The box office is open daily from 9am to 8pm. On the South Bank, SE1. Box office ✆ **0844/875-0073.** www.rfh.org.uk. Tickets £8–£60. Tube: Waterloo or Embankment.

Wigmore Hall An intimate auditorium, Wigmore Hall offers an excellent series of voice recitals, piano and chamber music, early and baroque music, and jazz. A cafe/bar and restaurant are on the premises; a cold supper can be preordered if you are attending a concert. Performances are held nightly, in addition to the "Sunday Morning Coffee Concerts" and Sunday concerts at 11:30am or 4pm. The box office is open Monday to Saturday 10am to 7pm and Sunday from 10:30am to 5pm. 36 Wigmore St., W1. ✆ **020/7935-2141.** www.wigmore-hall.org.uk. Tickets £10–£35. Tube: Bond St. or Oxford Circus.

Outside Central London

Kenwood Lakeside Concerts These band and orchestral concerts on the north side of Hampstead Heath have been a British tradition for more than half a century. In recent years, laser shows and fireworks have been added to a repertoire that includes everything from rousing versions of the *1812 Overture* to jazz to operas such as *Carmen*. The final concert of the season always features some of the "Pomp and Circumstance" marches of Sir Edward Elgar. Music drifts across the lake to serenade wine-and-cheese parties on the grass. Concerts take place in July and August, Saturday at 7:30pm. The box office is open Monday to Saturday from 9:30am to 6:30pm. Kenwood, Hampstead Lane, Hampstead Heath, London NW3. ✆ **0844/412-2706.** www.picnicconcerts.com. Tickets £20 for lawn seats, £30 for reserved deck chairs. Discounts of 13% for students and persons older than 60. Tube: Northern Line to Golders Green or Archway, then bus 210, a 30–45-min. jaunt to the north of London.

THE CLUB & MUSIC SCENE
Comedy

The Comedy Store This is London's showcase for established and rising comic talent. Inspired by comedy clubs in the U.S., the club has given many comics their start, and today a number of them are established TV personalities. Even if their names are unfamiliar, you'll enjoy the spontaneity of live comedy before a British audience. Visitors must be 18 and older; dress is casual. Reserve through **Ticketmaster** (✆ **0844/847-1637**); the club opens 1½ hours before each show. *Insider's tip:* Go on Tuesday when the humor is more cutting edge. Tuesday to Sunday, doors open at 6:30pm and the show starts at 8pm; on Friday and Saturday, an extra show starts at midnight (doors open at 11pm). 1A Oxendon St., off Piccadilly Circus, SW1. ℂ **0844/847-1728.** www.thecomedystore.co.uk. Cover £16. Tube: Leicester Sq. or Piccadilly Circus.

Live Music

The Bull & Gate   Outside central London, and smaller, cheaper, and often more animated and less touristy than many of its competitors, the Bull & Gate is the unofficial headquarters of London's pub rock scene. Indie and relatively unknown rock bands are served up in back-to-back handfuls at this somewhat battered Victorian pub. The place attracts a young crowd, mainly in their 20s. If you like spilled beer, this is off-the-beaten-track London at its most authentic. Bands that have played here and later ascended to fame on Europe's club scene have included Madness, Blur, and Pulp. There's music nightly from 8pm to midnight. 389 Kentish Town Rd., NW5. ℂ **020/8826-5000.** www.bullandgate.co.uk. Cover from £5. Tube: Northern Line to Kentish Town.

The Fridge   It's more fun at this grunge night spot if you get caught in a police raid. Otherwise, expect hard house or trance, a hard dance venue with an occasional gay night featuring live music. Instead of the Fridge, this club should be called "the Fringe," as it's on the far fringe indeed—way out in Brixton, where all colors are gray at night. The *Evening Standard* called it London's ultimate melting pot. There are some dull nights here, but when the joint's jumping, it leaps. Townhall Parade, SW2, Brixton. ℂ **020/7326-5100.** www.fridge.co.uk. Cover £10–£20. Tube: Brixton.

Roundhouse   Housed in a Victorian steam engine–repair shed, the Roadhouse in Camden is once again a cultural venue, presenting live music from emerging young talent, and even theater or dance. It once gained fame in the 1960s and reopened in 2006, attracting young London. At its peak it can house 3,300 patrons standing. In days of yore, Jimi Hendrix, Paul McCartney, and The Who performed here. At the on-site cafe you can order fresh, seasonal food, all at a reasonable price. Phone bookings Monday to Friday 9am to 6pm; Saturday 9am to 4pm. Chalk Farm Rd., NW1. ℂ **0844/482-8008.** www.roundhouse.org.uk. Price depends on the event. Tube: Camden Town.

The Roxy   This is an eclectic club featuring more traditional recorded pop, rock, soul, and disco. Ambience wins out over decor. During the week, a social lounge atmosphere pervades; on the weekends, this place is pure dance club. Open Monday to Thursday from 5pm to 3am, Friday 5pm to 3:30am, and Saturday 9:30pm to 3:30am. 3 Rathbone Place, W1. ℂ **020/7255-1098.** www.theroxy.co.uk. Cover £3–£9. Tube: Tottenham Court Rd.

Shepherd's Bush Empire   Located in an old BBC television theater with great acoustics, this is a major venue for big-name pop and rock stars. Announcements appear in the local press. There's a seating capacity of 2,000. The spot mostly attracts fans in their 20s. The box office is open Monday to Friday from noon to 4pm, but you can book 24 hours through **Ticketweb** at ℂ **0870/771-2000.** Shepherd's Bush Green, W12. ℂ **020/8354-3300.** www.02shepherdsbushempire.co.uk. Ticket prices vary according to show. Tube: Hammersmith & City Line to Shepherd's Bush or Goldhawk Rd.

Sound In the heart of London, this 700-seat venue has booked the big acts, everybody from Sinéad O'Connor to Diddy to the Spice Girls. Sound functions as a restaurant and bar every night, with limited live music and a DJ until 11pm; after 11pm, the mood changes, the menu is simplified to include only bar snacks, and the site focuses much more heavily on live music and dancing. The music program is forever changing; call to see what's on at the time of your visit and to reserve tickets. Crowds and age levels can vary here depending on what act is featured. Reservations are recommended for dinner, but reservations after 11pm are not accepted. The box office is open Monday to Saturday 10am to 6pm. 1 Leicester Sq., W1. ✆ **020/7287-1010.** www.soundlondon.com. Free admission until 9pm daily; £10 9–10pm, £10–£12 10–11pm, £15 from 11pm. Tube: Leicester Sq.

Windmill ★★ It's the music that lures devotees to the back streets of Brixton. This unpretentious club, whose reputation went from ground zero to great, is now hailed as one of the top 10 music venues in the U.K. Entry is cheap, and so is the beer. The staff is friendly, the atmosphere candlelit. The beer garden overflows with a hip, young crowd of Londoners and foreigners come to hear groups such as the Black Lips. Sounds embrace psycho beats, punk, Goth rock, and music as yet unlabeled. This place is open Monday to Saturday from 8pm to 2am. 22 Blenheim Gardens, SW2. ✆ **020/8671-0700.** www.windmillbrixton.co.uk. Cover £3–£5. Tube: Brixton.

Traditional English Music

Cecil Sharpe House CSH was the focal point of the folk revival in the 1960s, and it continues to treasure and nurture folk music and dance. You'll find a whole range of traditional music and dance here, with different evenings devoted to, among others, Irish set dances, English barn dances (similar to American square dances), dances from Louisiana's Cajun country, even reenactment of 18th-century quadrilles. Although many of the regular patrons of this bar and dance club know these arcane dances by heart, they're usually charitable toward quick-learning and agile newcomers who can pick up the steps and the beat quickly. Call to see what's happening on the nights that you're in town. The box office is open Monday to Friday 9:30am to 5:30pm. 2 Regent's Park Rd., NW1. ✆ **020/7485-2206.** www.efdss.org. Tickets £5–£30. Tube: Northern Line to Camden Town.

Jazz & Blues

Ain't Nothin' But Blues Bar This club, which bills itself as the only true blues venue in town, features local acts and occasional touring American bands. On weekends, be prepared to wait in line for a while. Open Monday to Wednesday 6pm to 1am, Thursday 6pm to 2am, Friday 6pm to 3am, Saturday 2pm to 3am, and Sunday 3pm to midnight. 20 Kingly St., W1. ✆ **020/7287-0514.** www.aintnothinbut.co.uk. Cover £5. Free Sun–Wed, free Thurs before 9:30pm, free Fri–Sat before 8:30pm. Tube: Oxford Circus or Piccadilly Circus. From the Oxford Circus Tube stop, walk south on Regent St., turn left on Great Marlborough St., and then make a quick right on Kingly St.

Bull's Head This club has showcased live modern jazz every night of the week for more than 40 years. One of the oldest hostelries in the area, it was a 19th-century staging post where travelers on their way to Hampton Court could rest while coach horses were changed. Today the bar features jazz by musicians from all over the world. Since it's way off the tourist trail, it attracts mainly locals in a wide age group, all of whom appreciate good music. Live jazz plays on Sunday from 1 to 3pm and 8:30 to 10:30pm, Monday to Saturday from 8:30 to 11pm. You can order lunch in the pub or dinner in Nuay's Thai Bistro. The club is open Monday to Saturday from noon to midnight, and Sunday from noon to 10:30pm. 373 Lonsdale Rd., Barnes, SW13. ✆ **020/8876-5241.** www.thebullshead.com. Cover £6–£15. Tube: Hammersmith, then bus 209 to Barnes Bridge, then retrace the path of the bus for some 91m (299 ft.) on foot; or take Weybridge train from Waterloo Station and get off at Barnes Bridge Station, then walk 5 min. to the club.

100 Club   Though less plush and expensive than some jazz clubs, 100 Club is a serious contender on the music front, with presentations of some remarkably good jazz. Its cavalcade of bands includes the best British jazz musicians and some of their Yankee brethren. Rock, R&B, and blues are also on tap. Serious devotees of jazz from ages 20 to 45 show up here. Open Monday to Thursday and Sunday 7:30 to 11:30pm, Friday noon to 3pm and 8:30pm to 2am, and Saturday 7:30pm to 1am. *Note:* These hours are subject to change. 100 Oxford St., W1. ✆ **020/7636-0933.** www.the100club.co.uk. Cover £6–£25. Club members get a £1 discount Sat nights. Tube: Tottenham Court Rd. or Oxford Circus.

Pizza Express   Don't let the name fool you: This restaurant/bar serves some of the best jazz in London by mainstream artists, along with thin-crust Italian pizza. You'll find local bands or visiting groups, often from the United States. The place draws an equal mix of Londoners and visitors in the 20-to-40 age bracket. Although the club has been enlarged, it's still important to reserve ahead of time. The restaurant is open daily from 11:30am to midnight; jazz plays from 7:30 to 11pm. 10 Dean St., W1. ✆ **020/7734-3220.** www.pizzaexpresslive.com. Cover £15–£35. Tube: Tottenham Court Rd.

Ronnie Scott's Jazz Club   Inquire about jazz in London, and people immediately think of Ronnie Scott's, the European vanguard for modern jazz. Only the best English and American combos, often fronted by top-notch vocalists, are booked here. The programs make for an entire evening of cool jazz. In the heart of Soho, Ronnie Scott's is a 10-minute walk from Piccadilly Circus along Shaftesbury Avenue. In the Main Room, you can watch the show from the bar or sit at a table, at which you can order dinner. The Downstairs Bar is more intimate; among the regulars at your elbow may be some of the world's most talented musicians. The club is open Monday to Saturday 6pm to 3am, Sunday 6pm to midnight. Reservations are recommended. 47 Frith St., W1. ✆ **020/7439-0747.** www.ronniescotts.co.uk. Tickets £5–£50, depending on the event. Tube: Leicester Sq. or Piccadilly Circus.

606 Club   Located in a discreet basement, the 606, a jazz supper club in the boondocks of Fulham, presents live music nightly. Predominantly a venue for modern jazz, its styles range from traditional to contemporary. Local musicians and some very big names play here, whether at planned gigs or informal jam sessions after they finish shows elsewhere in town. Because of license requirements, patrons can order alcohol only with food. Locals show up here along with a trendy crowd from more posh neighborhoods in London. Open Monday to Wednesday 7:30pm to 1am, Thursday to Saturday 8pm to 1:30am, and selected Sundays noon to 4pm and 8pm to midnight. 90 Lots Rd., SW10. ✆ **020/7352-5953.** www.606club.co.uk. Cover Mon–Thurs £10, Fri–Sat £12, Sun lunch £10, Sun night £10. Bus: 11, 19, 22, 31, 39, C1, or C3. Tube: Earl's Court.

Macy Grey performing at Ronnie Scott's Jazz Club.

Dance floor at Ministry of Sound.

DANCE, DISCO & ECLECTIC

Bar Rumba   Despite its location on Shaftesbury Avenue, this Latin bar and music club could be featured in a book of underground London. A hush-hush address, it leans toward radical jazz-fusion on some nights and phat funk on other occasions. It boasts two full bars and a different musical theme every night. All the music here is live. On weeknights you have to be 18 or older; on Saturday and Sunday, nobody younger than 21 is allowed in. 36 Shaftesbury Ave., W1. ✆ **020/7287-6933.** www.barrumba.co.uk. Cover £4–£20. Free Sat before 10pm. Tube: Piccadilly Circus.

Cargo   This watering hole in ultratrendy Hoxton draws a smart urban crowd from their expensive West End flats. Its habitués assure us it's the place to go for a "wicked time" and great live bands. If there are no bands on a particular night, then great DJs dominate the club. Music and dancing start at 6pm, and the joint is jumping by 9:30pm nightly. It's fun and funky, with two big arched rooms, fantastic acoustics, and a parade of videos. Open Monday to Thursday noon to 1am, Friday noon to 3am, Saturday 6pm to 3am, and Sunday 1pm to midnight. Kingsland Viaduct, 83 Rivington St., Shoreditch, EC2. ✆ **020/7739-3440.** www.cargo-london.com. Cover £6–£35 after 10pm. Tube: Liverpool St.

Egg ★   There's a wild party going on here for serious clubbers drawn to the somewhat seedy location across from King's Cross. Spread over three floors, the joint is warehouse-style, with music that embraces everything from electro-disco beats to house (its specialty). Egg is a leading contender in London's underground scene, complete with a large garden and balcony terrace. Sexy clubbers show up for such events as "Playtime" on Friday nights. Open Friday 10pm to 6am and Saturday from 10pm until noon on Sunday. 200 York Way, N7. ✆ **020/7609-8364.** www.egglondon.net. Tube: King's Cross.

The End This club is better than ever after its enlargement. You'll find a trio of large dance floors, along with four bars and a chill-out area. Speaker walls will blast you into orbit. The End is the best club in London for live house and garage music. From its drinking fountain to its swanky toilets, the club is alluring. Dress for glam and to be seen on the circuit. Some big names in London appear on the weekends to entertain. Open Monday and Wednesday 9pm to 3am, Tuesday 6pm to 3am, Thursday 8pm to 3am, Friday 6pm to 3:30am, Saturday 9pm to 3:30am, and Sunday 9pm to 1:30am. 18 W. Central St., WC1. *C* **020/7419-9199.** www. endclub.com. Cover £5–£20. Tube: Tottenham Court Rd.

Fabric While other competitors have come and gone, Fabric continues to draw crowds since opening in 1999. Its main allure is that it has a license for 24-hour music and dancing from Thursday to Sunday night. This is one of the most famous clubs in the increasingly trendy East London sector. On some crazed nights, at least 2,500 members of young London, plus a medley of inter-national visitors, crowd into this mammoth place. It has a trio of dance floors, bars wherever you look, unisex toilets, chill-out beds, and even a roof terrace. Live acts are presented every Friday, with DJs reigning on weekends. You'll hear house, garage, soca, reggae, and whatever else is on the cutting edge of London's underground music scene at the time. Open Thursday and Friday 9:30pm to 5am, Saturday 10pm to 7am. 77A Charterhouse St., EC1. *C* **020/7336-8898.** www.fabric london.com. Cover £8–£16. Tube: Farringdon.

Ministry of Sound Removed from the city center, this club remains hot. With a large bar and huge sound system, it blasts garage and house music for the ener-getic crowds that pack the two dance floors. If music and lights in the rest of the club have gone to your head, you can chill in the lounge. *Note:* The cover charge is stiff, and bouncers decide who is cool enough to enter, so slip into your grooviest and most glamorous club gear. Open Friday 10pm to 5am and Saturday 11pm to 7am. Student night is Tuesday 10pm to 4am. 103 Gaunt St., SE1. *C* **44870/060-0010.** www.ministryofsound.com. Cover £12–£20. Tube: Northern Line to Elephant & Castle.

Notting Hill Arts Club This is one of the hippest nighttime venues in Lon-don, with the action taking place in a no-frills basement in Notting Hill Gate. Yes, that was Liam Gallagher you spotted dancing with Courtney Love. To justify the name of the club, art exhibitions are sometimes staged here. Most of the clients are younger than 35, and they come from a wide range of backgrounds. The music is eclectic, varying from night to night—jazz, salsa, hip-hop, indie, and so on. Open Monday to Friday from 6pm to 2am, Saturday 4pm to 2am, and Sun-day 4pm to 1am. Bands perform Monday to Thursday, Saturday, and Sunday. 21 Notting Hill Gate, W11. *C* **020/7460-4459.** www.nottinghillartsclub.com. Cover £5–£15. Tube: Notting Hill Gate.

151 Down in Chelsea, pretty young things of both sexes are attracted to this basement night club that hosts a variety of themed nights. There's a bustling bar and a dance floor looking out onto the DJ booth. The room is surrounded by alcoves where you can sit . . . or whatever. You may enjoy dancing to the cheesy pop music, or otherwise just quaffing the champagne. It's open Monday through Saturday 10pm to 3:30am. 151 King's Rd., SW3. *C* **029/7351-6826.** Cover £10. Tube: S. Kensington.

Studio Valbonne ★ This is a throwback to those glamorous old supper clubs with elegant ambience installed at the same address that used to be patronized by the likes of Madonna, Boy George, and George Michael when they were

Dance, Disco & Eclectic

Las Vegas Nights in the Heart of London

If James Bond were to arrive in town with his latest girl, he might invite her to spend a night at **Casino at the Empire ★★**, Leicester Sq., WC2 (𝒞 020/3014-1000; www.thecasinolsq. com; Tube: Leicester Sq.), in the heart of London. For ages the Empire, with its iconic Art Deco decor, was one of the most famous dance palaces in the U.K. But the foxtrot and tango have given way to gaming tables, chic bars, and dining enclaves.

It succeeds in recreating the classy days of gaming, and you expect Frank Sinatra and his Rat Pack in tuxes to show up at any minute. Choose your spot for the evening's debauchery; ours is the Icon Room on the second landing, a cocktail lounge with a balcony overlooking the masses of Leicester Square. It

evokes a French boudoir with its crimson furnishings.

The Shadow Bar nearby features live entertainment and evokes Las Vegas with its deep seat lounges and illuminated dance floor. FuLuShou serves decent Asian fusion cuisine, with exotic teas a feature. Or else sample the succulent grilled meats and fresh seafood in Flame. There's even an ice cream parlor and coffee bar upstairs.

State-of-the-art electronic games include roulette, punto banco, blackjack, three-card poker, and other ways to lose your money in the glamorous ground floor casino. To become a member, you can present a driver's license or passport to the reception. The club is open Sunday to Friday noon to 6am and Saturday noon to 4am.

young. With its underlit dance floor and VIP section, it is a good place for chic dining or drinking expensive cocktails. A three-course dinner costs £45, with such main dishes as a Mediterranean steak with a tomato hollandaise sauce or penne with a tangy sauce for vegetarians. In such a setting only a fruit salad laced with champagne will do. Open Monday and Wednesday to Saturday 7:30pm to midnight. 62 Kingly St., W1. 𝒞 **020/7434-0888.** Cover £15 for women, £20 for men. Tube: Oxford Circus.

Vibe Bar As more and more of hip London heads east, bypassing even Clerkenwell for Hoxton, Vibe has been put on the map. The *Evening Standard* named it among the top five DJ bars in London. The paper compared it to an "expensively distressed pair of designer jeans." In summer the action overflows onto a courtyard. Patrons check their e-mail, lounge on comfortable couches, and listen to diverse music such as reggae, Latin, jazz, R&B, Northern Soul, African, or hip-hop. Hours are Sunday to Thursday 1:30 to 11:30pm, Friday and Saturday 5pm to 1am. 91 Brick Lane, E1. 𝒞 **020/7426-0491.** www.vibe-bar.co.uk. Cover free to £5 sometimes assessed after 6pm. Tube: Liverpool St.

Zoo Bar The owners spent millions of pounds outfitting this club in the slickest, flashiest, and most psychedelic decor in London. If you're looking for a true Euro nightlife experience replete with gorgeous au pairs and trendy Europeans, this is it. Zoo Bar upstairs is a menagerie of mosaic animals beneath a glassed-in ceiling dome. Downstairs, the music is intrusive enough to make conversation futile. Clients range in age from 18 to 35; androgyny is the look of choice. Hours are daily 4pm to 3am. 13–17 Bear St., WC2. 𝒞 **020/7839-4188.** www.zoobar.co.uk. Cover £2–£15 after 10pm. Tube: Leicester Sq.

The Gay & Lesbian Scene

Time Out London magazine also carries listings on gay and lesbian clubs. Another good place for finding out what's hot and hip is **Prowler Soho,** 5–7 Brewer St., Soho, W1 (✆ **020/7734-4031;** Tube: Piccadilly Circus), the largest gay life-style store in London. (You can also buy anything from jewelry to CDs and books, fashion, and sex toys.) It's open until 10pm Monday to Saturday, Sunday noon to 8pm. On the Web, **www.gingerbeer.co.uk** is the best site for lesbians to find out what's going on in London, and the magazine that all bona fide lesbians read is *G3* (www.g3magazine.co.uk).

Admiral Duncan Gay men and their friends go here to drink, have a good time, and make a political statement. British tabloids shocked the world in 1999 when they reported that this pub had been bombed, with three people dying in the attack. Within 6 weeks, the pub reopened its doors. We're happy to report that the bar is better than ever, now also attracting nongays showing their support. Open Monday through Thursday noon to 11pm, Friday through Saturday noon to 11:30pm, and Sunday noon to 10:30pm. 54 Old Compton St., W1. ✆ **020/ 7437-5300.** Tube: Piccadilly Circus or Leicester Sq.

The Box Adjacent to one of Covent Garden's best-known junctions, Seven Dials, this sophisticated Mediterranean-style bar attracts all kinds of men. In the afternoon, it is primarily a restaurant, serving meal-size salads, club sandwiches, and soups. Food service ends abruptly at 5pm, after which the place reveals its core: a cheerful, popular rendezvous for London's gay and counterculture crowds. The Box considers itself a "summer bar," throwing open doors and windows to a cluster of outdoor tables at the slightest hint of sunshine. Open Monday to Saturday 11am to 11:30pm and Sunday 11am to 11pm. 32–34 Monmouth St. (at Seven Dials), WC2. ✆ **020/7240-5828.** www.boxbar.com. Tube: Leicester Sq.

Candy Bar This is the most popular lesbian bar in London at the moment. It has an extremely mixed clientele, ranging from butch to femme and young to old. There are a bar and a club downstairs. Design is simple, with bright colors and lots of mirrors upstairs and darker, more flirtatious decor downstairs. Men are welcome as long as a woman escorts them. Open Monday to Thursday 5 to 11:30pm, Friday and Saturday 5pm to 2am, and Sunday 5 to 11pm. 4 Carlisle St., W1. ✆ **020/7494-4041.** www.candybarsoho.com. Cover Fri £5, Sat £6. Tube: Tottenham Court Rd.

The Edge Few bars in London can rival the tolerance, humor, and sexual sophistication found here. The first two floors are done up with decorations that, like an English garden, change with the seasons. Dance music can be found on the crowded, high-energy lower floors. Three menus are featured: a funky day-time menu, a cafe menu, and a late-night menu. Dancers hit the floors starting around 7:30pm. Clientele ranges from flamboyantly gay to hetero pub-crawlers. One downside: A reader claims the bartenders water down the drinks. Open Monday to Saturday noon to 1am and Sunday 2 to 11:30pm. 11 Soho Sq., W1. ✆ **020/7439-1313.** www.edgesoho.co.uk. Tube: Tottenham Court Rd.

First Out Café Bar First Out prides itself on being London's first (est. 1986) all-gay coffee shop. Set in a 19th-century building whose wood panels have been painted the colors of the gay-liberation rainbow, the bar and cafe are not particularly cruisy. Cappuccino and whisky are the preferred libations, and an exclusively vegetarian menu includes curry dishes, potted pies in phyllo pastries, and salads. Don't expect a raucous atmosphere—some clients come here with their grandmothers. Look for the bulletin board with leaflets and business cards of gay and gay-friendly entrepreneurs. Open Monday to Saturday 10am to 11pm and Sunday 11am to 10:30pm. 52 St. Giles High St., W1. ☏ **020/7240-8042.** www. firstoutcafebar.com. Tube: Tottenham Court Rd.

G.A.Y. Name notwithstanding, the clientele here is mixed, and on a Saturday night this could be the most rollicking club in London. You may not find love here, but you could discover a partner for the evening. Patrons have been known to strip down to their briefs or shorts. A mammoth place, this club draws a young crowd to dance beneath its mirrored disco balls. Open Monday, Thursday, and Friday 11pm to 4am; and Saturday 10:30pm to 5am. London Astoria, 157 Charing Cross Rd., WC2. ☏ **020/7434-9592.** www.g-a-y.co.uk. Cover £1–£15. Tube: Tottenham Court Rd.

George & Dragon A great deal of "Queer as Folk" life is shifting from Vauxhall and Soho to increasingly fashionable Shoreditch. Its epicenter is this pub where the late Alexander McQueen used to show up; Boy George still drops in. Even London's tabloid press has discovered it, *The Evening Standard* raving, "it's possibly the best pub in the world . . . ever." It's also been accused of "attracting flotsam," of being "grotty," and of looking "green and slimy." Regardless of what the spin is, the place is a subcultural phenomenon. Expect a kitschy decor of pink walls, a talking horse head on the wall, cowboy hats, and a sequined guitar worthy of Elvis. 2–4 Hackney Rd. ☏ **020/7012-1100.** www.myspace.com/georgeanddragon. Tube: Old St.

Heaven This club, housed in the vaulted cellars of Charing Cross Railway Station, is a London landmark. Heaven is one of the biggest and best-established gay venues in Britain. Painted black and reminiscent of an air-raid shelter, the club is divided into at least four areas, connected by a labyrinth of catwalk stairs and hallways. Each room offers a different type of music, from hip-hop to rock. Heaven also has theme nights, which are frequented at different times by gays, lesbians, or a mostly heterosexual crowd. Thursday in particular seems open to anything, but on Saturday it's gays only. Call before you go. Open daily 10pm to 6am. The Arches, Villiers, and Craven sts., WC2. ☏ **020/7930-2020.** www.heaven-london. com. Cover £12–£20. Tube: Charing Cross or Embankment.

Ku Bar The Happy Hour here lasts from noon to 9pm, and the bartenders assure us that their watering hole attracts "the tastiest men in London." Those bartenders serve up some of the tastiest drinks too, including peach, melon, apple, lemon, and butterscotch schnapps. On Sunday the staff hosts a gay tea dance. Come here for a fab time, to throw a bash, and to cruise. 30 Lisle St., WC2. ☏ **020/7437-4303.** www.ku-bar.co.uk. Tube: Leicester Sq.

Shadow Lounge This is the current hot spot for gay men in Soho. Shadow Lounge is in the vanguard of gay life in London, which is showing a tendency to shift from gargantuan dance palaces like Heaven to more intimate rendezvous points. Young men, who look like the cast of the British version of "Queer as Folk," meet here at 9pm for drinks. Some return after dinner for dance to raucous house music. Open Monday and Wednesday 10pm to 3am; Tuesday, Thursday, and Saturday 9pm to 3am; and Friday 9pm to 4am. 5 Brewer St., W1. ☏ **020/7287-7988.** www. theshadowlounge.co.uk. Cover £5–£10. Tube: Piccadilly Circus.

BARS & COCKTAIL LOUNGES

Absolut Icebar   You might say that this watering hole is the coolest joint in town. The temperature is always kept at 5°F (−15°C) year-round, with everything inside made out of crystal-clear ice from the Torne River in Sweden. You've got to make a reservation to chill out for 40 minutes, and you're given a silver cape and hood to wear for the experience. Inside you're offered a vodka cocktail to warm your soul. Open Monday to Wednesday 3:30 to 10pm, Thursday 3:30 to 11pm, Friday 3:30 to 11:45pm, Saturday 12:30pm to 12:30am, and Sunday 3:30 to 10pm. 31–33 Heddon St., W1. ✆ **020/7478-8910.** www.belowzerolondon.com. Cover Mon–Wed and Sun £12; Thurs–Sat £15. Tube: Oxford Circus.

Artesian at the Langham   In the Langham hotel, this chic (and pricey) lounge is perfect for a rendezvous. It attracts patrons who enjoy the bartender's specialty of hot buttered rum. The dark rum is blended with apple cider, spices, and a clove-infused apricot brandy, among other ingredients. The lilac-hued salon boasts more than 50 types of rum, a drink you associate more with the Caribbean than London. Open daily 10:30am to 2am. 1C Portland Place, W18. ✆ **020/7636-1000.** www.artesian-bar.co.uk. Tube: Oxford Circus.

Bartok ★ 🎁   It's been around for about a decade, but still isn't very well known—and it should be. It's the hippest bar in Camden, specializing in classical music (of all things) and named for the Hungarian composer, Bela Bartok. It's been called the ultimate chill-out bar in London, ideal for a romantic evening. Crystal chandeliers and the flicker of candles set the rather decadent, hedonistic mood. Visitors sprawl out on tapestry-covered couches, enjoying actual conversation, the music, the food, the drink, and each other. Open Monday to Thursday 5pm to 3am, Friday 5pm to 4am, Saturday 1pm to 4am, and Sunday 1pm to 3am. 78–79 Chalk Farm Rd. (opposite the Roundhouse), NW1. ✆ **020/7916-0595.** Tube: Chalk Farm.

Interior of Absolut Icebar.

Beach Blanket Babylon   Come here if you're looking for a hot singles bar that attracts a crowd in their 20s and 30s. The decor is a bit wacky, no doubt designed by an aspiring Salvador Dalí who decided to make it a fairy-tale grotto (or was he going for a medieval dungeon look?). It's close to the Portobello Market. Friday and Saturday nights are the hot, crowded times for bacchanalian revelry. Open daily noon to midnight. 45 Ledbury Rd., W11. ✆ **020/7229-2907.** www. beachblanket.co.uk. Tube: Notting Hill Gate.

Cantaloupe   This bustling pub and restaurant is hailed as the bar that jump-started the increasingly fashionable Shoreditch scene. Businesspeople commuting from their jobs in the City mix with East End trendoids in the early evening at what has been called a "gastro-pub/preclub bar." The urban beat is courtesy of the house DJ. The restaurant and tapas menus are first-rate. Open Thursday to Saturday noon to midnight, Sunday to Wednesday noon to 11pm. 35 Charlotte Rd., Shoreditch, EC2. ✆ **020/7729-5566.** Tube: Old St.

Claridge's Macanudo Fumoir   The most stylish and luxurious venue for cigar aficionados is sheltered at London's poshest address, Claridge's Hotel in Mayfair. Both sumptuous and moody, this eggplant-colored, leather-clad bar seats only 17. It features the largest selection of Macanudo cigars in the country, plus more than 20 different Cuban cigars. Along with your smoke, you can enjoy London's most revered selection of cognacs, Armagnacs, tequilas, and ports. At Brook St., W1. ✆ **020/7629-8860.** www.claridges.co.uk. Tube: Bond St.

Club Aquarium   Bring your bathing suit to this club with its swimming pool and Jacuzzi. Partygoers flock here in the scantiest of clothing, the more outrageously kitsch the better. Revelers go from one bar to the other—four in all—or else chill out in the two sofa-filled living rooms. Our favorite is the funky 1970s "Carwash" area, a retro glam place, though you may prefer Crème de la Kremlin with Russian pop and funky house. Dress like a tart (male or female), and you'll fit in just fine. Open daily 10pm to 3:30am. 256 Old St., EC1. ✆ **020/7253-3558.** www. clubaquarium.co.uk. Cover £10–£15. Tube: Old St.

Dream Bags Jaguar Shoes   What to do with the commercial signs from two long-gone shops? Turn it into the name of your hot new club, a bar and "gallery" filled with Shoreditch hipsters. Who would ever have thought that dreary Shoreditch would ever become cool? The joint has been packing them in for 5 years. Open Tuesday to Sunday 5pm to 1am. 34-36 Kingsland Rd., EC2, Shoreditch. ✆ **0871/7729-5830.** www.jaguarshoes.com. Cover £2. Tube: Old St.

Lab ★   Perhaps the best mixologists in London are found right in the heart of the city at this '70s kitsch-inspired cocktail bar, where bartenders will whip you up the best Feijon Flip or Red Hot Chili Pepper in town. Come here for the ultimate in intoxication, hanging out in an interior of leather and Formica spread over two floors. A thick cocktail book lies on every table; if you're in London long enough, you may want to work your way through all the drinks from the classic to house specialties. In a glam, glossy setting, DJs keep the mood relaxed. Open Monday to Saturday 4pm to midnight and Sunday 4 to 10:30pm. 12 Old Compton St., W1. ✆ **020/7437-7820.** www.lab-townhouse.com. Tube: Leicester Sq.

The Library   One of London's poshest drinking retreats, this deluxe bar boasts high ceilings, leather Chesterfields, respectable oil paintings, and grand windows.

Its collection of ancient cognacs and rare cigars is unparalleled in London. In the Lanesborough Hotel, 1 Lanesborough Place, SW1. ✆ **020/7259-5599.** www.lanesborough. com. Tube: Hyde Park Corner.

The Lobby Bar & the Axis Bar   These bars are found in one of London's best deluxe hotels. We advise that you check out the dramatic visuals of both bars before selecting your preferred nesting place. The Lobby Bar occupies what was built in 1907 as the grand, high-ceilinged reception area for one of London's premier newspapers. If the Lobby Bar setting doesn't appeal, take a look at the travertine, hardwood, and leather-sheathed bar in the Axis restaurant. The Lobby Bar is open Monday to Saturday 9am to midnight, Sunday 8am to 6:30pm; the Axis bar is open Monday through Saturday from 5:45 to 11pm. In the Hotel One Aldwych, 1 Aldwych, WC2. ✆ **020/7300-1000.** www.campbellgrayhotels.com. Tube: Covent Garden.

Loungelover ★★   The top cocktail bar for London fashionista types is Loungelover in Shoreditch, which was created from a dreary meat-packing factory. It's draws patrons from the chic restaurant, Les Trois Garçons, which is in front. It's a warren of rooms, each with its own identity; the effect has been compared to a walk through a film set. The elegant cocktails are among the most original creations in London, often with quirky names. Food is available on tapas-like platters. Even if you're only stopping in for a drink, you should make a reservation because space is limited. Open Monday to Thursday and Sunday 6pm to midnight, Friday 5:30pm to 1am, and Saturday 6pm to 1am. 1 Whitby St., E1. ✆ **020/7012-1234.** Tube: Liverpool St.

Match EC1   This epicenter for the fashionable 20s-to-30s set in London has put the *P* in partying in the once-staid Clerkenwell district. Drinkers sit on elegant sofas or retreat to one of the cozy booths for a late snack. The bar claims to be the home of the Cosmopolitan cocktail, which swept across the drinking establishments of New York. The bartenders make some of the best drinks in London but warn you "there is no such thing as a chocolate martini." Open Monday to Thursday 11am to midnight, Friday 11am to 2am, and Saturday 6pm to 2am. 45–47 Clerkenwell Rd., EC1. ✆ **020/7250-4002.** www.matchbar.com. Tube: Farringdon.

The Met Bar   Very much the place to be seen, this is one of the hottest bars in London. Mix with the elite of the fashion, TV, and music worlds. A lot of American celebrities have been seen here sipping on a martini. Despite the caliber of the clientele, the bar has managed to maintain a relaxed and unpretentious atmosphere. In the Metropolitan Hotel, 19 Old Park Lane, W1. ✆ **020/7447-1000.** www. metropolitan.co.uk. Members and hotel guests only after 6pm. Tube: Hyde Park Corner.

The Phoenix Artist Club   What's something so old it's new again? This is where Laurence Olivier made his stage debut in 1930, although he couldn't stop giggling even though the play was a drama. Live music is featured, but it's the hearty welcome, the good beer, and the friendly patrons from ages 20 to 50 who make this rediscovered theater bar worth a detour. It's open to the general public from 5 to 8pm only—it's "members only" after 8pm, but if it's relatively quiet at that time, the club will also admit nonmembers. 1 Phoenix St., WC2. ✆ **020/7836-1077.** www.phoenixartistclub.com. Tube: Tottenham Court Rd.

THE BEST OF LONDON'S PUBS: THE WORLD'S GREATEST PUB-CRAWL

Dropping into the local pub for a pint of real ale or bitter is the best way to soak up the character of the different villages that make up London. You'll hear local accents and slang, and see firsthand how far removed upper-crust Kensington is from blue-collar Wapping. Catch the local gossip or football talk—and, of course, enjoy some of the finest ales, stouts, ciders, and malt whiskies in the world. General open hours are noon to 11pm.

Belgravia

Grenadier Tucked away in a mews, the Grenadier is one of London's reputedly haunted pubs, the ghost here being an 18th-century British soldier. Aside from the poltergeist, the basement houses the original bar and skittles alley used by the Duke of Wellington's officers. The scarlet front door of the one-time officers' mess is guarded by a scarlet sentry box and shaded by a vine. The bar is nearly always crowded. Lunch and dinner are offered daily—even on Sunday, when it's a tradition to drink Bloody Marys (made from a well-guarded recipe) here. In the stalls along the side, you can order good-tasting fare based on seasonal ingredients. Well-prepared dishes include pork Grenadier, beef Wellington, and a chicken-and-Stilton roulade. Snacks such as fish and chips are available at the bar. 18 Wilton Row, SW1. ✆ **020/7235-3074.** Tube: Hyde Park Corner.

Blackfriars

Black Friar The Black Friar will transport you to the Edwardian era. The wedge-shape pub is swimming in marble and bronze Art Nouveau, featuring bas-reliefs of monks, a low-vaulted mosaic ceiling, and seating recesses carved out of gold marble. It's popular with the City's after-work crowd, and it features Adams, London Pride, and Speckled Hen on tap. 174 Queen Victoria St., EC4. ✆ **020/7236-5474.** Tube: Blackfriars.

Bloomsbury

Museum Tavern Across the street from the British Museum, this pub (ca. 1703) retains most of its antique trappings: velvet, oak paneling, and cut glass. It lies right in the center of the University of London area and is popular with writers, publishers, and researchers from the museum. Supposedly, Karl Marx wrote while dining here. Traditional English food is served: shepherd's pie, sausages cooked in English cider, turkey-and-ham pie, ploughman's lunch, and salads. Several English ales, cold lagers, cider, Guinness, wines, and spirits are available. Food and coffee are served all day. The pub gets crowded at lunchtime. 49 Great Russell St., WC1. ✆ **020/7242-8987.** www.mypubheaven.com/museumtavernlondon. Tube: Holborn or Tottenham Court Rd.

The City

Bow Wine Vaults Bow Wine Vaults has existed since long before the wine-bar craze began in the 1970s. One of the most famous in London, the bar attracts cost-conscious diners and drinkers to its vaulted cellars for such traditional fare as deep-fried Camembert, lobster ravioli, and a mixed grill, along with fish. The cocktail bar is popular with City employees after work (weekdays 11:30am–11pm).

More elegant meals, served in the street-level dining room, include Thai green mussels in curry sauce, escallop of veal Milanese garnished with pasta, and haddock Monte Carlo. Wines from around the world are available; the last time we were there, the wine of the day was a Chilean chardonnay. 10 Bow Churchyard, EC4. ✆ **020/7248-1121.** www.bowwinevaults.com. Tube: Mansion House, Bank, or St. Paul's.

Jamaica Wine House   This was one of the first coffeehouses in England and, reputedly, the Western world. For years, merchants and sea captains came here to make deals over rum and coffee. Nowadays, the two-level house dispenses coffee, beer, ale, lager, and fine wines, among them a variety of ports. The oak-paneled bar is on the street level and attracts crowds of investment bankers. You can order standard but filling dishes such as a ploughman's lunch and toasted sandwiches. 12 St. Michael's Alley, off Cornhill, EC3. ✆ **020/7929-6972.** Tube: Bank.

Covent Garden

Lamb & Flag   Dickens once frequented this pub, which has changed little from the days when he prowled the neighborhood. The pub has an amazing and scandalous history. Poet and author Dryden was almost killed by a band of thugs outside its doors in December 1679, and the pub gained the nickname the "Bucket of Blood" during the Regency era (1811–20) because of the bare-knuckled prizefights here. Tap beers include Courage Best and Directors, Old Speckled Hen, John Smiths, and Wadworths 6X. 33 Rose St., off Garrick St., WC2. ✆ **020/7497-9504.** Tube: Leicester Sq.

Nags Head   This Nags Head is one of London's most famous Edwardian pubs. In days of yore, patrons had to make their way through a fruit-and-flower market to drink here. Today, the pub is popular with young people. The draft Guinness is very good. Lunch (served noon–4pm) is typical pub grub: sandwiches, salads, pork cooked in cider, and garlic prawns. Snacks are available all afternoon. 10 James St., WC2. ✆ **020/7836-4678.** Tube: Covent Garden.

East End (Wapping)

Prospect of Whitby   One of London's most historic pubs, Prospect was founded in the days of the Tudors, taking its name from a coal barge that made

Interior of Prospect of Whitby pub.

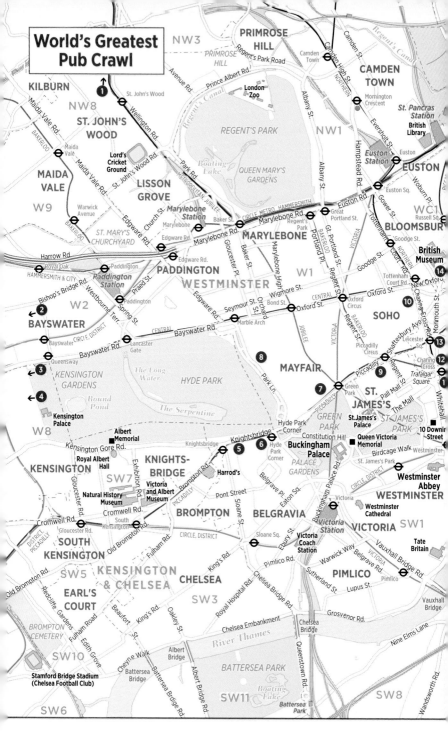

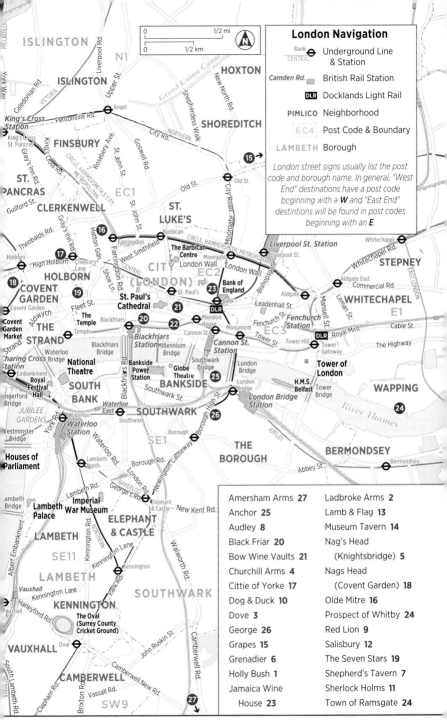

trips between Yorkshire and London. Come here for a tot, a noggin, or whatever it is you drink, and soak up the atmosphere. The pub has got quite a pedigree. Dickens and diarist Samuel Pepys used to drop in, and painter Turner came here for weeks at a time studying views of the Thames. In the 17th century, the notorious Hanging Judge Jeffreys used to get drunk here while overseeing hangings at the adjoining Execution Dock. Tables in the courtyard overlook the river. You can order a Morlands Old Speckled Hen from a hand-pump or a malt whisky. 57 Wapping Wall, E1. © **020/7481-1095.** www.fancyapint.com. Tube: Wapping.

Town of Ramsgate   At this old-world pub overlooking King Edward's Stairs and the Thames, you can enjoy Youngs Billing and Fullers London Pride on tap. 62 Wapping High St., E1. © **020/7481-8000.** Tube: E. London Line to Wapping.

Deptford

Amersham Arms   Those adventurous travelers who want to venture far from the beaten path might take the Tube to Deptford, situated on a desolate corner in deepest, darkest New Cross in an emerging section of southeast London. A local who comes here every night told us, "This gaff is undoubtedly the best drinker for miles." On weekends local students and even "trippers" from North London show up here to fill the sweaty backroom where live music is presented, or else some of the best DJs in London. Up front is a typical Irish boozer. Their free Friday night dance party is always packed. Drink specialties are the "Bloody Hell" Bloody Mary and a cocktail made with ginger beer and vodka, each guaranteed to make you completely "knackered." The food is nothing special—burgers, sandwiches, and other pub grub at £4.25 to £8 a platter. Open Sunday to Wednesday noon to midnight, Thursday noon to 2am, Friday and Saturday 10am to 12:30am. 388 New Cross Rd., SE14. © **020/8469-1499.** Tube: London Bridge.

Hampstead

Holly Bush   The Holly Bush is the real thing: authentic Edwardian gas lamps, open fires, private booths, and a tap selection of Fuller's London Pride, Adnams, and Harveys. 22 Holly Mount, NW3. © **020/7435-2892.** www.hollybushpub.com. Tube: Northern Line to Hampstead.

Holborn

Cittie of Yorke   This pub boasts the longest bar in all of Britain, rafters ascending to the heavens, and a long row of immense wine vats, all of which give it the air of a great medieval hall—appropriate because a pub has existed at this location since 1430. Samuel Smith's is on tap. 22 High Holborn, WC1. © **020/7242-7670.** Tube: Holborn or Chancery Lane.

Olde Mitre   Olde Mitre is the name of a working-class inn built here in 1547, when the Bishops of Ely controlled the district. It's a small pub with an odd assortment of customers. Adnams and Tetley are on tap. 1 Ely Court, EC1. © **020/ 7405-4751.** Tube: Chancery Lane.

The Seven Stars   This tranquil little pub facing the back of the Royal Courts of Justice dates back to 1602 and is now run by Roxy Beaujolais, author of the pub cookbook *Home From the Inn Contented,* whose former pub was voted the Soho Society's Pub of the Year. Within the ancient charm of two narrow rooms that are listed landmarks, drinking in Queer Street (as Carey St. was once called because of the bankruptcy courts) is pleasant. One can linger over pub food and real ales behind Irish-linen lace curtains with litigants, barristers, reporters, and pit musicians from West End shows. Then try to navigate to the lavatories up some comically narrow Elizabethan stairs. In mild weather, the law courts' stone balustrade under the trees provides customers with a long bar and beer garden. 53 Carey St., WC2. (C) **020/7242-8521.** Tube: Chancery Lane or Temple.

Kensington

Churchill Arms   Stop here for a nod to the Empire's end. Loaded with Churchill memorabilia, the pub hosts a week of celebration leading up to Churchill's birthday on November 30. Show up at the right time and you may be recruited to help decorate the place—visitors are often welcomed like regulars. Decorations and festivities are featured for Halloween, Christmas, and St. Paddy's Day, as well as for Churchill's birthday, helping to create the homiest village pub atmosphere you're likely to find in London. 119 Kensington Church St., W8. (C) **020/7727-4242.** Tube: Notting Hill Gate or High St. Kensington.

Knightsbridge

Nag's Head   This Nag's Head (not to be confused with the more renowned one at 10 James's St.; see above) is on a back street a short walk from the Berkeley Hotel. Previously a jail dating from 1780, it's said to be the smallest pub in London. In 1921, it was sold for £12 and 6p. Have a drink up front or wander to the tiny bar in the rear. For food, you might enjoy "real ale sausage" (made with pork and ale), shepherd's pie, or the quiche of the day, all served by the welcoming staff. A cosmopolitan clientele—newspaper people, musicians, and travelers—patronizes this warm, cozy pub. The pub touts itself as an "independent," or able to serve any "real ale" they choose because of their lack of affiliation. 53 Kinnerton St., SW1. (C) **020/7235-1135.** Tube: Hyde Park.

Leicester Square

Salisbury   An original gin palace, Salisbury's cut-glass mirrors reflect the faces of English stage stars (and hopefuls) sitting around the curved buffet-style bar. A less prominent place to dine is the old-fashioned wall banquette with its copper-topped tables and Art Nouveau decor. The pub's specialties, home-cooked pies set out in a buffet cabinet with salads, or fish and chips, are quite good and inexpensive. 90 St. Martin's Lane, WC2. (C) **020/7836-5863.** Tube: Leicester Sq.

Mayfair

Audley   While in Mayfair, especially if the weather's fine, head for this old Victorian pub. You can sit out enjoying a Pimm's cup at one of the wooden picnic tables. If the weather's foul, head inside behind the large arched windows, enjoying the dark wood paneling and the crystal chandeliers. There's a good selection of pub grub, with meals democratically priced from £7.50 to £9.50. Otherwise, try a lager for your tipple. You may become addicted to Hurliman on draught. 41 Mont St., W1. (C) **020/7499-1843.** http://the-audley.pub.mayfair.tel. Tube: Green Park.

Shepherd's Tavern   One of the focal points of the all-pedestrian shopping zone of Shepherd's Market, this pub occupies an 18th-century town house amid a warren of narrow, cobble-covered streets behind Park Lane. The street-level bar is cramped but congenial. Many of the regulars recall this tavern's popularity with the pilots of the Battle of Britain. Bar snacks include simple plates of shepherd's pie, and fish and chips. More formal dining is available upstairs in the cozy, cedar-lined, Georgian-style restaurant. The classic British menu probably hasn't changed much since the 1950s, and you can always get honey-roasted ham or roast beef with Yorkshire pudding. 50 Hertford St., W1. ✆ **020/7499-3017.** www.beer intheevening.com. Tube: Green Park.

Notting Hill Gate

Ladbroke Arms Previously honored as London's "Dining Pub of the Year," Ladbroke Arms is that rare pub known for its food. A changing menu includes roast cod filet with lentils and salsa verde; and aged bone-in rib steak with mustard, peppercorn, and herb and garlic butter. With background jazz and rotating art prints, the place strays from the traditional pub environment. This place makes for a pleasant stop and a good meal. The excellent Eldridge Pope Royal is on tap, as well as John Smiths, Courage Directors, and several malt whiskies. 54 Ladbroke Rd., W11. ✆ **020/7727-6648.** www.capitalpubcompany.com. Tube: Notting Hill Gate.

St. James's

Red Lion This Victorian pub, with its early-1900s decorations and 150-year-old mirrors, has been compared to Manet's painting *A Bar at the Folies-Bergère* (on display at the Courtauld Gallery). You can order premade sandwiches, and on Saturday, homemade fish and chips are served. Wash down your meal with Ind Coope's fine ales or the house's special beer, Burton's, a brew made of spring water from the Midlands town of Burton-on-Trent. 2 Duke of York St. (off Jermyn St.), SW1. ✆ **020/7321-0782.** Tube: Piccadilly Circus.

Soho

Dog & Duck This snug little joint, a Soho landmark, is the most intimate pub in London. A former patron was the author George Orwell, who came here to celebrate his sales of *Animal Farm* in the United States. A wide mixture of ages and persuasions flock here, usually chatting amiably. Publicans here stock an interesting assortment of English beers, including Tetleys, Fuller London, and Timothy Taylor Landlord. In autumn, customers will ask for Addlestone's Cider. A lot of patrons head to Ronnie Scott's Jazz Club, which is close by, after having a few pints here. The cozy upstairs bar is also open. 18 Bateman St. (corner of Frith St.), W1. ✆ **020/7494-0697.** Tube: Tottenham Court Rd. or Leicester Sq.

Southbank

Anchor You can follow in the footsteps of Shakespeare and Dickens by quenching your thirst at this pub. If literary heroes are not your bag, then perhaps you'll enjoy knowing that Tom Cruise had a pint or two here during the filming of *Mission Impossible*. Rebuilt in the mid–18th century to replace an earlier pub that managed to withstand the Great Fire of 1666, the rooms are worn and comfortable. You can choose from Scottish and Newcastle brews on tap. 34 Park St., SE1. ✆ **020/7407-1577.** Tube: Jubilee Line to London Bridge.

Southwark

George   The existing structure was built in 1877 to replace the original pub, which was destroyed in the Great Fire of 1666. That pub's accolades date from 1598, when it was reviewed as a "faire inn for the receipt of travelers." The present pub was built in the typical "traditional Victorian" style, with stripped oak floors, paneled walls, a curved bar counter, brass ceiling lights, and windows with etched and cut glass. Three huge mirrors decorate the walls. It's still a great place to enjoy Flowers Original, Boddingtons, and London Pride Abbot on tap. 77 Borough High St., SE1. © **020/7407-2056.** Tube: Northern Line to London Bridge or Borough.

Thameside

The Dove   You can relax by the Thames at the place where James Thomson composed "Rule Britannia" and part of his lesser-known "The Seasons." To toast Britannia, you can hoist a Fullers London Pride or ESB. 19 Upper Mall, W6. © **020/ 8748-9474.** Tube: District Line to Ravenscourt Park.

Grapes   This rustic 16th-century pub served as Dickens's inspiration for "Six Jolly Fellowship Porters" in *Our Mutual Friend.* Whistler came here, too, inspired by the view of the river. Taps include Friary Meux, Pedigree, and Tetleys; there are several single-malt whiskies to choose from as well. 76 Narrow St., E14. © **020/ 7987-4396.** Tube: Docks Light Railway, W. Ferry.

Trafalgar Square

Sherlock Holmes   The Sherlock Holmes was the gathering spot for the Baker Street Irregulars, a clan of mystery lovers who met to honor the genius of Sir Arthur Conan Doyle's famous fictional character. Upstairs, you'll find a re-creation of the living room at 221B Baker St. and such "Holmesiana" as the serpent from *The Speckled Band* and a faux beast's head from *The Hound of the Baskervilles.* In the upstairs dining room, you can order complete meals with wine, and then select dessert from the trolley. Downstairs is mainly for drinking, but there's a good snack bar. 10 Northumberland St., WC1. © **020/7930-2644.** www.sherlockholmes pub.com. Tube: Charing Cross or Embankment.

Sherlock Holmes pub.

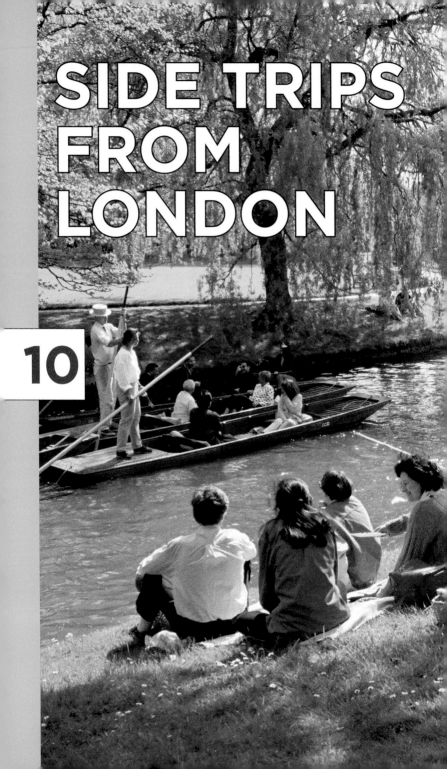

SIDE TRIPS FROM LONDON

10

You could spend the best part of a year—or a lifetime—exploring London, without risking boredom or repetition. But there's much more to England than just London. We advise you to tear yourself away from Big Ben for at least a day or two to explore some of the easily accessible and wonderfully memorable spots that surround the city.

WINDSOR & ETON ★

34km (21 miles) W of London

Windsor—the site of England's best-known and greatest castle and its most famous boys' school, Eton—would be a captivating Thames-side town to visit even if it were not associated with the royal Windsors.

Though a disastrous fire raged through the building in 1992, things are on the mend at Windsor Castle. But not without controversy—some of the new designs being unveiled have been called "Gothic shockers" and "ghastly." If you visit, you can decide for yourself. In summer it's overrun with tourists, which tends to obscure its charm, so plan your visit for spring or fall, if possible.

PREVIOUS PAGE: **Punting on the River Cam in Cambridge.**; RIGHT: **Windsor Castle.**

Essentials

GETTING THERE   More than a dozen trains per day make the 30-minute trip from Waterloo or Paddington Station in London (you'll have to transfer at Slough to the Slough-Windsor shuttle train). The cost is £7.70 round-trip. Call ✆ **0845/748-4950** or visit **www.nationalrail.co.uk** for more information.

    Green Line coach no. 702 (✆ **0844/801-7261;** www.greenline. co.uk) from Victoria Station in London takes about 1¼ hours. A same-day round-trip costs between £7 and £10, depending on the time of the day and week. The bus drops you near the parish church, across the street from the castle.

    If you're driving from London, take the M4 west.

VISITOR INFORMATION   A **Tourist Information Centre** is at Booking Hall, Windsor Royal Shopping Center, 5 Goswell Hill, Windsor, Berkshire SL4 1RH (✆ **01753/743900;** www.windsor.gov.uk). It is open May to September Monday to Saturday 9:30am to 5pm and Sunday 10am to 4pm; from October to April Monday to Saturday 10am to 5pm and Sunday 11am to 4pm. It also books walking tours for the Oxford Guild of Guides.

Castle Hill Sights

Jubilee Gardens   To celebrate Queen Elizabeth's Jubilee, the .8-hectare (2-acre) Jubilee Gardens were created inside the castle's main entrance. Filled with trees, roses, and flowering shrubs, they were designed by Tom Stuart-Smith, a Chelsea Flower Show gold medalist. The gardens are the first to have been

Jubilee Gardens.

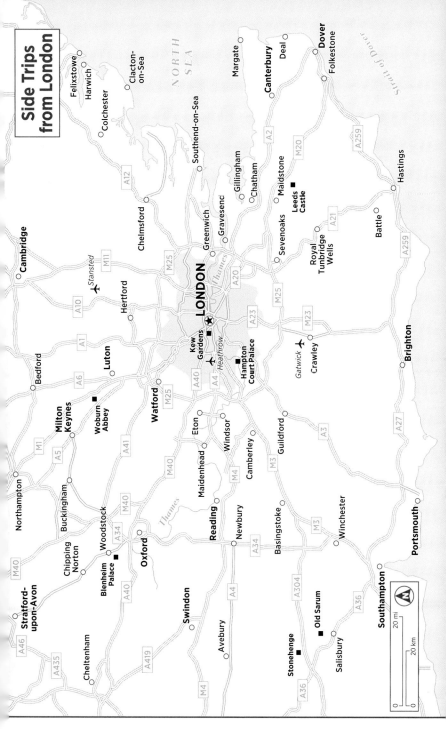

Side Trips from London

NORTH SEA

Strait of Dover

Felixstowe
Harwich
Clacton-on-Sea
Colchester

Cambridge

Stansted ✈

M11
A10
A1
Hertford
Bedford
Luton
A6
Milton Keynes
Woburn Abbey
A5
M1
Northampton
Buckingham
Chipping Norton
Stratford-upon-Avon
A46
A435
Cheltenham
Woodstock
Blenheim Palace
A34
Oxford
A40
M40
Swindon
A4
A419
Avebury
M4
Stonehenge
A36
Salisbury
Old Sarum
A304
A36
Southampton
Portsmouth

Margate
Canterbury
Deal
Dover
Folkestone
A2
M20
A259
Hastings
Maidstone
Leeds Castle
Gillingham
Chatham
Sevenoaks
Royal Tunbridge Wells
A21
Battle
A259
Southend-on-Sea
Chelmsford
A12
Greenwich
Gravesenc
Thames
LONDON
M25
A20
A23
M25
A23
M2
Gatwick ✈
Crawley
Brighton
A27
Kew Gardens
Heathrow ✈
Hampton Court Palace
A4
A40
Watford
M25
A41
Eton
Windsor
Maidenhead
M4
Camberley
Guildford
M3
A3
Reading
Newbury
A34
Basingstoke
M3
Winchester

Thames

20 mi
20 km
0
0

established at Windsor Castle since the days of George IV in the 1820s. They extend from the main gates of Windsor to St. George's Gate on Castle Hill. Color is provided by broad swaths of woodland perennials. White rambling roses clothing the old stone walls are particularly romantic.

Same hours and admission as for castle. www.jubileewalkway.com.

Queen Mary's Dolls' House   A palace in perfect miniature, the Dolls' House was given to Queen Mary in 1923 as a gift by members of the royal family, including the king. The house, designed by Sir Edwin Lutyens, was created on a scale of 1:12. It took 3 years to complete and involved the work of 1,500 tradesmen and artists. It is a miniature masterpiece; each room is exquisitely furnished, and every item is made exactly to scale. Working elevators stop on every floor, and there is running water in all five bathrooms.

Castle Hill. ⓒ **01753/831118** for recorded information. Admission is included in entrance to Windsor Castle. Mar–Oct daily 9:45am–4pm; Nov–Feb daily 9:45am–4:15pm. As with Windsor Castle, it's best to call ahead to confirm opening times.

St. George's Chapel ★★★   A gem of the Perpendicular style, this chapel shares the distinction with Westminster Abbey of being a pantheon of English monarchs (Victoria is a notable exception). The present St. George's was founded in the late 15th century by Edward IV on the site of the original Chapel of the Order of the Garter (Edward III, 1348). You first enter the nave, which contains the tomb of George V and Queen Mary, designed by Sir William Reid Dick. Off the nave in the Urswick Chapel, the Princess Charlotte memorial provides an ironic touch; if she had survived childbirth in 1817, she, and not her cousin Victoria, would have ruled the British Empire. In the aisle are tombs of George VI and Edward IV. The latest royal burial in this chapel was an urn containing the ashes of the late Princess Margaret. The Edward IV "Quire," with its imaginatively carved 15th-century choir stalls, evokes the pomp and pageantry of medieval days. In the center is a flat tomb, containing the vault of the beheaded Charles I, along with Henry VIII and his third wife, Jane Seymour. Finally, you may want to inspect the Prince Albert Memorial Chapel, reflecting the opulent tastes of the Victorian era.

Castle Hill. ⓒ **01753/848888.** www.stgeorges-windsor.org. Admission is included in entrance to Windsor Castle. Mon–Sat 10am–4:15pm, last admission 4pm. Closed Sun and for a few days in June and Dec.

Prince Albert Memorial Chapel.

Windsor Castle ★★★   William the Conqueror first ordered a castle built on this location, and since his day it has been a fateful spot for English sovereigns: King John cooled his heels at Windsor while waiting to put his signature on the Magna Carta at nearby Runnymede; Charles I was imprisoned here before losing his head; Queen Bess did some renovations; Victoria mourned her beloved Albert, who died at the castle in 1861; the royal family rode out much of World War II behind its sheltering walls; and when Queen Elizabeth II is in residence, the royal standard flies. With 1,000 rooms, Windsor is the world's largest inhabited castle.

The apartments display many works of art, armor, three Verrio ceilings, and several 17th-century Gibbons carvings. Several works by Rubens adorn the King's Drawing Room, and the King's Dressing Room contains a Dürer, along with Rembrandt's portrait of his mother and Van Dyck's triple portrait of Charles I. Of the apartments, the grand reception room, with its Gobelin tapestries, is the most spectacular.

George IV's elegant **Semi-State Chambers ★★** are open only from the end of September until the end of March. They were created by the king in the 1820s as part of a series of Royal Apartments designed for his personal use. Seriously damaged in 1992, they have been returned to their former glory, with lovely antiques, paintings, and decorative objects. The Crimson Drawing room is evocative of the king's flamboyant taste with gilt, crimson silk damask hangings, and sumptuous artworks.

It is recommended that you take a free guided tour of the castle grounds, including the Jubilee Gardens. Guides are very well informed and capture the rich historical background of the castle.

In our opinion, the Windsor **changing of the guard ★** is a more exciting experience than the London exercise. The guard marches through the town whether the court is in residence or not, stopping traffic as it wheels into the castle to the tunes of a full regimental band; when the Queen is not here, a drum-and-pipe band is mustered. From April to July, the ceremony takes place Monday to Saturday at 11:30am. In winter, the guard is changed every 48 hours Monday to Saturday. It's best to call ✆ **020/7766-7304** for a schedule.

Castle Hill. ✆ **01753/83118.** www.royalcollection.org.uk. Admission £15 adults, £13 students and seniors, £8.50 children 16 and younger, £38 family (2 adults and 3 children 16 and younger). Mar–Oct daily 9:45am–5:15pm; Nov–Feb daily 9:45am–4:15pm. Last admission 1 hr. before closing. Closed for periods in Apr, June, and Dec when the royal family is in residence.

Windsor Farm Shop ★ 🏠   Had any of the Queen's jars of jam lately, or maybe her homemade pork pie or a bottle of her special brew? If not, head for this outlet, which sells items from her estates outside Windsor, including pheasants and partridges bagged at royal shoots, produce bearing the seal of the Royal Farms, and cream, yogurt, and milk from the two Royal Dairy farms. This shop is located in converted Victorian potting sheds on the edge of the royal estate. This latest make-a-pound scheme is the brainchild of Prince Philip. The meat counter is especially awesome, with its cooked hams and massive beef ribs. The steak-and-ale pies are very tasty. You can stock up on the Queen's vittles and head for a picnic in the area. You can also purchase 15-year-old whisky from Balmoral Castle in Scotland.

Datchet Rd., Old Windsor. ✆ **01753/623800.** www.windsorfarmshop.co.uk. Free admission. Mon–Sat 9am–5pm; Sun 10am–5pm.

Eton Schoolboys make their way to class.   Peascod Street in Windsor.

Exploring the Town

Windsor is a largely Victorian town of brick buildings, with a few remnants of Georgian architecture. Antiques shops, silversmiths, and pubs line cobblestone Church and Market streets near the castle. Charles II's mistress, Nell Gwynne, supposedly lived on Church Street, which allowed her to be within shouting distance of her beau's chambers. After lunch or tea, you may want to stroll the 4.8km (3 miles) along the aptly named Long Walk.

On Sunday, in Windsor Great Park and at Ham Common, you may see Prince Charles playing polo and Prince Philip serving as umpire while the Queen watches. The park is also the site of Her Majesty's occasional equestrian jaunts. On Sunday she attends a little church near the Royal Lodge. Traditionally, she prefers to drive herself there, later returning to the castle for Sunday lunch.

Exploring Eton College

From Windsor, Eton is an easy stroll across the Thames Bridge. Follow Eton High Street to the college.

Organized Tours of Windsor & Eton

BOAT TOURS   The best way to see the area around Windsor is from the water. Informative **boat tours** depart from Windsor's main embarkation point along Windsor Promenade, Barry Avenue, for a 40-minute round-trip to Boveney Lock. The cost is £5 for adults, £2.50 for children. You can also take a 2-hour tour through the Boveney Lock and up past stately private riverside homes, the Bray Film Studios, Queens Eyot, and Monkey Island for £8 for adults, £4 for children. Of all the tours offered, we find this one the most scenic, insightful, and evocative. There's also a 45-minute tour

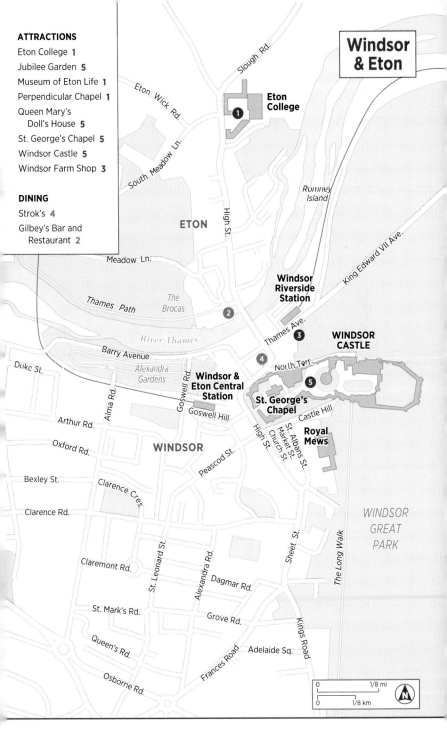

Windsor & Eton

ATTRACTIONS

Eton College **1**
Jubilee Garden **5**
Museum of Eton Life **1**
Perpendicular Chapel **1**
Queen Mary's
  Doll's House **5**
St. George's Chapel **5**
Windsor Castle **5**
Windsor Farm Shop **3**

DINING

Strok's **4**
Gilbey's Bar and
  Restaurant **2**

Eton College

ETON

Romney Island

Slough Rd.
Eton Wick Rd.
South Meadow Ln.
High St.
Meadow Ln.
Thames Path
The Brocas
River Thames
Barry Avenue
Alexandra Gardens
Duke St.
Alma Rd.
Goswell Rd.
Goswell Hill
Arthur Rd.
Oxford Rd.
Bexley St.
Clarence Cres.
Clarence Rd.
Claremont Rd.
St. Leonard St.
St. Mark's Rd.
Queen's Rd.
Osborne Rd.
Alexandra Rd.
Dagmar Rd.
Grove Rd.
Frances Road
Adelaide Sq.
Kings Road
Sheet St.

Windsor Riverside Station
Thames Ave.
King Edward VII Ave.

WINDSOR CASTLE
North Terr.
Windsor & Eton Central Station
St. George's Chapel
Castle Hill
St. Albans St.
Market St.
Church St.
High St.
Royal Mews

WINDSOR

The Long Walk

WINDSOR GREAT PARK

Peascod St.

0   1/8 mi
0   1/8 km

from Runnymede on board the *Lucy Fisher*, a replica of a Victorian paddle steamer. You pass Magna Carta Island, among other sights. This tour costs £5 for adults, £2.50 for children. In addition, longer tours between Maidenhead and Hampton Court are offered. The boats offer light refreshments and have well-stocked bars; plus the decks are covered in case of an unexpected shower. Tours are operated by **French Brothers, Ltd.,** Clewer Boathouse, Clewer Court Road, Windsor (✆ **01753/851900;** www. boattrips.co.uk).

Where to Dine

EXPENSIVE

Strok's MODERN BRITISH/CONTINENTAL   This restaurant, located near the castle, is Windsor's most elegant. Possessing garden terraces, a conservatory, and a dining room designed a bit like a greenhouse. Chef Stephen Boucher selects an individual garnish to complement each well-prepared dish. For starters, try the tower of smoked salmon and asparagus. For a main course, enjoy the halibut with a ginger and prawn crust, tiger prawns with crispy wontons and lime cream foam, or breast of guinea fowl with a sweet potato purée and truffle sausage.

In Sir Christopher Wren's House Hotel, Thames St., Windsor. ✆ **01753/442422.** www.sirchristopher wren.co.uk. Main courses £17–£27. AE, DC, MC, V. Daily 12:30–2:15pm and 6:30–10pm.

MODERATE

Gilbey's Bar and Restaurant MODERN BRITISH/CONTINENTAL   Just across the bridge from Windsor, this charming place is located on Eton's main street, among the antiques shops. Furnished with pinewood tables and simple chairs, a glassed-in conservatory is out back. A brigade of seven chefs turns out quite good Modern British dishes. Begin with one of the well-prepared soups. Some of the main-dish temptations include slow-braised venison with a chestnut ravioli, or pan-fried rump steak with an onion and thyme-flavored compote. For dessert, try sticky toffee pudding with butterscotch sauce and a crème fraîche.

82–83 High St., Eton. ✆ **01753/854921.** www.gilbeygroup.com/eton-wine.htm. Reservations recommended. Main courses £13–£23; fixed-price 2-course menu £15, 3-course menu £20. AE, MC, V. Sun–Thurs noon–2:30pm and 6–9:30pm; Fri–Sat noon–2:30pm and 6–10:30pm.

OXFORD: THE CITY OF DREAMING SPIRES ★★

87km (54 miles) NW of London; 87km (54 miles) SE of Coventry

A walk down the long sweep of the High, one of the most striking streets in England; a mug of cider in one of the old student pubs; the sound of May Day dawn when choristers sing in Latin from Magdalen Tower; students in traditional gowns whizzing past on rickety bikes; towers and spires rising majestically; nude swimming at Parson's Pleasure; the roar of a cannon launching the bumping races; a tiny, dusty bookstall where you can pick up a valuable first edition—all that is Oxford, home of one of the greatest universities in the world.

Romantic Oxford is still here, but to get to it, you have to experience the bustling and crowded city that is also Oxford. You may be surprised by the never-ending stream of polluting buses and fast-flowing pedestrian traffic—the city

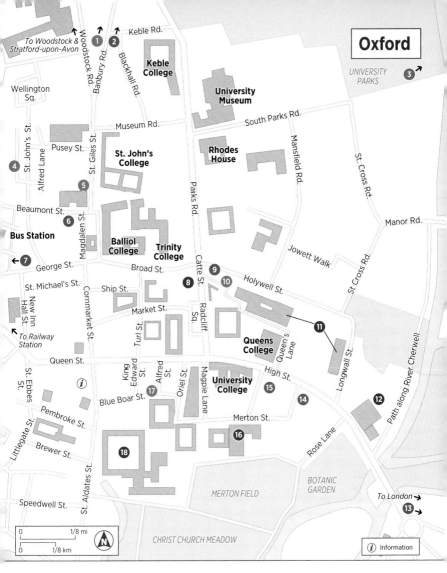

Oxford

To Woodstock & Stratford-upon-Avon

Keble Rd.

Woodstock Rd.
Banbury Rd.
Blackhall Rd.

1
2

UNIVERSITY PARKS **3**

Keble College

University Museum

Wellington Sq.

Museum Rd.
South Parks Rd.

Mansfield Rd.

St. Cross Rd.

St. John's St.
Pusey St.
Alfred Lane
4

St. Giles' St.
5

St. John's College

Rhodes House

Parks Rd.

Manor Rd.

Beaumont St.
6

Magdalen St.

Bus Station

7
George St.
Broad St.

Balliol College

Trinity College

Catte St.
9
8
10
Holywell St.

Jowett Walk

St. Cross Rd.

St. Michael's St.
New Inn Hall St.

Cornmarket St.

Ship St.
Market St.

Turl St.

Radcliff Sq.

11

To Railway Station

Queen St.

Queens College

Queen's Lane

Longwall St.

Path along River Cherwell

St. Ebbes St.

King Edward St.
Alfred St.
Oriel St.
Magpie Lane

17

Blue Boar St.

Pembroke St.
Littlegate St.
Brewer St.

18

University College

15

High St.

14

12

Merton St.

16

Rose Lane

BOTANIC GARDEN

Speedwell St.
St. Aldates St.

MERTON FIELD

To London **13**

0   1/8 mi
0   1/8 km

N

CHRIST CHURCH MEADOW

ⓘ Information

ATTRACTIONS

The Old Bodleian
   Library **8**
Christ Church
   College **18**
Magdalen College **12**
Merton College **16**
New College **11**

ACCOMMODATIONS

Bath Place Hotel **9**
Dial House **13**
The Galaxie Hotel **2**
Macdonald Randolph Hotel **6**
Malmaison Oxford Castle **7**
Mercure Eastgate Hotel **14**
Old Bank Hotel **15**
Old Parsonage Hotel **2**

DINING

The Bear Inn **17**
Brasserie Blanc **4**
Browns **5**
Cherwell Boathouse
   Restaurant **3**
Gee's Restaurant **1**
The Turf Tavern **10**

Rooftop view of Oxford.

core feels more like London than once-sleepy Oxford. Surrounding the university are suburbs that keep growing, and not in a particularly attractive manner.

Any time of the year, you can enjoy a tour of the colleges, many of which represent a peak in England's architectural history, as well as a valley of Victorian contributions. The Oxford Tourist Information Centre (see below) offers guided walking tours daily throughout the year. Just don't mention the other place (Cambridge), and you shouldn't have any trouble. Comparisons between the two universities are inevitable: Oxford is better known for the arts, Cambridge more for the sciences.

The city predates the university—in fact, it was a Saxon town in the early part of the 10th century. By the 12th century, Oxford was growing in reputation as a seat of learning, and the first colleges were founded in the 13th century. The story of Oxford is filled with conflicts too complex and detailed to elaborate upon here. Suffice it to say, the relationship between town and gown wasn't always as peaceful as it is today. Riots often flared, and both sides were guilty of abuses. Nowadays, the young people of Oxford take out their aggressions in sporting competitions.

Ultimately, the test of a great university lies in the caliber of the people it turns out. Oxford can name-drop a mouthful: Roger Bacon, Sir Walter Raleigh, John Donne, Sir Christopher Wren, Samuel Johnson, William Penn, John Wesley, William Pitt, Matthew Arnold, Lewis Carroll, Harold Macmillan, Graham Greene, A. E. Housman, T. E. Lawrence, and many others. Women were not allowed until 1920, but since then many have graduated from Oxford and gone on to fame—Indira Gandhi and Margaret Thatcher both graduated from Somerville College.

Essentials

GETTING THERE   Trains from Paddington Station reach Oxford in 1½ hours. Five trains run every hour. A cheap, same-day round-trip ticket costs £27. For more information, call ✆ **0845/748-4950** or visit **www.nationalrail. co.uk**.

    Stagecoach (✆ **01865/772250;** www.stagecoachbus.com) operates the Oxford Tube, with buses leaving London at the rate of three to five per hour, costing £16 one-way or £13 if you're a student.

    If you're driving, take the M40 west from London and just follow the signs. Traffic and parking are a disaster in Oxford. However, there are four large park-and-ride parking lots on the north, south, east, and west of the city's ring road, all well marked. Parking is £2 to £2.50 per hour. From 9:30am on and all day Saturday, you pay £2 for a round-trip ticket for a bus ride into the city, which drops you off at St. Aldate's Cornmarket or Queen Street to see the city center. The buses run every 8 to 10 minutes in each direction. There is no service on Sunday. The parking lots are on the Woodstock road near the Peartree traffic circle, on the Botley road toward Farringdon, on the Abingdon road in the southeast, and on the A40 toward London.

VISITOR INFORMATION   The **Oxford Tourist Information Centre** is at 15–16 Broad St., Oxford OX1 3AS (✆ **01865/252200;** www.visitoxford. org). The center sells a comprehensive range of maps, brochures, and souvenir items, as well as the famous Oxford University T-shirt. Guided walking tours leave from the center daily (see "Guided Tours," below). The center is open Monday to Saturday 9:30am to 5pm, and Sunday and bank holidays 10am to 4pm.

Oxford's High Street.

Exploring Oxford University

Many visitors arriving at Oxford ask, "Where's the campus?" If a local chortles when answering, it's because Oxford University is made up of 35 widely dispersed colleges. To tour all of these would be a formidable task—it's best to focus on a handful of the better-known colleges.

Guided Tours

The best way to get a running commentary on the important sights is to take a 2-hour **walking tour** through the city and the major colleges. The tours leave daily from the Oxford Tourist Information Centre at 11am, and 1 and 2pm. Tours costs £7 for adults and £3.50 for children 15 and younger; the tours do not include New College or Christ Church. There are two tours that leave the Oxford Tourist Information Centre on Saturday at 10:30am and 1:30pm; these tours include admission to Christ Church. They cost £7.50 adults, £4 children 15 and younger. Call ℂ **01865/252200** (www.visitoxford.org) for more information.

For a good orientation, hour-long, open-top bus tours around Oxford are available from **City Sightseeing Oxford** (ℂ **01865/790522;** www.citysightseeingoxford.com), whose office is at the railway station (tours also start from the railway station; other pickup points are Sheldonian Theatre, Gloucester Green Bus Station, and Pembroke College). Buses leave every 10 to 15 minutes daily. Tickets are good for the day. Tours run daily from 9:30am to 3:40pm November to February, daily from 9:30am to 4:40pm in March, and daily 9:30am to 6:30pm April to October. The cost is £12 for adults, £9.50 for students and seniors, £6 for children 5 to 14 years old; a family ticket for two adults and three children is £31. Children 4 and younger get to ride free. Tickets can be purchased from the driver and are valid for 24 hours.

Christ Church College.

The Colleges

Christ Church ★★ ☺ Begun by Cardinal Wolsey as Cardinal College in 1525, Christ Church (ℂ **01865/276492;** www.chch.ox.ac.uk), known as the House, was founded by Henry VIII in 1546. Facing St. Aldate's Street, Christ Church has the largest quadrangle of any college in Oxford. Tom Tower houses Great Tom, an 8,165km (18,000-pound) bell. It rings at 9:05pm nightly, signaling the closing of the college gates. The 101 times it peals originally signified the number of students

Magdalen College.

in residence at the time the college was founded. Although the student body has grown significantly, Oxford traditions live forever. There are some portraits in the 16th-century Great Hall, including works by Gainsborough and Reynolds. There's also a separate portrait gallery.

The college chapel was constructed over a period of centuries, beginning in the 12th century. (Incidentally, it's not only the college chapel but also the cathedral of the diocese of Oxford.) The cathedral's most distinguishing features are its Norman pillars and the vaulting of the choir, dating from the 15th century. In the center of the great quadrangle is a statue of Mercury mounted in the center of a fishpond. Many scenes from the Harry Potter films have been shot with the cloisters, quads, and staircases of Christ Church standing in for Hogwarts, making this a popular stop for kids of all ages. The college is open Monday to Saturday 9am to 5pm and Sunday 1 to 5pm, charging £4.90 for adults or £3.90 for students, seniors, and ages 5 to 17.

Magdalen College Pronounced *Maud*-lin, Magdalen College, High Street (*©* **01865/276000;** www.magd.ox.ac.uk), was founded in 1458 by William of Waynflete, bishop of Winchester and later chancellor of England. Its alumni range from Wolsey to Wilde. Opposite the botanic garden, the oldest in England, is the bell tower, where the choristers sing in Latin at dawn on May Day. Charles I, his days numbered, watched the oncoming Roundheads from this tower. Visit the 15th-century chapel, in spite of many of its latter-day trappings. Ask when the hall and other places of special interest are open. The grounds of Magdalen are the most extensive of any Oxford college; there's even a deer park. From July to September it is open daily noon to 6pm, from October to June daily 1 to 6pm. Admission is £4 adults; £3 seniors, students, and children.

Merton College ★★ Founded in 1264, Merton College, Merton Street (☏ **01865/276310;** www.merton.ox.ac.uk), is among the three oldest colleges at the university. It stands near Corpus Christi College on Merton Street, the sole survivor of Oxford's medieval cobbled streets. Merton College is noted for its library, built between 1371 and 1379 and said to be the oldest college library in England. Though a tradition once kept some of its most valuable books chained, now only one book is secured in that manner to illustrate that historical custom. One of the library's treasures is an astrolabe (an astronomical instrument used for measuring the altitude of the sun and stars) thought to have belonged to Chaucer. You pay £2 to visit the ancient library as well as the Max Beerbohm Room (the satirical English caricaturist who died in 1956). Call ahead for information. The library and college are open Monday to Friday 2 to 4pm, and Saturday and Sunday 10am to 4pm. It's closed for 1 week at Easter and Christmas and on weekends during the winter.

New College New College, Holywell Street (☏ **01865/279555;** www.new. ox.ac.uk), was founded in 1379 by William of Wykeham, bishop of Winchester and later lord chancellor of England. His college at Winchester supplied a constant stream of students. The first quadrangle, dating from before the end of the 14th century, was the initial quadrangle to be built in Oxford and formed the architectural design for the other colleges. In the antechapel is Sir Jacob Epstein's remarkable modern sculpture of Lazarus and a fine El Greco painting of St.

James. One of the treasures of the college is a crosier (pastoral staff of a bishop) belonging to the founding father. Don't miss the beautiful garden outside the college, where you can stroll among the remains of the old city wall. It's an evocative, romantic site. The college (entered at New College Lane) can be visited from Easter to October daily between 11am and 5pm, and in the off season daily between 2 and 4pm. Admission is £2 from Easter to October and free off season.

The Old Bodleian Library ★★
This famed library on Catte Street (☏ **01865/277000;** www.bodley.ox. ac.uk) was launched in 1602, initially funded by Sir Thomas Bodley. It is home to some 50,000 manuscripts and more than five million books. Over the years the library has expanded from the Old Library complex to other buildings, including the Radcliffe Camera next door. The easiest way to visit the library is by taking a guided tour, leaving from the Divinity School across the street from the main entrance. In summer there are four tours Monday to

Radcliffe Camera.

Friday and two on Saturday; in winter, two tours leave per day. Call for specific times.

Where to Stay

The **Oxford Tourist Information Centre** (✆ **01865/252200**), operates a year-round room-booking service for a £5 fee, plus a 10% refundable deposit. If you'd like to seek lodgings on your own, the center has a list of accommodations, maps, and guidebooks.

EXPENSIVE

Macdonald Randolph Hotel ★   Since 1864, the Randolph has overlooked St. Giles, the Ashmolean Museum, and the Cornmarket. The hotel is an example of how historic surroundings can be combined with modern conveniences to make for elegant accommodations. The lounges, though modernized, are cavernous enough for dozens of separate and intimate conversational groupings. The furnishings are traditional. Some rooms are quite large; others are a bit cramped. The double-glazing on the windows appears inadequate to keep out the noise of midtown traffic. We'd opt first for the more stylish and intimate Old Parsonage (see below) before checking in here.

Beaumont St., Oxford, Oxfordshire OX1 2LN. ✆ **888/892-0038** or 01865/256-400. Fax 01865/791678. www.macdonaldhotels.co.uk/randolph. 151 units. £164–£284 double; from £279–£559 suite. AE, DC, MC, V. Parking £25. Bus: 7. **Amenities:** Restaurant; 2 bars; babysitting; concierge; room service; Wi-Fi (£5 per hour). *In room:* TV, CD player, hair dryer.

Malmaison Oxford Castle ★★ 👜   In a TripAdvisor poll of the top 10 quirkiest hotels in the world, the Malmaison in Oxford made the list. Formerly it was for inmates detained at Her Majesty's pleasure, and many aspects of prison life, including barred windows, have been retained. In a converted Victorian building, guest rooms are remodeled "cells" that flank two sides of a large central atrium, a space that rises three stories and is crisscrossed by narrow walkways like in one of those George Raft prison movies of the '30s. The former inmates never had it so good—great beds, mood lighting, power showers, satellite TV, and serious wines. In spite of its former origins, this is a stylish and comfortable place to stay.

3 Oxford Castle, Oxford OXI 1AY. ✆ **01865/268400.** Fax 01845/3654247. www.malmaison.com. 94 units. £170–£240 double; £255–£505 suite. AE, DC, MC, V. Parking (prebooking required) £20. **Amenities:** Restaurant; bar; exercise room; room service. *In room:* TV/DVD, CD player, minibar, Wi-Fi (free).

Old Bank Hotel ★★   The first hotel created in the center of Oxford in 135 years, the Old Bank opened late in 1999 and immediately surpassed the traditional favorite, the Randolph (not reviewed), in style and amenities. Located on Oxford's main street and surrounded by some of its oldest colleges and sights, the building dates back to the 18th century and was indeed once a bank. The hotel currently features a collection of 20th-century British art handpicked by the owners. The bedrooms are comfortably and elegantly appointed, often opening onto views. A combination of velvet and shantung silk-trimmed linen bedcovers gives the accommodations added style.

92–94 High St., Oxford OX1 4BN. ✆ **01865/799599.** Fax 01865/799598. www.oldbank-hotel.co.uk. 42 units. £230–£270 double; £370 suite. AE, DC, MC, V. Free parking. Bus: 7. **Amenities:** Restaurant; bar; babysitting; room service. *In room:* A/C, TV, CD player, hair dryer, Wi-Fi (free).

Old Parsonage Hotel ★★ This extensively renovated hotel, near St. Giles Church and Keble College, looks like an extension of one of the ancient colleges. Originally a 13th-century hospital, it was restored in the early 17th century. In the 20th century, a modern wing was added, and in 1991 it was completely renovated and made into a first-rate hotel. This intimate old hotel is filled with hidden charms such as tiny gardens in its courtyard and on its roof terrace. In this tranquil area of Oxford, you feel like you're living at one of the colleges yourself. The rooms are individually designed but not large; each of them opens onto the private gardens.

1 Banbury Rd., Oxford OX2 6NN. ⓒ **01865/310210.** Fax 01865/311262. www.oldparsonage-hotel.co.uk. 30 units. £175–£230 double; £240–£260 suite. AE, DC, MC, V. Free parking. Bus: 7. **Amenities:** Restaurant; bar; room service. *In room:* A/C, TV, hair dryer, Internet (free).

MODERATE

Bath Place Hotel ★★ 🎁 Its owners took these 17th-century weavers' cottages and converted them into a small inn of charm and grace, one of the "secret addresses" of Oxford. Bath Place lies on a cobbled alleyway off Holywell Street in the center of Oxford between New College and Hertford College. Flemish weavers built the cottages around a tiny flagstone courtyard. The Turf Tavern, adjacent to the hotel, is the oldest in Oxford. The site has had a notorious history, especially when it was the Spotted Cow, known as a center for illicit gambling, bear baiting, and cockfighting. Thomas Hardy mentioned the cottages in his novel *Jude the Obscure.* The address became a secret hideaway for the married Richard Burton and his "mistress," Elizabeth Taylor, when he was acting at the Oxford Playhouse. Completely refurbished to a high standard, the inn today offers comfortable and well-appointed bedrooms.

4–5 Bath Place, Oxford OX1 3SU. ⓒ **01865/791812.** Fax 01865/791834. www.bathplace.co.uk. 13 units. £99–£160 double; £165–£200 family suite. Rates include continental buffet or room-service breakfast. AE, DC, MC, V. Free parking. **Amenities:** Room service. *In room:* TV, Internet (free), minibar.

Mercure Eastgate Hotel ★ The Eastgate, built on the site of a 1600s structure, stands within walking distance of Oxford College and the city center. Recently refurbished, it offers modern facilities while somewhat retaining the atmosphere of an English country house. The bedrooms are well worn but still cozy and range in size from small to medium.

73 the High St., Oxford, Oxfordshire, OX1 4BE. ⓒ **1865/248332.** Fax 01865/791681. www.mercure.com. 63 units. £128–£209 double. AE, DC, MC, V. Parking £13. Bus: 3, 4, 7, or 52. **Amenities:** Bar; babysitting; room service. *In room:* A/C, TV, hair dryer, Internet (free), minibar.

INEXPENSIVE

Dial House 🏷 Three kilometers (1¾ miles) east of the heart of Oxford, beside the main highway leading to London, is this country-style house originally built between 1924 and 1927. Graced with mock Tudor half-timbering and a prominent blue-faced sundial (from which it derives its name), it has cozy and recently renovated rooms. The owners, the Morris family, serve only breakfast in their bright dining room.

25 London Rd., Headington, Oxford, Oxfordshire OX3 7RE. ⓒ **01865/425100.** Fax 01865/427388. www.dialhouseoxford.co.uk. 8 units. £80–£85 double; £90–£125 family room. Rates include English breakfast. AE, MC, V. Free parking. Bus: 2, 7, 7A, 7B, or 22. *In room:* TV, hair dryer, no phone, Wi-Fi (in some; free).

The Galaxie Hotel   When it was built about a century ago, this redbrick hotel served as a plush private mansion for a prosperous local family. This little hotel is better than ever following a refurbishment when a conservatory lounge was added. Each of the well-maintained bedrooms is well furnished to a high standard. Although no meals other than breakfast are served, the hotel is within a short walk of at least five restaurants and two pubs. A public bus runs down Banbury Road to the center of Oxford.

180 Banbury Rd., Oxford, Oxfordshire OX2 7BT. ☎ **01865/515688.** Fax 01865/556824. www. galaxie.co.uk. 32 units, 28 with bathroom. £98–£125 double. Rates include English breakfast. MC, V. Limited street parking. **Amenities:** Breakfast room; lounge. *In room:* TV, hair dryer, Wi-Fi (free).

Where to Dine

EXPENSIVE

Cherwell Boathouse Restaurant ★ FRENCH/MODERN BRITISH   An Oxford landmark on the River Cherwell, this restaurant is owned by Anthony Verdin, who is assisted by a young crew. With an intriguing fixed-price menu, the cooks change the fare every 2 weeks to take advantage of the availability of fresh vegetables, fish, and meat. There is a very reasonable and exciting wine list. The kitchen is often cited for its "sensible combinations" of ingredients. The success of the main dishes is founded on savory treats such as pork belly with a foie gras terrine or crispy pork cutlets with a Provençal sauce. A special treat is the grilled gray mullet with ratatouille accompanied by a basil-and-chili sauce. For dessert, indulge in the lemon-and-almond roulade. The style is sophisticated yet understated, with a heavy reliance on quality ingredients that are cooked in such a way that natural flavors are always preserved.

Bardwell Rd. ☎ **01865/552746.** www.cherwellboathouse.co.uk. Reservations recommended. Main courses £15–£22; fixed-price dinner Fri–Sat £25; Mon–Fri set lunch 2-course £16, 3-course £20. AE, MC, V. Daily noon–2:30pm and 6–9:30pm. Closed Dec 24–30.

MODERATE

Brasserie Blanc ★ MODERN BRITISH/FRENCH   Master restaurateur Raymond Blanc took a former piano shop and converted it into a stylish place for dining, one of the best in Oxford. The informal brasserie, with its striking modern interior, bustles with diners, ranging from visitors to students. Here you get a taste of this famous chef's creations without paying the high prices of his swanky restaurant Le Manoir aux Quat' Saisons. The menu is more straightforward at the brasserie, the chefs using fresh ingredients and savory recipes. Some dishes winning the highest praise include slow-cooked beef and onions with a parsnip puree or roast Barbary duck breast with blackberry sauce.

71072 Walton St. ☎ **01865/510999.** www.brasserieblanc.com. Reservations recommended. Main courses £8.50–£27. AE, MC, V. Mon–Fri noon–2:45pm and 5:30–10:30pm; Sat noon–11pm; Sun noon–10pm.

Gee's Restaurant ★ MEDITERRANEAN/INTERNATIONAL   This restaurant, in a spacious Victorian glass conservatory, was converted from what for 80 years was the leading florist of Oxford. Its original features were retained by the owners, also of the Old Parsonage Hotel (p. 404), who have turned it into one of the most nostalgic and delightful places to dine in the city. Based on fine ingredients and a skilled preparation, the meals are likely to include smoked eel with horseradish potatoes or lamb sweetbreads with pearl barley, perhaps deep-fried haddock and chips with a warm caper sauce. A good dessert choice is the lemon tart with blackberries.

61 Banbury Rd. ℭ **01865/553540.** www.gees-restaurant.co.uk. Reservations recommended. Main courses £15–£22; 2-course fixed-price menu £22, 3 courses £25; set lunch and pretheater menu £22–£25. AE, MC, V. Mon–Sat noon–2:30pm; Sun noon–3:30pm; daily 6–10:30pm.

INEXPENSIVE

Browns 🔥 BROWNS/CONTINENTAL   Oxford's busiest and most bustling English brasserie suits all groups, from babies to undergraduates to grandmas. A 10-minute walk north of the town center, it occupies the premises of five Victorian shops whose walls were removed to create one large, echoing, and very popular space. A thriving bar trade (where lots of people seem to order Pimm's) makes the place an evening destination in its own right. A young and enthusiastic staff serves traditional British cuisine. Your meal may include meat pies, hot salads, burgers, pastas, steaks, or poultry. Afternoon tea here is a justly celebrated Oxford institution. Reservations are not accepted, so if you want to avoid a delay, arrive here during off-peak dining hours.

5–11 Woodstock Rd. ℭ **01865/511995.** www.browns-restaurants.co.uk. Main courses £7.95–£19. AE, MC, V. Mon–Thurs 9:30am–11pm; Fri–Sat 9:30am–11:30pm; Sun 9:30am–10:30pm.

Pubs

The Bear Inn   A short block from High Street, overlooking the north side of Christ Church College, this village pub is an Oxford tradition. Its swinging sign depicts a bear and a ragged staff, the old insignia of the Earls of Warwick, who were among its early patrons. Many famous Oxford students and residents have caroused within the pub's walls since the 13th century, earning it a well-worn place in English literature. Some past owners developed the prankish habit of clipping their guests' neckties. Around the lounge bar you'll see the remains of thousands of ties, all labeled with their owners' names.

6 Alfred St. ℭ **01865/728164.** Snacks and bar meals £3.50–£11. MC, V. Mon–Sat 11am–11pm; Sun noon–10:30pm.

The Turf Tavern   This 13th-century tavern, the oldest in Oxford, stands on a very narrow

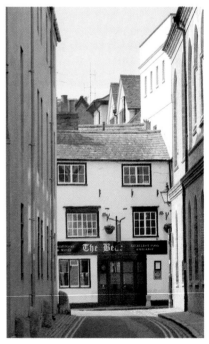

The Bear Inn.

passageway near the Bodleian Library. Thomas Hardy used it as a setting in *Jude the Obscure*. Today's patrons include a healthy sampling of the university's students and faculty. During warm weather you can choose a table in one of the three separate gardens that radiate outward from the pub's core. For wintertime warmth, braziers are lit in the courtyard and in the gardens. A separate food counter, set behind a glass case, displays the day's fare. The pub is reached via St. Helen's Passage, which stretches between Holywell Street and New College Lane.

7 Bath Place (off Holywell St.). ℰ **01865/243235.** Main courses £6–£12. MC, V. Mon–Sat 11am–11pm; Sun noon–10:30pm; last meal served at 7:30pm.

THE PURSUIT OF SCIENCE: CAMBRIDGE ★★★

89km (55 miles) N of London, 129km (80 miles) NE of Oxford

The university town of Cambridge is a collage of images: the Bridge of Sighs; spires and turrets; willows; dusty secondhand bookshops; lanes where Darwin, Newton, and Cromwell walked; the grassy Backs of the colleges, sweeping down to the banks of the Cam; punters; and the tattered robes of hurried upperclassmen flying in the wind.

Along with Oxford, Cambridge is one of Britain's ancient seats of knowledge. In many ways their stories are similar. However, beyond its campus, Cambridge has a thriving, high-tech industry. And while Oxford concentrates on the arts, Cambridge has embraced the sciences. Both Isaac Newton and Stephen Hawking are graduates, joined by luminaries in every field.

There is much to explore in Cambridge, so give yourself time to wander.

Essentials

GETTING THERE Trains depart frequently from London's Liverpool Street and Kings Cross stations, arriving an hour later. For inquiries, call ℰ **0845/748-4950.** A one-way ticket costs £19 to £35.

National Express buses leave hourly from London's Victoria Coach Station for the 2-hour trip to Drummer Street Station in Cambridge. A one-way ticket costs £12. For schedules and information, call ℰ **0871/781-81-81.**

If you're driving from London, head north on the M11.

Punting near the Bridge of Sighs.

407

GETTING AROUND The center of Cambridge is made for pedestrians, so park your car at one of the car parks (rates increase as you approach the city center) and stroll the widely dispersed colleges. Follow the courtyards through to the Backs (the college lawns) and walk through to Trinity (where Prince Charles studied) and St. John's colleges, where you'll find the Bridge of Sighs.

Another popular way of getting around is by bicycle. **Station Cycles** (© **01223/307125;** www.stationcycles.co.uk) has bikes for rent for £8 per half-day, £10 per day, or £20 per week. A deposit of £50 is required. Call in advance to reserve a bike; at that time you'll be told the address at which to pick up the bike. The shop is open Monday to Friday 8am to 6pm, Saturday 9am to 5pm, and Sunday 10am to 4pm.

Stagecoach, 100 Cowley Rd. (© **01223/423-578;** www.stagecoach bus.com), services the Cambridge area with a network of buses, with fares ranging in price from 3£ to £5 for a day pass. The local tourist office has bus schedules.

VISITOR INFORMATION In back of the guildhall, the **Cambridge Tourist Information Centre,** Wheeler Street, Cambridge CB2 3QB (© **1223/ 464-732;** www.visitcambridge.org), has a wide range of information, including data on public transportation and sightseeing attractions. Year-round, the office is open Monday to Friday 10am to 5:30pm and Saturday 10am to 5pm; April to September, the office is also open Sunday 11am to 4pm.

City Sightseeing at Cambridge Railway Station (© **01223/457574;** www.cambridgetmtours.co.uk), on the concourse of the railway station, sells brochures and maps. Also available is a full range of tourist services, including accommodations booking. It's open in summer daily from 8:45am to 7pm (closes at 5pm off season). Guided tours of Cambridge leave the center daily.

SPECIAL EVENTS Cambridge's artistic bent peaks at the end of July during the **Cambridge Folk Festival** (www.cambridgefolkfestival.co.uk). Event tickets are generally from £10 to £25.

Exploring the University

Oxford University predates Cambridge, but by the early 13th-century scholars began gathering here. Eventually, Cambridge won partial recognition and received funds from Henry III. After Henry III's reign, approval and funding rose and fell depending on the monarch. Cambridge consists of 31 colleges for both men and women. Colleges are closed to the public during exams from mid-April until the end of June.

The following listing is only a sample of some of the more interesting colleges. If you're planning to be in Cambridge awhile, you might also want to visit **Magdalene College,** on Magdalene Street, founded in 1542; **Pembroke College,** on Trumpington Street, founded in 1347; **Christ's College,** on St. Andrew's Street, founded in 1505; and **Corpus Christi College,** on King's Parade, which dates from 1352.

Emmanuel College On St. Andrew's Street, Emmanuel (© **01223/334200;** www.emma.cam.ac.uk) was founded in 1584 by Sir Walter Mildmay, a chancellor of the exchequer to Elizabeth I. John Harvard, of the university that bears his

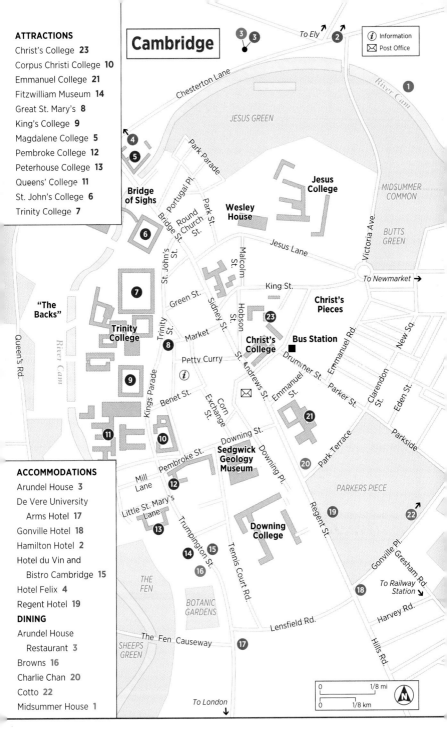

Cambridge

ATTRACTIONS

Christ's College **23**
Corpus Christi College **10**
Emmanuel College **21**
Fitzwilliam Museum **14**
Great St. Mary's **8**
King's College **9**
Magdalene College **5**
Pembroke College **12**
Peterhouse College **13**
Queens' College **11**
St. John's College **6**
Trinity College **7**

ACCOMMODATIONS

Arundel House **3**
De Vere University
  Arms Hotel **17**
Gonville Hotel **18**
Hamilton Hotel **2**
Hotel du Vin and
  Bistro Cambridge **15**
Hotel Felix **4**
Regent Hotel **19**

DINING

Arundel House
  Restaurant **3**
Browns **16**
Charlie Chan **20**
Cotto **22**
Midsummer House **1**

(i) Information
✉ Post Office

To Ely
To Newmarket →
To Railway Station ↘
To London ↓

Chesterton Lane
JESUS GREEN
River Cam
MIDSUMMER COMMON
BUTTS GREEN
Park Parade
Jesus College
Wesley House
Portugal Pl.
Park St.
Round Church St.
Bridge St.
St. John's St.
Bridge of Sighs
"The Backs"
River Cam
Queen's Rd.
Kings Parade
Green St.
Trinity St.
Trinity College
Market
Petty Curry
Benet St.
Corn Exchange St.
Pembroke St.
Mill Lane
Little St. Mary's Lane
Trumpington St.
Tennis Court Rd.
THE FEN
BOTANIC GARDENS
SHEEPS GREEN
The Fen Causeway
Sidney St.
Malcolm St.
Jesus Lane
King St.
Hobson St.
Christ's Pieces
Christ's College
Bus Station
St. Andrews St.
Emmanuel St.
Drummer St.
Downing St.
Sedgwick Geology Museum
Downing Pl.
Downing College
Regent St.
Victoria Ave.
Emmanuel Rd.
Parker St.
Park Terrace
PARKERS PIECE
New Sq.
Clarendon St.
Eden St.
Parkside
Gonville Pl.
Gresham Rd.
Harvey Rd.
Hills Rd.
Lensfield Rd.

0   1/8 mi
0   1/8 km

Woman sitting on a wall outside King's College Chapel.

name in another city called Cambridge, studied here. You can stroll around Emmanuel's attractive gardens and visit the chapel designed by Sir Christopher Wren, consecrated in 1677. Both the chapel and the college are open daily during sunlight hours.

Insider's tip: Harvard men and women, and those who love them, can look for a memorial window in Wren's chapel dedicated to John Harvard, an alumnus of Emmanuel who lent his name to that other university.

King's College ★★   The adolescent Henry VI founded King's College on King's Parade (✆ **01223/331100;** www.kings.cam.ac.uk) in 1441. Most of its buildings today date from the 19th century, but the construction of its crowning glory, the **Perpendicular King's College Chapel ★★★**, began in the Middle Ages. Owing to the whims of royalty, the chapel wasn't completed until the early 16th century.

Henry James called King's College Chapel "the most beautiful in England." Its most striking features are its magnificent fan vaulting, all in stone, and its great windows, most of which were fashioned by Flemish artisans between 1517 and 1531 (the west window dates from the late Victorian period). The chapel also boasts Rubens's *Adoration of the Magi* and an ornamental screen from the early 16th century. The chapel is famous for its choir and musical concerts. You can call the college (phone number above) for concert dates and times.

Insider's tip: For a classic view of the chapel, you can admire the architectural complex from the rear, which is an ideal picnic spot along the river. To acquire the makings of a picnic, head for the vendors who peddle inexpensive food, including fresh fruit, at **Market Square,** open Monday to Saturday 9:30am to 4:30pm. You can also get the makings of a picnic at a major grocery store, **Sainsbury's,** 44 Sidney St. (✆ **01223/366891;** www.sainsburys.co.uk), open Monday to Saturday 8am to 10pm and Sunday 11am to 5pm. E. M. Forster came here to contemplate scenes for his novel *Maurice.*

The chapel is open during college term, Monday to Friday 9:30am to 3:30pm, Saturday 9:30am to 3:15pm, and Sunday 1:15 to 2:15pm and 5 to 5:30pm. During the term, the public is welcome to attend choral services Monday to Saturday at 5:30pm and on Sunday at 10:30am and 3:30pm. During school vacations, the chapel is open to visitors Monday to Saturday 9:30am to 4:30pm and on Sunday 10am to 5pm; it is closed from December 23 to January 1. It may be closed at other times for recording sessions, broadcasts, and concerts.

An exhibition in the seven northern side chapels shows why and how the chapel was built. Admission to the college and chapel, including the exhibition, is £5 for adults, £3 for students and seniors, and free for children 11 and younger.

Peterhouse College On Trumpington Street, Peterhouse College (*©* **01223/338200;** www.pet.cam.ac.uk) attracts visitors because it's the oldest Cambridge college, founded in 1284 by Hugh de Balsham, the bishop of Ely. Of the original buildings, only the hall remains. It was restored in the 19th century and has stained-glass windows by William Morris. The chapel, called Old Court, dates from 1632 and was renovated in 1754. Ask to enter at the porter's lodge.

Insider's tip: Now almost sadly neglected, the Little Church of St. Mary's next door was the college chapel until 1632. Pay it the honor of a visit.

Queens' College ★★ On Silver Street, Queens' College (*©* **01223/335511;** www.quns.cam.ac.uk) is the loveliest of Cambridge's colleges. Dating back to 1448, it was founded by two English queens, Margaret of Anjou, the wife of Henry VI, and Elizabeth Woodville, the wife of Edward IV. Its second cloister is the most interesting, flanked by the early-16th-century half-timbered President's Lodge.

Admission is £2 for adults, free for children 11 and younger accompanied by parents. A printed guide is issued. From October 27 to March 14, hours are daily 1:45 to 4:30pm; March 15 to May 18 Monday to Friday 11am to 3pm, Saturday and Sunday 10am to 4:30pm; May 19 to June 21 closed; June 22 to September 28 daily 10am to 4:30pm; and September 29 to October 26 Monday to Friday 10:45am to 4:30pm, Saturday and Sunday 10am to 4:30pm. Entry and exit is by the old porter's lodge in Queens' Lane only. The old hall and chapel are usually open to the public when not in use.

Insider's tip: Queens' College's wide lawns lead down to the "Backs" (the backs of the colleges), where you can stroll, sit, or go punting. Take in Mathematical Bridge, best viewed from the Silver Street bridge, dating from 1902.

Cloister Court at Queens' College.

St. John's College ★★   On St. John's Street, this college (🕾 **01223/338600;** www.joh.cam.ac.uk) was founded in 1511 by Lady Margaret Beaufort, mother of Henry VII, who had launched Christ's College a few years earlier. The impressive gateway bears the Tudor coat of arms, and the Second Court is a fine example of late Tudor brickwork. The college's best-known feature is the Bridge of Sighs crossing the Cam. Built in the 19th century, it was patterned after the covered bridge in Venice. It connects the older part of the college with New Court, a Gothic Revival on the opposite bank, where there is an outstanding view of the famous Backs. The Bridge of Sighs is closed to visitors but can be seen from neighboring Kitchen Bridge. Wordsworth was an alumnus of this college. Visitors are admitted from March 3 to October 28 daily 10am to 5:30pm; it is also open Saturday and Sunday in November and again in February at the hours given. Admission is £2.80 for adults, £1.70 for seniors and children 12 to 17, free for children 11 and younger. Visitors are welcome to attend choral services in the chapel.

Insider's tip: The Bridge of Sighs links the old college with an architectural "folly" of the 19th century, the elaborate New Court, which is a crenellated neo-Gothic fantasy. It's adorned with a "riot" of pinnacles and a main cupola. Students call it "the wedding cake."

Trinity College ★★   On Trinity Street, Trinity College (not to be confused with Trinity Hall; 🕾 **01223/338400;** www.trin.cam.ac.uk) is the largest college in Cambridge. It was founded in 1546 by Henry VIII, who consolidated a number of smaller colleges that had existed on the site. The courtyard is the most spacious in Cambridge, built when Thomas Neville was master. Sir Christopher Wren designed the library.

Insider's tip: What's fun to do here is to contemplate what went on here before you arrived. Pause at Neville's Court where Isaac Newton first calculated the speed of sound. Take in the delicate fountain of the Great Court where Lord Byron used to bathe naked with his pet bear. Why a bear? The university forbade

Quadrangle at Trinity College.

students from having dogs, but there was no proviso for bears. Years later, Vladimir Nabokov walked through that same courtyard dreaming of the young lady he would later immortalize as *Lolita*. For admission to the college, apply at the porter's lodge. Trinity College is open to visitors March to November Monday to Friday from 10am to 5pm. There's a charge of £2.20 adults, £1.30 seniors and children, and £4.40 for families.

Cambridge students waiting to receive their degrees.

Cambridge's Other Attractions

Fitzwilliam Museum ★★ This is one of Britain's finest museums, founded by the bequest of the seventh viscount Fitzwilliam of Merrion to the University of Cambridge in 1816. The permanent collections contain remarkable antiquities from ancient Egypt, Greece, and Rome. Galleries display Roman and Romano-Egyptian art along with Western-Asiatic exhibits. The Fitzwilliam's Applied Arts section showcases English and European pottery and glass, as well as furniture, clocks, armor, fans, rugs and samplers, Chinese jades, and ceramics from Japan and Korea. The museum also has married a rare ancient and medieval coin collection with a host of medals created from the Renaissance onward. The Fitzwilliam is best loved for its collection of paintings, which includes masterpieces by Simone Martini, Titian, Veronese, Rubens, Van Dyck, Canaletto, Hogarth, Gainsborough, Constable, Monet, Degas, Renoir, Cézanne, and Picasso. There is also a fine collection of other 20th-century art, miniatures, drawings, watercolors, and prints. The Fitzwilliam stages occasional musical events, including evening concerts, in Gallery III. Throughout the year, it plays host to some of the best lectures in England.

Trumpington St., near Peterhouse. (✆ **01223/332900.** www.fitzmuseum.cam.ac.uk. Free admission, donations appreciated; guided tours £6 per person. Tues–Sat 10am–5pm; Sun noon–5pm; tours Sat 2:45pm. Closed Jan 1, Good Friday, May Day, and Dec 24–31.

Great St. Mary's Closely associated with events of the Reformation because the leaders of the movement (Erasmus, Cranmer, Latimer, and Ridley) preached here, this university church was built mostly in 1478 on the site of an 11th-century church. The cloth that covered the hearse of King Henry VII is on display in the church. There is a fine view of Cambridge from the top of the tower.

King's Parade. (✆ **01223/741716.** www.gsm.cam.ac.uk. Admission to tower £2 adults, £1 children. Church open May–Aug Mon–Sat 9:30am–5pm; Sun 12:30–5pm; Sept–Apr Mon–Sat 9–4, Sun 12:30–4. Tower open May–Aug Tues–Sat 10am–4:30pm, Sun 12:45–4:30, Sept–Apr Tues–Sat 10am–3:30pm, Sun 12:45–3:30pm.

Where to Stay

EXPENSIVE

De Vere University Arms Hotel ★ This 1834 hotel maintains much of its antique charm and many original architectural features despite modernization over the years. Near the city center and the university, it offers suitable bed-rooms. Rooms range from small to midsize, each with bedside controls; the pre-mium rooms also have slippers and robes. Many of the bedrooms have been recently refurbished; eight have four-poster beds. Rooms in front are smaller but more up-to-date and have double-glazed windows. Three rooms are suitable for families.

Regent St., Cambridge, Cambridgeshire CB2 1AD. ✆ **01223/273000.** Fax 01223/273037. www.
devere.co.uk. 119 units. £145–£205 double; £275–£350 suite. Rates include English breakfast. AE,
DC, MC, V. Parking £12. Bus: 1. **Amenities:** Restaurant; bar; babysitting; room service. *In room:* TV,
hair dryer, minibar, Wi-Fi (free in some).

Hotel du Vin and Bistro Cambridge ★★   This upmarket chain has taken a historic building in the heart of Cambridge and turned it into a plush hotel. Spe-cial features include some suites with private gardens and the chain's trademark bistro and champagne bar. The hotel is completely up to date, after millions of pounds were poured into its restoration, yet it is also a classic, as the building on this site dates from medieval times. Two wells from the Middle Ages were glassed over as a focal point for one of the larger rooms. Rooms are elegant and beauti-fully furnished, some with private terraces. The hotel bar lies in the vaulted cel-lar. For afternoon tea, ever had a drink of hibiscus flowers, sweet blackberry leaves, apple, licorice root, and poppy flowers? You can here.

Trumpington St., Cambridge, Cambridgeshire CB2 1QA. ✆ **01223/227-330.** www.hotelduvin.
com. 41 units. £160–£190 double; £240–£390 suite. AE, DC, MC, V. **Amenities:** Restaurant; bar;
room service. *In room:* A/C, TV, hair dryer, minibar, Wi-Fi (£10 per day).

Hotel Felix ★★   Although it lies about 1.6km (1 mile) from the city center, this contemporary hotel has shot up to the top of the heap as the best in Cam-bridge. Set in more than 1.2 hectares (3 acres) of landscaped gardens, its stylish design and tasteful decor have brought luxury to the often staid accommodations of this university city. A chic boutique hotel, the Felix arises from a Victorian mansion to which two new wings were added. The *Daily Telegraph* called it "a work of art," and the *Sunday Times* hailed it as "one of the country's choicest boltholes." We like the way the Felix, Cambridge's first designer hotel, harmoni-ously blended the old and new, all while maintaining a cozy atmosphere through-out. Imbued with specially commissioned modern art, the bedrooms have wide beds and unfussy decor.

Whitehouse Lane, Huntingdon Rd., Cambridge CB3 0LX. ✆ **01223/277977.** Fax 01223/277973.
www.hotelfelix.co.uk. 52 units. £190–£265 double; £285–£345 suite. Rates include breakfast. AE,
DC, MC, V. Free parking. **Amenities:** Restaurant; bar; access to health club; room service.
In room: TV, CD player, hair dryer, minibar, Wi-Fi (£10).

MODERATE

Arundel House   Occupying one of the most desirable sites in Cambridge, this hotel consists of six interconnected identical Victorian row houses—all fronted with dark-yellow local bricks. In 1994, after two additional houses were pur-chased, the hotel was enlarged, upgraded, and expanded into the well-main-tained hostelry you'll see today. Though not as well appointed as the University Arms or the Felix (see above), it competes successfully with the Gonville (see below) and has the best cuisine of the hotels. Rooms overlooking the River Cam and Jesus Green cost more, as do those on lower floors (there's no elevator). All rooms are simple but comfortable, with upholstered chairs and carpeting.

53 Chesterton Rd., Cambridge, Cambridgeshire CB4 3AN. ✆ **01223/367701.** Fax 01223/367721. www.arundelhousehotels.co.uk. 103 units. £95–£150 double; £135–£160 family bedroom. Rates include continental breakfast. AE, DC, MC, V. Free parking. Bus: 1 or 3. **Amenities:** Restaurant (see review below); bar. *In room:* A/C, TV, hair dryer, Wi-Fi (free in some).

Gonville Hotel This hotel and its grounds are opposite Parker's Piece park, only a 5-minute walk from the center of town. The Gonville has been much improved in recent years and is better than ever, although not yet the equal of the Hotel Felix (see above). It's like an ivy-covered country house, with shade trees and a formal car entry. The recently refurbished rooms are comfortable and modern in style.

Gonville Place, Cambridge, Cambridgeshire CB1 1LY. ✆ **800/780-7234** in the U.S. and Canada, or 01223/366611. Fax 01223/315470. www.gonvillehotel.co.uk. 73 units. £119–£140 double. AE, DC, MC, V. Free parking. **Amenities:** Restaurant; bar; room service. *In room:* TV, hair dryer, Wi-Fi (free).

INEXPENSIVE

Hamilton Hotel 🏆 One of the better and more reasonably priced of the small hotels of Cambridge, this redbrick establishment lies about 1.6km (1 mile) northeast of the city center, close to the River Cam. Well run and modestly accessorized, the hotel stands on a busy highway, but there's a parking area out back. The well-furnished bedrooms contain reasonably comfortable twin or double beds. Bathrooms are compact with shower stalls. The hotel has a small, traditionally styled licensed bar, offering standard pub food and snacks.

156 Chesterton Rd., Cambridge, Cambridgeshire CB4 1DA. ✆ **01223/365664.** Fax 01223/314866. www.hamiltonhotelcambridge.co.uk. 25 units. £56 double with shared bathroom; £60–£70 double with bathroom. Rates include English breakfast. AE, DC, MC, V. Free parking. Bus: 3 or 3A. **Amenities:** Bar. *In room:* TV, hair dryer, Wi-Fi (free).

Regent Hotel This is one of the most desirable of Cambridge's reasonably priced small hotels. Right in the city center, overlooking Parker's Piece Park, the house was built in the 1840s as the original site of Newnham College. It became a hotel when the college outgrew its quarters. Bedrooms are on the small side but are redecorated frequently in traditional Georgian style.

41 Regent St., Cambridge, Cambridgeshire CB2 1AB. ✆ **01223/351470.** Fax 01223/464937. www.regenthotel.co.uk. 22 units. £105–£136 double; £147 suite. Rates include continental breakfast. AE, DC, MC, V. Parking £10. Closed Dec 22–Jan 2. Bus: 1. **Amenities:** Bar. *In room:* A/C, TV, hair dryer, Internet (£2).

Where to Dine

Drop down into the cozy **Rainbow Vegetarian Cafe,** King's Parade, across from King's College (✆ **01223/321551;** www.rainbowcafe.co.uk), for coffee, a slice of fresh-baked cake, or a meal from their selection of whole-food and vegetarian offerings. A main course lunch or dinner goes for only £8.95. It is open Tuesday to Saturday 10am to 10pm. The cafe lies at the end of a lily-lined path.

VERY EXPENSIVE

Midsummer House ★★ 🎁 MEDITERRANEAN Located in an Edwardian-era cottage near the River Cam, the Midsummer House is a real find. We prefer to dine in the elegant conservatory, but you can also find a smartly laid table upstairs. The fixed-price menus are wisely limited, and quality control and high standards are much in evidence here. Daniel Clifford is the master chef, and he has created such specialties as filet of beef Rossini with braised winter vegetables and sauce Perigourdine; and roast squab pigeon, *pomme* Anna, *tarte tatin* of onions, caramelized endives, and jus of morels.

Midsummer Common. ✆ **01223/369299.** www.midsummerhouse.co.uk. Reservations required. 2-course set lunch £30; 3-course set lunch £35; 3-course fixed-price dinner £65. AE, MC, V. Tues–Sat noon–2pm and 7–10pm.

MODERATE

Arundel House Restaurant ★ BRITISH/FRENCH/VEGETARIAN   One of the best and most acclaimed restaurants in Cambridge is in a hotel overlooking the River Cam and Jesus Green, a short walk from the city center. Winner of many awards, it's noted not only for its excellence and use of fresh produce, but also for its good value. The decor is warmly inviting with Sanderson curtains, Louis XV–upholstered chairs, and spacious tables. The menu changes frequently, and you can dine either a la carte or from the set menu. Perhaps you'll sample such dishes as filet of plaice in lime-and-basil butter or grilled salmon wrapped in Parma of ham. Medallions of pork are sautéed with sweet peppers and served in a Dijon-mustard-and-cream sauce, and supreme of chicken appears with wild mushrooms in a cream-and-brandy sauce.

In the Arundel House hotel, 53 Chesterton Rd. ✆ **01223/367701.** Reservations required. Main courses £10–£20; 2-course fixed-price menu £19, 3 courses £24. AE, DC, MC, V. Daily 7:30–10am, 12:15–1:45pm, and 6:30–9:30pm. Bus: 3 or 5.

Browns ★ 🍴 CONTINENTAL/BRITISH   After wowing them at Oxford, Browns now lures Cambridge students in equal numbers. The building lies opposite the Fitzwilliam Museum and was constructed in 1914 as the outpatient department of a hospital dedicated to Edward VII; that era's grandeur is apparent in the building's neoclassical colonnade. Today, it's the most lighthearted place for dining in the city, with wicker chairs, high ceilings, pre–World War I woodwork, and a long bar covered with bottles of wine. The extensive bill of fare includes pastas, scores of fresh salads, several selections of meat and fish (from chargrilled leg of lamb with rosemary to fresh fish in season), hot sandwiches, and the chef's daily specials. If you drop by in the afternoon, you can also order thick milkshakes or natural fruit juices. In fair weather, outdoor seats are prized possessions.

23 Trumpington St. (5 min. from King's College and opposite the Fitzwilliam Museum). ✆ **01223/461655.** www.browns-restaurants.com. Reservations not accepted on weekends. Main courses £7.95–£19. AE, MC, V. Mon–Sat 10am–11pm; Sun 11:30am–10pm. Bus: 2.

Cotto ★ BRITISH/CONTINENTAL   This innovative restaurant lies above a small deli-bakery, attracting a youthful clientele to its contemporary, wood-filled interior decorated with modern paintings for sale. Its success stems from its "no frills, no choice" three-course fixed-price dinners. That menu is based on quality ingredients freshly cooked to order. A typical evening meal might begin with carpaccio of Cornish monkfish, followed with a soup of wood-roasted Fenland spaghetti squash with pesto. For a main, perhaps slow-roasted Suffolk partridge might appear with a beet salad, followed by a selection of cheese and poached prunes. For dessert, perhaps a tart of Willingham pear and almond. Much of the produce that goes into these meals comes from local organic farmers. Lunch is less elaborate, featuring such dishes as Pollock and leek fish cakes or roasted pigeon breast. You can also try Cotto for breakfast (have a slice of their sourdough bread).

183 East Rd. (✆ **01223/302010.** www.cottocambridge.co.uk. Reservations recommended for dinner. Fixed-price dinner £35; lunch main courses £8.50–£16. AE, MC, V. Tues–Fri 9am–3pm; Thurs–Sat 7–10pm.

INEXPENSIVE

Charlie Chan CHINESE   Most people say that this is the finest Chinese restaurant in Cambridge, and we agree. We've always found Charlie Chan reliable and capable, which is remarkable given its huge menu. Downstairs is a long corridor-like restaurant, with pristine decor. The ambience is more lush in the Blue Lagoon upstairs. Most of the dishes here are inspired by the traditional cuisine of Beijing. The specialties we've most enjoyed include an aromatic and crispy duck, lemon chicken, and prawns with garlic and ginger. Most of the dishes are affordably priced except for the expensive shellfish specialties, especially lobster.

14 Regent St. (✆ **01223/361763.** Reservations recommended. Main courses £6–£38. AE, MC, V. Daily noon–5pm and 6–11pm.

Cambridge After Dark

Nightlife in this university city revolves around the new and improved complex, **Cambridge Leisure Park** (✆ **01223/511511**), lying behind the Cambridge Station. The complex features a multiscreen cinema; a bowling alley; numerous chain restaurants; and bars, some of which offer live entertainment. Saturday night is the big blast here, attracting hundreds of university students. There is also a theater presenting comedy, drama, and even children's shows.

You can take in a production where Emma Thompson and other well-known thespians got their start at the **Amateur Dramatic Club,** Park Street near Jesus Lane (✆ **01223/359547,** or 01223/300085 for box office; www.cuadc.org). It presents two student productions nightly, Tuesday through Saturday, with the main show tending toward classic and modern drama or opera, and the late show being of a comic or experimental nature. The theater is open nearly year-round, closing in September, and tickets run from £3.50 to £10.

The most popular Cantabrigian activity is the **pub-crawl** (www.cambridge pubs.co.uk). With too many pubs in the city to list, you may as well start at Cambridge's oldest pub, the **Pickerel,** on Magdalene Street (✆ **01223/355068**), dating from 1432. English pubs don't get more traditional than this. If the ceiling beams or floorboards groan occasionally—well, they've certainly earned the right over the years. Real ales on tap include Bulmer's Traditional Cider, Old Speckled Hen, Theakston's 6X, Old Peculiar, and Best Bitter. The **Maypole,** Portugal Place at Park Street (✆ **01223/352999**), is the local hangout for actors from the nearby ADC Theatre. Known for cocktails and not ales, you can still get a Tetley's 6X or Castle Eden.

The **Eagle,** Benet Street off King's Parade (✆ **01223/505020**), will be forever famous as the place where Nobel Laureates Watson and Crick first announced their discovery of the DNA double helix. Real ales include Icebreaker and local brewery Greene King's Abbott, so make your order and raise a pint to the wonders of modern science.

The Pickerel Inn.

To meet up with current Cambridge students, join the locals at the **Anchor,** Silver Street (✆ **01223/353554**), or **Tap and Spiel (the Mill),** 14 Mill Lane, off Silver Street Bridge (✆ **01223/357026**), for a pint of Greene King's IPA or Abbott. The crowd at the Anchor spills out onto the bridge in fair weather, whereas the Tap and Spiel's clientele lays claim to the entire riverside park.

For a gay and lesbian hangout, your best bet is to head for **Five Bells,** 126 Newmarket St. (✆ **01223/314019**), especially on a Friday or Saturday night when the joint is packed. In summer the action overflows into the garden in the rear. You might also check out **Fleur-de-Lys,** 73 Humberstone Rd. (✆ **01223/470401**), which features everything from drag shows to striptease, dance music, and karaoke.

For musical entertainment, you can find out who's playing by checking out fliers posted around town or by reading the *Varsity.* The **Corn Exchange,** Wheeler Street and Corn Exchange (✆ **01223/357851**), hosts everything from classical concerts to bigger-name rock shows. The **Graduate,** 16 Chesterton Rd. (✆ **01223/301416**), is a pub located in a former movie theater.

Entertainment in some form can be found nightly at the **Junction,** Clifton Road, near the train station (✆ **01223/511511**), where an eclectic mix of acts takes the stage weeknights to perform all genres of music, comedy, and theater, and DJs take over on the weekend. Cover charges vary from £5 to £25, depending on the event.

Ballare, Lion Yard (✆ **01223/364222**), a second-story club, has a huge dance floor and plays everything from house to the latest pop hits, Monday to Saturday 9pm until 2am. Sometimes they even DJ the old-fashioned way, by taking requests. The cover charge ranges from £3 to £10, depending on what night you're here.

SHAKESPEARE'S STRATFORD-UPON-AVON ★★

147km (91 miles) NW of London, 65km (40 miles) NW of Oxford

Crowds of visitors overrun this market town on the River Avon during the summer months. In fact, Stratford so aggressively hustles its Shakespeare connection

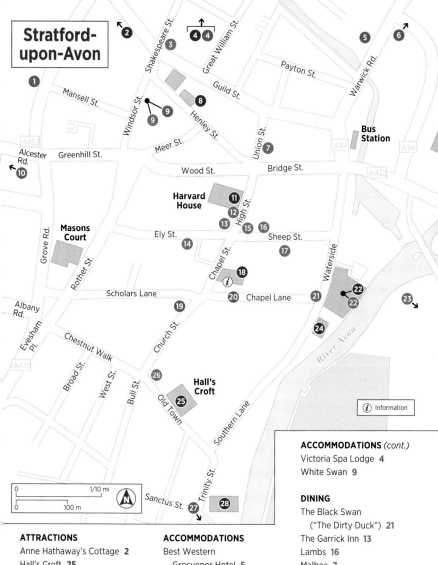

Stratford-upon-Avon

that it seems at times that everybody here is trying to make a buck off the Bard. If he could return today, Shakespeare would be inundated with T-shirts bearing his likeness and china models of Anne Hathaway's cottage. He might look for a less trampled town in which to pen his masterpieces.

One visitor magnet is the Royal Shakespeare Theatre, where Britain's foremost actors perform. Other than the theater, Stratford is nearly devoid of cultural life, and you may want to rush back to London after you've done the literary pilgrimage and seen a show. If you can, visit in winter, when the throngs dwindle.

Essentials

GETTING THERE The journey from London to Stratford-upon-Avon takes about 2¼ hours, and a round-trip ticket costs £28 to £69 depending on the train. For schedules and information, call 𝄐 **0845/748-4950,** or go to **www. nationalrail.co.uk**. The train station at Stratford is on Alcester Road.

Four **National Express** buses a day leave from London's Victoria Station, with a trip time of 3¼ hours. A single-day round-trip ticket costs £19. For schedules and information, call 𝄐 **0871/781-81-81** (www.national express.com).

If you're driving from London, take the M40 toward Oxford and continue to Stratford-upon-Avon on the A34.

VISITOR INFORMATION The **Tourist Information Centre,** Bridgefoot, Stratford-upon-Avon, Warwickshire CV37 6GW (𝄐 **0870/160-7930;** www. shakespeare-country.co.uk), provides any details you may wish to know about the Shakespeare houses and properties, and will assist in booking rooms (see "Where to Stay," below). Call and ask for a copy of their free *Shakespeare Country Holiday* guide. They also operate a Thomas Cook currency-exchange office (𝄐 **01789/269750**). It's open April to September Monday to Saturday 9am to 5:30pm and Sunday 10am to 4pm, and October to March Monday to Saturday 9am to 5pm and Sunday 10am to 3pm.

To contact **Shakespeare Birthplace Trust,** which administrates many of the attractions, call the Shakespeare Centre (𝄐 **01789/204016;** www.shakespeare.org.uk).

Visiting the Shrines

Besides the attractions on the periphery of Stratford, many Elizabethan and Jacobean buildings are in town, a number of them administrated by the **Shakespeare Birthplace Trust** (𝄐 **01789/204016;** www.shakespeare.org.uk). One ticket—costing £15 for adults, £13 for seniors and students, and £7.50 for children—lets you visit the five most important sights. You can also buy a family ticket to all five sights (good for two adults and three children) for £40—a good deal. Pick up the ticket if you're planning to do much sightseeing (obtainable at your first stopover at any one of the Trust properties).

Guided tours of Stratford-upon-Avon are conducted by **City Sightseeing** (𝄐 **01789/412680;** www.citysightseeing-stratford.com), Civic Hall, Rother Street. In summer, open-top double-decker buses depart every 15 minutes daily from 9:30am to 6pm. You can take a 1-hour ride without stops, or you can get off at any or all of the town's five Shakespeare properties. Though the bus stops are clearly marked along the historic route, the most logical starting point is the sidewalk in front of the Pen & Parchment Pub, at the bottom of Bridge Street. Tour

The Pen and Parchment Public House.

tickets are valid all day so you can hop on and off the buses as many times as you want. The tours cost £11 for adults, £9 for seniors or students, and £6 for children 5 to 15 (children 4 and younger ride for free). A family ticket sells for £28. Tour frequency depends on the time of the year; call for information.

Anne Hathaway's Cottage ★   Before she married Shakespeare, Anne Hathaway lived in this thatched, wattle-and-daub cottage in the hamlet of Shottery, 1.6km (1 mile) from Stratford. It's the most interesting and the most photographed of the Trust properties. The Hathaways were yeoman farmers, and their descendants lived in the cottage until 1892. As a result, it was never renovated and provides a rare insight into the life of a family in Shakespearean times. The Bard was only 18 when he married Anne, who was much older. Many original furnishings, including the courting settle (the bench on which Shakespeare is said to have wooed Anne) and various kitchen utensils, are preserved inside the house. After visiting the house, take time to linger in the garden and orchard.

Cottage Lane, Shottery. ✆ **01789/292100.** www.shakespeare.org.uk. Admission £7 adults, £6 seniors and students, £4 children, £18 family ticket (2 adults, 3 children). Nov–Mar daily 10am–4pm; Apr–May and Sept–Oct Mon–Sat 9:30am–5pm, Sun 10am–5pm; June–Aug Mon–Sat 9am–5pm, Sun 9:30am–5pm. Closed Dec 23–26. Take a bus from Bridge St. or walk via a marked pathway from Evesham Place in Stratford across the meadow to Shottery.

Hall's Croft   This house is on Old Town Street, not far from the parish church, Holy Trinity. It was here that Shakespeare's daughter Susanna probably lived with her husband, Dr. John Hall. Hall's Croft is an outstanding Tudor house with a walled garden, furnished in the style of a middle-class home of the time. Dr. Hall was widely respected and built up a large medical practice in the area. Fascinating exhibits illustrate the theory and practice of medicine in Dr. Hall's time.

Old Town St. (near Holy Trinity Church). ✆ **01789/292107.** Admission £12 adults, £11 seniors and students, £7.50 children, £31 family ticket (2 adults, 3 children). Nov–Mar daily 11am–4pm; Apr–May daily 11am–5pm; June–Aug Mon–Sat 9:30am–5pm, Sun 10am–5pm; Sept–Oct daily 11am–5pm. Closed Dec 23–28. To reach Hall's Croft, walk west from High St., which becomes Chapel St. and Church St. At the intersection with Old Town St., go left.

Harvard House The most ornate home in Stratford, Harvard House is a fine example of an Elizabethan town house. Rebuilt in 1596, it was once the home of Katherine Rogers, mother of John Harvard, founder of Harvard University. In 1909, the house was purchased by a Chicago millionaire, Edward Morris, who presented it as a gift to the famous American university. Today, following a restoration, it has reopened as the Museum of British Pewter. The museum displays trace the use of pewter from the Roman era until modern times. Pewter, as you learn, used to be the most common choice for household items. Even kiddie toys were made from pewter. Highlights include a tankard engraved with the images of William and Mary, a teapot inspired by the Portland Vase, and a rare bell-based Elizabethan candlestick. Two "hands-on" activities allow children to examine original items.

High St. ✆ **01789/204507.** Admission £3.50 adults, free for children under 16. May–June and Sept–Oct Fri–Sun noon–5pm; July–Aug Wed–Sun noon–5pm.

Harvard House.

Holy Trinity Church (Shakespeare's Tomb) In an attractive setting near the River Avon is the parish church where Shakespeare is buried ("and curst be he who moves my bones"). The Parish Register records his baptism in 1564 and burial in 1616 (copies of the original documents are on display). The church is one of the most beautiful parish churches in England.

Shakespeare's tomb lies in the chancel, a privilege bestowed upon him when he became a lay rector in 1605. Alongside his grave are those of his widow, Anne, and other members of his family. You can also see the graves of Susanna, his daughter, and those of Thomas Nash and Dr. John Hall. Nearby on the north wall is a bust of Shakespeare that was erected approximately 7 years after his death—within the lifetime of his widow and many of his friends.

Old Town St. ✆ **01789/290128.** Free admission to church; Shakespeare's tomb £2 adults, £1 students. Apr–Sept Mon–Sat 8:30am–6pm, Sun 12:30–5pm; Mar and Oct Mon–Sat 9am–5pm, Sun 12:30–5pm; Nov–Feb Mon–Sat 9am–4pm, Sun 12:30–5pm. Walk 4 min. past the Royal Shakespeare Theatre with the river on your left.

Mary Arden's House (Glebe Farm)/Palmer's Farm ★ So what if millions of visitors have been tricked into thinking this timber-framed farmhouse with its old stone dovecote and various outbuildings was the girlhood home of Shakespeare's mother, Mary Arden? It's still one of the most intriguing sights outside Stratford, even if local historian Dr. Nat Alcock discovered in 2000 that the actual childhood home of Arden was the dull-looking brick-built farmhouse,

Glebe Farm, next door. Glebe Farm has now been properly renamed Mary Arden's House. It was all the trick of an 18th-century tour guide, John Jordan, who decided Glebe Farm was too unimpressive to be the home of the Bard's mother, so he told tourists it was this farmstead instead. What was known for years as "Mary Arden's House" has been renamed Palmer's Farm. Actually, this farm wasn't constructed until the late 16th century, a little late to be Mary Arden's actual home. After the name confusion, local authorities have converted Palmer's Farm into a working farm. Visitors can tour the property seeing firsthand how a farming household functioned in the 1570s—yes, cows to be milked, bread to be baked, and vegetables cultivated in an authentic 16th-century manner. In the barns, stable, cowshed, and farmyard is an extensive collection of farming implements illustrating life and work in the local countryside from Shakespeare's time to the present.

Wilmcote. ✆ **01789/293455.** Admission £8 adults, £7 students and seniors, £5 children, £21 family ticket, free for children 4 and younger. Nov–Mar daily 10am–4pm; Apr–May and Sept–Oct daily 10am–5pm; June–Aug daily 9:30am–5pm. Closed Dec 23–26. Take A3400 (Birmingham) for 5.5km (3½ miles).

New Place/Nash's House   Shakespeare retired to New Place in 1610 (a prosperous man by the standards of his day) and died here 6 years later. Regrettably, the house was torn down, so only the garden remains. A mulberry tree planted by the Bard was so popular with latter-day visitors to Stratford that the garden's owner chopped it down. It is said that the mulberry tree that grows here today was planted from a cutting of the original tree. You enter the gardens through Nash's House (Thomas Nash married Elizabeth Hall, a granddaughter of the poet). Nash's House has 16th-century period rooms and an exhibition illustrating the history of Stratford. The popular Knott Garden adjoins the site and represents the style of a fashionable Elizabethan garden.

Chapel St. ✆ **01789/292325.** Admission £12 adults, £11 seniors and students, £7.50 children, £31 family ticket (2 adults, 3 children). Nov–Mar daily 11am–4pm; Apr–May and Sept–Oct daily 11am–5pm; June–Aug Mon–Sat 9:30am–5pm, Sun 10am–5pm. Closed Dec 23–26. Walk west down High St.; Chapel St. is a continuation of High St.

Shakespeare's Birthplace ★   The son of a glover and whittawer (leather worker), the Bard was born on St. George's Day, April 23, 1564, and died on the same date 52 years later. Filled with Shakespeare memorabilia, including a portrait and furnishings of the writer's time, the Trust property is a half-timbered structure, dating from the early 16th century. The house was bought by public donors in 1847 and preserved as a national shrine. You can visit the living room, the bedroom where Shakespeare was probably born, a fully equipped kitchen of the period (look for the "babyminder"), and a Shakespeare museum, illustrating his life and times. Later, you can walk through the garden. You won't be alone: It's estimated that some 660,000 visitors pass through the house annually.

Built next door to commemorate the 400th anniversary of the Bard's birth, the modern **Shakespeare Centre** serves both as the administrative headquarters of the Birthplace Trust and as a library and study center. An extension houses a visitor center, which acts as a reception area for those coming to the birthplace.

Henley St. (in the town center near the post office, close to Union St.). ✆ **01789/204016.** www. shakespeare.org.uk. Admission £12 adults, £11 students and seniors, £7.50 children, £31 family ticket (2 adults, 3 children). Nov–Mar Mon–Sat 10am–4pm, Sun 10:30am–4pm; Apr–May and Sept–Oct daily 10am–5pm; June–Aug Mon–Sat 9am–5pm, Sun 9am–5pm. Closed Dec 23–26.

The Stratford Brass Rubbing Centre   This is a brass-rubbing center, where medieval and Tudor brasses illustrate the knights and ladies, scholars, merchants, and priests of a bygone era. The Stratford collection includes a large assortment of exact replicas of brasses. Entrance is free, but visitors are charged depending on which brass they choose to rub. According to size, the cost ranges from £2 to make a rubbing of a small brass, to a maximum of £20 for a rubbing of the largest brass.

The Royal Shakespeare Theatre Summer House, Avon Bank Gardens. ℂ **01789/297671.** www. stratfordbrassrubbing.co.uk. Free admission. Mar–Oct daily 10am–6pm; Nov–Feb daily 11am–4pm.

The Royal Shakespeare Theatre

On the banks of the Avon, the **Royal Shakespeare Theatre (RST),** Waterside, Stratford-upon-Avon CV37 6BB (ℂ **01789/403444;** www.rsc.org.uk), is a major showcase for the Royal Shakespeare Company and seats 1,500 patrons. The theater's season runs from April to November and typically features five Shakespearean plays. The company has some of the finest actors on the British stage.

You usually need **ticket reservations,** with two successive booking periods, each one opening about 2 months in advance. You can pick these up from a North American or English travel agent. A small number of tickets are always held for sale on the day of a performance, but it may be too late to get a good seat if you wait until you arrive in Stratford. Tickets can be booked through **Keith Prowse** (ℂ **800/669-8687** in North America, or 0870/840-1111 in England; www.keithprowse.com).

You can also call the **theater box office** directly (ℂ **0844/800-1110**) and charge your tickets. The box office is open Monday to Saturday 9am to 8pm, although it closes at 6pm on days when there are no performances. Seat prices range from £5 to £45. You can make a credit card reservation and pick up your tickets on the performance day, but you must cancel at least 1 full week in advance to get a refund.

Where to Stay

During the theater season, it's best to reserve in advance. The Tourist Information Centre (part of the national "Book-a-Bed-Ahead" service, which enables visitors to make reservations in advance) will help find accommodations in all ranges. The fee for any room reservations the service makes is 10% of the first night's stay (bed-and-breakfast rate only), deductible from the visitor's final bill.

VERY EXPENSIVE

Menzies Welcombe Hotel Spa & Golf Club ★★★   For a formal, historic hotel in Stratford, there's nothing

Performance of *Love's Labour's Lost* at Royal Shakespeare Theatre.

better than the Welcombe. One of England's great Jacobean country houses, this hotel is a 10-minute ride from the heart of Stratford-upon-Avon. Its key feature is an 18-hole golf course. It's surrounded by 63 hectares (156 acres) of grounds and has a formal entrance on Warwick Road, a winding driveway leading to the main hall. Bedrooms are luxuriously furnished in traditional Jacobean style, with fine antiques and elegant fabrics. Most bedrooms are seemingly big enough for tennis matches, but those in the garden wing, although comfortable, are small. Some of the bedrooms are sumptuously furnished with elegant four-posters.

Warwick Rd., Stratford-upon-Avon, Warwickshire CV37 0NR. ✆ **01789/295252.** Fax 01789/414666. www.menzies-hotels.co.uk. 78 units. £161–£270 double; £250–£600 suite. Rates include English breakfast. AE, DC, MC, V. Free parking. Take A439 2km (1¼ miles) northeast of the town center. **Amenities:** 2 restaurants; bar; health club & spa; pool (indoor); room service; tennis court. *In room:* TV, hair dryer, Wi-Fi (£10).

EXPENSIVE

Macdonald Alveston Manor Hotel ★★ This Tudor manor is perfect for theatergoers—it's just a 5-minute walk from the theaters. The hotel has a wealth of chimneys and gables, and everything from an Elizabethan gazebo to Queen Anne windows. Mentioned in the *Domesday Book,* the building predates the arrival of William the Conqueror. The rooms in the manor will appeal to those who appreciate the old-world charm of slanted floors, overhead beams, and antique furnishings. Some triples or quads are available in the modern section, connected by a covered walk through the rear garden. Most rooms here are original and have built-in walnut furniture and a color-coordinated decor. You can live in luxury in the original rooms with their walnut furniture or be assigned a rather routine standard twin that, though comfortable, will lack romance.

Clopton Bridge (off B4066), Stratford-upon-Avon, Warwickshire CV37 7HP. ✆ **0844/879-9138.** Fax 01789/414095. www.macdonaldhotels.co.uk. 113 units. £137–£153 double; £179–£239 suite. Rates include breakfast. AE, MC, V. Free parking. **Amenities:** Restaurant; bar; babysitting; pool (indoor); room service; Wi-Fi (£10). *In room:* TV, hair dryer, minibar, Wi-Fi (£12 per day).

MODERATE

Best Western Grosvenor Hotel A pair of Georgian town houses, built in 1832 and 1843, join together to form this hotel. In the center of town, with lawns and gardens to the rear, it is a short stroll from the intersection of Bridge Street and Waterside, allowing easy access to the Avon River, Bancroft Gardens, and the Royal Shakespeare Theatre. There is a rambling ground floor that has tremendous character—it reminds us of an elegant English country house, with small intimate lounges and open fires. Bedrooms are midsize to spacious, each personally designed with a high standard of tasteful modern furnishings. Rooms are not overly adorned or stylish, but they're snug and cozy.

12–14 Warwick Rd., Stratford-upon-Avon, Warwickshire CV37 6YT. ✆ **01789/269213.** Fax 01789/266087. www.bwgh.co.uk. 73 units. £79–£114 double; £104–£140 suite. AE, MC, V. Free parking. **Amenities:** Restaurant; bar; babysitting; access to health club; room service. *In room:* TV, hair dryer, Wi-Fi (free).

Legacy Falcon This inn blends the very old and the very new. The black-and-white timbered inn was licensed a quarter of a century after Shakespeare's death; connected to its rear by a glass passageway is a more sterile bedroom extension added in 1970. In the heart of Stratford, the inn faces the Guild Chapel and the

New Place Gardens. The recently upgraded rooms in the older section have oak beams, diamond leaded-glass windows, antiques, and good reproductions. In the inn's intimate Merlin Lounge, you'll find an open copper-hooded fireplace where fires are stoked under beams salvaged from old ships.

Chapel St., Stratford-upon-Avon, Warwickshire CV37 6HA. ✆ **0844/411-9005.** Fax 0844/411-9006. www.legacy-hotels.co.uk. 83 units. £90–£150 double; from £165 suite. AE, DC, MC, V. Free parking. **Amenities:** 2 restaurants; 2 bars; room service. *In room:* TV, hair dryer, Wi-Fi (free).

Mercure Shakespeare Hotel ★★   Filled with historical associations, the original core of this hotel, dating from the 1400s, has seen many additions in its long life. Quieter and plusher than the Falcon (see above), it is equaled in the central core of Stratford only by the Macdonald Alveston Manor (see above). Residents relax in the post-and-timber-studded public rooms, within sight of fireplaces and playbills from 19th-century productions of Shakespeare's plays. Bedrooms are named in honor of noteworthy actors, Shakespeare's plays, or Shakespearean characters. The oldest are capped with hewn timbers, and all have modern comforts. Even the newer accommodations are at least 40 to 50 years old and have rose-and-thistle patterns carved into many of their exposed timbers. Bathrooms range in size.

Chapel St., Stratford-upon-Avon, Warwickshire CV37 6ER. ✆ **01789/294997.** Fax 01789/415411. www.mercure.com. 74 units. £99–£202 double; from £240 suite. Rates include buffet breakfast. Children 12 and younger stay free in parent's room. AE, DC, MC, V. Parking £10. **Amenities:** Restaurant; bar; room service; Wi-Fi (75p per 10 min.). *In room:* A/C, TV, hair dryer, minibar (in some).

The Stratford ★   This is definitely not one of the atmospheric inns of Stratford-upon-Avon. But if you prefer a modern hotel with up-to-date conveniences when paying your call to the Bard, the Stratford is for you. It lacks personality but has just about everything else. The bedrooms are spaciously and elegantly appointed. Some of the units come with four-poster beds, as in Tudor days, but others are more geared to commercial travelers seeking streamlined conveniences—not romance. The hotel lies only a short walk from the banks of the River Avon. Market-fresh dishes deftly prepared change with the seasons in the on-site Quills Restaurant.

Arden St., Stratford-upon-Avon, Warwickshire CV37 6QQ. ✆ **01789/271-000.** Fax 01789/271-001. www.qhotels.co.uk. £79–£114 double. AE, DC, MC, V. Free parking. **Amenities:** Restaurant; bar; small exercise room; room service. *In room:* TV, hair dryer, Wi-Fi (2 free hr., £12 per 24 hr.).

White Swan   This cozy, intimate hotel, housed in Stratford's oldest building, is one of the most atmospheric in Stratford. In business for more than a century before Shakespeare appeared on the scene, it competes successfully with the Legacy Falcon (see above) in offering an ancient atmosphere. The gabled medieval front would present the Bard with no surprises, but the modern comforts inside would surely astonish him. Many of the rooms have been well preserved despite the addition of modern conveniences. Paintings dating from 1550 hang on the lounge walls. All bedrooms are well appointed.

Rother St., Stratford-upon-Avon, Warwickshire CV37 6NH. ✆ **01789/297022.** Fax 01789/268773. www.pebblehotels.com. 41 units. £95–£120 double. Rates include English breakfast. AE, DC, MC, V. Parking £5. **Amenities:** Restaurant; bar (p. 431); room service. *In room:* TV, hair dryer, Wi-Fi (free).

INEXPENSIVE

Heron Lodge ★ 🏷️   Bob and Chris Heaps run one of the better B&Bs in Stratford, their lodge lying a kilometer (⅔ mile) outside the heart of town. Their midsize bedrooms have individual character, and the furnishings are both tasteful
and comfortable. They still practice the old-fashioned custom of an afternoon
"cuppa" served in their conservatory. Like Penryn House (see below), the Heaps
serves one of the town's best breakfasts, using local products when available.

260 Alcester Rd., Stratford-upon-Avon, Warwickshire CV37 9JQ. ℂ **01789/299169.** www.
heronlodge.com. 5 units. £58–£88 double. Rates include English breakfast. MC, V. Free parking.
In room: TV, hair dryer, Wi-Fi (free), no phone.

Moonraker Guest House ★ 🏨   Privately owned and personally managed by
Ruth and Morris Masaaki, this is a delightful discovery, lying midway between
Anne Hathaway's House Cottage and Shakespeare's birthplace. Each bedroom is
comfortably and attractively furnished. A luxury suite is available with a bedroom,
lounge, and kitchenette, plus two more suites, each having two rooms. Among the
amenities are four-poster beds, a lounge area, and garden patios. A hearty English
breakfast is followed by toast and homemade marmalade and jams.

40 Alcester Rd., Stratford-upon-Avon, Warwickshire CV37 9DB. ℂ/fax **01789/268774.** www.
moonrakerhouse.com. 7 units. £70–£95 double. Rates include English breakfast. MC, V. Free parking. 2 min. by car from the heart of town on A422. **Amenities:** Breakfast room; Wi-Fi (free).
In room: TV, hair dryer.

Penryn House ★ 🏷️   The location is convenient and the price is right at this
B&B, where hosts Anne and Robert Dawkes are among the most welcoming in
town. Their bedrooms are a bit small but well furnished and comfortable. They
justifiably take special pride in their breakfasts right down to their superb "Harvest of Arden" English apple juice. Free-range Worchestershire eggs are served
along with fresh seasonal fruit and locally produced bacon and sausage. They
even prepare a vegetarian breakfast if requested. The location is close to the rail
station, Anne Hathaway's Cottage, and the heart of town.

126 Alcester Rd., Stratford-upon-Avon, Warwickshire CV37 9DP. ℂ **01789/293718.** Fax 01789/
266077. www.penrynguesthouse.co.uk. 7 units. £60–£75 double. Rates include English breakfast.
MC, V. Free parking. **Amenities:** Breakfast room. *In room:* TV, hair dryer, Wi-Fi (free).

Victoria Spa Lodge   This B&B is old-fashioned and atmospheric. Opened in
1837, the year Queen Victoria ascended the throne, this was the first establishment to be given her name, and it is still going strong. The lodge was originally a
spa frequented by the queen's eldest daughter, Princess Vicky. The accommodating hosts offer tastefully decorated, comfortable bedrooms.

Bishopton Lane (2.5km/1½ miles north of the town center where A3400 intersects A46),
Stratford-upon-Avon, Warwickshire CV37 9QY. ℂ **01789/267985.** Fax 01789/204728. www.
victoriaspa.co.uk. 7 units. £65–£70 double. Rates include English breakfast. MC, V. Free parking.
Amenities: Breakfast room. *In room:* TV, hair dryer, Wi-Fi (£10 per day).

Where to Dine

After visiting the birthplace of Shakespeare, pop across the street for tea at **Brasserie,** Henley Street (ℂ **01789/262189**). This airy tearoom is tremendously
popular, but the very attentive staff more than compensates for the throngs of

Stratford-upon-Avon

patrons. Choose from an array of tea blends, cream teas, and various cakes, pastries, and tea cakes—all freshly baked in their own kitchen.

EXPENSIVE TO MODERATE

Lambs ★ CONTINENTAL/BRITISH   A stone's throw from the Royal Shakespeare Theatre, this cafe-bistro is housed in a building dating from 1547 (and with connections to Lewis Carroll). For a quick, light meal or pretheater dinner, it's ideal. The menu changes monthly. Begin with such starters as an English muffin with smoked haddock and creamed leeks, or else Serrano ham with fresh figs and a basil salad. Then you can tuck into such mains as filet of Scottish beef with portobello mushrooms or else rack of Cornish lamb with dauphinoise potatoes, perhaps roast Gressingham duck with Puy lentils. For dessert, why not the dark-chocolate truffle cake with white-chocolate ice cream? Look to the blackboard for daily specials. The chef takes chances (no doubt inspired by trips to the Continent), and it's a nice departure from the bland tearoom food served for decades in Stratford.

12 Sheep St. ✆ **01789/292554.** www.lambsrestaurant.co.uk. Reservations required for dinner Fri–Sat. Main courses £10–£16; fixed-price menu £17 for 2 courses, £20 for 3 courses. MC, V. Mon 5:30–10pm; Tues–Sat noon–2pm and 5–10pm; Sun noon–2:30pm.

Malbec Petit Bistro ★★ BRITISH/FRENCH   Many savvy local foodies cite this as the best restaurant in Stratford-upon-Avon, and we're inclined to agree. The chef and owner, Simon Malin, offers market-fresh and unpretentious cuisine in fashionable surroundings. His produce is fresh, his seasonings on target, and his imagination active. On the ground floor is an intimate restaurant of character, and on the lower level is a charming cellar with vaulted ceilings and flagstone floors. You'll be impressed with such starters as sautéed lamb's kidneys with thyme-roasted onions or crispy fried squid with almond and a roasted-pepper dipping sauce. You might also savor such mains as rump of local lamb with a butternut-squash gnocchi or free-range pork belly with chorizo sausages and butter beans. Desserts are made fresh daily. How about champagne-laced rhubarb with whipped vanilla shortcake?

6 Union St. ✆ **01789/269106.** www.malbecrestaurant.co.uk. Reservations required. Main courses £10–£17. AE, MC, V. Daily noon–2pm; Mon–Sat 7–9:30pm.

Marlowe's Restaurant BRITISH   Many famous actors appearing in Shakespeare plays have made their way here for dinner, including Paul Schofield, Vanessa Redgrave, Sir Ralph Richardson, and Sir John Gielgud. You can dine formally in the Elizabethan Room or more casually in the Bistro. A large bar in winter has a fireplace blazing with logs, and it opens into a splendid oak-paneled room. In summer there is a spacious courtyard for alfresco dining. Starters are a harmonious blend of flavors, including terrine of guinea fowl and oyster mushrooms with sherry and a red-onion marmalade. Among the fish dishes, grilled sea bass emerges from the kitchen with roasted fennel and a tomato fondue, or else you can opt for one of the chargrilled dishes such as a filet steak with pan-fried mushrooms and grilled tomatoes. Drunken duck has been a longtime specialty here. It's marinated in gin, red wine, and juniper berries before it's roasted in the oven.

18 High St. ✆ **01789/204999.** www.marlowes.biz. Reservations recommended. Main courses £14–£43. AE, MC, V. Elizabethan Room Mon–Thurs 5:30–10pm; Fri 5:30–10:30pm; Sat 5:30–11pm. Bistro daily noon–2:15pm and Mon–Sat 5:30–11pm.

The One Elm BRITISH   This is a convenient stopover because of its long hours of food service. Guests enjoy its pub atmosphere, ground-floor restaurant, or its courtyard for dining and drinking. The cooks pride themselves on serving dishes fresh from their suppliers, including free-range chicken and eggs and high-quality Scottish beef. You can see these chefs at work in an open kitchen, so you know they are preparing everything to order. A special feature is the Elm's "Deli Board," featuring all sorts of antipasti and charcuterie, such as a hot chorizo-and-butter-bean salad. Both starters and mains are an appetizing array of market freshness. Begin with shredded beef samosa or else smoked Scottish salmon with horserad-ish blinis. Among the most enticing main dishes are fish cakes of salmon and smoked haddock with sautéed spinach or else whole roast black bream with kum-quat potatoes. A Catalan fish stew is made from the catch of the day.

1 Guild St. ✆ **01789/404919.** www.oneelmstratford.co.uk. Reservations not needed. Main courses £10–£17. MC, V. Mon–Sat 11am–10pm; Sun noon–3pm and 6:30–9:30pm.

RSC Courtyard Theatre Café Bar BRITISH/CONTINENTAL   This restau-rant enjoys the best location in town—it's in the Royal Shakespeare Theatre itself—with glass walls providing an unobstructed view of the swans on the Avon. You can enjoy an intermission snack of smoked salmon or champagne. Consider the cafe a venue for lunch, pre-show dining, or a supper. The food is prepared with market-fresh ingredients. Light meals feature a chicken liver parfait with apple chutney or the homemade soup of the day. A meat pie special is offered daily, or else you can order "shareboards," platters for two including a meze plat-ter of various appetizers ranging from hummus to zucchini and basil tapenades. Sandwiches are also available, and for dessert you can order a classic hot apple and cinnamon crumble with ice cream.

In the Royal Shakespeare Theatre, Waterside. ✆ **01789/412654.** www.rsc.org.uk. Reservations recommended. Platters for two £8.95–£9.95; bar snacks £2.50; light meals £3.95–£7.95. AE, MC. Mon–Sat 10:30am–8:30pm; Sun 10:30am–5pm.

Sorrento ★ ITALIAN   For a taste of Italy, visit this family-run restaurant, where Jackie and Tony de Angelis welcome you at a location only a 4-minute walk from the Shakespeare Theatre. Guests seated on leather furniture enjoy a predinner aperitif in the lounge before heading into the stylish yet informal res-taurant itself. Everything is cooked to order using market-fresh ingredients, so you need to allow time for each dish to be prepared. In summer those dishes may be enjoyed alfresco on the patio. A selection of well-chosen Italian wines comple-ments the meal, which might begin with such starters as the chef's homemade chicken-liver pâté or else a roast-pepper-and-artichoke salad dressed with olive oil, basil, and capers. The filet steak is flamed in brandy and served in a creamy sauce of black peppercorns, and the pastas are among the best in town.

8 Ely St. ✆ **01789/297999.** www.sorrentorestaurant.co.uk. Reservations recommended. Main courses £5.90–£20; set lunch £13 for 2 courses, £17 for 3 courses. MC, V. Tues–Wed 11:30am–1:45pm; Mon–Sat 5–10:30pm.

Thai Boathouse ★ THAI   The only restaurant set on the Avon, this charming choice is reached by crossing Clopton Bridge toward Oxford and Banbury. The second-floor dining room opens onto vistas of the river. This restaurant, originally established 4 decades ago in Bangkok, has brought spice and zest to Stratford's lazy restaurant scene. The decor comes from Thailand itself, with elephants, woodcarvings, and Buddhas adorning the restaurant. Seasonal specialties such as wild duck and pheasant are a special feature of the menu. Fresh produce, great skill in the kitchen, and exquisite presentations are the hallmarks of this restaurant. Sample a selection of authentic Thai appetizers before continuing on to the delectable main courses, which include stir-fried mixed seafood with fresh chili and sweet Thai basil, or chicken stir-fried with sweet peppers, pineapple, and onion in a sweet-and-sour sauce.

Swan's Nest Lane. © **01789/297733.** www.thaigroup.co.uk/restaurants/boathouse.html. Reservations recommended. Main courses £3–£16; fixed-price menus £21–£26. MC, V. Sun–Fri noon–2:30pm and daily 5:30–10:30pm.

INEXPENSIVE

The Oppo INTERNATIONAL   Located in the heart of Stratford within a 16th-century building, this refreshingly unpretentious restaurant serves up good bistro cooking at reasonable prices. The menu often includes local farm products. Salmon fish cakes are served on a bed of spinach with a sorrel sauce, and pork filet is slow-roasted with fondant potatoes. The most exotic item on the menu is chicken roasted with banana in lime butter and served with basmati rice and a mild curry sauce.

13 Sheep St. © **01789/269980.** www.theoppo.co.uk. Reservations recommended. Main courses £5.50–£20; 2-course lunch £12; 3-course lunch £15. DC, MC, V. Daily noon–2pm; Mon–Sat 5–10pm; Sun 6–9:30pm.

Russons INTERNATIONAL   Because the theater is a short stroll away, this is a great place for a preshow meal. The restaurant is housed in a 400-year-old building, and the two simply furnished dining rooms both feature inglenook fireplaces. The menu changes monthly, reflecting the availability of seasonal ingredients. Fresh seafood is the specialty here, with different choices every day. Daily specials are posted on a blackboard and include shoulder of lamb, Norfolk duck, and numerous vegetarian dishes. Finish with one of the delicious homemade desserts.

8 Church St. © **01789/268822.** Reservations recommended. Lunch and pretheater main courses £5.50; dinner main courses £11–£16. AE, MC, V. Tues–Sat 11:30am–1:45pm and 5:15–9pm.

The Vintner BRITISH/CONTINENTAL   In a timber-framed structure little altered since its construction in the late 15th century, the Vintner may very well be the place where William Shakespeare went to purchase his wine. It derives its name from John Smith, who traded as a wine merchant (vintner) during the 1600s. Close to the Shakespeare Theatre, the Vintner is both a cafe/bar and a restaurant owned by the same family for 5 centuries; its location makes it ideal for a pretheater lunch or supper. When possible, fresh local produce is used. Good-tasting mains include breast of chicken with mango and slow-roasted lamb shank with parsley mashed potatoes. Escalopes of pork filet are made more enticing by caper butter, and a rib-eye comes in a peppercorn sauce. For dessert, try that British nursery favorite, toffee pudding with vanilla ice cream.

4–5 Sheep St. © **01789/297259.** www.the-vintner.co.uk. Reservations not needed. Main courses £5.50–£20. DC, MC, V. Mon–Sat 9:30am–10pm; Sun 9:30am–9pm.

The Best Places for a Pint

The Black Swan ("the Dirty Duck") ★★ BRITISH   Affectionately known as the Dirty Duck, this has been a popular hangout for Stratford players since the

Sign outside the Black Swan pub.

18th century. The wall is lined with autographed photos of its many famous patrons. Typical English grills, among other dishes, are featured in the Dirty Duck Grill Room, though no one has ever accused it of serving the best food in Stratford. You'll have a choice of a dozen appetizers, most of which would make a meal themselves. In fair weather, you can have drinks in the front garden and watch the swans glide by on the Avon.

Waterside. ✆ **01789/297312.** Reservations required for dining. Main courses £6.85–£11; bar snacks £4–£9.95. AE, DC, MC, V (in restaurant only). Restaurant daily noon–10pm. Bar daily 11am–1am.

The Garrick Inn BRITISH   Near Harvard House, this black-and-white timbered Elizabethan pub has an unpretentious charm. The front bar is decorated with tapestry-covered settles, an old oak refectory table, and an open fireplace that attracts the locals. The back bar has a circular fireplace with a copper hood and mementos of the triumphs of the English stage. The specialty is homemade pies such as steak and kidney or chicken and mushroom. Wild boar and venison are other specialties.

25 High St. ✆ **01789/292186.** Main courses £6.85–£11. MC, V. Meals Mon–Sat noon–10pm; Sun noon–9pm. Pub Mon–Thurs 11am–11pm; Fri–Sat 11am–midnight; Sun noon–10:30pm.

The White Swan BRITISH   In the town's oldest building is this atmospheric pub, with cushioned leather armchairs, oak paneling, and fireplaces. You're likely to meet amiable fellow drinkers, who revel in a setting once enjoyed by Will Shakespeare himself when it was known as the Kings Head. At lunch, you can partake of hot dishes of the day, along with fresh salads and sandwiches. Typical mains include a warm brie salad with tomatoes and walnuts, or else salmon with savoy cabbage and potatoes. You can also enjoy the chef's fried chicken served with a red-wine sauce.

In the White Swan hotel, Rother St. ✆ **01789/297022.** Bar snacks £2–£15; main courses £13–£17. AE, DC, MC, V. Daily noon–9pm.

SALISBURY ★★ & STONEHENGE ★★★

Long before you enter Salisbury, the spire of its cathedral comes into view—just as John Constable captured it on canvas. The 121m (397-ft.) pinnacle of the Early English and Gothic cathedral is the tallest in England.

Salisbury, or New Sarum, lies in the valley of the River Avon. Filled with Tudor inns and tearooms, it is the only true city in Wiltshire. It's an excellent base for visitors anxious to explore Stonehenge or Avebury, who, unfortunately, tend to visit the cathedral and then rush on their way. But the old market town is an interesting destination on its own, and if you choose to linger here for a day or two, you find that its pub-to-citizen ratio is perhaps the highest in the country.

Essentials

GETTING THERE **Network Express trains** depart for Salisbury hourly from Waterloo Station in London; the trip takes 1½ hours. Sprinter trains offer fast, efficient service every hour from Portsmouth, Bristol, and South Wales. Also, direct rail service is available from Exeter, Plymouth, Brighton, and Reading. For rail information, call ☎ **0845/748-4950** or visit **www.nationalrail.co.uk**.

Three **National Express buses** (☎ **0871/781-81-81;** www.nationalexpress.com) make a 3-hour run daily from London, costing £16 for a one-way ticket.

If you're driving from London, head west on the M3 to the end of the run, continuing the rest of the way on the A30.

VISITOR INFORMATION The **Tourist Information Centre** is at Fish Row (☎ **01722/334956;** www.visitsalisbury.com) and is open October to April Monday to Saturday 9:30am to 5pm; May Monday to Saturday 9:30am to 5pm and Sunday 10am to 4pm; and June to September Monday to Saturday 9:30am to 6pm and Sunday 10am to 4pm.

The Chief Attraction

Salisbury Cathedral ★★★ You'll find no better example of the Early English pointed architectural style than Salisbury Cathedral. Construction on this magnificent building began as early as 1220 and took only 45 years to complete. (Most of Europe's grandest cathedrals took 3 centuries to build.) Salisbury Cathedral is one of the most homogenous of all the great European cathedrals.

The cathedral's 13th-century octagonal chapter house possesses one of the four surviving original texts of the Magna Carta, along with treasures from the diocese of Salisbury and manuscripts and artifacts belonging to the cathedral. The cloisters enhance the cathedral's beauty, along with an exceptionally large close. At least 75 buildings are in the compound, some from the early 18th century and others from much earlier.

Insider's tip: The 121m (397-ft.) spire was one of the tallest structures in the world when completed in 1315. In its day, this was far more advanced technology than the world's tallest skyscrapers. Amazingly, the spire was not part of the original design and was conceived and added some 30 years after the rest. The name of the master mason is lost to history. In 1668, Sir Christopher Wren expressed alarm at the tilt of the spire, but no further shift

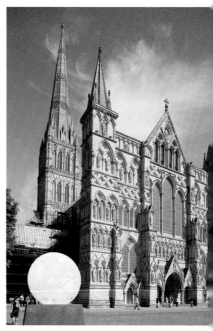

Salisbury Cathedral.

has since been measured. The entire ensemble is still standing; if you trust towering architecture from 700 years ago, you can explore the tower on 1½-hour guided visits costing £8 for adults, £6 for children and seniors. Between March and October there are two to four tours a day depending on demand. From November to February there is only one tour a day at 2:15pm.

The Close, Salisbury. © **01722/555120.** www.salisburycathedral.org.uk. Suggested donation £6, £4.50 students and seniors, £4 children, £13 family. Sept to mid-June Mon–Sat 7:15am–6:15pm; mid-June to Aug Mon–Sat 7:15am–7:15pm; year-round Sun 7:15am–6:15pm.

A Side Trip to Stonehenge

Stonehenge ★★★   This huge circle of lintels and megalithic pillars is considered by many to be the most important prehistoric monument in Britain.

Some visitors are disappointed when they see that Stonehenge is nothing more than concentric circles of stones. But perhaps they don't understand that Stonehenge represents an amazing engineering feat because many of the boulders, the bluestones in particular, were moved many miles (perhaps from southern Wales) to this site. If you're a romantic, you'll see the ruins in the early glow of dawn or else when shadows fall at sunset. The light is most dramatic at these times, the shadows longer, and the effect is often far more mesmerizing than it is in the glaring light of midday.

The widely held view of 18th- and 19th-century Romantics that Stonehenge was the work of the Druids is without foundation. The boulders, many weighing several tons, are believed to have predated the arrival in Britain of the Celtic culture. Controversy surrounds the prehistoric site, especially since the publication of *Stonehenge Decoded* by Gerald S. Hawkins and John B. White, which maintains that Stonehenge was an astronomical observatory—that is, a Neolithic "computing machine" capable of predicting eclipses.

In 2008 Stonehenge made world headlines when part of its eternal mystery may have been solved. From the beginning, it was a monument to the dead, as revealed by radiocarbon dating from human cremation burials around the brooding stones. The site was used as a cemetery from 3000 B.C. until after the monuments were erected in 2500 B.C.

In yet another development, archaeologists uncovered hearths, timbers, and other remains of what was probably the village of workers who erected the monoliths on the Salisbury Plain. These ancient ruins appear to form the largest Neolithic village ever found in Britain. The trenches of this discovery, Durrington Walls, lie 3.2km (2 miles) from Stonehenge.

Your ticket permits you to go inside the fence surrounding the site that protects the stones from vandals and souvenir hunters. You can go all the way up to a short rope barrier, about 15m (49 ft.) from the stones.

A full circular tour around Stonehenge is possible. A modular walkway was introduced to cross the archaeologically important avenue, the area that runs between the Heel Stone and the main circle of stones. This enables visitors to complete a full circuit of the stones and to see one of the best views of a completed section of Stonehenge as they pass by, an excellent addition to the informative audio tour.

Insider's tip: From the road, if you don't mind the noise from traffic, you can get a good view of Stonehenge without paying admission to go for a close-up encounter. What we like to do is climb **Amesbury Hill,** clearly visible and lying 2.4km (1½ miles) up the A303. From here, you'll get a free panoramic view.

Stonehenge.

Wilts & Dorset (*℡* **01722/336855;** www.wdbus.co.uk) runs several buses daily (depending on demand) from Salisbury to Stonehenge, as well as buses from the Salisbury train station to Stonehenge. The bus trip to Stonehenge takes 40 minutes, and a round-trip ticket costs £11 for adults, £5 for children ages 5 to 15 (4 and younger ride free), £6 seniors, and £15 family ticket.

At the junction of A303 and A344/A360. *℡* **01980/623108** for information. www.stonehenge. co.uk. Admission £6.40 adults, £5.10 students and seniors, £3.20 children 5–15, £16 family ticket. June–Aug daily 9am–7pm; Mar 16–May and Sept–Oct 15 daily 9:30am–6pm; Oct 16–Mar 15 daily 9:30am–4pm. If you're driving, head north on Castle Rd. from the center of Salisbury. At the first roundabout (traffic circle), take the exit toward Amesbury (A345) and Old Sarum. Continue along this road for 13km (8 miles) and then turn left onto A303 in the direction of Exeter. You'll see signs for Stonehenge, leading you up A344 to the right. It's 3km (1¾ miles) west of Amesbury.

Where to Lunch

Salisbury Haunch of Venison BRITISH   Right in the heart of Salisbury, this creaky-timbered chophouse (it dates from 1320) serves excellent dishes, especially English roasts and grills. Stick to its specialties and you'll rarely go wrong. Begin with a tasty warm salad of venison sausages with garlic croutons and then follow with the time-honored roast haunch of venison with parsnips and juniper berries. Other dishes likely to tempt you include pan-fried orange-glazed duck breast with a beetroot salsa, and smoked mackerel salad with roasted cherry tomatoes and a sweet chili dressing (a dish of cabbage and potatoes).

1 Minster St. *℡* **01722/411313.** www.haunchofvenison.uk.com. Fixed-price menu £11 served daily noon–2pm and 6–8pm; main courses £8.35–£16. MC, V. Mon–Sat 11:30am–11pm; Sun noon–10:30pm.

11

FAST FACTS: LONDON

Area Codes The country code for England and Wales is **44.** The area code for London is **020.**

ATM Networks/Cashpoints See "Money & Costs," p. 66.

Business Hours With many, many exceptions, business hours are Monday to Friday 9am to 5pm. In general, stores are open Monday to Saturday 9am to 5:30pm. In country towns, there is usually an early closing day (often Wed or Thurs), when the shops close at 1pm.

Car Rentals See "Airline, Hotel & Car-Rental Websites," p. 439.

Drinking Laws The legal drinking age is 18. Children younger than 16 aren't allowed in pubs, except in certain rooms, and then only when accompanied by a parent or guardian. Don't drink and drive. Penalties are stiff.

Breaking decades of tradition, England in 2005 abandoned its strict, often draconian, liquor laws, allowing 24-hour alcohol sales in England and Wales. Many pubs no longer close at 11pm, which used to be "last call." Of course, it's up to the publicans, but many, if they elect to do so, could stay open day and night.

Driving Rules See "Getting There & Getting Around," p. 57.

Drugstores In Britain, they're called "chemists." Ask at your hotel for the nearest location. For an emergency chemist, dial "0" (zero) and ask the operator for the local police, who will give you the name of one nearest you.

Electricity British electricity is 240 volts AC (50 cycles), roughly twice the voltage in North America, which is 115 to 120 volts AC (60 cycles). American plugs don't fit British wall outlets. Always bring suitable transformers and/or adapters—if you plug an American appliance directly into a European electrical outlet without a transformer, you'll destroy your appliance and possibly start a fire. Electronic equipment with motors intended to revolve at a fixed number of revolutions per minute probably won't work properly even with transformers.

Embassies & Consulates The **U.S. Embassy** is at 24 Grosvenor Sq., W1 (℡ **020/7499-9000;** www.usembassy.org.uk; Tube: Bond St.). Hours are Monday to Friday 8am to 5:30pm, Saturday 10am to 4pm. However, for passport and visa information, go to the **U.S. Passport and Citizenship Unit,** 55–56 Upper Grosvenor St., London, W1 (℡ **020/7894-0563;** http://london.usembassy.gov; Tube: Marble Arch or Bond St.). Passport and Citizenship Unit hours are Monday to Friday 8:30am to 12:30pm.

The **Canadian High Commission,** MacDonald House, 38 Grosvenor St., W1 (℡ **020/ 7258-6600;** www.canadainternational.gc.ca/united_kingdom-royaume_uni/index. aspx; Tube: Bond St.), handles visas for Canada. Hours are Monday to Friday 8 to 11am for immigration services.

The **Australian High Commission** is at Australia House, the Strand, WC2 (℡ **020/ 7379-4334;** www.australia.org.uk; Tube: Charing Cross or Aldwych). Hours are Monday to Friday 9am to 5pm, 9 to 11am for immigration services, passports 9:30am to 3:30pm.

The **New Zealand High Commission** is at New Zealand House, 80 Haymarket at Pall Mall, SW1 (℡ **020/7930-8422;** www.nzembassy.com; Tube: Charing Cross or Piccadilly Circus). Hours are Monday to Friday 10am to 4pm.

The **Irish Embassy** is at 17 Grosvenor Place, SW1 (℡ **020/7235-2171;** http://ireland. embassyhomepage.com; Tube: Hyde Park Corner). Hours are Monday to Friday 9:30am to 1pm and 2 to 5pm.

Emergencies Dial ℡ **999** for police, fire, or ambulance. Give your name, address, and telephone number and state the nature of the emergency.

Holidays Britain observes New Year's Day, Good Friday, Easter Monday, May Day (first Mon in May), spring and summer bank holidays (the last Mon in May and Aug, respectively), Christmas Day, and Boxing Day (Dec 26).

Hotlines If you're in some sort of substance abuse or legal emergency, call **Release** (℡ **020/7729-9904**), open Monday to Friday 11am to 1pm. **The Rape and Sexual Abuse Hotline** (℡ **0845/122-1331**) is open daily Monday to Friday noon to 2:30pm and 7 to 9:30pm, and on weekends and bank holidays 2:30 to 5pm. **Alcoholics Anonymous** (℡ **020/7833-0022**) answers its helpline daily 10am to 10pm. For issues related to sexual health and sexually transmitted diseases, call the **Sexual Health Information Line** at ℡ **0800/567-123.**

Insurance For information on traveler's insurance, trip cancelation insurance, and medical insurance while traveling, please visit www.frommers.com/tips.

Internet Access It's hard nowadays to find a city that *doesn't* have a few cybercafes. Although there's no definitive directory for cybercafes—these are independent businesses, after all—two places to start looking are at **www.cybercaptive.com** and **www.cybercafe.com**.

London, of course, has great Internet access. If you've brought your laptop, the quest will be easier, since many hotels are wired; rates run from £10 to £20 a day, although £12 is probably the average. Countless Internet cafes and coin-operated kiosks can be found around town. Libraries are reserved for residents, so you can't rely on them. The most common Internet cafe chain is **easyInternetcafe** (www.easyinternetcafe.com). Fifteen locations are around town, with West End locations in Burger King's basement at Piccadilly Circus (46 Regent St., W1; Tube: Piccadilly Circus; 358 Oxford St., W1;

Tube: Bond Street; 9–16 Tottenham Court Rd., W1; Tube: Tottenham Court Road; and east of Trafalgar Square 456–459 Strand, WC2; Tube: Charing Cross).

Legal Aid The American Services section of the U.S. Consulate (see above) will give you advice if you run into trouble abroad. They can advise you of your rights and will even provide a list of attorneys (for which you'll have to pay if services are used). But they cannot interfere on your behalf in the legal processes of Great Britain. For questions about American citizens who are arrested abroad, including ways of getting money to them, telephone the **Citizens Emergency Center** of the Office of Special Consulate Services in Washington, D.C. (© **202/647-5225**). Citizens of other nations should go to their London-based consulate for advice.

Lost & Found Be sure to tell all of your credit card companies the minute you discover your wallet has been lost or stolen, and file a report at the nearest police precinct. Your credit card company or insurer may require a police report number or record of the loss. Most credit card companies have an emergency toll-free number to call if your card is lost or stolen; they may be able to wire you a cash advance immediately or deliver an emergency credit card in a day or two. American cardholders can call these toll-free numbers in case of an emergency—**Visa** at © **0800/891-725, American Express** at © **0800/587-6023,** and **MasterCard** at © **020/7557-5000.** (The last is not a toll-free number.)

If you need emergency cash over the weekend when all banks and American Express offices are closed, you can have money wired to you via **Western Union** (© **800/325-6000;** www.westernunion.com).

Mail An airmail letter to North America costs 56p for 10 grams (⅓ oz.); postcards also require a 56p stamp; letters generally take 7 to 10 days to arrive to the United States. The British postal system is among the most reliable in the world, so you don't need to depend on Federal Express or some other carrier unless you're in a great hurry.

Measurements See the chart on the inside front cover of this book for details on converting metric measurements to nonmetric equivalents.

Newspapers & Magazines In London *The Times, Daily Telegraph, Daily Mail,* and *Guardian* are dailies carrying the latest news. The *International Herald Tribune,* published in Paris, and an international edition of *USA Today,* beamed via satellite, are available daily. Copies of *Time* and *Newsweek* are sold at most newsstands. Magazines such as *Time Out* and *Where* contain useful information about the latest happenings in London.

Passports **For Residents of the United States:** Whether you're applying in person or by mail, you can download passport applications from the U.S. Department of State website at http://travel.state.gov. To find your regional passport office, either check the U.S. Department of State website or call the toll-free number of the **National Passport Information Center** (© **877/487-2778**) for automated information.

For Residents of Canada: Passport applications are available at travel agencies throughout Canada or from the central **Passport Office,** Department of Foreign Affairs and International Trade, Ottawa, ON K1A 0G3 (© **800/567-6868;** www.ppt.gc.ca). *Note:* Canadian children who travel must have their own passports. However, if you hold a valid Canadian passport issued before December 11, 2001, that bears the name of your child, the passport remains valid for you and your child until the document expires.

For Residents of Ireland: You can apply for a 10-year passport at the **Passport Office,** Setanta Centre, Molesworth Street, Dublin 2 (☏ **01/671-1633;** www.foreignaffairs.gov. ie). Those under age 18 and over 65 must apply for a 3-year passport. You can also apply at 1A South Mall, Cork (☏ **021/494-4700**) or at most main post offices.

For Residents of Australia: You can pick up an application from your local post office or any branch of passports Australia, but you must schedule an interview at the passport office to present your application materials. Call the **Australian Passport Information Service** at ☏ **131-232** or visit the government website at **www.passports.gov.au**.

For Residents of New Zealand: You can pick up a passport application at any New Zealand Passports Office or download it from their website. Contact the **Passports Office** at ☏ **0800/225-050** in New Zealand or 04/474-8100, or log on to **www.dia. govt.nz**.

Police Dial ☏ **999** if the matter is serious. Losses, thefts, and other criminal matters should be reported to the police immediately.

Smoking As of July 1, 2007, a smoking ban went into effect in England. Smoking is now banned in all indoor public places such as pubs, restaurants, and clubs.

Taxes To encourage energy conservation, the British government levies a 25% tax on gasoline (petrol). There is also a 17.5% national value-added tax (VAT) that is added to all hotel and restaurant bills and is included in the price of many items you purchase. This can be refunded if you shop at stores that participate in the Retail Export Scheme (signs are posted in the window).

Telephones See "Staying Connected" in chapter 3.

Time Britain follows Greenwich Mean Time (5 hr. ahead of Eastern Standard Time), with British summertime lasting (roughly) from the end of March to the end of October. Because of different daylight saving time practices in the two nations, there's a brief period (about a week) in autumn when Britain is only 4 hours ahead of New York and a brief period in spring when it's 6 hours ahead of New York.

Tipping For cab drivers, add about 10% to 15% to the fare on the meter. However, if the driver loads or unloads your luggage, add something extra.

In hotels, porters receive 75p per bag, even if you have only one small suitcase. Hall porters are tipped only for special services. Maids receive £1 per day. In top-ranking hotels, the concierge will often submit a separate bill showing charges for newspapers and other items; if he or she has been particularly helpful, tip extra.

Hotels often add a service charge of 10% to 15% to most bills. In smaller bed-and-breakfasts, the tip is not likely to be included. Therefore, tip people for special services, such as the waiter who serves you breakfast. If several people have served you in a bed-and-breakfast, you may ask that 10% to 15% be added to the bill and divided among the staff.

In both restaurants and nightclubs, a 15% service charge is added to the bill, which is distributed among all the help. To that, add another 3% to 5%, depending on the service. Waiters in deluxe restaurants and nightclubs are accustomed to the extra 5%. Sommeliers (wine stewards) get about £1 per bottle of wine served. Tipping in pubs isn't common, but in wine bars, the server usually gets about 75p per round of drinks.

Barbers and hairdressers expect 10% to 15%. Tour guides expect £2, though it's not mandatory. Gas station attendants are rarely tipped, and theater ushers don't expect tips.

Toilets They're marked by public toilets signs in streets, parks, and Tube stations; many are automatically sterilized after each use. The English often call toilets "loos." You'll also find well-maintained lavatories in all larger public buildings, such as museums and art galleries, large department stores, and railway stations. It's not really acceptable to use the lavatories in hotels, restaurants, and pubs if you're not a customer, but we can't say that we always stick to this rule. Public lavatories are usually free, but you may need a small coin to get in or to use a proper washroom.

AIRLINE, HOTEL & CAR-RENTAL WEBSITES

MAJOR U.S. AIRLINES
(all offer service to London)

American Airlines
www.aa.com

Continental Airlines
www.continental.com

Delta Air Lines
www.delta.com

United Airlines
www.united.com

US Airways
www.usairways.com

MAJOR INTERNATIONAL AIRLINES

Aer Lingus
www.aerlingus.com

Aeroméxico
www.aeromexico.com

Air Berlin
www.airberlin.com

Air Canada
www.aircanada.com

Air France
www.airfrance.com

Air India
www.airindia.com

Air New Zealand
www.airnewzealand.com

Air Transat
www.airtransat.com

Alitalia
www.alitalia.com

American Airlines
www.aa.com

Austrian Airlines
www.aua.com

BMI
www.flybmi.com

British Airways
www.british-airways.com

Cathay Pacific
www.cathaypacific.com

Continental Airlines
www.continental.com

Delta Air Lines
www.delta.com

Emirates Airlines
www.emirates.com

Finnair
www.finnair.com

Germanwings Airlines
www.germanwings.com

Iberia Airlines
www.iberia.com

Icelandair
www.icelandair.com
www.icelandair.co.uk (in U.K.)

Korean Airlines
www.koreanair.com

Lufthansa
www.lufthansa.com

Meridiana
www.meridiana.it

Monarch Flights
http://flights.monarch.co.uk

North American Airlines
www.flynaa.com

Norwegian Airlines
www.norwegian.no

Olympic Airlines
www.olympicairlines.com

Qatar Airlines
www.qatarairways.com

Quantas Airlines
www.quantas.com

Royal Dutch Airlines
www.klm.com

SAS (Scandinavian Airlines)
www.flysas.com

Singapore Airlines
www.singaporeair.com

South African Airways
www.flysaa.com

Swiss Air
www.swiss.com

Thai Airways International
www.thaiair.com

Tunisair
www.tunisair.com

Turkish Airlines
www.thy.com

United Airlines
www.united.com

US Airways
www.usairways.com

Virgin Atlantic Airways
www.virgin-atlantic.com

BUDGET AIRLINES

Aer Arann
www.aerarann.com

Aer Lingus
www.aerlingus.com

Air Berlin
www.airberlin.com

Aurigny
www.aurigny.com

BMI Baby
www.bmibaby.com

Brussels Airlines
www.brusselsairlines.com

Cimber Air
www.cimber.dk

Cirrus Airlines
www.cirrusairlines.de

Condor
www.condor.com

Croatia Airlines
www.croatiaairlines.com

Czech Airlines
www.czechairlines.com

Ryanair
www.ryanair.com

Tap Airlines
www.flytap.com

Ted (part of United Airlines)
www.flyted.com

VLM
www.flyvlm.com

Wizz Air
www.wizzair.com

MAJOR HOTEL & MOTEL CHAINS

Accor Hotels
www.accorhotels.com

Best Western International
www.bestwestern.com

Britannia Hotels
www.britanniahotels.com

Carlson Hotels
www.carlson.com

Clarion Hotels
www.choicehotels.com

Comfort Inns
www.comfortinn.com

Courtyard by Marriott
www.marriott.com/courtyard

Crowne Plaza Hotels
www.ichotelsgroup.com

Holiday Inn Hotels
www.holidayinn.com

Days Inn Hotels
www.daysinn.com

Firmdale Hotels
www.firmdale.com

Four Seasons
www.fourseasons.com

Grange Hotels
www.grangehotels.com

Hilton Hotels
www1.hilton.com

Hotel Formule 1
www.hotelformule1.com

Hyatt
www.hyatt.com

Ibis Hotels
www.ibishotel.com

Imperial Hotels
www.imperialhotels.co.uk

InterContinental Hotels & Resorts
www.interconti.com

Leading Hotels of the World
www.lhw.com

Marriott
www.marriott.com

Mercure Hotels
www.mercure.com

Millennium Hotels
www.millenniumhotels.com

Novotel Hotels
www.novotel.com

Preferred Hotels & Resorts
www.preferredhotels.com

Premier Inn Hotels
www.premierinn.com

Quality
www.choicehotels.com

Radisson Hotels & Resorts
www.radisson.com

Ramada Worldwide
www.ramada.com

Red Carnation Hotels
www.redcarnationhotels.com

Residence Inn by Marriott
www.marriott.com/residenceinn

Rocco Forte Collection
www.roccofortecollection.com

Shaftesbury Hotels
www.shaftesburyhotels.com

Sheraton Hotels & Resorts
www.starwoodhotels.com/sheraton

Small Luxury Hotels of the World
www.slh.com

Sol Melia Hotels & Resorts
www.solmelia.com

Thistle Hotels
www.thistle.com

Travelodge Hotels
www.travelodge.com

Westin Hotels & Resorts
www.starwoodhotels.com/westin

CAR-RENTAL AGENCIES

Alamo
www.alamo.com

Auto Europe
www.autoeurope.com

Avis
www.avis.com

Budget
www.budget.com

Dollar
www.dollar.com

Enterprise
www.enterprise.com

Hertz
www.hertz.com

Kemwel (KHA)
www.kemwel.com

National
www.nationalcar.com

Thrifty
www.thrifty.com

Index

Restaurants Index

Photo Credits

p. i: © Bo Zaunders/Corbis; p. iii, vi: © Travel Library Limited/SuperStock; p. iv-v: © Axiom Photographic Limited/SuperStock; p. 1: © Mark Mawson/Robert Harding World Imagery; p. 2: © Kord.com/AGE Fotostock; p. 4, left: © Adam Woolfitt/Robert Harding World Imagery; p. 4, right: © Prisma/SuperStock; p. 5: © Jon Arnold Images/AGE Fotostock; p. 6: © Alan Klehr/Danita Delmont Stock Photography; p. 7, left: © Axiom Photographic/SuperStock; p. 7, right: Photo courtesy of 41 Hotel; p. 8: Photo courtesy of Firmdale Hotels; p. 9: © PSL Images/Alamy; p. 10: © Karl Johaentges/Look/AGE Fotostock; p. 11: © David Pearson/Alamy; p. 12: © Bernard Friel/DanitaDelimont.com; p. 13, top: © Alastair Muir/Rex USA; p. 13, middle: © Sandro Vannini/Corbis; p. 14, left: © Zute Lightfoot/Impact/AGE Fotostock; p. 14, right: © Charles Bowman/Robert Harding World Imagery/Corbis; p. 15, left: © Polka Dot Images/SuperStock; p. 15, right: © Mike Abrahams/Alamy; p. 16: © Adrian Dennis/Rex USA; p. 18: © Andy Rain/epa/Corbis; p. 23: © Gustavo Tomsich/Corbis; p. 26: © Underwood & Underwood/Corbis; p. 28: © David Bebber/Reuters/Corbis; p. 30: © The Bridgeman Art Library International; p. 33: © The Print Collector/Impact/AGE Fotostock; p. 34: © Duncan Phillips/Alamy; p. 35: © Axiom Photographic Limited/SuperStock; p. 36: © Heeb Christian/Prisma/AGE Fotostock; p. 38: © Bettmann/Corbis; p. 40, top: © Jonathan Player/Rex USA; p. 40, bottom: © Universal Pictures/Photofest; p. 42: © Simone Joyner/Getty Images; p. 44, top: © View Pictures Ltd/SuperStock; p. 44, bottom: © FoodPix/Alamy; p. 45: © Food Features/Alamy; p. 48: © Micha Theiner/UPPA/Photoshot; p. 84: © Vidler/Mauritius Images/AGE Fotostock; p. 88: © AGE Fotostock/SuperStock; p. 89: © Jonathan Player/Rex USA; p. 91, left: © Pawel Libera/Alamy; p. 91, right: © Jaume Gual/AGE Fotostock; p. 92: © Dennis Johnson/Lonely Planet Images; p. 93: © Eric Nathan/Alamy; p. 95: © Terry Harris Just Greece Photo Library/Alamy; p. 96: © Photononstop/SuperStock; p. 97: © Robert Read/Alamy; p. 99: © Prisma/SuperStock; p. 100: © Steve Vidler/Mauritius Images/Photolibrary; p. 101: © Alex Segre/Alamy; p. 107: © Steve Vidler/ImageState/AGE Fotostock; p. 109: © Paul Carstairs/Alamy; p. 110: © Tom Steventon/Alamy; p. 111: © Spectrum/Impact/AGE Fotostock; p. 112: © David Noble Photography/Alamy; p. 114: © F. Monheim/R. von Göt/Bildarchiv Monheim/AGE Fotostock; p. 115: © Shane Aurousseau/Alamy Images; p. 116: Photo courtesy of Firmdale Hotels; p. 167: © Alex Segre/Alamy; p. 235: © Geoff A. Howard/Alamy; p. 238, left: © Mark Thomas/Axiom Photographic; p. 238, right: © Rex USA; p. 243: © Eric Lewis/SuperStock; p. 244, left: © Stuart Forster/Alamy; p. 244, right: © Jonathan Hordle/Rex USA; p. 247: © Ian Murray/AGE Fotostock; p. 248: © Markku Murto/art/Alamy; p. 249: © Alessia Pierdomenico/Reuters/Corbis; p. 250, left: © John Norman/Alamy; p. 250, right: © Dynamic Graphics 32/JupiterImages/Creatas/Alamy; p. 252: © brianengland/Alamy; p. 253: © AGE Fotostock/SuperStock; p. 254: © Kathy deWitt/Alamy; p. 255: © Carlos S. Pereyra/AGE Fotostock; p. 256: © Peter Phipp/Travel Shots/AGE Fotostock; p. 258: © The Print Collector/Alamy; p. 259: © Sandro Vannini/Corbis; p. 260: © William Helsel/AGE Fotostock; p. 262: © Britain on View/Photolibrary; p. 266: © Eric Nathan/Alamy; p. 270, top: © Frank Monaco/Rex USA; p. 270, bottom: © Mike Booth/Alamy; p. 270: © Pictures/Alamy; p. 273: © Alain Schroeder/Nomad/AGE Fotostock; p. 274, left: © Eric Nathan/Alamy; p. 274, right: © Robert Stainforth/Alamy; p. 275: © Mike Booth/Alamy; p. 276: © Mark Beton/Alamy; p. 277: © Alex Segre/Alamy; p. 278, left: © AA World Travel Library/Alamy; p. 278, right: © R. Kiedrowski/Arco Images/AGE Fotostock; p. 279: © Roberto Herrett/Alamy; p. 280: © Michael Jenner/Robert Harding World Imagery; p. 281: © Mike Booth/Alamy; p. 282: © Bettmann/Corbis; p. 283, top: © Lebrecht Music and Arts Photo Library/Alamy; p. 283, bottom: © Kathy deWitt/Alamy; p. 285, left: © Steve Forrest/Rex USA; p. 285, right: © Clare Kendall/Rex USA; p. 286, left: © Giacomo Giannini/Marka/AGE Fotostock; p. 286, right: © Nick Hufton/View Pictures/AGE Fotostock; p. 287: © The Bridgeman Art Library International; p. 289: © Roberto Herrett/Alamy; p. 290: © Steve Vidler/Prisma/AGE Fotostock; p. 291: © Massimo Listri/Corbis; p. 292: © Pawel Wysocki/Hemis/AGE Fotostock; p. 294, left: © Nigel Lloyd/Alamy; p. 294, right: © Nils Jorgensen/Rex USA; p. 295: © Timothy Allen/Axiom Photographic; p. 296: © Britain on View/Photolibrary; p. 297: © Travelshots/Alamy; p. 298: © Robert Stainforth/Alamy; p. 299: © Horst & Daniel Zielske/Laif/Aurora Photos; p. 300: © Andrew Holt/Alamy; p. 301, top left: Jacky Parker/Alamy; p. 301, top right: samc/Alamy; p. 301, bottom: © Pawel Libera/Alamy; p. 302: © Jon Arnold Images/AGE Fotostock; p. 303: © John Glover/Gap Photos/AGE Fotostock; p. 304: © David Hoffman Photo Library/Alamy; p. 305: © Eric Nathan/Alamy; p. 306: © Peter Barritt/Alamy; p. 307, left: © Robert Harding Picture Library/

NOTES